"For Madge"

The Clan Feuds

Of

The MacDonalds

Ross Dickinson

Printed in Dorset by:
Creeds, Printers by Design
Broadoak
Bridport
Dorset
DT6 5NL
www.creedsuk.com

Ross Dickinson
thanefarm@hotmail.com

First edition published 2010

© Ross Dickinson

ISBN 978 0 956 5095-0-5

Acknowledgements

A considerable number of people have contributed to shape this book. In terms of source material every chapter relied heavily on the three volume Clan Donald written by the Reverend A. MacDonald and Reverend A. MacDonald whose detailed study of all aspects of the history of MacDonalds has never been surpassed by any later work. N.H. MacDonald's detailed grasp of the source material has been vital to my interpretation of events especially with regard to those chapters concerned with the feuds of the Clanranald. The description of the massacre of Glencoe drew heavily on John Prebble's Glencoe. J. M. Hill's Fire and Sword was invaluable when writing about the history of the Clan Iain Mor in Ireland. A debt is also owed to all the authors listed in the select bibliography.

During my travels in the western Highlands I was given directions to places of interest by so many local people, shopkeepers, farmers, fishermen, walkers, local historians, hoteliers and librarians. They often offered me their own insights into local events and their views of the MacDonalds. There are too many to thank individually but I would like to thank them all for their friendly efforts to help me. Two challenging conversations stick in my mind; one on Islay with Mrs MacEachern who wondered why I bothered as these stories had all been recorded before and Randel MacDonell from Cushendun who was not convinced by my "obsession" with the details of the sequence of events. I thank them both for making me question my project.

I owe a debt to my friend Henry Elliot who first encouraged me to record some of the stories of clan feuds. The onerous task of reading, correcting and commenting on the text was done by Robert Nantes and Clive Organ. I am indebted to them both for their thoughtful comments and the many alterations they had to make to the spelling and grammar. It goes without saying that any that remain in the text are entirely my own responsibility.

Thanks to Cliff Towler, www.creative-studios.com, for the art work on the cover and to Tim Beer for bringing together all the disparate computer files and constructing the book. I would also like to thank my mother Anne for her encouragement.

To a greater or lesser degree my children, Euan and Lydia have had to live with the consequences of their father committing himself to this project. For their encouragement and understanding I am indeed grateful.

The greatest debt I owe is to my wife, Madge who has been involved with this book for three years. Although progress was spasmodic and work done on it was intermittent it was always in the background. Madge spent many a stormy night with me in our tent as we travelled throughout the western highlands and islands and no doubt saw too many crumbling ruins. She drew all the maps and genealogical tables in this book. Above all else she was supportive and encouraging when it was taking up my time and attention and when it was not she prompted me into getting on with it.

All intellectual, grammatical and factual errors that readers come across in this book are entirely my own responsibility and are despite the best efforts of all those who have helped me.

Preface

As a child being driven through the Highlands to visit relatives I would look out at the dramatic and desolate landscape and wonder who lived there and what were their lives like? The characters of a childish imagination were out matched by those that actually lived there in the sixteenth century.

This book is intended for the general reader; it is for those interested in the history of the MacDonalds after the fall of the Lordship of the Isles in the last years of the fifteenth century till the early years of the seventeenth century. This was a period of great social and political instability which fostered an environment in which there was only fragmentary order above the level of the clan. A power vacuum was created, in which the power of the Lords of the Isles was not replaced by that of the Scottish state. In turn this led to a period of anarchy in which raiding and feuding flourished in the western highlands.

A history of this period in the western highlands is beset by many problems. The political landscape is complicated by the many contending influences on the region; first and foremost were the clans themselves, all struggling for aggrandizement or survival. The continual, if somewhat spasmodic and ineffectual, efforts of the Scottish state to establish control over the region and the instability caused by English foreign policy, both in Scotland and Ireland, was also a contributory factor. This period of history in the western highlands is dominated by feuds between rival clans. These feuds were exacerbated by the social nature of clans, a scarcity of resources and the clan's own Gaelic heritage.

Any attempt to write a history of clan feuds has a serious problem with the source material. The material that derives from state papers presents the same difficulties as for any subject of the period. The information derived from clan histories is more problematic as the contemporary clan historians were primarily interested in promoting their own agenda; they tend to be partisan and were written for the edification of their own people. Some of the feuds are only recorded by one of the contending clans and their descriptions of events are often liberally dosed with propaganda.

However, the greatest dilema is the contribution made by the oral tradition in the highlands. These "histories" were passed down by word of mouth through many generations and it is clear these stories altered in the telling. Apart from the natural affect of "Chinese whispers" it is very understandable that the historian might be tempted to alter the tale to suit either, his own or his audience's inclinations. Amongst the clan feuds of the MacDonalds there are several important feuds that have survived into the nineteenth century only via the oral tradition. It is clear that some aspects of the feuds which have only come down to us by this source are wrong or at least highly suspect. The writer is left with the conundrum of how to deal with them. In this book I have included them where I believe they best fit the known chronology. I have attempted to make clear when descriptions are based on the oral tradition and where there are two conflicting oral accounts, I have usually followed the one that is more favourable to the MacDonalds. I felt that the only alternative was either to relegate them to an appendix or miss them out all together. This has somewhat damaged the historical accuracy of this book, but hopefully added to the colour and detail of events. These stories were in the end too significant to leave out and I believe, in themselves, offer an insight into the nature of clan societies in the sixteenth century.

There is also the insurmountable problem that the actions and passions of half the adult population is almost entirely neglected by all of the histories whether they are written or oral. With the exception of a few notable examples; like Agnes Campbell, the part women played in these great feuds is not recorded. Given that the women were exposed to the same political, economic and social circumstances as the male population it seems reasonable to assume that they were equally committed to feuding. Where there are descriptions of women taking part in feuds they are no less ruthless than their male counterparts. Sixteenth century Gaelic culture denied them the ability to take part in the actual violence so they had to employ more subtle means. They risked losing their husbands, brothers and children in these feuds. They had no less to lose than the men, their sense of clan, their hatred, fear and sorrow were in no way diminished by their inability to take part on the battlefield. In any family the wife and mother has enormous influence and it seems reasonable to assume that these feuds could not have taken place without their active support.

This book is somewhat old fashioned in its approach; in that it has followed the nineteenth century tradition of examining the history of one clan and has taken an overall view that there was a conflict between the interests of the western highland clans and the Scottish state. While it has attempted to avoid the nineteenth century interpretation of the history of the highlands as being primarily a struggle between Gaelic and lowland Scots culture, it does acknowledge that this is an important theme during this period. This is particularly true of the MacDonalds who were primarily interested in a Gaelic semi-independent "kingdom" in the western highlands ruled by themselves. This history has hopefully avoided any misconception that this period was in the main a struggle between the MacDonalds and Campbells for control over the western highlands or indeed that the Campbells were in some way a non-Gaelic clan. However, it does interpret Campbell policy as being distinctive from those of the MacDonalds in that it saw its best opportunities for aggrandizement emerging from acting as the Government's "policeman" in the western isles.

All the branches of this clan have here been referred to as MacDonalds while I am aware that many MacDonalds spell or have spelt their name in many other ways. Some of these include McDonald, MacDonell, Donalds, etc. In the sixteenth century many of the MacDonalds referred to themselves by their chief's name, for example the MacIains of Ardnamurchan, after the name of their progenitor MacIain. The MacDonalds refer to themselves in several different ways, including the clan Cholla (the first identifiable ancestor of Somerled), or in descriptive terms, for example, as the bountiful people. I have used the name MacDonald for all those who would have considered themselves to be descended from Donald the grandson of Somerled in an attempt to simplify a complex nomenclature.

The first chapter describes the sixteenth century world the people lived in. When writing a history of a particular feud, with its often interminable bloodletting I became concerned that even an interested reader might tire of their violence. I felt it was necessary to attempt to explain why these people were so unremittingly violent. By describing the climate, topography and economy of the western highlands in the sixteenth century it would demonstrate how difficult their lives were and that they lived life on the "edge" with little room for material losses. Their social structures in clans and their cultural history predisposed them to feud with their neighbours. While their belief in folklore and witchcraft made their interpretation of the world so different from ours.

The second chapter is a brief history of the MacDonalds up to the fall of the Lordship. It is just "one damn thing after another"; however I felt that for those readers who were not familiar with the origins of the MacDonalds it would help to put the feuds in context. A recurring question has been when is a feud not only a feud but also part of a larger sequence of events?

It is clear that the feud between the Clanranald and the Frasers, in chapter three, was part of a wider conflagration concerned with Donald Dubh's efforts to re-establish the Lordship. However the events clearly were, whatever else, embraced by what is considered to be a feud. When considering the feuds of the MacDonalds of Glencoe I felt that I could not omit the massacre which occurred in the late seventeenth century. This massacre was not part of a feud however I believe that some readers would expect an account of the massacre in any history of the MacDonalds of Glencoe.

Chapter twelve is a history of the extinction of the Clan Iain Mor (the MacDonalds of Isla) at the hands of the Campbells in the early seventeenth century. There are many aspects of these events which are not a feud between two clans. However, it was, at least in some sense a struggle between the Campbells and MacDonalds. While the extinction of the Clan Iain Mor was in part due to the ineptness of their chief and an avaricious and unsympathetic James VI, it was also caused by Campbell ambition and power.

A chapter on the history of the MacDonalds in Ireland has been placed in the appendix. It is not directly concerned with clan feuds in Scotland. However, the struggle between the MacDonalds and O'Neills for mastery over Gaelic Ulster has many elements of feud within it. Of more importance is the profound significance of Ulster and especially Antrim to the western highlands and in particular to the history of the Clan Iain Mor.

Should any Gaelic speakers pick up this book, I ask them to forgive my errors where I have attempted to use the language incorrectly. I have been concerned what professional historians will make of this history especially in the realm of interpretation. I hope that despite the book's inadequacies my enthusiasm for the history of the western highlands in the sixteenth century will be some mitigation.

Contents

Chapter 1

Through The Looking Glass

Clan Feuds – their causes and characteristics. Geography and climate of the western Highlands- its effect on sixteenth century Highland societies. The flora and fauna in the sixteenth century- the economic basis for these agrarian societies. Social structure- clachans-runrig-castles. The economy- trade-monopolies-coinage-imports and exports-raiding and piracy. Economic poverty and isolation. Clans-chiefs-tacksmen-commonality-their nature and interrelationship. Specialization-smiths-historians-poets-musicians-physicians. Warfare-Gallowglasses-mass mobilization-weapons-battles. Religion-Celtic routes. Gaelic law-succession to the chiefship-daughters-political marriages. Superstitions-wells-blessings-rituals-signs-animals. Witchcraft-Hector Munro-ancestral memory-seers-Dubh Sith-the Great Men. Politics-fall of the Lordship-subsequent anarchy-western and eastern clans-relationship between the western clans and the Scottish State-a country divided by language and culture. The human cost of feuding.

Chapter 2

By Sea By Land

Political situation after the fall of the Lordship. The arrival of the Scots. The Dalriadic Kingdom. Gaels-Norse-Picts-Saxons. Emergence of the Kingdom of Scotland. Emergence of Augustinian Catholicism and feudalism in Lowland Scotland-origins of a divided nation. Somerled and the origins of the MacDonalds-struggles with the Norse-marriage to Ragnhilda-King of the Isles-Somerled's legacy. The sons of Somerled-rift with the MacDougals. Angus Mor and Angus Og 1249-1330. Norway cedes the western isles to Scotland. Bruces versus Comyns-the interference of the English-relationship between the MacDonalds, Bruces and the English. Friendship between Angus Og and Bruce-Bruces gift of the MacDougal lands to Angus Og. John, first Lord of the Isles 1330-1386-his relationship with the Scottish and English Kings- an independent Kingdom-marriage to Amie MacRuarie-the MacRuarie inheritance-marriage to Margaret Stewart. Donald, second Lord of the Isles 1389-1423-relationships with Scottish and English Kings-claim to the Earldom of Ross-Battle of Harlaw and its consequences. Alexander, third Lord of the Isles 1423-1449-relationship with James I-Alexander imprisoned-his humiliation-Battle of Inverlochy-obtains the Earldom of Ross. John, fourth Lord of the Isles 1449-1493-alliance with the Earls of Crawford and Douglas-James II defeats the rebels-John isolated-the Treaty of Ardtornish-John humbled by James III-loss of the Earldom of Ross-Angus Og- Battle of Lagabraad- civil war within the Lordship-Battle of Bloody Bay-death of Angus Og-MacDonalds of Lochalsh assume control of the Lordship-Battle of Park-forfeiture of the Lordship by James IV 1493-

the consequences. James IV's policy in the western highlands-rebellion of Alexander of Lochalsh-Campbells and Gordons as royal instruments-escape of Donald Dubh-his capture-Battle of Flodden 1514 and its consequences-rebellion of Donald Galda-destruction of the Maclains of Ardnamurchan-Campbell power expanding. Donald Dubh escapes-the western clans rise to support him-his relationship with Henry VIII of England-rebellion disintegrates-death of Donald Dubh.

Chapter 3

The Mound of Pain

Origins of the Clanranald-the MacRuarie inheritance-support for the Lordship-Allan's feud with the MacKintoshes-Ranald Ban-Dugall's chiefship and subsequent murder. Election of Alexander as "captain" of Clanranald-the inheritance of John Moydartach. The Clanranald's relationship with the Frasers-Ranald Galda and the Fraser influence. Moydartach's relationship with James V-the claims of Moydartach and Ranald Galda to the chiefship of the Clanranald-their relationship with the Clanranald. Imprisonment of Moydartach by James V-imposition of Ranald Galda on the Clanranald- release of Moydartach-Ranald Galda abandons the chiefship. Donald Dubh's second rebellion-Donald Dudh supported by Moydartach. Earl of Gordon and the Frasers invade Lochaber –Frasers return alone up the Great Glen-confronted by the Clanranald at Kinlochlochy-prelude to battle-Battle of Kinlochlochy-the arrival of the Master of Lovat-death of Hugh fifth Lord Lovat chief of the Frasers-death of Ranald Galda-the role of Ben Clearch-the consequences of the battle. Earl of Gordon invades Lochaber –execution of Keppoch and Locheil. Moydartach joins Donald Dubh-he ignores overtures from Arran-Campbells invade Moidart-fail to capture Tioram. Moydartach-captured by the Queen Dowager-escapes and continues to resist Royal authority-death and legacy of Moydartach.

Chapter 4

Fire and Sword

Allan (the son of Moydartach) abandons the daughter of Alastair Crotach in favour of Janet MacLean-the MacLeods anger. Violence on Chathustail-MacLeods invade Eigg-Clanranalds on Eigg hide in Uamh Fhraing-they are discovered-they are asphyxiated by the MacLeods-description of their remains-who was responsible. The Clanranald invade Skye-MacLeods alerted-massacre at Trumpan-the fairy flag-the Battle of the Spoiling of the Dyke. The Clanranald invade Skye-Battle of the Blacksmiths Hill. Death of Allan Og-MacLeods determined on vengeance. Clanranald join the Clan Iain Mor in their feud with the MacLeans-Canna, Rum and

Eigg ravaged. Angus assumes the chiefship-MacLeods invade South Uist-Battle of Amhainn Roag-death of Angus-role of Angus's brother Donald-consequences of the feud.

Chapter 5

A House Divided

Origins of the Maclains of Ardnamurchan-history during the Lordship. John Brayach's accession to the chiefship-his relationship with James IV. Enmity between John Brayach and John Cathanach of the Clan Iain Mor over clan territories-John Brayach captures John Cathanach and sends them to James IV for trial-John Brayach overruns Isla-pursues Alexander to Antrim-John Brayach kills Alexander of Lochalsh-John rewarded further by James. The consequences of James IV's death for John Brayach-defeat of Maclains in Antrim by the Clan Iain Mor-Alexander returns to Isla-John Brayach captured-Alexander marries his daughter. Invasion of Ardnamurchan by the Clan Iain Mor and the MacLeods-Battle of Creag-an-Airgid-death of John Brayach and his sons-consideration of John Brayach's character and strategy. Campbells gain influence in Ardnamurchan through control of a Maclain heiress-Campbells gain legal title to Ardnamurchan. John Maclain supports the Clan Iain Mor in their feud with the MacLeans-MacLeans invade Ardnamurchan-Maclains in Ulster. John Og murdered by his uncle Donald-Donald killed at Battle of Leachd-nan-Saighead. Grim Faced Archibald makes his move on Ardnamurchan-Maclains become ensnared in Campbell subtlety-Campbell of Brabreck takes control of Ardnamurchan-Maclains oppressed-they join Sir James MacDonald's rebellion. Brabreck begins evictions on Ardnamurchan-Maclains rebel-their persecution by Brabreck-they turn to piracy-Campbells clear Ardnamurchan of Maclains-postscript in Kingussie.

Chapter 6

Trotternish the Crucible

The early settlement of the MacDonalds on Skye-the first chiefs of the MacDonalds of Sleat – their occupation of Trotternish and their first attempts to gain legal title to the district. They lose control to the MacLeods of Harris-they invade Trotternish-Battle of Glendale-Donald Gruamach losses control of Trotternish. Donald Gorm invades Trotternish-Donald Gorm's death at Eilean Donan-childhood of Donald Gormson-he obtains legal title to Trotternish-how this came about through Campbell auspices. The feud with the MacLeods is rekindled-separation of Donald Gorm Mor and Mary MacLeod-MacLeods invade Trotternish-Harris devastated. MacLeods invade North Uist-Sheumus-Battle of Carinish-Sheumus at Rodil-Donald

Gorm Mor invades MacLeod lands on Skye-Battle of Ben-a Chuilin-the state acts to enforce an end to the feud. Legal claim and counter claim-a settlement is reached-the emerging power of the state- the consequences of the feud.

Chapter 7

Cain and Able

Hugh the progenitor of the MacDonalds of Sleat- his marriages and unions and their offspring. Donald Gallach becomes chief-his provision for his brothers-their envy and disunity. The murder of Donald Herrach-the murder of Donald Gallach by Archibald Dubh- Archibald Dudh flees. Angus Collach outrages the people of North Uist-his execution. The death of Angus Dubh-the sons of Donald Gallach and Donald Herrach have revenge on Archibald Dubh-Donald Gruamach becomes chief-death of Paul na h-eille on North Uist-murder of Donald Gruamach's wife's relatives-her revenge. Hugh MacGilleasbuig Cleirich-his inheritance-his piracy-his entrapment of Donald Gorm Mor on Jura. Hugh appointed Baillie of Trotternish-he builds Castle Uisdean-his plotting-he is captured by Sheumus-his death and the exposure of his bones.

Chapter 8

By The Strong Arm

Origins of the MacDonalds of Keppoch-their clan lands. Their history under the Lordship-the intitial causes of their feud with the MacKintoshes. Their early raiding-Battle of Loch Earn-death of Donald. Iain Aluinn-deposed as chief. Donald Glas assumes the chiefship-raid of Clan Chattan. Ranald Mor-his part in the feud between the Clanranald and the Frasers. Feud with the Camerons-Ranald Og's relationship with the Campbells. Alasdair nan Cleas leads his clan in a raid against the MacKintoshes and Grants-capture and surrender of Inverness Castle. Alasdair joins the Catholic rebellion-accommodation with the Campbells. Feud with the MacKintoshes continues-Alasdair joins Sir James MacDonald's rebellion-he continues his raiding-his persecution of the MacGregors. He supports Sir James's last attempts to save the Clan Iain Mor-he is forced to flee abroad. The clan join Montrose-Cambells occupy Glen Spean-they are driven out. Battle of Stronachlachan. Clan join the Scottish invasion of England-disaster at Worcester-the Protectorate. Alexander becomes chief-discontent in the Clan-murder of Alexander-Iain Lom appeals for revenge. He gains support from the MacDonalds of Sleat-the Well of Heads. Clan again raid MacKintoshes and their allies-MacKintosh counter raid. Archibald becomes chief-his support of the MacLeans in their attempts to resist the Campbells- Campbells devastate clan lands. MacKintosh attempts to gain control over Glen Spean by use of the law-he is thwarted. Coll imprisoned by MacKintosh-his release. MacKintosh invades Glen Spean backed by Government troops-successful occupation-Coll prepares to drive him out. Battle of Mulroy-capture of MacKintosh-his release. Government troops occupy Glen Spean-Coll raids MacKintosh lands-Dundee intercedes. A final settlement.

Chapter 9

The Bitter Legacy of Lochalsh

The emergence of the MacDonalds of Glengarry as an independent clan. Their support for the MacDonalds of Lochalsh-Sir Donald Galda's rebellion. The inheritance of Lochalsh, Loch Carron and Loch Broom. Alexander MacDonald's imprisonment and subsequent escape- Donald Dubh's rebellion. The clan's support for John Moydartach- Kinlochlochy. MacKenzies acquire an interest in Glen Carron-their antagonism to MacDonald interests in Ross. Origins of the feud with the MacKenzies- the Mathesons and the Clan Iain Uidhir. Raid and counter raid-ambush and death of Donald of Glengarry. Bloodshed on the shores of Loch Carron- MacKenzies gain and then lose control over Strome Castle. MacDonalds raid Kishorn- legal disputes over Lochalsh. Angus MacDonald raids Torridon-MacDonalds outmanoeuvred in the courts. MacKenzies devastate Morar- Lochalsh and Glen Carron "cleansed" of MacDonalds. Angus counter attacks by invading Applecross- MacDonalds again raid Applecross. Death of Alexander MacGorrie-Angus defies his father. Angus ravages Glenshiel while Allan of Lundy raids Glenelchaig. Both clans seek allies- Angus raids Glen Carron- death of Angus. Fall and destruction of Strome Castle- Allan of Lundy raids Easter Ross- supposed massacre at Kilchrist church- MacKenzie pursuit of Allan- their retreat. Glengarry gains control Knoydart- death of Donald. The loss of Glengarry in the nineteenth century.

Chapter 10

The Lowlanders Great Hatred

The origins of the MacDonalds of Glencoe-the topography of Glencoe. The release of Donald Dubh. Raids on the Campbells- the vengeance of "mad" Colin Campbell. Further raiding against the Drummonds, MacAulays and Campbells- Battle of Glenfruin. Feud with the Stewarts of Appin- the death of Iain Abrach. Why they were so embroiled in raiding at such a late date and the shift in view of the neighbouring clans. Alastair Ruadh raids the Campbells- encounter on the slopes of Sron a'Chlachain- the Bloody Burn- further raids on the Campbells. Ranald of the Shield and the exploits of Archibald MacPhail-Archibald's raid on Strathspey.

Campbell support for Monmouth- state sanctioned retribution. James VIII deposed- Dundee's rebellion-Maclains defy King William. The Earl of Breadalbane- the Master of Stair- William demands submission. James delays releasing the loyal clans so they can submit- an example is to be made- Stair makes his plans. Alasdair is finally released by James VIII- he is delayed on his way to Inveraray- Ardkinglas takes his oath. Stair will have his example-Alasdair feels secure- Captain Robert Campbell. Argyle militia move into Glencoe- the trap is set. The massacre of Glencoe- the aftermath.

Chapter 11

Dubh Sith

Origins of the Clan Iain Mor- their role in the history of the Lordship. John Mor and John Cathanach rebel- their capture by John Brayach and their subsequent execution. Feud with the Maclains- death of James IV. The MacLeans and their territorial possessions- events on Gigha. Hector MacLean refuses to vacate the Rinnes of Isla- MacDonalds invade Mull- Privy Council rule that the Rinnes of Isla belong to the Clan Iain Mor. Further raiding- Sir James dies at the Battle of Glentasie. Angus MacDonald's and Lachlan Mor MacLean's character. Angus fails to capture Fort Gorm- MacLeans devastate Gigha- the Clan Iain Mor retaliate. MacDonalds of Sleat embroiled in the feud by Hugh- Lachlan slaughters the unsuspecting MacDonalds on Jura- MacDonald clans act in concert against the MacLeans. Angus visits Lachlan- he is held captive- he has to leave hostages and agree to MacLean ownership of the Rinnes before he is released. Lachlan captured at Mullintrae- many MacLeans beheaded- Angus releases Lachlan who is forced to give up his claim to the Rinnes. Angus devastates Tiree and invades Mull- Battle of Lecklee- MacLeans invade Kintrye- almost all the clans of the western highlands take sides. Maclain marries Janet Campbell- massacre at the wedding- Lachlan invades the small isles and Ardnamurchan- Angus invades Coll and Tiree. The loss of the Florida- the Parliament of Peace- Angus defies James VI. Angus is forced to submit by his son James. James assumes the chiefship of the Clan Iain Mor- Lachlan invades Isla- the witches warning- James prepares to meet the MacLeans. Dubh Sith- the Battle of Gruinneart- the death of Lachlan. MacLeans invade Isla- Battle of Ben Bigrie- the feud peters out.

Chapter 12

No Joy With Out Clan Donald

The inexorable rise of the Campbells- Campbell policy. The relationship between the Clan Iain Mor and the Campbells in the early sixteenth century. Archibald

Campbell exposed- the zenith of the Clan Iain Mor- James claims the Lordship- his marriage to Agnes Campbell. Angus becomes chief- war with the MacLeans and in Ireland. The Clan Iain Mor and the MacLeans weakened- the deteriorating political situation and the increasing power of the Scottish state. Angus refuses to surrender Kintrye to James VI- Angus is seized at Askomull- his son James becomes chief. James forced to cede Kintrye- Campbell intrigue. Angus duped by the Campbells- his son James held captive- Angus regains control. Internal stresses in the Clan Iain Mor- Grim faced Archibald shows his hand- the Campbells given Kintrye and Jura by James VI. Angus rebels- the rebellion falters. James MacDonald's captivity and trial- the Campbell web. Angus sells Isla to the Campbells- Dunnyveg Castle occupied — the castle is captured by MacDonald rebels- Angus Og MacDonald suppresses the rebellion- James MacDonald desperate to be set at liberty to help his clan. Angus Og deceived by the Campbells- he resists Bishop Knox- the Bishop forced to retreat. The Campbells prepare to invade Isla- James MacDonald makes some desperate offers- Angus Og defies the King- the Campbells invade Isla- the fall of Dunnyveg Castle. James MacDonald escapes- he is joined by Coll Coitach- rebellion on Isla- Dunnyveg captured. James takes control of Kintyre- the Campbells prepare to do the King's will. James's forces in Kintrye collapse- Campbells invade Isla- James flees from Isla.

Appendix

Ireland The Maelstrom

The Gallowglasses- methods of warfare and maintenance. The early Gallowglass settlements in Ireland- the disinheritance of Alastair Og. Black John and his descendents- decline of the use of Galowglasses. The Clan Iain Mor in Ireland- political reality and aspirations. The origins of their possessions in Antrim- the Bisset legacy. Alexander flees to the Glens- John Brayach fails to capture him. Alexander establishes a firm hold on the Glens- he reaches an accord with James V. Alexander threatens English interests in Ireland- Conn O'Neill is forced to submit to Henry VIII. The Clan Iain Mor desire the Route- Donald Dubh's rebellion. Sorley Boy emerges as an effective leader of the Clan Iain Mor in Ireland. Croft's campaign- disaster at Rathlin- it disintegrates. Sorley Boy defeats the English at Carrickfergus and conquers the Route. Sydney's campaign- battle in the passes- Glenarm falls to the English. Failure of Fitzwalter's campaign- Sorley Boy appointed Captain of the Route. Sussex's campaign of 1588- Rathlin occupied- Kintrye attacked- English exhaustion. MacQuillins attempt to regain control of the Route- Battle of Slieve-an-Aura. The rise of Shane O'Neill- his hostility to the Clan Iain Mor. Sussex's invasion of 1561- Battle of Monaghan. The Clan Iain Mor under pressure- the English seek an understanding with Sorley Boy- Shane discomforts another English invasion. Shane recognized as The O'Neill by the English- he attacks the Clan Iain Mor in 1564- diversions on the Bann- Shane strikes 1565. MacDonalds overrun in the Glens- Battle of Glentasie-death of James and the capture of Sorley Boy. Elizabeth I acts to curb Shane's power- Sydney attacks Shane in 1566. Shane asks the Clan Iain Mor for an alliance- he is killed at Cushendun and Sorley Boy released. Sorley Boy re-establishes his clan's power base- his support for Turlough O'Neill. Essex's campaign of 1573- his army is worn down. Essex's campaign of 1575- the massacre on Rathlin- English defeated at Carrickfergus. The emergence of Irish and Scottish branches of the Clan Iain Mor- O'Neills and MacDonalds unite against the English- Turlough loses his nerve. Perott's campaign of 1584- he occupies Dunluce Castle. Sorley Boy counter attacks and drives Sydney and Bagenal out of the Glens and Route. The English and the Clan Iain Mor are exhausted- the death of Sorley's son. Sorley Boy reaches terms with the English- the Clan Iain Mor is granted legal title to the Glens and Route. Sorley's death- the emergence of the MacDonalds of Antrim.

Chapter 1

Through The Looking Glass

To resent some action which one regards as harmful, whether real or imaginary, is a characteristic which makes us human. To plan and then possibly execute some form of retaliation is a process which lies close to most of our hearts. This desire for retribution and as we see it justice is tempered by our logic, our fear of further retaliation and the constraints imposed by society, whether directly by constructs such as the law, or indirectly by our moral sense which has been formed by our cultural legacy, whether it is by religion or our understanding of reason and tolerance. To-day there is a significant gap between desiring retribution and attempting to enforce it, although in the simpler world of the play ground the unrestrained ability to act is more self-evident. How many of us have enjoyed the idea of achieving justice for ourselves by our own actions, even if in the cold grey light of day our reason prevents it?

This book describes the clan feuds the MacDonalds[1] after the fall of the Lordship of the Isles in 1494 to the early seventeenth century when various factors led to the end of open clan warfare. It is therefore concerned largely with the sixteenth century although some understanding of the influence of the preceding centuries is essential.[2] The sixteenth century was a time of great turbulence for all the clans and is known as Linn nan Creach (The Age of Forays); it saw the gradual emergence of the clans into those entities which are recognized today and which were so cruelly broken at Culloden Moor in 1746 and the years that followed.

When one reads of the feuds that erupted between the clans in the sixteenth century, with their apparently trivial causes, their violence, degradation and suffering one is often left with a sense of bewilderment as to why these people hazarded everything to support their mutual dignity. The reader can develop an attitude of "a plague on all their houses" as these peoples behaviour seems to be relentlessly ruthless and violent. When compared to their world, we (those of us that live in western democracies) live in an environment of material plenty in which many of us do not even know the price of basic necessities like bread or milk; we are part of well ordered and complex society. This society is supported by global economic systems and is suffused with a cultural legacy based on those of the renaissance and thus ultimately on our heritage from ancient Rome and Greece. This legacy, embraces the rights of the individual, democracy, self-determination and for Christians the emphasis placed on forgiveness and love in the New Testament. These rights are supported by a complex plethora of laws which are in

---

[1] Throughout this book the spelling used is MacDonald although many differing spellings were used, for example, MacDonnell, MacConnell and Donalds. The MacDonalds often referred to themselves as the Clan Cholla, while some of the clans were known by the name of their founder, for example, the MacIains of Glencoe, the MacIains of Ardnamurchan and the Clan Iain Mor.

[2] Some of the feuds spill over into the seventeenth century while a few events described in this book take place towards the end of the seventeenth century.

their turn accepted, in the main, by the societies in which we live. The world inhabited by the clans at the beginning of the sixteenth century was very different, and this chapter attempts to give some explanation as to why their history was so unremittingly violent and self- destructive.

Clan feuds were brutal and unforgiving, they were fuelled by a complex web of personnel and family relationships, and for the participants they were inescapable and terrifying. By their nature they involved extended family groups either tearing at each other or struggling with other families for revenge, honour, power and economic resources. They involved murder, betrayal, massacre and full scale war which on occasions led to the annihilation of clans.

The participants lived in a time when anarchy,[3] starvation and disease were an ever present threat, and their lives were, by our standards, unremittingly hard. Clan feuds were often on a small scale; one would know who it was, who had murdered your father or who had cut down your son in battle. Even if one could not lay the blame at any individual's door you would know which clan was responsible. To add to this heady mix the clansmen knew that defeat would expose their families to enormous hardship and possibly starvation, because all of these societies were operating on the economic margins.

The history of clan feuds is not unremittingly gloomy; they include notable examples of heroism, generosity, self-sacrifice and loyalty. Events are usually suffused with a clan's loyalty to their own kindred,[4] right or wrong, and willingness to hazard all for ones own people. Clan feuds provided the environment in which heroes like John Moydartach[5] and villains such as Hugh Gilleasbuig[6] were able to express their personalities to the full. An account of clan feuds exposes human nature at its most raw.

The various clans of MacDonalds[7] which emerged after the fall of the Lordship of the Isles[8] occupied territories from the Glens of Antrim in Ireland to the areas around Loch Broom which border Assynt in the far north. They were present along almost the entire western seaboard of the highlands.

---

[3] The inability of the Scottish executive to maintain its authority in the western highlands is a recurring theme throughout this period.

[4] This was at least true of the commonality but their are notable exceptions amongst the leading families

[5] See chapter 3

[6] See chapter7

[7] These were the Clan Iain Mor, the MacIains of Ardnamurchan, the MacDonalds of Keppoch, the MacIains of Glencoe, the MacDonalds of Glengarry, the MacDonalds of Sleat, the Clanranald and the MacDonalds of Lochalsh.

[8] See chapter 2

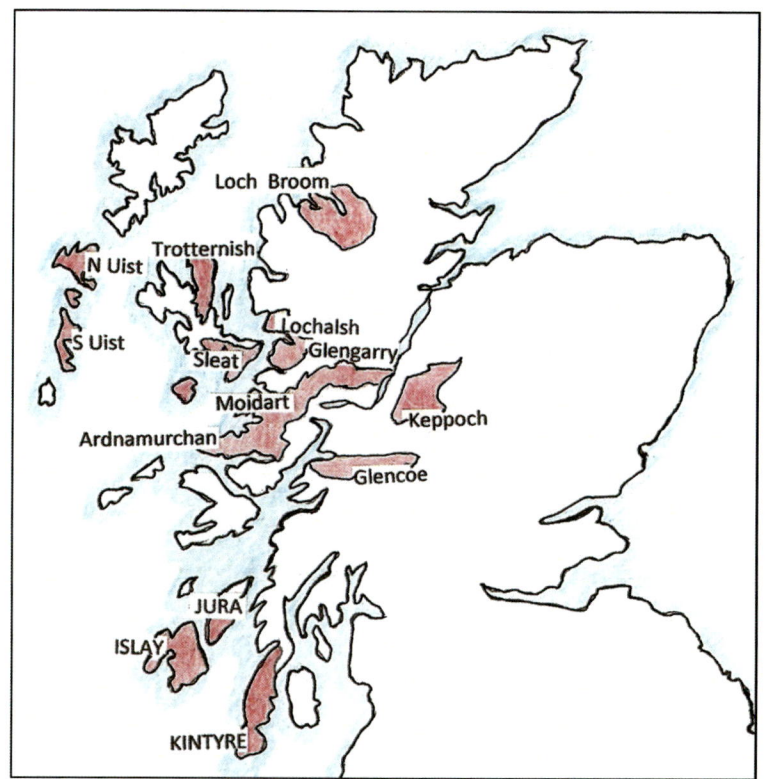

Territories of the Clan Donald c1510

To understand something of their lives and how they interpreted their world, a brief description of the geography of the western highlands, the sixteenth century economy in the region, their social organization and aspects of their culture is necessary.

The western highlands of Scotland are on the same latitude as central Canada and southern Norway. Although the climate is greatly ameliorated by the effects of the North Atlantic, especially the warm currents of the Gulf Stream, this northerly latitude causes long dark winters and short summers. In the depths of winter there are only a few short hours of daylight while in the summer there is up to twenty hours, the sun hardly slipping below the horizon. The amount of daylight and temperatures mean that the growing season is at least two months shorter than the south of the British Isles, starting in late May and finishing in September.[9]

The North Atlantic was also a major influence on their lives; throughout the autumn and winter there is often a continual series of low pressure systems with their resulting storms which can continue with unabated fury for weeks at a time.

---

[9] The wild grasses which were the basis of agriculture in the sixteenth century are much slower to respond to the seasonal changes than the hybrid ryegrasses which cover more than 90% of Britain's grasslands to-day. These grasses also yield considerably less energy value for the livestock than their modern cousins.

On the more low lying and exposed islands these storms would give rise to severe flooding especially when combined with a spring high tide. The Exchequer Rolls of 1542 mention that the rentals due for North Uist were reduced due to extensive flooding. These weather systems can also be active even in the height of summer as they smash into the western highlands. The long dark sterile winters which were dominated by Atlantic storms had a profound effect on the daily lives of the population with their primitive agriculture. It placed an enormous emphasis on agricultural success in the short summer months as any failure would result in hunger, even starvation, by the late winter. The storms prevented any communication between the island communities for weeks at a time and increased their isolation and vulnerability.

The topography of the western highlands is an intricate pattern of islands bordered by a rugged coast cut into by many drowned glacial valleys; this complex pattern is further fragmented by the ancient Cambrian Mountains which dominate the landscape, and often rise to a height of several thousand feet, they are interspersed with steep valleys (glens). These turbulent seas, the islands, and the mountain ranges, when combined with the bleak peat bogs and rocky glens had a profound impact on the development of human societies. It tended to lead to small scale and isolated communities who had to be largely self-sufficient. The highlands have been parcelled up into districts since the early medieval period.

Islands and Traditional Districts of the Western Isles

By the sixteenth century there was already some deforestation of the landscape especially on the Outer Hebrides; however the ancient Caledonian Forest dominated by the Scots fir but also containing oak, ash and hazel held sway over the majority of the land.[10] The peat bogs and moor land were less extensive than they are today as the tree root systems facilitated drainage of the large quantities of rain water. Areas of fertile grassland were very limited and usually

---

[10] Fragments of the ancient forest still survive, for example, the Black Wood of Rannoch in Glenstrathfarrar.

confined to the sea shore,[11] or the sheltered edges of the streams that are found in the bottom of every glen.

The natural fauna of the highlands was more diverse and plentiful in the sixteenth century than it is today, due in part to the forest and the limited technologies available to the population. Herds of red deer were jealously guarded by the chiefs;[12] while venison did not contribute a significant element to the economy it made a welcome supply of fresh meat in the hard winter months. Rabbit and hare were snared at every opportunity. Wolves were still common in the highlands, their howling adding to the fear and loathing the highlands engendered in travellers from the lowlands of Scotland. Wolves were sufficiently common for a burgess of Inverness to blame them for the disappearance of one of his cattle on the outskirts of the town in 1569. They would have been an ever present threat to livestock in the highlands.

Seals were hunted with bow and arrow in the rocky inlets,[13] providing a high calorie addition to the food supply. At low tide cockles and whelks were gathered from the exposed sands as they had been since the time of earliest hunter gatherers.[14] The seas which are so intimately interlaced with the land contained many species of fish, which formed an important source of protein for the coastal populations. Herring, mackerel and bass were among the more common coastal species caught; there were, for example, regulations on Raasay that all the fishing rods should be of the same length so that all the men should have an equal chance.[15] Salmon were also caught in the rivers when they returned from the Atlantic to spawn.

The hunting of the prolific numbers of sea birds that breed on the cliffs was a common activity in the spring months. The men would be lowered over the cliff edges in small baskets, and while swinging precariously would snare the birds and collect the eggs from the nests.[16] In the remotest communities like the island of Saint Kilda wildfowling formed the most important source of food.

Despite the useful incrementation to the diet by the products of hunting and fishing, agriculture was the mainstay of the highlanders food supply. Apart from the difficulties imposed upon them by the short growing season the communities had

---

[11] An example of this is the distinctive vegetation of the Machair which grows on the sand dunes of the Outer Hebrides.

[12] A dispute between a gamekeeper and some poachers lit the fuse which ignited a bitter feud between the MacKenzies and the MacDonalds of Glengarry, see chapter 9.

[13] There is a reference to the sons of the chief of Clanranald murdering their brother while out hunting seals.

[14] During the sixteenth century Ruari the Turbulent (chief of the McNeills of Barra) was kidnapped and taken to Edinburgh to face justice. A near contemporary document describes the lamentations of the women of the clan who were gathering cockles on the sea shore as they saw their chief taken from them.

[15] In 1583 during an attack on the MacLeods of Harris by the Clanranald the initial warning of their presence was given by five McLeods who were out fishing (see chapter 4).

[16] There are descriptions of boats returning to Lewis from the outlying islands laden with birds and eggs.

to contend with thin acidic soils,[17] which were often waterlogged and liberally dosed with rocks and boulders. Oats and barley were sown, wheat being unsuitable to the difficult environment. The small plots of land known as rigs would bare little resemblance to fields of cereals we see today. The crop would have been much thinner, interspersed with many types of weed. Today one seed of oats will return approximately thirty while in the sixteenth century in the highlands one would expect a return of no more than three or four. This was of course assuming that one was able to successfully harvest the crop which the storms and short growing season always put at risk. Cereals were not only sown in the rigs but also on any small patch of viable ground which could be as small as a couple of square meters.

A problem faced by all farmers in the western highlands is the inability of the cereals to ripen. Even today it is not an uncommon sight to watch the combines harvesting the cereals with snow on the ground. Often the harvest was not started till October. There are several nineteenth century accounts of the sheaths of oats been blown into the sea or onto a neighbours land by the violent autumnal gales.[18] In the worst years the oats had to be left to be desiccated by the first frosts rather than by ripening. The oats and barley were ground on small hand querns and made into small round cakes to be cooked over the smouldering peat fires. The problems of preserving the meagre store of grain over the winter would have been immense with the continual rain, the depredations of the rodent population and the materials available to them to build their grain stores.

Barley and oats were also used to produce beer and whisky. Brogac was a sweetened malt liquor which roughly translates as "the stimulation"; this was easy to produce and was common to many houses in the sixteenth century.[19]Whisky was also consumed in copious quantities; there was a milder blend which was known as trestarig which was distilled three times and then there was "stop the breath" whisky which was more common in the Isles, and was distilled four times. Both brogac and trestarig were consumed in excessive quantities during feasts put on by the chief. These feasts could last for several days and formed an important element in the cohesion between the chief and his clansmen. It has been argued that one of the underlying causes of clan feuds was to deprive clans of the ability to have feasts by stealing their cattle. This would have diminished the prestige of the chief of the clan and thus of the clan itself.[20]

There is a description of a feast given by a chief of the seventeenth century which gives a flavour of these occasions. "When the Hebridean chiefs and captains returned...after a successful expedition, they summoned their friends and clients to

---

[17] The acidity of the soil was reduced by the manuring of the land with large quantities of seaweed.

[18] The sheaths could be recovered by the owner as each family had a distinctive way of tying the sheaths.

[19] There was a steady stream of laws produced by the burgesses of Inverness to restrict the manufacture of brogac. This was because large quantities of barley were being diverted from food production.

[20] R.A.Dodgshon. "From Chiefs to Landlords."

a grand entertainment. Bards…pipers and harpists had an undisputed right to appear… These entertainments were wild and cheerful… The bards sang, and the young women danced. The old warrior related the gallant actions of his youth, and struck the young men with ambition and fire. The whole tribe filled the chieftain's hall. Trunks of trees covered with moss were laid, in the order of a table, from one end of the hall to the other. Whole deer and oxen were roasted and laid before (the crowd).After the feast was over they had… entertainments… Then the females retired, and the old and young warriors sat down in order from the chief, according to their proximity in blood to him. The harp was then touched, the song was raised and the sliga-crechin, or drinking shell, went round." [21]

Given the problems associated with cereal production and their cultural preferences, livestock, especially cattle, were the joy of the highland husbandman in the sixteenth century. Besides cattle, sheep and goats were also kept. The livestock were kept in the "infield" during the winter which was more sheltered and fertile. Apart from the grazing which had been laid up during the summer the cattle were kept alive by being fed any available fodder such as hay and even the old thatch from the roofs. Occasionally they were bled, the blood being mixed with the oats to make "black puddings". During the summer months the cattle were taken to the higher and more remote pastures by the women and children. The pastures were known as shielings (an airdh); the women lived in small remote shacks which they refurbished each season. Here in the high pastures they milked the cows and made butter and cheese in this short time of plenty for man and beast. The men stayed behind repairing the houses, hunting and fishing.

Most of the non-breeding stock was slaughtered in the autumn; the beef either being salted in barrels or dry salted and smoked while hanging in the roof rafters. When an animal was slaughtered nothing was wasted; for example, traditionally a haggis skin is made from the stomach of a sheep. The hides were tanned and cured and used for a variety of purposes, including shoes, belts and armour or exported to the lowlands.

The sheep were much smaller than those we see today and would have resembled the Soay sheep. They were also taken to the higher ground in the summer and brought back in the winter; at low tide they were driven down to the sea shore to graze on the seaweed. They were sheared or plucked[22] in early summer, the wool was waulked (this was a process by which the wool was cleaned and separated by continual treading), it was then carded (separated by combing) and then spun. The wool was then dyed using local plants and woven into a series of patterns of different thickness.

This last process was the origin of tartan which today is so intimately connected with all things Scottish. These tartans were not rigidly set out like the Victorian tartans used today to demonstrate which clan an individual belongs to. The style and pattern of weave was handed done from mother to daughter, so that patterns

---

[21] Martin.

[22] Soay sheep moult their wool in early summer, so that the wool can be just pulled of them.

were very similar in family groups. Districts tended to have similar coloured tartans as the plants used to dye the cloth varied from place to place.[23] In the sixteenth century the main method of recognition of the clansmen was the use of specific plants worn on their clothing; for the MacDonalds it was heather.

The wide variety of food resources exploited by the highlanders gave them a healthy diet in times of plenty. However, during the winter months the population was often stalked by hunger and diseases associated with malnutrition and climate.[24] They had to give every care to their cattle to nurse them through the winter months, these animals being of huge importance to the survival of the family.

There were no towns in the highlands in the sixteenth century, although there were several market towns on the edge of the highland line.[25] In the north the largest town was Inverness, which in the sixteenth century comprised of no more than a few hundred houses. It was dominated by its castle and surrounded by a foul smelling ditch into which all the towns refuse was dumped. The town was populated by artisans and merchants who provided services and markets for the highlanders. The inhabitants spoke English and sometimes Gaelic as a second language. Within a few miles of the town the population spoke no English and were fully immersed in Gaelic culture. The townspeople rarely travelled to these areas regarding them as strange and frightening. A contemporary English observer wrote, "The highlands of Scotland are but little known even to the inhabitants of the low country of Scotland, for they have ever dreaded the difficulties and dangers of travelling among the mountains; and when some ordinary occasion has obliged any one of them to such a progress, he has, generally speaking, made his testament before setting out, as though he were entering upon a long and dangerous sea voyage, wherein it was very doubtful if he should ever return." In many respects Inverness was a frontier town.

The highland population lived in small clusters of round houses with their associated sheds, called clachans.[26] They consisted of about six houses all built closely together and sometimes interconnected by the adjoining sheds. Clachans would have had a population of between thirty and sixty souls, and probably represented extended family groups. Their distribution was determined by the available local resources and were randomly scattered over every type of land.

---

[23] Some clans may have had identifiable tartans. This is suggested by a sixteenth century document, which states that, the MacLeans had an annual rent payable in black, white and green cloth, the colours of their present tartan.

[24] It is probable that given the cold, the damp and the scarcity of food that TB was a major contributor to premature death.

[25] The highland line was the border between Gaelic highland Scotland and the lowlands; it should be seen as an area of cultural overlap, often dozens of miles wide, where the traveller gradually passed from one world to the other.

[26] The Black Houses which so readily spring to mind when one thinks of highland houses did not develop for several centuries and are associated with crofting.

The clachans disappeared in the early nineteenth century when the crofting system was introduced into the highlands.[27] The abandonment of the clachans exacerbated the break down in the social cohesion of the clans and was often fiercely resisted by the community. In the New Statistical Account[28] there are descriptions of this change of settlement pattern. The main emphasis of the work is to emphasize the increased levels of efficiency in agricultural production as the runrig system, associated with the clachans (see below), was abandoned for individual crofts.[29] The emphasis is on the reward to the industrious individual who is no longer held back by their less capable neighbours. The early emigrants to America (especially the women) cited the disintegration of social groups associated with the clachans, as one of the main reasons for them emigrating.[30] The New Statistical Account also comments in the decline in incidences of typhus once the people had moved into crofts. It is clear that the cramped and unsanitary conditions which pervaded in the clachans exposed the inhabitants to the risk of catching this terrible disease during the sixteenth century.

The house walls were constructed using dressed stone on the sides, the centre being filled with rubble. They were several feet thick to prevent the penetration of the wind and rain. The roofs were made of turfs or/and straw which were then held down by ropes which in their turn were held in place by rocks tied to each end. There were no chimneys the peat smoke either escaping from a small hole in the roof or through the doorway.[31]

These communities were surrounded by rigs (ploughable strips in the "infield"); these were small irregular plots which were delineated by shallow ditches whose other purpose was to drain the soil. Each clachan was surrounded by many dozens of rigs, each family being allotted a different series of rigs perhaps on an annual basis by the maor (village officer). The advantage of the continual redistribution of the rigs and the irregularity of the rigs themselves was that each family would receive a mixture of the good and bad land available to the community. This system is known as runrig.

Beyond these rigs, known as the infield because of its more intensive cultivation was the head dyke. The dyke delineated the boundary between the infield and the outfield. The head dyke was built of layers of turf and stood about six feet high. In the spring a breach was made in the head dyke and the livestock were driven onto the outfield and then later were taken to the shieling. The outfield was less

---

[27] It is this settlement pattern which we see today with individual houses sitting in some sixty acres.

[28] Rev. F. MacRae 1837.

[29] It does not comment on the problems faced by the weaker members of clan society once the communal life style of clachans and runrig were abandoned.

[30] B. Lawson

[31] During the 45 rising one highlander was exasperated by the Prince's inability to stay in his house or to stay outside. It is likely that he found the smoky environment inside the house hard to bare.

intensively farmed and was used mainly for grazing, certain areas being left fallow to slowly recuperate while new areas were broken in.

Castle Tioram

At the centre of clan life were the various castles. There were usually several castles in a clan's territory; for example, the MacDonalds of Sleat had up to four castles that were occupied at any one time.[32] They were either held directly by the chief or held by an important sept of the clan.[33] By the sixteenth century the castles of the western isles had been occupied for hundreds of years, for example, Castle Tioram, which was built in the late thirteenth century by the MacRuaries (the ancestors of the Clanranald).

One exception to this general rule is Castle Uisdean which was built by the infamous Hugh Gilleasbuig in the sixteenth century; it is a bleak block house structure on the shores of Skye. The clan castles were relatively small and usually situated on a rocky promontory on the coast, controlling strategic areas of water whether they were the entrance to lochs like Strome Castle, or narrows between land masses, like Castle Camus. Due to the rugged terrain, the sea was used as the medium of communication and bound the whole area together; galleys would continually sail between these coastal castles. Castles were rarely besieged as clans

---

[32] For their names and location see chapter 6.
[33] Septs were family branches of the clan or represented other families who were allied to the clan.

usually lacked either the will or the resources to undergo a long siege.[34] The main purpose of castles was to passively control the surrounding districts by their very presence. For the clan they also reflected the prestige of their chief and therefore of themselves as well as providing the background for clan feasts. For long periods the castles were left with only a couple of watchmen the most senior of whom was known as the Cockman,[35] Martin, in his travels through the western highlands in the late seventeenth century recounts that the Cockman of the MacNeill's castle of Castlebay would still not allow him access to the castle despite it being in a fairly ruinous condition without the permission of the chief.

In the sixteenth century the chiefs were starting to construct substantial houses for themselves which they occupied during the breaks in the violence. One rare surviving example is The Laird's House at Pitcastle in Atholl, built by Duncan Robertson in the sixteenth century. The ground floor has a sitting room and a public room while the upper floor contained the bedrooms.

The economy of the highlands in the sixteenth century was undeveloped and the overriding element was that of self-sufficiency and barter over short distances. There was always a shortage of coinage and the chiefs and gentlemen of the clans were becoming aware of their financial poverty when they compared themselves to the magnates of the Scottish lowlands. They were hampered in their attempts to trade by their different culture and language, and the complete lack of any roads in the highlands during this period,[36] the lowlands being only accessible by twisting mountain tracks. A more tangible hindrance to them was the monopoly of trade that the burgesses of towns like Inverness held over large tracts of the highlands.

There is an account in the sixteenth century records of Inverness of a MacGregor trading between Glen Urquhart and Perth; the burgesses arrested the unfortunate entrepreneur and he was forced to recall his goods. These goods give us a useful insight into the type of small scale trade which occurred between many individuals and the markets of the south. They included twenty dozen lamb skins, twelve dozen kid skins, six dozen calf skins and five stones of wool.

The burgesses were usually trading on a grander scale, acting as the middle men in the trade in timber,[37] seal oil for lamps, salted beef, hides, salmon and some cattle when the clans were within a reasonable distance of the markets.[38] Barrels of salted fish were also exported and further money was raised by the chiefs selling the right to anchor in safe bays like Lochmaddy in North Uist. The income from these relatively low value exports was not enough to satisfy the growing demand

---

[34] An exception was the MacKenzie siege of Castle Strome, see chapter 9.

[35] In 1539 when Donald Gorm MacDonald besieged Eilean Donnan, it was only defended by three men.

[36] There were no roads until General Wade built the military roads in the early eighteenth century.

[37] There are accounts of timber being floated down Loch Ness from the forests of Glengarry in the eighteenth century.

[38] The droving system which embraced the entire highland region was not to be developed for another century.

for imports from the upper echelons of highland society, quite apart from the needs of the "common" people. These included high quality steel from as far away as Toledo in central Spain, linen, books and large quantities of wine from France for the chiefs and gentlemen while the clansmen could not afford to buy grain in times of scarcity. Money was also required for maintaining their dignity when the chiefs made their ever more frequent visits to the Scottish court during the later sixteenth century.

Different clans attempted to increase their income in many diverse and often imaginative ways. The clans near the highland line like the MacGregors were not adverse to the odd protection racket, while others took to piracy and raided any passing merchantman. Amongst these pirates; the most feared were the McIains of Ardnamurchan and the MacNeills of Barra. Even the Lords of the Isles were highly susceptible to English gold, receiving considerable sums in exchange for military intervention against Scotland. The arrival of the battered remnants of the Spanish Armada saw the chiefs employing the sailors as auxiliaries in their feuds while stripping the galleons of useful articles. The consequences of shipwreck were enjoyed by the whole community and no doubt ships were lured onto the rocks on occasions.

Compared to the rest of the British Isles the economy of the highlands was rudimentary, being agrarian and largely self-sufficient. The population lived in material poverty; the lack of agricultural surpluses resulted in the inability of these societies to become more complex by specialization. When this was combined with the highlanders love of their cultural heritage this led to relative stagnation. Although the clan system did evolve it did not keep pace with the rate of change in the rest of the British Isles. The relative simplicity of their essentially self-sufficient economy meant that they were impervious to any form of economic manipulation by the Scottish state. It was one of the factors which rendered the power of the state ineffectual in the western highlands until the early seventeenth century. A recurring theme of this book will be the inability of the Scottish state to act effectively in the western highlands. Apart from the difficult topography and the bellicosity of the clans the main reason may have been that the Kings of Scotland did not regard any advantages they would achieve to be worth the cost; given their own impoverished condition.

The Gaelic word, clan, translates as children, and this reflects the view the highlanders took of the way their society was constructed. The social organization of highland society in the sixteenth century was based on a series of complex webs of interrelationships which they had brought with them from Ireland a thousand years before. During this period highland social structure regressed to a form which in many aspects was more similar to Iron Age Ireland than their own immediate past. In the preceding two centuries the Lords of the Isles had had political interaction not only with Edinburgh, but also England and the continent.[39] The

---

[39] An example of this was the capture of John, first Lord of the Isles, at the battle of Poitiers in 1356 while fighting as an ally of the King of France against Edward III (see chapter2).

chiefs of the western highlands during the sixteenth century were often isolated from the political intrigue in Edinburgh let alone events in London or Paris. The initial penetration of feudalism into the highlands during the reign of Malcolm Canmore had been diluted with many of the Anglo-Norman families establishing their own clans and becoming indistinguishable from the original Gaelic families.[40]

During the sixteenth century there were innumerable problems caused by the differences between Feudal and Gaelic law; a failure by various parties to appreciate the differences between the two legal systems, even by the Scottish state. This duality in the legal system was the cause of much bad feeling and many feuds. Without getting bogged down in the detail it is useful to understand the fundamental differences. The feudal system was maintained on the principle of service, an individual received rights which were determined by his service. This relationship was practised from the king down to the lowest levels of society. This in its turn meant that the superior at any given level of society had complete power of those below him. This power was reinforced by a strict adherence to the practice of primogenitor.

The clan system was maintained on the principle of blood relationship, in which the interests of one were the interests of all. Clan societies believed that all levels of society had inalienable rights and that ultimately a chief governed by the consent of the clan. There are many examples of chiefs being deposed by their clans because in some way they were regarded as being unfit.[41]

The interpretation of the relationship between the chief as "father" and the clansmen as "children" can only be taken so far, as unlike a patriarchal family; their society was based on a mutuality of interest. However this interpretation of clan society was to endure well after the period covered by this book. During the battle of Culloden in 1746, Alexander seventeenth chief of the MacDonalds of Keppoch advanced alone when the clan hung back, shouting, "My God, have the children of my clan forsaken me?"

The commonality of the clan can best be descrbed by the ancient Irish word Tuath; they were connected to the chief either by varying degrees of blood relationship or by mutually agreed absorption.[42] The people of the clan regarded themselves as having duthchas which translates as kindness, this in its turn meant that they had an inalienable right to a part of the clan lands and they had a direct link with the chief's ancestral lineage. These rights were in exchange for their loyalty and military service to the chief. As the century went on a discrepancy developed between the clan's belief in duthchas and the leases (tacks) granted by the chief to the gentlemen of the clan. The chiefs and gentlemen (tacksmen) were, by the mid-seventeenth century becoming involved more and more intimately with

---

[40] For example, the Frasers.
[41] The Clanranald deposed Dugall, their chief, and forbade his descendents from the chiefship. They then elected his uncle as chief. This was legitimate under Gaelic law but clearly not under Feudal law.
[42] Families from clans which had been destroyed agreed to become members of other clans in exchange for protection.

the monetary economy of the south, while the commonality were still immersed in the rights and obligations of the past.

The chief provided land for his people, protection in time of war, and was the anchor point for their own understanding of their past. He was also expected to be generous to his clan by providing days of feasting[43] and by his courage to uphold the dignity of his people. The clan would support the chief in his position by supplying him with all the products and services he required. This exchange is known as calp, the rules of which were well understood by the people, for example, on the death of the clansman the chief was entitled to the best horse or cow in the family's possession. On the other hand if a family fell into destitution the chief was expected to help them with a gift of livestock.[44] The clan's main obligation was to support him in time of war, their loyalty knew few bounds and they were usually prepared to sacrifice everything in support of their chief. There is nobility in the way the clan adhered to their chief, despite the deaths of fathers, brother, sons and uncles, and the murder, eviction and starvation of the women and children, and on occasions clans would support their chief and each other till they were exterminated. This degree of loyalty was only achieved by each member of the clan believing that they were part of one larger family.

During the sixteenth century the Cinntighe, the gentry of the clan, held a position in clan society between the chief and his family and the tuath (commonality).[45] They were described as tacksmen from their being granted tacks (leases), of extensive lands within the clan territory. These tacks were often of considerable size and could be several thousand acres. The tacksmen were usually close blood relatives[46] of the chief, being uncles or cousins, and were responsible not only for administering the clan lands but also for commanding clan "regiments" during war. In the subsequent chapters they will be referred to as gentlemen. The gentlemen would also form a body guard for the chief, they would advise him on policy and maintain the interests of the clan should the chief become incompetent. The chief would often foster his children with the family of a gentleman. This practice would greatly strengthen the bonds which held the clan together.

In clan society there was a significant degree of specialization, although the vast majority of the people were occupied with agriculture. The clan would have one or more families of smiths who were responsible for the manufacture and repair of weapons as well as agricultural implements such as hand scythes. This occupation was hereditary, the knowledge being handed down from father to son. Each smith

---

[43] The unfortunate comment by Ranald Galda that perhaps a few chickens would have done instead of the roasting oxen at a feast at Castle Tioram did not endear him to the Clanranald. See chapter three.

[44] The practice of calp was to continue in the Outer Hebrides till the eighteenth century.

[45] It was not till later that other classes of clansmen evolved, for example, wadstters and the system of steelbow.

[46] This was not always the case, for example, amongst the McDonalds of Sleat some of the tacksmen came from other septs of the clan, like the Nicolsons and McQueen, who were not related by blood.

was supported by a farm, for example, the family of MacRuarii were the smiths to the MacDonalds of Sleat in the district of Trotternish and were supported from the farm at Balvicilleriabhaich. The smith was held in awe by his community, due to his ability to convert iron ore into steel, and took on a mystical significance when they were involved in folk tales which recounted ancient clan battles like Beinn a Ghoba.[47]

From a cultural perspective the most important position was occupied by the clan bards who also performed the role of historian. This post was also hereditary, the son learning by heart the poems, which recorded the origins and the history of the clan, from his father. These poems were extremely long and they would take days to recite during the feasts held in the halls of the castle. The poets would often lie on the ground for many hours in a trancelike condition either memorizing poems or composing new ones. If the line should fail then the resident bard would take on a nephew to be an apprentice. The most famous line of bards was the family of MacVurich who were retained by the chiefs of the Clanranald. Throughout this book MacVurich is often cited as a source, these references will refer to one or other of this family.

During the Lordship of the Isles the MacVurichs were bards to the island lords, but after their fall they adhered to the Clanranald. They received their education in Ireland and were fluent in Gaelic, English and Latin. They were maintained by the farm of Stelligarry in Moidart, this farm was made available to them for generation after generation.[48] The MacVurichs were not only poets but also historians; they were responsible for recording clan history in the Red and Black Books of Clanranald. For the modern reader there is a problem of interpretation of all clan histories from the time of the MacVurichs to the Victorians, in that they are permeated with a liberal amount of subjectivity. They are written with a desire to please and entertain a readership which was assumed to be partisan. A clan's defeats or the atrocities they committed are often glossed over, while their victories are described in detail and the discomfort of their enemies is described with relish. This book, although written from a MacDonald perspective and being sympathetic to this great clan, has attempted to avoid the worst excesses of this tradition.

Sixteenth century Gaelic poetry, while continually evolving, was generally archaic in style and content. Its function was not only to amuse and inform but also to inspire the people by drawing on a "golden past", a view shared by the audience. The style of this poetry was repetitious and hyperbolic, as was the ancient poetry of Ireland. MacVurich writes on the death of Donald Dubh,[49]

---

[47] See chapter 5.
[48] This tradition continued till 1746. By the early 1800's the family was completely illiterate.
[49] The death of Donald Dubh was the end of the direct line of the Lords of the Isles, see chapter 2.

Alas for those who have lost that company; alas for those who
have parted from that society; for no race is as Clan Donald, a
noble race, strong of courage.
There was no counting of their bounty; there was no
Reckoning of their gifts; their nobles knew...no end of
generosity...
For sorrow and for sadness, I have forsaken wisdom and
Learning; on their account, I have forsaken all things; it is no
joy without Clan Donald.

Another famous MacDonald poet, Iain Lom, writing two centuries later,
followed the traditional heroic style. This extract cruelly celebrates the catastrophe
which befell the Campbells at Inverlochy. During the civil war they were cut to
pieces by the clans they had ousted, under the command of Alasdair MacColla, the
fearsome MacDonald general who returned for vengeance from Ireland. One can
imagine his audiences delight at hearing it.

You remember the place called the Tawny Field?
It got a fine dose of manure;
not the dung of sheep or goats,
but Campbell blood well congealed.

To Hell with you if I care for your plight,
as I listen to your children's distress,
lamenting the band that went to battle,
the howling of the women of Argyll.

Alasdair of the sharp, biting blades,
if you had the heroes of Mull with you,
you would have stopped those that got away
as the dulse-eating rabble took to their heels.

Alasdair, son of handsome Colla,
skilled hand at cleaving castles,
you put to flight the Lowland pale-face;
what kale they had taken came out again.

During the sixteenth century a new style of song poetry developed, in which each line had a fixed number of stressed syllables which gave a rhythm to the stanzas. One of the most beautiful of these is "Clan Gregor outlawed" which in many ways soulfully captures the dislocation felt by so many highland communities.

I sit here alone by the level roadway,
Trying to meet in with a fugitive
Coming from Ben Cruachan of the Mist
One who will give me news of Clan Gregor
Or word of where they have gone.

During the long feasts, the clan was also entertained by the harpist who played a small richly interlaced Clarsach (harp).[50] The harp was the preferred musical instrument of the chiefs and gentlemen, and was often used to accompany the poets as they recited their poetry. The music of the harp was only suited to the castle halls although there is evidence that they were taken on campaign.[51] Like the smiths and poets the harpists were also maintained by a farm, in several parishes there are farms called Croit-a-Chlarsair (the harper's croft). By the end of the seventeenth century the professional harper had almost entirely disappeared from the social life of the Isles. The last of his profession is believed to have been Murdoch MacDonald, harper to MacLean of Coll, who died in 1739.

The bagpipes became widely used in the later sixteenth century. They were used to inspire the clan as they mustered for war and in the heat of battle. There is little mention of them in this context prior to this period and it is likely that they were highly suited to the mass mobilization of clans which was a new feature of this century. Jean de Beaugue, while serving with a detachment of French auxiliaries in the 1540's commented that, "the wild Scots encouraged themselves to arms by the sound of their bagpipes." The sixteenth century saw the development of complex tunes known as piobaireachd whose haunting sounds told of traumatic events. The piobaireachd of the MacDonalds of Glengarry is known as "Kilchrist", and is a celebration of the supposed massacre of a congregation of MacKenzie worshipers at a church of that name.[52] The clan had an intimate knowledge of the meaning of each piobaireachd; no doubt many of these tunes were only suitable for certain audiences. The most famous family of pipers were the MacCrimmons who played for the MacLeods of Harris at their castle of Dunvegan. The most famous of the MacDonald pipers were the MacArthurs of

---

[50] A fine example of the Clarsach is known as Queen Mary's Harp which dates to the beginning of the sixteenth century.
[51] Angus Og, the son of John last Lord of the Isles was murdered by his harpist while on campaign against the MacKenzies, see chapter 2.
[52] For a discussion of this event see chapter 8.

Hunglater in Trotternish, Skye. The three hundred surviving piobaireachd tunes are collectively known as the ceol mor, or great music.

The physicians were also a hereditary caste. They were well embedded in clan society by the sixteenth century. Amongst whom were the MacBeths, who were later known as the Beatons. Cathelus MacVurich refers to them as "of the ancient race of Isla," and they were the physicians to the Lords of the Isles. They were maintained by the produce from the lands of Balinbeg, Arest, Howe and Saligo on Isla.[53] Several other members of the family held similar positions in other parts of the Hebrides. The Beatons wrote many voluminous Gaelic texts on medical maters, some of which survive. Their teachings on the efficacy of different plants were learnt by the people and handed down through the generations as folklore. Medical treatment was extremely limited, many people dying from relatively minor conditions or injuries. For women childbirth was not only to be hoped for but also dreaded.

There were attempts in some districts to control the grinding of corn at the chief's mills that were run by millers, their status was not hereditary and it is uncertain as to how they were appointed. Laws were enacted to prevent the private grinding of corn, the miller being empowered to break private querns. From the issue of exemption licences we know that there were no mills on Skye or in the Outer Hebrides. It may well be that this oppressive situation only applied to those districts nearer the highland line at this period, and thus more influenced by feudal law. In any event the private grinding of corn is amply attested to by the many querns recovered from clachans.

The economy and social structure show strong elements of continuity with the past. Other elements of clan culture such as dress, religion, warfare and the political landscape show the sixteenth century as a period of transition.

The women of the highlands were dressed as their predecessors with long dresses and shawls, only wearing shoes on special occasions. The men came to wear a plaid, which was a large "blanket" of wool which was wrapped around the body, fastened over the shoulder and belted at the waist. These plaids were extremely practical in the wet cold climate of the highlands, suffused with lanolin[54] they were relatively waterproof, unless completely soaked they were warm and easy to dry. For most of this period the clansmen were known as redshanks or caterans by those beyond the highland line. In a letter to Henry VIII of England, John Elder writes, "goynge always bair leggide and bair footide…. The tendir gentillmen of Scotland call us Redshanks." The ancient saffron shirt was still widely worn either under the plaid or on its own.[55]

---

[53] These lands were held by the Beatons into the seventeenth century; James VI confirmed their rights to these farms in 1609.

[54] Lanolin is the natural grease in sheep wool.

[55] It is said that at the battle of Blair-na-Leine (the battle of the shirts) describes a clan battle in 1544 on a hot summer's day. The protagonists threw aside their plaids and fought in their shirts, see chapter 3. N.H. MacDonald has demonstrated that this is a misinterpretation of Leine.

The sixteenth century saw a dramatic change in the nature of warfare in the highlands. At the beginning of the century warfare was dominated by the Gallowglasses.[56] They were professional heavy infantry dressed in a thickly padded and quilted jacket which was overlain with chain mail. They were armed with two-handed swords called claymores (great swords) or two-handed axes. The Gallowglass fought in dense masses several ranks deep, their elite status as professional troops inclined them to give and receive no quarter their casualties were consequently high when defeated. Gallowglass societies were common in Ulster were they were maintained by the Irish chieftains as mercenaries. The Gallowglass was supported by light infantry who were armed with bows or javelins. The early clan battles would have included Gallowglass type infantry which was drawn from the gentlemen of the clan.

The anarchy of the period encouraged a drift towards "total war." This led to a demand for mass mobilization of the clan's manpower and a more mobile force. The consequence was that, as the century progressed, the clansmen were armed with lighter and cheaper weapons. The bow and arrow was used extensively for skirmishing. They were still used in the battle of Carinish at the end of the century.[57] Guns were used in clan warfare from the middle of the century, but due to their cumbersome nature and their slow rate of fire, not to mention their expense, they made little impact on the highland battlefield.[58]

Slowly the great claymores were abandoned in favour of basket hilted swords which could be wielded with great effect with one hand.[59] The other arm was left free to hold a targe (shield) and dirk (dagger). The targe was made of overlapping layers of oak wood covered in several layers of hide. The poorer members of the clan were armed with such deadly weapons as the Lochaber Axe a wickedly designed bill hook on a long shaft which was capable of slashing and stabbing. All these weapon types were to remain in use till their last appearance at Culloden in 1746.

At the political level strategy was based on a complex series of calculations of the intentions of other clans. The MacDonalds usually acted in concert, although the feud between the Maclains and The Clan Iain Mor is a notable exception.[60] It was fear of an attack by all the MacDonald clans which led Kenneth MacKenzie to seek the aid of the MacLeans of Duart during his feud with the MacDonalds of Glengarry over the lands of Lochalsh and Glen Carron.[61] At its height, the feud between Clan Iain Mor and the MacLeans over the Rinns of Isla had sucked in most of the clans on the western seaboard of the highlands.

---

[56] Gallowglass is the anglicised version of the Gaelic Galloglach.

[57] See chapter 6.

[58] Two centuries later regular British infantry were often overwhelmed by the sudden onrush of the highlanders.

[59] Alasdair MacColla beheaded some of his Campbell prisoners after the battle of Inverlochy with one sweep of his arm.

[60] See chapter 5.

[61] See chapter 9.

During a feud the strategy of the clans was to break the military power of the opposition by any means available to them. These included the subtle use diplomacy whether at the Scottish court or in a neighbour's castle, or by direct confrontation in battle. Attempts were made to undermine the economic position of the opposing clan by raiding or even to exterminate the enemy population, for example, the massacres at Trumpan and on the Island of Eigg.[62]

Battle tactics had to be simple as the bulk of clan armies were made up of ordinary clansmen who were only semi-professional soldiers. The subtle use of topography is well attested to, for example, at the battle of Blair-na-Parc the MacDonald army was tempted into attacking the MacKenzies over impenetrable bog. In all clan armies there were champions who no doubt sought each other out on the battlefield.[63] At the battle of Beinn a Ghobha the two smiths were locked in mortal combat and were an inspiration to their clans. One of the most detailed descriptions of a clan battle is that for Kinlochlochy between the Clanranald, Camerons, MacDonalds of Keppoch and Ardnamurchan on one side and the Frasers and Grants on the other. The MacDonald forces were organized into "regiments" drawn from distinctive areas[64] of the clan territory and led by the local gentlemen of the clan. The chief was surrounded by his body guard which was drawn from the gentlemen who were most closely related to him.

Battles often began with skirmishing between the opposing archers, and were followed by an all out attack by the main body of the clan. The use of the "highland charge" was a new feature of highland warfare and was a tactic suitable to the consequences of mass mobilization. The battle would then be decided in a chaotic whirl of hand to hand fighting which was fuelled by the courage and hatred of the participants. Due to the local nature of the feuds the combatants were often known to each other, so it was personal, and each man risked not only his own life but those of his family. This led to little mercy being shown to the vanquished, the enemy wounded being dispatched without compassion. Often the consequence of one of these bloody encounters was that yet more hatred was created, and the desire for revenge burnt brighter.

Religion in the highlands in the early sixteenth century comprised of a unique mixture of Roman Catholicism and the practises of the early Celtic church of the Irish saints. It was unlike the austere Augustinian tradition of the rest of the British mainland with its monasteries and unbending moral code.

The priests while representing the teachings of Rome were also clansmen and highlanders. They condoned many Celtic practises like "handfast marriages." These ceremonies harked back to an ancient pagan world which had been absorbed into Christian society. A couple would pledge their love and union for a specified time

---

[62] See chapter 4.

[63] There was an ancient tradition in Gaelic societies of individual combat between the heroes of opposing clans.

[64] The areas from which these clan "regiments" were drawn, were usually controlled by a family closely related to the chief, for example, the men of Knoydart were formed into a distinctive unit led by their own gentlemen when fighting for the Clanranald.

after which the relationship could be dissolved. This type of marriage was strictly forbidden south of the highland line. Hand fasting allowed couples to see if they were compatible and if the union was capable of producing children. This later characteristic was of great use to chiefs as it allowed them to dispose of wives who were infertile as well as producing many offspring.

Gaelic law was not as rigid about the rights of succession as its feudal neighbour. Hand fasting allowed for a large number of sons to be potentially eligible for the chiefship, usually the eldest legitimate son became chief but in the event of some severe character defect he could be replaced with another son whether legitimate or not. For a chief to have many sons also led to an increase in the number of gentlemen of the clan who were closely connected to the chief by blood. Occasionally this number of sons, each with some claim on the chiefship could lead to internecine conflict. Sons born of this type of relationship could feel aggrieved that they were not the first choice for chief and could act against the clan structure. At its worst this could lead to a civil war within the clan. This situation occurred amongst the MacDonalds of Sleat; Hugh the progenitor of this clan had many sons, some by hand fast marriages. Partly due to the circumstances of their birth and partly due to their own dark natures they assassinated the rightful chief and the clan was ripped apart by internal feuding.[65]

There was also an advantage in a chief having many daughters. These women were equally loyal to their clan and when they were married to other clan chiefs they often continued to act in the interests of their clan as well as the union forming an alliance between the two clans. They often had the "ear" of the chief and would attempt to influence their husband to support their people. There are examples of these women celebrating the defeat of their husbands at the hands of their father's clan. An example of this was Catherine Maclain who was married to Alexander the chief of the Clan Iain Mor. Her father and brothers had been killed in battle by her husband's clan and in revenge she prayed that their first born son would be born blind. In due course Donald Malaicht (the cursed) was indeed born blind.

The role of these women has been much underrated in highland history and their story is largely unrecorded. Clans from the west did not generally marry into those of the east. In the western highlands there were also traditional relationships between certain clans. These patterns were broken for the sake of expediency, for example, to patch up a truce.[66] The MacDonalds tended to intermarry with other branches of the clan as well as with the Camerons, the MacLeods of Lewis and Raasey, the MacNeills of Barra, and the Stewarts of Appin.

Organized Roman Catholicism began to break down in the highlands in the later sixteenth century due to the effects of the Reformation which had swept across the rest of Scotland. Especially in the west, the population began to revert to a more Gaelic style of worship and more emphasis than ever was given to ancient sacred

---

[65] See chapter 7.
[66] Alexander chief of the Clan Iain Mor agreed that his daughter should marry his mortal enemy John Brayach of Ardnamurchan.

sites and superstitions. Society became permeated with belief in ghosts, seers, and witchcraft. These beliefs ranged from the harmless, for example, fishermen believed that if the wind was in a certain direction then they could not land on certain islands, to the dangerous, witchcraft was used extensively in an internal Campbell struggle which was to lead to many deaths.

The most pervasive superstitions were associated with wells. Is it possible that the ancient pagan Celtic belief that water was the gateway to the afterlife had survived a thousand years of Christianity? The people would visit the wells to relieve a wide variety of conditions by performing some simple ceremony. Martin; during his travels in the Hebrides in the late seventeenth century, recounts how the well at Loch Saint on Skye was famous for its ability to cure all diseases. He describes how the islanders made a procession around the well, called a deasil. "They move thrice round the well, proceeding sunways from east to west, and so on. This is done after drinking the water; and, when one goes away from the well, it is a neverfailing custom to leave some small offering on the stone which covers the well." The stream next to the well was full of salmon, but these were never taken as they were regarded as holy fish. There was the well of Saint Molochus on Lewis which cured the supplicant of insanity if he managed to spend a peaceful night sleeping on the altar of the adjacent chapel. The most remarkable well of all was the well of Tobar na Cnaber which translates as "the well that sallied about from place to place." This well is currently on Isla but the people firmly believed that it originally came from Colonsay.

Superstition embraced every aspect of highland life, boats were regularly blessed before sailing, a fine example of this is Alexander MacDonald's beannachadh (blessing) of the galley of Clanranald. Fishermen trapped by a contrary wind on the Island of Fladda-Chuan would go to the Columban chapel and wash a certain blue stone, this action would quickly cause the wind direction to change.

The commonalty of the period sincerely believed that, a man coming towards you was a good sign, a standing man denoted the recovery of a neighbour from illness. Birds in flight were looked upon as a good omen, especially if they were flying towards you as this meant that you would receive good news. Sightings of larks were known to be especially lucky. They were often referred to as Uiseag Mhoire (the lark of the Virgin Mary).

The cat was considered to be only lucky for the MacKintoshes (perhaps because of their close association with the Clan Chattan whose motto is "beware the cat"). There was a cruel practise which involved the local witch roasting a cat alive, its screams were said to draw neighbouring cats to the fire. These cats were believed to be the familiars of other witches and the witch could influence these cats to gain power over her rivals. For all other clans the cat was considered "rosadach" or untoward. The ritual of tagharim[67] (yell of the cats) involved spitting a live cat and roasting it over a fire. The cat's screams were said to draw all the neighbourhood

---

[67] Tagharim was last practised on Mull in the seventeenth century.

cats to the fire, among them would be several gigantic cats that were thought to be emanations of the devil. These cats could be asked for two boons which they would grant. The chiefs of the Camerons performed this ritual and were granted a silver slipper which was placed on the left foot of every son born into the family. This ritual was said to imbue the Cameron chiefs with great courage.[68] In the same way the pig was only lucky for the Campbells (whose crest includes a boar's head). Witches were known to turn themselves into hares so meeting a hare could be a daunting experience.

The widespread use of witchcraft in the sixteenth century was not confined to the commonality or the remote districts of the highlands. It was widely used by the gentlemen of Clan Campbell during an internal feud. That such a well educated and widely travelled man as Campbell of Ardkinglass should hang on every word issued by notable witches from Argyle demonstrates the pervasive belief in witchcraft in the sixteenth century.

The people of the clachan of Bravas, on the island of Lewis, would send a man very early in the morning of Latha bealtainn or Beltane, which is the first of May, to cross the Bravas river because they believed that should a woman be the first to cross on this day the salmon would not return to the river. The ordinary clansmen firmly believed that his livestock were under continual threat from witchcraft practiced or paid for by jealous neighbours. In the Shetlands, Marion Pardown was convicted of witchcraft; "Ye the sd. Marion Pardown ar indyttit and accusit for that zeers syne James Halcro having a cow that ye allegit had pushed a cow of yours, ye in revenge therof by yr. devilish art of witchcraft made the sd. James his cow milk nothing but blood, whereas your awin cow had na harm in her milk."[69]

A belief in witchcraft permeated the higher echelons of highland society in the sixteenth century. A notorious example of this involved Hector Munro of Foulis, chief of the Munros. Hector called in the assistance of some local warlocks and witches to save his ailing life. The witches cast a spell on his half-brother George Munro with the aim of using him as a substitute victim. The principal witch, Marion MacIngarrath dug a grave in which the Munro chief lay down at midnight, wrapped in blankets, and was covered over with green turf. The turfs were fastened down with withies, probably cut from a rowan tree which was thought to guard against evil spirits. His foster mother then ran nine rigs (over a mile) to consult with the local devil. When she returned Marion asked her if the devil had made his choice, Hector's foster-mother then spoke the grim doom that "Mr.[70] Hector was to live and his brother George to die."

Hector returned from his grave to Castle Foulis to await events. His brother George duly died in 1590, and he recovered from his long illness in time to be brought before the court and charged with murder and witchcraft. Due to the jury consisting of his own clansmen he was acquitted, but Marion MacIngarrath and the

---

[68] Only one child could not fit the slipper on his foot due to its size and he subsequently disgraced himself by fleeing from the English at the Battle of Sheriffmuir.

[69] From the symptoms described, James Halcro's cow probably had severe mastitis.

[70] The title of Mister implies that he was a graduate of a university.

rest of her coven confessed under torture and were condemned. They were taken to the market square (probably at Dingwall, the nearest market town to Foulis) and publicly strangled and burnt at the stake.[71]

Another aspect of pre-Christian beliefs were the enigmatic "shiela-na-gig" figures that were built into the walls of medieval churches, they were fertility symbols who helped members of the congregation have children. Some of the best preserved "shiela-na-gigs" are found in the walls of the church of Rodil, the ancient burial place of the MacLeods of Harris.[72]

Sheila-na-gig at Rodil

There is a fascinating theory that some clansmen inherited ancestral memory from their ancestors. Some anthropologists believe that Neanderthals passed on their learnt behaviour to their progeny. We know that family resemblances can be very strong even after a gap of several generations. Clansmen were often closely genetically related on both sides for generation after generation. Is it possible that they could develop an ancestral memory? A possible example of this was James Fraser, who was a nineteenth century cartwright from Beauly. He recounted to Charles Ian Fraser, a respected local historian, a recurring dream that he had.

[71] The ritual practised in this instance is similar to an old Norse ritual which may well have lingered in the folk memory.
[72] They were not a great favourite of Victorian ladies who regarded them as being reminders of a licentious past.

James then described in great detail a clan battle, his description included the dress of the highlanders, their equipment and the events of the battle. Charles recognized the dream as describing the battle of Kinlochlochy in 1544[73] in which the Frasers were almost annihilated by the Clanranald. Charles researched the detailed Fraser histories and found that even the minutia of the description was accurate in every respect. Charles Fraser found it very hard to believe that this semi-literate workman would have had access to any of this material. Rather reluctantly he was drawn to the conclusion that this dream might be an example of ancestral memory. Was it possible that one of James Fraser's relatives had been one of the few survivors of the carnage of Kinlochlochy and that through the continual re-combination of Fraser DNA the memory of the battle had re-surfaced?

All elements of highland society believed in seers, that is, individuals who were able to see into the future. Their predictions were often open to interpretation, rather like the oracles of Delphi. This ability was often handed down from generation to generation. The MacVicars of Kilmun in Argyle, who predicted the fate of many a Campbell gentleman and the Brahan seers who were used by the MacKenzies, are examples of individuals who were blessed with "the second sight". The Brahan seer successfully predicted the way in which the MacKenzies would eventually lose much of their power.

One of the most well known stories of the use of a seer in the western highlands occurred during the great feud between the Clan Iain Mor (the McDonalds of Isla) and the MacLeans of Mull over the Rinns of Isla.[74] Lachlan Mor MacLean consulted a wise woman before invading Isla. She warned him that he had to avoid three things to avert his death. She told him not to land on Isla on a Thursday, to avoid Loch Gruinart and not to drink from the well known as Tobar Niall Neonaich, or the well of strange Neil. Lachlan intended to arrive on the shores of Isla on a Wednesday but was delayed by a storm and landed a day later than he planned. He was attacked by the MacDonalds at the head of Loch Gruinart, and during the battle took a drink from a well which he was told was called Tobar Niall Neonich. Shortly afterwards Lachlan lay dead a crossbow bolt having entered the back of his skull, the tip coming out at his eye.

Local folklore told that his killer was a dark-skinned, hunch-backed dwarf of a black and hairy appearance. The dwarf's name was Dubh Sith which translates as, black fairy. This character was probably a MacDuffie from Colonsay, not some misshapen dwarf, as Sith is very nearly the same as the Gaelic for Shaw the family name of the MacDuffies of Colonsay who were also traditional allies of The Clan Iain Mor. Dubh (dark) being a common description of an individual's complexion or temperament. This story is recounted in more detail in chapter eleven. What is interesting in this context is the firm belief that a highland chief could be killed in battle by a malevolent fairy and that Lachlan had encompassed his own doom by failing to abide by the advice of the seer.

---

[73] See chapter 3.
[74] See chapter 11.

The belief that supernatural beings could directly intervene in their world was also associated with specific places. When Martin visited the Uists, he learnt that a fertile shieling was haunted by ghosts known as, the Great Men. The women and children who drove their livestock to this shieling in the summer months would renounce their claim to earthly things by reciting an invocation to the Great Men. The women then considered themselves as under the guidance and protection of the Great Men. Martin was assured that once a woman had entered the shieling without knowing about the Great Men and had been found wondering out of her mind because she had failed to perform the proper procedure.

There was a belief by all elements of highland society in a world which was full of supernatural forces which could have a direct and profound impact on their lives. These beliefs added a great deal of colour to their world and meant that their reasoning was not merely a matter of analysing facts. This very different belief system to our scientific and empirical reasoning was a significant factor in their behaviour which to us often seems almost inexplicable.

The internal and external political environment of the period and the preceding century had a profound impact on the events that are described in this book. The fall of the MacDonald Lords of the Isles and the repeated attempts by their adherents to restore them during the first half of the century are discussed in chapter two. The consequences of the fall of the Lordship for the clans of the western highlands were profound. They were left in a power vacuum with each clan attempting to establish their own independent identity and power base. There were ties of association between the clans of MacDonalds and also between them and some of the other clans of the Lordship, for example, the MacLeods of Lewis. Other clans like the Camerons and MacLeans established their own identities, and while they long supported attempts to re-establish the Lordship they also had their own agenda.

The clans of the central and eastern highlands like the MacKenzies and Frasers were hostile to any encroachment of MacDonald power. The Earls of Argyle and Huntley, using their respective power bases of their clans, the Campbells and Gordons were willing instruments of Royal policy. This proxy use of clans with their own strong ambitions by the kings, queens and regents of Scotland was a significant cause of the anarchy and bloodshed of the period.

The most important external cause of this lawlessness was the nature of the Scottish state. Between the battle of Flodden in 1513[75] and James VI achieving his majority in 1587 there were thirty three years when the sovereign was a minor. The regents who were appointed to govern Scotland ruled with varying degrees of success. Whether it was the implacable Mary of Guise or the vacillating Arran all the regents lacked the economic and military power to extend their influence into the western highlands. These weaknesses were exacerbated by the transient nature of their rule, much of their attention being taken up with intrigues in the

---

[75] Flodden was a disaster for Scotland, the King and a high proportion of the nobility were killed thus removing the very magnates who might have been able to ensure that the highlands were quickly and peacefully integrated into the Scottish state.

Scottish court. For much of the sixteenth century sovereigns and regents were reduced to issuing impotent threats to their recalcitrant subjects in the highlands. There were long periods in which it was clear to all that the executive was unable to enforce its will; this merely encouraged the endemic anarchy to flourish.

James IV appointed the Campbell Earls of Argyle as lieutenants over the fallen Lordship in 1500. Unwittingly he had introduced an arrangement which was to have disastrous consequences under less able rulers. Due to the weakness of succeeding Kings, Queens and Regents, the Campbells and Gordons were used to attempt to enforce the state's will in the highlands. The paramount interest of these clans was, their own aggrandisement, the national policies coming a poor second. Their manipulation of feudal charter rights, their control of access to the regent, and their ability to continually expand their territories in the guise of carrying out the wishes of the state led to immense bitterness amongst their victims. While this policy was one of the few options available to the state, it fuelled the violence and anarchy; due to a lack of intelligent supervision.

After the accession to the throne of James VI a new and destructive royal policy was promulgated. James found himself short of money and bitterly resented the wealth of Elizabethan England. The highlands were still regarded at this time as the "wild west" of Scotland; it was inhabited by "savages" who were considered to have little or no role to play in the future development of the country. The King and the more credulous members of the court were encouraged to believe that the western highlands were potentially hugely fertile and capable of producing copious amounts of many agricultural products. James, wanting to believe the veracity of the reports was soon convinced that it was only the "savage Irish" inhabitants who stood between him and large rental incomes supported by a productive tenentry.

An early example of this absurdly optimistic attitude was Sir Donald Munro's report on the Western Isles in 1549. The report is full of descriptions such as, "incredible fertilitie of cornis" and stating that they were "of auld, the maistconstant and suire rent and patrimonie of the Croun". Presumably this type of report, which so flagrantly ignored the facts, was drawn up with the sole purpose of pleasing the Scottish court. The King needed little encouragement to raise the rental values of the western isles.[76] In a letter of 1614 Sir Alexander Hay marvelled at the high rents demanded in the western isles when compared to the infinitely more fertile lands of Fife.

This wilful misconception of conditions in the western highlands led to several attempts at "colonization" by lowland settlers encouraged by the Scottish state. Some, like the Fife Adventures, ended in bloody disaster, while others like the settlement of Kintyre by farmers from Galloway were more successful. Either way they were yet another destabilizing factor which added to the hatred and violence.

The governing class of sixteenth century Scotland with the King or Regent at their head regarded highland society with growing dislike. Their ambition was to

---

[76] His ability to collect any income from the western isles was subject to the agreement of the chiefs till the late sixteenth century or early seventeenth century.

create a nation state which would be able to compete with England. The most important contributor to a vibrant, cohesive state was a degree of social uniformity which in its turn was built on elements such as language, law and social organization. With the fall of the Lordship, Gaelic Scotland ceased to be a military or political threat to the state. The governing classes were to strive with increasing success to undermine and eradicate the Gaelic culture of the highlands as it was regarded as an impediment to a vibrant and successful Scottish nation state. In the sixteenth century the methods were generally rather crude, with the granting of clan lands to the clans who were willing and able to enforce the will of the crown, to "colonization," and the establishment of royal garrisons in clan castles[77] and the occasional use of a Scottish fleet in the remote seas of the Hebrides.[78]

The highland clans of the sixteenth century lived in an essentially closed system, they were isolated from the rest of Scotland, by the topography, their language, their social organization and their cultural legacy. They existed in a power vacuum caused by the fall of the Lordship which the Scottish state was unable to replace with its own feudal systems. They had a rich cultural legacy which reached back to their Irish roots while living in economic poverty. The lack of economic resources was exacerbated by an increasing population, who were unable to emigrate apart from in a few particular circumstances.[79] Due to this dearth of resources, the loss of livestock to a family could mean the difference between life and death and was in itself a reason to start a conflict. Underlying many feuds was a struggle to control resources. Their sense of isolation was increased by an unsympathetic government which only added to the anarchy with its, inefficiency, ill-advised policies, ignorance, greed and corruption.

The clan system itself, which was based on blood relationships, meant that feuds were easily started, and were conducted with the utmost ferocity. The feuds were conducted with a relentless tenacity, the main reason for this was that in a period of economic poverty and social anarchy the blood ties of the clan were all that stood between individual families and certain death. The highlanders understanding of their "heroic" cultural past in which their ancestors were thought to always act with courage and determination meant that pride was another important factor in the feuds.

The continual feuding of the period meant that almost no generation spent their lives in peace, which, however hard, must have been longed for by the commonality. The violent events described in these pages would, for those caught up in them, have been terrifying, and full of sorrow. Clan feuds not only led to the premature death of promising young men in battle but also the suffering, hunger, disease and starvation of the rest of the population. An individual knew that when

---

[77] Examples include Dunaverty on the southern tip of Kintyre.
[78] The Scottish fleet was based at Leith and therefore had to sail around the north of Scotland to reach the western seaboard.
[79] Ulster was one of the main destinations for emigration, for example, the Gallowglass communities that settled there. Later MacDonalds from The Clan Iain Mor settled in large numbers in the Glens and Route of Antrim.

he became enmeshed in a feud that everything was at stake. He could not only see his male relatives die in battle, but defeat would at the very least bring great hardship to his family. In some cases the defeat of his clan could also see the extinction of his entire extended family and their ancient lands being occupied by the victor. By the losses of kindred and their place in the world defeat could signal the cultural and genetic annihilation of an individual's past. The stakes were high indeed.

THE LORDS OF THE ISLES

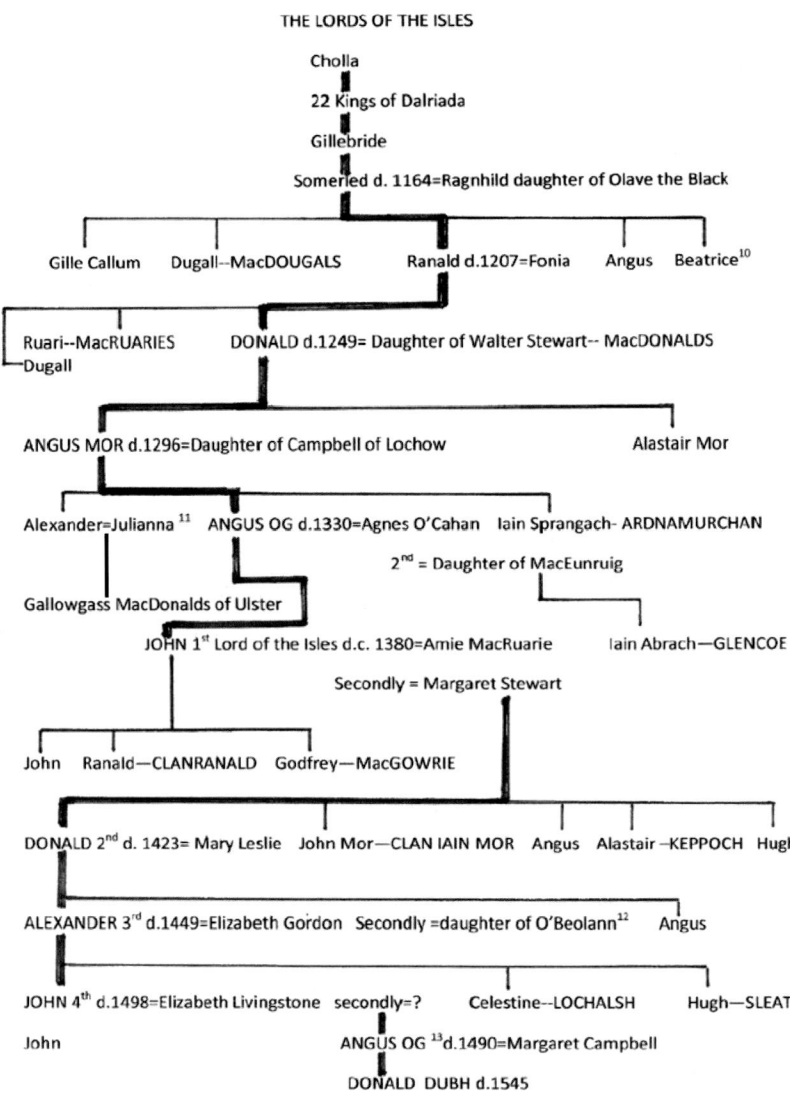

Cholla

22 Kings of Dalriada

Gillebride

Somerled d. 1164=Ragnhild daughter of Olave the Black

Gille Callum   Dugall--MacDOUGALS   Ranald d.1207=Fonia   Angus   Beatrice[10]

Ruari--MacRUARIES   DONALD d.1249= Daughter of Walter Stewart-- MacDONALDS
Dugall

ANGUS MOR d.1296=Daughter of Campbell of Lochow   Alastair Mor

Alexander=Julianna [11]   ANGUS OG d.1330=Agnes O'Cahan   Iain Sprangach- ARDNAMURCHAN

2[nd] = Daughter of MacEunruig

Gallowgass MacDonalds of Ulster

JOHN 1st Lord of the Isles d.c. 1380=Amie MacRuarie   Iain Abrach—GLENCOE

Secondly = Margaret Stewart

John   Ranald—CLANRANALD   Godfrey—MacGOWRIE

DONALD 2nd d. 1423= Mary Leslie   John Mor—CLAN IAIN MOR   Angus   Alastair –KEPPOCH   Hugh

ALEXANDER 3rd d.1449=Elizabeth Gordon   Secondly =daughter of O'Beolann[12]   Angus

JOHN 4th d.1498=Elizabeth Livingstone   secondly=?   Celestine--LOCHALSH   Hugh—SLEAT

John   ANGUS OG [13]d.1490=Margaret Campbell

DONALD DUBH d.1545

---

[10] Beatrice who was prioress of Iona.
[11] MacDougal
[12] The O'Beolans were the abbots of Applecross.
[13] Angus Og was legitimized as the son of John 4th Lord of the Isles by feudal charter.

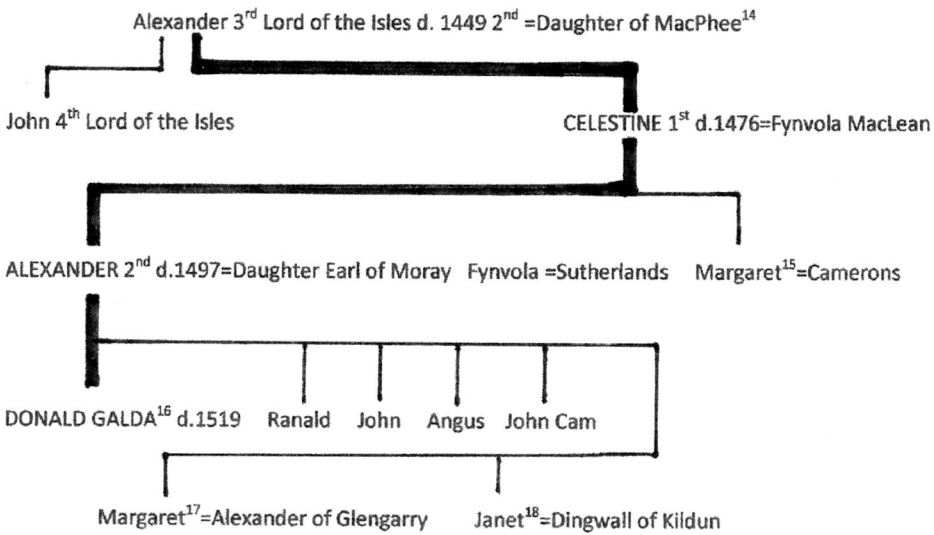

---

[14] It was from his father Alexander (as Earl of Ross) that Celestine inherited his lands of Lochalsh, Lochcarron and Lochbroom.

[15] Margaret married Ewen Cameron of Lochiel who was appointed keeper of the Castle of Strome by Celistine.

[16] After the death of Donald Galda his sisters inherited the lands of Lochalsh.

[17] It was through Margaret that the MacDonalds of Glengarry came into their possessions in Lochalsh.

[18] It was through Janet that the MacKenzies ultimately came into possession of their lands in Lochalsh.

Chapter 2

By Sea by Land

By the beginning of the sixteenth century the ancient hegemony of the MacDonald Lords of the Isles had been broken and the MacDonalds had split into seven separate clans.[1] They occupied lands down the entire western seaboard of the highlands from Loch Broom to the southern tip of Kintrye. The MacDonalds were already well established in the Glens of Antrim[2] and many inland districts of Lochaber.

This history of clan feuds does not cover in any depth, the more profound processes which are the fundamental movers of history, for example, economic and social change. The history of the Scottish state and that of the other clans of the western highlands are only considered as they become relevant from a MacDonald perspective.

Clan feuds were not only caused by the economic, cultural and social conditions in the highlands in the sixteenth century,[3] but also by the historical legacy of the preceding centuries. An underlying theme of this period is the lack of any coherent political order above the level of the clan in the western highlands. The MacDonald Lords of the Isles had been swept away by the Scottish kings who had then been unable to exert any control over the region. The Scottish state exacerbated the ensuing anarchy by its inept and corrupt attempts to exert its authority in the western highlands. As a rule they resorted to a strategy which encouraged compliant clans (for example, the Campbells) to implement Royal policy. These clans were of course primarily concerned with their own agenda and often interpreted their instructions in a highly subjective manner. This led to an almost uninterrupted expansion of the power of the compliant clans who extended their territories at the expense of the original possessors of the land. The consequences of this Royal policy were that the directives of the Kings and Regents of Scotland were often put into effect in an unsympathetic and unjust manner.

The western clans longed for a re-establishment of the Gaelic "kingdom" of the Lords of the Isles and were involved in a series of rebellions aimed at its restitution. These rebellions merely increased the dependence of the state on the compliant clans. The rebellions and the unjust application of Royal authority fed on each other and created a situation whereby Scottish Kings would often describe their subjects in the western highlands as "barbarous" and would issue instructions that a certain clan should be exterminated. This total breach between the monarch and his subjects meant that whatever limited authority the Scottish Kings were able to exert in the western highlands caused, in effect, a persecution of some of his subjects while favouring their local rivals. It is clear that the anarchy caused by the

---

[1] The MacDonalds of Lochalsh, Sleat, Clanranald, Glengarry, Keppoch, Glencoe, Ardnamurchan and Isla.
[2] Northern Ireland.
[3] See chapter 1.

fall of the Lordship and the policies of the Scottish court were major factors in many of the clan feuds. This chapter will briefly describe the origins, history and downfall of the Lordship of the Isles.

The Gaels first began migrating to Scotland, from Ulster, in the fifth century.[4]They settled in what is now known as Argyllshire and established an initially small and vulnerable kingdom called Dalraida. The early settlers brought with them a rich and distinctive Gaelic culture from Ireland. While much of the British Isles was descending into chaos caused by the collapse of the Roman Empire, Ireland was entering a period of sustained economic and cultural development.[5] The new settlers were culturally and linguistically distinctive from the Picts who had been settled in the highlands for centuries. These enigmatic people have left only faint traces of their world except for their forts (brochs) and beautifully carved stones. The Gaelic settlers became known as Scots after the Roman description of the Celtic inhabitants of Ulster.[6] They brought with them the full legacy of their culture in Ireland including, their law, history, poetry and art.

The clan historians were often descended from each other for many generations, for example the MacVurichs who recorded much of the history of the Clanranald. These histories were passed down orally; one of the most important aspects of these histories was to establish that the ancestors of the chief were of royal blood, this trail always led back to Ireland for the western clans.[7] The poetry of the western highland clans was similar to that constructed in Ireland a thousand years before; it is full of heroism, suffering, and revenge in its descriptions of its society.[8] It was this culture that the highlanders of later centuries were to regard as their cultural heritage despite profound interaction with the Picts and the Norse. This culture although of fundamental importance to the future identity of the highlanders of the sixteenth century was not preserved in aspic, it adapted to the new conditions it found in Scotland. This process continued over the centuries and by the late sixteenth century we find the people of Isla complaining to the government about the strange customs i.e. Irish customs [9]imposed by the MacDonalds of Antrim on the island.

---

[4] The earliest recorded settlement being that of Fergus Mor MacErc in about 500A.D.
[5] The evidence for this is extensive; the main source for this revival was the early Irish church which preserved Latin both in speech and writing by producing beautifully engraved manuscripts. Although late Celtic societies are not renowned for their material remains, due to their extensive use of wood and leather, the fifth and sixth century excavations at Tara suggest that under such kings as Niall of the Nine Hostages there was a considerable concentration of political power.
[6] The Scotii.
[7] This desire to have as ancient and royal descent as possible even led clans to claim that they were descended from the Pharaohs of ancient Egypt.
[8] A good example of this poetic style is Ian Lom's description of the triumph of his clan (the MacDonalds) over the Campbells at the battle of Inverlochy in 1645.
[9] The MacDonalds of Antrim had purchased large tracts of Isla, partly in an attempt to prevent the whole island falling under the sway of the Campbells. Here they organized their tenentry under the same lines as in Ulster. The style of land tenure was completely foreign to

The Dalriadic Kingdom clung with varying degrees of fortune to its new homeland in the face of fierce opposition from the Picts. It faced another severe threat with the Norse invasions in the Hebrides in the late eight century. These raids devastated much of Ireland, the Hebrides and large tracts of the northern Scottish mainland. Over time the pattern of Norse incursion changed and there was an increased emphasis on settlement and trade. A new culture developed due to the intermingling of Norse and Gaelic elements and from the mid-ninth century the annalists begin to refer to the Gall- Ghaidheal (the Norse Gaels). The Gaelic language and culture remained dominant in both the Hebrides and the western highland coast. The Gaels were over the next two centuries able to acculturate the Norse settlers and create an essentially Gaelic society which was, however, starting to show characteristics which were unique to the western highlands.

In part, due to the Norse raids the centre of government of the Scots was moved further east to Scone and the ancient capital of Dalraida at Dunadd with all its traditions was forgotten. In 844 the kingdoms of Dalriada and Pictland were united under Kenneth Mac Alpine, king of Dalriada. The Pictish Kingdom appears to have been absorbed peacefully[10] and the Kingdom of Scotland emerges for the first time. In 872 Harold Harfagr became the first king of Norway, and by 888 the Norse settlements in the western highlands of Scotland were incorporated into his kingdom. Shortly afterwards the inhabitants of this region threw off the direct rule of Norway and under Ketil Fletneb established a semi-autonomous kingdom which stretched from Lewis to the Isle of Man and whose leaders styled themselves Kings of the Isles. These kings were men who played a significant role on the international stage, for example, Aulaf MacSitric who died in battle against the Angles at the battle of Brunaburh, and Sigurd who died in Ireland at the battle of Clontarf in 1014.

In the tenth century the early Kingdom of Scotland was involved in the processes of melding together the Scots and Picts to form a single cohesive society and a continual struggle to resist the relentless pressure of the Norse incursions. It was not until the eleventh century with the defeat of the Angles of Lothian by Malcolm II's victory at Carham in 1018 and the absorption of the Britons of Strathclyde by marriage under Duncan in 1034, that the rough form of modern Scotland took shape. Duncan was slain by Macbeth, who by the strength of his rule proved a good king for the vulnerable early Kingdom of Scotland.[11] Duncan's son Malcolm fled to the Anglo-Saxon Kingdom of England; he later returned to Scotland and after avenging his father was crowned at Scone in April 1057. Nine years later

---

the inhabitants of Isla, who were still largely MacDonalds. Given that both populations had been part of the same clan (the Clan Iain Mor) only sixty years before it is remarkable how quickly the two societies had diverged.

[10] The absorption of Pictland may have been by marriage; the Picts allowed for inheritance to be passed down through the female line, so their kingdom could have passed to the Scots by a royal marriage.

[11] Macbeth's reputation has suffered severely due to Shakespeare's Macbeth.

Harold Godwinson fell with his huscarls and the fryds[12] of the south east of England at Hastings and Norman hegemony was established in England. The profound implications of that day in 1066 could not have been appreciated by any of the protagonists, and the ripples were to spread out until they eventually lapped on the shores of the Hebrides.

Members of the Anglo-Saxon court and Harold's family fled to the safety of Scotland where under Malcolm's rule they knew they would receive a welcome and might escape the grim power of William. Amongst this group of refugees were Edgar Atheling and his sister Margaret. Malcolm fell in love with Margaret and soon they were married. Ever since his time as a refugee in England Malcolm had been an admirer of Anglo-Saxon England, and this combined with the influence of his strong minded wife led Malcolm to change the nature of the Scottish state by anglicising its institutions.

The Columban Church of Scotland had its routes in the Celtic west while Margaret's lay in the Augustinian tradition of Rome. Malcolm initiated reforms in the Scottish church which led to its Anglicization and a dilution of its traditions. The Gaelic language was superseded by English at court and in the course of the next century became the language of power; in that to climb the slippery pole of political success a Scottish courtier must be at least bilingual. Gaelic was gradually replaced by English in the lowlands and by the opening years of the sixteenth century was mainly restricted to the north of the highland line. Malcolm's admiration for Anglo-Saxon England led him to encourage refugees from William's harsh rule and to settle large numbers of them in Scotland. Malcolm and Margaret had initiated a process of change which was to lead to the spread of such processes as feudalism and ultimately to the English and Scottish courts being virtually indistinguishable with many Scottish nobles owing allegiance to the Kings of both countries.

This process of Anglicization created a Scotland which had two different cultures; a feudalized, Anglo-Norman lowlands and a somewhat marginalized Gaelic highlands. In 1384 Fordun described a Scotland in which two different languages were spoken; the people of the lowlands he describes as "of civilized habits, trusty, patient and urbane..." while the highlanders are described as "a savage and untamed nation, rude and independent, given to rapine, ease-loving, of a docile and warm disposition, comely of person but unsightly in dress, hostile to the English people and language....". By the fourteenth century Scotland was clearly divided by language, law and culture.

To the south of the highland line was a society which was part, in every sense, of the western European tradition. Its church was controlled from Rome, the people spoke English and the entire fabric of their society was suffused with feudalism. To the north and west the old Gaelic way of life held sway although always slowly retreating to the north and west as the Scottish state's power increased. Despite its

---

[12] The huscarls were the professional heavy infantry of late Anglo-Saxon armies while the fryds were the local county levies who were called upon to do service for a limited period.

gradual retreat Gaelic culture had some notable successes, for example, the acculturation of Norman feudal families like the Frasers and Chisolms whose highland branches became Gallicised and these families went on to lead clans who took their name. Highland society was evolving from its Gaelic routes and although affected by the spread of feudalism it was still vibrant and capable of maintaining a rich culture of its own. The retreat of Gaelic culture was a long and intermittent process which would halt for long periods when there was political or economic weakness in the Scottish state; the sixteenth century is an example of this. The MacDonalds formed a fundamental part of this Gaelic culture and in the fifteenth century through their rule as the Lords of the Isles, its institutions created the building blocks for an alternative Gaelic society.

Somerled and the origins of the MacDonalds.

Somerled the progenitor of the MacDonalds and MacDougals was the son of Gille Bride and was born in the early twelfth century. Somerled was descended from the Clan Cholla who originated in Ulster; the Clan Cholla was later used by MacDonald historians and poets as a description of all the branches of the MacDonalds. Somerled (Norse for summer voyager), would have been thought of as Gall-Ghaedheal that heady mix of Norse and Gaelic culture; one of the legacies of which was to view the sea as the medium which held the tapestry of islands and lochs into one interconnected region.

The history of the early twelfth century is an intertwined mix of legend and fact. It appears that Somerled and his father had to flee from the Scottish mainland to Ireland, in the face of fierce opposition from the Viking supporters of the Kings of Norway. Here among their relatives of the Clan Cholla they recruited a new band of retainers and returned to Scotland. Gille Bride and his son Somerled carried out a series of hit and run attacks against the Vikings. It was during this gorilla war that Somerled established a reputation as a brave and skilful leader of men. As more Gall-Ghaedheal came to join him he was able to switch from gorilla to conventional warfare. Somerled defeated a Viking invasion of Morvern, and then went on to clear the entire mainland of Viking settlements. Due to the force of his personality and his skill in leading the Gall-Ghaedheal against the Norse on the mainland of ancient Dalriada he quickly built up a significant power base of his own followers and allied clans. Somerled was elected to be head of a new clan which comprised of the inhabitants of the mainland and the men who had followed him from Ireland.

Somerled attention now focused on the Hebrides where his own kinfolk lived under the rule of the kings of Norway. Norwegian rule stretched from the Shetlands to the Isle of Man, the control of this area by the Norwegian kings was often tenuous, due to internal weakness which was exacerbated by the remoteness of this region from the centre of their power. The control of this area was often reasserted with great ferocity, for example, the invasion of Magnus Barefoot in 1102. The Norse and Gaelic inhabitants of the Hebrides would both have suffered severely when they attempted to break away from Norwegian hegemony.

In 1140 Somerled married Ragnhilda the daughter of Olaf the Red, the King of Man.[13] This marriage greatly increased Somerled's power and influence in the Hebrides, on the death of Olaf in 1153 Somerled was able to strengthen his position still further by taking full advantage of the power struggle that erupted. In 1156 Godfrey the King of Man ceded all the islands south of Ardnamurchan and the peninsular of Kintyre to Somerled.

While Somerled was laying the foundations of what was to become the semi-independent Lordship of the Isles, the process of Anglicization was continuing in the Kingdom of Scotland during the reign of David I. Partly in response to this there was a rebellion by Malcolm MacHeth who was an illegitimate son of David's predecessor Alexander I. Malcolm MacHeth was the Mormaer (Celtic earl) of Moray and represented the interests of the old Celtic Scotland and opposed the erosion of the old order. Malcolm MacHeth was strongly supported by Somerled who even gave him his sister in marriage. In 1160 Somerled signed a treaty with Malcolm the Maiden who had succeeded David as King of Scotland. This treaty recognizes Somerled's control over large tracts of the south-western highland seaboard.

Somerled now styles himself as King of the Isles as he ruled an independent kingdom nominally holding his island possessions from the king of Norway and his mainland possessions from the King of Scotland. Somerled was murdered while mounting an expedition against the King of Scotland in 1164. One probable reason for this conflict was the friction created when two expanding powers collided; one was becoming feudalized, centralized and looked to Rome for religious instruction, the other was steeped in the very different culture of the Celtic west.

Somerled had created a political structure which was to have an enduring appeal for his MacDonald descendents. In their eyes they were the inheritors of an independent Gaelic kingdom which was the only true embodiment of the legacy of the ancient Kingdom of Dalriada. Somerled left three sons, Dougall who become the progenitor of the MacDougals, Reginald, whose son Donald was to leave his name to the greatest of all the clans, and Allan. Reginald inherited Islay and Kintyre which were to form the heartland of the Lordship of the Isles. Allan inherited Bute, Arran and the lands of Moidart, Morar and Knoydart. On the death of Allan and his sons, Arran and Bute passed into the possession of the Stewarts[14] due to the marriage of the heiress Janet to Walter the High Steward of Scotland. From now on it was to be the Scottish Kings policy to prevent the heirs of Somerled from possessing these islands as they controlled the access to the Clyde estuary; they

---

[13] The Kingdom of Man was a semi-independent kingdom which at the zenith of its power stretched from the Orkneys, down through the Inner and Outer Hebrides to the Isle of Man and into Ireland.

[14] The highland clans of Stewarts and their lowland relatives derive their origin from an Anglo-Norman family who were stewards to the Kings of Scotland. It was in this role that they were given possession of Bute and Arran. They were charged with preventing either the Norse or the descendents of Somerled from gaining control over these strategic islands.

were to be left in the more reliable hands of the Stewerts. Allan's lands of Moidart, Morar and Knoydart were divided equally between Reginald and Dugall.

Reginald the second son of Somerled had a happy combination of attributes, in that he was a man who enjoyed peace while being successful in war. He is described by MacVurich as "the most distinguished....of the Gaels for prosperity, sway of generosity, and feats of arms," Reginald's seal describes him as Reginaldus Rex Insularum Dominus de Argile (Reginald King of the Isles and Lord of Argyle), it also shows a galley which is the ancient galley of the Kingdom of Man.[15]

Reginald died in 1207 and was succeeded by his son Donald who gave his name to all the branches of the house of MacDonald. Donald and his brother Ruarie (who was to found the MacRuarie clan[16]) were involved in aiding another rebellion by the MacHeths probably for the same reason as their grandfather Somerled had done. The reigning monarch of Scotland was Alexander II who led several expeditions into the western highlands. He probably received the submission of Donald, but both would have understood the impermanence of such contrition. During Donald's turbulent life he murdered his uncle Dougal and went to visit Rome as an act of penance. This act of violence against a member of his own kindred led to a rift between the MacDougals and the MacDonalds and this was the first of the seeds of discord which was sown amongst the descendents of Somerled. During his life Donald walked the difficult path between being truly subservient to either the Kings of Norway or the Kings of Scotland; he died at Skipness in 1267 and was buried on Iona.

Angus Mor and Angus, 1249-1330, the foundations of the Lordship.

Sometime before Donald's death his eldest son Angus Mor MacDonald had become acting King of the Isles. By 1262 Angus Mor was coming under severe pressure from King Alexander III, who wanted to expand the area of influence of the Scottish state. Angus Mor supported Haakon the King of Norway when he sailed into Hebridean waters to re-establish the authority of Norway in this region. No doubt Angus saw in Haakon a useful counter weight to the emerging power of the Scottish state. A year later Haakon was defeated at the Battle of Largs and nominal superiority over the Isles passed to the Kingdom of Scotland in the subsequent treaty of 1266.

Angus Mor's difficult position had been exacerbated by his association with the Norwegians and he made his submission to Alexander. At the time of the death of Alexander we find that Angus Mor is living peacefully enjoying the privileges that would come with his position. As was to happen so many times in the future, the King of Scotland had come to an accommodation with a powerful and semi-independent ruler who he was unable to control by force. Despite the almost

---

[15] The galley is represented in the later heraldic devices of all the clans of the MacDonalds and other clans who were, at least in part, descended from Reginald.

[16] The MacRuarie lands were later to form a major part of the territories of the Clanranald.

continual challenges thrown down by the MacDonald Lords of the Isles, the repeated evidence for the unusual toleration of the state for the island lords was a reflection of the state's weakness and of the power of the MacDonald lordship.

With the death of Alexander in1286, Scotland entered a dark period in which various factions contended for the crown, this lack of cohesion within the state allowed the English to meddle in Scottish affairs and for periods to control Scotland. Angus Mor was by now an old man who although he favoured the claims of the Bruce family to the crown he took no active part in the coming struggle. Angus Mor died circa 1300 having successfully steered the MacDonalds between the rock and the hard place which were represented by the Kingdoms of Norway and Scotland.

The extensive territories of Angus Mor were divided among his three sons. Alexander his eldest son received Islay and mainland territories in Argyle; Angus Og received Kintyre while his youngest son John Sprangach[17] (the bold) received the peninsular of Ardnamurchan. Alexander had the misfortune to back the losing side in what was in effect a Scottish civil war; he compounded his error by staying loyal to the losing side. Alexander was closely related by marriage to the MacDougals who were in their turn related to the Comyns the most powerful supporters of the Balliol faction who were ultimately backed by the English. In 1291 Alexander gave his allegiance to the English and as the struggle between the houses of the Bruces and Balliols intensified he threw his whole weight behind the latter.

To the modern reader his behaviour may appear treacherous. However, from his perspective the right of the over lordship of Scotland was at best tenuous, and he may well have regarded the newly emerged feudal Scottish state as an interloper which had no right to command his loyalty. In 1296 the Scottish nobility submitted to Edward, and Alexander, as one of the loyal supporters of the English faction was rewarded by being appointed Admiral of the Western Isles.

Bruce was crowned King of Scotland at Scone in 1306. Alexander took to the field on behalf of his English allies, but he was defeated in Galloway and taken prisoner by Robert Bruce's younger brother Edward. Alexander escaped to Castle Swein where he was besieged by Bruce and again captured. Alexander was imprisoned in Dundonald Castle where he died shortly afterwards. His sons although belonging to the senior branch of the family found themselves dispossessed by Bruce; they fled to Ireland and established many families of Gallowglasses (professional heavy infantry mercenaries) who fought with great bravery for various Irish chieftains in the maelstrom of warfare in Ulster.[18]

Angus Og the second son of Angus Mor succeeded to the estates of his dispossessed elder brother in 1308. Initially he had followed his brother's example and supported the English interest. It is not clear why Angus Og switched his allegiance to Bruce although some contributing factors were his father's predilections and the feud that had developed with the MacDougals (the main

---

[17] John (Iain) Sprangach was the founder of the MacIains of Ardnamurchan.
[18] One of the notable characteristics of these Gallowglass families was that few of them died in their beds.

highland opponents of Bruce) over the ownership of the island of Mull. When Bruce's fortunes were at their lowest ebb after the defeat at Methven he found that he had the full support of Angus Og who hid him in the MacDonald castles of Sadell and Dunaverty. Angus Og was intimately involved in the gradual re-emergence of Bruce's power and after becoming chief of the MacDonalds he was able to throw the whole weight of his people behind Bruce. Angus Og at the head of five thousand Islesmen fought on the right of Bruce's battle line at Bannockburn. Bruce said to Angus Og as he ordered him to go to the assistance of his brother Edward "my hope is constant in thee," these words were later to become the motto of the Clanranald.

With the defeat of his enemies Bruce was able to distribute the spoils to his loyal supporters. Angus Og was a principle beneficiary of this largesse, the territories he received came from the highland opponents of the Bruces namely the Comyns and the MacDougals. He was gifted besides his own possessions of Isla and Kintyre the islands of Mull, Jura, Coll and Tiree as well as the mainland districts of Morvern and Glencoe. Lochaber was divided between Angus Og and his uncle Ruarie who sprung from another branch of the house of Somerled, and already held sway over Moidart, Morar, Knoydart and North and South Uist in the Outer Hebrides. It was these gifts by Bruce to Angus Og that were, when combined to the territories already held by the MacDonalds to form the power base for the Lords of the Isles and later for the independent clans of MacDonalds.

Angus Og married Agnes, a daughter of O'Cahan one of the most powerful men in Ulster. It is interesting to note that despite Angus's intimate involvement in Scottish politics he chose a bride and thus made an alliance with a chieftain in Ulster. Throughout the centuries of MacDonald power in the west they always felt more at ease with the people of Ulster and other western clans than they did with the central or northern highland clans let alone the Scottish state. This situation led to very limited ties with the clans of the central and eastern highlands, and when ties were established the relationship usually ended badly. A good example of this is the marriage of a chief of the Clanranald[19] to the daughter of the chief of the Frasers. After many twists and turns, events led both clans to the bloody field of Kinlochlochy.[20] For a MacDonald chieftain living on Isla his world was much more closely bound to Ulster than Scotland; his clan's cultural routes as well geographical proximity meant that events in Ulster were often of more significance to him than those in Edinburgh. When one looks out to sea from the southern tip of Kintyre, Ulster is only a few hours sailing away. It is so close that some of the fields can be made out. This part of Ulster is known as the Glens and formed part of the MacDonald hegemony from the middle of the fifteenth century.

Angus Og remained loyal to Bruce for the remainder of his days dying shortly after Bruce, who died in 1329. Angus had two sons by Agnes O'Cahan, the first, John, was destined to become the first Lord of the Isles.

---

[19] The Clanranald are one of the most ancient MacDonald clans, they were founded by Ranald (died 1389) the eldest surviving son of John first Lord of the Isles.
[20] See chapter 3.

John, first Lord of the Isles, 1330-1386.

John of Isla (known as good John) succeeded to his father's vast possessions at a time when both the internal and external political environment were favourable to the existence of an independent Gaelic state on the western seaboard of the Scottish highlands. From what limited evidence there is available, John's power appears to have had no significant internal threats with the MacDonalds forming a cohesive political entity. On a regional level the destruction of the power base of the MacDougals and the Comyns during the Scottish civil war had eliminated the threat from their rivals. As yet the Campbells were not a force to be reckoned with. Under a long succession of gifted chiefs they were establishing their power base, centred on Loch Awe. At the national level the Norse threat had long since evaporated, Ulster was in its usual state of chaos and the Kingdom of Scotland was riven by anarchy and confusion. John's succession was almost contemporaneous with the accession of David II[21] to the throne. David's minority led to internal power struggles in Scotland and the re-emergence of English influence under Edward III, which ultimately led to Edward Balliol being crowned at Scone and soon afterwards paying homage to Edward.

During this stormy period of Scottish history John of Isla was an ally of the Balliol faction and Edward, this culminated in a treaty being signed at Perth in December 1335 between John and Edward in which Edward grants John feudal title to his ancestral lands, the lands gifted to his father by Bruce and some additions which included the Isle of Lewis and the Isle of Skye. It is from this date the MacDonald Lords of the Isles held sway over the Outer Hebrides, however the gift of Skye was in these terms not within the remit of any king. Skye was an integral part of the Earldom of Ross which was not to become part of the Lordship for several decades. John's alliance with the English does not fit comfortably with modern nationalistic views on the struggle for Scottish independence, as indeed does much of the future conduct of the Lords of the Isles.

They were often in league with either Scottish forces plotting against the crown or directly with the English. They led a series of rebellions which erupted with great violence from their remote fastnesses. From the perspective of the Lords of the Isles, they represented a semi-independent kingdom in which they were regarded as ancient kings. This "Kingdom" had all the institutions in place which were required by the Gaels. The Lords of the Isles were governed in their political judgements by the interests of the MacDonalds, and this overrode any considerations of the national interest. By the early fourteenth century, the complete separation between the two parts of Scotland was already well under way with the main representatives of the two parts, the King of Scotland and the Lord of the Isles, having very different perspectives.

---

[21] David II was still a child.

In 1341 David II was able to return from France and resume his position as King of Scotland. John avoided any serious punishment, David was a pragmatist and knew that John was beyond the reach of his power, and besides he wanted John's support for his proposed invasion of England. David assembled his army at Perth; among those present was Ranald MacRuarie (whose ancestor was Reginald, brother of Donald the progenitor of the MacDonalds). Ranald was at feud with the Earl of Ross over certain lands in Western Ross. The Earl of Ross seized his opportunity and murdered Ranald as he slept despite Ranald being protected by the sanctuary of the church.

John was married to Amie MacRuarie, sister of the murdered Ranald; she was the rightful heiress to the MacRuarie lands as Ranald had no offspring. John was refused legal title to his wife's inheritance by David who regarded John as already wielding too much power and influence. David marched south with the Scottish host only to meet with disaster at Neville's Cross and begin a long period of captivity. It is surprising that David's denial of John's rights to the MacRuarie lands did not lead the latter into open rebellion. John had actual undisturbed possession of the MacRuarie lands during the eleven years of David's captivity and may have considered confirmation of his rights on "sheepskin"[22] as relatively unimportant. In negotiations with the MacDougals in 1354; there is the first recorded use by John of the title "Lord of the Isles".

With the immanent release of David due, the French, who were involved in a life and death struggle with Edward III in the continuing Hundred Years War, paid the Scottish nobility a large bribe to assist them against the English. A considerable Scottish contingent sailed for France in 1355, among them was John Lord of the Isles with his wild army of highland warriors. The only plausible explanations for this volte face in his policy is that significant quantities of the French gold had found its way to Isla or that John believed that only recognition by the King of Scotland would give true legitimacy to the MacRuarie inheritance. In September 1356 the French and their Scottish allies were catastrophically defeated at the Battle of Poitiers; John was among the many hundreds of nobles taken prisoner. Due to John's usefulness to Edward as a counter weight against the Scots he was soon released to resume his control over the western highlands. John played an active part in raising the ransom for David, and amongst the terms for David's release John was required to honour a truce with the English. This last piece of evidence implies that John had come to believe that his interests were best served by a rapprochement with the Scottish crown.

On David's return from England there was a fundamental realignment of Scottish politics, with the Balliol faction supporting David's now pro-English policies and the Steward's[23] faction becoming the national party. John managed to steer a

---

[22] The term "sheepskin" denotes a written charter, they were commonly used by the Scottish kings but were relatively unknown in the territories of the Lordship.

[23] The Stewarts derived their name from being Stewards to the Kings of Scotland. By the fourteenth century they had become one of the most powerful families in Scotland, owning extensive tracts of lands in both the highlands and lowlands.

path between these two camps while promoting his own interests. John divorced his wife Amie MacRuarie and married Lady Margaret, daughter of the Steward. John was now in secure possession of Amie's MacRuarie inheritance and reasoned that an alliance with the rising star of the Stewards (who had intimate access to the King and controlled amongst other territories the vital districts of Arran and Bute which dominated the entrance to the Clyde) would further increase his power. Whatever the political advantages of abandoning Amie were; John's actions are deplorable at a personal level. John's biographers describe Amie as "a good and virtuous gentlewoman", and the MacRuarie inheritance was to prove a far more loyal supporter of the Lordship of the Isles than any legacy of his union with Margaret.

John was clearly in favour at the Scottish court, due no doubt to his power in the west, his own abilities and to the influence of the Steward, John eventually becoming High Steward of the King's Household. It was in this capacity that John visited Flanders as an emissary of the King. John was the only Lord of the Isles or later MacDonald chief to reach such heights on the international stage.

Shortly afterwards we find a more familiar situation in which John is refusing to pay his part of David's ransom, this ransom put an enormous strain on the people of Scotland who were impoverished by years of war with England. After years of open and successful defiance of the King, John submitted to David's authority at Inverness in 1369.Two years later David died and was succeeded by Robert II. Relations between Robert and John were cordial. In 1371 John finally received legal title to the MacRuarie inheritance and the lands of Moidart, Arisaig, Morar, Knoydart and the islands of Uist, Barra, Rum, Egg and Lewis became part of the MacDonald hegemony.

The right of over lordship of these islands and mainland districts by both Gaelic and

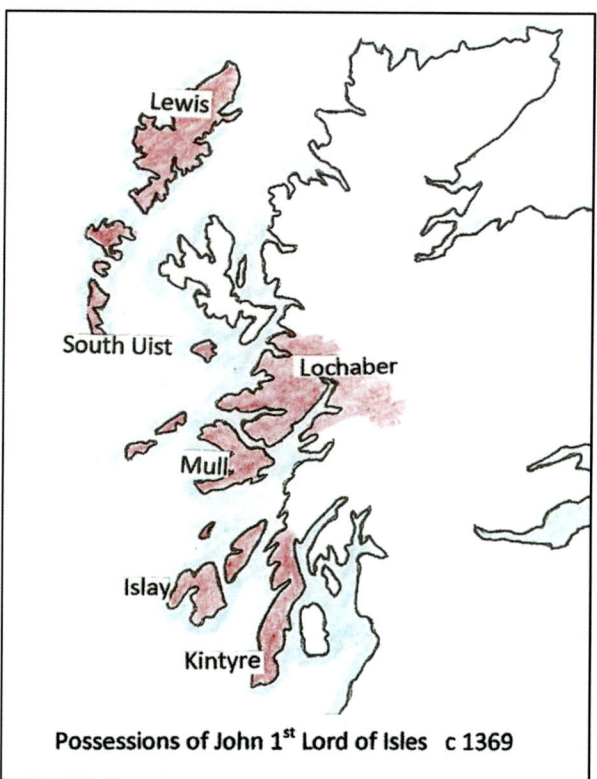

Possessions of John 1st Lord of Isles c 1369

feudal law[24] is extremely significant in that apart from the large areas occupied by the MacDonalds, the other clans owed the Lord of the Isles their allegiance which left no room for manoeuvre.[25] While with the decline in the power of the Lordship the loyalty of the eastern clans fell away, the clans of the west rose time and again in support of the Lords of the Isles and later the claimants to the title.

The last fourteen years of John's life leaves little trace in the historical record; which may well be an indication of a peaceful and contented old age. John died at his castle of Ardtornish in Morven in 1386 leaving numerous surviving offspring who would go on to establish many of the independent MacDonald clans of the sixteenth century (see genealogical tables for the Lords of the Isles). John left a legacy of a strong Gaelic semi-autonomous kingdom whose memory was to fuel the aspirations of the MacDonalds in the years after the fall of the Lordship. It was to be remembered with great affection by the MacDonald poets, for example, Iain Lom.

Donald, second Lord of the Isles, 1389-1423.

Ranald was the eldest of John's sons but was passed over for the Lordship in favour of Donald the eldest son of John's second marriage to Margaret. There was a combination of reasons why Ranald accepted that he should only inherit the ancient lands of his mother's people. Donald was backed by the King[26] and also his father who had already settled the MacRuarie lands on Ranald. The explanation as to why Ranald accepted the situation may also lie in his own character, he was either peace loving or unambitious or wise, or a combination of all three, to forgo the power associated with the Lordship.

Ranald as High Steward of the Isles gave over all his rights to Donald when he came of age. MacVurich states that despite the preference for Ranald among a significant element of the principal men of the Isles, Donald was elected as the second Lord of the Isles at Kildonan on the island of Eigg. Donald eradicated any internal opposition by generous grants of land to his brothers; and by a firm but just rule he cemented the clans under his sway into a unified and cohesive political body.

Soon after Donald had acceded to the Lordship his brother John Mor Tannister, who had already been granted large parts of Isla and Kintyre by Donald married Margery Bisset the daughter of the Lord of Antrim and heiress of the Glens in Ulster. By this advantageous marriage John Mor Tannister extended The Clan Iain

---

[24] It was becoming ever more important that the state should recognize the legal right to lands claimed by The Lords of the Isles as the verbal Gaelic arrangements of the Lordship were not recognized or understood in Edinburgh.

[25] Even the MacKintoshes whose territories were in the eastern highlands owed their allegiance (they were bound to support the Lords of the Isles against all except the King), for their possessions in Lochaber and fought with John's son at the battle of Harlaw in 1411.

[26] The King may well have been influenced by the Steward who was Margaret's father.

Mor's[27] land holdings into Ulster. The ownership of significant territories in Ulster extended the power of the MacDonalds and was to be both a blessing and a curse. It had the obvious advantages of increasing the financial and military power of the Clan Iain Mor as well as the more subtle benefits of being able to minimize the danger posed in later years by the Scottish and English crowns, the Campbells and their Irish opponents. As these various opponents were rarely united The Clan Iain Mor could retreat or counter attack from either Scotland or Ulster. Even at the height of their power the Campbells were unwilling to mount any major expeditions to Ulster, while usually the Kingdoms of Scotland and England could to some degree be played off against each other. However the ownership of the Glens in Ulster also meant that the chief of Clan Iain Mor was involved in both Scottish and Ulster politics and could not devote the entirety of his efforts to either region.

As a child Donald had been held hostage at Dumbarton Castle for the good behaviour of his father. This could not have endeared him to the Scottish state. Donald followed the same political stance as his father; he was encouraged in his attitude by a series of English Kings. The late fourteenth century was a period of continual friction between England and Scotland; the Lords of the Isles were a useful counter weight for the English against the Franco-Scottish alliance. Donald visited the English court on several occasions where he formed alliances with both Richard II and Henry IV. With the benefit of hindsight this pro-English policy may appear short sighted. However, Scottish independence often hung on a knife edge and the Lords of the Isles commanding the Gaelic power of the west from the Glens of Ulster to the Isle of Lewis, felt that with English aid they could match the power of the Scottish state. The catalyst for open hostilities was an accusation by Robert III that Donald and his brother Alasdair Carrach had been mistreating their mother, the king's sister. This accusation may well have been promulgated by the family of the Stewards, their power and influence was continually growing and in a few years they were to form a dynasty of Scottish kings as the house of Stewart. Alasdair Carrach broke out in open rebellion in 1394 and sacked the royal castles of Inverness and Urquhart. Alasdair's occupation of these castles was short lived; he was captured by forces loyal to the crown and only released after Donald gave a pledge for his good behaviour.

Donald did not take an active part in Scottish politics after the death of Robert III, and only reappears on the national stage when his own interests require him to do so. It was Donald's claim to the Earldom of Ross which led him into open conflict with the Scottish state.[28] Both Donald and the Stewarts had tenuous claims to the

---

[27] The Clan Iain Mor was named after John (in Gaelic Iain) Mor Tannister who was their progenitor.

[28] The Earldom of Ross had passed out of the hands of the Celtic Mormaers (the last of whom there is any record is Macbeth) in the middle of the eleventh century. The Earldom was then ruled by the O'Beolans (the progenitors of Clan Ross). With the death of the fifth earl, the Earldom of Ross passed ultimately to an heiress Euphemia who in turn gave up her claims when she entered a nunnery. The Earldom was then claimed by Euphemia's mother Isabel Stewart who was the daughter of the powerful Duke of Albany. It was also claimed by

Earldom, both through the female line. The Stewart claim was backed by the Duke of Albany (father of the Stewart claimant); he was Chamberlain to the feeble Robert III and essentially ruled Scotland. The issue of the Earldom of Ross was not merely one of whether it should be ruled by a Stewart or a MacDonald; it affected the security of the Scottish state.

The claims of both of the contending factions were tenuous, but the Duke of Albany was not about to abandon his own claim to the Earldom; no ruler of Scotland could feel comfortable if Ross should fall into the already powerful hands of the Lord of the Isles. Donald would also not give up his claim as the Earldom of Ross, with its extensive possessions stretching from Skye to the Black Isle, Ross, would make him master of the entire western seaboard of the highlands of Scotland; as well as becoming the feudal superior of many clans like the Frasers, Rosses, and MacKenzies who opposed any further expansion of the Lordship. A clash between Donald and the Albany was inevitable.

Donald marshalled his host at Ardtornish Castle, it comprised of all the clans of the western isles and from this gathering of ten thousand he selected the best six thousand. Landing at Strome Castle in Lochalsh Donald led his army by way of Loch Carron to the east coast of Scotland. As Donald approached Dingwall his way was bared by Angus Dubh Mackay at the head of his clan. After a fierce engagement Angus was defeated and the levies of the isles flooded down to Inverness. At Inverness Donald issued a summons to the clans of the Earldom of Ross to join his army. The response was at best mixed, the MacKintoshes, Roses, Chisolms and the Clan Chattan came out with varying degrees of enthusiasm for Donald either because they regarded him as their rightful feudal superior or through fear of his long reach. The MacKenzies were divided with their chief being imprisoned while a contingent were present in Donald's army, other clans like the Rosses stayed sullenly at home while the Frasers joined the forces opposing Donald. In general the clans of the central and eastern highlands were not enthusiastic about any further increases in the power of the Lordship. Donald's expedition should not be interpreted as a struggle between feudal and Gaelic Scotland as there were many clans who were opposed to him.

Donald put Inverness to the flames before setting out with his host now totalling ten thousand on a circuitous route via the Laigh of Moray towards Aberdeen. It is remarkable that Donald took this direction as it was longer, more heavily defended, and on the very edge of the area which could be considered as Gaelic. The answer may lie in the fact that the Earls of Ross were the feudal superiors of this district and Donald wanted to emphasize his claim to them.

Albany's nephew the Earl of Mar had assembled an army to oppose Donald; it included the levies of three other earls, a sheriff and the burgesses of the town of Aberdeen. Mar's army although numerically inferior were better armed and included a fair number of knights from amongst the local nobility. On the twenty

---

Margaret her aunt and nearest blood relative to the senior branch of the O'Beolan Earls, Margaret was married to Donald second Lord of the Isles.

fourth of July 1411 the opposing forces met on the bloody field of Harlaw, the struggle continued all day with the impetuous rushes of the highlanders being stoutly resisted by the armoured troops of Mar. Highland chief engaged lowland earl in single combat. The conflict ebbed and flowed with the greatest ferocity neither army prepared to give way. Casualties were high on both sides and the conflict ended in exhausted stalemate with both sides claiming victory.

Donald withdrew into the remote fastnesses of his realm, while Albany raised an army and soon established control over the Earldom of Ross. In the following year of 1412 Albany campaigned against Donald's mainland possessions, the islands being invulnerable at this time because Donald had complete control of the sea. John of Fourdun recounts how, after Albany's campaign; Donald made his submission at Lochgilphead and consented to becoming a vassal of the crown.[29] Whether one accepts the lowland or highland traditions as to which of the two protagonists achieved the ascendancy, Donald was not able to enforce his claims to the Earldom of Ross and it was not until the time of his son Alexander that the Earldom came within the orbit of the Lords of the Isles. Albany was able to ensure that, on the resignation of the earldom by Euphemia, it passed not to Donald but to the Stewarts.[30]

In his later years Donald joined a religious order and spent his life in prayer and contemplation. Donald died at Ardtornish Castle in the early 1420's, and was buried among his ancestors on Iona. His eldest son Alexander became the third Lord of the Isles. Donald had exhibited the qualities so admired by his clan, those of courage and upholding Gaelic culture against the relentless pressure of feudal Scotland. But Donald's greatest achievements lay in the field of diplomacy; he held a firm grip on the Lordship which could so easily have dissolved into anarchy. Donald, although unsuccessful, understood the pivotal role the control the Earldom of Ross played in establishing the Lordship's domination of the north of Scotland. If the Lordship was able to establish complete hegemony over the Earldom of Ross then it would hold not only have complete mastery of the western highland seaboard but also dominate the north of Scotland. Control of these vast possessions would have meant that the Lordship would be by far the most powerful element in Scotland and could, during periods of weakness, challenge the authority of the Scottish state. He was also involved in a series of treaties with

---

[29] There are some problems with this account, Donald was already a vassal of the crown (at least nominally), and any submission on this basis did not alter the status quo. Some doubt as to the accurateness of Fordun's account must exist as Donald's submission is not recorded in either the Chamberlain or Exchequer Roles although both mention Albany's campaign.

[30] Donald was next involved in a brief but bitter feud with his brother John Mor Tannister, the cause of the dispute was the ownership of certain lands in Kintrye. The Lordship was divided, with the MacLeods of Harris and the MacLeans supporting John Mor Tannister while the other clans supported Donald. John Mor was defeated and fled to his clan's possessions in the Glens of Antrim. Shortly afterwards the two brothers were reconciled and harmony was re-established in the Lordship.

England which might well have led to the Lordship occupying half of Scotland.[31] It is only with the benefit of hindsight that we know that this relationship with England was to sow the seeds of destruction of the Lordship.

Alexander, third Lord of the Isles, 1423-1449.

Alexander was proclaimed third Lord of the Isles in 1423. Only a year later, Albany's son, the Earl of Buchan, who had been created the Earl of Ross by his father, was killed at the Battle of Verneuil fighting with his French allies against the English. Once again the issue as to who had the right to the Earldom was open to debate. Alexander considered that his claim to the Earldom was just through the rights of his mother as heiress. This claim was yet again to be one of the main sources of tension between the Lordship and the Scottish Crown.

After the payment of a ransom, James I returned from captivity in England, and took control of government. James understood that in order to transform Scotland into a state that could resist English pressure he must break the semi-autominous power of the great nobles of Scotland, amongst whom was Alexander. James was an astute statesman and by the end of his reign he had largely succeeded in his designs against enormous difficulties. In order to achieve his objectives he did not scruple from all forms of deception and violence including murder. Initially Alexander's relationship with James was cordial, Alexander even appearing on a jury which condemned some nobles who had been plotting against James. The initial break between the two men was caused by the death of John Mor Tannister, Alexander's uncle. Some of the courtiers that surrounded James drew up a plot to break the power of Alexander, by installing a compliant John Mor Tannister as Lord of the Isles.

John rejected any idea of betraying Alexander and was clearly not going to be the instrument for overthrowing the Lordship. John Mor Tannister received a message from a certain James Campbell to meet him on Isla as he wished to give him a message from James. The unsuspecting John arrived at the meeting with only a few attendants and was promptly murdered by the agents of the crown. The level of James's involvement in this affair is unclear. However, given the nature of the dark side of his personality it is likely that he was intimately involved. This murder caused widespread anger throughout the highlands and especially in the lands of the Lordship. James strongly denied any involvement, although his stance was weakened by Campbell, who continued to assert that he had verbal orders from James till the day he was led to the gallows. The involvement of James Campbell is the first recorded incident in what was to be a long and bitter relationship between the Clan Campbell and the MacDonalds, especially with regards to the Clan Iain Mor.

---

[31] These treaties provide for the dismemberment of Scotland, the English would have annexed the south while the Lordship would have controlled all the land north of Stirling.

Shortly after this James called a convention at Inverness at which all the clan chiefs were ordered to attend. His stated aim was to form a view as how best to establish a greater control by the Scottish state over the highlands, what the chiefs did not know was the means by which he intended to exert his authority. When all the chiefs had gathered at Inverness they were either imprisoned in solitary confinement or were hanged on the gallows.[32] The unlawful execution of many of Alexander's relatives and supporters can only have fuelled the resentment of the imprisoned Alexander. James showed no remorse for his treachery, quite the contrary he is described as being delighted by the consequences of his plot.

Alexander was soon released, but had to accompany James to Perth where he was further humiliated by having to abase himself before James who admonished him before the court. Alexander's mother Margaret was held a prisoner on the island of Inchcolm in the Firth of Forth. It comes as no surprise that on Alexander's return to the Isles a large scale rebellion erupted. With ten thousand men gathered from his considerable domains Alexander sacked Inverness and devastated the surrounding countryside in 1429. James raised a royal army and marched north to intercept his rebellious subject, James, despite his underhand methods was a strong minded and resourceful monarch who was determined to establish his authority throughout Scotland. As James approached, Alexander was deserted by two of his most powerful supporters, the Camerons and the MacKintoshes, who, to compound Alexander's problems joined James's army. With this defection the balance of power had shifted and Alexander made his submission to James.

Alexander was forced to do homage to James at Holyrood Palace, on bended knee and holding his bonnet in one hand and holding his sword pointing towards his chest in the other. The implications of this ritualistic submission were well understood by the Scottish court; James was publicly exerting his authority over the powerful island lord. Alexander was imprisoned in Tantallon Castle, where he joined another of James's opponents William Douglas.

If James had calculated that by imprisoning Alexander he would gain the acquiescence of the isles he was mistaken. After the murder of John Mor Tannister his son Donald Balloch had quickly established a firm grip on the Clan Iain Mor, and after Alexander's imprisonment he was accepted by the vassals of Alexander as their leader. Donald Balloch assembled the power of the isles and marched on Inverlochy Castle, to engage the royal army led by the Earl of Mar who had encountered Donald second Lord of the Isles at Harlaw in 1411. The royal army was routed after they failed to withstand a ferocious charge of the highland army.[33] Donald Balloch then swept through the lands of the Camerons and MacKintoshes laying them waste in revenge for them deserting Alexander, he then returned to the Isles to evade retribution.

---

[32] Among those executed was Alexander MacGorrie the chief of the Clan Gorrie, who was descended from Gorrie the third son of Alexander's grandfather John first Lord of the Isles. He died on the gallows without any trial or explanation.
[33] Amongst the nine hundred dead of the royal army were the Earl of Caithness and the Master of Lovat.

James hurried north with the flower of the Scottish nobility and was soon at Dunstaffnage where he slacked his thirst for revenge on dozens of the local rebels. Donald Balloch retreated to his clan lands in the Glens of Antrim to avoid any possibility of falling within the compass of James's long reach. On learning that Donald Balloch had fled to Ireland James sent a message to O'Neil, Lord of Antrim, urging him to send him the head of Donald Balloch. By this period the MacDonalds were a significant factor in the politics of Ulster being both represented by the Clan Iain Mor and the gallowglass communities that had settled there during the reign of Robert the Bruce. O'Neil not wanting to disturb the fragile balance of power in Ulster or to defy James sent the Scottish King the head of some poor unfortunate with the claim that it belonged to Donald Balloch. James allowed himself to be satisfied that Donald Balloch had met the fate reserved for rebels and let the matter rest. Donald Balloch went on to marry O'Neil's daughter and was to outlive James.

In October 1431 a son was born to the King and to celebrate this event, James released Alexander and restored not only his freedom but also his dignities and possessions. Although the birth of his son was a convenient pretext, the reasons for Alexander's release lay elsewhere. James faced emerging problems both internally and externally, Donald Balloch had amply demonstrated that the imprisonment of Alexander was no guarantee that the territories of the Lordship would submit peacefully to the authority of the Scottish state. In the fifteenth century the Kings of Scotland did not possess the military power to suppress a significant uprising in the Isles, nor could they afford a large scale military campaign in such a remote region. Alexander did live at peace with the Scottish state for the rest of James's rule both men had perhaps learnt the limits of their power. James I was assassinated in February 1437; Alexander standing aloof from court politics in his remote island realm was not implicated in the plot.

James II was only six at the time of his father's death and thus there was to be a long period of regencies before he obtained his majority. Alexander was appointed High Sheriff of Scotland north of the Forth and carried out his duties with fairness and diligence. It was during this period that Alexander laid the foundations for a long and bitter feud between the MacDonalds of Keppoch and the MacKintoshes.[34] On the information available he capriciously bestowed Keppoch's lands in Brae Lochaber on the chief of the MacKintoshes; this seems an extraordinary decision as he gave his own relative's lands into the hands of a clan that had deserted him in his struggle with James I. Possibly it was an attempt to firmly commit the MacKintoshes to the cause of the Isles, and thus to establish a powerful bulwark in the eastern highlands.[35]

---

[34] See chapter 8.
[35] The charter that Alexander granted to the MacKintoshes for the lands in Glen Spean seems to translate in a way which refers to MacKintosh as "our faithful servant", although the medieval Latin allows room for differing translations. In any event this description of MacKintosh must have caused much bitterness amongst the MacDonalds of Keppoch whose lands Alexander had gifted away to the clan which deserted Alexander's standard in 1429.

It was during the period of the Regency that Alexander became not only third Lord of the Isles but also the Earl of Ross. The long coveted Earldom was at last in MacDonald hands and the clan had reached the apogee of their power. The territories owing their allegiance to the MacDonald Lord of the Isles stretched from the Glens of Ulster to the northern tip of Lewis, and from the remote shores of the islands of Uist to the fertile peninsular of Easter Ross. The final acceptance of the claims of the Lords of the Isles by the regency does reflect its own weakness and its fear of the island lord.

Alexander seems in his later years to have come to an accommodation with the Scottish state no doubt in part due to him obtaining the Earldom of Ross. Alexander died on the eight of May 1449 and was buried at Dingwall, breaking with the tradition of being buried on Iona; this may have been his final act to reinforce the MacDonald claim to Ross. He left John his eldest son who was to succeed him, Celestine who was gifted lands in Lochalsh where he founded his own family, and Hugh who was given the lands of Sleat in Skye where he founded his own

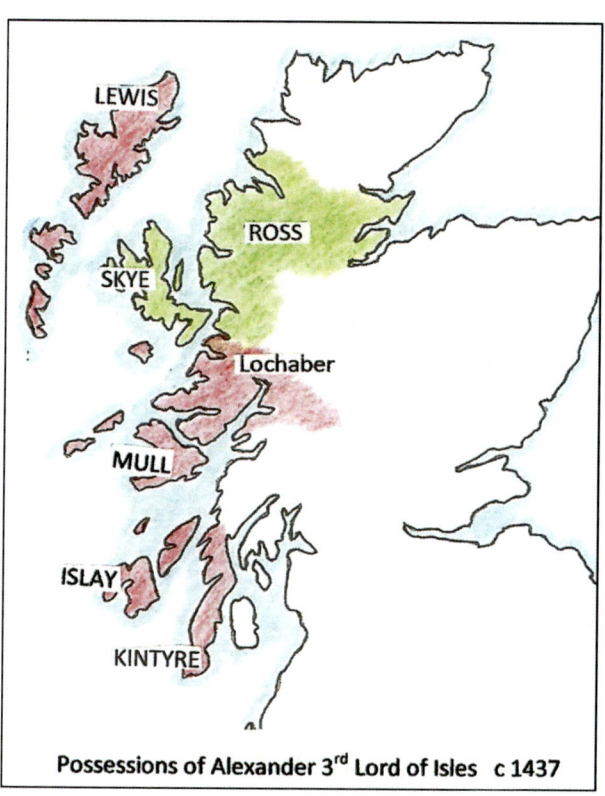

Possessions of Alexander 3rd Lord of Isles c 1437

clan; the MacDonalds of Sleat. Alexander vacillated between rebellion and submission during his rule as third Lord of the Isles. However, in the circumstances both seem understandable, and by the end of his life the power of his people held sway over an area that even the Campbells were unable to achieve at the height of their power. For a short period the MacDonald Lords of the Isles held sway over half of the highlands of Scotland and were the most powerful magnates in the Kingdom of Scotland.

John, fourth Lord of the Isles, 1449-1493.

John, Alexander's eldest son succeeded him to become the fourth Lord of the Isles. He inherited an enviable situation, he had the absolute loyalty of the clans which belonged to the territories of the original Lordship, and was feudal superior of the clans of the Earldom of Ross. Amongst the latter were a majority which had opposed an expansion of the power of the MacDonald Lords. However, under feudal law they were obliged to support their Earl against all excepting only the

King. To the south of the highland line, Scotland was being torn apart as the Douglases, Livingstones and Crichtons struggled for supremacy during the minority of James II. The highlands by comparison were relatively tranquil with John being by far the most powerful magnate in the region. The powerful hand of James I had been removed from the tiller of state, and there was no authority that threatened John's position, John's best course would have been to stay aloof from Scottish politics and advance the interests of the MacDonalds by masterly inactivity. John was only eighteen when he succeeded to the Lordship, but his inexperience should have been countered by the counsel given to him by Donald Balloch and the other chiefs of the clans. John held an almost regal court at Ardtornish or Dingwall, with a President of the Council, Treasurer and Chamberlain, as well as the traditional Gaelic posts.

John entered into an alliance with the Earls of Douglas and Crawford with no less an aim than to dismember Scotland. There is no existing evidence to say whether he was badly advised or was too headstrong to listen. In any event he committed himself to the one course of action which could threaten his position. John stormed the castles of Inverness and Urquhart, he then marched south through Moray committing the Castle of Ruthven to the flames as he passed. James II had just achieved his majority and acted quickly with skill and determination. James murdered Douglas[36] with his own hands at a meeting at which Douglas had been promised his safety. James then turned his attention on the Earl of Crawford and supported by the Earl of Huntley, defeated him at the Battle of Brechin. Huntley then marched north to encounter John who was still in Moray; however he withdrew when he realized the size of John's host. John did not intervene in the south as his Douglas and Crawford allies were picked off one at a time by the royal army. By this inaction he achieved the worst possible outcome in that he did not help his co-conspirators and yet he earned the enmity of James and became isolated in his northern possessions. The power of the Douglases was broken at the Battle of Arkinholme and the new Earl of Douglas fled to John for protection. Douglas, after being assured of John's support, fled to England where he was welcomed by the Duke of York.

John gave Donald Balloch command of five thousand clansmen and a fleet of one hundred galleys. Donald Balloch proceeded to invade the islands of Bute and Arran. The castles on both islands were stormed and the highland army laid waste the land, and carried off an enormous plunder. This invasion of Arran and Bute was a deliberate act of revenge on James because they had been Stewart possessions for over a century. The raids on Arran and Bute did not alter the strategic situation; John was isolated and although formidable would not be able to resist the full weight of the Scottish state. John's nerve broke and he sent ambassadors to James asking for clemency if he repaired the damage he had caused. James mastered his resentment and in effect put John on probation. The relationship between John

---

[36] William fifth Earl of Douglas was murdered by James II on 22 February 1452. He led the Black Douglas faction who had amassed a vast power base in the borders and lowlands.

and the King had evolved into a stand off, neither were able to administer a knock out blow, however both knew that time was on the side of the king, as he alone had the power to determine whether the possessions of the Lords of the Isles would stay intact. John was sincere in regretting his part in the recent upheavals and was rewarded by James with further increments to his titles and possessions. These gifts only served to reinforce the view of the western clans that Royal authority could be flouted with impunity.

In 1460 James invaded England; he was joined by John Lord of the Isles and Earl of Ross at the head of three hundred men,[37] John offered to act as the vanguard of the Scottish army. Shortly afterwards, at the siege of Roxburgh Castle, James was killed when one of the Scottish siege guns exploded. The untimely death of James II yet again exposed Scotland to a long royal minority with all the associated risks of chaos.

Soon after James's death, John received ambassadors from England amongst whom was the exiled Earl of Douglas. The treaty proposed by the English was nothing less than the dismemberment of the Scottish state, by John, the Earl of Douglas and the English. The terms of the treaty were that John was to become the vassal of the King of England and was to receive in return for this submission and his aid in the break up of Scotland all the land north of the Forth. John sent ambassadors to England and ratified the compact, thus becoming a signatory to the Treaty of Ardtornish in 1461. John's decision to agree to this wild scheme was critical to the history of the MacDonalds, and many of the adversities they were to face in the future can be traced back to this extremely unwise decision.

John was already the most powerful magnate in Scotland, while it had already been demonstrated that this power could not successfully resist a determined Scottish monarch.[38] John had enjoyed increments to his power as a reward for his loyalty during the later years of James II. The explanation as to why John allowed himself to sign such a risky document lay in his own weak and greedy nature and the self-interested advice of the dispossessed Earl of Douglas, which was backed up by that of the wild Donald Balloch, whose world view was encompassed by his own Gaelic legacy, and to whom the concept of Scotland as a nation state was of no interest.

The treaty of Ardtornish was kept a secret by the two signatories and for twelve years lay hidden from James III. During this period John's domains enjoyed a respite from the usual cycle of rebellion and the consequent retribution. James was made aware of the treaty while negotiating with England about the marriage of his son to the daughter of Edward IV. James was profoundly shocked and angered when he discovered the contents of this document, which exposed this plot to dismember Scotland. Only John lay within his reach as Douglas was still in exile and Donald

---

[37] It is clear that judging by the numbers of followers John brought with him he did not over exert himself on behalf of his King.

[38] The monarch's power was often achieved by default. The endemic disunity of the great magnates offered plenty of scope for playing of one or more against any which might directly confront him.

Balloch was on his own clan lands in the glens of Ulster. John was condemned in his absence and sentenced to death as well as being stripped of all his offices and titles. James then started assembling an army led by Colin Campbell, Earl of Argyll, to exact his revenge on John.

On hearing of the preparations that were being made against him John lost his nerve and in July 1476 he appeared before James with all the semblance of humility and contrition. The queen interceded on John's behalf and with the express consent of the nobility John was pardoned and reinstated to all his possessions.[39] On the same day John resigned his right to the Earldom of Ross while still retaining his title as Lord of the Isles. The events of this day were pure theatre for the benefit of the court, all the details of which had been carefully worked out before. John had forfeited the Earldom of Ross due to his inept political intriguing, and lost without a struggle the prize which the MacDonalds had striven for, for over a century. John's submission to James and his surrender of Ross was regarded with dismay by all the clans of MacDonalds and no one was more outraged at this supine surrender than John's own proud and warlike son Angus Og.

The position of the other clans within the Lordship was more opaque. Although they valued the Lordship and were in later years to rise time and again in support of it, they had witnessed a continual expansion of the MacDonald influence at their expense.[40] The diminution of MacDonald power allowed the possibility that they could achieve greater independence for themselves. The political consensus of the Lordship was breaking down with the MacDonald clans[41] supporting Angus Og in his opposition to the loss of the Earldom of Ross, while the other clans of the original Lordship adhered to John.

Apart from the loss of the Earldom of Ross, John had been forced to cede the ancient MacDonald patrimony of northern Kintyre and Knapdale which were later restored to him, but only for his lifetime. This region was an area of special concern to the kings of Scotland as it controlled access to the Clyde estuary and was a particularly sensitive area as it also formed part of the original MacDonald territories. There was an uneasy tranquillity in the western highlands between 1478 and 1481 during which both factions brooded on the future. In 1481 Angus Og gathered a large force of isles men and carried fire and sword into Ross. His aim was to re-establish MacDonald hegemony in that region and to curb the emerging power of the MacKenzies. James commissioned the Earl of Athol to march north and check Angus Og. When he arrived in Ross he was joined by contingents of

---

[39] The reason for these continual pardons for what were clearly acts of treachery was the complete inability of the King to enforce his will in the heartland of the Lordship i.e. the western highlands and islands.

[40] The MacLeods had witnessed the grant of lands in Skye, to Hugh, by his father Alexander third Lord of the Isles, Alexander had also gifted large tracts of the western coast of the Earldom of Ross to Celestine his second son. Celestine became the founder of the MacDonalds of Lochalsh.

[41] By this date all the clans of MacDonalds had formed as distinctive social units, Lochalsh, Sleat, Clanranald, Glengarry, Keppoch, Glencoe and the Clan Iain Mor.

those clans who did not wish to see the restoration of MacDonald hegemony; they included, the MacKenzies, MacKays, Brodies, Rosses and Frasers. A sanguinary battle was fought at Lagabraad in which Angus Og was victorious with Athol and the chief of the MacKenzies barely escaping with their lives. This encounter only served to reinforce the esteem in which Angus Og was held by his people; however it did not result in the restoration of MacDonald power in the region. Matters were brought to a head when the two opposing factions within the Lordship met in the Sound of Mull with their accompanying fleets.

On one side were ranged the MacDonald clans under the command of Angus Og and on the other was the fleet of the other clans of the Lordship under the command of his father John, fourth Lord of the Isles. After some delay caused by the prevailing winds, the two fleets engaged each other in a deadly clash in which many supporters of both sides lost their lives. Eventually Angus Og was victorious and John's battered forces were forced to withdraw. The Battle of Bloody Bay was fought in 1484 and established Angus Og as the new captain of the MacDonalds. This civil war was a disaster for the Lordship and heralded the beginning of the end of the MacDonald hegemony in the western highlands, because it had put an end to the consensus that had been in place since the time of Bruce.

Oil was poured on troubled waters by the subsequent actions of the Earls of Argyll and Athol. Angus Og had married a daughter of Colin Campbell, Earl of Argyll and she had bore him a son called Donald Dubh. The Earl of Athol with the connivance of Argyll abducted Donald Dubh, who was only a child, from his home at Finlaggen. The unfortunate infant was delivered into the hands of Colin Campbell who immediately incarcerated him in the grim Castle of Inchconnel which sits on a small island in Loch Awe. Colin, Earl of Argyll, had seized his opportunity to possess the heir to the Lordship and saw that he could not only gain favour with James, but also advance his own clan's interests. Under the leadership of a succession of able chiefs the Campbells had established themselves as the paramount clan in Argyllshire and were now casting their ambitions further a field. As part of his plan to disrupt the succession of the Lordship Colin concocted a story that Donald Dubh was illegitimate. This fabrication was ultimately accepted by the Scottish government. It will be noted that Colin did not stoop from casting aspersions on the morality of his own daughter in order to fulfil his ambitions.

Angus Og was not a man to let such a deed go unpunished; he invaded the Campbell country and laid it waste before moving on to Athol. However he was not able to release his son from Inchconnel. This fact gives a hint that the balance of power in Argyllshire was already shifting in favour of the Campbells for it would have been inconceivable that they would have been able to resist the power of the Lord of the Isles even fifty years before. A few years later Angus Og was reconciled to John and for a brief moment in the twilight of its existence the Lordship was at peace.

MacKenzie power and influence had meanwhile been spreading in Ross and as this clan had long been opposed to the Lordship, Angus Og invaded the Earldom at the head of a large force of islanders. At this time the MaKenzies were not able to resist the power of the Lordship so they played the only viable hand which was available to them. Angus Og's harper a certain O'Cabe had developed a passion for the daughter of MacKenzie; he was offered her hand in exchange for murdering Angus Og. MacVurich records that O'Cabe would sing a couplet he had written prior to the assassination.

> Rider of the dappled steed, thy soul to God commend,
> If there is poison in my blade, thy life right soon shall end.

One night as Angus Og was sleeping O'Cabe slit his throat and the man most likely to able to restore the Lordship to its past glories or even to save it from disintegration, was dead.

Angus Og was a hero to his people who admired his courage and determination and with his death something of the ancient dignity of the MacDonalds was lost for ever. The Irish Annuls record that in 1490 "MacDhomnaill of Alba, the best man in Erin or in Alba of his time, was unfortunately slain by an Irish harper...". Shortly after the murder of Angus Og, John retired from the active rule of the Lordship perhaps broken in spirit by the death of his son, the abduction of his grandson and the bitter divisions within the Lordship. John handed control over to Celestine of Lochalsh to whom he had gifted the lands of Lochbroom, Lochcarron and Lochalsh. John retired to the monastery of Paisley, although he still travelled widely among his old possessions and due to events to be described shortly he was stripped of his title of Lord of the Isles and died a broken man in 1503 at Dundee.

In his later years John exhibited an inability to curb the rash excesses of Celestine and failed to act in any way which would have prevented the political disintegration of the Lordship. It is ironic that on the occasions that he did act, for example, in his plotting with the English, it would have been better if he had not. John through his susceptibility to ill considered advice, his inability to stem the political fractures within the Lordship, and ultimately his failure to either support his son Angus Og or curb Alexander of Lochalsh was largely responsible for the demise of the Lordship.

Alexander of Lochalsh was the son of Celestine (John's younger brother), who after John's abdication took on the role as Lord of the Isles. He acted on behalf of Donald Dubh who was still incarcerated in Inchconnel, although by this period his superiority over the western highlands was restricted to only some of the adherents of the Lordship. The MacLeans and MacLeods were by this time starting to carve out their own destinies. Due in part to Alexander's possessions lying on the western mainland of Ross and the historical legacy he had inherited, Alexander resolved to claim Ross by force of arms. With the support of all the clans of MacDonalds and the Camerons he invaded Ross in 1491. Alexander marched as his forefathers had done through Lochaber and Badenoch where he was joined by the MacKintoshes, he then moved on and stormed Inverness. Here he was joined by the Roses of Kilravock, who were the only clan in the area to rise in his support. Unwisely he then sent half his army home with the spoils they had amassed, while he preceded to Strathconnan so that he could humble the MacKenzies and check their growing power. Kenneth MacKenzie had assembled his clan and routed Alexander's force at the Battle of Park, after a surprise night attack.

Alexander retired from Ross having to abandon his dreams of conquest. James IV had come to the throne in 1488, and for him this act of rebellion was the last straw. John had either acquiesced to the rebellion or was too ineffectual to have stopped it. After a long history of rebellion and treachery (at least from the crown's perspective) James felt strong enough to act decisively. In May 1493 John was forfeited in all his estates and titles, John formally implemented this decision by making a voluntary surrender of all the lands of the Lordship in 1494.

The fall of the Lordship was a disaster for the western highlands if not for the Scottish state. A power vacuum was created in the region which the state was not able to replace with its own different style of authority. The door was left open to a prolonged period of anarchy during which the clans which had followed the Lords of the Isles struggled to maintain their independence and aspired to gain mastery over their neighbours. The situation was exacerbated by a weak and venal Scottish state which suffered from prolonged periods of infighting caused by self-serving regents who controlled the reins of power during the minorities of several kings and queens.

With the fall of the Lordship in 1494 the period covered by this book begins. However, alongside the clan feuds which almost immediately erupted in many districts of the western highlands there were the contemporaneous attempts to re-establish the Lordship. These continual risings formed the backdrop to the internecine local struggles. Many clan feuds were intimately bound up with the final agonies of the moribund Lordship; for example, the feud between the Frasers and the Clanranald.[42] It is clear that the clans would on occasion put aside their feuds for a while in order to support an attempt to re-establish the Lordship. These rebellions represented the higher political aspirations of the western clans. As each rebellion failed, the anarchy increased, and pressure increased on the clans from the state and its instruments. They gradually abandoned their larger vision and settled down to the grim business of struggling for their survival.

The MacDonalds of Lochalsh, 1503-1519.

After John's death in 1503, the MacDonalds and other supporters of the Lordship settled their support on the hapless Donald Dubh who was still languishing in the dungeons of Inchconnel.

James IV was blessed with both a strong hand and the wisdom to know when not to use it. In 1493 he held court at Dunstaffnage Castle; here in an atmosphere of conciliation he met with the west highland chiefs. The chiefs of the MacDonald clans held aloof from his overtures with one important exception, Maclain of Ardnamurchan. In the following year James rebuilt and garrisoned the strategic castles of Tarbert and Dunaverty in Kintyre, no doubt in order to overawe the

---

[42] See chapter 3.

recalcitrant MacDonalds. John Mor and his son John Cathenach were incensed at this intrusion into the territories of the Clan Iain Mor. They laid siege to Dunaverty and after storming the castle, hung the newly installed governor in full view of James's returning fleet. James could not allow such a flagrant act of defiance to go unpunished and had a willing accomplice in Maclain.[43]

In 1495 James tightened his hold on the west coast by garrisoning the castles of Mingarry in Ardnamurchan, and Cairnburgh in the Treshnish Isles. The chiefs were at last compliant to his authority and all the chiefs of the MacDonalds made their submission to James at Mingarry, with the notable exceptions of Glencoe and the Clan Iain Mor. On James's return to Edinburgh he passed a series of acts which made the chiefs responsible for their clans. James then went on a northern progress; he was well received by the clans of the Earldom of Ross when he held council at Dingwall.

It was not long before Alexander of Lochalsh was in open rebellion, ostensibly on behalf of Donald Dubh. The MacKenzies and Munros encountered him at the Battle of Drumchatt, where they defeated Alexander's force and he was again forced to retire. Alexander fled to the island of Colonsay from where he hoped to renew his struggle to re-establish the Lordship. The effects of James's firm but judicious policies were beginning to have a pronounced effect on the dispositions of the chiefs and he failed to attract the necessary support to continue his defiance. The MacDonalds of Ardnamurchan had by now fully abandoned any support for the old order, and Maclain slew Alexander to curry favour with the King.[44]

James had a change of policy shortly after this; perhaps this last attempt by Alexander had convinced him that a more drastic tack was required. He was also influenced by some of the great magnates who were ever present at his shoulder, the Gordon, Earl of Huntley and more particularly the Campbell, Earl of Argyll. It was greatly to their disadvantage that those representing the interests of the MacDonalds were rarely at court. James's new policy was to use these great houses as the instruments of royal policy as the state still lacked the ability to campaign for lengthy periods in the western isles. This policy was disastrous for the western clans especially the MacDonalds, as the Gordons and Campbells furthered their own interests while carrying out royal policies. These policies had often been drawn up, or at least initiated by Huntley and Argyll. As the power of the Campbells inexorably grew, the violent attempts of the western clans to resist them only served to further prejudice the state against them. This policy was continued for over a century and eventually led to the last MacDonald chief of the Clan Iain Mor fleeing Isla in 1615 under relentless pressure from the Campbells.[45]

The immediate consequences of this new policy was that vast tracts of the ancient MacDonald heritage were gifted (at least on paper) to those who had proved their loyalty. Amongst these beneficiaries were the Maclains, the Gordons and the Campbells. The injustice was compounded when the MacDonald chiefs

---

[43] See chapter 5.
[44] See chapter 5.
[45] See chapter 12.

were asked to produce their charters for their remaining lands. Few of them could show charters for their ancestral lands as charters were an aspect of feudal law and although some were used during the period of the Lordship most grants were given verbally under the Gaelic system. Some of the feuds of the sixteenth century were at least in part caused or fuelled by a lack of legal title to clan lands; for example, the struggle between the MacLeods of Harris and the MacDonalds of Sleat over the district of Trotternish in Skye.[46]

The rightful heir to the inheritance of the Lordship, Donald Dubh was still held captive by the Campbells in the dark depths of Inchconnel. The western highlands were again put into a state of turmoil when Donald Dubh escaped from his long captivity. He was released after a party of MacDonalds of Glencoe penetrated into the heart of Campbell country and released him from his dreary confinement. On gaining his freedom Donald Dubh immediately raised the standard of revolt in an attempt to re-establish the Lordship. His legitimate claim, as the rightful heir to the Lordship and his understandable bitterness not only towards his Campbell tormentors, but also James IV on whose behalf they claimed to act left him with few other options. The news of the escape of Donald Dubh spread like wildfire in the lands of the old Lordship, and soon most of the ancient supporters of the Lordship had flocked to his side, including the MacLeods, MacLeans, MaKinnons, MacQuarries, MacNeills, and some of the branches of the MacDonalds. There were some notable exceptions to this confederation; the MacKintoshes, the Maclains of Ardnamurchan, and the Clanranald and predictably none of the clans of Ross joined him. By the beginning of the sixteenth century the various clans of the MacDonalds were no longer acting in unison and were carving out their own individual policies. The risks that the rebel clans took were immense especially when faced by the formidable personality of James IV commanding the resources of an ever more powerful Scottish state. The longing for the Gaelic world for the old order must have been strong for these chiefs to hazard everything in their support for Donald Dubh. As his ancestors had done before him Donald Dubh swept through Badenoch committing it to the flames.

In 1505 James prepared a major expedition against the rebels, a previous attempt at suppressing them having failed. James prepared not only an army led by the Earl of Arran but also a fleet which could strike with ease at the island possessions of the rebels. The appearance of a powerful royal fleet in the Hebrides exposed the vulnerability of the rebel clans to the power of the Scottish navy. The rebel chiefs made their submissions to James; one notable exception was Torquil MacLeod of Lewis who refused to submit and subsequently led the remainder of his life as a fugitive. The hapless Donald Dubh was captured when MacLean of Duart made his submission; he was imprisoned in Edinburgh Castle. After the capture of Donald Dubh the highlands enjoyed a period of tranquillity. This was partly caused by the growing reach of James's authority by using the Gordons and Campbells. The other reason was that the raft of judicious legislation James had

---

[46] See chapter 6.

drawn up in 1503 was beginning to be effectively implemented in the region. Had he lived longer, James's powerful personality and his energetic enforcement of the law might well have altered the relationship between the Scottish state and many of the western clans.

1n 1514 James IV and the flower of the Scottish nobility were cut down on the field of Flodden having fallen victim to the deadly English billmen. The strong hand which had kept the peace in the highlands was removed and rebellion broke out again with renewed violence. Sir Donald Galda the son of Alexander of Lochalsh raised the western clans in another attempt to re-establish the Lordship; like his father he also claimed to be representing Donald Dubh who was imprisoned in Edinburgh Castle. Donald Galda was supported by the MacLeods of Lewis and Harris, MacLean of Duart, the Clan Iain Mor and the MacDonalds of Glengarry and Keppoch. With each successive rising the list of rebel clans was diminishing as the belief in the re-establishment of the Lordship began to fade in the hearts of their ancient supporters.

Donald Galda occupied Glen Urquhart and stormed the royal castle there, while MacLean took the castle of Cairnburgh and MacLeod occupied Dunskaith Castle[47] on Skye. The Regent Albany let loose the new and old opponents to a re-establishment of the Lordship, the MacKenzies operating in the north, and the Campbells in the south. MacIain of Ardnamurchan was sent to bribe or coerce the less recalcitrant clans. Faced by the formidable forces arrayed against them the rebels sued for peace and Donald Galda's support ebbed away. During August 1515 Donald Galda submitted to Albany and due to the vulnerability of Scotland after the devastating losses of Flodden, was given lenient terms.

The restless Donald Galda was soon in open rebellion again due to his disputes with MacIain of Ardnamurchan and the opportunity provided by the rebellion of Lord Home on the borders. Donald Galda captured MacIain's stronghold of Mingarry and then proceeded to lay waste the entire district. The chiefs of the MacLeods and MacLeans had wearied of this continual cycle of violence and feared that retribution would also fall on them. They offered to hunt down Donald Galda in return for a pardon for past offences. The Regent Albany accepted their terms while at the same time giving yet more power to Argyll to suppress the rebellion. Argyll had little success in reducing the rebels; however he had accrued even greater authority over the southern isles. MacLean captured Donald Galda's two brothers who were later executed at Edinburgh. Despite the flow of events against him Donald Galda with his allies The Clan Iain Mor and the MacLeods of Lewis again invaded Ardnamurchan and utterly defeated MacIain, killing both him and his two sons,[48] the relentless pursuit of this feud was caused by MacIain being regarded as a traitor by the other branches of Clan Donald.

This victory and the removal of MacIain encouraged others to join Donald Galda and the rebellion was re-invigorated. Before retribution could catch up with Donald

---

[47] Both castle had been garrisoned by James IV.
[48] See chapter 5.

Galda he died on Mull in 1519. Donald Galda's brief and turbulent life during which he was knighted by James IV the day before the Battle of Flodden, before plunging with reckless abandon into attempting to re-establish the Lordship, was full of contradictions. He had been a favourite of James while held as a hostage at court; he had upheld the belief in the ancient independence of the Lordship and had exacted terrible retribution on those he saw as betraying the MacDonald legacy. He was single-minded and strong willed but his judgment must be in question as his violence and lack of political skill alienated many of the old supporters of the MacDonalds. With the death of Donald Galda the house of Lochalsh ended. The Lochalsh MacDonalds were all remarkable for their courage, and their violence. They demonstrated an inability to comprehend the changing kaleidoscope of political inter-relationships which was emerging with the disintegration of the Lordship.

The early part of the sixteenth century was a period of rapid expansion of Campbell power and influence; this was facilitated by weak central government under a series of regents who were often only too glad to have the Campbells acting on their behalf in the "lawless" regions of the west. The regents had more pressing problems than concerning themselves whether the Campbells were mainly serving their own interests. The model which the Campbells used was a combination of legal obligation backed by their own military power which was in its turn ultimately supported by the full weight of the state. With some notable exceptions this model was to prove highly successful and within a century had led to the Campbells controlling vast tracts of the south-west highlands and tying in the remainder with varying degrees of success through feudal forms of obligation. The legal instrument they used was the Bond of Manrent which was based on the feudal system. It engaged the vassal to provide certain services to their superior in exchange for protection. In the sixteenth century the vast majority of manrents drawn up in the western highlands are between the chiefs of the clans and one of the ever growing cadet branches of the Campbells. A considerable number of the feuds of this period were caused by two differing interpretations of what was the significance of these agreements. To the Campbells and the state they were strictly binding arrangements between a vassal and his superior. The fact that they were often infused with corruption was due usually to Argyll's influence at court where he was able to draw up their terms to suit his own ambitions. Few of the clan chiefs who signed these manrents understood the full implications of these agreements; they saw them as short term necessary evils in order to achieve some local advantage over their rivals or as a method of resisting Campbell pressure. Amongst the manrents signed in the sixteenth century were some involving the Clanranald, the MacDonalds of Sleat and the Clan Iain Mor.

Donald Dubh; the final agony.

With the death of James V in 1542, Scotland once again entered a period of weak government which created an environment which would allow violence and anarchy to flourish. James had for a time halted the ever increasing power of the

Campbells and had been well disposed towards the Clan Iain Mor and had even pardoned John Moydartach captain of the Clanranald for his long defiance of Royal authority. A year later Donald Dubh escaped from Edinburgh Castle amidst the confusion of political intrigue created by the magnates jockeying for position in the vacuum created by James's death. He was accepted with enthusiasm by most of the clans which had belonged to the old Lordship. Within months several other chiefs who were at this time being held at Edinburgh including John Moydartach were, on the ill considered advice of the Earl of Glencairn, released.[49]

Donald Dubh at the head of an army consisting of all the western clans, with the exception of the Clan Iain Mor, swept into the lands of the Campbells plundering, laying waste and killing. Donald Dubh's bitterness at the course of his life, being held as a captive since he was a young child first by the Campbells and then after his first escape by the state can only be imagined. No doubt he exacted what vengeance he could on the hapless inhabitants of the quiet glens of Argyll. John Moydartach was involved in his own country in a bitter feud with Hugh Lord Lovat chief of the Frasers.[50] This feud was bound up with the rising of Donald Dubh in that, John Moydartach as chief of the Clanranald was supported by the MacDonalds of Keppoch and the Camerons while the Frasers were supported by the Gordons. John Moydartach exacted a terrible price on the Frasers for their scheming over the Clanranald inheritance at the bloody field of Kinlochlochy in July 1544.His defeat of the Frasers and the fact that the Gordons were occupied with trying to suppress him greatly assisted Donald Dubh's efforts in Argyllshire.

As the relationship between Scotland and England deteriorated the Regent Arran offered Donald Dubh favourable terms for peace in the west. With the benefit of hindsight this was the chance for Donald Dubh to set the MacDonalds and the other western clans on a new and more favourable footing with the Scottish state. The Campbells were defeated or hiding in their strong castles while the state was weak and divided, it was now also threatened by an aggressive and opportunistic English foreign policy. Donald Dubh did not respond to Arran's overtures, his ambition was to re-establish the MacDonald hegemony over the Isles and the Earldom of Ross. He had spent most of his life in prison and it may well be that he was out of touch with the real state of the political situation in the western highlands. Donald summoned a council of the Lord of the Isles which was to convene on the Island of Eigg. At this meeting all the clans which had belonged to the Lordship were represented even the MacIains of Ardnamurchan, who had, up till now acted as loyal supporters of the state. They decided to treat with Henry VIII of England in order to form an alliance which would restore the Lordship of the Isles to its old glory.

After appointing commissioners to draw up a treaty with Henry, Donald Dubh and the council moved to Knockfergus in Ireland with a fleet of one hundred and eighty galleys and four thousand men. This host is described as " three thousand of

---

[49]   The Earl of Glencairn's motive for releasing John Moydartach was to provide a counter-weight to the power of the Campbells and Gordons.
[50]   See chapter 3.

them very tall men, clothed for the most part in habergeons of mail, armed with long swords and long bows, but with few guns: the other thousand, tall mariners, that rowed the galleys." The commissioners were dispatched to Henry with their terms for an alliance; in exchange for the creation of an independent Lordship in the Isles, Donald Dubh would assist Henry in the subjugation of Scotland. On the fourth of September 1545 agreement was reached on the terms that Donald had set out and the policy of his ancestors was once more put in place.

The policy of the island clans is hard to understand with the cold logic enimating from historical precedent, and from the perspective of nationalistic history. The chiefs no doubt had a different world view, in which Edinburgh was still a remote power which did not uphold the same culture as that still in place in the west. They believed that in their remote and extensive territories that the re-establishment of an independent Gaelic Kingdom was still possible. This remarkable union of all the western clans was also a sign of desperation and anger at the ever increasing, and threatening power of the Campbells. The chiefs may have felt that this moment was their last opportunity to reverse the encroachment on their lands and the presence of a power which would eventually threaten their very existence. If this was the case then their fears were to be realized in the coming century when the Maclains of Ardnamurchan, The Clan Iain Mor and the MacLeods of Lewis were to be swept away due to the encroachment of their ancient foes.

The grand scheme soon began to unravel; Donald was to be supported by the Earl of Lennox with English troops, and inexplicably Lennox delayed his arrival on the west coast. The highland and Irish levies of Donald Dubh's army began to loose heart and drift away, in an attempt to halt this gradual diminution of his forces Donald returned to the Isles. When Henry's gold subsidies arrived there were disputes as to their allocation and the army began to disintegrate. When eventually Lennox did arrive in the Irish Sea the west highland host had melted away and Donald Dubh was in no position to assist him. Donald Dubh returned to Ireland in an attempt to raise a fresh army from his Irish supporters especially from the considerable possessions of the Clan Iain Mor who now held lands not only in the Glens but also the Route of Antrim. On his way to Dublin, Donald Dubh caught a fever and died at Drogheda in 1545. With his death the direct line of Somerled came to an end and any realistic hope of the re-emergence of The Lordship of the Isles had ended. The clans of the western highlands were never again to be united, they were all caught up in a struggle to survive as distinct entities. Each clan attempted to secure legal title to their lands and resist the encroachment of their neighbours in the anarchy which was so prevalent in the sixteenth century. Beyond these local trials they had to attempt to survive the ever increasing power of the Campbells in the south and the MacKenzies in the north. With the loss of any hope of a restoration of the Lordship the MacDonalds were diminished in their political and cultural aspirations.

MACDONALDS OF CLANNRANALD TO 1594

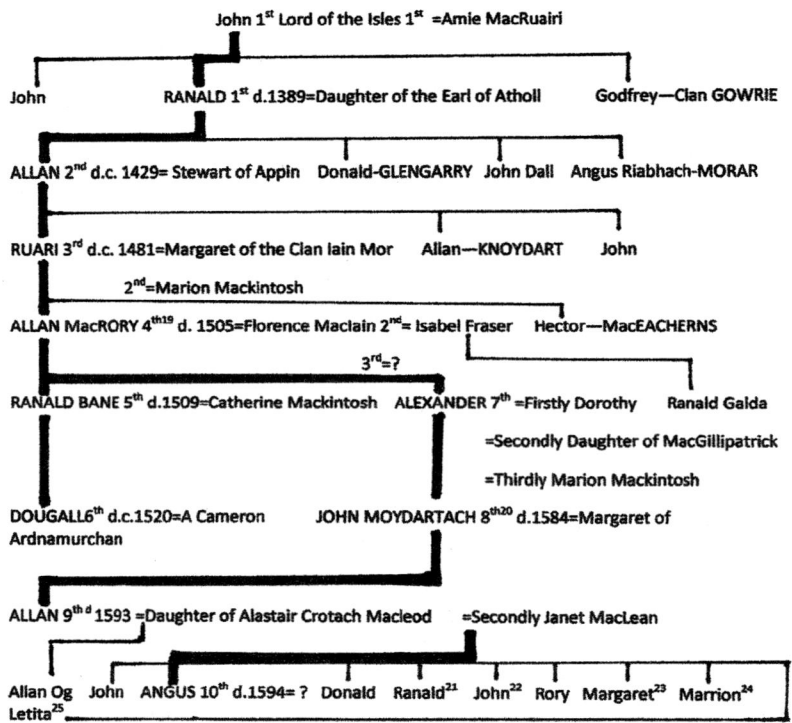

John 1st Lord of the Isles 1[st] =Amie MacRuairi

John   RANALD 1st d.1389=Daughter of the Earl of Atholl   Godfrey—Clan GOWRIE

ALLAN 2nd d.c. 1429= Stewart of Appin   Donald-GLENGARRY   John Dall   Angus Riabhach-MORAR

RUARI 3rd d.c. 1481=Margaret of the Clan Iain Mor   Allan—KNOYDART   John

2[nd]=Marion Mackintosh

ALLAN MacRORY 4[th19] d. 1505=Florence Maclain 2[nd]= Isabel Fraser   Hector—MacEACHERNS

3[rd]=?

RANALD BANE 5th d.1509=Catherine Mackintosh   ALEXANDER 7[th] =Firstly Dorothy   Ranald Galda

=Secondly Daughter of MacGillipatrick

=Thirdly Marion Mackintosh

DOUGALL6[th] d.c.1520=A Cameron   JOHN MOYDARTACH 8[th20] d.1584=Margaret of
Ardnamurchan

ALLAN 9[th d] 1593 =Daughter of Alastair Crotach Macleod   =Secondly Janet MacLean

Allan Og   John   ANGUS 10th d.1594= ?   Donald   Ranald[21]   John[22]   Rory   Margaret[23]   Marrion[24]
Letita[25]

=Secondly Janet of Clanranald

---

[19] For a more detailed genealogy of this period, see THE CLANRAŃALD INHERITANCE.
[20] John Moydartach also had unions with a daughter of Knoydart, Neill and Penelope of the Stewarts of Appin
[21] Ranald's descendants are the MacDonalds of Benbecula.
[22] John's descendants are the MacDonalds of Kinlochmoidart.
[23] Margaret married Donald MacDonald of Glengarry.
[24] Marion married Roderick MacNeill of Barra.
[25] Letita married MacDonald of Glenaladale.

THE CLANRANALD INHERITANCE OF JOHN MOIDART

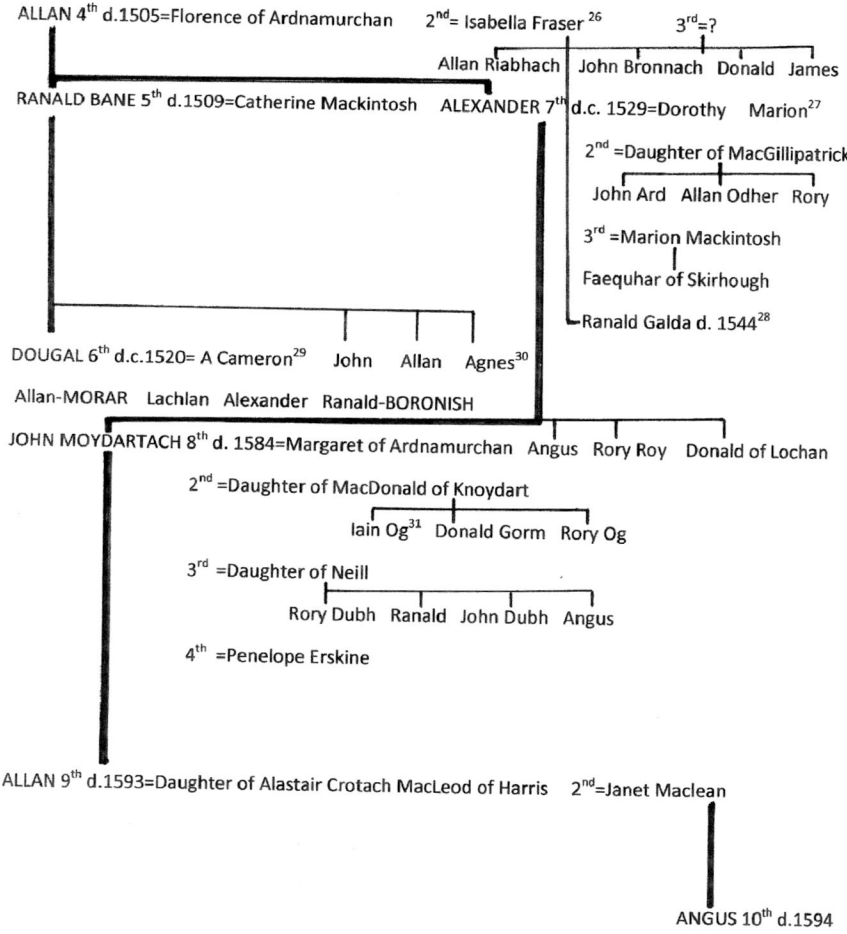

ALLAN 4th d.1505=Florence of Ardnamurchan   2nd= Isabella Fraser [26]   3rd=?

Allan Riabhach | John Bronnach Donald James

RANALD BANE 5th d.1509=Catherine Mackintosh   ALEXANDER 7th d.c. 1529=Dorothy   Marion [27]

2nd =Daughter of MacGillipatrick

John Ard   Allan Odher Rory

3rd =Marion Mackintosh

Faequhar of Skirhough

Ranald Galda d. 1544 [28]

DOUGAL 6th d.c.1520= A Cameron [29]   John   Allan   Agnes [30]

Allan-MORAR   Lachlan   Alexander   Ranald-BORONISH

JOHN MOYDARTACH 8th d. 1584=Margaret of Ardnamurchan   Angus Rory Roy   Donald of Lochan

2nd =Daughter of MacDonald of Knoydart

Iain Og [31]   Donald Gorm   Rory Og

3rd =Daughter of Neill

Rory Dubh   Ranald   John Dubh   Angus

4th =Penelope Erskine

ALLAN 9th d.1593=Daughter of Alastair Crotach MacLeod of Harris   2nd=Janet Maclean

ANGUS 10th d.1594

---

[26] Daughter of Thomas Lord Lovat Fraser.

[27] Marion married Donald Herrach MacDonald of North Uist.

[28] Ranald Galda was the protégé of the Frasers in their attempt to gain influence over the Clanranald.

[29] Other traditions assert that he married either a daughter of the O'Beolans or a daughter of MacLeod of Lewis.

[30] Agnes married Robert Robertson of Struan.

[31] Iain Og's descendants are the MacDonalds of Glenaladale

Chapter 3

The Mound of Pain

The Clanranald were the most ancient branch of all the MacDonald clans which were descended from Somerled through the eldest son. The founder of the Clanranald was Ranald (died 1389), who was the eldest son of John; first Lord of the Isles, and his first wife, the heiress Amie MacRuarie.[1] During John's later years, Ranald acted as the High Steward and effectively governed the Lordship. His father abandoned his first wife Amie to marry Margaret Stewart. Whether or not John's marriage had been of a "handfast"[2] nature, his abandonment of Amie was a shameful example of opportunism, in that, having secured the MacRuarie inheritance, John then went on to secure further influence at the Scottish court through his marriage into the powerful Stewart family who were stewards to the Kings of Scotland.

In order to settle his inheritance John called a meeting of all the principal men of the Lordship and it was agreed that Ranald would surrender his claim to the Lordship in favour of Donald (the eldest son of John's second marriage),in exchange for receiving his mother's inheritance, the ancient lands of the MacRuaries. The Clanranald historians[3] record that this was done only after considerable resistance from the council, who regarded Ranald as the rightful heir to the Lordship. They had seen that Ranald could govern the Lordship and in Gaelic law John's first marriage to Amie was legal even if it had not been officially sanctioned by the Church. Ranald accepted his father's wishes and gave up his rightful claim to the Lordship. He went on to found the Clanranald. Ranald's acceptance of his father's wishes is remarkable and demonstrates a character which was able to forgo his own interests for the sake of the general benefit of the Lordship.

Ranald's acceptance was to have a profound impact on the history of the western highlands. It led to the creation of the Clanranald which had peacefully adsorbed the lands of the MacRuaries. His possessions stretched from South Uist in the Outer Hebrides to the forbidding glens of Morar.

---

[1] Amie MacRuarie came to inherit the MacRuarie possessions of South Uist and Benbecula, the islands of Eigg and Rum and Moidart, Morar, Knoydart and Arisaig; after her brother Ranald was murdered by the Earl of Ross at the monastery of Elcho and her other brother Alan died without issue.

[2] Handfast marriages were unions which had a specified period (usually a year and a day); they were used so that a couple could see if they were compatible. They did not carry as much validity as marriages but were recognized as a valid union by Gaelic societies.

[3] The historians of the Clanranald were the family of the MacVurichs who for generations recorded the history of the clan in the Red and Black books of Clanranald. Much of their work has been lost as it was passed down orally. The MacVurichs could recite the clan's history and the genealogy of their chiefs in long speeches which could last for several days during clan feasts.

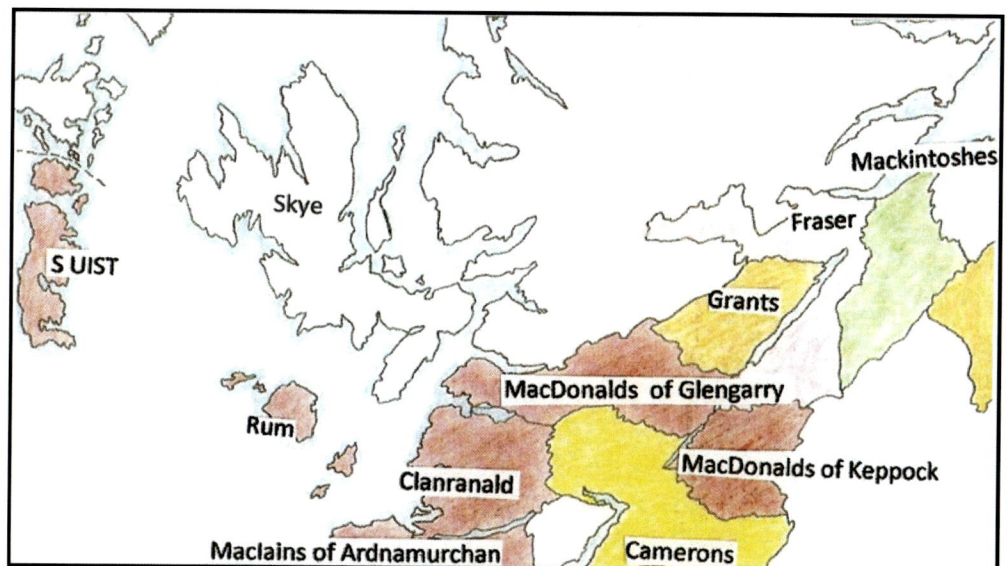

Territories of the Clan Ranald c1540

Ranald's acquiescence meant that the Clanranald stayed peacefully within the polity of the Lordship and actively supported the Lords of the Isles in all their future struggles to maintain a Gaelic kingdom in the western highlands. Although the evidence is lacking, it is probable that Margaret Stewart campaigned tirelessly for her son Donald to be acknowledged as the second Lord of the Isles. The abandoned Amie would at least have had the satisfaction of seeing her family lands pass to her own son. Ranald's moderation was a crucial factor in securing the unity of the Lordship and ensuring that it would go on to grow into a power which could maintain its independence for another hundred and fifty years.

The history of the Clanranald is intimately bound up with that of the Lordship till its demise in the late fifteenth century. The clan supported the Lords of the Isles in their efforts to gain control over the Earldom of Ross and their resistance to the spread of Royal authority into the western highlands. Under the command of their chiefs the clan was present at the bloody Battles of Harlaw and Inverlochy. It was during the struggle of the Lords of the Isles for control of the Earldom of Ross that a fundamental rift in the Gaelic world first became apparent. The MacDonald Lords of the Isles were supported by all the island clans[4] as well as the Camerons, Chisholms and the Clan Chattan. With the exception of the Camerons the mainland clans support for the Lordship was to be intermittent and unreliable. Whether they supported or opposed the Lordship these clans were attempting to carve out their own destiny and their policies were determined by political expediency.

---

[4] These included all the branches of the MacDonalds, the MacLeods of Harris and Lewis, the Morrisons, the MacNeills of Barra and Gigha, the MacLeans, the MacQuarries, and the MacKinnons.

The Lords of the Isles were resisted by most of the mainland clans in the Earldom amongst whom were the MacKenzies, Frasers, Grants and Rosses. Although there was an ever shifting pattern of clan alliances during the period it is clear that most of the clans from the central highlands were opposed to any further expansion of MacDonald power and did not wish to become the feudal vassals of the Lords o the Isles. It is during this period that enmity developed between the MacDonalds and many of these clans and in the case of the MacKenzies and Frasers this would lead to a long history of bitter feuding.

In 1481 Ruairi the third chief of the Clanranald died and he was succeeded by his son Allan, who was known to his clan as "Allan the mighty deeded". Allan supported Angus Og in his attempts to regain control of the Earldom of Ross after it had been forfeited by John fourth Lord of the Isles. After the death of Angus Og, Allan switched his support to the MacDonalds of Lochalsh who continued the struggle to regain the Earldom and later to re-establish the Lordship after its fall in 1494.[5] During these rebellions the Fraser lands of Stratherrick and the Ard were repeatedly devastated. The Frasers were subjected to casual murder, fire-raising and the loss of all their livestock. These communities were often left in a state of utter destitution which added to the enmity felt by the Frasers towards the western clans.

MacKenzie histories[6] describe how Allan, at the head of the Clanranald laid waste Kintail in the ongoing feud; this raid was part of a wider struggle between those clans that supported the Lordship and those that opposed it. Despite his involvement in the rebellions of Angus Og and the MacDonalds of Lochalsh, Allan still found time for extensive feuding with other clans. Local tradition has it that at one time, Allan had the chiefs of the MacLeods, MacKays and the MacKintoshes held prisoner in the dungeons of Castle Tioram.[7]

When the chief of the MacKintoshes[8] returned to his own country he built a stronghold on one of the small islands of Loch Moy. To celebrate its completion he invited his clan to a feast. Fortified by copious quantities of whisky and the security of his new construction he fell to boasting of his defiance of Allan and the Clanranald. The feast was attended by a wandering Irish harper[9] who noted what was said. During the course of his travels the harper found himself in the hall of Castle Tioram. When the harper recounted what he had heard at the MacKintosh feast Allan was enraged and vowed that even in the distant security of his stronghold MacKintosh would fear the Clanranald. Allan led a party of the Clanranald to Loch Moy and surprised MacKintosh in bed. The unfortunate

---

[5] See chapter 2.
[6] The Earl of Cromarty's History of the MacKenzies.
[7] Castle Tioram was the ancient seat of the MacRuaries and later became the seat of the Clanranald chiefs.
[8] Probably Ferquhard twelfth chief of the MacKintoshes.
[9] Harpists were an important element to any clan gathering at this date.

chieftain was hauled back to Tioram where he was imprisoned for a year and a day. Allan released him only after instructing him never to forget to fear the reach of the Clanranald. [10]

Another tale relates how Allan was sailing in his galley to visit his possessions in South Uist when he was intercepted by a fleet of ten MacLean galleys. At this time he was at feud with the MacLeans and he realized he was facing overwhelming odds. Allan ordered his men to make a bier and place him upon it; they were then to make sure the MacLeans saw them mourning their late chief. The MacLean galleys pulled alongside and on hearing of Allan's death they sailed on delighted. During his later years this turbulent chief seems to have had a peaceful retirement as the Clan was led by his son Ranald Ban.[11]

Allan married twice, his first wife was Florence Maclain with whom he had Ranald Ban and Alexander, later he married Isabel Fraser with whom he had Ranald Galda. Allan died in 1505, the actions of his life and the nature of his character created strong and opposing opinions in those that wrote about him. In the Book of the Dean of Lismore, Allan is described as a destroyer of churches whose pedigree is traced straight to the devil; "First of all from hell he came, the tale's an easy tale to tell."[12] While to his own historians Allan "was a hero by whom the board of monks was maintained, and by whom the plain of the Fingalls[13] was defended."

In 1503 Donald Dubh[14] escaped from his Campbell gaolers and began a revolt to re-establish the Lordship. He was enthusiastically joined by most of the western clans. Under the leadership of Ranald Ban, the fifth chief, the Clanranald stayed aloof from the rebellion. As a reward for the Clanranald's neutrality during the rebellion, Ranald Ban was granted charters by King James IV to extensive possessions belonging to the MacDonalds of Sleat and the MacLeods of Lewis. Ranald Ban did not attempt to exert his authority in these areas which is a testament to his acumen as any attempt by the Clanranald to occupy these lands would have embroiled them in bitter feuding.   Ranald Ban died at Perth in 1509,[15] the clan historians refer to him as a chief who managed the affairs of his people with good governance "for exalted was his position, and great was his sway, and good were the laws and regulations of his country during the short time he lived."

---

[10] From the Clanranald History of 1819.

[11] From the Clanranald History of 1819.

[12] The Book of the Dean of Lismore is an early sixteenth manuscript said to have been written by Finlay, chief of the MacNabs who may well have suffered the attentions of the Clanranald, thus Finlay may have had a personal motive for writing such a derogatory passage.

[13] The Fingalls were the semi-mythical ancestors of the Scots when they were establishing Dalraida.

[14] Donald Dubh was the son of Angus Og and was acknowledged by the western clans as the rightful heir to the Lordship.

[15] Gregory in his History of the Western Highlands asserts that Ranald Ban was executed. However, as there is no mention of this in the clan histories this seems unlikely.

Ranald Ban was succeeded by his son Dugall who became the sixth chief of the Clanranald. The history of the Clanranald during Dugall's chiefship (1509-1520) was relatively peaceful. During this turbulent period of Scottish history; Dugall only appears occasionally in the state records. The Council attempted to call him to account for stripping a shipwrecked Spanish ship of all its goods.[16] Dugall ignored their efforts to bring him to justice and the Council had to drop the matter as they had no way of exerting their authority.

After the disaster of Flodden in 1514 the whole Scottish polity was thrown into confusion. The most pertinent aspect of this in the Western Highlands was the rising of Donald Galda of Lochalsh, and although the Clanranald held aloof, the entire fabric of power in the Highlands appeared to be rending apart. With internal tensions developing in the Clanranald and the virtual collapse of Royal authority in the Highlands, the political environment was ripe for the extraordinary events that followed.

Dugall became extremely unpopular with his own clan; the reason for this is not fully explained by the extant sources. Dugall entered into a bond of manrent with Sir John Campbell of Calder.[17] It has been suggested[18] that the subservient nature of the wording by which Dugall bound himself to Calder was part of the reason for his unpopularity with his own people. In the document, Dugall describes Calder as "dearest and most beloved." Not too much emphasis should be placed on this language as this form of wording was common in bonds of manrent of this period and was no doubt entered into by Dugall as a matter of short term expediency. In any event any disquiet brought about by this agreement does not fully explain future events.

The best clue as to why Dugall was hated by his clan is in an eighteenth century Clanranald manuscript which describes Dugall as "a jealous and bad tempered man who put to death his two brothers John and Allan, and was afterwards himself killed". The usually detailed sources for the history of the Clanranald are surprisingly unhelpful. MacVurich in the Red Book of Clanranald merely says "I leave it to another certain man to relate how he spent and ended his life". The Black Book of Clanranald is even less helpful just stating that Dougal inherited the chiefship from his father. The events of Dugall's death in 1520 are obscure and confused. Hugh MacDonald, the Sleat historian, writes that Dougal was murdered by his cousins John Moydartach and Alan while Dougal's sons were killed by Alexander, fifth Chief of Glengarry.[19] This explanation is at least in part incorrect as we know that Alan, one of Dougal's sons, inherited lands in Morar some twenty

---

[16] Until the eighteenth century any shipwreck was considered fair game by the impoverished communities of the western highlands.
[17] During the sixteenth century it was part of Campbell policy to create a web of these bonds of manrent throughout the western highlands.
[18] The MacDonald brothers.
[19] Hugh's source is the Knock MS.

years later. There was a tradition in Moidart that Dougal was a victim of a plot by his cousins. He was ambushed at Polnish by a gang led by the infamous villain Alan-nan- Core and murdered. Whatever the exact truth of the death of Dougal we can be confident that it was violent and that senior members of the Clanranald, even if not involved, certainly acquiesced to it, and that his sons were disinherited from the chiefship. It is clear from the drastic actions taken by the Clanranald especially with regards to Dugall's descendants that Dugall committed a crime which was completely unacceptable in clan society, the full story of which is lost.

Alexander, Dougall's uncle, was elected by the Clanranald to the chiefship and was styled Captain of Clanranald probably because the direct line of inheritance had been broken. In Gaelic law the Clanranald had the right in extreme circumstances to depose a chief and disinherit his offspring, although the latter is almost unheard off. Feudal law which was pervasive in the lowlands and beginning to penetrate the highlands did not recognize clans and certainly not their right to depose a chief and disinherit his offspring. It was this interpretation of feudal law which was later to challenge John Moydartach's legitimacy as chief of Clanranald.

We may be sure that Alexander was a popular choice as he and his son John Moydartach had the unswerving loyalty of the clan. Alexander died some time before 1530, and was succeeded by his son John Moydartach, who was to become the greatest of all the chiefs of Clanranald. The Clanranald with other western clans was soon in rebellion against the Crown primarily due to some ill conceived land tenure legislation of James V.[20] After the threat of a Royal expedition against them they submitted, and were pardoned in 1531. The Clanranald charter chest contains a long series of conflicting charters and appears to be the product of an inconsistent and dishonest process or at worst a deliberate, illegal attempt by James V to undermine John Moydartach.

In 1539 Donald Gorm MacDonald of Sleat backed by most of the clans, which had belonged to the old Lordship of the Isles, started another rebellion with aim of re-establishing the Lordship and even laying claim to the Earldom of Ross. The rebellion petered out quickly with the death of Donald Gorm before the walls of the castle of Eilean Donan.

The consequences of this rebellion were to be profound for both the Clanranald and the Frasers. In 1540 Hugh, fifth Lord Lovat and tenth Chief of the Frasers, probably encouraged by the Scottish government, began to meddle in the affairs of Clanranald. He attempted to gain influence in the western highlands, an area which at this time was usually closed to the eastern clans. Hugh already had some interests in the west and possibly his interest in the Clanranald succession was an extension of this. In 1533 Alexander MacLeod VII of Harris had sold one third of the two thirds of Glenelg which belonged to the MacLeods. The money paid seems to have represented a debt incurred by him. In 1535 the remaining McLeod lands

---

[20] James revoked all the land charters drawn up during his minority, this effectively left many clans with no legal title to their lands.

in Glenelg were sold to Hugh under the terms that Hugh was to return the lands of Glenelg if Alexander repaid the money within seven years. In 1540 Hugh resigned these lands to the King who then granted them back to Alexander. This grant represented Agnes Fraser's dowry, when she married Alexander's son William.

Hugh, known as MacShimi[21] to the Frasers, might have calculated that the lands of the Clanranald with their often rebellious people and the consequent approbation of the Crown offered much more potential for the expansion of Fraser influence than the immediate lands surrounding him occupied by his powerful and more law abiding neighbours. That he should cast his eye on the Clanranald rather than a weaker clan was because he held the card of Ranald Galda (the Stranger).Ranald Galda was the son of Alan, fourth chief of the Clanranald and his second wife Isabella daughter of Thomas Lord Lovet chief of the Frasers. He was known as Ranald the Stranger by the Clanranald probably because he had spent much of his life with his Fraser relatives in the Aird.[22]

The first years of John Moydartach's chiefship saw him embroiled in large scale disturbances caused by James V's revocation of many of the charters granted by his mother Queen Margaret and the Regent Angus during his minority. The western clans anger was increased when the King proclaimed that only charters agreed to by the Campbell Earls of Argyle would be valid. The Clan Iain Mor, the MacLeans and the Clanranald under the leadership of John Moydartach invaded Campbell lands, carrying devastation into Argyle. The Campbells retaliated with raids into the MacLean lands of Mull and Tiree. After the King had agreed to reduce the influence of the Campbells the western clans made their submission to him in 1531. A few months later John Moydartach was formally recognized as the chief of the Clanranald by James V.

In 1540 James V attempted to overawe the western clans by a naval demonstration in the Hebrides. After the chiefs had come abroad his ship, James imprisoned them. The chiefs, amongst whom was John Moydartach, who had been betrayed[23] by their sovereign were taken to Edinburgh and imprisoned. The Clanranald was leaderless and Hugh fifth Lord Lovat, no doubt with James's approval, seized his opportunity. In 1540, backed by the military might of the Gordons, who acted as the King's lieutenants in the North, Hugh imposed Ranald Galda on the Clanranald as their new chief. Ranald Galda was a relatively old man when he assumed the chiefship of the Clanranald. He had spent most of his life amongst his Fraser relatives and although this was a Gaelic culture it was different to the culture of the western highlands.[24] Hugh then unleashed a massive legal

---

[21] Shimi is Gaelic for Simon.
[22] The Aird is the fertile district around Beauly.
[23] This betrayal of trust and hospitality was completely abhorrent in Gaelic societies, the offence being compounded by the fact it was committed by the King.
[24] By the middle of the sixteenth century the Aird was becoming heavily influenced by lowland Scotland. The region had continual contact with Edinburgh and even London

campaign on behalf of his protégée Ranald Galda. He persuaded James to grant royal charters to Ranald Galda while simultaneously revoking the charters he had issued to John Moydartach. James V may well have understood the dubious legality of these machinations but it should be remembered that a pliant chief of Clanranald under the influence of the Frasers would have suited the policy of the crown much better than a turbulent John Moydartach.

Hugh also claimed that Ranald Galda was the legitimate heir to the chiefship of the Clanranald, and that John Moydartach had no right to the chiefship. Hugh's contention has been accepted by many writers on the subject ever since. The arguments set out by the MacDonald brothers seem irrefutable.[25] The Gaelic law of Tanistry[26] which was followed by the Clanranald accepted John Moydartach as legitimate, so in the eyes of the clan there was no doubt as to John Moydartach's right to the chiefship. Hugh's argument following feudal law could only place legitimacy on Ranald Galda's claim by demonstrating that Allan's first marriage to Florence Maclain was void. This would then exclude all the descendents of Ranald Bane and Alexander (including John Moydartach) from the chiefship. The validity of Allan's marriage to Florence was never successfully challenged by anybody.

While it is likely that John Moydartach was the illegitimate eldest son of Alexander[27] he had every right to assume the chiefship of the Clanranald as he had been elected by the polity of the Clanranald under the laws of Tanistry.

On the succession of Ranald Galda, MacVurich relates a story of his parsimony and states that this was the cause of his unpopularity with the Clanranald. A day or two after the arrival of Ranald Galda at Castle Tioram preparations were made for a traditional feast to be given to the clan to celebrate his succession. This feasting was an important aspect of the dignity of the chief and had been part of Gaelic culture for many centuries as one of the means of cementing the relationship

---

through the burgh of Inverness. Its fertile fields and exposure to national and international trading meant it was a far cry from the remote shores of Moidart.

[25] Allan the fourth chief was first married to Florence MacIain, to whom was born Ranald Bane who became the fifth chief. Secondly Allan married Isabel Fraser to whom was born Ranald Galda. Ranald Bane married Catherine MacKintosh to whom was born Dugall, who became the sixth chief of Clanranald. Dugall was killed and his descendents were barred from the chiefship. This was legal under Gaelic law although not under feudal law. Hugh's challenge to the legitimacy of John Moydartach is based on feudal law, by following feudal law it is the descendents of Dugall who have the right to the chiefship of the Clanranald. The Clanranald then elected Dugall's uncle Alexander to be chief, it was his eldest son John Moydartach who became the eight chief of Clanranald.

[26] Tanistry was the Gaelic legal system by which a clan could elect a new chief if the incumbent chief had given serious offence to his people.

[27] N.H. MacDonald writes that according to local traditions John Moydartach was the child of Alexander and a local girl called Diorbhail (Dorothy) whose father was a clansman from Kinlochmoidart.

between the clan and the new chief.[28] Ranald on seeing the large fires with oxen and sheep roasting over them, the copious supplies of whiskey, beer and wine and all the other necessities asked what the cause of so much consumption was. On being told it was to celebrate his succession he was unfortunately heard to comment that a few hens would have done just as well. This "foreign" attitude exhibited not only parsimoniousness but a failure to understand the tradition of the Clanranald, a tradition which the chief above all others was duty bound to uphold. Feasting was one of the main mechanisms by which the social ties of the clan were reinforced (especially between the chief and the commonality). [29]

View from the Courtyard of Castle Tioram

This story although showing the cultural gap between Ranald and his clan does not address the root cause of their hostility towards him. The main reason must have been his dubious legitimacy as chief especially as he had been imposed upon them by outsiders who appeared to have considerable influence over him, and that

---

[28] Archaeological evidence of clan feasting was found during recent excavations at Finlaggen on Isla. The large quantity of animal bones attests to the fondness of the Lords of the Isles for celebrating in the traditional Gaelic way.
[29] This story comes from the Clanranald History of 1819 and some aspects of this tale are inaccurate, for example, Ranald Galda is described as a boy when he must have been about fifty years old.

they had a chief already who they all regarded as legitimate. Ranald Galda was disliked by the entire Clanranald because his claim to the chiefship failed on every possible count and when combined with the heady mix of clan prejudice on such a vital matter and of his cultural alienation from them caused by his upbringing, the unity of the clan in their opposition to him is not surprising. To the Clanranald, not only did he have no claim under Gaelic law but it has been demonstrated that as there was no challenge to the legality of the marriage of Allan and Florence, Ranald Galda had no claim under feudal law, as he was the son of the second marriage. These facts would have been well understood by the clansman as they sat around the fires of the courtyard of castle Tioram.[30]

In 1542 James V died at Falkland at the young age of thirty. The consequences for the Clanranald and Ranald Galda were both unexpected and profound. At court, the Earl of Glencairn's rival was Mac Calien Mor or as he was known in the lowlands the Duke of Argyle, chief of the Clan Campbell. The wily Glencairn saw an opportunity to cause difficulties for Argyle if he could persuade the regent Arran to release the highland chiefs captured by James V. In due course Arran released the chiefs of the western clans. From the perspective of the stability of the Scottish state this was a disaster and such a poor decision reflects the chaotic state of Scottish Government as the principal men at court jockeyed for position after the King's death.

The Gordon Earls of Huntley as the Royal Lieutenants of the North were preoccupied with the escape from prison of Donald Dubh in the spring of 1543. After Donald Dubh had escaped he was enthusiastically welcomed by most of the western clans and launched a second rebellion to re-establish the Lordship. Hugh Fraser, fifth Lord Lovat would have been well aware of the threat that John Moydartach's release posed to Ranald Galda but was unable to protect his protégée. Once John Moydartach had been released and returned to the Clanranald events in the west were outside of his control as his writ did not run in the western glens and islands of the Clanranald territory.

John Moydartach, on gaining his freedom immediately returned to Castle Tioram where he was enthusiastically welcomed by the whole polity of his clan. Ranald Galda fled back to his mother's people and joined Lord Lovat at Beauly. Moydartach was a man of many accomplishments, as well as those so admired by the senecharies of the Clanranald he was imbued with a subtle understanding of the consequences of his actions. He knew that in time he would have to resist the pressure of both the Gordons and the Frasers who would be willing to go to war on behalf of Ranald Galda. John Moydartach also knew that his struggle with Ranald Galda over the chiefship of the Clanranald was part of a wider conflagration (the rebellion of Donald Dubh). John Moydartach and the people of the Clanranald (along with the other western clans) supported Donald Dubh in his second rebellion

---

[30] For a detailed examination of the claims to the Clanranald see the genealogical tables at the beginning of this chapter.

to re-establish the Lordship. The Frasers not only wanted to see Ranald Galda as chief of the Clanranald but were also strongly opposed to any re-emergence of the Lordship. To the Gordon Earls of Huntley the major concern was the rebellion of Donald Dubh and the threat this posed to Royal influence in the highlands. The struggle for the chiefship of the Clanranald was to them, an important aspect of this wider problem. They wanted Ranald Galda as chief of the Clanranald as his compliance would have neutralized one of the most powerful clans which supported Donald Dubh.

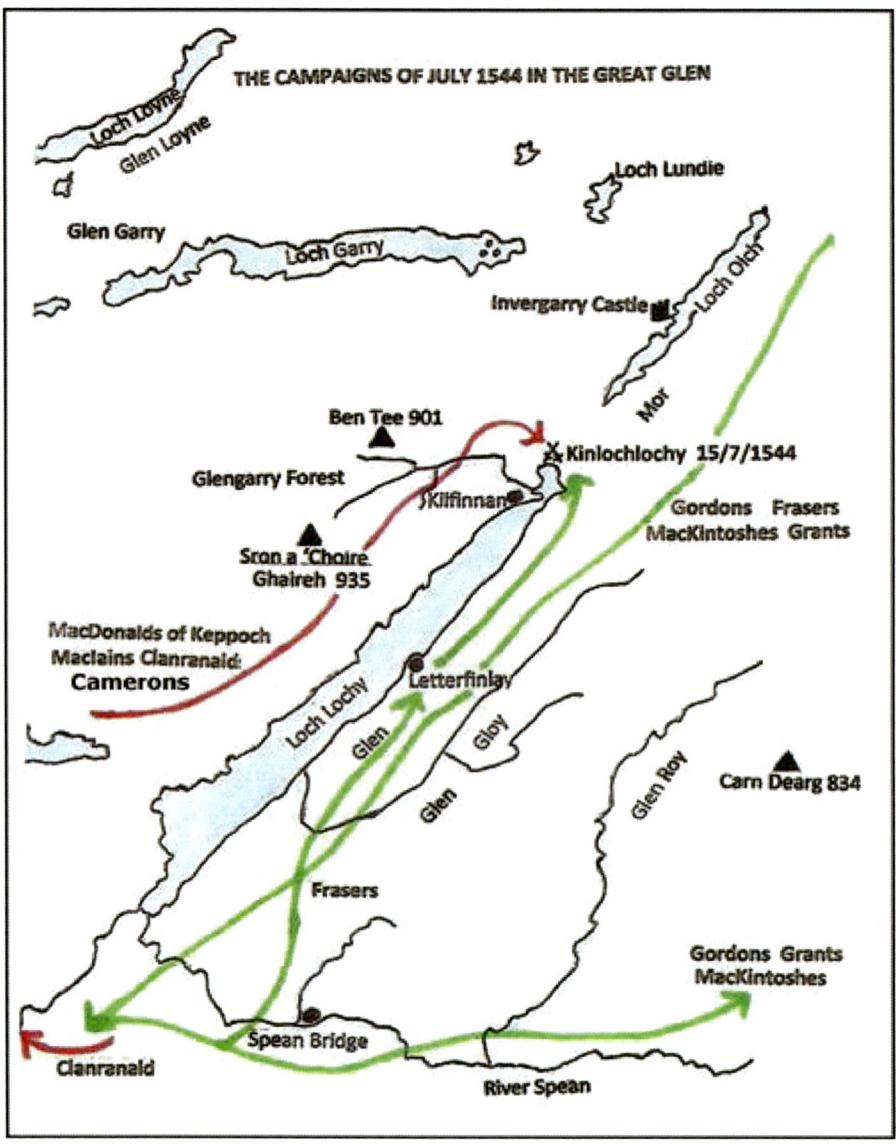

It has been widely understood that John Moydartach led the Clanranald and other western clans on a large scale raid into the Fraser lands of Abertaaf and

Stratherrick. They stormed Urquhart castle and even attempted to settle permanently in Glenmoriston. But a careful examination of the source material[31] shows that this raid took place immediately after the Battle of Kinlochlochy and that John Moydartach and the Clanranald were not involved.

The Gordon Earl of Huntley as Lieutenant of the North gathered his clan and his feudal vassals and prepared to invade the territories of the clans which supported the insurrection of Donald Dubh in the district of Lochaber. The disaffected clans in this region included the Clanranald, the MacDonalds of Keppoch, the Maclains of Ardnamurchan, the MacDonalds of Glencoe and the Camerons. Huntley's feudal vassals included the Grants of Freuchie, the MacKintoshes and the Frasers. The motives of the clans which followed Huntley were complex and their support for him went further than merely their feudal obligations. They all opposed any re-emergence of MacDonald power in the central and eastern highlands in the form of a resuscitated Lordship lead by Donald Dubh.

Each of these clans also had their own specific reasons for supporting Huntley. The Grants wished to maintain their hold over their newly acquired possessions in Glenmoriston which they would be unlikely to do if the Lordship was re-established. The MacKintoshes wished to impose their legal right to Glen Spean which they had never able to gain access to as they were held by the "sword" by the MacDonalds of Keppoch. The Frasers wished to re-impose their protégé Ranald Galda on the Clanranald. It is clear that the clan army led by Huntley was united not only by its feudal obligations but also by many individual agendas. It is also true that the clans that opposed Huntley (the MacDonald clans and the Camerons) were also motivated by the broader desire for the re-emergence of the Lordship but also their own policies. The Clanranald were at feud with the Frasers over who was to be chief of their clan. The Camerons opposed Huntley's claims on their lands, while the MacDonalds of Keppoch were determined to resist the claims of the MacKintoshes.

Hugh gathered the Fraser clansmen at Tomnahurich[32] and set out, accompanied by Ranald Galda to join up with Huntley. After the clans had coalesced during the early summer months of 1544 they advanced through Badenoch and emerged through Glen Spean into the heart of Lochaber.

It has been claimed[33] that Huntley, after restoring order in the wasted areas advanced through Moidart and put Ranald Galda in possession of the Clanranald country. There must be some doubts over this statement, he must presumably have been referring only to their mainland territories and even these during the sixteenth century were a mountain fastness which was very inaccessible to those who were not familiar with the topography. The force that George fourth Earl of

---

[31] N.H. Macdonald, The Clanranald of Gamoran.
[32] Tomnahurich is a hill which in the sixteenth century would have been a mile from Inverness; this yew covered hill was the gathering point for Fraser clansmen.
[33] D. Gregory in his History of the Western Highlands and Islands.

Gordon, Hugh fifth Lord Lovat and William fifteenth chief of Clan MacKintosh led was probably too large and unwieldy to penetrate decisively into Moidart. The difficulties of moving such a large force through this type of terrain and supplying them would have been enormous in the sixteenth century. A century later a royal expedition to the more accessible areas of Kintyre and Islay had great difficulty with its logistics. If Huntley had achieved this he would have still had to storm Castle Tioram which, as there is no evidence he possessed artillery this would have meant a siege; only exacerbating his logistical difficulties. There is no record of Huntley and John Moydartach clashing in the Clanranald country and this, combined with the above reasons makes it unlikely that Huntley went much further west than the area of Loch Eil. One would also have to speculate on Ranald Galda's position; although it is stated that he accompanied Hugh back along the great Glen is it credible that he was able to, or would have wished to be in occupation of Tioram having been previously expelled by the Clanranald? The only forces on which he could count were withdrawing. There is also no record of him being given a garrison for Tioram. Bishop Lesley offers some support for this view when he writes, "The Earl (Huntley) marching forward with his company made them (the MacDonalds and Camerons) to retreat and run to their own country upon the western sea, where lowland men could have no access and so placed the Lord Lovat and the Laird of Grant in their own lands." Some weight must be placed on this statement as Bishop Lesley occupied the local see off Ross and was writing only a few decades after Kinlochlochy. If this speculation is correct then none of the leaders of Huntley's force could have felt satisfied with the result especially Ranald Galda.

Hugh would have known that there was still a real threat from John Moydartach and their lands were still vulnerable to a catastrophic invasion. Having forced John Moydartach's forces to withdraw into the fastnesses of the west, the allies arrived at the opening of Glenroy at the point where the Spean joins the Lochy and it was here that their forces divided. George Gordon and William chief of the MacKintoshes with their clansmen went up Glen Spean; the age old route from the west to Badenoch, the Gordons then going on to their home country. Hugh and the Frasers accompanied by the Grants of Glen Urquhart and Glenmoriston carried on up the Great Glen.[34] During this period the relationship between the Frasers and this branch of the Grants was very close[35] and in part explains why Grant territories in the Great Glen were to suffer so severely. Lord Lovat was probably accompanied by Patrick Grant chief of this branch of the Grants; his interest in this affair was reinforced by the fact that he was Ranald Galda's half brother as Isabelle Fraser had

---

[34] There is no record of the Grants at the Battle of Kinlochlochy, and the majority would have returned through Badenoch with their chief Grant of Freuchie. However it does seem reasonable to assume that the Grants of Glenmoriston would have accompanied the Frasers up the Great Glen as it was the direct way to their homes.
[35] There was a considerable amount of inter-marriage between the two clans.

married the chief of the Grants of Glenmoriston after the death Alan fourth of Clanranald.

The forthcoming battle is referred to here as the Battle of Kinlochlochy. It is more commonly known as the Battle of Blair-na-Leine (the Battle of the Shirts). Following the cogent arguments of N.H. MacDonald it is clear that Blair-na-Leine is a misnomer. The battle took place at the head of Loch Lochy on an area of marshy meadows (in Gaelic Leana) and it is from this word that the area was known for centuries as Leny.[36] It seems clear that Blair-na-Leine translates as the Battle of the Marshy Meadows not the Battle of the Shirts.

The source material for Kinlochlochy is contradictory and problematic. However it is clear that an exceptionally brutal encounter took place between the forces of John Moydartach and the Frasers at the head of Loch Lochy in the summer of 1544. The Frasers were all but exterminated in the encounter and their ambitions on the chiefship of the Clanranald ended forever. The sources[37] vary in their reliability and although Kinlochlochy is one of the best documented clan battles they are confused, contradictory, and subjective. The events described below have been drawn on a wide variety of sources of varying quality from both the Fraser and MacDonald traditions.

According to Fraser historians Hugh received messages of warning from MacKintosh and Grant of Freuchie while at Letterfinley about the intensions of John Moydartach. If it is correct that Hugh was at Letterfinley when he received these warnings then the allies had already divided, and Hugh's forces would have been two days march away from the MacKintoshes and Gordons. They advised Hugh that the MacDonalds and Camerons were preparing to intercept him on his way home. They suggested that he either took another route home, presumably for Hugh the circuitous route through Badenoch to Inverness, or that he waited till they could march with him up the Great Glen.

It is understandable that Hugh did not take this apposite advice; he was only a day's march from the nearest Fraser territories of Abertaaf and Stratherrick. There was also a psychological reason; Hugh was the tenth chief of his clan, the fifth Lord Lovat and Mac Shimi to his people and all that that implied. He may well have felt that he could not be seen to be escorted home, like a weak and frightened youth which would have been hard for his Gaelic pride to swallow. Their fate may have been decided by his brother, Fraser of Foyness who was said to have been a head strong and obstinate man who railed loudly that it would be cowardice to take any

---

[36] N.H. MacDonald has pointed out that Blair-na-Leine translates as the Battle of the Shirt (Leine is singular) and the Battle of the Shirts should be Blair-na-Leintean.
[37] Rev. James Fraser, the Wardlaw Manuscripts (early eighteenth century), Bishop Leslie (1570's), Robert Lindsay (late 16th century), Sir Robert Gordon, History of the Earldom of Sutherland (early 17th century), John MacRae, History of the Mackenzies (late 17th century), Dr. Mackintosh MacKay, Blair Leine, Rev. Father Allan MacDonald, Moidart or Among the Clanranalds. This source material was taken from N.M. MacDonalds The Clanranald of Gamoran.

other route and that they were more than capable of forcing their way past John Moydartach to get home.

While Hugh was at Letterfinely John Moydartach had marched up on the north side of Loch Lochy behind a range of hills and was camped at a small loch which was later to be called Lochan-nam-Bata or the Loch of Staves. John Moydartach had surveyed the topography and had decided the best place to engage the Frasers was at the north end of Loch Lochy. The advantages to John of this site was that it left the Frasers little option but to stand and fight and they would have been out of reach of their own country and any aid from George Gordon. On the cold muddy edge of Lochan-nam-Bata each MacDonald clansman left his stave; when they returned from the battle each man would reclaim it. Clearly the staves left in the Loch would represent their fallen clansmen. On the morning of the fifteenth of July 1544 John led the MacDonalds and Camerons down through Glengarry forest to Kilfinnan.[38] At this point John Moydartach's forces would have seen the Frasers making their way up the south side of Loch Lochy from Letterfinely.

If these records are correct then as the Frasers and Grants set out on a warm summer's morning they knew that there was a probability that they were heading for a clash with John Moydartach's forces. John Moydartach had kept a close watch on Huntley's expedition and would have known that Hugh's army could not be reinforced by the Gordons in time.

The Frasers numbered approximately four hundred and there were perhaps also about one hundred Grants. The Fraser force would have included all the gentlemen of the clan representing every family of note from all their lands; they would have been well equipped, for example, with broad swords of the finest steel.[39] John's force was about seven hundred strong and again would have consisted of most of the gentlemen of the clans he commanded. John's forces would, on the whole have had somewhat inferior weapons and been less protected by armour.[40] When Hugh reached Laggan-acha-droma near the head of Loch Lochy he saw John Moydartach's force coming down on the north side of the Loch. John's force was divided into seven columns at the head of each column a banner fluttered in the gentle breeze. It is probable that each banner represented the clan or sept of the men behind it, and that each clan formed a column which was led by the chief and

---

[38] By this period an area at the head of Loch Lochy (now mostly submerged) was already the traditional burial ground of the chiefs of the MacDonalds of Glengarry. One of the old tombstones was saved from the rising water levels and can be seen in the old cemetery of Kilfinnan.

[39] There were already some imports of sword blades from Toledo, city renown for the quality of its steel.

[40] Steel used in weapons and armour was extremely expensive in the impoverished highlands. It is clear from descriptions of battles involving the clans that many of the men fought unarmoured and that their weapons varied greatly in quality. The Frasers, through their economic contact with Inverness and their more fertile lands were able to afford both higher quality and a greater quantity weapons.

his immediate family.[41] Hugh called a halt and consulted with the gentlemen of his clan and after a brief discussion it was agreed they would fight. As previously mentioned, this may have been resolved the night before, in any case he now had little choice because John's forces were going to intercept him before he could reach Fraser country and the only alternative was a rapid withdrawal down the south side of the glen.

Putting aside the vital aspect of clan pride this would not have been a viable option as he would have been withdrawing back towards the lands of the MacDonalds of Keppoch and the Camerons. There was also no possibility of Huntley retracing his steps in time even if he had known about Hugh's situation. One manuscript records an address by Hugh to the Frasers just before the conflict. I have quoted the manuscript[42] verbatim as it gives a good sense of the type of oration that Hugh would almost certainly have addressed his clan with before the clash.

"Gentlemen, you are my guard-de-corps whom I have chosen out of many to accompany me in this honourable expedition for the services of my sovereign. You are most of you my flesh and blood, the offspring of those heroes who signalise themselves so often in defence of their country. Remember the honour of your noble ancestors, of who you are descended, some of whom will be forever on record as illustrious examples of Scotland's pristine bravery. The several branches of our ancient family have upon all occasions distinguished themselves and to this day never brought the least stain upon the name they bare. The time is short to speak of each of them in particular; methinks I see them all alive in you, and that they have transmitted their courage and bravery as well as their blood and name to you. You are indeed but a handful to encounter yonder formidable crew but consider the difference in other respects. They are rebels, you are loyal subjects, they outlaws, you are free subjects. I go on before you. I will hazard my life with you and for you. I by far prefer a noble death to an inglorious retreat, or anything that sullies the glory of my house; and are not you as much concerned in its glory as I am. We have from others the characters of men of fortitude and resolution; we carry our lives on the points of our swords. Let us act as men. Fall on and refer the event to almighty god; for the battle is the Lord's who can save with few as with many."

There must of course be doubt as to the authenticity of this speech as it smacks of later propaganda written by Fraser historians for the edification of their clan, and clearly few men would be able to recall a lengthy speech under the stress of

---

[41] The seven columns tie in with the seven distinct clan or cadet units under the command of John Moydartach. They were the Clanranald of Moidart, Knoydart and Morar, the MacIains, the MacDonalds of Keppoch and Glengarry and the Camerons. For the chiefs who led these columns see footnote 18.

[42] Much of the primary source material for the Battle of Kinlochlochy comes from the Fraser Wardlaw Manuscripts.

preparing for hand to hand combat. It should also be remembered that few men who heard Hugh's address survived. Despite all these caveats it is certain that Hugh would have addressed his clan before the battle, and that the Frasers would have considered the MacDonalds as rebels in the wider context of Scottish history. But despite the broader picture of Donald Dubh, the Lordship, and the authority of the Scottish state both clan armies knew that the coming struggle was primarily a clan feud. The Frasers were fighting for the dignity and safety of "MacShimi". To the Frasers on the battlefield the rights of Ranald Galda to the chiefship of the Clanranald or the wider political aspects of the conflict would not have loomed large in their reasons for fighting.

John Moydartach would also have addressed his clansmen; he would have inspired them with a longing for a re-establishment of the Lordship and reminded them of their illustrious ancestors. John's address would have differed significantly in style to that of Hugh and would have been similar to Lachlan MacVurich's poem which was composed to incite the MacDonalds before the Battle of Harlaw in 1411.[43]

> O children of Conn,[44] remember
> Hardihood in time of battle;
> Be watchful, daring,
> Be dextrous, wining renown,
> Be vigorous, pre-eminent,
> Be strong, nursing your wrath,
> Be stout, brave,......
> O children of Conn of the Hundred Battles
> Now is the time for you to win recognition,
> O raging whelps
> O sturdy heroes,
> O most sprightly lions,
> O battle-loving warriors,
> O brave, heroic firebrands,
> The children of Conn of the Hundred Battles,
> O children of Conn, remember
> Hardihood in time of battle.

Like their opponents the struggle between John Moydartach and Hugh, through his proxy Ranald Galda, for control of the Clanranald would have been uppermost

---

[43] Gaelic poetry was remarkably conservative and remained relatively unchanged over centuries, so although this poem was written over a century earlier it would still have been enjoyed by MacDonalds in the mid-sixteenth century.
[44] Conn was believed by the MacDonalds to have been amongst their ancestors as well as being a great Gaelic hero.

in the minds of the men of the Clanranald as they prepared for this desperate encounter with the Frasers.

The Battlefield at Kinlochlochy

The two forces moved towards each other at the northern end of Loch Lochy, one can only imagine the fear and excitement that must have coursed through every man. It must be remembered not only was it the fearful nature of the conflict in which they were about to become engaged but also that the stakes were so high because you fought with your son or father with cousins and nephews and in a very real sense your whole male family was at risk. The terrible brutality of clan battles was fuelled by seeing your son or father cut down by your side. Each man would also have been aware of the consequences for the female members of their family if they were defeated.[45] The battle of Kinlochlochy began on a hot summer's day at about midday.

The topography of the battlefield has been altered by the expansion of Loch Lochy to the north and east and also it is now dissected by the Caledonian Canal. In 1544 the encounter took place in an area about half a square mile delineated on

---

[45] Widows and orphans were to some extent looked after by the rest of the clan, or the widows quickly looked for a new husband. But despite these attempts to mitigate the effects of the loss of husbands and fathers these wives and children were extremely vulnerable to starvation without the help of sons and fathers.

the south side by the Loch and on the north side by a bog; on the other sides by the hills of Kinloch and Kilianan. Still visible today are two small hillocks which were within the parameters of the conflict; on the north side was Cnocan-nan-creuchd and on the south side Cnocan-oich-oich. This hillock whose name roughly translates into English as the mound of pain, received its name from the local people after the battle.

Just before the engagement Hugh ordered a gentleman called Bean Cleireach to take a small band of Frasers and guard a pass on the eastern side of the Loch through which they could escape. This pass ultimately led over the mountains and down into Glen Roy, and from there to Glen Spean where Hugh's forces could have coalesced with Huntley's forces. It was said of Bean Cleireach that he was a great favourite of Hugh's but the nature of his character is ambiguous as later events will show.

As the two clans moved towards each other the clansmen threw off their plaids which was the usual custom before conflict as the plaids were heavy and restricted movement. As it was a hot day many also took off their coats and some their shirts and it is thought by many that it is from this peculiarity that the battle was known as Blair-na-Leine i.e. the Battle of the Shirts.[46] The MacDonald's came down from the north side probably still in seven columns. Hugh organised his best armed troops to form the front line of the Fraser battle. Each of the Highland chiefs would have been surrounded by their bodyguard of gentlemen who were closely related to the chief and were honour bound to protect him. They often also included men of a similar age to themselves who had been fostered[47] with the chiefs' family when they were children.

The battle began by each side firing their arrows as they advanced towards a collision. After the archers had expended their arrows the two sides rushed at each other with their two-handed swords (claymores) and Lochaber axes.[48]

The first stage of the struggle was described by Fraser historians, "the fronts of both armies engaged so closely without either side yielding or giving way, that they were felled down either side like trees in a wood till room was made by their breaches on each side, and at last all came to fight hand to fist. There were some there but met with his match to encounter him, many were seen to fall but none to fly, they all fought for victory, which still remained uncertain." If this had been a normal clan battle this initial onset would normally have been decisive, usually one clan or the other broke and ran after a short but devastating encounter like this, at Kinlochlochy this was not to be the case; the battle was to rage till dusk, which at

---

[46] It has been pointed out earlier in this chapter that this interpretation is incorrect.

[47] Fostering was a common practice amongst the clans; it was used as a mechanism to reinforce the close bonds between the chief and the gentlemen of the clan or allied clans.

[48] The mid-sixteenth century was a period of transition in terms of military tactics and weapons. The protagonists at the battle of Kinlochlochy would have been a mixture of heavy infantry protected by chain mail and armed with claymores (two handed swords) and unarmoured men armed with such deadly weapons as Lochaber axes.

that time of year would have been around midnight. This initial clash would not have lasted longer than an hour due to exhaustion. The clansmen would have been extremely fit and due to the high quality of the men involved, they all would have trained for this very event; however they would have been unlikely to keep up this level of physical exertion for any longer.[49] Over that hot afternoon groups or individuals would pull back to rest while others would engage in mortal conflict.

Shortly after the initial onrush the stakes were raised even higher for Hugh when he was joined by his son the Master of Lovat. Seeing his son come onto the battlefield must have filled Lovat's heart with dread and desperation. It is acknowledged by both Fraser and MacDonald historians that the Master of Lovat was a young man of many talents and was blessed with all the personal qualities which were as much admired in his day as in ours. He was also well educated having spent time at the university of Paris and was only nineteen when he arrived on this blood soaked field with his twelve companions.

Hugh had expressly forbidden his son to accompany him on this expedition because he did not want to risk his eldest son, who was the heir to the chiefship of the Frasers, in what he knew to be a potentially dangerous campaign against a protagonist like John Moydartach. Hugh had left his son in charge of all the cares of the Fraser country while he was away. How the Master of Lovat and his companions arrived at this place is a pithy example of human frailty.

Lord Lovat had first married Anne, daughter of John Grant of Grant and it was from this marriage that the Master was born; later he married Janet Ross daughter of Walter Ross of Balnagown, and they also had children. A few days before the Master and his companions had been out hunting in the forest of Corricharbie and had returned to Beauly with game. On meeting him, Lady Lovat (Janet Ross) told him that she hoped he was having fun and that he enjoyed his comfortable bed while old men where fighting in the fields. The obvious insincerity of her words were not lost on him.

The Master was cut to the quick by these biting words and immediately decided to join his father and clan. He and twelve companions rode with all speed down the Great Glen to find the Frasers.

The Master of Lovat and his companions fought valiantly but soon the Master fell mortally wounded. One can only conjecture whether Lady Lovat's bitter words were just a loss of temper caused by anxiety for her husband or were they a deliberate attempt to clear the path for her own children? Probably they were the former as she had no idea that such a bloody encounter was imminent.

One can only imagine the sorrow and rage that must surged through Hugh when he saw his much loved son fall. It is said that Hugh surrounded by his bodyguards moved with bitter determination through the battlefield slaying all in his path. Mac Vurich (the historian of Clanranald) refers to Hugh as 'Chruaidh Choscar' or in

---

[49] It is clear from watching professional boxers that even the fittest individual cannot fight for more than a few minutes without becoming exhausted.

English as the hardy slaughterer. It was late in the afternoon when Hugh fifth Lord Lovat, tenth chief of Clan Fraser, Mac Shimi to his people fell amongst his own bodyguards. The MacDonald shouted out that the cutter of men had fallen and invigorated by the news they renewed their attacks on the shrinking bands of Frasers. As they rushed forward some were wounded or killed by prostrate Frasers driven to one last desperate act on hearing of the death of their chief. As the day wore on the ranks of Frasers and MacDonalds thinned and the battlefield was one of utter carnage. The survivors on both sides must have been exhausted and one can only imagine the scene in which the remaining clansmen would be leaning on their weapons panting for breath while small groups or individuals continued the bitter conflict.

Ranald Galda was no young man in 1544; he was in his fifties as his father died in 1505. Despite his unsuitability to becoming the chief of the Clanranald, and his acquiescence to the spider's web of intrigue over the inheritance of the Clanranald territories, Ranald at this moment of catharsis faced his predicament with great courage and determination. Ranald was said (at least by the Fraser historians) to have been the best swordsman who fought at Kinlochlochy. Whether the circumstances related below were true, it is certain that he fought bravely by the side of his mother's people. This description of him is also acknowledged by Mac Vurich.

Amongst the forces gathered in Moidart there was a MacDonald of great strength and courage who had joined John with his seven sons and had followed him to the shores of Loch Lochy. He like Hugh was distressed to find that he had been joined by an eighth son from a second marriage; he dearly loved his wife and knew that if this son was lost, then she would have no immediate family to support her. He tried all his powers of persuasion to induce this young man to return to Moidart before the encounter. After all his inducements had failed he tried taunting his son saying, "I hate to see in battle a beardless youth, escaped from the spoon-feeding care of his mother" The young man said nothing but descended down to the field by the side of his veteran father and his seven brothers. Ranald Galda and his bodyguard attempted to engage John Moydartach but due to the absolute chaos of this type of conflict failed to find him. It is said that John Moydartach was wounded and that the old veteran's duty was to stand over him till he could recover or be carried from the field. At an earlier stage of the battle he had already lost three of his sons only to see the last four fall before the compact and deadly group led by Ranald Galda. The old man driven on by motives of hate and revenge attacked Ranald. However, due to Ranald's skill he was quickly forced onto the defence and began to give ground.

His youngest son who had been running over the desolate and forlorn field searching for his father saw him being driven back by Ranald. The wily old veteran had been giving ground but it was at least in part a stratagem to lure Ranald Galda towards the main concentration of MacDonalds. Not understanding his father's tactics he shouted out, "I hate the site which meets my eyes, the backward step of an old man in battle." Sword and targe in hand he instantly dashed in and stood between Ranald and his father and said, "Cothrium na Feinne" (the equal combat of the Fingalians). This was an expression understood by all highlanders which could be interpreted as meaning a fair fight with no mercy to be shown. The old man could see that his son was no match for Ranald and in his anxiety resorted to a trick in an attempt to save his son's life. He shouted out, "I will not be traitor to you Ranald, they are at you behind." Ranald instinctively looked over his shoulder and was instantly struck in the back of the head, a part of his skull being shattered by the old man's broad sword. The old man bellowed out in triumph and relief and rapidly the news spread amongst all the surviving contestants that Ranald had fallen.

The evening was drawing on and dusk was falling on the exhausted remnants of the Frasers. They retreated to the south east part of the battle field in an effort to slip through the passes that should have been guarded by Ben Clearch. The fall of Ranald Galda was the last straw for the survivors as he was at least superficially the reason for the conflict, MacShimi and the Master of Lovat were already dead and the ties which held the Frasers had all been broken. There was no sign of Ben Clearch and the gaps in the hills were now occupied by the MacDonalds. They must have felt utter dismay at this final turning of the screw as there was now no escape. The MacDonalds mustered all their strength at the opposite side of the battlefield and then launched an exterminating assault on the remnant of the Frasers. A few survivors who broke and fled for safety towards their own territory were pursued for about ten miles, and of these pitiful few all but a handful were cut down.

The severely wounded Ranald Galda crawled to a hut built on the side of the hillock of Cnocan-oich-oich. He was examined by the physician of Clanranald who was described as 'wild and hair-brained'; he also acted as a seer for his clan. The physician reported to John Moydartach on Ranald's condition. On being asked whether he would survive the physician was said to have replied, "He might live, but so small is his hold of life that the point of a dealg (pin) which fastens your plaid were sufficient to send him to eternity, for his brain is laid open by the wound." John drew his dealg in silence from his plaid and handed it to the physician. As the physician lent over Ranald he held Ranald's arm, as Ranald was attempting to draw his dirk and drove the broach pin into Ranald's brain. This is the story of how Ranald died; its veracity cannot be confirmed but it is beyond doubt that he died fighting with fortitude. Few people apart from his immediate family would morn his passing yet on the last day of his life he had exhibited all the qualities so admired by clan societies, if circumstances had been different perhaps he would have made an admired and feared chief of Clanranald.

There is disagreement over the actions and character of Ben Clearch the favourite of Hugh who had been sent to guard the escape route. Gregory states that he lost his way and was unable to come to the aid of his kinsman. This seems unlikely as he would have probably been familiar with the topography. It should also be born in mind that Kinlochlochy was an unusually long battle for this period lasting ten to twelve hours. This would have given him plenty of time to find the passes or failing this to return to the battlefield. It has been suggested[50] that Alexander[51] sixth Lord Lovat who came to the chiefship on the death of Hugh and the Master gifted Ben Clearch the bailieship of Stratherrick and that this implies that this was a reward for easing his way to the chiefship. We do not know what Alexander's motives were, however there is no hint of an internal Fraser plot to bring about Hugh's destruction. One explanation for the appointment of Ben Clearch was that if there was no proof of cowardice or betrayal then he was the only surviving man of note among his clan and would have been the obvious choice for such an important position in guarding the borders of their country. Ben Clearch's actions on July 15th are covered now with obscurity but there must at least be some question as to his character.

As night fell the battlefield was covered with bodies lying thickest in the centre but the entire area had groups or individuals lying where they had fallen including on the shore of Loch Lochy. A number of clansmen had crawled towards the hut built on the slope of Cnocan-oich-oich where they had sought sanctuary before dying of their wounds. The losses for the Frasers were devastating; apart from Hugh fifth Lord Lovat, the Master of Lovat, eighty gentlemen of the clan had died. William Fraser of Foyers was the only gentleman that survived. He was carried to safety by Norman Gow his foster brother. Norman Gow died about ten miles from the battlefield having bled to death after attempting to extract an arrow from his side.[52] Fraser of Foyers must have died of his wounds a few days later for it is recorded that at the funeral service of his son in 1563 his father died in the month of July 1544.

It seems fairly certain that every branch of the Frasers lost the head of the family and many would have lost the next in line. As a proportion, the losses of Fraser clansmen were significantly less, however still considerable. The scene throughout the Fraser lands must have been pitiful after the runners had arrived with the news, with desperate heartbroken women seeing the world they had known fall apart. Almost immediately large numbers of Fraser men and women set out for Loch Lochy to collect their fallen kinsmen. Andrew Roy of Kirkhill the brother of Hugh looked so similar to him that his body was mistakenly identified as Hugh's. It was not until the sad procession reached Cillichuiman that he was correctly identified by Hugh's nurse. Andrew Roy and a considerable number of the Fraser gentlemen were buried here.

Hugh, Ranald Galda and the Master of Lovat were carried to the Aird and interred at Beauly priory. Until 1746 the inscription on Hugh's tomb was still legible, it read, 'Hic jacet Hugo Dominus Fraser de Lovat qui fortissime pugnans

---

50 Mr Fraser-Mackintosh.
51 Janet Ross saw her son Alexander assume the chiefship of the Frasers.
52 Norman Gow's descendents were gifted a croft as a recognition by the Frasers of his loyalty to his laird. They farmed the croft for over two centuries after Kinlochlochy.

contra Reginalinos occuidit July 17th 1544' It translates as 'Here lies Hugh Lord Fraser of Lovat who fell fighting gallantly against the Clanranalds, July 17th 1544' It will be noticed that the inscription on Hugh's tomb has the wrong date by two days. The lesser ranks of the Frasers and MacDonalds, Grants and Camerons are said to be buried in communal pits around Cnocan-oich-oich.

The losses suffered by the MacDonalds and Camerons were also extremely severe and traditionally it is said that only five Frasers and eight MacDonalds survived the battle. It can be shown that certainly on the MacDonald side these losses are exaggerated but they do reflect the heavy losses incurred during this battle. The MacDonalds and Camerons lost perhaps three to four hundred men but John's army was not annihilated. This can be implied from the fact that all the leaders of John's force survived the battle. In a document dated August 5th 1545 drawn up by the council of Donald Dubh all the leaders can be shown to be still living over a year after the battle. The only leaders missing from this document are Keppoch and Locheil and we know from other events that they too survived. The inference must be that if all the MacDonald chiefs survived then a certain proportion of clansmen must also have survived. Most of the accounts of the battle come from Fraser sources as the MacDonalds tended to pass down their histories orally from generation to generation and many were lost when the MacVurichs lost their position as poets and historians to the Clanranald in the eighteenth century. There is one telling sentence in a Mac Donald manuscript "The captain of Clanranald the last year ago in his defence slew the Lord Lowett, his son and heir, his thre brother with XIII score of men." One can only wish that we knew more about this conflict from the perspective of John Moydartach and the Clanranald. The exact numbers of survivors is a rather sterile debate. The exaggerated losses, telling us that no more than thirteen men survived the battle, is an indication that contemporary Highland society viewed this fatal clash as unusually brutal and the losses were extremely high on both sides. The battle had much less severe consequences for the MacDonalds and Camerons, than the Frasers, as they lost a much smaller proportion of their fighting strength, none of their chiefs and a significantly fewer number of their gentlemen. However throughout their clan territories many hundreds of individuals were bereft of fathers, husbands and sons.

The regent Arran on hearing the news must have bitterly regretted releasing John Moydartach and immediately ordered the Gordons and MacKintoshes to invade the lands of the clans involved at Kinlochlochy. George Gordon, Earl of Huntley, led an expedition into Lochaber and caused a great deal of destruction in Keppoch and in the glens of the Camerons. He captured both Ewen Cameron of Locheil and Ranald Mor MacDonald of Keppoch. He appears to have made no serious attempt on Moidart probably for the same reasons as previously discussed.[53] Huntley returned through Glen Spean. Keppoch and Locheil were

---

[53] Even in 1746 after the Battle of Culloden the Clanranald were deeply shocked when Hanoverian troops penetrated the remote fastnesses of Moidart.

imprisoned for a while at Ruthven in Badenoch; later they were taken to Elgin and put on trial for the slaughter of Hugh Lord Lovat. They were of course found guilty, they were beheaded and several of there clansmen hanged. For Keppoch and Locheil this was not the end of the state's revenge; their heads were impaled on spikes over the gates of the town. One of the clansmen hung was a brother of Keppoch and was married to the sister of William MacKintosh XV chief. Believing that MacKintosh had a hand in the conviction of her husband the wife of this clansman cursed her brother praying that no father should be succeeded by his son for several generations of MacKintosh chiefs. It may have been coincidence but due to an unfortunate set of circumstances this did come to pass amongst the MacKintoshes.

John Moydartach joined the rebellion of Donald Dubh and travelled with Donald's army of four thousand men to Ireland. It is said that four thousand were left in the western highlands to protect their homeland from Argyle. If these figures are anywhere near accurate then it shows that when the western clans coalesced for a single purpose they could at least match in men the size of the force available at short notice to the Scottish crown. Donald Dubh was the last viable claimant to the Lordship to the Isles; he died at Drogherda in the winter of 1545 leaving no heir. After Donald's death the rebellion disintegrated and John Moydartach returned to Scotland. In September 1545 John was again declared a rebel and all the territories of the Clanranald were given as grants to the most powerful clans in the highlands. With the unswerving loyalty of the Clanranald behind him, he was again to frustrate the Regent and may well have gone onto the offensive.

At this time Huntley enters into a bond with MacKintosh, MacKenzie of Kintail, Ross of Balnagowan and Munro of Fowlis to assist each other against the Clanranald. It will be noted that this bond does not include the Frasers presumably because of their shattering losses at Kinlochlochy. John Moydartach conveyed his support to James MacDonald chief of the clan Iain Mor[54] when he took up the claims of Donald Dubh to the Lordship. He may well have calculated that however unlikely the restoration of the Lordship it was his best hope as he was so hopelessly compromised in the eyes of the crown.

The Regent Arran knowing that war with England was again brewing withdrew the charge of treason from John, who was ordered to join the Scottish host at Fala Muir with the strength of the Clanranald in the summer of 1547. Unsurprisingly John did not respond to the summons and remained out in his remote fastnesses. The regency was further weakened by the defeat at Pinkie and Arran felt compelled to offer John a full pardon in August 1548. This pardon was to last for seventeen years and not only included his failure to appear at Fala Muir but also for "Ye slaughter of ye Lord Lovat and his complices." John doggedly continued to defy both the Scottish state and the Earl of Huntley; he again failed to appear after a summons from Arran at Aberdeen and again later at Inverness. Of all the western

---

[54] Otherwise known as the Clan Donald South or the MacDonalds of Dunnyveg.

clans the Clanranald were the most obdurate in defying Arran, who was not able to find any solution to John's aloofness as he had no way of imposing his will on John Moydartach. At last the Campbells under the Duke of Argyle were induced to act against the Clanranald, Argyle attempted to lure John with assurances of protection. John steadfastly refused to submit his safety to the Campbells and Argyle was also forced to abandon his attempts to ensnare John.

In 1553 John eventually had a meeting with the Earl of Huntley at which both men swore to forgive and forget the past. The impotence of the Scottish state and this agreement must have been a bitter pill to swallow for the Frasers. During the regency of the Queen Dowager, Mary of Guise, John's relationship with the state again deteriorated, probably due to the endemic raiding of cattle so favoured by the western clans. Mary resolved to bring the Clanranald to heal and ordered the Earl of Huntley to invade Moidart by land and the Earl of Argyle by sea. George Gordon amassed a large force consisting of his own clan and other vassals as well as a contingent of lowland cavalry. On reaching the district of Abertaaff his force fell into confusion with the cavalry and Clan Chattan refusing to advance any further.

The loyalty of the Clan Chattan to Huntley at this time was extremely questionable as he had only recently executed their chief. Huntley had no choice and abandoned another expedition to Moidart. John had drawn up the Clanranald at the head of Lochmoidart, on hearing of Huntley's withdrawal he returned to Castle Tioram to await Argyle. After Argyle had been provided with some artillery he immediately set sail for Moidart. On arriving at Castle Tioram he established a battery under the Dorlin cliffs and bombarded the castle from both land and sea. The Clanranald held out till Argyle had exhausted his ammunition, Argyle then abandoned the siege. The Queen Dowager was incensed by their failure; Huntley was thrown into prison.

In 1555 she ordered the Earl of Athole to deal with the Clanranald; his forces faced the same problem as Huntley when they reached district of Abertaaff and his expedition had to be abandoned. One wonders why it was at Abertaaff where both Huntley and Athole encountered mutiny? Perhaps it was because this region marked the boundary between what some clans regarded as the limit of civilization it being on the periphery of the Fraser lands. Eventually John submitted to the blandishments of Athole and the Queen Dowager; he accompanied Athole to Perth where Mary was holding court. Mary immediately broke her guarantee of safe passage and arrested John and his two sons. John and his sons soon escaped and returned to Moidart. Predictably John refused to have any further communication with Mary. Mary then unleashed another storm of charters by which she gifted away all the lands of the Clanranald. Amongst the supposed beneficiaries of this largesse was Allan the son of Ranald Galda who was to receive Moidart, Arisaig and Eigg. It says a great deal for John Moydartach's power of leadership and the cohesion of the Clanranald that none of the beneficiaries of these charters established themselves in Clanranald territory. On the contrary, John must have gone on to the offensive as there are bonds of support for Grant of Freuchie against the Clanranald.

Shortly after this period John retired from the captaincy of Clanranald and made way for his son, Allan eighth of Clanranald. Mac Vurich records that John "spent the end of his life godly and mercifully", he erected several churches in his last years. In 1584 John Moydartach died peacefully in his bed and was buried at Howsmore in South Uist.

Howsmore Church. South Uist

John exhibited all the qualities so admired by his clan, courage, loyalty, uprightness, generosity and a love for his people. What made John the greatest of all the chiefs of Clanranald and amongst the greatest of all the chiefs of the MacDonalds throughout their history was not only his courage and decisiveness but his talents as a wily politician and astute strategist. He must have been a charismatic character to have commanded the unswerving loyalty of his clan through such difficult times. He knew when to avoid conflict and when to strike with ruthlessness and for the most part he had the courage and good sense to ignore the blandishments and threats of his enemies.

The terrible events of this feud which culminated on that bloody day in July 1544 left a deep scar on that part of the highlands. It seems that the boil of rancour that had festered between the two clans was lanced at Kinlochlochy; the Frasers and the Clanranald never engaged in open battle again. The Frasers quickly recovered, thanks in part to the fact that many of the widows of the Fraser gentlemen killed at Kinlochlochy were pregnant and it is said that they all had sons. Even if this is not strictly accurate, the land charters demonstrate that within twenty years of the battle there was a new generation of Frasers reaching adulthood. Despite the loss of manpower the clan did not suffer too greatly in terms of their wealth, in part no doubt due to the fertile land of the Aird and there advantageous trading position with Inverness. The descendants of Ranald Galda made many attempts to obtain possession of what they believed to be their rightful inheritance. All of these efforts ended in failure although when they pass out of history in 1615 they are, ironically, living in Moidart.

Hugh fifth Lord Lovat was with others attempting to gain influence both for the Frasers and possibly the Scottish government over the Clanranald, by imposing Ranald Galda on the Clanranald. The circumstances were in his favour and he had the support of powerful allies. If the Clanranald had been led by a lesser man than John Moydartach then Hugh may well have been successful. He acted in an environment which was favourable to his plans but was undone by a situation which spiralled out of his control. His protégée Ranald Galda died fighting bravely at the head of his mother's clan when fate had decided against him.

The Clanranald also suffered a great loss of life, and the aftermath of loss and sorrow would also have spread like a dark cloud over the glens of the west. Under John's leadership the Clanranald stood up to the enormous pressure of their situation of which the Frasers were only a part. Their achievement in surviving these tests intact can be measured by a comparison with other clans of MacDonalds who failed under similar circumstances; for example the Maclains of Ardnamurchan or the Clan Iain Mor.

With the backing of the Clanranald, John Moydartach successfully resisted the efforts of the greatest magnates in Scotland to replace him as chief of the Clanranald. He defied the Regent Arran and the Dowager Queen Mary and destroyed the military power of the Frasers. It was to be two hundred years before a British monarch could impose his will with any confidence on the Clanranald.

Chapter 4

Fire and Sword

There are many problems with the events described in this chapter as they are not recorded in any state papers of the time or in the Clanranald's own histories. There are serious doubts about the dates at which these conflicts took place which clearly has implications as to which characters were involved and the underlying reasons behind the feuds. The descriptions of these events are preserved in documents whose date and accuracy are disputed and in the oral traditions of Skye and the Outer Hebrides. This chapter has assumed that a "Description of the Isles of Scotland", which was the first document to record the events on Eigg, places them in the early months of 1577. Many of the oral traditions place these same events some forty years earlier, when Alastair Crotach was chief of the MacLeods of Harris. The date of 1577 has been followed for the massacre on Eigg as it allows for a chronology which fits in with the history of the Clanranald.[1] One fine summer's morning early in the 1570's Allan, the son of John Moydartach, accompanied by his wife sailed for the island of Mull. Allan, although he was in his forties had not yet become the seventh captain of the Clanranald as his father was still alive, John Moydartach not dying till 1584. At some point during John's later years it is probable that Allan took over the active leadership of the clan and it is certain that by this date Allan was a man of great influence within the Clanranald. Allan was the son of John and Margaret (a daughter of MacIain of Ardnamurchan) and had married a daughter of Alastair Crotach (the hunchbacked) MacLeod, the chief of the MacLeods of Harris.[2] Allan has been overshadowed by his father the great John Moydartach, but as events were to show he possessed many of the qualities so admired in highland societies of this period. He was already well versed in the brutal nature of clan feuds; Allan was present at the bloody field of Kinlochlochy.

It was to be during the period of Allan's chiefship that the Clanranald became embroiled in a bitter feud with the MacLeods of Harris. The seeds of this feud may well go back to the first half of the sixteenth century, when the Clanranald leased part of Glenelg from, ironically, the Frasers. Glenelg was amongst the most ancient possessions of the MacLeods and they could not have looked favourably on this encroachment on their ancestral lands by a rival clan, especially as they were MacDonalds; another branch of whom (the MacDonalds of Sleat) had been

---

[1] Some writers do not accept the date of 1577 for the events on Eigg and place them in the early sixteenth century, when Alastair Crotach was chief of the MacLeods of Harris. Almost all the oral traditions describe Alastair Crotach and his William as being the perpetrators of the massacre on Eigg. J. L. Campbell claimed that the date of 1577 had been miscopied and should read 1517. While others express doubts that the massacre even took place.

[2] This branch of the MacLeods was known as the Siol Tormod and is not to be confused with the MacLeods of Lewis who were known as the Siol Torquil.

expanding their territories on Skye since the fifteenth century at the expense of the MacLeods.[3]

Allan and his wife were on a social visit to Hector Mor MacLean the chief of the MacLeans of Duart. On arriving they were entertained in the traditional manner which included much feasting and drinking; during these festivities Hector Mor's seven daughters were present. Allan became captivated by Janet, Hector's fifth daughter. When the wind was set fair for Castle Tioram he set sail with Janet for his own lands, abandoning his wife in Mull. Allan's wife must have experienced all the pain and humiliation which is reserved for those who are betrayed in public by their spouse. She (we do not know her name) returned to her own people in Skye and complained with justifiable anger to her own people.[4] The MacLeods were deeply offended by the treatment given by Allan to the daughter of their late chief. An insult of this magnitude given to a person so closely related to their chief was regarded as an insult to the whole clan who it should be remembered considered themselves to be one family.

Allan's behaviour was rash and headstrong and reflects poorly on his political judgement. It should have been clear to him that he ran a very real risk of embroiling his clan in a bitter feud with the MacLeods of Harris.

In the spring of 1577 a MacLeod galley containing thirty or forty men was driven by bad weather to the shores of to the small and remote island of Chathustail near the island of Eigg.[5] The crew asked for provisions for which they offered to pay but the MacDonalds who occupied this small island refused them.

This lack of hospitality was unusual and may well have been connected with the dispute between their chief Allan and the MacLeods. The MacLeods killed a cow and began to roast the carcass on the beach; the MacDonalds were incensed at this act. They assembled all the available fighting men on Eigg and attacked the MacLeods, killing many and capturing the rest. This may seem like a complete over reaction to such an incident but one must bear in mind how limited their resources were and how often they must have been exposed to near starvation especially after struggling through a long winter.[6] The surviving MacLeods were bound hand and foot and cast adrift in their ship without a sail, oars or a rudder so that they were entirely at the mercy of the treacherous currents. By chance they were picked up by a MacLeod galley at the head of Loch Dunvegan which was returning from a

---

[3] MacLeod traditions state that the origins of the feud lay in the claims by the Clanranald chiefs that the MacLeod genealogy was tainted by their Norse origins and that this was exacerbated by the slaughter of some Clanranalds that landed on Harris, N. H. MacDonald has pointed out the implausibility of this particular story. It will also be remembered that the two clans had supported opposing sides during the "civil war" within the Lordship, which culminated at the Battle of Bloody Bay (see chapter 2).

[4] It is likely that the MacLeods were led by Tormod MacLeod.

[5] MacLeod traditions assert that the feud broke out after the crew of a Clanranald galley were massacred after they ran ashore on Harris.

[6] In another version of this feud the MacLeods molested some MacDonald women.

trip to the Orkneys. For the MacLeods this was the pretext they had been waiting for to exact revenge on the Clanranald. The MacLeods sent out the fiery cross and assembled a considerable fighting force under the walls of Dunvegan. They had waited patiently for several years and now they had been given the opportunity to revenge the events in Mull and no doubt they believed the maxim that, "revenge is a dish best served cold."

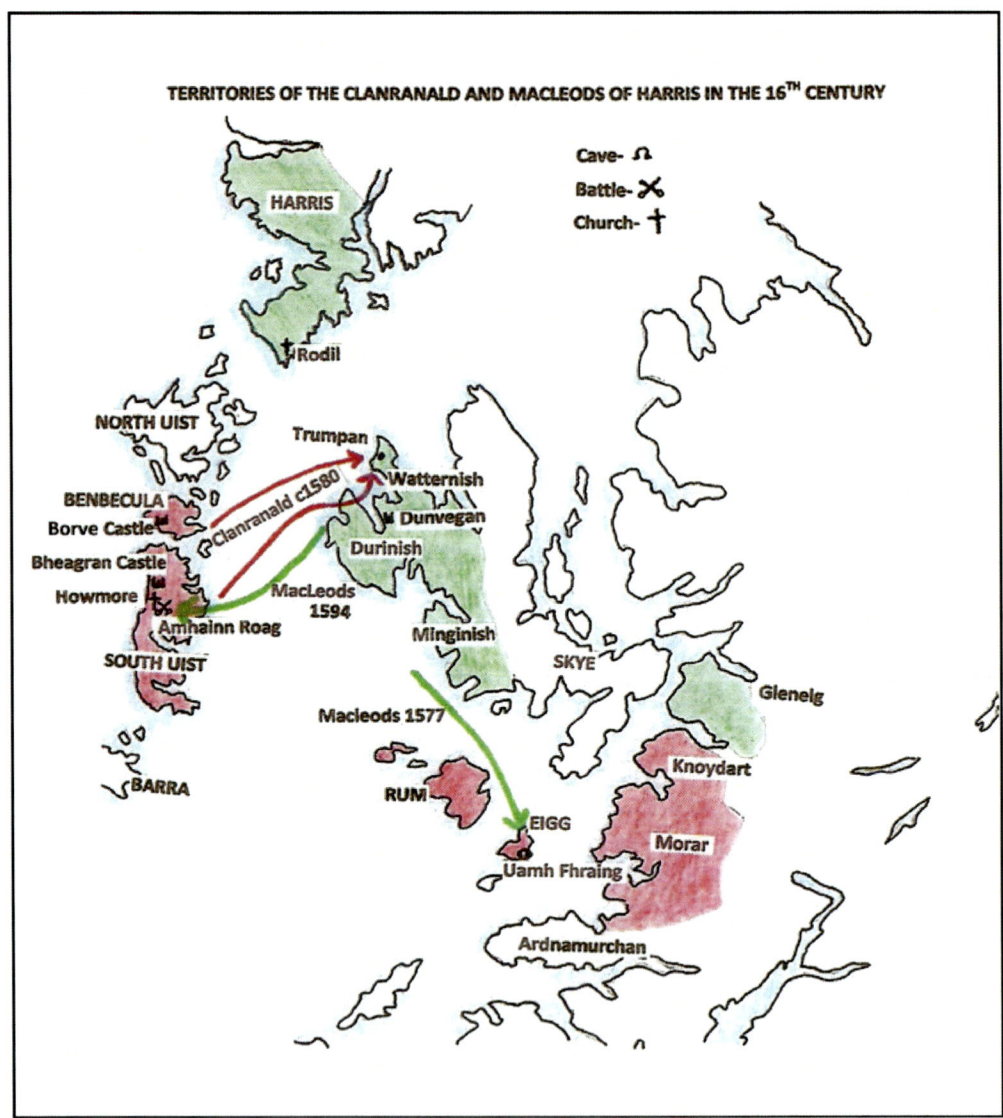

TERRITORIES OF THE CLANRANALD AND MACLEODS OF HARRIS IN THE 16TH CENTURY

The MacLeods sailed for Eigg in March 1577.[7] Eigg is described as fertile and suitable at least in parts to the rearing of livestock and the growing of crops. The island is five miles long by two miles wide, with many caves which it says were used by the inhabitants as "strengths" where the people could gather and hide in times of emergency.

The MacDonalds of Eigg would have been well aware of the complete breakdown in the relationship between their chief and the MacLeods and would have known that there was a chance that the MacLeods they had cast adrift might have survived. They were alerted to the fleet bearing down on them by lookouts they had posted. The population of Eigg in 1577 was said to be three hundred and ninety five men women and children and their leader was Angus fourth son of John Moydartach who lived on the island and was able to raise sixty men to fight for the Canranald from among the population.

Uamh Fhraing

On counting the number of ships heading for the island it was clear to Angus that the MacLeods numbered several hundred and that he could not hope to resist this invasion with the few dozen men he could muster from the island's population. The population of Eigg quickly coalesced and Angus led them to one of their ancient and secret refuges. This was a cave called Uamh Fhraing (the Cave of Saint Francis), it had only one entrance and this entrance was partly obscured by a waterfall.

The islanders hid in the cave for two days while the MacLeods ravaged the whole island. They were unable to find any trace of the MacDonalds except for one old woman who had been too lame to reach Uamh Fhraing.[8] The old woman refused to tell the MacLeods where the islanders were hiding always answering "if it comes from my knee, it can't be helped but it shall not come through my mouth." She maintained her defiance despite having her house burnt down and her crops destroyed. Finally when the MacLeods left her she cursed them "humpbacked is

---

[7] This date is mentioned in a "Description of the Isles of Scotland" which Skene demonstrates could not have been written after 1595.

[8] It is likely that some of the islanders found other refuges other than Uamh Fhraing.

the heir of MacLeod today and as long as dry straw will burn, many a hump and a crook there will be in the clan hereafter."[9]

Failing to find any MacDonalds on whom to exact their revenge; they reluctantly drew the conclusion that the inhabitants had had enough time to flee either to another island or the mainland. The three days the MacDonalds had hidden in the cave trying to keep the children quiet passed very slowly and eventually a scout was sent out to see if the MacLeods had left. As the scout looked out from a high vantage point he was spotted by the MacLeods at the same moment that he saw them. He quickly made his way back to the cave making sure he was not followed. There was however one critical factor which he overlooked, there had been a light sprinkling of snow since he had left the cave which to compound things had stopped shortly after he had reached his lookout position. When the MacLeods reached the place they had seen him they could clearly see his footprints in the snow. They followed the fresh prints and of course they were led to the mouth of the cave.[10] The MacLeods proposed to the trapped community that they hand over the "perpetrators" of the attack on Eilean Cathastail and that the rest of the people would be unharmed. Shrieks of despair rose from the mouth of the cave as the MacDonalds knew that they were trapped by an overwhelming force and yet they could not abandon their fathers, brothers and sons to the tender mercy of the MacLeods. The ties of this small community would have been immeasurably greater than a comparable community to-day. Even putting aside the intricate web of family ties all the people would have worked together and close co-operation would have been vital to their very survival. They would have shared in all the vicissitudes of life including the most profound, birth, love and death.

The MacLeods set to work and in a short while they cut a channel and diverted the stream above the cave so that it no longer flowed over the entrance. They then cut vast quantities of heather, bracken and gorse and piled it at the mouth of the cave.[11] After they had set fire to the heap of combustibles, they stood back in readiness for any attempt at escape by the ensnared islanders. As the conflagration took hold vast quantities of smoke were generated and were blown into the cave. It was many hours before all three hundred and ninety five souls had died of

---

[9] It is clear that in this tradition the raid took place during the chiefship of Alastair Crotach (the hunchback).

[10] One tradition asserts that the scout was aware that he would leave a trail in the snow and attempted to confuse the MacLeods by walking backwards, however this clearly makes little sense.

[11] One story recounts how Alasdair Crotach prevaricated before committing this terrible act and told his men to await God's judgement, if after six hours the wind was blowing away from the cave then he would spare the islanders. After six hours the wind direction had not changed and actually blew with greater force into the mouth of the cave, Alasdair Crotach sailed away leaving his son William to give the orders to light the fire. William was later known as Uilleam na h-Uamha (William of the Cave).

asphyxiation. Almost the entire population of the island had been swept away in this massacre; it was some years before human voices were heard again on Eigg.[12]

Their pitiful remains were to lie undisturbed in the cave for two hundred years. When the cave was examined the bones were found in small groups, the skeletons in each group were male and female, mature and immature. Pathetically each family had stayed together and died in each others arms. This quote from the New Statistical Account for Invernesshire is one of the first recorded visits to the cave, "We stood on the very ground where the tragedy was acted, and felt our sensibility increased by the sequestered and dreary place in which the deed was done. But even this interest was faint when compared to that we felt when, after creeping a considerable way through a low and narrow entrance, half-covered with brushwood, we found ourselves at last within a large and gloomy cave, the extent and height of which we could not distinguish and perceived the gleams of the lights we carried reflected from the bones and skulls of the unhappy MacDonalds. The force with which the truth and all the circumstances of this dreadful tale struck at this moment upon our minds, and the strange variety of sensations excited by an event so extraordinary it is not easy to find words to express. The entrance to the cave is low and narrow for about twelve feet, the breadth fourteen feet, and in length it extends inwards two hundred and thirteen feet. The air was damp and now our lights on the blank sides of the cave without dispelling that deep and solemn gloom which harmonized so well with the melancholy story. The projecting masses of rock were dimly illuminated while the skulls and bones catched a strong light. Our figures too touched with the pale flame showed the features of an outstretched arm, while parts of the body removed from the light were lost in the gloom. The whole scene was admirably adapted to the canvas, but it would require a very rare talent in the painter who could attempt it." Shortly after this visit the bones of the people of Eigg were removed from the cave and respectfully buried under a cairn nearby.[13]

Eigg today is a beautiful splash of green and brown set in the treacherous and dramatic seas of the sound of Mull. The small hamlet of Clealdale is joined by scattered crofts all of which are overlooked by the ancient mountains of An Sgurr and An Cruachan. Today the tranquil nature of Eigg gives no clue to the tragedy which occurred in the late sixteenth century. The whole community with all their hopes, fears, loves and disputes had been exterminated. The population of Eigg

---

[12] N.H. MacDonald has demonstrated that the Description of the Isles of Scotland was probably written before 1588. In this document the island of Eigg is said to be able to raise some sixty fighting men for the Clanranald, this implies a population of a few hundred individuals on Eigg less than a decade after the massacre. Given the land hunger and lack of resources it seems plausible that Eigg was quickly re-settled after the massacre. However the fact that the bones of the victims were left in the cave suggests that the newcomers were not closely related to the original inhabitants.

[13] By the nineteenth century many of the skulls of the victims had been removed by the early visitors to the site, including Sir Walter Scott.

would have had a culturally distinctive way of life which was swept way in a single day and was lost to the Clanranald and ultimately to all of us forever.

There is a song which was preserved on the island of Benbecula which was written by a Clanranald poet from South Uist who morns the extirpation of his clan on Eigg.

Distant is the view that I can see
I can see Rum and Eigg and Islay
Where MacLeod has wrought destruction
He has slacked his thirst in bloodshed
I see Barra low lying land.
I see Uist of the bountiful people[14]
Where they keep the feast of St Michael
Hi Hoireann o
Who will be mirthful
Who will carry the slender gun
Sad is the climbing,
E ho a ho, sad is the climbing.[15]

This atrocious event which by its unusual set of circumstances had led to the annihilation of a whole society was unparalleled even in the violent and anarchic environment of the western highlands in the sixteenth century. During the many feuds and creachs (raids) of this period there were many examples of the killing of the old, the innocent, women and children but this deliberate mass murder was to plunge the Clanranald and the MacLeods of Harris into a cycle of revenge atrocities which led to the surviving population being reduced to a state of starvation and complete degradation.

At the end of this feud the populations of certain areas of both clans were reduced to eating anything they could lay their hands on including cats and dogs. There are some real problems as to who was responsible for the massacre on Eigg; many writers (including most of the oral traditions) point the finger at Alastair Crotach eight chief of the MacLeods of Harris and his son William. If we accept that the massacre took place in 1577, then clearly Alastair Crotach who died in 1547 nor his son William who died in 1552 can have been involved in the massacre. Alistair Crotach and his son William were buried in the church of Saint Clements at Rodil in Harris, the inscription on Alistair's tomb reads "Here lies Alistair son of William Macleod of Dunvegan who died in the year 1547".

---

[14] The bountiful people is the descriptive term used by MacDonald poets to describe their clan.

[15] This poem was taken from Dressler's Eigg The Story of an Island whose source was J. L. Campbell's Hebridean Folksongs.

MacLeod historians[16] suggest that the responsibility may lie with a certain Ian Dubh MacLeod who committed many dark deeds in the MacLeod lands of Skye and ultimately crowned his life of betrayal and murder by assassinating his own chief Donald MacLeod, tenth of Dunvegan. Ian Dubh died a criminal's death in Ireland where he was executed by having a red hot poker thrust into his bowels on the orders of the O'Donnell[17] chief. The date of Ian Dubh's death is unknown but it must have been after 1557 when he his mentioned in a document dated 1557 written for the queen dowager Mary. This document demonstrates that in May 1557 Iain Dubh had control of Dunvegan Castle; the principal residence of the MacLeods of Harris. It is possible that during this period that Iain Dubh held authority over a significant element of the MacLeods. However by 1577 if Iain Dubh was still alive he was a fugitive on the run from the justice of his own clan and would have been unable to mount a large scale operation against the island of Eigg. From the available evidence (if one accepts the date of 1577 for the massacre) this feud took place when Tormod was the eleventh chief of the MacLeods of Harris.

The extirpation of the people of Eigg[18] did not happen in isolation, they were part of the polity of the Clanranald. Many members of the clan would have lost relatives and friends, Angus; Allan's brother had died in the flames. The Clanranald now had another and more justifiable reason for revenge and nursed a deep seated hatred for the MacLeods of Harris.

The events that followed are recorded only by the MacLeod historians and although they are clear in outline the details have to be read with caution because no clan history was written with historical accuracy as the primary objective. It was to record the history of the clan in such a way that the clan was seen in the best possible light. This style was at least to a degree continued in the great Victorian histories. The other problem was that this aspect of this feud was embedded in the folklore of Skye and as the stories were passed down orally they may well have become intermingled with local legends; for example, when the fight between two blacksmiths is described it should be borne in mind that smiths were for centuries considered to have magical powers due to there ability to transform ores into metal.

Approximately three years after the massacre on Eigg, circa 1580 the Clanranald acted to quench their thirst for revenge. The men of South Uist set sail for Skye on a Saturday night; their approach to the island from the west was cloaked by a thick bank of fog.

---

[16] Alexander MacKenzie.

[17] The O'Donnells were an Irish tribe and are not to be confused with the MacDonalds.

[18] Apart from the oral tradition about the old woman who would not tell where the islanders were hiding there is one other fact which suggests that there were a few survivors on Eigg. Irish Franciscans who visited Eigg in 1625 mention one old woman who remembered hearing mass there in her youth. Given that this was only forty eight years after the massacre could she have been a survivor?

Their first contact was with five fishermen off Dunvegan head. The MacDonalds dispatched a fast sixteen oared boat to deal with them before they could give the alarm. The MacLeods cut away their fishing lines and rowed with all their strength for the shore. The Clanranald boat although gaining on them could not prevent them reaching land. The MacLeods raced up the beach amidst a hail of arrows, four of the MacLeods rushed into a cave where they were trapped by the Clanranalds and killed. The fifth fisherman who was called Finley MacLeod, a man renowned for his physical

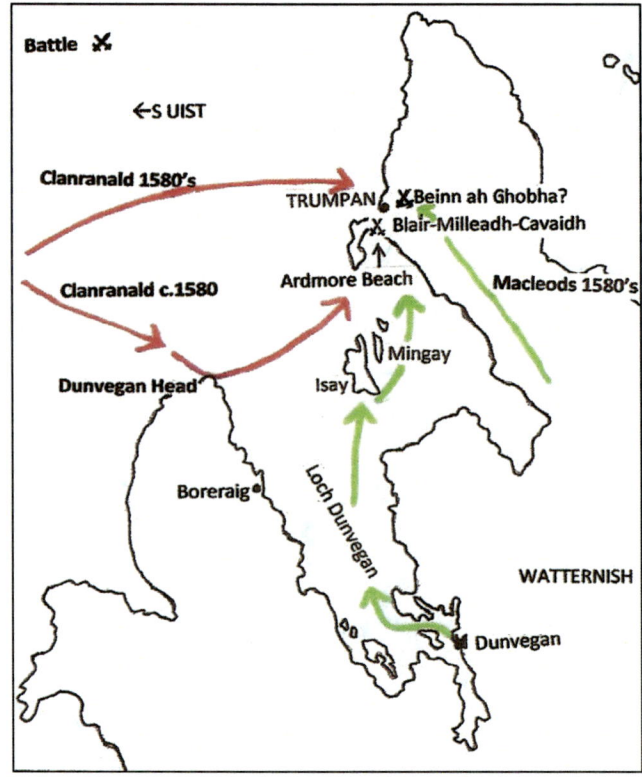

prowess scrambled up the steep slope and was gradually able to increase the distance between himself and his pursuers. It is said that he was able to alert the watchman at Dunvegan by three shouts when he was five miles away. Although the distance may be somewhat exaggerated it should be remembered that without all the paraphernalia of modern life the highlands would have been extremely quiet and sound would have travelled a long way especially as the weather was foggy there would have been no noise from the wind.

The Crann Tairc (the fiery cross) was sent out amongst all the MacLeod clachans (hamlets) to raise the clan for their defence. The fiery cross was an ancient method of warning used by the clans, it was passed from one runner to the next and could cover over eighty miles a day. It was two pieces of wood tied together one end was burnt and the other was dripping in blood to signify fire and sword. As soon as a significant number of clansmen (a few hundred) had rallied at Dunvegan the MacLeods launched their galleys and sailed up Loch Dunvegan. Due to the fog and the considerable expanse of sea it is no surprise that they were unable to make contact with the Clanranald. The MacDonalds knowing that they had been discovered reembarked from Durinish and sailed across the loch to the long beach at Ardmore. It was a good site to land their ships as the galleys were sheltered from bad weather and as the shore was overshadowed by steep cliffs the raiding party could not be seen until they climbed the steep path from the beach. Merely to steel cattle and sheep would not have satisfied the Clanranalds thirst for revenge and shortly after dawn they resolved on a much more terrible form of retribution. In the quiet morning air they could hear the beautiful sound of the Gaelic hymns coming from the congregation of the church of Trumpan.[19]

Trumpan Church

The MacDonalds crept up the ridge and surrounded the church. The small door was barricaded and the thatched roof was set on fire, the men from South Uist surrounded the burning church and waited for the congregation to attempt to force their way out. The desperate MacLeods eventually managed to prize the door open but as they ran from the church they were cut down with ease by the men waiting outside for them. Some of the surviving congregation on seeing the fate of those who tried to escape stayed inside and were burnt to death when the roof collapsed. The killing of the innocent MacLeods was made a simple task due to the small size of the medieval doorway at Trumpan which would only provide enough

---

[19] N.H. MacDonald has pointed out that there is a problem with the events in the Trumpan district in that, Trumpan is in Watternish which belonged to the MacLeods of Lewis (who were allied to the MacDonalds) and did not pass into the hands of the MacLeods of Harris until the seventeenth century. However during the mid-sixteenth century Watternish was gifted to Iain Dubh MacLeod's (of Harris) grandfather after he married the niece of Roderick MacLeod of Lewis and thus it may be that in the 1580's Watternish was occupied by the MacLeods of Harris.

room for one person to run through at a time. Apart from one young woman the entire congregation of men, women and children was massacred. The scene that summer's morning would have been terrible with some of the bodies of the community lying scattered over the churchyard and the charred remains of the others intertwined amongst the blackened beams of the roof. The dimensions of the church suggest that, assuming it was full at the time of the service, between fifty and sixty souls were murdered at Trumpan church.

There is a local tradition that one young woman escaped the conflagration by jumping from one of the church windows. She was said to have had one breast severed from the slash of a sword as she darted amongst her tormentors. The windows of the church are only a few inches wide and any survivor must have escaped by some other means.[20] She died from loss of blood two miles from the church and the place is still called Mararat MacLeod after her. Another tradition asserts that she ran all the way to Dunvegan and alerted the castle at which point the fairy flag was unfurled, the MacLeods assembled with miraculous speed and swept down on the Clanranald. Standing in the churchyard of Trumpan and considering the distance and the terrain that Mararat had to run, and the time it would have taken to muster a sufficient number of MacLeod clansmen and their subsequent return journey the story has an air of implausibility about it. The description of this feud will follow the other tradition; with the MacLeods searching Loch Dunvegan for the Clanranalds and Mararat dying a few miles from the church. Towards dawn they landed on the Isle of Isay and in the cold grey light of dawn saw the smoke and flames rising above Trumpan.

It must have seemed like an eternity as they sailed from Isay towards Trumpan unable to protect their people. The same advantage of obscurity now benefited the MacLeods as their ships approached the beach under the lee of the cliffs as it had the Clanranald. The MacDonalds continued with their butchery and plundering unaware that their doom was sailing sedately towards them across the loch. They were thrown into complete confusion when they were attacked with great fury by the MacLeods. The fierceness of the MacLeod onslaught was exacerbated by the terrible site they witnessed in the graveyard of the church, the bodies of men, women and children lying scattered and mutilated.

Local tradition asserts that the MacLeods unfurled the fairy flag which it was said greatly added to their resolve. Even if one discounts the magical powers attributable to it by the clansmen the display of this ancient relic of their house can only have added to their determination to revenge themselves on the men from South Uist.

The fairy flag is a piece of finely woven silk cloth which has been dated to between the fourth and seventh centuries AD, and came from the middle east. How this ancient banner found its way to Dunvegan is unclear, two possibilities

---

[20] One tradition states that Mararat had been left for dead amongst the congregation inside the church.

have been suggested with a historical basis as well as many tales which have been associated with the fairies. One suggested origin is that it was the war banner of Harald Hardrada who fell at the battle of Stamford Bridge in 1066. This suggestion is supported by the access the Swedish Vikings[21] had to Byzantium and the middle east via the river systems of the Dneiper and Dynester rivers in what is now Russia. There are also known associations between the progenitors of the MacLeods and the Viking kings of Man and Norway. Is it possible that some of the ancestors of the MacLeods fought with Harald Hardrada at Stamford Bridge? The other possibility is that the flag was bought back from the middle east by a MacLeod crusader. If one accepts this explanation then the cloth would already have been at least four hundred years old and would have been bought back to Skye as a holy relic, this acquisition of holy relics was widespread and is well documented.[22]

The Skye traditions are associated with the mythical belief in the sith (fairies) and their powers. These tales have a theme of contact by a MacLeod with the sith who then for various reasons gifts the flag to the MacLeods. In any event the MacLeods believed that the unfurling of the fairy flag would bring them the support of magical powers. Whether or not the sith did come to the aid of the MacLeods their belief in the flag can only have greatly increased their moral.

The MacDonalds rushed down the steep slopes hoping to launch their boats, abandoning the livestock they had gathered together the night before. When they reached the beach they saw that the tide was out and their ships were stranded on the shore. Some of the Uist men had already been cut down by the MacLeods who were in hot pursuit. The survivors of the Clanranalds grimly formed a defensive line behind a stone wall at the edge of the beach. After the events at the church they knew that there would be no quarter given and that they would have to stand and die together where they stood. The MacLeods halted and organized their forces for the final struggle and then in one mass rushed at the wall. A long and merciless struggle was fought at the top of the beach which only ended when all the MacDonalds were slain.

The MacLeods would have buried their own dead from the battle and the victims of the massacre with great respect in the little churchyard of Trumpan and tended with every care to the wounded. The MacDonald wounded who had survived were slaughtered without mercy where they lay on the beach. The corpses of the men from Uist were laid out behind the wall they had used as a defence and the wall of stones and turf was dragged down over them and it was from this action that the battle derived its name, Blair-Milleadh-Cavaidh (The Battle of the Spoiling of the Dyke). The story of this murderous encounter was told to Alexander MacKenzie in the mid-nineteenth century by Major MacLeod of Skye who recalled

---

[21] Harald Hardrada was King of the Norwegian Vikings, but it is likely that he had contact with his Swedish neighbours.
[22] Runciman's History of the Crusades.

that his father had told him that as a young man he had seen the bleached bones of the men of Clanranald on the shoreline.

Ardmore Beach

A few years after Blair-Milleadh-Cavaidh there was another clash between the Clanranald and the MacLeods of Harris. The year of the battle is unknown but would have occurred in the 1580's. The Clanranald again landed in Watternish. They landed at night in an attempt to take the MacLeods by surprise but were quickly detected by the lookouts which every clan must have had on a permanent basis in times of feud. Knowing that they had been discovered the MacDonalds withdrew through the peninsular collecting all the sheep and cattle as they went. At dawn the two clan armies made contact two miles from the clachan of Trumpan.

The MacLeod historians record that few of the combatants survived on both sideS and this clash was also another example of the clansmen of both the Clanranald and the MacLeods of Harris refusing to give way at whatever cost. Due to the location it is likely that it again involved clansmen from South Uist and local MacLeod levies from Watternish. A local tradition records that among the last survivors were two blacksmiths, one from each clan. The two smiths were equally matched and protected by full armour. They fought each other all through the morning; at last the MacLeod smith was badly wounded and was weakening from a severe loss of blood. His wife having heard news that her husband had been killed, rushed to the battlefield despite the danger, to recover his corpse.

She saw her husband starting to fail under the repeated blows of the Clanranald smith; she moved behind the MacDonald and struck him on the head with her staff, at the same time shouting out "turn to me". He was momentarily distracted and glanced over his shoulder, her husband seized his opportunity and drove his broadsword through a joint in his opponents armour and the MacDonald fell dying to the ground. The spot where he fell is still known as Beinn a Ghobha (The Blacksmith's Hill). Two leaders of the MacLeods died during the battle of Beinn a Ghobha, one was John, who was the son of Alexander MacLeod of Trumpan; in the clan histories he is described as being in full plate armour. While it is possible that this description may originally have described combatants who were Gallowglasses[23] with a saffron coloured coat with chain mail across the shoulders, the mention of plate mail must be wrong.

John did much execution amongst the Clanranald but eventually on becoming separated from his clan fell under a multitude of dirk thrusts. John's death is described as being caused when a group of MacDonalds rushed him and drove their dirks between the chinks in his armour. This seems somewhat unlikely as John as a son of a tacksman would not have been able to afford the expense of full body armour nor would he have wanted to be virtually immobilized on such a fluid battle field. Later his family erected a huge cross where he fell and even in the nineteenth century the place was known as Crois Mhic Alastair (the Cross of Alexander's son).

The other MacLeod of rank who died that day was Roderick of Unish; he was a man of immense physical strength who strode around the field putting any of the Clanranald he encountered to the sword. Eventually he died in a frenzied assault by a group of his enemies. The MacLeod historians describe how his enemies fell like wheat before the scythe "under the irresistible heavy sweep of his sword and his powerful arm". Eventually a MacDonald with a lunge of his claymore hewed off both his legs at the knee and he fell to the ground on a small grassy knoll. As he knelt before his foes he continued in his work of execution before being finally dispatched. The place where he died was called Crocan Mhic Iain (The Knoll of John's Son). For many years a large white cross marked the spot where he fell, the whiteness either being caused by whitewashing or perhaps it was made from a piece of bleached wood from the sea shore.

There is no evidence that Allan the chief of the Clanranald was present at either of these encounters,[24] but it is unlikely that either raid would have taken place without his knowledge and agreement. The battles of The Spoiling Of The Dyke and The Battle Of The Smiths are somewhat enigmatic we know only that they occurred

---

[23] The gallowglasses were heavy infantry who often acted as mercenaries in the continual warfare of Ireland. They wore protective chain mail which covered their torso and hung down to their knees. It is highly unlikely that any of the combatants were in full plate armour, which was unheard of amongst the highlanders. Given that the stories of these encounters were handed down by word of mouth for generations it is probable that they were embellished in the telling. For more information on Gallowglasses see Appendix I.

[24] Indeed these clan battles in Watternish are not recorded at all in the Clanranald histories.

in the 1580's, there is no information as to the numbers involved but we may infer that they were relatively small perhaps involving a few hundred men from the absence of Allan and the participation of clansmen from only parts of the Clanranald and MacLeod lands. The two conflicts are not mentioned in the histories of the Clanranald or more significantly in the public records emanating from the Scottish court.

These conflicts would have had profound implications for the Clanranald lands of South Uist and the MacLeod lands of Watternish. Both areas would have lost a very high proportion of their able bodied men as well as the entire MacLeod community of Trumpan. Many hundreds had died and large tracts of land had felt the effect of fire and sword, but unlike some other feuds as only a part of the clan were involved they did not threaten the social cohesiveness of the either clan.

During these turbulent times Allan lived with Janet his second wife (daughter of Hector Mor MacLean of Duart) at Castle Tioram. Allan's eldest son by this marriage was known as John of Strome, he died in a tragic accident while practising using a sling with a servant. Allan was also fated to lose his eldest son and heir, Allan Og, who was the only child born to Allan and his first wife (the daughter of Alasdair Crotach MacLeod, who Allan had abandoned on Mull). Allan and Janet would regularly visit a place called Keppoch (not to be confused with the Keppoch in Lochabar) in Arisaig during the summer months. Near Keppoch at the head of Lochnakaul Allan's sons would hunt the seals as they basked on the rocks with bows and arrows. It was during one of these hunting expeditions that Allan Og was murdered. As Allan Og was aiming at a seal he was transfixed by two or three arrows; he fell dying amongst the rocks on the shore. His brothers all claimed that it was an accident. Clearly this was not the case as he was hit by ay least two arrows simultaneously. Their motive was of course to clear the way for them to take control of the Clanranald on the death of Allan. The brothers were all the children of Janet. Is it possible that Janet was involved in this despicable murder to clear the way for her sons to inherit the chiefship of the Clanranald?

One can be sure that the murder of Allan Og did not pass unnoticed amongst the MacLeods. Potentially it would have been greatly to their advantage if Allan Og had assumed the chiefship of the Clanranald as it was quite possible that they would have been able to exert some influence on him because of their blood connections. The MacLeods must have considered this as yet another outrage committed against their clan by Allan and Janet, Tormod gathered the gentlemen of the clan and plotted his revenge in the halls of Dunvegan. Allan the old chief of the Clanranald and Angus his son were both held responsible for the murder of Allan Og and declared rebels by the state and interestingly their lands were gifted to the descendants of Ranald Galda. This legal loss of title to their lands was of no concern as they maintained absolute control of their ancient patrimony and were never successfully challenged by the descendants of Ranald Galda.

In 1588 the Clanranald became embroiled in the great feud between the Clan Iain Mor and the MacLeans over the Rinnes of Isla.[25] It is probable that Allan led his clan to support the Clan Iain Mor after the treacherous attack on the Maclains at Torlisk. John Maclain and his attendants had been attacked by the MacLeans during John's wedding to Lachlan's mother. Allan would already have been predisposed to support his fellow MacDonalds against the MacLeans, but the attack on John Maclain would have led him to commit the Clanranald to a feud with the MacLeans. Allan's family life may well have been difficult during this period because his mother was a Maclain while his wife was a MacLean.

The Clanranald joined the Clan Iain Mor and the Maclains in an invasion of the MacLean territories of Mull, Coll and Tiree.[26] In revenge Lachlan Mor MacLean led the MacLeans (assisted by the Spanish sailors from the Juan de Sicilia[27]) in an attack on Canna, Rum and Eigg. The inhabitants of the islands were massacred and all their houses set on fire, their livestock were slaughtered and their goods carried back to Mull. The Register of the Privy Council of Scotland records "....and in maist barbarous, shameful and creull maner, byrnt the same illis, with the hail men, weimen and children being therintill, not spairing the pupillis and infantis...". If it is correct that the massacre at Uamh Fhraing took place in 1577 then the population of Eigg had been massacred twice in eleven years.[28]

Allan of Moidart seventh chief of the Clanranald died in 1593. MacVurich the Clanranald sennicherie describes him as "generous, open hearted, hospitable and desirous to maintain and establish a good name". To these qualities it would not be unreasonable to add that he could be irresponsible and thoughtless and that by indulging his personnel predilections (by abandoning his first wife) he had embroiled his people in a desperate feud with the powerful and proud MacLeods. Among the listed achievements of his life was the errection of a chapel at Kildonan on the island of Eigg, this may have been to commemorate his brother Angus and the people of Eigg.

Allan's son Angus assumed the chiefship as the eighth chief of Clanranald although he had been the acting head of the clan during the last few years of Allan's life. Angus was to hold the chiefship for less than a year as he fell in battle in 1594. Tormod MacLeod had died in 1585 and had been succeeded as chief of the MacLeods of Harris by William MacLeod. During the 1580's the MacLeods of Harris and the Clanranald were involved in a vast conflagration between the MacLeans of

---

[25] See chapter 11.

[26] See chapter 11.

[27] This Spanish galleon had been part of the Spanish Armada and had been blown ashore on Mull.

[28] It has been argued that it was not possible for Eigg to have been re-populated only eleven years after the first massacre at Uamh Fhraing. However given the paucity of resources in the western highlands the relatively fertile island would have been an attractive proposition for the poorer members of the Clanranald.

Mull and the Clan Iain Mor.[29] As one would expect they supported different sides; the Clanranald lending their weight to the Clan Iain Mor. The rancour between the two clans was nourished by their opposing positions in this feud and the memories associated with the murder of Allan Og and the atrocities and battles of the preceding years.

In 1594 Angus and his brother Donald were living at Ormiclate in South Uist. Due to the widely dispersed nature of the Clanranald territories the chiefs travelled frequently between their possessions in the summer months. The main purpose of this itinerant lifestyle was to maintain a close personal relationship between the chief and his people which was essential to the cohesion of the clan.

Runners arrived with the news that the MacLeods had landed at Acarsaid Fhalaich (the Hidden Anchorage) in six ships. The total number of the invaders was estimated at one hundred and twenty. Angus immediately organised precautionary measures to protect the cattle on the island. The cows in milk and their calves were sent to the south of the island while the other cattle were hidden on the east of the island at a place called Bualde Ghaill (the fold of the lowlander). Angus ordered Donald to take twenty picked men and protect these cattle while at the same time to keep in sight of the force that Angus was assembling and come to their aid if necessary. Angus mustered all the forces available to him including young boys and old men. The backbone of his army were a few well armed gentlemen (tacksmen) who as his close relatives travelled with him to South Uist from Castle Tioram. South Uist was short of fighting men due to the heavy losses that had befallen the island in previous encounters with the MacLeods. The MacDonalds concentrated at the base of a hill called Harsal where they built a bank and ditch to help them withstand the onslaught of the MacLeods. Traces of this earthwork were still visible in the late nineteenth century.[30]

The MacLeods immediately sent out scouts after they had landed. They returned mid-morning with a detailed description of the Clanranalds location and described the building of the earthwork. They set out by a circuitous route in an attempt to keep out of sight of the Uist men and to negate any value the bank and ditch may have had by emerging behind the Clanranald. The topography of South Uist is, in the main fairly flat on the western side of the island. In the late sixteenth century there would have been little tree cover so that the MacLeods were unable to avoid detection and their movements were soon reported back to Angus by the local population. Angus knew of their location and the speed and direction of their approach. When the MacLeods came into view the Clanranald were expecting them.

As the two clans drew closer the leader of the MacLeods threw off his chain mail, the hillock where it landed was later known as Maol na Luirich (the mound of

---

[29] The Clan Iain Mor was also known as the Clan Donald South or the MacDonalds of Dunnyveg.

[30] MacDonald brothers.

mail).[31] The MacDonalds were mustered in a bend of the river Amhainn Roag; Angus had allowed himself to be placed at a disadvantage even though he had known of the exact dispositions of the enemy. There is no mention in the description of the battle of the earthworks, which were presumably rendered obsolete due to the direction of approach of the MacLeods. What is harder to understand is why Angus allowed himself to be trapped in a bend in the river with his back to the banks which now, instead of strengthening his deployment actually meant that the Amhainn Roag hemmed him in on three sides. The battle of Amhainn Roag was one of the bloodiest clan battles ever fought in the Outer Hebrides; it was the usual merciless anarchic slugging match of terrifying butchery.

As the two clans continued to slaughter each other Angus came face to face with the leader of the MacLeods. During the ensuing struggle Angus's foot slipped on the river bank and loosing his balance he fell into the river, the MacLeod seizing his momentary advantage lifted up his broadsword and with a huge double handed sweep separated Angus's head from his body. His head; followed at a more sedate pace by his torso; floated down the fast flowing Amhainn Roag. The situation was becoming desperate for the Clanranald, they had lost a large number of men, their chief had fallen and they were in effect hemmed in by the river, as any attempt to escape would give the enemy a huge advantage as they struggled through the fast flowing water. The battle continued to rage until a group of the Clanranald who had not been able to arrive at the start of the encounter swept down on the MacLeods and killed several of them before they knew they were there. The scales were slowly tipping in favour of the MacDonalds. The conflict settled down to its dreadful rhythm of pain, fear, hatred and exhaustion. A MacLeod called Ronald Mor chased three MacDonalds and one by one he overtook them and cut them down.[32]

Local tradition relates that as Ronald Mor was returning to the battlefield he came across two severely wounded MacLeods who were dying from loss of blood. On reaching his clan he sent some of his men to help them if they could and if not to bury them. The place where they buried them was known as Glaic nam fear Iota (the hollow of the wounded men). Again there is a problem with this scrap of description from Amhainn Roag. We are told that there was a great loss of life on both sides and that it was one of the severest clan encounters ever fought in the outer isles. Eventually the MacLeods were defeated. It seems most unlikely that

---

[31] This description of the Battle of Amhainn Roag was given to the MacDonald brothers who wrote the seminal three volume Clan Donald by Farquhar Beaton, a shepherd from Drimsdale, South Uist. This description was collected in the nineteenth century and no doubt had already been altered and embellished as it had been retold and passed down through the generations.

[32] It has been pointed out that this description of the deeds of Ronald Mor should be read with some caution as it has close similarities with the classical description of the encounter between the Horatti and the Curattii. Clan historians of the sixteenth century were often fluent in Latin and may have wished to embellish their description of the battle.

Ronald Mor would have wanted to spare some of his men during the battle and as his clan was defeated there would have been no time for anything but attempting to save their own lives as they rushed to the ships. These problematic descriptions should not be given too much weight as no doubt the story of this battle was embellished as it was handed down from generation to generation. These descriptions can either be dismissed or enjoyed as part of a rich Gaelic tradition of story telling. Eventually the MacLeods broke and fled for the safety of their ships. The MacDonalds were too exhausted to follow them. Of the one hundred and twenty MacLeods who had landed on the island only thirty remained. Instead of the large plunder they had expected they found one old cow which had inadvertently been left behind. They built a fire and roasted the carcass on the beach before returning to Skye in their empty ships.

Donald, Angus's brother played a less than distinguished role in the dramatic events of that summer's day. Donald with the twenty picked men who had been chosen to protect the cattle did not come to his brother's aid in his hour of need; he stood aloof and watched as the battle raged in clear view of his group of men. One can only speculate as to what difference they would have made other than to surmise that in a conflict of that scale they would have been a very welcome addition to the Clanranald forces. It is likely that Donald coldly calculated that the death of his brother would open the way to him becoming chief. Angus had no children and their other brother Ranald was younger and therefore Donald would have had precedence over him.

Donald did succeed to the captaincy of the Clanranald to become the ninth chief of the Clanranald and clearly possessed the qualities required by the clan or after his self-serving behaviour at Amhainn Roag he would not have been elected by his people. In later years Donald was to become involved in other feuds both with the MacLeans and the MacKenzies. The part the Clanranald played in these will be discussed elsewhere.[33] Donald was among many highland chiefs who were in 1608, kidnapped by James VI on his ship the Moon. His great adversary Rory Mor MacLeod suspecting a trap could not be inveigled aboard the Moon and escaped the fate planned for him; Donald and the other chiefs were imprisoned in Blackness Castle. After the union of the Scottish and English crowns James was no longer the impecunious king of an impoverished state and he was able to exert his authority with much greater efficiency into the western highlands.

Donald of the Clanranald and Rory Mor of the MacLeods of Harris were cowed by the increasing power of the state and this bitter feud faded from history. No doubt there were minor incidents involving the two clans and all those on both sides who had lost relatives and friends nursed their resentment, but the days when these two proud clans could engage each other in full-scale warfare were over. This feud which started in the early 1570's had burnt itself out by the early

---

[33] See chapters 9 and 11.

1600's. The preservation of the major events in the folk memory of the people of Watternish and South Uist attest to the trauma these areas suffered.

The Macleod district of Watternish and the Clanranald district of South Uist had been devastated with a high proportion of their livestock either slaughtered or driven off, a large number of their ships had been lost and numerous clachans burnt. The human losses were of course the most serious consequence of the feud. There had been the extermination of the entire population of the island of Eigg and the congregation of the church at Trumpan had been slaughtered as well as many other men, women and children in the raids and counter raids. These two districts had lost an appallingly high proportion of their able bodied men with all that that implied for communities living in such a difficult environment. After the casualties suffered by the men of South Uist at Blair-Milleadh-Cavaidh and Amhainn Roag this part of the territories of the Clanranald would not have been able to make any significant contribution to the forces of the Clanranald for a generation. This feud ended with no definite marker and the two clans were swept on by the flow of events which soon commanded all their attention. [34]

---

[34] In the nineteenth century, stories were still told in which all the MacLeod and MacDonald participants emerged from their graves and aided by one mortal from each clan re-fought their battles on the island of Lewis.

THE MACIAINS OF ARDNAMURCHAN

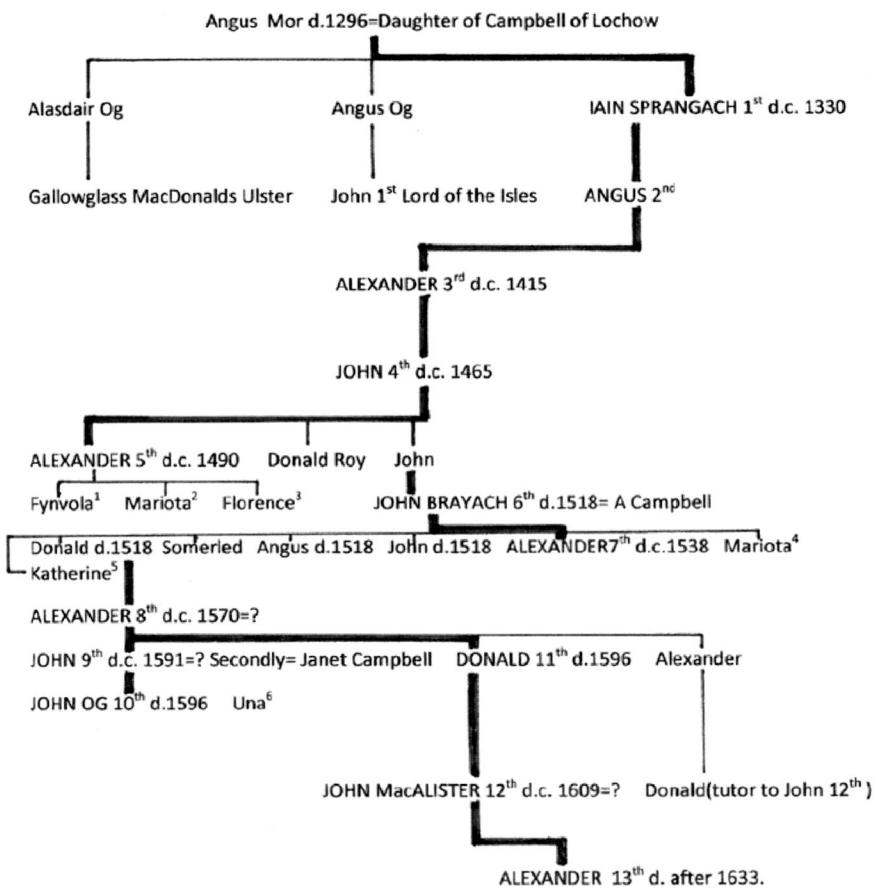

Angus Mor d.1296=Daughter of Campbell of Lochow

Alasdair Og   Angus Og   IAIN SPRANGACH 1st d.c. 1330

Gallowglass MacDonalds Ulster   John 1st Lord of the Isles   ANGUS 2nd

ALEXANDER 3rd d.c. 1415

JOHN 4th d.c. 1465

ALEXANDER 5th d.c. 1490   Donald Roy   John

Fynvola[1]   Mariota[2]   Florence[3]   JOHN BRAYACH 6th d.1518= A Campbell

Donald d.1518 Somerled Angus d.1518 John d.1518 ALEXANDER7th d.c.1538 Mariota[4]
Katherine[5]

ALEXANDER 8th d.c. 1570=?

JOHN 9th d.c. 1591=? Secondly= Janet Campbell   DONALD 11th d.1596   Alexander

JOHN OG 10th d.1596   Una[6]

JOHN MacALISTER 12th d.c. 1609=?   Donald(tutor to John 12th)

ALEXANDER 13th d. after 1633.

---

[1] Fynvola married Hugh 1st MacDonalds of Sleat.
[2] Mariota married MacDuffie of Colonsay
[3] Florence married Allan 4th of Clanranald.
[4] Mariota married Robertson of Struan and as the heiress took her feudal deeds to her husband and thence to the Campbells.
[5] Katherine married Alexander 5th of Clan Iain Mor.
[6] Una married Allan MacLean of Ardtornish

Chapter 5

A House Divided

No description of the clan feuds of the MacDonald's would be complete without a history of the Maclains of Ardnamurchan; from their rise to being for a brief moment the most powerful of all the branches of the Clan Donald, to their utter ruin. The Maclains became a broken and disposed clan when the ancient lineage of their chiefs became extinct over three hundred years ago. This chapter discusses their adoption of a different policy to the rest of their people and its consequences, and their desperate struggle to maintain their identity in the face of remorseless Campbell pressure. Unlike many other chapters it is not an account of one particular feud but of a series of feuds both with their own kindred and later with the Campbells.

The rugged peninsular of Ardnamurchan was their most ancient possession; Ardnamurchan had been in the patrimony of the MacDonalds since the time of Somerled.[1] It was one of the principal territories which made up their mainland possessions. After the forfeiture of the MacDougal Lords of Lorn by Robert the Bruce, Ardnamurchan was bestowed on Angus Og MacDonald his faithful supporter. In his turn Angus Og gifted Ardnamurchan and Sunart to his younger brother Iain Sprangach (the bold), Iain Sprangach become the progenitor of the Maclains of Ardnamurchan. It is from Iain Sprangach that this branch of the clan derived their name.

During the period of the Lordship of the Isles the Maclains loyally supported the policies of their lords, John, Donald, Alexander and John. Their chief at the head of his clan was present at all the dramatic encounters of the period including the battles of Harlaw and Inverlochy. As with all the branches of the MacDonalds they supported the Lords of the Isles in their efforts to maintain the semi-regal authority of the MacDonald hegemony, including their close ties to England when it suited them. While the Lordship existed the Maclains served it loyally, holding their lands not by charter from the King but by Gaelic tradition as the gift of the Lord of the Isles. There was one exception to this form of land tenure.

Iain Sprangach's son Angus was given a charter to certain lands in Isla by David II when he was restored to the throne in 1341. This gift was to reduce the power of John first Lord of the Isles. The reason why David bestowed these lands on Isla to Angus has been lost to us, but if it was to sow disunity amongst the MacDonalds it was ultimately only too successful. In later years disputes with the Clan Iain Mor over these lands was to be one of the causes of a bitter feud between the two clans. The Maclains although having legal title to these lands may well not have been able to establish tenure of them as they were situated in the heartland of their powerful cousins the Clan Iain Mor.

---

[1] See chapter1.

For their loyal support of Alexander's (third Lord of the Isles) attempts to establish his claim to the Earldom of Ross, the Maclains were gifted yet more lands in Isla and possessions on the island of Jura by Donald Balloch and later by Alexander himself. These lands were at this time directly held by Alexander and whether under feudal or Gaelic law rightfully belonged to the Maclains. It is again unlikely that the Maclains established any lasting control over these lands due to the intransigent resistance of the Clan Iain Mor. There is a striking similarity with the position the MacKintoshes found themselves in with regard to the gift of lands by the Lord of the Isles to lands in Lochaber which were occupied by the Camerons and the MacDonalds of Keppoch.

During the closing years of the Lordship in the late fifteenth century the Maclains had reached a position of considerable power, having not only their traditional lands of Ardnamurchan and Sunart, but also legal title to lands on Isla and Jura. Their chiefs were respected members of the council of the Isles, and their influence was further enhanced when Fynvola daughter of Alexander Maclain married Hugh the progenitor of the MacDonalds of Sleat. It was during the chiefship of John Brayach[2] the sixth of Ardnamurchan that the Lordship was abolished by James IV in 1494.

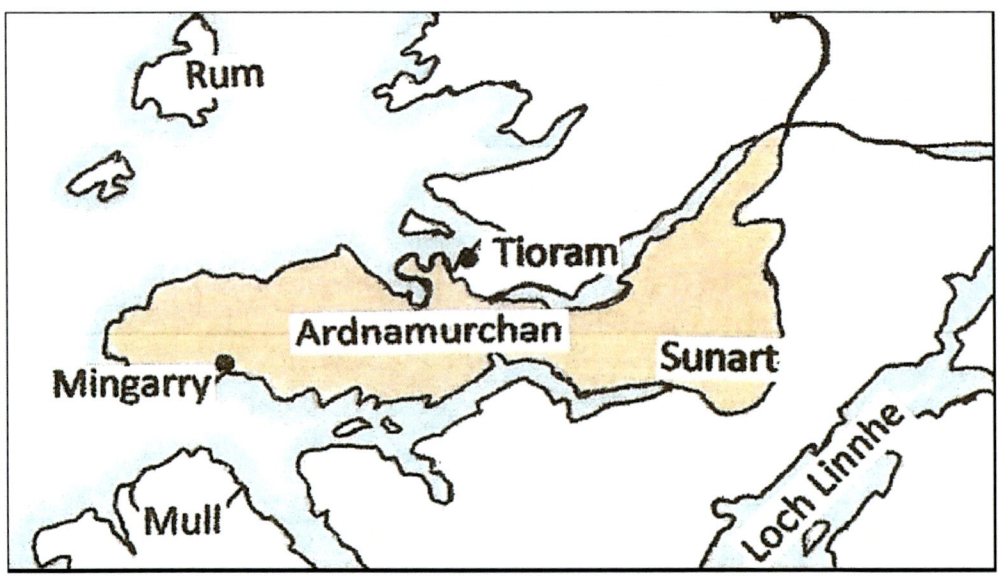

Maclain influence circa 1500

---

[2] John VI of Ardnamurchan is described as John Brayach (the bastard) by Hugh MacDonald the Sleat historian. The MacDonald brothers assert there is no justification for this adjective. Here John VI of Ardnamurchan will be referred to as John Brayach to emphasize the importance of this pivotal character.

He is described[3] as a "bold, intrepid man, and not altogether sound in his mind." While John Brayach exhibited the characteristics of violence and cunning so prevalent amongst many of his peers, he was a man who pragmatically adapted to the changed circumstances of the early sixteenth century and raised his clan to be, for a time, the most powerful of all the branches of the Clan Donald. Hugh no doubt considered him as being almost insane because he abandoned the old order of the MacDonald hegemony and supported James IV in preference to any loyalty to the re-establishment of the Lords of the Isles. John Brayach stands out as a unique individual in the early history of the MacDonalds in that he was a hard headed pragmatist who abandoned his longing for the past and seeing the new opportunities seized them and allowed no sense of past loyalties to stand in his way. By his MacDonald contemporaries he was regarded as a traitor, and was held in contempt for his adaptability, and feared for his clever ruthlessness.

James IV forfeited John the fourth and last recognized Lord of the Isles in 1493, although the forfeiture was finally put into effect in the following year. Knowing that the dissolution of the Lordship was likely to result in widespread unrest, this able and energetic king hastened to the highlands and received the submission of Alexander of Lochalsh, John Cathanach the acting chief of the Clan Iain Mor and John Brayach; of whom only the later was sincerely attached to the new order. A year later John Brayach was confirmed in the possessions that the Maclains held under the Lords of the Isles by a charter he received from James. John's loyalty was transferred from that of the Lordship to that of the King irrevocably, earning for him the hatred of the other adherents of the Lordship.

John Brayach was immediately involved in a bitter dispute with the Clan Iain Mor over not only the possessions in Isla but also his ancient patrimony of Sunart. It may be that John Cathanach laid claim to the Maclain lands of Sunart to divert attention from John Brayach's legal title to a significant proportion of the heartland of the Clan Iain Mor on Isla. The hatred the two men bore for each other was fuelled by this dispute but was greatly intensified by their strong and intolerant personalities and their diametrically opposed loyalties after the fall of the Lordship. John Cathanach was pronounced a rebel by James after he had stormed the Castle of Dunaverty and hung James's governor in full view of the royal fleet. To be declared a rebel by the king meant that not only could the individual be executed for treason but also that all his possessions were forfeit and could be gifted by the king to whomsoever he pleased. Clearly the latter aspect of being declared a rebel was of great concern to the whole of the Clan Iain Mor.

There is no doubt of John Brayach's loyalty to James, and this combined with the opportunity of successfully concluding his dispute with John Cathanach over the lands on Isla and Sunart led John to act quickly to bring John Cathanach to justice. The gulf between the two men was also widened by their backgrounds and relationships. John Cathanach derived his name Cathanach from the time when he

---

[3] Hugh MacDonald

had been fostered by his mother's people the O'Cathans in Ulster who were neighbours of the Clan Iain Mor in Ulster.[4] The O'Cathans along with the other Irish clans of Ulster had been under sustained pressure from the Anglo-Irish and their influence can only have strengthened John Cathanach's resentment of the ever increasing power of feudal national states whether they were English or Scottish. John Brayach had married a daughter of the Campbell Earl of Argyle, it has been suggested that John acted,[5] at least in part, at the instigation of Argyle, although there is no surviving evidence of Argyle's involvement.

Feigning friendship, John Brayach arranged to meet with John Cathanach and his aged father Sir John of Dunnyveg[6] at Finlaggan in Isla the ancient residence of the Lords of the Isles. Taking a strong party of his clansmen John Brayach captured the unsuspecting John Cathanach, his father and some gentlemen of the Clan Iain Mor. John Brayach brought the captives to Edinburgh and presented them to James. All the captives were quickly condemned and were hung at the Borrowmuir on the outskirts of the capital. The Clan Iain Mor and to a lesser extent all the clans of MacDonalds were outraged at this treacherous behaviour by one of their own, John Cathanach's sons escaped to their clan lands in the Glens of Antrim resolving to have revenge.

After crushing any resistance by the Clan Iain Mor on Isla, John Brayach pursued Alexander the son of John Cathanach to the Glens of Antrim. The ferocity of the struggle in Ulster is attested to in comments made by MacVurich in the Books of Clanranald, in which he refers to the considerable expense John Brayach incurred in procuring large quantities of axes. The Glens were densely wooded during this period and the Maclains deforested large tracts to deprive Alexander and the surviving members of Clan Iain Mor of cover. Ultimately John Brayach was unsuccessful in his attempts to capture Alexander and retired to Isla.

James confirmed John in all of the disputed lands on Isla and Jura, and then rewarded him with more extensive possessions on Isla. In effect through the legal title to most of Isla and his occupation of the Castle of Dunnyveg John had gained control of the ancient heartland of the Lordship. For the time being he had destroyed the power of the Clan Iain Mor in western Scotland, Alexander did not return to Scotland during the lifetime of James IV.

In the summer of 1495 James IV held court at the Maclain castle of Mingarry in Ardnamurchan, and it was here that he received the submission of almost all the western highland clans. John Brayach's policy as acting as an instrument of the King's will had elevated the Maclains of Ardnamurchan to being the most powerful of all the branches of the MacDonalds. Shortly after James held court at Mingarry

---

[4] By this period the Clan Iain Mor occupied extensive areas of Ulster including the Glens of Antrim.

[5] Hugh MacDonald.

[6] Dunnyveg was the main castle and seat of the Clan Iain Mor, the clan are sometimes referred to as the MacDonalds of Dunnyveg.

Castle, Alexander of Lochalsh launched a second rebellion to re-establish the Lordship.[7]

Castle of Mingarry

He was defeated by the MacKenzies and Munros at the Battle of Drumchatt; Alexander fled to the west and established himself on the island of Colonsay. Here he attempted to rally support from the remnants of the Clan Iain Mor and the other southern clans. On the small neighbouring island of Oronsay he was hunted down by John Brayach with a strong party of Maclains and put to death. John acting on behalf of James IV and possibly encouraged by the Campbells had killed a MacDonald chief who was directly descended from the Lords of the Isles. The clans loyal to the Lordship, especially the various branches of the MacDonalds thirsted for revenge against the Maclains who they regarded as betraying the legacy of Somerled and acting as the hirelings of the crown, or worse, the Campbells. Even James in Edinburgh was aware of the threat to the Maclains and attempted to counter act it and to protect the Maclains from the revenge of their neighbours. In October 1496 the west highland chiefs including the Maclains, gathered in the presence of the Earl of Argyle and were coerced into an agreement of mutual

---

[7] See chapter 2.

defence. This agreement was in effect a forced alliance of different clans to protect the Maclains from their MacDonald kinsmen.

John Brayach Maclain was given more lands on Jura and Isla by James, who also confirmed him in his possession of Sunart after a dispute over its control with Allan of Clanranald. He had become the most powerful of all the MacDonald chiefs despite the questionable loyalty of his tenants on Isla and Jura. The MacDonalds of these islands sympathized with John Cathanach's son Alexander, and regarded themselves as belonging to the Clan Iain Mor. The fact that they had had John Brayach imposed upon them by James's feudal charters did not affect their loyalty to Alexander. John was regularly in touch with James who made frequent visits to the castle of Mingarry. There are also frequent records of the payment of messengers who carried letters between the two parties. But however close the level of contact was between John Brayach and James IV it was clear that the Maclains were isolated and exposed in the remote peninsular of Ardnamurchan.

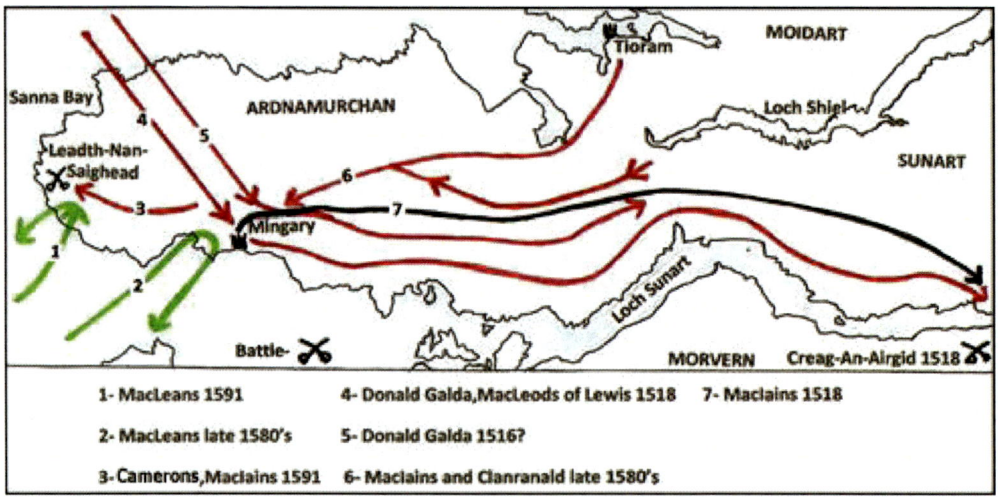

1- MacLeans 1591	4- Donald Galda,MacLeods of Lewis 1518	7- Maclains 1518
2- MacLeans late 1580's	5- Donald Galda 1516?	
3- Camerons,Maclains 1591	6- Maclains and Clanranald late 1580's	

In 1501 Donald Dubh was liberated from the forbidding castle of Inchconnel and immediately led a revolt to re-establish the Lordship.[8] John Brayach continued his policy of supporting the crown and assisted the royal forces to suppress the rebellion. Due to his loyalty to James, John was rewarded with further land charters, and the bond between the King and his willing instrument strengthened further. This close tie is demonstrated at a personnel level by some extant correspondence between the two men; James begins his letters "dear John Makkane of Ardnamurchane".

John Brayach was present at the Battle of Flodden at the head of his clan along with many other highland chiefs and the flower of the Scottish nobility. He was listed among the huge Scottish losses by the English but he clearly survived as he

---

[8] See chapter 2.

was soon active in the western highlands attempting to suppress another rebellion. The storm clouds were gathering and casting a long shadow over all that John had achieved. His friend and protector the able James IV lay dead amongst mounds of corpses on the field of Flodden. There also lay many of the great Scottish nobles who would have been able to run the machinery of state during the minority of James V. His enemies were gathering all around him, and the state for which he had risked so much was paralysed by the losses at Flodden. Even his uneasy relationship with the Campbells was weakened by the loss of their chief Archibald second Earl of Argyle on the battlefield.

John Brayach acted swiftly in an attempt to pre-empt his enemies, he sent his two sons Donald and Somerled at the head of a large force to Ireland to intercept and defeat Alexander (chief of clan Iain Mor) before he could reach Isla and raise his people against the Maclains. When they landed Alexander was in Glenseich with one hundred and forty men. He immediately decided to give battle to his family's persecutors.

"When Mac Iain's sons saw him and his men advance they asked their own men (seeing Alexander's party so small) whether they believed he had a mind to fight. The men answered in the affirmative, and a smith of Isla said that few as they were in number they would be a veminous thorn in their side that day, and that he for his own part would rather be on their side than on the side of the Maclains. Maclain said it was much better for them to want any man who thought so at heart than have him in their company. The smith singling himself from the rest, asked if any other that pleased to follow him should be hindered, Maclain said they would not. Upon this fifty men more separated themselves from the company, and following the smith made straight for Alexander. The attack immediately commenced on both sides. The Maclains were routed, the most of whom, including Mac Iain's two sons were killed."[9]

From this account it is clear that the Maclain force not only comprised of clansmen from Ardnamurchan and Sunart but also from Isla. The men from Isla were still loyal to the Clan Iain Mor and deserted the Maclains to fight by the side of their chief. Alexander then took one of the enemy's boats and sailed with all haste for Isla. On arriving at the Castle of Dunnyveg he was asked by the constable of the castle whether he knew what had happened to the unfortunate Alexander Cathanach, and whether he had survived the Maclain raiding party. This enquiry showed that the constable's sympathies lay with the Clan Iain Mor, and once Alexander had exposed his identity the castle was surrendered to him. The constable also told him that John Brayach was at a small fort in Lochgorm on the other side of the island.

Alexander marched rapidly across Isla gathering his loyal clansmen on his way. John Brayach was taken by surprise and after a lengthy siege he surrendered to Alexander. The speed of Alexander's movements after the victory in Ireland had

---

[9] Hugh MacDonald.

caught John isolated and cut off from support from his own clan in Ardnamurchan. John only surrendered to Alexander on condition that his life should be spared. Although this was agreed, John had to cede back to Alexander all the lands which had belonged to the Clan Iain Mor on Isla and Jura, and the two men agreed that Alexander should marry John's daughter and the feud between the two clans should be ended.

John was in a desperate position isolated on Lochgorm so any terms he could achieve with Alexander would have to be acceptable. Alexander shows a profound level of political skill when drawing up these terms. He understood that he was still exposed to the power of the Campbells and ultimately the state, as he was still a declared rebel. By mastering his desire for revenge he had regained his clan lands on Isla and Jura and by his marriage to John's daughter he hoped to remove the threat from the Maclains.

Although there was an attempt by the Regency to protect John Brayach from his many enemies the state was too weak after Flodden to influence events in the western highlands. Great raids on Maclain lands both on Isla and Ardnamurchan were carried out while the Regent stood by helplessly, writing ineffectual letters to John's tenants on Isla ordering them "to rise and support him (John) in whatever actions he may be engaged, under full penalty." During the rebellion of Sir Donald of Lochalsh, Alexander seized his opportunity and invaded Ardnamurchan with a force comprising of his own clan, Sir Donald of Lochalsh, and the MacLeods of Lewis and Raasay. The consequences of his past actions had caught up with John Brayach and after assembling all of his clan he was powerless to stop the formidable host from committing Ardnamurchan to the flames. The ancient Maclain stronghold of Mingarry was sacked and left a ruin.

In 1518 there was a second invasion by John's inveterate enemies, and again John's force was unable to resist them. The MacDonalds and MacLeods pursued the Maclains till they stood at bay at Creag- an-Airgid in Morven.The battle was fought with the greatest ferocity by both sides, Alexander's men being driven by the hatred of those who had betrayed their own kin, and the Maclains grimly fighting for their very survival. After a long and brutal encounter the Maclains were almost annihilated. John Brayach and his three remaining adult sons were found lying among the dead. The Maclains never recovered from Creag-an-Airgid, Ardnamurchan and Sunart lay desolate, their ancient castle of Mingarry had been stormed and their military strength reduced to a pitiable remnant.

John Brayach was regarded by his MacDonald contempories as a traitor. The only explanation that their historians can offer is that he was to a greater or lesser degree insane. John Brayach's policy of abandoning the past in favour of the new order after the fall of the Lordship was pragmatic and showed a clear grasp of the consequences of the new political landscape at the dawn of the sixteenth century. By using his clan as an instrument of royal policy in return for influence and power, he took the same path as the Campbells. This policy ultimately led to his ruin because he lacked the depth of resources that the Campbells had already amassed, in land, men, wealth and political influence. By acting against his own people, he was marked out for special retribution as a traitor, the isolated location of Ardnamurchan making the Maclains especially vulnerable. Added to this, John Brayach was unlucky; had James been less rash and not personally led his army in battle there is every likelihood that James's rule would have continued for decades. Had this able and subtle monarch ruled Scotland for another twenty years there is every chance that he would have extended the power of the state into the western highlands permanently. The Maclains would have been further rewarded for their loyalty to the crown and would have gone on to prosper in a similar way, albeit on a smaller scale, to the Campbells. John Brayach; an unattractive personality from a MacDonald perspective, was a chief who saw more clearly the political realities after the fall of the Lordship than any of the MacDonald chiefs during the sixteenth century. He was buried among his ancestors on Iona where his beautifully engraved coffin is preserved.

John was succeeded by his son, Alexander who was only a child in 1518. Colin Campbell third Earl of Argyle was appointed Alexander's guardian and was given power over all the territories of the Maclains during his minority. In effect the Maclains and their vast estates were in the hands of the Campbells, who were now the only surviving power which could be effectively used in the western highlands by the state. The remaining Maclain possessions on Isla were never recovered by Alexander; gradually passing into the hands of his Campbell guardians.[10] Alexander's attitude to his Campbell "guardians" is made clear when he is mentioned, at the head of his clan, as joining with the MacLeans in an attack on them caused by the murder of Lachlan MacLean.

Alexander died as a young man shortly before 1538. His alliance with the MacLeans suggests that he was aware that the Campbells were gradually usurping the Maclain lands and he led his people back into the fold of traditional MacDonald policy. Alexander died childless and in 1538 his sister Mariot became heiress to the Maclain inheritance. Two years later Mariot, with the consent of her husband, Robertson of Struan, resigned all the ancient lands of her people into the hands of the Campbells. There is no surviving explanation as to why Mariot surrendered the independence of her people other than that Archibald the fourth Earl of Argyle was her uncle. Possibly her husband's clan, the Robertsons, were ensnared by debt to the Campbells or her uncle put Mariot under severe pressure to surrender the documents. As the daughter of a chief she would have been well aware of the seriousness of her gift to the Campbells.

The following year James V paid five thousand pounds to the Earl of Argyle for possession of the Macalain inheritance. In 1543 Queen Mary granted a charter to

---

[10] Although the Campbells obtained charters which bestowed the MacIain lands on Isla on themselves, it is clear that their only relevance was that of a pretext for Campbell interference on Isla. The Campbells did not gain control of these lands until the fall of the Clan Iain Mor in the early seventeenth century.

Archibald which granted him a tenancy over Ardnamurchan, which he sub-let to James MacDonald the sixth chief of the Clan Iain Mor. During these legal manoeuvrings the Campbells failed to establish any actual occupation of either the lands on Isla or Ardnamurchan, and may even have been unable to extract any rental income from these estates. However they had established a degree of legal control and were even able to sub-let Ardnamurchan to another branch of the MacDonalds, as well as being paid a handsome figure by the king to relinquish land over which they had no right. It is remarkable that Archibald should have achieved so much by subtle diplomacy by his clever use of the well oiled Campbell machine. During these years the effective ownership of the Maclain inheritance on Isla was in the hands of the Clan Iain Mor while those of Ardnamurchan and Sunart were still occupied by the Maclains. By not attempting to take actual possession of either territory the Campbells exhibited their usual subtlety and patience; they would wait till they judged there was every chance of success before encompassing the fate of the Maclains.

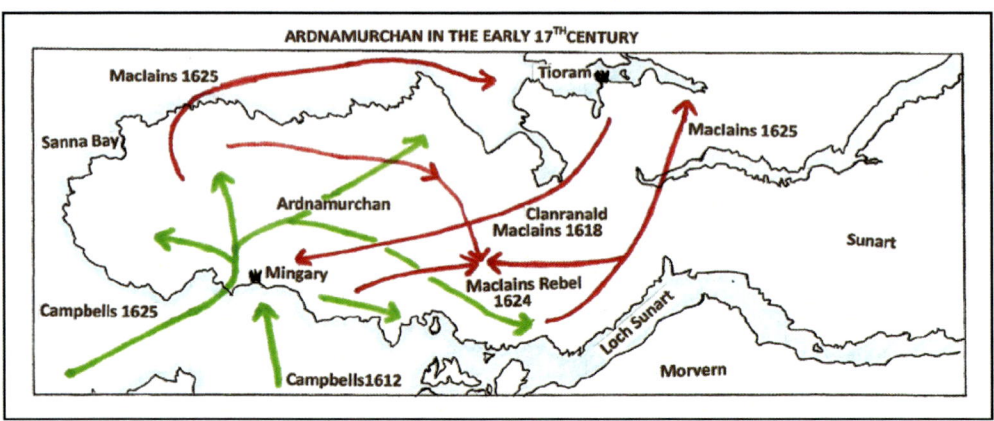

In feudal law the possessions of the Maclains had passed to Mariot on the death of Alexander. However in Gaelic law they were assumed by his cousin also called Alexander when he was elected to the chiefship. Alexander MacDonald Vclain of Ardnamurchan as he was styled by contemporary chroniclers, developed a more traditional policy in supporting John Moydartach of the Clanranald on the bloody field of Kinlochlochy in 1544,[11] and the rebellion of Donald Dubh the rightful heir to the Lordship of the Isles. Alexander's stance was in part due to the unjust dispossession of the Maclains by James V, and judging by his enthusiastic role in the above conflicts, in part due to his own inclination. Alexander died about the year 1570 having played a more traditional role in west highland history than his uncle John Brayach.

---

[11] See chapter 3.

Alexander was succeeded by his son John the ninth chief of the Maclains. John was deeply involved in the great feud between the Clan Iain Mor and the MacLeans.[12] John's support for his MacDonald kinsmen led to Ardnamurchan being ravaged by the MacLeans of Morven, peace only being established after the marriage of Alan MacLean to John's daughter Una. The chief of the senior branch of the MacLeans of Duart at this time was Lachlan Mor Maclean whose violent and turbulent nature was not one inclined towards peace, especially as John was still assisting the Clan Iain Mor in the continuing feud. John sought the hand of Lachlan Mor MacLean's mother in marriage. Lachlan trapped John at Torloisk on Mull during the wedding celebrations. All of John's train (bodyguard) of gentlemen were murdered and his own life was only spared after the desperate entreaties of Lachlan's mother, the new bride.

Aware that he now faced invasion by the combined forces of the Clanranald and the Maclains, Lachlan Mor MacLean took the initiative and invaded Ardnamurchan. Initially he was successful, devastating large tracts of the peninsular and laying siege to Mingarry. Eventually he was defeated by the combined forces of the Clanranald and the Maclains and retreated to Mull. These events form part of the feud between the Clan Iain Mor and the MacLeans and will be discussed in more detail in chapter eleven. John died in 1591 and was succeeded by his son John Og Maclain.

John Og soon found himself playing a small supporting role in events in Ulster in which the prime movers were Queen Elizabeth of England and James VI of Scotland. Elizabeth had bribed Lachlan Mor MacLean to invade Ulster and support English efforts to crush the Earl of Tyrone's rebellion. A formidable army of west highland clans had assembled to aid the Earl of Tyrone. The clans involved were the MacLeods of Harris, the MacDonalds of Sleat, the Clanranald and the Maclains led by John Og. This army had the tacit approval of James VI who wanted to halt the continual expansion of English influence in Ulster.

By the late sixteenth century the Maclains often fought under the banner of the Clanranald MacDonalds as the events of the early decades of the century had reduced their numbers and they were unable to raise an adequate force to operate independently. It was as part of the Clanranald effort that the Maclains sailed to Ulster. Due to inclement weather they landed on the shores of Mull hoping to avoid detection from their old adversary Lachlan Mor MacLean. Their presence was however soon discovered and the chief of the Clanranald and Angus Og were incarcerated in the dungeon of Duart Castle. King James applied pressure on Lachlan Mor and the two chiefs were released.

John Og was to be married to Cameron of Locheil's daughter and on his return from visiting the Camerons he and his small bodyguard were attacked and slaughtered at a place ever since called Faoghail Dhomhnuill Chonulluich. This ambush was carried out by John Og's uncle Donald, who would inherit the Maclain

---

[12] See chapter 11.

patrimony should John Og die childless. Allan Cameron swore to have revenge on Donald, who on hearing of the preparations of the Camerons fled to Mull to have the protection of Lachlan Mor MacLean. As the Camerons marched through Sunart and Ardnamurchan they were joined by the Maclains who were outraged at the fate of John Og. When Lachlan Mor saw the Camerons and Maclains gathered on the opposite side of the sound of Mull he gathered the MacLeans and sent them to engage them. This force of MacLeans numbered two hundred and twenty men which he placed under the joint command of his eldest son Hector and Donald Maclain, John Og's uncle. A fierce battle took place on the shore line at a place known afterwards as Leachd-nan-Saighead in which the MacLeans were defeated and Donald Maclain killed. A local tradition[13] describes his death. "One of the Clan Cameron on seeing him uplifting his helmet, instantly bent his bow, took aim, and drove his arrow into Maclain's head, pinioning his hand, to his skull. He fell, but for a moment regaining his strength he arose and expressed a desire, it is feared a treacherous one, to deliver his sword to Locheil. But the last spark of life was fast expiring. He clenched the huge weapon, and in the ire of death, transfixed it to the hilt in the opposite bank, and fell on it to rise no more."

Since the death of John Brayach a succession of Maclain chiefs had had policies which had supported the other branches of the MacDonalds as well as their own interests. They had however failed to address the risks to their position from the charters which stated that the Campbells were the feudal superiors of Sunart and Ardnamurchan. After the interregnum caused by John Og's murder, John MacAllister was elected as chief of the Maclains. The Maclains had been in almost continual conflict with neighbouring clans for eighty years. This had depleted their economic and military resources, but of more significance they were not represented at the Scottish court while their new and deadly enemy the Campbells were usually hovering by the throne.

John MacAllister's right to the succession to the lands of Ardnamurchan was disputed by Archibald Campbell the Earl of Argyle, whose nick name, Grim Faced Archie, gives a hint of what was in store for the Maclains. Archibald still had the charters in which Mariot had gifted her feudal right as heiress to the Maclain patrimony to the Earls of Argyle. These charters had been held by the Campbells for over fifty years; Archibald at last seized the opportunity created by the weakened state of the Maclains.

Archibald forced John Maclain into a contract which stipulated that in exchange for Campbell "protection", John would resign his rights to Ardnamurchan to Archibald, who would then feu Ardnamurchan back to John and his descendents who would become tenants of the Earls of Argyle. Archibald stipulated that as one of the prerequisites for this contract to become effective, John Maclain must submit his charter for Ardnamurchan which had been granted to the Maclains by James IV in 1499. This charter was never returned to John and remained in the

---

[13] The Clan Donald.

hands of the Earls of Argyle and still resides in their charter chest.[14] Archibald not only held onto the old Maclain charters but did not give John the charter by which he and his descendents became tenants to the Earls of Argyle for Ardnamurchan. To John these legal manoeuvrings may well have seemed relatively trivial when attempting to maintain his clan's inheritance against his vengeful neighbours in remote Ardnamurchan. However the political environment was changing at the beginning of the seventeenth century and the importance of a legal right by the possession of charters was becoming vital to all the clans if they were to maintain their hold on their ancient possessions.

The Maclains were now ensnared by the manoeuvrings of the Campbells, and they were already legally dispossessed. They were granted some respite from the Campbells as Archibald was distracted by the new circumstances created by the accession of James to the English throne. There were several attempts by the Privy Council to persuade the west highland clans to demonstrate that they had legal title to their territories by exhibiting their charters, John Maclain failed to attend any of these meetings as he now had no legal title to Ardnamurchan in his possession. John was sparred having to witness the final overthrow of his people; he died at Mingarry Castle in 1609 with the Maclains still in actual possession of Ardnamurchan. But the Maclains did not even enjoy the rights of sitting tenants under Scottish law. John left a son, Alexander, who was still a child at the time of his father's death. The Maclains were now led by Alexander's uncle, Donald, who became the Tutor of Ardnamurchan till Alexander achieved his majority.

In 1612 Archibald was ready to extend Campbell power into Ardnamurchan. Early in the year he granted a commission to Campbell of Brabreck[15] "to take and receive the Castle and place of Meigarie and upon our expenses to put keepers thereinto," Barbreck was given legal powers to fix and extract rents from the Maclain tenants and to expel any refractory tenants. Campbell of Brabreck was a man of great ability, being a brave and skilful soldier who was known for his stern and even cruel disposition, which he had amply demonstrated when hunting down his father's killers. Barbreck was seen by Archibald as the ideal sub-tenant to bring the Maclains to obedience and to deal with the expected resistance to the new order.

---

[14] Alastair Campbell, the Clan Campbell volume two.

[15] Brabreck was a tough and ruthless individual who was used by Archibald when Campbell policy required a more direct approach than the intricacies of the law.

Ardnamurchan with Skye in the background

Brabreck stayed within the bounds of the law while extracting onerous rents on his new tenants. The Maclains deeply resented the imposition of this "foreigner" who relentlessly pursued them for dues which for centuries they had paid to their own chief. The common people knew nothing of charters and their implications and saw only that they were being relentlessly oppressed by this hard and efficient overseer. It was not long before the Maclains broke out in open rebellion against Brabreck's factorship. Brabreck appealed to the Privy Council who compelled the Tutor of Ardnamurchan to sign a bond, on Alexander's behalf, in which he was responsible for the good behaviour of the Maclains. James was by now king of both Scotland and England and had to concern himself with the rule of both countries. He resided in London from where events in Ardnamurchan were hopelessly remote. There was to be no royal restraint upon the Campbells.

The Tutor of Ardnamurchan saw the bond which he had signed, under which he was to pay a large fine if he could not control the Maclains, as a temporary expedient to avoid any direct conflict with the state. He fundamentally failed to grasp that the balance of power in the western highlands had shifted in favour of both the state and the Campbells both of whom had greatly increased their ability to influence events in this region. It is understandable that the Tutor thought he could defy both the Campbells and the state. A cavalier attitude to the law, and the inability of the crown to enforce it, had allowed all the western clans to pursue their own interests since the fall of the Lordship of the Isles in 1494. The Tutor then compounded the dire situation that the Maclains found themselves in, by joining Sir James MacDonald's rebellion in his own desperate attempt to salvage the fortunes of his own branch of the MacDonalds the Clan Iain Mor.[16]

James MacDonald had escaped from Edinburgh Castle and after travelling through Lochaber and Skye he was joined by the Maclains as he made his way to the lands of the Clan Iain Mor on Isla, amongst scenes of wild rejoicing. The enthusiasm with which the Maclains joined such a forlorn rebellion demonstrates how parlous their own circumstances were becoming. The Tutor led the Maclains during James's blighted campaign which ended with such tragic consequences, their determined support for James bringing them to the attention of the Privy Council and making them ever more vulnerable to Campbell authority. Predictably the Tutor was fined for his actions; the Maclains were outlawed thus giving Brabreck the opportunity to strike a decisive blow for his master. He began violent attempts to extract the fines and rents levied on the Maclains, as they could not pay; Brabreck began a series of large scale and brutal evictions. The Maclains withdrew to an isolated area of Ardnamurchan called the Rough Bounds; from there they witnessed the occupation of their lands by Campbell colonists. This land had been held by the MacDonalds since the time of Somerled and had been gifted by Angus Og to John Sprangach the first chief of the Maclains in the early fourteenth century. Given the nature of Celtic society during this period there was only one response which they would adopt however hopeless their situation and however harsh the consequences would be.

The situation for the Maclains became increasingly desperate, and soon they were in such a hopeless and destitute position that the Tutor was forced to attempt to appeal to Archibald Earl of Argyle to spare the Maclains from the cruelty of Brabreck. The Tutor sent his son to Edinburgh to gain an audience with Archibald; here he was met by William Sterling who was acting for Archibald who was not resident in Edinburgh at the time. William Sterling wrote to Brabreck urging him to be more lenient to the Maclains, "it is not without reason and some foirknowledge in preventing further inconvenience I have written to you which I am assured ye will consider out of our own wisdom. I hope ye will press to win the people with kindness rather nor with extremitie specially at first." William Sterling, although urging Brabreck to be more lenient with the Maclains, was driven primarily by his anxiety not to cause his master the Earl of Argyle any inconvenience; force however was always an option if a softer approach failed. It is poignant to reflect that the descendents of Iain Sprangach, who was the uncle of John first Lord of the Isles, had been reduced to pleading to the chief of the Campbells to spare them from the actions of one of his cadets.

Brabreck clearly heeded the advice proffered by Stirling, Ardnamurchan enjoyed a two year respite from the continual upheavals till the summer of 1618. John MacDonald who had just become the twelfth chief of the Clanranald invaded

---

[16] See chapter 12.

Ardnamurchan and with the aid of the surviving Maclains expelled Brabreck and his Campbell garrison. John had been granted a lease of Ardnamurchan by the Earl of Argyle in exchange for a considerable payment. This lease was granted several years before Brabreck's lease was due to expire. John and Brabreck had leases to Ardnamurchan which ran contemporaneously. The explanation as to why Archibald undermined Brabreck's position was in part because of the impecunious position Archibald was in at this time. By exacerbating an already violent and unstable situation, Archibald could, by exerting his political and military power, reinforce his control over Ardnamurchan. The dispute was put before a panel of arbitration which decided in favour of Brabreck and ordered that the Clanranald should abandon Ardnamurchan when they had been compensated by Archibald.

The Maclains again found themselves to be at the dubious mercy of Brabreck who now not only demanded the outstanding rents but also reparation for the damage caused in this latest outbreak of violence. Archibald attempted to prevent any further outbreaks of violent dissatisfaction by compelling the Clanranald, the MacLeods of Harris and the MacLeans of Coll to stand surety for the good behaviour of the Maclains. The bitterness that the chiefs of these clans must have felt at having to agree to suppress the Maclains on behalf of the Campbells can only be imagined.[17] This surety of by now fairly compliant clans is a demonstration of Archibald's ever expanding power and the fact that the Maclains had nothing left to constrain them.

Within a few months the Maclains were again in open rebellion. A list of the principal offenders[18] was drawn up, and when presented to the authorities they were denounced as rebels by the Privy Council. This new attempt by the Maclains to regain their independence may well have been associated with Alexander the thirteenth chief of the Maclains gaining his majority. Ardnamurchan was now in a continual state of unrest. Two years later Brabreck complained to the Privy Council that Alexander had held a meeting of the Maclains at which they had pledged to support him in recovering his possession either by law or by force. In 1624 Alexander raised his clan in a last desperate attempt to throw off Campbell hegemony. The Maclains broke loose from all conventional forms of warfare, and they became pirates and spread terror to all their foes in the waters around Ardnamurchan. They sailed out of remote lochs and acted out revenge in the only way left open to them.

The clans that had stood surety for them were either unwilling or unable to prevent these latest desperate actions by the Maclains. When they failed to appear before the Privy Council the chiefs were all declared rebels. The documents that

---

[17] All of these clans had been in conflict with the Campbells as their long reach stretched into the Hebrides.

[18] This list contained all the surviving gentlemen of Clan MacIain, it is notable that even under this sustained and continual pressure that the cohesiveness of the clan remained intact at this date.

refer to the Clanranald are of particular interest when referring to the Maclains "pretend to be a branch of the Captain of Clanranald's House, quhilk he lykwayes acknowledgeit and takis the patrocine and defence of thame in all their ados." This reference to the absorption of the Maclains by the Clanranald is an example of the merger of two clans. This form of compact entailed that a clan which was faced with extermination would surrender its independence and even its identity in exchange for the protection afforded to the individuals of the "broken" clan. In exchange for the protection of the Clanranald the Maclains would adopt the name Clanranald and support the captains of the Clanranald in all their disputes. This type of arrangement had occurred throughout highland history when a particular clan was facing annihilation.

The plight of the Maclains had now sunk to a new low. They had been unjustly deprived of their ancient patrimony, the Privy Council was only interested in a strict interpretation of possession by legal charter, James was out of reach in London, and their was nobody in the Scottish executive who was prepared to challenge the power of Archibald Earl of Argyle and chief of the powerful clan Campbell. The unjust way in which the Maclains were legally deprived of their ancient possession of Ardnamurchan is commented on by Alistair Campbell in his history of that clan, "The apparent inability of Maclain to produce his charter, in 1605, after he had been induced to resign his lands to the seventh Earl of Argyll, suggests deliberate procrastination on the part of the latter in producing formal evidence of the promised regrant. The leasing of Ardnamurchan to Clanranald, when it had already been set to Mr Donald Campbell of Barbreck-Lochawe, can only have been a deliberate attempt to stir up trouble for due exploitation …".

The Maclains soon failed to distinguish between ships which were involved with the Campbell estates and begun to plunder any merchantmen they came across. The Maclains captured an English ship which they manned and armed. This action bought them to the attention of James in London. The town of Ayr was ordered to fit out two frigates to hunt down the Maclains, while the Campbell Lord Lorn and the Campbell lairds of Lochnell, Auchinbreck, Calder and Ardkinglass were given commissions of fire and sword to bring the Maclains to bay on land.

The Maclains were now faced by an overwhelming force, this however did not alter their activities and despite some Royal successes they continued to plunder shipping, on an even greater scale. Their piratical activities which had, in part been forced upon them and in part they regarded as acts of revenge against a state which had acquiesced to their unjust dispossession from Ardnamurchan brought down the full approbation of the state. In 1625 the Scottish Council wrote to James in London, in which they are referred to as, "rebillis of the Clan Eane be whom not only your maiesties awne subjectis, bot the subjectis of otheris princes yo maiesties friends and confederates were havelie distrest and robbed of thair shippis and goodis and some of them cruellie and barbarouslie slain".

The Campbells now prepared for the extirpation of the last remnants of the Maclains; on April the thirteenth 1625 they convened at Inveraray. They made arrangements for watches to be set on the coast lines of Argyle and Lorne to give early warning of any raids. On the twenty first of the same month a commission of fire and sword was granted to the Campbell chiefs with the only proviso that the eighteen year old Lord Lorne was to be among their number. The Campbell forces assembled at Dunstaffnage Castle, and soon drove the Maclains from their last refuges on Ardnamurchan. The Maclains fled to Skye; here they were attacked by Rory Mor MacLeod at the head of his clan and again forced to flee.

The Maclains took refuge in the woods and caves of Arisaig and Moidart, hoping to find protection in the lands of their kinsmen the Clanranald. The Campbell and MacLeod forces coalesced and followed them to their last refuge. The Maclains were hunted down and exterminated in this remote fastness; a few survivors escaped and threw in their lot with the Clanranald.

With this last sad episode the Clan Iain ceased to exist as a viable social entity, this ancient and proud branch of the MacDonalds had been cut of from the great tree of Somerled. The legal claim of the Campbells was clearly under much suspicion and it appears that Alexander Maclain (who survived the events of 1625) was paid a large sum of money to abandon any claim to Ardnamurchan. He is found making a bond for £40,000 Scots to a burgess in Fortrose in 1629. The most likely explanation as to how he was in possession of such a large fortune was that he had reached a final understanding with the Campbells. The Campbells (if they were the source of this money) had thought it expedient to reinforce their title by some form of compensation to Alexander; clearly this would not have been undertaken without some reason.

Donald Campbell still did not enjoy his occupation of Ardnamurchan without intermittent outbreaks of violence by the ancient possessors of the land. In 1633 he exonerates Alexander Maclain from any involvement in various "sundrie wrangis" committed in the peninsular. Alexander was now no longer the chief of a recognized clan, as the remnants of the Maclains had thrown in their lot with the Clanranald. His probable acceptance of a Campbell pay off could be seen as a betrayal of his heritage or from a more pragmatic point of view it was merely retrieving something from the wreckage. Alexander the twelfth and last chief of the Maclains of Ardnamurchan passes into obscurity and we know nothing of the rest of his life or the date of his death.

The MacDonald brothers mention an interesting post script to the history of this once powerful clan. In the late nineteenth century when the old churchyard at Kingussie in Badenoch was being restored, the workmen came across an old tombstone which bore a fascinating inscription. This inscription roughly translates, "here lies Alexander MacDonald son of Iain MacDonald in Ruthven who died thirteenth of April 1719 also Alexander and Alexander MacDonald his father and uncle sometime representing the ancient family of Ardnamurchan". If one goes back three generations from 1719 then it is possible that the first Alexander mentioned on the tomb is Alexander the last chief of the Maclains. It is at least possible that the last descendents of Iain Sprangach fled to Kingussie after the diaspora of their clan. If this was the case then the line of the house of Ardnamurchan can be traced for a further three generations living in peaceful obscurity in Kingussie.

The Maclains of Ardnamurchan have a unique place in the history of the MacDonalds during this period. They were the first of the MacDonald clans to form, being a distinctive social entity before the Lordship of the Isles became a recognized political entity. Under the able and perceptive John Brayach they followed a different policy to the other MacDonalds. After the collapse of the Lordship, John Brayach led his people to extend their power and territorial possessions by a policy of co-operation with the Scottish State even if it meant opposing their own kindred. There are many similarities with the policies adopted so successfully by the Campbells. Ultimately the Maclains failed because they did not have the political or economic resources which the Campbells were so effective in manipulating. John Brayach's policy exposed the Maclains to the greatest animosity of the other branches of the MacDonalds. The consequences of this were exacerbated by their territory of Ardnamurchan being geographically situated in the heart of the territories held by the MacDonalds. This made this relatively small clan vulnerable to attack on all sides and with no place of safe refuge from their own people.

After the failure of John Brayach's policy they weakened themselves still further becoming embroiled in the bitter feud between the Clan Iain Mor and the MacLeans. They were also unlucky that the Campbell Earls of Argyle managed to gain a feudal over lordship to Ardnamurchan which eventually led to them being legally dispossessed and outlawed in their own land. When the Maclains responded in the predictably violent fashion of their culture its only effect was to strengthen the already strong grasp of the Campbells. When all the guile of grim faced Archibald was combined with his political and military power and ably supported by such men as Barbreck and Donald Campbell it is only surprising that the Maclains held out for so long. There is some poignancy in the motto of the Maclans, IN HOPE I BYDE, for in all the history of the MacDonalds there was never a clan which had less reason to hope than the Maclains.

Chapter 6

Trotternish the Crucible

The struggle between the MacDonalds of Sleat and the MacLeods of Harris extended over two centuries to gain control of the district of Trotternish. The ownership of this peninsular would give either clan a dominant position on the island of Skye.[1] The feud continued intermittently for over a century and was interspersed by brief periods of peace, other feuds and by the continual risings to re-establish the Lordship of the Isles. In these both the MacLeods of Harris and the MacDonalds of Sleat were loyal supporters of the claimants to the Lordship.[2]

The MacLeods of Harris (the Siol Tormod) are the first named clan to possess Skye; they held the island first of the Norwegian kings of Man and later as part of the Earldom of Ross as vassals of the Scottish kings. The MacDonalds established a presence in Skye in the later years of the fifteenth century when the Lords of the Isles had become the Earls of Ross and thus became the feudal superiors of Skye. The seeds of rancour were sown between the two clans by the grant of Sleat to the MacDonalds by Alexander; Lord of the Isles in 1463.The MacLeods can not have been pleased at this grant of land to the MacDonalds and their arrival on Skye which till then had been their sole preserve.

A traditional story amongst the MacLeods tells that the MacDonalds drove out all the male MacLeods and forced all the women to stay.[3] One of these tales recounts that when a MacDonald slipped on the cliff edge and was hanging over the precipice, he only saved himself by grasping at a clump of grass. A MacLeod woman on investigating the urgent cries for help saw his precarious situation and said "Ah well you've taken everything else, so I suppose you had better take this with you"; she gave the clump of grass a good kick and sent the MacDonald flailing to his death.

The MacDonalds of Sleat are descended from Hugh third son of Alexander Lord of the Isles and it is from Hugh that they are also known as Clan Uisdean (Gaelic for Hugh). In 1469 Hugh received a grant of land from Alexander which included all the lands which were regarded as the patrimony of the Clan Uisdean; the islands of North Uist in the Outer Hebrides and the territory of Sleat on the island of Skye. The district of Trotternish is not included in this grant. However, by 1482 Trotternish was in MacDonald hands as Angus Og MacDonald (son of John fourth Lord of the Isles) is specifically referred to as "Master of the Isles and Lord of Trotternish" in a charter he issues to the monks of Iona.

---

[1] It was also a conflict to control extremely limited resources for their expanding populations.

[2] See chapter 2.

[3] Both Carthage and Rome were both populated in their early days by the capture of local women and this story may be attributable the clan historians knowledge of classical authors.

On the death of Angus Og in 1490, Hugh as his heir claimed and took possession of Trotternish. At the end of the fifthteenth century Skye was divided between three clans, the MacLeods were occupying Watternish, Durinish, Minginish and Glamaig. The MacDonalds held Sleat and Trotternish while the MacKinnons were settled in Strathaird.

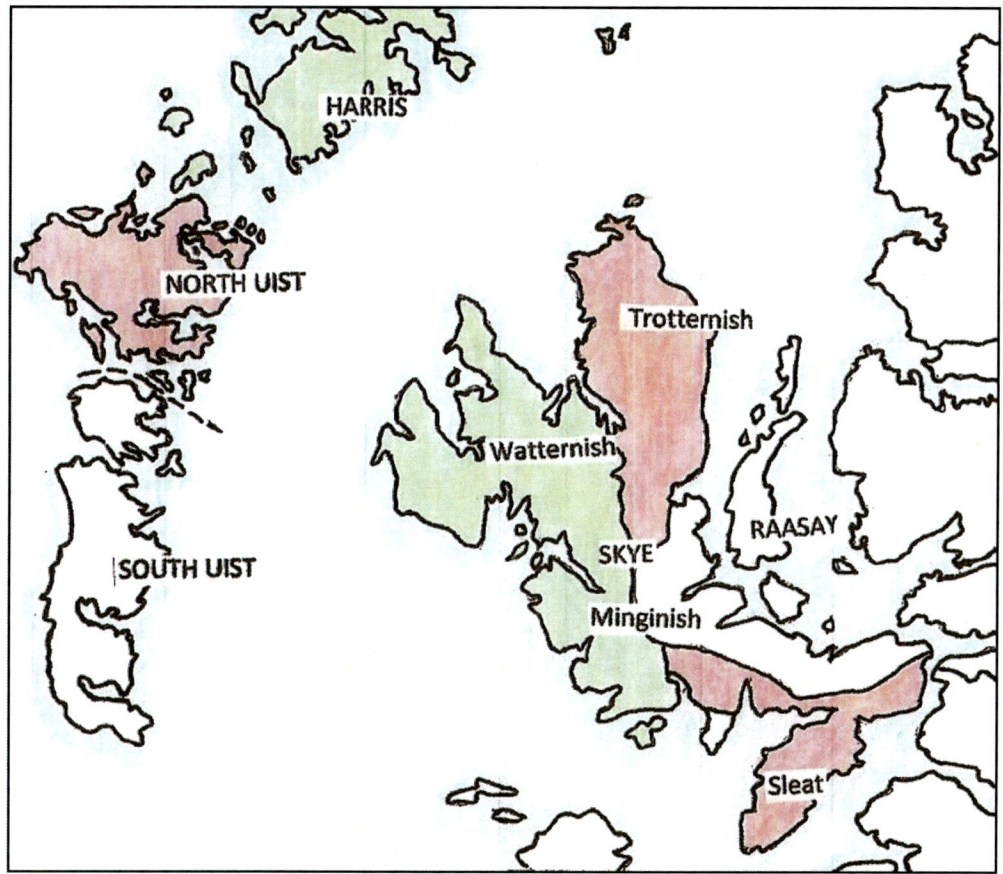

Territories of the MacDonalds of Sleat c.1560

After the forfeiture of the Lordship of the Isles in 1494 Hugh obtained a Crown charter confirming him in possession of all the lands granted to him by Alexander in 1469. The status of Trotternish is unclear as it is not mentioned in the Crown charter, with the historians of both clans claiming that their people were in occupation. Hugh died in 1498 leaving six sons by six different women. Some of his sons were amongst the darkest characters to appear in the history of the western highlands and were to lead the Clan Uisdean into decades of treacherous upheavals.[4] In the course of thirty years Hugh had established a new branch of the Clan Donald and had obtained Crown charters for their lands, he had firmly

---

[4] See chapter 7.

established the Clan Uisdean in Sleat and had occupied Trotternish with at least some justification. The possession of lands in Skye was a great achievement as it must have been done in the face of bitter opposition from the powerful MacLeods of Harris.

He was succeeded by his eldest son John Hucheonson, whose mother was Fynvola daughter of Alexander Maclain of Ardnamurchan. John's time as chief of the Clan Uisdean was one of complete disaster for his people in that he resigned almost the entire possessions of the clan to Ranald Bane the chief of the Clanranald.It is now unclear why John should have alienated the entire patrimony of his people with such reckless abandon. John had no children and may have had such a strong dislike of his half-brothers that he preferred that Ranald Bane should gain at least legal control of the clan lands rather than his own family. Ironically the only lands which John was not able to gift away were those of Trotternish as he had no charters for the district.

In June 1498 during the minority of James IV the Regent granted charters to Trotternish to both Alistair Crotach MacLeod of Harris and in October to Torquil MacLeod of Lewis (the Siol Torquil). It is extraordinary that the government should have granted Trotternish to both of the branches of the MacLeods in the same year, with another clan (the MacDonalds of Sleat) probably in actual occupation. This cavalier approach to the legal ownership of vast tracts of the western highlands was bound to lead to inveterate disputes between the clans and in this case did not bode well for future peace on Skye. It may well have been that bribes or court intrigues could lead to the granting of charters even when the claim was backed by the flimsiest of evidence and certainly did not always reflect ancient rights or the situation on the ground. Some support for this argument is given by the fact that when James assumed the crown he cancelled all the charters issued in his minority.

John died in 1502 after four catastrophic years as chief and was succeeded by Donald Gallach his half-brother. Donald Gallach inherited a desperate situation in which all the lands of the MacDonalds of Sleat had legally been entailed to their competitors or even worse their rivals. His position was made even more precarious by Hugh's many marriages or liaisons which had resulted in four other surviving half-brothers three of which had a deep-seated resentment of him. Donald Gallach derived his name from the fact that he had spent a considerable amount of time with his mother's people the Gunns of Caithness. He is described by a clan historian "Donald Gallach was a moderate man inclined to peace, black haired and fair skinned." He took up residence at the castle of Dunskaith in Sleat which became the seat of the MacDonalds of Sleat.

Castle of Dunskaith

Only four years later Donald Galllach was dead, having been murdered by his infamous half-brother Archibald Dubh in 1506.[5] During the dark days of the minority of Donald Gruamach when the clan was under the sway of Archibald Dubh the MacDonalds of Sleat lost control of Trotternish and some time before 1517 a charter was granted to Alistair Crotach MacLeod of Dunvegan for the occupation of the peninsular.Doanald Gruamach (the grim) was not a man who would take the occupation of what he considered his birthright lying down. He formed an alliance with John MacLeod of Lewis[6] and they planned a joint invasion of Trotternish in the following year. John MacLeod was struggling to regain his own inheritance on the island of Lewis, so he and Donald Gruamach made natural allies as they both considered that they had been wrongfully dispossessed of their patrimony.

In the winter of 1528 the forces of the MacDonalds of Sleat and the MacLeods of Lewis coalesced and they fell on the unsuspecting MacLeods of Harris in Trotternish. Alistair Crotach was unable to resist such a formidable coalition and his clan was expelled from Trotternish with catastrophic losses of livestock. In the summons issued by Alistair Crotach in March 1528 he claims compensation for six

---

[5] For a more detailed examination of the internal power struggles of the clan, see chapter 7.
[6] John Macleod's sister was the mother of Archibald Dubh. Archibald Dubh was an uncle to Donald Gruamach.

thousand sheep and goats, nine hundred cattle and two hundred and eighty horses. Even allowing for the exaggeration which is likely in such a claim, it is clear that this was a successful attempt to clear the whole peninsular of the MacLeods of Harris. Judging by the number of livestock listed it is clear that Trotternish was relatively productive by the standards of the western highlands and would have been a very significant factor in the economies of either clan.

It is likely that it was during this period that there was another encounter between the two rival clans which culminated at the battle of Glendale. There is no surviving evidence for this event other than in MacLeod traditions and even in these it is unclear when the events took place. According to these traditions Donald Gruamach was killed in the battle. However this cannot have been the case since he did not die till 1534. Donald Gruamach's campaign which ended at the battle of Glendale has been placed here in the text as it is during this period that it seems most likely to have occurred.[7] The MacLeod traditions relate how a large force of MacDonalds landed at Loch Eynort in Minginish and then marched north towards Dunvegan, devastating the land as they advanced. On hearing the news of the invasion Alastair Crotach hurried back to Dunvegan[8] with a large number of MacLeods. The MacLeods sailed up Loch Pooltiel and landed at the head of the loch. It was here, at the end of the Glendale valley that the two clans engaged each other. Initially the MacDonalds had the upper hand and were pushing the MacLeods back into the sea. However it was at this moment that Alistair Crotach ordered the fairy flag[9] to be unfurled, this ancient talisman of the MacLeods lent them new heart and eventually the tide of battle turned and the MacDonalds were forced to retreat.

Donald Gruamach then helped John MacLeod of Lewis to obtain effective control over the island of Lewis. In 1530 Donald Gruamach with eight other chiefs was summoned to appear before the king, to consult with him on the good rule of the isles. Donald and Alistair Crotach submitted themselves to James's will at this meeting and it must have been that while Donald was in Edinburgh that he was forced to cede Trotternish to his old rival, Alistair Crotach. This enforced loss of Trotternish was a bitter pill to swallow, it is unclear as to what pressures were brought to bear on Donald Gruamach but certainly his son Donald Gorm believed that MacKenzie of Kintail played a significant role by intriguing for the restoration of the MacLeods. Was it at this time that Donald Gruamach's son by his second marriage, John Og, married a daughter of Alistair Crotach?

---

[7] MacLeod tradition suggests that Donald Gruamach's campaign took place around 1490. This cannot be correct as in the 1490's it was Donald Gruamach's great uncle Hugh who was chief of the MacDonalds of Sleat. Glendale is unlikely to have taken place before the chiefship of Donald Gruamach as prior to this the MacDonalds of Sleat were paralysed by internal power struggles. It is also certain that a date in the 1490's is too early for the other protagonist; Alistair Crotach.

[8] It is highly likely that he was on Harris at the time.

[9] For a discussion of the fairy flag see chapter 4.

If this marriage did take place at this date then we may see in this unexpected union an attempt by the two chiefs to end the feud over Trotternish. For Donald Gruamach to try to end this feud with the MacLeods in possession of Trotternish there must have been some very compelling reasons other than fear of royal authority which have been lost to us. Donald Gruamach's later years seem to have been peaceful and uneventful; in any event he does not appear in the records until his death in 1534.

The chiefship of the MacDonalds of Sleat was inherited by Donald Gorm the eldest son of Donald Gruamach.Donald Gorm inherited all the dark brooding determination of his forbears and deeply resented his clan's loss of Trotternish and the role MacKenzie of Kintail had played in it. He also regarded himself as the rightful heir to the Lordship of the Isles after the failure of the MacDonalds of Lochalsh to re-establish the Lordship.[10] This branch of the MacDonalds led a continual series of rebellions against the state which viewed with a modern perspective seem almost insanely violent and hopeless. To Alexander of Lochalsh and his son Donald Galda plotting in the secure fastnesses of castles like Strome with the power of the MacDonalds and their allies stretching over almost the entire western highlands the chances of success must have seemed very real.

In May 1539 Donald Gorm raised the standard of rebellion, and with his allies the MacLeods of Lewis invaded Trotternish. The chroniclers simply comment that "he laid it waste before sailing with fifty galleys to the shores of Kinlochewe to besiege MacKenzie's castle of Eilean Donan." Donald Gorm had observed the gradual rise in the power of the MacKenzies, a clan who had always opposed the Lordship of the MacDonalds. He would have regarded the storming of their stronghold of Eilean Donan as an essential prerequisite to a successful rebellion as its close proximity to Skye would threaten his communications during any invasion of the Earldom of Ross. It should be remembered that there was also a personal element to this assault in that he believed that John MacKenzie ninth baron of Kintail had aided Alistair Crotach MacLeod regain control of Trotternish in 1530.

---

[10] See chapter2.

Eilean Donan Castle

The story of how Donald Gorm met his death is recorded by the historian of the MacRaes, the hereditary constables of the castle, which even if one allows for a certain amount of hyperbole records the main facts of Donald Gorm's fate. "in John MacKenzie's time, Donald Gorm, came with a strong party to the south side of Kintail, carried away a great many cattle, and killed several of the inhabitants,...Donald Gorm ,afterwards hearing that the castle was but slightly guarded, thought to have taken it by surprise. So, with seven or eight large boats or berlins full of men towards Islandonan, was observed by the sentinel....Only this Duncan MacGichrist hearing the cry and being very ready to do his master's service, in time of greatest danger, came directly, and standing at the gate of the old tower, continued shooting his arrows at MacDonald's men, until those of the first boat of them landed, by which time he had killed and wounded several of them. Upon his entering the tower he found none there but Matheson the constable and the Cryer. MacDonald and his men by this time had landed and were attempting to break the castle gate, which being strongly secured by a back door of iron, and they within throwing stones upon the assailants, they were obliged to give up the attempt, and begun to shoot their arrows at the windows, by which John Du Matheson the constable was killed; so that Duncan had now but the Cryer and one arrow to defend the fort. MacDonald having taken down the masts of some of the berlins, was looking where he might easiest make a breach and mount the wall, when Duncan took the opportunity of shooting the only arrow he had, which happened to be a barbed one, and wounded MacDonald in the master vein of the foot, he became impatient of the pain, and pulled out the arrow, not adverting that it was barbed, by which means he cut the artery called in Gaelic "strurossach" and finding the blooding could not be stopped, desisted from the attack and took to their boats. MacDonald being carried to one of them by his men, few of whom escaped being killed or wounded, and before he was out of sight of the garrison he died…".

The Sleat historian records that the dying chief was taken to a sand bank (which was later named after him) and it was here that Donald Gorm's life ebbed away in a crimson stream. He was buried at Ardleve on the opposite side of Loch Loung. His short time as chief of the MacDonalds of Sleat inevitably leaves one pondering what he might have accomplished had he not irritably pulled the arrow from his foot.

Donald Gorm was succeeded by his son Donald Gormson who was a child at the time. During his minority the MacDonalds of Sleat were led by his uncle, Archibald the Clerk, a son of Donald Gruamach. Donald Gormson although only a child, was regarded as a threat by the Scottish state because of his late father's claim to the Lordship. Archibald the Clerk initially secreted Donald Gormson with his mother's people the MacLeods of Lewis. After a short while Archibald decided that even the remote island of Lewis was no longer safe for the future chief and took the extraordinary precaution of sending him to the safety of the English court. Archibald's action demonstrates the expanding political horizons of the island clans.

Donald Gormson spent several years at the English court and became a firm favourite of Queen Mary. Donald Gormson must have struck a very exotic figure at Hampton Court with his strange language and manner of dress. The England of the mid-sixteenth century regarded the "wild Irish" with as much amazement as the North American Indians.[11] For Donald Gormson his time at the English court would have been an invaluable education into the political dynamics of the wider European scene. When he returned to the north his political perspective must have been intriguing to the clever but somewhat isolated Archibald the Clerk. It was from his long sojourn in England that he was known as Donald Gorm Sassenach (the Englishman).

In 1542 Alexander MacLeod of Dunvegan was granted another charter to Trotternish; surprisingly he was also granted charters to Sleat and North Uist "for good, faithfull and free service". What these services were is unclear but the charters were never put into effect for Trotternish never mind the ancient and undisputed lands of the MacDonalds on Sleat and North Uist. The charters were

---

[11] There are many recorded descriptions of highland and Irish deputations to the English court in the sixteenth century. They refer to the highlanders with a mixture of fascination and contempt and it is clear that the people of the Celtic fringe belonged to a world which was utterly alien to the courtiers in London.

made even more ineffectual by the death of James shortly afterwards. Instead of the charters being of benefit to the MacLeods they were in fact a poisoned chalice as they threatened the legal position of the MacDonalds of Sleat and thus added to their simmering resentment over the loss of Trotternish. In the decade between 1542 and 1552 the MacLeod senecharies record that Trotternish frequently changed hands.

The minority of Donald Gorm Sassenach came to an end when he assumed the chiefship of the clan sometime before 1553. The exact year is not known but in a document of 1553 Kenneth MacKenzie of Kintail requires the Council to prevent Donald Gormson from stealing timber from his forests. A year later, Mary the Queen Dowager assumed the regency; she was determined to re-establish order in the highlands which had fallen into its usual state of near anarchy when there was a weak executive. Some chiefs remained defiant like John Moydartach, but Donald Gormson along with the vast majority of chiefs made his submission.

In the decade of the 1560's Donald Gormson became embroiled in the feud between the MacDonalds of Dunnyveg and the MacLeans of Duart over the Rinns of Isla.[12] In 1566 he laid claim to the patrimony of the MacLeods of Lewis, claiming to be the nearest living heir (through his mother[13]).This claim was thwarted by Ruairi MacLeod re-marrying and producing another heir. The MacDonalds of Sleat and the MacLeods of Lewis were closely connected by marriage and by alliances since the breakup of the Lordship of the Isles. It was only to be expected that Donald Gormson would take a keen interest in events on Lewis and to take advantage of opportunities presented by internal disputes amongst the MacLeods of Lewis. He would have known that any claim through the female line had little weight in Gaelic law but was he practising a degree of political flexibility that he had learned at the English court as a child? During this period the MacDonald claims to Trotternish were certainly not forgotten and Donald Gormson eventually obtained legal title to North Uist, Sleat and Trotternish in 1567.

Donald Gormson obtained title to all the lands of his clan by agreeing to a contract with the Archibald Gillasbuig Donn fifth Earl of Argyll. The salient points of this agreement were that Argyll should get legal title to all the lands occupied by the MacDonalds of Sleat and would then make Donald Gormson and his descendents his vassals for which they would pay the Earl a penny more than the Earl paid the crown. It is unlikely that Donald Gormson realized to what extent he was playing with fire, however because of his desperate need for legal title to his lands he was prepared to tolerate a degree of Campbell interference. To have the increasingly important legal title to his clan's land Donald Gormson agreed to pay the Earl of

---

[12] See chapter11.
[13] Margret was the daughter of Torquil MacLeod of Lewis.

Argyll fifteen hundred merks and bound himself to be his vassal and to support the Earl against all his enemies excepting only the crown.[14]

Donald Gormson had no intention of supporting the Campbells against their enemies, but this unpalatable aspect of this agreement was outweighed by obtaining legal title to the ancestral lands of his clan including Trotternish. With the increasing effectiveness of the Scottish state it was becoming ever more vital to have legal ownership and very few clans were able to hold onto their territories without it, one notable exception were the MacDonalds of Keppoch in Lochaber.[15] This charter is also of broader interest, in that it demonstrates how Campbell power was inexorably growing in the sixteenth century. The Campbell Dukes of Argyll were the conduit by which most of the west highland chiefs could gain access to the Scottish court. It was by acting as a go-between that the Campbells were continually able to find opportunities to forward their own interests while ostensibly facilitating both the state and the clans involved. By the later sixteenth century the whole of the western seaboard of the highlands was covered with a legal web of theoretical obligations and superiorities almost all of which involved the Campbells in one way or another.

Archibald Donn Duke of Argyll had managed to obtain charters to the lands of the MacDonalds of Sleat from Tormod MacLeod by obtaining control over a MacLeod heiress. The legal heir under feudal law to the lands of the MacLeods of Harris was a young girl called Mary MacLeod who was exchanged in a series of agreements between the great magnates of the western highlands. Mary eventually became the ward of the Duke of Argyll. The Earl of Argyll came to an agreement with Tormod MacLeod to the effect that on payment of one thousand merks and a renunciation of the MacLeod rights to the lands of North Uist, Sleat and Trotternish he would procure from Mary and any future husband a revocation of her title to the MacLeod lands. This revocation would allow Tormod to claim the feudal right to the MacLeod inheritance.[16] It was by this agreement that the Earl of Argyll obtained the charters for the territories of the MacDonalds of Sleat. Archibald Gillasbuig Donn fifth Earl of Argyll had by the subtlety of his intellect managed to secure significant payments from both the MacLeods of Harris and the MacDonalds of Sleat. He had also obtained obligations of support from Tormod of Dunvegan and Donald Gormson of Sleat. Finally to seal his achievement, at least from a Campbell perspective, he married Mary MacLeod, the feudal heiress to the lands of the MacLeods of Harris to Duncan Campbell of Castle Swynie. One can only admire the crafty way Archibald Gillesbuig Donn's manoeuvring at the outset of

---

[14] This agreement is known as a bond of manrent. The Campbells used these bonds to build up a complex web of feudal relationships with many clans throughout the western highlands during the sixteenth century.

[15] See chapter 8.

[16] To his own clan there was already no question that he was the rightful heir to the chiefship of the MacLeods.

this series of agreements between the MacLeods and the MacDonalds led to such a favourable conclusion with both clans, when initially none of the issues had any connection with the Campbells.

Donald Gormson Sassenach died in 1575. He had led his clan back from the brink of disaster; in that without legal title to their lands and in being involved in a bitter feud with the MacLeods of Harris the MacDonalds of Sleat could have become a broken clan like their neighbours the Maclains of Ardnamurchan.[17] He had held in check the growing power of the MacKenzies, maintained his clan's hold on Trotternish by occupation. He had also secured legal title to all of his patrimony including Trotternish. Donald Gormson had laid the firm foundations for his clan by which they were able to survive the severe test of the coming generation.

On his death Donald Gormson left three sons, who were still children and the Clan Uistean was again led by tutors. The eldest son of Donald Gormson was Donald Gorm Mor, who did not assume the chiefship of his clan till 1585.During the decade of the minority of Donald Gorm Mor the clan initially chose James of Castle Camus to lead them. James, probably due to his weak position agreed to share power with Donald and Hugh Mac Gilleasbuig Chleirich whose family were pre-eminent in Trotternish. The evil nature of Hugh's character and the subsequent events will be discussed in chapter 7.

The feud between the MacDonalds of Sleat and the MacLeods of Harris was resumed with greater intensity in the 1590's when Donald Gorm Mor was in his late twenties.He had been married in a "hand fast" ceremony to Mary MacLeod the eldest sister of Ruairi Mor MacLeod of Dunvegan, (this Mary is not to be confused with Mary MacLeod the heiress previously mentioned). Hand fast marriages had been common practice in the western highlands for centuries and although not sanctioned by the established church they were accepted as respectable by the whole structure of highland society. The tradition in Skye was that Donald Gorm Mor sent her back to her own people, having tired of her. Mary had only one eye, and the insult was greatly increased by Donald sending her back to her brother on a one eyed horse, accompanied by a one eyed servant who was followed by a one eyed dog.

Ruari Mor tried to persuade Donald Gorm to take Mary back, but Donald would have none of it. Instead he poured more fuel on the fire of Ruari's resentment by almost immediately marrying Mary, daughter of Colin Cam MacKenzie of Kintail. No alternative bride could have been more damaging to the relationship between the two clans as the MacLeods and the MacKenzies were at bitter feud over the lands of Glenelg. Ruairi Mor was filled with rage and vowed revenge on Donald Gorm and the MacDonalds of Sleat. The personal insult he had received was real enough but the MacDonald occupation of Trotternish and his own restless spirit can only have increased the pitch of the crisis now about to engulf the two clans.

---

[17] See chapter 5.

Ruari Mor assembled all the available strength of his people and carried fire and sword into the long disputed lands of Trotternish. He vented his resentment upon every living thing that crossed his path sparing neither man nor beast. The old sores had been reopened and the feud had been rekindled for the MacDonalds of Sleat. On the face of it the conflagration had been caused by some very undiplomatic and indulgent behaviour by Donald Gorm. Although only conjecture, is it possible that Donald's actions had a subtlety that was not apparent to the people of Skye? Had he come to the conclusion that the MacKenzies would be more useful allies than the MacLeods of Harris? He had observed what would have seemed like the inexorable rise of the MacKenzies during his lifetime. During this period the ancient allies of his house the MacLeods of Lewis were becoming increasingly ensnared in a web of intrigue at the heart of which the MacKenzie Lords of Kintail sat and waited. He would also have seen another branch of the house of Somerled the MacDonalds of Glengarry gradually losing ground in their bitter feud with the MacKenzies over the lands of Glen Carron and Lochalsh.

It seems improbable that Donald Gorm was so irresponsible as to deliberately incense Ruari Mor and condemn his people to more years of warfare, sorrow, starvation and destitution. The inevitable retaliation for the invasion of Trotternish quickly followed when Donald Gorm gathered the fighting strength of the clan and invaded Harris. Harris was devastated, many of the inhabitants were killed and almost all the cattle were either slaughtered or carried off. The viscous cycle of mayhem turned again when the MacLeods launched a counter strike by invading North Uist. Ruari Mor had chosen his target with care; he struck at the most isolated territories of the MacDonalds of Sleat knowing that the island could not be supported from Skye in time. He was also aware that the allies of the MacDonalds of Sleat, the Clanranald, who occupied South Uist had lost a high proportion of its manpower in its own feuds with his clan[18] and would be unable to send many men to help in North Uist.

In 1601 Ruari landed on the shores of Loch Ephort with sixty men on a cold winter's day, the raiding party comprised of picked men all of whom were experts with the bow. Ruari remained with twenty men by the shore to guard the boats, while he sent his kinsman Donald Glass MacLeod of Drynoch with the other forty clansmen to exact retribution on the unsuspecting island. The MacDonalds however had seen the sails approaching from Skye and guessing the worst had attempted to protect their cattle and other possessions by concentrating them at the church of Kiltrynad. They had also sent runners with an urgent request to Domhnull Mac Ian Ic Sheumus for assistance (who will from now on be referred to as Sheumus). Sheumus had already established a considerable reputation for himself as a redoubtable warrior. He was the the grandson of James of Castle Camus, the late tutor to Donald Gorm during his minority.

---

[18] See chapter 4.

As soon as word reached Sheumus he set out for North Uist accompanied by his bodyguard of twelve men. At the time Sheumus was living on Eriskay a small island off South Uist and as the small band moved up through the island his force was augmented by a few members of the Clanranald. In the morning light as he approached North Uist Sheumus learnt that the MacLeods had successfully gathered all the cattle on the island and had assembled them at the Church of the Trinity at Carinish.

Temple of Carinish

Allowing for the time it would have taken Sheumus to move north, the MacLeods would have been on the island for at least two days, as it is thirty five miles as the crow flies from Carinish. In the short winter days it would have taken the runners a day to reach Sheumus and assuming he left almost immediately it would have taken him another day to arrive at Carinish. They may well have felt secure being so far from the centre of power of the MacDonalds in Sleat, and were feasting in the outhouses of the church.

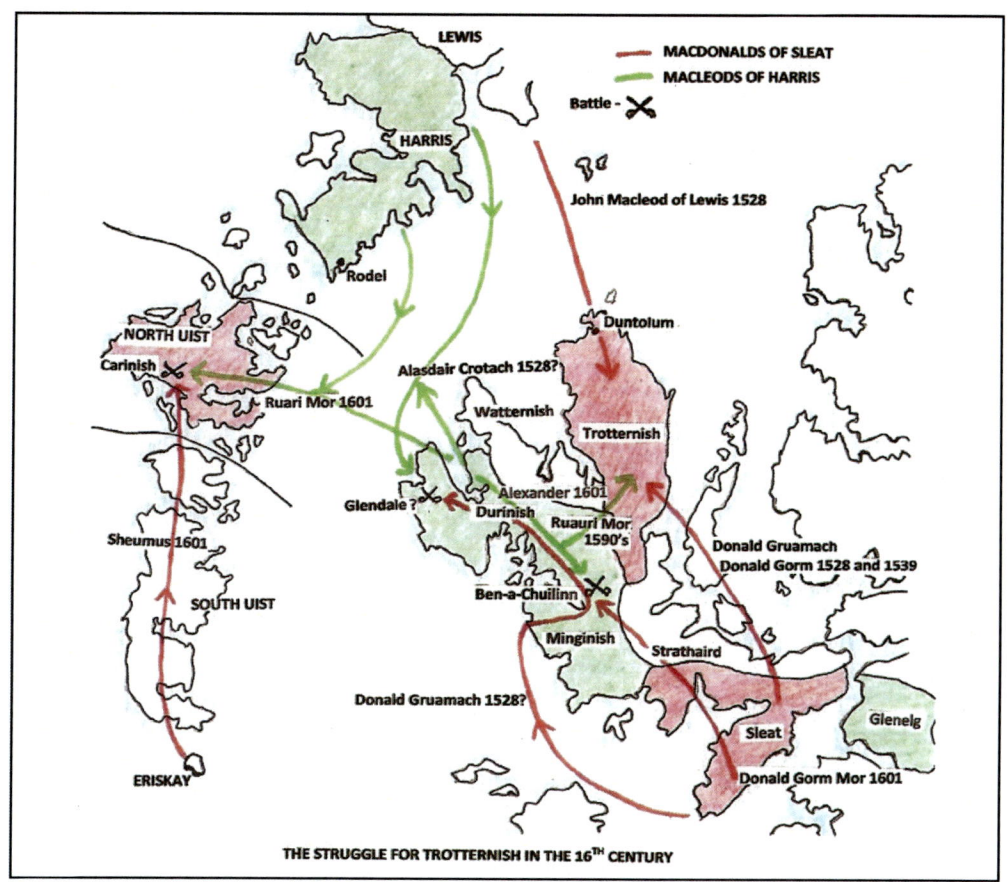

When Sheumus landed in North Uist he divided his small band into three groups. The first consisted of seven men who took position behind the rising ground north-east of the church and south of a marshy stream. The next group of four men he ordered to conceal themselves behind a knoll half-way between the first group and the church. Sheumus led the remaining four clansmen to the outhouses to announce his arrival, Sheumus stood back on a small rise and shouted to the MacLeods. As they rushed out in confusion four of them fell pierced by arrows let loose by the first group of MacDonalds. These men immediately ran back to the knoll where the second contingent of men were waiting. The MacLeods on seeing the paltry size of the opposing force ran forward to engage them, they were hit by eight arrows and more fell transfixed to the ground. The MacDonalds quickly retreated to the rising ground where they were reinforced by the seven men who were waiting there. Donald Glass the leader of the MacLeods did not check his men but maddened by the loss of so many of his people, led the MacLeods in a disorganized charge against their persecutors. They were met by yet more arrows as all the MacDonalds let loose their bows simultaneously and more MacLeods fell.

The MacDonalds moved forward quickly across the hollow where the road now runs and braced themselves to take the onrush of the MacLeods. The enraged

MacLeods attacked with great fury and started to drive Sheumus and his bodyguard back towards the rise, at this critical moment Sheumus was joined by his foster brother who was among the MacLeod raiding party. The immense strength of the bond between men who had been fostered together is attested to throughout highland history; for example, Ranald Galda was clearly much closer to the Frasers than his father's people the Clanranald.[19] The bonds of love, familiarity and obligation created by being brought up with a particular family were often able to override even the sense of loyalty to the individual's clan and certainly led to foster brothers taking enormous risks for each other. Sheumus and his foster brother fought side by side in the ensuing conflict protecting each other to the utmost of their ability in the terrifying chaos of hand to hand combat. After a while, due to exhaustion, the two clans separated from each other and began exchanging arrow fire. During these exchanges Sheumus noticed that the bows of his men were more powerful than those of the MacLeods. Sheumus ordered his men to continually withdraw so that they kept a distance between the two clans which meant that the arrows of the MacDonalds continued to inflict casualties on the enemy while those of the MacLeods fell spent a few yards short.

Donald Glas was becoming exasperated at the predicament he found himself in, the ranks of the MacLeods were growing thinner and he was well aware that defeat would be extremely serious as his men would be very vulnerable while attempting to launch their ships to escape (as it was for the Clanranald at the Battle of the Spoiling of the Dykes[20]). The situation was exacerbated for him by the knowledge that his chief was waiting for him on the shores of Loch Ephort. He asked his men for one last supreme effort as they moved forward to engage the enemy at close quarters.

Sheumus moved forward to help his men in the immanent struggle; he was hit by an arrow and fell full length into the brook. The crisis for both protagonists had arrived, the conflict hung in the balance. The MacDonalds saw their leader fall and were filled with a berserk rage; they fell upon the MacLeods with unremitting hatred. The MacLeods were cut to pieces and after a short and desperate resistance, broke and fled to the shores of Loch Ephort. One of them, who was renowned for his athletic prowess soon increased the distance between himself and both pursued and pursuers, was the first to bring the sad news to his chief. Due to his speed the clansman was known ever after as Glas nam Bean (the swift footed); he bought Ruari Mor enough time to launch his ship and to put out to sea.

Donald Glas realizing that he could not launch his galley in time raced with the other survivors for the safety of the Island of Baleshare. The vengeful MacDonalds overtook them all and one at a time dispatched them on the strand leading to the island. It was here that Donald Glas met his fate, the strand is known as Oitir Mhic Dhomhnuill Ghlais (the Strand of Donald Glas) after him. The wounded MacLeods

---

[19] See chapter 3.
[20] See chapter 4.

were quickly dispatched and collected near a swampy ditch. Here the corpses were decapitated and they were then slung into the ditch which was afterwards known as Feithe-na-fala (the morass of blood). Their skulls were exhibited on the windowsills of the church of Carinish and were to stay there as a bloody reminder to the parishioners of their clan's victory till the early years of the nineteenth century.

Sheumus although pierced by an arrow in the thigh had survived. His god mother Nic Coisean a famous healing woman was called for. Nic Coisean carefully removed the arrow and applied her concoctions of plant pastes to prevent infection and to reduce the pain. To distract his attention she sang a song, the words were still preserved in the folk memory of the people of Uist in the nineteenth century. The song is in the ancient style of her ancestors and follows the traditions of the formalized poetry of a thousand years before.

> Your noble body's blood
> Lay on the surface of the ground
>
> Your fragrant body's blood
> Seeped through the linen
>
> I sucked it up
> Until my breath grew husky

In "Traditions of the Isle of Skye"[21] there is an interesting postscript to the Battle of Carinish. After three weeks care at the hands of Nic Coisean, Sheumus was sufficiently recovered to set out for Sleat to report to his chief Donald Gorm. While Sheumus was crossing the treacherous stretch of water between the Uists and Skye a storm blew up and he was forced to land at Rodil on Harris, the ancient burial place of the MacLeods of Harris.

Rodil House was one of the seats of the chiefs of the MacLeods of Harris and by chance Ruari Mor was in residence at the time. It was dusk when Sheumus landed at Rodil, the only person who knew that he had arrived was MacLeod's page MacCrimmon who was Sheumus's godson. It is remarkable how despite the continual eruptions of bloodshed between the clans there are also many examples of close personnel relationships such as this. Ruari Mor was feasting in the hall at Rodil with the gentlemen of his clan from Harris. The severity of the storm that howled around the walls made Ruari uneasy, he paced up and down and eventually he removed a wooden panel from one of the apertures in the wall. There was an icy blast of wind and a flurry of snow blew into the room. He quickly replaced the panel and said; "I would not refuse shelter to my greatest enemy even Domhnull Mac Ian Ic Sheumus on such a night". MacCrimmon immediately seized his

---

[21] Alexander Cameron.

opportunity and replied "I take you at your word; Domnhull Mac Ian Ic Sheumus is here".

Ruari was profoundly shocked by this news and was torn between his desire for revenge and the obligation of hospitality incumbent on all highland societies. After a while he asked one of his gentlemen to invite Sheumus and his retinue into the hall. The long table groaned under the weight of the food supplied for the feast as the MacLeods and MacDonalds stared at each other in the flickering candle light. The tense atmosphere was so thick that it could have been cut with a knife, as all present were well aware of what had happened at Carinish a few weeks earlier. Eventually one of the MacLeods said "remember this day three weeks was fought the Battle of Carinish", in a loud voice. Ruari Mor gave his clansman a withering stare but the man's hatred overcame his respect for his chief and he repeated his words. The MacLeod's words acted like a spark from a tinder box and all the MacLeods drew their dirks.[22] Ruari Mor immediately called for them to sheath their weapons and reminded them of his own obligation of hospitality and asked them not to dishonour their clan. They quickly obeyed him and a bloody scene was averted.

The mood quickly changed and the MacLeods laughingly asked Sheumus why he had drawn his sword. He grimly replied "an t-eun as aired tha'san ealtuim" (I intended to have secured first the highest bird in the air) by this of course he meant Ruairi Mor. After the feast the MacDonalds were shown to an outer house to sleep while Sheumus was offered a bedroom in the main house, he wisely declined saying that he preferred the company of his own men. During the night MacCrimmon woke Sheumus and told him that there was a fair wind for Skye. Sheumus understood the warning, woke his men and they set sail for the castle of Duntulm[23] in Trotternish.

As they reached the entrance to the bay of Rodil they saw that the house where they had been sleeping was a mass of flames, clearly some of their hosts had not been able to master their desire for revenge for the events of Carinish. Sheumus was accompanied by his piper who struck up a pibroch which was afterwards known as "Tha an dubhthuil air MacLeod" (the MacLeods are disgraced[24]).

While Ruari Mor MacLeod was absent from Skye, Donald Gorm Mor seized his opportunity and mustering all the power of his clan invaded the MacLeod lands. Ruari Mor was in Argyll possibly attempting to entice the Campbells into assisting him in his feud with Donald Gorm. Donald Gorm crossed the Snizort River with all the fighting strength of his clan behind him. The Snizort was traditionally the

---

[22] A type of dagger.

[23] By this date the Castle of Duntulm had become the principal seat of the chiefs of the MacDonalds of Sleat. It is quite possible that they chose Duntulm as their principal residence to emphasize their ownership of Trotternish.

[24] This must be a piece of later oral embellishment as pibrochs took a great deal of time to compose.

boundary between the two clans and to cross it in force could only be taken as an act of war.[25]

Alexander MacLeod of Minginish the brother of Ruari Mor, was the acting head of the clan during the absence of their chief. Alexander sent out the fiery cross as soon as news reached him of the invasion and dispatched his fastest ships to Harris with an urgent request for help. The MacLeods of Harris and a small contingent of reinforcements from the MacLeods of Lewis coalesced at the foot of Ben-a-Chuilinn. For the small contingent from Lewis to join Alexander there must have been a period of at least a week during which Donald Gorm was able to range over the Macleod lands leaving death and destruction in his wake. The MacDonalds swept through Bracadale and Minginish carrying away a huge amount of plunder during those critical days when the MacLeods were concentrating their forces. Donald Gorm gathered all the captured cattle in a corrie afterwards known as Coire- na-Creiche (the ravine of the raid). The MacLeods moved out from Ben-a-Chuilinn and came up with the MacDonalds in the late afternoon. Both clans spent an uneasy night waiting for dawn.

Alexander is described by a near contemporary writer as being "encased in full armour" at the head of his people. This description, as with similar descriptions at the battles around Trumpan[26] does not fit with what we know of sixteenth century battle dress and is probably the effect of oral licence. The details of this battle have been lost to us, however we do know that the battle lasted most of the day and was fought with great tenacity by both clans. The conflict probably followed the same pattern as that of Kinlochlochy with an initial exchange between the archers before a collision of the two forces in which terrible execution was done on both sides by the deadly broadswords and Lochaber axes. The battle then settled down to a series of individual or small group encounters with a large proportion of the combatants either trying to draw breath or tending their wounds.

The encounter was a disaster for the MacLeods, many were killed. Amongst the slain were John Mac Tormod and Tormod Mac Tormoid, two close relatives of Ruari Mor, while thirty other leading men of the clan were wounded and captured including Neil Mac Alistair Roy and Alexander himself .Sheumus commanding the MacDonalds of North Uist fought with great distinction under the gaze of his chief Donald Gorm Mor. This battle of Chuilinn was commemorated by a pibroch called An Cath Gailbheach (the desperate battle).

The Privy Council at last intervened to halt this catastrophic cycle of violence between the two great island clans. A document dated twenty second of August 1601 refers to Donald Gorm Mor and Ruari Mor as "continuing their wicked and evil dispositions to prosecute their particular revenge", and had " massed together

---

[25] The significance of the Snizort as a boundary bears great similarity to the role played by the Rubicon during the Roman Republic. When Caesar crossed the Rubicon it was well understood by all that he was declaring war on the Senate.

[26] See chapter 4.

great numerous forces of their kin and friends" and had pursued each other "with fire and sword and other hostility by sea and land". Both chiefs were ordered to disband their forces and to observe the King's peace. Ruari Mor was ordered to submit himself to the Duke of Argyll and Donald Gorm Mor to the Marquis of Huntley, a situation that both magnates must have relished. Both chiefs were ordered to stay with their respective keepers. To all intents and purposes they were hostages for their own good behaviour .The council also stated that if either of them broke their security they would be charged with treason, a crime that would not only condemn them but would also include their clan lands becoming forfeit to the state.

Angus MacDonald of Dunnyveg and MacLean of Coll acting as intermediaries between the two proud chiefs persuaded them to meet first at Eilean Donan and later in Glasgow. Eventually Donald Gorm and Ruari Mor were reconciled and they both agreed to submit their differences to the arbitration of the state. Mary MacLeod whose rejection by Donald Gorm had lit the fuse to the latest outbreak of feuding was allowed to pursue any claim she might wish to make in the courts against her husband. The Scottish executive in the early seventeenth century was a far more formidable instrument than it had been a century before and both Donald Gorm and Ruairi Mor knew that they defied it at their peril. The lands of both clans had been devastated in the endemic raiding and both clans had been reduced to a state of utter destitution. It was said that in certain districts of Skye the people only averted starvation by eating dogs, cats and rats.

After the two chiefs had been reconciled Donald Gorm was invited to Dunvegan for a banquet. When Donald Gorm was in sight of the castle he was met by Ruari's famous piper Donald Mor MacCrimmon who welcomed him by playing a pibroch he had composed called The MacDonald's Salute.

On the twenty third of August 1609 the statutes of Iona were formulated by Bishop Knox, these statutes were a legal obligation upon the chiefs of the western highlands and in essence drew them inexorably into the main framework of the Scottish polity. These statutes were another demonstration of the increased power and efficiency of the state. Within a few years this expanding state power brought an end to the anarchy and feuding endemic in the western highlands. A day after the Statutes of Iona were put into effect Ruari Mor and Donald Gorm were made to reconfirm their agreement of 1601.

The military option had been closed to Ruari Mor to re-establish control over Trotternish, but the restless chief could still resort to the law. In 1613 he succeeded in having himself made heir to his uncle William MacLeod of Harris which gave him a tenuous claim on all of the lands of the MacDonalds of Sleat including Trotternish. It is unclear how strong these claims were and how they compared to the arrangements made by Archibald Donn Duke of Argyll in the 1560's. However, on the twelfth of June 1614 Ruari succeeded in taking sasine of Trotternish at Duntulum Castle. It is very hard to understand how Ruari was able to do this, as sasine is a legal formality which requires the physical presence of the claimant and the handling of "earth and stone" however the possibility that he did take sasine of Trotternish is supported by the document stating that it was witnessed at Duntulum! How was it that Ruari Mor Macleod was signing charters from Duntulum, which by this date was the main residence of the MacDonalds of Sleat?

Donald Gorm instead of invading Ruari's lands with fire and sword went to Edinburgh and in 1614 and secured legal title to all the lands of his clan except Trotternish which however he had re-occupied. The next year Ruari sought "justice" against Donald Gorm for dispossessing him of his claim, but his petition received no response from the council. Ruari then attempted to implicate Donald Gorm in the rising of Sir James MacDonald of Dunnyveg[27] and more specifically of harbouring Col Ciotach, Sir James's right hand man and a cause for much concern to the government. Ruari's intrigues again met with no response and both chiefs were bound by another set of ordinances which were even more stringent than the statutes of Iona. Among the six requirements of the act was one which required the chiefs to educate their children in such a way that by the age of nine they were to be able to read, write and speak English. There is a sense that with the creeping influence of English law and customs backed up by power of the state, which was now dominated by England after the union the days of the highland chiefs as independent autocrats with the power of "pit and gallows" was coming to an end.

When Donald Gorm signed these new requirements he was resident in Duntulum which he described as his principle residence thus negating Ruari's claim of sasine. Donald Gorm Mor died in December 1616. He was no great age but no doubt the strains and exertions of his life had taken their toll. He had married three times but left no children and the chiefship was taken by the son of his brother Archibald. Donald Gorm deserved his sobriquet of Mor (great) as he had steered the MacDonalds of Sleat through desperate times and was pitted against one of the greatest chiefs the MacLeods of Harris were ever to produce in the form of Ruari Mor. He also had to contend with serious dissension within the clan and the treachery of Hugh Gillesbeagh[28]. Had Ruairi Mor and Donald Gorm not been pitted against each other one wonders what these two great chiefs could have achieved?

Ruari Mor would still not let his claims to Trotternish lapse and in 1618 there is more correspondence between him and Sir Donald Gorm Og MacDonald eighth of Sleat, the son of Donald Gorm Mor's brother, and the Scottish council. At last the dispute between the two clans over Trotternish came to an end when after arbitration, the chiefs accepted terms proposed by the council. It was agreed that Ruari would receive the rents from Trotternish for a number of years until they matched the sum agreed (which is not specified) between Ruari and Sir Donald, and then finally Trotternish would pass to Sir Donald and his descendents. The

---

[27] This rising were the last efforts of the Clan Iain Mor to maintain its existence in the face of remorseless Campbell pressure.
[28] See chapter7.

struggle for the control of Trotternish had lasted for over a century and had been the cause of a continual festering resentment between the two clans.

This resentment had intermittently erupted into open clan warfare in which significant areas of their territories had been laid waste. there had also been the loss of hundreds of young men killed in battle. The consequences of this continual unrest were that in large areas of Skye the MacLeods and MacDonalds had been made utterly destitute. With the benefit of historical hindsight and the reasonable views formulated in a liberal western democracy it may seem that this long struggle by the two protagonists was unnecessary and that they should have accepted arbitration at the outset.

The political landscape had changed beyond all recognition between the end of the fifthteenth century and the beginning of the seventeenth century. The power and prestige of the MacDonald Lords of the Isles had faded into memories, the Scottish and latterly the British state's power and effectiveness had, despite setbacks increased enormously and with the ever increasing reach of the Campbells, as the quasi instrument of the executive the ability of the island chiefs to act as semi-autominous autocrats was coming to an end. At the beginning of the sixteenth century the chiefs of both clans would have known that it was possible to gain control over Trotternish by military might and that they had every chance of avoiding any retribution from or on behalf of the Scottish Kings. During this period it was possible to obtain complete military victory due to the regions remoteness from Edinburgh, the often weak and corrupt nature of the Scottish executive and it's absorption in its own internal and external difficulties. At a time when their was a continual dearth of resources and the people of both clans lived in abject material poverty the control of Trotternish would have been considered pivotal to the survival and well being of the both clans. When these factors were blended with clan pride and previous losses incurred in the feud it is clear why this feud over Trotternish lasted for over one hundred years.

By 1618 neither clan had achieved military superiority nor despite the almost continual production of charters from Edinburgh did either of them establish an indisputable legal claim to Trotternish. During most of the sixteenth century the MacDonalds had been in actual occupation of Trotternish and in the time of Donald Gorm the Castle of Duntulm in Trotternish became the principle residence of the chiefs of the MacDonalds of Sleat. In the centuries to come both clans were badly affected by migration, the clearances, and economic poverty. Both the chiefs of the MacLeods of Harris and the MacDonalds of Sleat retained some of their clan lands. However more damage was done to both clans by the slow grinding of economic and political processes than was ever achieved by the strong arm of their clan armies   in   war.

THE MACDONALDS OF SLEAT TO 1695

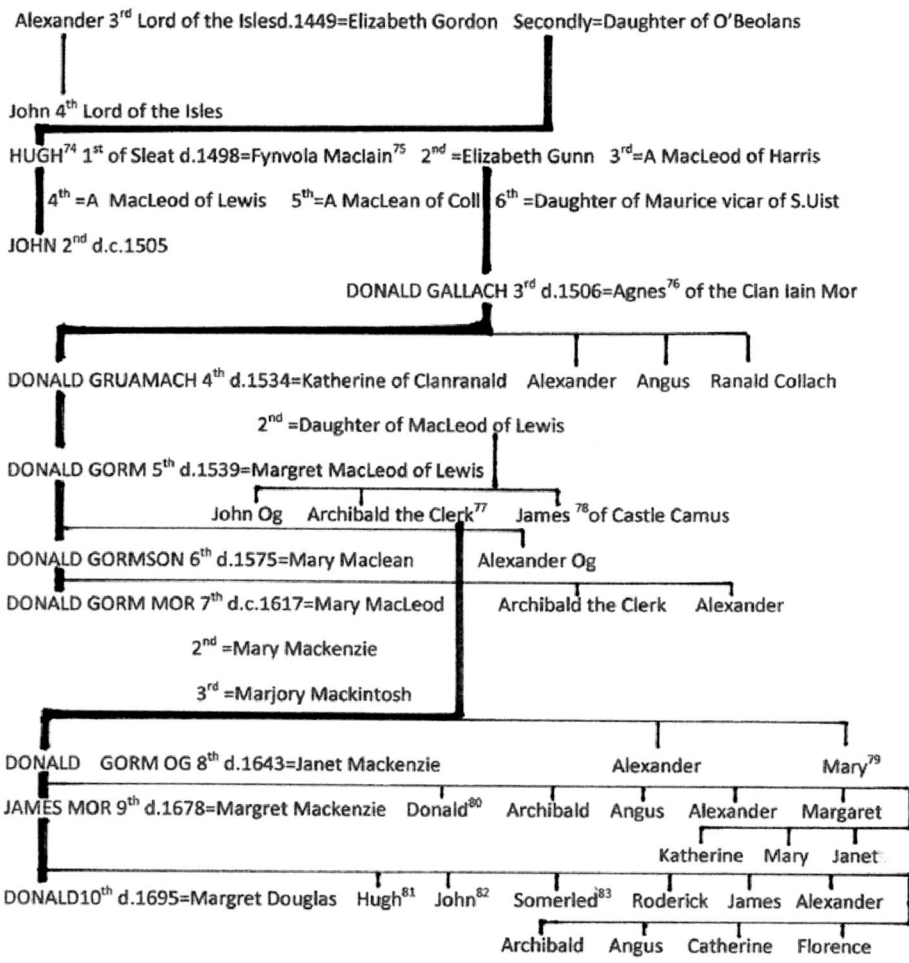

Alexander 3rd Lord of the Isles d.1449=Elizabeth Gordon   Secondly=Daughter of O'Beolans

John 4th Lord of the Isles

HUGH[74] 1st of Sleat d.1498=Fynvola Maclain[75]   2[nd] =Elizabeth Gunn   3[rd]=A MacLeod of Harris

4[th] =A MacLeod of Lewis   5[th]=A MacLean of Coll   6[th] =Daughter of Maurice vicar of S.Uist

JOHN 2nd d.c.1505

DONALD GALLACH 3rd d.1506=Agnes[76] of the Clan Iain Mor

DONALD GRUAMACH 4th d.1534=Katherine of Clanranald   Alexander   Angus   Ranald Collach

2[nd] =Daughter of MacLeod of Lewis

DONALD GORM 5th d.1539=Margret MacLeod of Lewis

John Og   Archibald the Clerk[77]   James [78]of Castle Camus

DONALD GORMSON 6th d.1575=Mary Maclean   Alexander Og

DONALD GORM MOR 7th d.c.1617=Mary MacLeod   Archibald the Clerk   Alexander

2[nd] =Mary Mackenzie

3[rd] =Marjory Mackintosh

DONALD   GORM OG 8th d.1643=Janet Mackenzie   Alexander   Mary[79]

JAMES MOR 9th d.1678=Margret Mackenzie   Donald[80]   Archibald   Angus   Alexander   Margaret

Katherine   Mary   Janet

DONALD 10th d.1695=Margret Douglas   Hugh[81]   John[82]   Somerled[83]   Roderick   James   Alexander

Archibald   Angus   Catherine   Florence

---

[74] For a more detailed examination of the descendents of Hugh 1st of Sleat, see The Legacy of Hugh 1st of Sleat.
[75] Maclains of Ardnamurchan.
[76] Agnes was the daughter of John Cathanach.
[77] Archibald was the father of the evil Hugh MacGilleasbuig Chleirich.
[78] James's descendants are the MacDonalds of Kingsburgh, Ostaig and Capstill.
[79] Mary married Ranald MacDonald of Benbecula.
[80] Donald's descendants are the MacDonalds of Caslteton.
[81] Hugh's descendants are the MacDonalds of Glenmore and Mugstot.
[82] John's descendants are the MacDonalds of Bernisdale and Sclapay.
[83] Somerled's descendants are the MacDonalds of Sartle.

THE LEGACY OF HUGH MACDONALD 1ST OF SLEAT

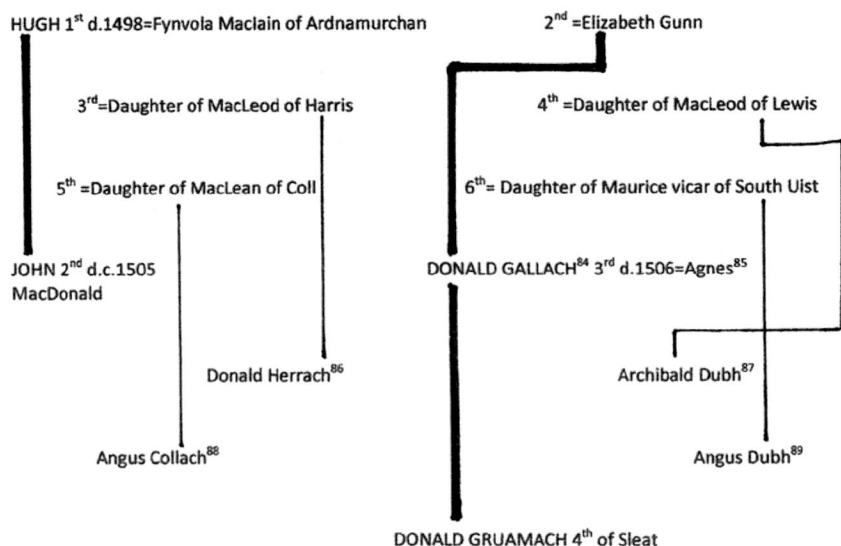

HUGH 1st d.1498=Fynvola MacIain of Ardnamurchan

2nd =Elizabeth Gunn

3rd=Daughter of MacLeod of Harris

4th =Daughter of MacLeod of Lewis

5th =Daughter of MacLean of Coll

6th= Daughter of Maurice vicar of South Uist

JOHN 2nd d.c.1505 MacDonald

DONALD GALLACH[84] 3rd d.1506=Agnes[85]

Donald Herrach[86]

Archibald Dubh[87]

Angus Collach[88]

Angus Dubh[89]

DONALD GRUAMACH 4th of Sleat

---

[84] Donald Gallach was murdered by Archibald Dubh while inspecting his galley.

[85] Agnes was the daughter of John Cathanach chief of the Clan Iain Mor.

[86] Donald Herrach's descendants are the MacDonalds of Griminish, Balranald, Heiskir and Skeabost. Donald Herrach was murdered by Paul of the thong at the behest of Archibald Dubh.

[87] Archibald Dubh was responsible for the murder of his brothers and was eventually killed by his nephews Donald Gruamach and Ranald (the son of Donald Herrach).

[88] Angus Collach was allied to Archibald Dubh and was an accomplice in the murder of Donald Gallach and Donald Herrach. He was drowned by the Clanranald for his crimes.

[89] Angus Dubh was also an accomplice of Archibald Dubh and accompanied on his piratical raiding. He was eventually captured by Donald Bane, chief of the Clanranald. He died while attempting to escape his captors.

Chapter 7

Cain and Abel

Hugh, the youngest son of Alexander, third Lord of the Isles, was the founder of the MacDonalds of Sleat. Hugh first appears in the historical record in 1460, when he is described as a "gentleman of the isles" during a raid on the Orkneys. This creach (raid) was his first major expedition and would have taken place when he was in his late teens or early twenties, which suggests a that he was born around 1440. Hugh was a man of considerable energy and ability, his great achievement being the establishment of his family on Skye which had long been the sole preserve of the MacLeods. This energy also found expression in his private life; he had three marriages and at least three other unions (which were either of the hand fast[1] type or had no claim at all to legitimacy). Each of these relationships were with women who came from proud and powerful clans and each woman bore Hugh at least one son. No doubt these women would have had a strong sense of their own identity and would have been bought up as girls with the political struggles that surrounded their fathers in their own clans. Did they as mothers inculcate their sons with a sense of their own importance and nurture the flame of ambition which later burned so strongly inside them?

The Marriages and Unions of Hugh First of Sleat

To Fynvola daughter of MacIain of Ardnamurchan ------ John

To Elizabeth daughter of the chief of the Gunns ------- Donald Gallach

To a daughter of William Dubh MacLeod of Harris ------- Donald Herriach

To a daughter of Torquil MacLeod of Lewis -------- Archibald Dubh

To a daughter of MacLean of Coll -------- Angus Collach

To a daughter of Maurice vicar of South Uist -------- Angus Dubh

Hugh died in 1498 and was succeeded by John his eldest son by his first marriage to Fynvola the daughter of MacIain of Ardnamurchan. The period of John's short reign was a disaster for the MacDonalds of Sleat. He gifted away to the Clanranald all the clan's land to which he had charters from Alexander third Lord of the Isles, and although the MacDonalds of Sleat remained in occupation of these territories it was to take a long and determined effort by future chiefs to re-

---

[1] Hand fast marriages were recognized as legally binding in highland society. They were a means whereby a couple could "try" each other out; they could be dissolved after a fixed term, usually one year. There is something peculiarly modern about them.

establish their legal right to these lands.[2] There is no hint in the records as to why John acted with such apparent folly, and one can only guess at what his motives were; perhaps he had a strong dislike of some or all of his half-brothers. Had he noticed the evil nature of Archibald Dubh and feared for the utter ruin of his people if Archibald should, by removing Donald Gallach and Donald Herriach, become chief of the MacDonalds of Sleat? After a short and inglorious period as head of his people John died in 1502.

Donald Gallach assumed the chief ship of the clan and established his main residence at Dunskaith Castle on the northern side of Sleat. Dunskaith was one of several castles occupied by the MacDonalds of Sleat.

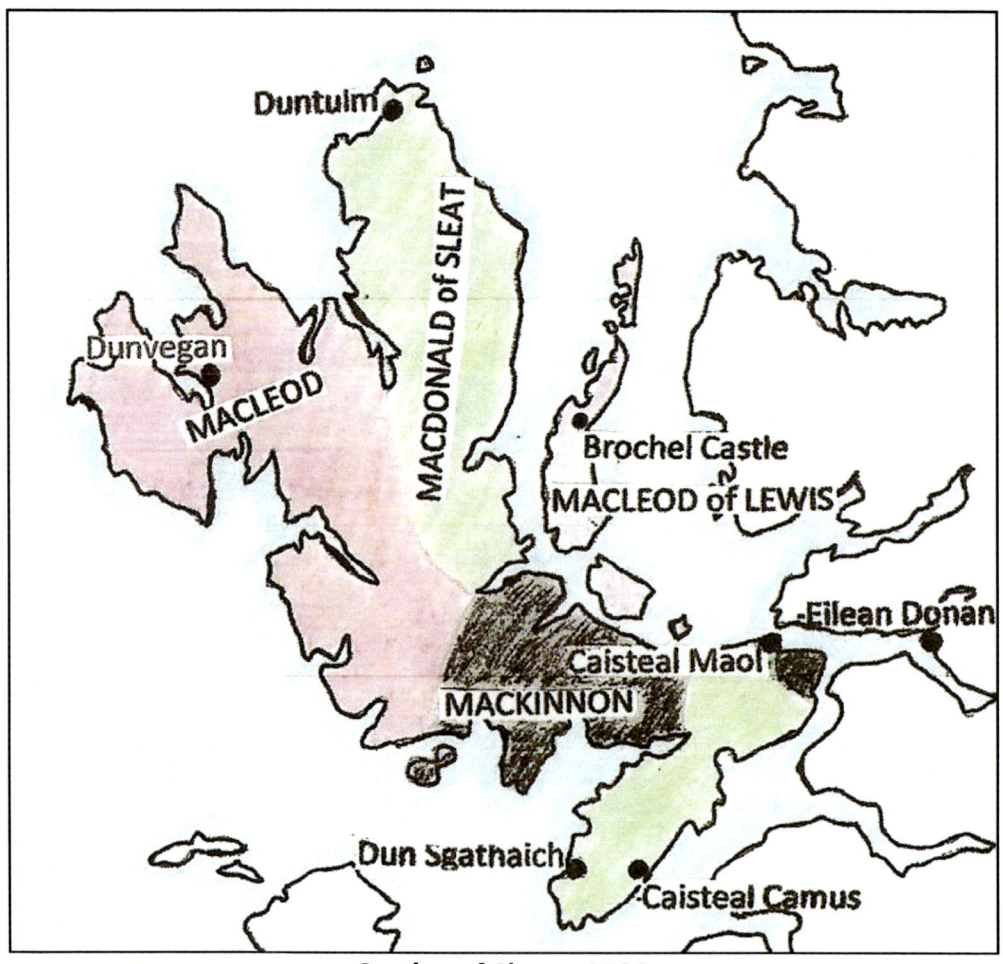

Castles of Skye c.1520

Donald was known to the clan as Donald Gallach, Gallach because he had spent a considerable proportion of his youth amongst his mother's people, the Gunns of Caithness. Donald Gallach is described[3] as, "... a moderate man, inclined to peace, black haired and fair skinned,...". He then goes on to record how Donald Gallach divided his patrimony with his half-brother, Donald Herrach (of Harris after his mother clan). He gave Donald Herrach the Island of North Uist and some lands in Sleat, while he retained the remainder of Sleat and kept the peninsular of Trotternish for his own support.

Hugh MacDonald also states that Donald Gallach was to provide for Archibald Dubh (black Archibald[4]) his half-brother the son of a daughter of MacLeod of Lewis, and Angus Collach (after his mothers clan) also his half-brother the son of a daughter of MacLean of Coll. Donald Herriach was to provide for his other half-brother Angus Dubh the son of a daughter of the vicar of South Uist. The scene was set for a bitter power struggle between Hugh's surviving offspring, which was to plunge the MacDonalds into a long period of anarchy which led to a severe weakening in the clan's power which was only torturously restored by the determination of future chiefs.[5]

Donald Gallach had made a generous and reasonable settlement for his half-brothers and this settlement should have ushered in a period of peace and stability. Instead it was the medium by which one of the darkest characters in highland history was to emerge upon the stage. Archibald Gilleasbuig Dubh's personality casts a long dark shadow over the house of Sleat in the early sixteenth century. Archibald Dubh (Black Archibald), whose soul was as dark as his complexion, was discontented with the provision made for him by Donald Gallach; this resentment was fanned into hatred by his foster-father, MacKinnon of Dunskeith. The MacKinnons had long been settled in parts of the south of Skye, and this intriguing may have been an attempt to weaken the growing power of the MacDonalds of Sleat. Archibald Dubh began to plot how he could clear his path to the chiefship. He found two willing instruments to carry out his schemes in the form of two of his half-brothers, Angus Collach,[6] and Angus Dubh,[7] on promising to increase the size of their inheritance.

The vicious cycle of fratricide began when Archibald encompassed the fate of Donald Herrach in 1506. Archibald and Angus Collach arranged that there should be a gymnastic competition on the Dun of Loch Scilpaig on the island of North Uist. They formed a plot with a certain Paul, he was to hide in the rafters of the barn where the competition was to take place, and murder Donald Herrach. Donald

---

[3] Hugh MacDonald.

[4] Dubh hear means black or dark featured and is not (although apposite) a reflection on his character.

[5] See chapter 6.

[6] The son of Hugh and a daughter of Maclean of Coll.

[7] The son of Hugh and a daughter of Maurice vicar of South Uist.

Herrach was renowned for his physical abilities, and eagerly entered into the competition. During the high jump event, Donald Herrach leapt high into the air, and Paul deftly dropped a noose around his neck and held him suspended above the ground. Archibald Dubh and Angus Collach rushed forward and held the struggling Donald Herrach, they then thrust a red hot iron through his bowels, and it was in this agonizing way that Donald Herrach met his death. After this brutal murder Paul was known as Pal na heille or Paul of the thong.

Archibald Dubh immediately set sail for Donald Gallach's residence of Dunskaith in Skye, knowing that he must accomplish the second phase of his plan before there was any possibility of the news of Donald Herrach's murder reaching Skye. The unsuspecting Donald Gallach was delighted to see him and invited him to a feast in the hall of Dunskaith. Afterwards Donald Gallach took Archibald Dubh down to the shore to show him the frame of a new galley that he was having constructed. Archibald examined the workmanship very carefully before commenting that the keel plank was rotten. Surprised at this major problem Donald Gallach bent down to inspect the faulty timber. Archibald quickly drew his dirk and stabbed Donald Gallach in the back, Donald fell mortally wounded onto the framework of the boat. As he lay dying he bitterly rebuked Archibald for his treachery, Archibald was struck with remorse at his act of fratricide and begged Donald to forgive him. This sense of guilt may seem surprising, but to murder your brother in cold blood clearly deeply affected Archibald, and he begged Donald for his forgiveness. Donald Gallach understood that his life was ebbing away and knowing that his only son was at the mercy of Archibald, made him swear that he would bring up his son as though he was his own.

Almost unbelievably Archibald Dubh brought up the two sons of Donald Gallach and Donald Herrach as though they were indeed his own on the island of Oronsay in North Uist. One can only assume that, having secured the control of the clan he was satisfied that one day the son of Donald Gallach would become chief of the clan. It is also strange that he did not consider the very real possibility that the sons of the two men he had so treacherously murdered would one day reach adulthood and seek revenge. Archibald Dubh while exhibiting a dark and murderous nature also had a strong sense of duty towards the sons of his half-brothers. This contradiction in his character only adds to the strangeness of this enigmatic individual.

Archibald Dubh did not enjoy the fruits of his actions for long; he was soon forced to flee to the southern Hebrides after coming under sustained pressure from Ranald Bane the chief of the Clanranald.[8] For the next three years Archibald and some MacAlisters[9] from Kintyre immersed themselves in many acts of piracy, their main prey being the merchantmen who plied their trade between the Clyde

---

[8] This was probably because of the gift of Sleat to the Clanranald by Archibald's half-brother, John.

[9] The oldest of the cadet branches of MacDonalds.

estuary and Ulster. He eventually returned to Skye after obtaining a pardon from the Crown by betraying the MacAlisters who he handed over to the authorities. The MacAlisters faced the full penalty of the law, the fate of all pirates who were captured. On his return he not only resumed the chiefship of the MacDonalds of Sleat but was granted legal control over Trotternish in 1510. The complicity of the state by association with Archibald Dubh is yet another example during this period of its venal weakness.

Even during the absence of Archibald Dubh the MacDonalds of Sleat were racked by internecine violence. Angus Collach, who had been an accomplice in the murder of Donald Herrach, paid a visit to North Uist accompanied by his tail (group of adherents). On a Sunday morning they attended the church of Saint Mary's. After the service he met the wife of Donald MacDonald of Balranald, and suggested that she might offer them hospitality, which she cheerfully agreed to. After a sumptuous meal during which copious quantities of whisky were consumed, Angus attempted to seduce his host. When his advances were rejected he resorted to force. She was able to dissemble until Angus was distracted; she then made her escape and sought refuge with her father's people the Clanranald of South Uist. The Clanranald were outraged at Angus's conduct and gathering sixty men landed on North Uist. They were reinforced by her husband's men soon after landing. They surprised Angus's party at Kirkibost, where after a vicious skirmish they captured Angus and left eighteen of his men either dead or dying. Angus was instantly put on trial for his crimes; it is uncertain whether they included the murder of Donald Herrach. In any event he was found guilty; he was tied up with ropes, forced into a large sack and thrown into the sea. Some weeks later the sack containing his putrefying remains was recovered on the beach at Carinish. He was buried on the seashore thereby denying him the sanctified burial of a church yard. Angus Collach was buried with no respect like any common criminal.

Angus Dubh the youngest son of Hugh was involved in Archibald Dubh's piratical activities in the southern Hebrides. He was apprehended by Donald Bane the chief of the Clanranald and placed in prison in South Uist, it is interesting to note how Donald Bane was enforcing law and order in an area which was outside the reach of the Crown and was consequently regarded as lawless. One day while taking exercise on the Strand of Askernish, Angus Dubh attempted to escape by running off. His gaolers immediately pursued him, one of them hitting him in the leg with an arrow. When he was recaptured the arrow was removed, the wound was examined and judged to be incurable. Angus Dubh was killed with a sword thrust by one of his captors. It is a possibility that his escape and subsequent wounding was a convenient pretext to be free of their tedious charge.

Archibald Dubh was the only surviving son of Hugh, all his brothers dying in the mayhem he had initiated. Once Archibald was sure of his control of the clan he exacted revenge on the men of North Uist[10] who had helped the Clanranald give

---

[10] The MacDonalds of Balranald.

justice to Angus Collach. There are no details as to how they were killed but whether it was by treachery or force the men of North Uist were put to the sword.

Local tradition in North Uist recorded that Archibald Dubh's two nephews the sons of the murdered Donald Gallach and Donald Herrach successfully hid their hatred of their uncle and that during the years of their childhood he suspected nothing. They nursed their hatred which no doubt was continually fanned by their weakness and vulnerability until they became young men.

On a beautiful summer's day, they all went on a hunting expedition in the Hills of Lea on North Uist. The three men waited for the game to be driven towards them at the pass of Bealach a Sgail, Archibald Dubh fell asleep amongst the heather; the two cousins quickly discussed whether they should take advantage of the opportunity that he had given them. Donald Gruamach (the grim), the son of Donald Gallach hesitated but his cousin, Ranald the son of Donald Herrach said that he would kill Archibald Dubh. On hearing this Donald Gruamach is said to have replied "Do, do, and remember my father and your own..." With one quick action Archibald Dubh's throat was slit open and he stared with utter surprise into the immense blueness of the sky. Archibald died as violently as he had lived, and ironically died at the hands of his own family when least suspecting any threat. With the death of Archibald Dubh which took place circa 1518, Donald Gruamach assumed his rightful place at the head of MacDonalds of Sleat.

Donald Gruamach found himself in an unenviable situation; his clan was "broken" having no legal title to the lands it occupied, and Donald was soon to be embroiled in a bitter feud with the MacLeods of Harris.[11] Donald Gruamach laid the foundations of the recovery of the MacDonalds of Sleat by maintaining his people's occupation of Trotternish and establishing a number of alliances with some of the eastern clans, including the MacKintoshes and the Munros. In all his endeavours Donald Guamach was loyally supported by his cousin Ranald,the son of the Donald Herrach who was the first to be treacherously murdered by strangulation by the assassin Pal na h-eille (Paul of the thong) at the behest of Archibald Dubh. Paul had been rewarded for the murder of Donald Herrach by Archibald Dubh with the gift of the farm of Balmore in North Uist. When news reached Paul of the death of his benefactor Archibald Dubh, Paul spent much of his time at the ancient Pictish fort of Dun Steinigarrry on Loch Paible. In late summer at harvest time Paul was building a stack in his corn-yard; from the top of the stack Paul saw two men approaching. Always being alert to danger Paul asked one of his workmen which way the wind blew yesterday, the man replied that it blew from the east. Paul immediately guessed that the approaching strangers were a threat; he understood that the easterly wind could well have brought a ship from Skye to North Uist. Paul jumped down from the corn stack and started to run for the sanctuary of Kilmuir churchyard, a distance of about three miles.

---

[11] See chapter 6.

Meanwhile Angus Fionn MacDonald Herrach (a son of Donald Herrach) and his companion, who were making their way towards Balmore Farm, had initially seen two men on the corn stack, one wearing a red waistcoat[12] and the other man a white one. Angus noticed that there was now only one man on the rick, and asked his companion, who presumably had better eyesight, which of the two had disappeared. He was told that it was the man in the red waistcoat. Angus, guessing that Paul was attempting to escape broke into a run in pursuit of his quarry. Soon he came in sight of Paul as he made for the safety of the sanctuary; Angus increased his speed and was soon close to Paul. Just as Paul was crossing a rivulet on the south side of the sanctuary Angus bent back his bow and with unerring accuracy pierced Paul's heel with an arrow. Paul stumbled and fell; Angus came up with him and was able to avenge the death of his father by driving his broadsword through Paul's torso.

Paibal Sanctuary

Ranald must have savoured the news that his brother Angus had "justified" the murderer of their father, but he also was soon to die in the murderous mayhem that formed so much of the early history of the MacDonalds of Sleat. Ranald went

---

[12] Presumably the description of the two men in "waistcoats are a later addition as this type of garment was not in use in the highlands in the sixteenth century.

on a visit to his cousin Donald Gruamach at his castle of Dunskaith. The two men were closely bound by the murder of their two fathers (Donald Collach and Donald Herrach) and the trials they had suffered together as boys under the tutorship of Archibald Dubh.

Donald Gruamach had married a daughter of the chief of the Clanranald[13] and was entertaining a large number of his wife's relatives when Ranald arrived. Ranald was mortally offended at what he took to be the arrogant and disrespectful behaviour of the relatives of the wife of his old friend Donald Gruamach. The importance of the dignity of the chief to his clansmen can not be overemphasized as they believed that the respect or lack of it shown to their chief reflected on them personally. Ranald resolved that a terrible retribution should fall on the people of the Clanranald. That night as the guests lay sleeping, Ranald crept into their chambers and moving quickly and quietly from bed to bed slit the throat of each occupant. Soon Ranald had murdered all twelve guests; he then opened the wooden shutter of the window and dragged the bodies over to the window and through them one after another onto the rocks below.

At first light Ranald prepared to leave for the safety of his home in Trotternish, Donald Gruamach on seeing that his cousin was packing urged him to stay, or at least to stay until his wife came down. To these kind words Ranald is said to have replied, "I must leave instantly for she will not bless me when she looks out her window and views my morning's work." Donald Gruamach's wife's heart was filled with hatred for Ranald on seeing their bodies lying on the rocks. She bribed the Black Finnon MacKinnon to murder Ranald when the opportunity arose. At New Year Ranald decided to visit Donald Gruamach who was at Kirkibost on North Uist. As Ranald went to meet the ship that was to carry him to North Uist he was set upon by Black Finnon and killed.

The history of the MacDonalds of Sleat in the later years of Donald Gruamach's rule and during the minorities and rule of his son Donald Gorm and following him his son Donald Gormson takes a welcome break from the vicious internal feuding. During the course of the next fifty years the clan's history is dominated by its struggle to establish legal title to its hereditary lands and to gain control over the district of Trotternish on Skye.[14] The clan was also involved in an attempt by Donald Gorm to re-establish the Lordship of the Isles.[15] By 1575 on the death of Donald Gormson the clan was well on the way to achieving these long held objectives.

In 1575 the eldest son of Donald Gormson, Donald Gorm Mor was a minor and James of castle Camus was appointed by the clan to be his guardians. It is with this appointment that one of the most sinister personalities ever to grace this dark period of west highland history emerges. James's two nephews were Donald and Hugh Mac Gilleasbuig Chleirich, the MacGilleasbuig sept of the MaDonalds of Sleat

---

[13] Catherine daughter of Alexander.
[14] See chapter 6.
[15] See chapters 2 and 6.

held sway over the district of Trotternish. Donald MacGilleasbuig died shortly before 1581 and Hugh was now the sole representative of the MacGilleasbuig sept as the tutor of the young Donald Gorm Mor.

Hugh MacGilleasbuig Cleaeirich (henceforward to be referred to as Hugh), was the son of Archibald the Clerk who had been the tutor of Donald Gormson when he had been a child. During the period that Archibald the Clerk had been the tutor of Donald Gormson he had greatly increased the power and influence of the MacGilleasbuigs, especially in Trotternish. His son Hugh was to bring untold suffering to many hundreds of his people in the course of his cruel and treacherous career.

James of castle Camus had divided his authority with Donald and Hugh who were given sway over the clan's interests in Trotternish. This dilution of his influence by this allocation of power is a clear indication of the rise in status of the MacGilleisbuigs during the preceding decades. By 1581 Hugh was the unchallenged leader of this branch of the MacDonalds of Sleat. Hugh's treachery to his own clan is almost unparralled in the annuls of highland history, there are two factors, which at least in part, explain his future behaviour. Hugh believed, with some justification, that Angus Og, the younger brother of Donald Gormson had assassinated his father Archibald the Clerk. Hugh also greatly resented the division of the tutorship of the clan, being convinced that he should have been the sole tutor to the young Donald Gorm Mor; and even his position of joint tutor had been granted as an afterthought by James of castle Camus who had been elected as sole tutor by the gentlemen of the clan. Hugh's views were based on the fact that his father had held sole sway over the clan when he had been appointed tutor to Donald Gormson. His resentment against his clan and future chief was further increased when he was forfeited by the crown for the failure of the clan to pay their rents to the Bishop of the Isles in 1581.

Hugh therefore became an outlaw in1581 or 1582 due to the failure of the clan to pay the arrears due to the bishop. Within the course of a few short months he had in effect lost his position as head of the MacGilleisbuig sept. His influence and power over both the young chief and the clan as one of the tutors of Donald Gorm Mor was negated by the fact that he had to flee Skye to evade the wrath of the bishop (for the non-payment of rents) who in turn was backed by the power of the state. Judging by the events that were to follow Hugh's heart was full of bitterness towards his young chief and the gentlemen of the clan. Hugh joined up with other "broken" men and took to piracy in the southern isles.

In 1585 Donald Gorm Mor achieved his majority and assumed the chiefship of the MacDonalds of Sleat. Hugh was still under the shadow of outlawry and his resentment can only have been fuelled by life continuing as normal on Skye. In the same year that Donald Gorm Mor became chief he set sail for Isla to visit Angus MacDonald of Dunnyveg the chief of the Clan Iain Mor. This clan was currently involved in a deadly feud with the MacLeans of Mull.[16] As Donald Gorm Mor sailed south with a considerable retinue the winds which had been blowing from a northerly direction changed to a strong south westerly. With conditions deteriorating and being unable to make any headway against the opposing wind Donald Gorm Mor ordered his fleet of galleys to take shelter in the inlet of the Speckled Hill in southern Jura. Jura was politically unstable during this period as both the MacDonalds and the MacLeans held land on the island.

It so happened that Donald Gorm Mor landed on the northern side of the loch. Hugh had been keeping an eye on the progress of his chief as he sailed south, and due to being placed in similar circumstances by the weather had also taken shelter near the inlet. Hugh had a detailed grasp of the politics and patterns of land ownership in the whole of the southern isles due to his four years of piracy in the region. He seized what he knew to be an opportunity to stir up trouble between the MacDonalds of Sleat and the MacLeans of Mull. Hugh and his followers drove off a number of cattle and slaughtered them during the night. These cattle belonged to the MacLeans. The next day the weather moderated and Hugh set sail for the south without Donald Gorm Mor ever having been aware that Hugh had been on Jura or that he had implicated him in the slaughter of the cattle.

When news reached Lachlan Mor MacLean the chief of the MacLeans this proud and warlike man resolved on instant retribution on the perpetrators of this act of pillaging; which he assumed were Donald Gorm Mor's men. Lachlan immediately set sail with a large body of his clansmen for Jura. Why Donald stayed for what must have been several days in the environs of the Speckled Hill; when the wind had changed to a favourable direction is unknown. In any event the hapless MacDonalds were asleep when they were attacked by the vengeful MacLeans. Sixty of the unsuspecting MacDonalds were killed while Donald Gorm Mor only escaped because he had decided to spend the night on his galley instead of on the shore.

It was by this act that Hugh embroiled his people in a sanguinary and disastrous feud which lasted several years. Donald Gorm Mor sailed from Jura deeply incensed at what appeared to be a gratuitous and unprovoked attack. The MacDonalds of Sleat were then to join the Clan Iain Mor in their feud with the MacLeans. By September of 1585 the pressure bought to bear on the MacLeans by the alliance of these two clans was enormous. This is attested to by a letter sent to Roderick MacLeod of Dunvegan by James VI in which he entreats Roderick to assist the MacLeans as "the Clan Donald, who had done him (Lachlan MacLean) much injury". In the course of this feud a network of alliances were bought into play, and at its height the whole of the western highlands were ablaze.[17]

The active involvement of the MacDonalds of Sleat in this feud ended in 1589 when all the principal gentlemen of the clan were granted a remission for their crime by James VI. Interestingly amongst the members of the clan who are

---

[16] See chapter 11.
[17] See chapter 11.

mentioned by name there is one Hugh Gilleasbuig Clearich. This remission is problematic in that it has been shown how Hugh had ensnared his people into the feud with the MacLeans, it can only be surmised that Hugh rejoined his own clan at some point during the feud. This supposition is supported by the fact that Donald Gorm Mor later appointed Hugh to be Baillie of Trotternish in 1586; this appointment must imply that Donald Gorm Mor believed that Hugh had mended his ways. Hugh's implied support for his own clan might be explained by the loyalty he bore his people overriding his hatred of Donald Gorm Mor, or, which is more likely, he could see that the Clan Donald was gaining the ascendancy and his actions were governed by opportunism and a shrewd calculation of his own self-interest.

Why Donald Gorm Mor appointed Hugh Baillie of Trotternish is hard to understand. Did he believe that Hugh had returned to the fold? Did he not know of Hugh's involvement in the events on Jura? Or was it because he needed Hugh's authority over the MacGilleasbuigs of Trotternish and merely reflected a necessary pragmatism which highland chiefs often had to adopt. Was Donald Gorm Mor's decision based on the social structure he knew in which clansmen were regarded as his "children" and a chief could usually rely on their devotion? In the sixteenth century it was understood that the clansmen regarded their clan as being their extended family and in exchange for this sense of belonging and the protection it offered in an anarchic world they would hazard all they had for their kin whether real or imaginary.

Hugh's bailieship of Trotternish was a disaster for the people of the district, Trotternish became infamous for lawlessness and the cruelty of his control. Eventually his actions reached the Scottish court. In1596 when Donald Gorm Mor was obtaining legal charters to his clan lands there is a stipulation in which Hugh is mentioned, and one of the conditions of the gift of the new charters is that Hugh was to be given no position of authority. Clearly Hugh's reputation was well known even in remote Edinburgh.

By 1600 Hugh was again an outlaw having being banished from Trotternish, in April of that year he is mentioned as committing various acts of piracy. This included boarding a ship belonging to a certain Thomas Inglis of Edinburgh and " wrongly, violently, and masterful against all order of law and justice, wrecked, stole, interfered with and took away from the aforementioned ship the whole merchandise, goods and gear." Interestingly in these papers he is described as " of Watternish". The significance of his place of residence is that Watternish was part of the MacLeod lands. The MacLeods were led at this time by Rory Mor Macleod the great rival of his own chief Donald Gorm Mor. It is clear that Hugh was living under the protection of Rory Mor, and was no doubt a useful pawn in the struggle between the two chiefs.

Whatever the defects in Hugh's character he clearly did not lack diplomatic skills, for shortly afterwards he was again taken back by Donald Gorm Mor. After Rory Mor and Donald Gorm Mor had made their uneasy peace in 1601, Hugh was accepted back by his chief and was even permitted to build a residence for himself at Criudeach in Trotternish. More surprisingly Hugh was allowed to build a small fort nearby called Castle Uisdean.[18] That Donald Gorm Mor should allow Hugh to return for a second time seems difficult to understand but that he also allowed him to build a small castle seems unfathomable. Did Hugh have some hold over Donald Gorm Mor? Or was he more powerful than history now records?

Castle Uisdean

The little fort of Castle Uisdean reflects in its appearance and style of construction Hugh's character. It is constructed of large basalt slabs, which combined with its simple rectangular shape gives it a dark forbidding nature as it sits broodingly on the cliff edge. The most notable feature of Castle Uisdean is that there is no entrance at ground level, the only access was by a ladder up to the second floor. Hugh had to be careful about his security, once the ladder had been pulled up behind them any occupant of the fort would have felt secure in the knowledge that no one else could enter.

After completing Castle Uisdean, Hugh once again started plotting against Donald Gorm Mor. Hugh had a power base in Trotternish which comprised of men who had sailed with him on his piratical expeditions, the Gilleasbuigs and local men

---

[18] The MacDonalds of Sleat were also known as Clan Uisdean.

who lived in fear of his power and malevolence. Hugh planned to invite all the leading men of his clan including his chief to a feast to celebrate the completion of Castle Uisdean. While Donald Gorm Mor and the gentlemen of the clan were enjoying the feast, Hugh, with the help of his henchmen planned to murder them all so that he could assume the leadership of the MacDonalds of Sleat. Hugh sent out a flurry of letters, some were invitations to the intended victims and some were addressed to his co-conspirators. By an oversight Hugh addressed the letter meant for his chief to one of his co-conspirators, a certain Martin who lived on Trotternish while a letter meant for Martin which described the plot in detail was sent to Donald Gorm Mor.

This clear evidence of treachery was the final straw for Donald Gorm Mor who ordered a renowned warrior of the clan called Domhnull Mac Ian Ic Sheumus to hunt Hugh down and bring him before his chief so that he might experience justice. By 1601 Domhnull Mac Ic Sheumus had already served his chief with great distinction in the bloody feud with the Macleods of Harris over Trotternish.[19]

Word reached Hugh that the plot had been discovered and that retribution was sailing towards him in the form of Sheumus and his men. Hugh fled Castle Uisdean and made for the safety of an ancient Pictish broch known as Dun-a-Sticir on North Uist.

The only access to this broch was a chain of stepping stones which were always covered by the sea even at low tide. Sheumus pursued Hugh to North Uist and besieged Hugh in Dun-a-Sticir. Hugh and his band of conspirators had had no time to prepare for a siege and were soon running out of provisions. They were only kept supplied by the efforts of an old woman, who would bring them a sack of corn on dark moonless nights. One night she stayed too long and Hugh was seen as he helped her back over the hidden stones.

---

[19] See chapter 6.

Dun-a-Sticir

Sheumus led his party in an immediate assault on Dun-a-Sticir and the broch was soon in his hands. All Hugh's men were captured but there was no sign of Hugh himself. Sheumus came across an old woman grinding corn, and judging by her powerful frame suspected that it was Hugh in disguise. Sheumus resorted to a ruse to see if the figure was all that she appeared to be. He threw a piece of bread for her to catch, the old woman having both her hands occupied brought her legs together to catch the bread. The dresses of highland women in the sixteenth century were long and voluminous and they always caught objects by pushing their legs apart so that the object was caught in the folds of their dress. Sheumus's suspicions were reinforced and he ordered his men to seize the old woman, Hugh who was a tall man with a powerful frame put up a severe struggle before he was overcome. He was bound hand and foot and taken Sheumus's galley. Sheumus sailed with his captive for Skye and the castle of Duntulm which by the end of the sixteenth century was the principal residence of the chiefs of the MacDonalds of Sleat.

Duntulum Castle

When Hugh was bought before Donald Gorm Mor he was grimly thanked for his invitation and was told that it was he who would be the guest of his chief. After this charged meeting Hugh was cast into the dungeon in the bowels of the castle. There is a tradition in Skye that Hugh was kept for several days without food before being given a large portion of beef and a flagon of water. Hugh ravenously devoured the beef which he found very salty, he then reached for the flagon which to his dismay he found was empty. Hugh suffered a slow and agonizing death while the object of his vindictive hatred led the clan just a few feet above him. On occasion, as Hugh lingered in his dungeon he would have heard the sounds of the clan feasting and dancing in the hall above him. Hugh's despair and agony of thirst was demonstrated some years later when the dungeon was opened to show a large skeleton grasping a pewter flagon which was completely distorted by Hugh in his death throws.

Hugh's bones were removed from Duntulum and taken to the local parish church of Kilmuir. Here Hugh's remains were exposed on the window ledges of the church. This act of vengeance by Donald Gorm Mor was no doubt to act as a salutary reminder to the congregation, or any curious passersby, as to the fate of traitors and the power of "pit and gallows" that the chiefs held over their people.

Hugh's bones lay for over a century on the window ledges as objects of curiosity to the people of Trotternish until eventually in 1827 his bones were interred in the graveyard. Hugh, who was known by the local people as Mac Mallach Chloim

Uisdean (the great devil of Clan Uisdean), had in his life cast a long shadow over the stability of his clan's hierarchy, but his actions had also caused grief and suffering to the common people. It was they that suffered the casualties in the feud with the MacLeans (that Hugh had caused) and the terrible poverty brought about by the cruelty of his administration of Trotternish.

The death of Hugh took place at the dawn of the seventeenth century, and within a few years the feuds of his clan, for example, with the MacLeods of Harris over Trotternish, were only to find expression at the court of the Kings of Scotland or as part of a national struggle. The most striking example of this was the vengeance wrecked by Alistair MacDonald on the Campbells, during the civil war, for what he regarded as the usurpation of the lands of Clan Iain Mor. The authority of the chiefs of the MacDonalds of Sleat increased dramatically at the turn of the seventeenth century and this combined with the rise in power of both the Campbells and the Scottish state left no place for characters like Archibald Dubh and Hugh Gilleasbuig to commit such open acts of piracy, treachery and murder. The seventeenth century was to see the MacDonalds of Sleat emerge as one of the successful clans of the MacDonalds while other older and more senior branches were swept away.[20] The characters of the chiefs of the MacDonalds of Sleat were forged in the fire of internal treachery and feuding. Without being brought up in this hard school would they have had the grim determination to overcome all the adversity of the clan's desperate situation and then go on to successfully steer their people through the dangers of the next two centuries?

---

[20] For example, the MacIains of Ardnamurchan and the Clan Iain Mor.

THE MACDONALDS OF KEPPOCH TO 1729

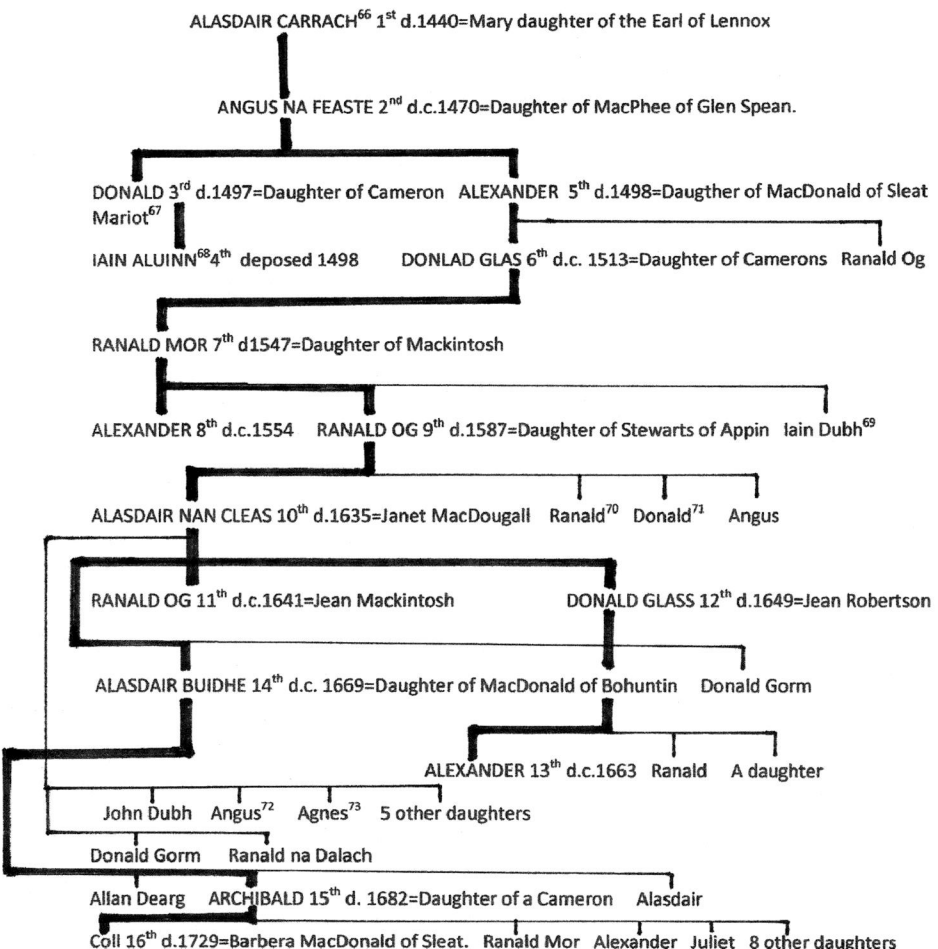

ALASDAIR CARRACH[66] 1st d.1440=Mary daughter of the Earl of Lennox

ANGUS NA FEASTE 2nd d.c.1470=Daughter of MacPhee of Glen Spean.

DONALD 3rd d.1497=Daughter of Cameron   ALEXANDER 5th d.1498=Daugther of MacDonald of Sleat
Mariot[67]

IAIN ALUINN[68]4th deposed 1498   DONLAD GLAS 6th d.c. 1513=Daughter of Camerons   Ranald Og

RANALD MOR 7th d1547=Daughter of Mackintosh

ALEXANDER 8th d.c.1554   RANALD OG 9th d.1587=Daughter of Stewarts of Appin   Iain Dubh[69]

ALASDAIR NAN CLEAS 10th d.1635=Janet MacDougall   Ranald[70]   Donald[71]   Angus

RANALD OG 11th d.c.1641=Jean Mackintosh   DONALD GLASS 12th d.1649=Jean Robertson

ALASDAIR BUIDHE 14th d.c. 1669=Daughter of MacDonald of Bohuntin   Donald Gorm

ALEXANDER 13th d.c.1663   Ranald   A daughter

John Dubh   Angus[72]   Agnes[73]   5 other daughters

Donald Gorm   Ranald na Dalach

Allan Dearg   ARCHIBALD 15th d. 1682=Daughter of a Cameron   Alasdair

Coll 16th d.1729=Barbera MacDonald of Sleat.   Ranald Mor   Alexander   Juliet   8 other daughters

---

[66] Alasdair Carrach was the fourth son of John 1st Lord of the Isles.

[67] Mariot married Allan Cameron of Locheil.

[68] Iain Alluin was the great great grandfather of the famous poet Iain Lom.

[69] Iain Dubh's descendants are the MacDonalds of Bohuntin and seven other cadet branches of Keppoch MacDonalds.

[70] Ranald's descendants are the MacDonalds of Inch.

[71] Donald's descendants are the MacDonalds of Fersit.

[72] Angus's descendants are the MacDonalds of Achnancoichean.

[73] Agnes married a Robertson of Struan while the others married into local clans.

Chapter 8

By the Strong Arm

The MacDonalds of Keppoch are descended from Alastair Carrach (the warty). Alastair Carrach was the fourth son of John first Lord of the Isles, he settled in Lochaber in the later fourteenth century. The Keppoch lands of Lochaber formed part of the patrimony of the Lords of the Isles. Lochaber had belonged to the MacDougals; they lost control over the district during the upheavals of the Bruce/Balliol dispute in the early fourteenth century.[1] Bruce gifted Lochaber to his loyal supporter Angus Og, the father of John first Lord of the Isles.

Alastair Carrach settled his Keppoch lands with his own extended family and other supporters from the isles. It is likely that some of the original inhabitants threw in their lot with the MacDonalds and were assimilated by changing their name or becoming an identifiable sept of the clan.[2] Alastair quickly established a powerful clan and is described as "Magnificus vir et potens" in a deed of 1398. Even allowing for a degree of hyperbole he had made extraordinary progress in no more than fifteen years.

The clan lands were to the east of Loch Lochy and included Glen Roy, but the pivotal territory was Glen Spean. This glen was one of the ancient routes which connected Badenoch and ultimately the Scottish east coast with the southern end of the Great Glen and from there to the western highlands. Glen Spean was used continually by the clan hosts to invade the central highlands and even the east coast and central lowlands. It provided the MacDonalds with quick easy access to unsuspecting victims when they set out to "lift" some cattle. However the glen's pivotal position was a two-edged sword for the Keppoch MacDonalds. They were the most exposed to reprisals of all the MacDonald clans after they had joined their cousins in supporting the Lords of the Isles or the later claimants to the Lordship in their continual clashes with Scottish authority. Their clan territories were also easily accessible to clans who opposed the Lords of the Isles, like the Frasers and MacKenzies. In the sixteenth and seventeenth century there was a long lasting feud between the MacDonalds of Keppoch and the MacKintoshes in which both clans used Glen Spean in their continual raiding.

---

[1] See chapter two.
[2] Septs were separate identifiable families who, although an integral part of a clan retained their own family names. One possible early example of this amongst the Keppoch MacDonalds was the Philipsons.

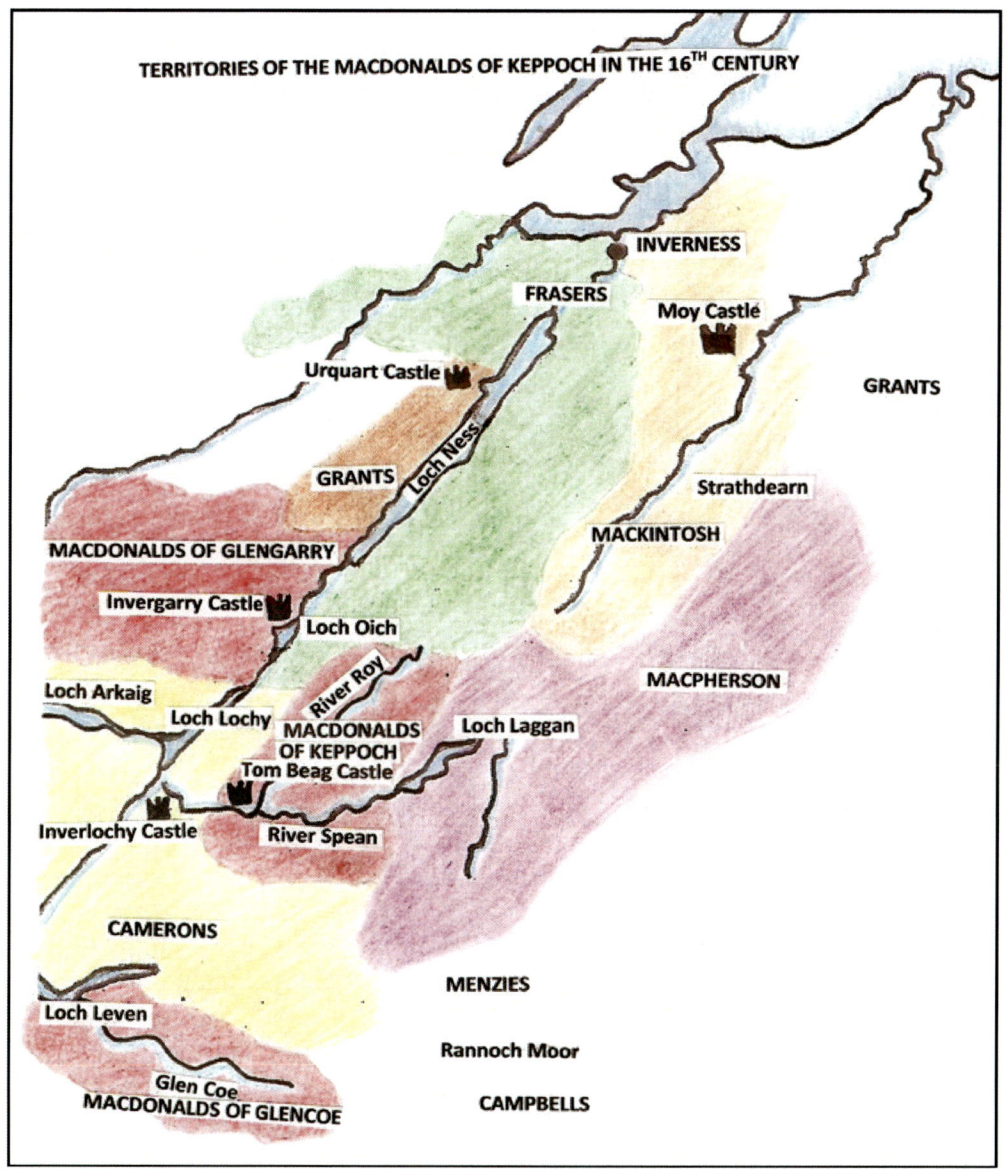

TERRITORIES OF THE MACDONALDS OF KEPPOCH IN THE 16TH CENTURY

INVERNESS

FRASERS

Moy Castle

Urquart Castle

GRANTS

GRANTS

Loch Ness

Strathdearn

MACDONALDS OF GLENGARRY

MACKINTOSH

Invergarry Castle

Loch Oich

River Roy

MACPHERSON

Loch Arkaig

Loch Lochy MACDONALDS
OF KEPPOCH Loch Laggan

Tom Beag Castle

Inverlochy Castle River Spean

CAMERONS

MENZIES

Loch Leven

Rannoch Moor

Glen Coe
MACDONALDS OF GLENCOE CAMPBELLS

Alastair Carrach's great grandson Donald Glas built a stronghold at a place called Tom Beag, where the rivers Roy and Spean meet. To-day there are only a few mounds to show where the old castle was, although the beautiful surroundings and the babble of the rivers is unchanged. Until the early nineteenth century the fruit trees of their old garden continued to blossom and bear fruit.

Tom Beag Castle

The MacDonalds of Keppoch supported the Lords of the Isles in all their struggles, and later were active in every attempt to restore it. They supported the Clan Iain Mor (the MacDonalds of Isla), in their struggles in Ireland and against the MacLeans. Despite enormous risks[3] they maintained their alliance with the Clan Iain Mor till the bitter end against the Campbells. The MacDonalds of Keppoch were the most loyal of all of the branches of their family to other clans of MacDonalds.

Alastair Carrach was with his brother Donald second Lord of the Isles at the bloody field of Harlaw in 1411. After another confrontation between Alexander third Lord of the Isles and royal authority, the island lord was forced to surrender and was subsequently imprisoned. Donald Balloch raised an island host and encountered the royal army at Inverlochy.[4] The description of the role of the MacDonalds of Keppoch during the battle offers some useful insights into their early battle tactics. "Alistair Carrach took possession of the hill above the enemy with two hundred and twenty archers, being unable by the smallness of his number to face the enemy,... As the combatants faced one another Alastair Carrach and his

---

[3] They were intermittently bound by "manrent" agreements with the Campbells who were their feudal superiors, and their near neighbours.
[4] See chapter 2.

archers poured down the brow of the hill..... and shot their arrows so thick on the flank of the royal army as to compel them to give way."

Throughout their history clans fought as distinctive units, so it is safe to assume that these two hundred and twenty archers were Alastair Carrach's clansmen. It is possible that this description of Inverlochy shows that the MacDonalds of Keppoch were specialists with the bow and arrow at this date. If we assume that Alastair could raise two hundred and twenty men then the entire population of the MacDonalds of Keppoch in the mid-fifteenth century would have been in the order of one thousand souls.

For his support of Donald Balloch, Alastair Carrach was declared a rebel and his lands were forfeit. These lands were granted to the MacKintoshes, in recognition of their services to the crown during its previous encounter with Alexander third Lord of the Isles. The MacKintoshes, along with the Camerons had deserted Alexander's standard and gone over to the Royal army. These defections had left Alexander unable to resist and forced him to surrender.

Alexander was released soon after the Battle of Inverlochy, and in 1443 issued a charter which was to have a profound impact on the MacDonalds of Keppoch. In this charter he confirms MacKintosh in possession of the lands of Lochaber, describing MacKintosh as "pro fideli servitor nobis". The medieval Latin allows for several differing translations, however the most likely approximation might be " our noble and faithful servant";[5] from a MacDonald perspective this is hardly a description which fits the chief of the MacKintoshes after their defection at the Battle of Inverlochy. Alexander had gifted the lands of his loyal uncle and his own people to a clan which had deserted him and were partly responsible for his abject surrender to Royal authority.

This perverse decision is hard to explain. Alexander may have taken a judgment that the support of the MacDonalds of Keppoch could be taken for granted and that the gift of the Lochaber lands would strengthen the loyalty of the MacKintoshes to the Lordship. The MacKintoshes were a powerful eastern clan whose support Alexander may have considered essential in his attempts to gain control over the Earldom of Ross. They were closely related to the Clan Chattan confederacy that controlled Badenoch and had considerable influence with the Gordon Earls of Huntley.[6] It is also possible that Alexander was forced to grant these strategic glens to the MacKintoshes as a condition of his release. This gift left the MacDonalds of Keppoch with no legal title to their lands, and was to embroil them in a feud with the MacKintoshes which lasted for two hundred and fifty years.

---

[5] Mr. R. Gore-Andrews.
[6] The Gordon Earls had been appointed by James IV as Royal lieutenants of the North.

They successfully resisted all attempts by the MacKintoshes[7] to gain control over Lochaber and held their lands by the strong arm.[8]

Alasdair Carrach died in the 1440's; his son Angus now led the MacDonalds of Keppoch, and after his death in 1478 the clan was led by his eldest son Donald. Both Angus and Donald were loyal supporters of John fourth Lord of the Isles and supported every political and military attempt to maintain or restore the integrity of the Lordship. Donald led the Keppoch men during the campaigns of the ferocious Alexander of Lochalsh.[9] The MacDonalds of Keppoch are largely absent from the records of the time.[10] This was not because they were living quietly in Glen Spean, but as they had no legal title to their lands they were considered to be a "broken" clan and thus not worthy of any legal consideration.

In 1497 a complaint against Donald was lodged at the court in Elgin, for "violence, and slaughter and distrucione", by a certain William Dallas. Even at this early date the MacDonalds of Keppoch were ranging far and wide in their "creachs". Donald fled to the island of Rathlin,[11] and later placed himself under the protection of the Maclains of Ardnamurchan whose power and influence were expanding under the leadership of the ruthless John Brayach.[12]

Within a few months Donald had returned to Lochaber, and had resumed his depredations over a wide area of the central highlands. Donald raised his clan and led a large raid into Moray some eighty miles to the south east, While the clansmen were away, Glen Spean was invaded by the MacLarens of Balquihidder; the valley was stripped of all its cattle and goods. When Donald returned from his own raid he immediately led the Keppoch men in pursuit of the MacLarens. He intercepted them at the head of Loch Earn; there was a brief struggle before the MacLarens abandoned their plunder. Donald set out for home via ancient tracks which wound around the foot of Ben Dorian.

They had not gone far when they in their turn were confronted by a force of the Stewarts of Appin.[13] The Stewarts of Appin had been pursuing the MacLarens with a view to relieving them of their plunder. On seeing the exhausted condition of the Keppoch men the temptation to relieve them of their cattle was too great. The two

---

[7] These attempts were supported with varying degrees of enthusiasm by Edinburgh.

[8] The expression "by the strong arm" meant that they held their lands by force against all comers including those that had a legal right which would have been expressed in a document written on parchment.

[9] See chapter 2.

[10] An exception is a reference to an Alexander who was brother to Donald, who was on his way to join the Lochalsh rebellion with 240 MacDonalds of Keppoch when news reached him of the collapse of the rebellion.

[11] Rathlin is a small island off the coast of Ulster; it was occupied by the Clan Iain Mor and was used as a sanctuary by the MacDonalds for centuries.

[12] See chapter 4.

[13] The Stewarts of Appin were the neighbours of the MacDonalds of Keppoch and they were usually on friendly terms with each other.

clans were equally matched in numbers and courage, the encounter was brutal and merciless. The two chiefs, Donald of Keppoch and Dugall of Appin fought each other to the death. Each chief was supported by his attendant gentlemen, neither side asking for or receiving any quarter. Eventually the Stewarts of Appin were driven off, the MacDonalds held the field and their cattle. The bodies of Donald and Dugall were found lying together in a grim embrace.

One of the victorious Keppoch men known as Domhnall Ruadh Beag (Little Red Donald) seeing the two prostrate corpses noted that the Stewart chief was considerably taller than that of his own. He bent down and cut of Dugall's head, remarking that if Donald was at least his equal in life, he would be no less equal in death. While this tale of endemic raiding is of only local historical significance it does demonstrate that as early as 1497 the authority of the Lordship had already lapsed in this part of its domain and the Crown was completely incapable of replacing it.

Donald was succeeded by his only son Iain Aluinn (Handsome John). Iain Aluinn was destined to be chief of the MacDonalds of Keppoch for less than a year. He was deposed by the gentlemen of the clan when his character was shown to be unsuitable to being the "father" of his "children". Within a few weeks of becoming chief, Iain Aluinn received a demand from MacKintosh to surrender Domhnall Ruadh Beg, who apart from supporting his own clan; had been conducting his own unsanctioned raids on the MacKintoshes.

Iain Aluinn meekly handed over the recalcitrant Domhnall to the MacKintoshes with the only proviso that Domhnall's blood should not be spilt. MacKintosh circumnavigated this stipulation by hanging the unfortunate Domhnall. To the clan this supine surrender of Domhnall was an affront to every member's dignity. Domhnall's raids on the MacKintoshes were regarded as bringing not only wealth to the people but also prestige. As chief, Iain Aluinn's role was to uphold the honour of his people, the surrender of Domhnull, a hero amongst his clan, to a clan which was at feud with them over their lands was unforgivable.

The clan met and deposed Iain Aluinn as he was judged unfit to lead them. Iain Aluinn accepted the decision of his people with calmness. He retired to Urchair and lived out his life in peace.[14] His temperament was not suited to the proud and violent age in which he lived; no doubt he would have been more at home amongst the politicians of to-day. This episode has been described in some detail as it demonstrates a fundamental difference between Celtic and Feudal law. In the feudal system which was in place in lowland Scotland this type of relatively democratic deposition of a magnate on the grounds of his unsuitability would have been unthinkable.

---

[14] Iain Aluinn's descendents lived in Lochaber for many generations, they were known as Slochd a Bhrathair bu Shine (Family of the Elder Brother). The famous poet Iain Lom was one of Iain Aluinn's descendents.

The MacDonalds of Keppoch were then divided into three strands of opinion. The most powerful sept,[15] who believed that they were related to the MacNeills of Barra, proposed that the son of the MacNeill chief should lead them. Another sept were descended from a branch of the MacDonalds of North Uist,[16] they wanted a member of this family to become chief. The majority of the clan were in favour of Iain Aluinn's uncle Alasdair, who was Donald's brother. The clan eventually settled the dispute in favour of Alasdair; Iain Aluinn's descendents were permanently barred from assuming the chiefship. This example of a clan electing a new chief who was the uncle of the chief who was disposed is known as Tanistry; under this law it was possible for the uncle's descendents to inherit the chiefship. If this happened they were called The Tanist or Captain. The most famous example of Tannistry was the election of John Moydartach to the chiefship of the Clanranald.[17]

Within a few months Alasdair[18] was killed while raiding the Camerons. He was ambushed while returning with his spoils; the place where he fell being ever after known as Carn Alasdair.

Donald Glas succeeded his father to the chiefship. The violence and insecurity of this period is amply demonstrated by the fact that Donald Glas was the fourth chief of the MacDonalds of Keppoch in less than three years. Donald Glas exhibited a more politically astute character than his predecessors. Soon after becoming chief he entered into bonds of mutual security with the Grants and Munros in an attempt to stabilize the situation after the anarchy caused by the rebellion of Alexander of Lochalsh.

In 1500, Alexander, Lord Gordon, became the feudal superior to the Keppoch lands; this over lordship replaced that of the Lordship of the Isles which had fallen six years earlier. Donald Glas ignored demands by Alexander for crown rents. This failure to acknowledge the superiority of the Gordons may well explain why a devastating raid was carried out by the Clan Chattan (who had feudal obligations to the Dukes of Gordon) on Glen Spean. This raid took place within a few months of Gordon assuming the superiority. The Clan Chattan were closely associated with Gordon interests at this period. They devastated Glen Spean acting as the agents of the Gordons. This view is supported by the fact that two of the ringleaders[19] were pardoned within a few weeks of the raid.

Donald Glas avoided embroiling his clan in the first rebellion of Donald Dubh,[20] and eventually secured a form of legal tenure to the lands of Keppoch from Alexander Gordon. This was achieved in the face of fierce opposition from the MacKintoshes who had their own charters to Keppoch. Donald Glas died in 1513.

---

[15] The Clan Mhic Ghillemhantich.
[16] The Clan Godfrey, who were descended from Godfrey, who was the third son of John first Lord of the Isles and his first wife Aimie MacRuari.
[17] See chapter 3.
[18] Alasdair was known by his people as Alastair nan Gleann (of the Glens).
[19] Gillies MacPhail and Patrick MacBane.
[20] See chapter 2.

He had a better understanding of the political landscape of his time than his predecessors or indeed of many of the chiefs who were to come after him. He had established some legal right to the clan lands and had helped them avoid the consequences of the rebellion of Donald Dubh.

He was succeeded by his son Ranald Mor, as seventh chief of the MacDonalds of Keppoch. Ranald is described in an early Gaelic poem as being blessed by a keen intellect and a courageous heart. Ranald Mor's life was intimately bound up with the great feud between the Clanranald and the Frasers.[21] He was a close and loyal ally to the great John Moydartach through triumph and adversity, ultimately paying for this alliance with his life. Ranald mustered his clan, and led them at the bloody field of Kinlochlochy.

After John Moydartach had been forced to retreat into the fastness of Morar by a punitive expedition led by the Gordons, Ranald was captured by MacKintosh and handed over to the Gordon Earl.[22] Ranald and Ewen Cameron were both imprisoned at the royal castle of Ruthven; they were then transported to Elgin. At Elgin they and some of their clansmen were tried for complicity in the slaughter of Lord Lovat. Both chiefs were found guilty and beheaded in 1547; their heads were to remain on spikes above the town gates for several years. The MacDonalds of Keppoch held the MacKintoshes responsible for the death of Ranald; their resentment was further fuelled by the fact that MacKintosh had made his own sister a widow.[23] The "justifying" of Ranald was enough to keep the flame of hatred burning brightly between the MacDonalds of Keppoch and the MacKintoshes.

Ranald was succeeded by his son Alastair. It was a custom amongst the clans that when a young man assumed the chiefship of his clan that he should lead a large scale raid on a neighbouring clan. This was designed to demonstrate the new chief's courage and ability in war. Alastair mustered his clansmen and swept through the fertile lands of Urquhart and Strathardle.

The usually friendly relationship between the MacDonalds of Keppoch and the Camerons broke down during the chiefship of Alastair. The reasons for this violent feud have been lost; the continual raiding of cattle by the clans is the most likely cause. In the winter of 1554 the Camerons invaded Glen Spean with a large force, burning and plundering as they advanced into the heart of Keppoch. Alastair retreated in the face of this sudden onslaught gathering his men. When he had the whole might of his clan assembled he faced the enemy at Bohenie behind Mulroy. The two clan armies rushed upon each other with great enthusiasm. Each clan fought with bravery and stubbornness. Casualties on both sides were heavy and the conflict was prolonged and murderous. Eventually the leader of the Camerons (the chief's son) was killed and they retreated back to their own lands of Loch Eil.

---

[21] See chapter 3.

[22] The Earls of Gordon were the King's Lieutenants in the North, and therefore represented Royal authority.

[23] Ranald's wife was Agnes Mackintosh sister to William Mackintosh chief of his clan.

Alastair was severely wounded and relinquished control of the clansmen to his brother John Dubh of Bohuntin who pursued the Camerons to the shores of Loch Lochy. The chronicle of Fortingall describes this feud; " Ewyn son of McEwin of Lochiel... abyr waryth againis Alexander of Keppoch.... Glas quhen mony war slayn on ...sydis and boyth their cuntries bryint."

The badly wounded Alastair was carried to a well known herbalist who lived at Kingussie, Alastair died shortly after being treated by the wise woman. There was a suspicion that due to some grudge she deliberately poisoned his wounds. No doubt Alastair's men insured that she soon followed the same road as her patient.

Ranald Og succeeded his brother as chief in 1554. Ranald Og's chiefship of the MacDonalds of Keppoch marks a significant break with the past. He developed a policy of co-operation with the Crown and his neighbours. For the first time the MacDonalds of Keppoch had a close and peaceable relationship with their Campbell neighbours.

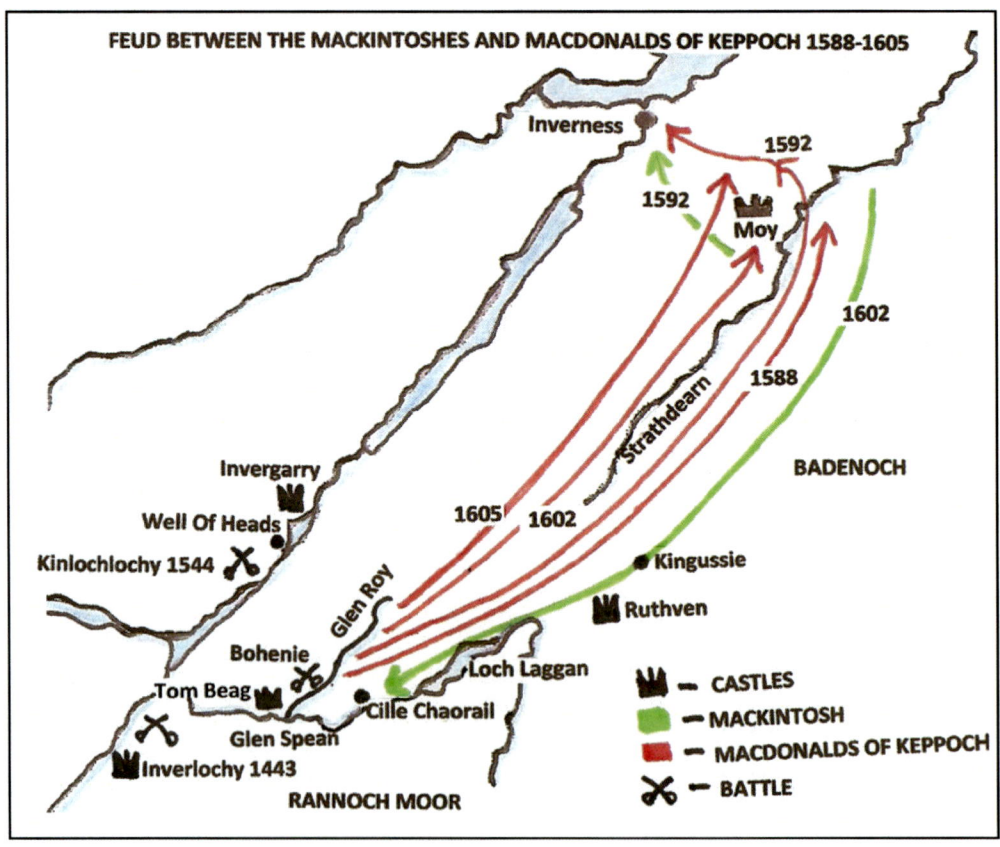

The nearest Campbell clan to the lands of Keppoch were the powerful Campbells of Glenorchy. The Lords of Glenorchy ruled their ever expanding possessions from their austere and impressive castle of Kilchurn. As the crow flies the two clans were in close proximity and at a superficial glance one may wonder why these two clans had had so little contact with each other. The reason why these two diametrically opposed clans, with their different histories and world view had not clashed lay in topography. They were isolated from each other by the high wastes of Rannoch Moor which formed a natural barrier between them.

In 1563 Ranald Og entered into a bond of manrent[24] with Colin Campbell of Glenorchy. Apart from the usual vows of mutual support and friendship, Ranald Og agrees to occupy the ancient lands of the MacGregors in Rannoch. Ranald agreed to cultivate the wastes, to make his principal residence there and to have no communication with the MacGregors. Ranald Og had calculated that with the help of the Campbells he would be able to deal with any recalcitrant MacGregors and expand his clan lands considerably.

The Children of the Mist, as the MacGregors were known; were having none of it. They were determined to resist any encroachment on their ancient patrimony by either the Campbells or the MacDonalds. Their hit and run tactics soon reduced Rannoch to a wasteland of destroyed clachans and burnt fields. The situation deteriorated to such an extent that Ranald Og MacDonald and Colin Campbell were issued with a joint commission of "fire and sword" against the MacGregors. Clan politics was nothing if not pragmatic, and although history is more palatable if seen as a series of black and white events, here we have Campbell and MacDonald hunting down The Children of the Mist with equal zeal.

The MacGregors clearly put up their usual stubborn and violent resistance to this encroachment. Six years later there is another agreement between Ranald Og and Colin Campbell in which the former renounces any claim to the lands of Rannoch.

Ranald even agreed to submit his clan's interests in their ancient lands to the arbitration of the Regent, Moray. Relying on the fact that he was now in favour with the authorities he gambled that he could obtain a favourable judgment in his dispute with MacKintosh over Glen Spean. Moray's arbitration was successful and Ranald and MacKintosh signed a bond of manrent which apart from the usual avowals of mutual support seemed to settle the long running dispute over the Keppoch lands. Ranald agreed to become MacKintosh's tenant on condition that his clan had legal security of tenure. When Ranald died in 1587 he had given his clan a generation of much needed peace. His failure to secure new territory in Rannoch was outweighed by his success in establishing the clan's legal right to their lands.

Ranald's son Alasdair nan Cleas (of the Tricks),[25] was made from entirely different clay. Alasdair soon found himself embroiled in the feud between the Gordon Earls of Huntley and the Earls of Moray. As the sixteenth century wore on

---

[24] These manrent agreements were used widely by the Campbells in the sixteenth century to create a series of agreements with other clans in which there was mutual support. They were a subtle way of expressing growing Campbell power and influence.
[25] Reputedly for his sleight of hand and his dexterity with cards.

clan relationships were becoming more complex; clan alliances and feuds encompassed a wider area with regional and even national implications. Huntley and Moray were feuding over not only personal matters but also their influence over vast tracts of the eastern highlands. Moray encouraged Huntley's vassals, the MacKintoshes and Grants to break away from his control. Huntley then called for the support of the Camerons and MacDonalds of Keppoch to put pressure on the MacKintoshes and Grants. Alasdair nan Cleas agreed to support Huntley. His motives were to weaken the MacKintosh hold over his lands, and it is also likely that Alasdair received a payment from Huntley.

The MacDonalds of Keppoch and the Camerons swept through the lands of the Grants and MacKintoshes with fire and sword. A Royal Commission empowered Huntley, MacKintosh and Grant to invade the lands of the MacDonalds and Camerons in retaliation. Huntley, of course, protected his allies by thwarting the efforts of the MacKintoshes and Grants. It is remarkable how ignorant the Royal Commission was of the relationship between Huntley and his allies, the MacDonalds and Camerons.

In January 1589 Alasdair nan Cleas and Lachlan MacKintosh patched up a truce between the two clans; the basis of which was that Alasdair should hold his lands as a permanent tenant of Lachlan. With the death of the Earl of Moray in early 1592 the central and eastern highlands were again engulfed in violence and anarchy. The MacKintoshes and Grants as supporters of the Earls of Moray swept down on the Gordon lands destroying everything in their path.

Alasdair nan Cleas mustered his own clan and fell upon the Grants. The MacDonalds set fire to houses, destroyed the grain stores and drove the cattle to Glen Spean; any resistance was brutally dealt with.[26] Alasdair led his men through the MacKintosh country again burning, killing and plundering. He entered Inverness, stormed the castle and held it for Huntley. Alasdair was soon besieged by the MacKintoshes. After a short siege he was forced to surrender due to a lack of provisions. He was allowed to return to Lochaber, although two of the clan were hung for their crimes during this raid.[27]

The raiding and counter raiding continued with unabated fury. Eventually the Government were forced to intervene. A commission of fire and sword was issued to the Frasers, MacKintoshes and Grants against the MacDonalds of Keppoch and the Camerons. Alasdair was accused of being "gilty of opin and manifest oppressioun, murther, slauchter, soirning, theft, and resseit thairof, and otheris odious and capitall crymes".

Clearly Alasdair had been giving full reign to his violent and restless disposition. The powerful combination of Frasers, Grants and MacKintoshes was shortly augmented by another commission which was issued to the Earl of Angus. The

---

[26] When Alasdair moved on to the MacKintosh country he left eighteen Grant clansmen dead.
[27] One of the MacDonalds who were executed was Gorrie Dubh, Alastair's brother.

raiding by the MacDonalds and Camerons seems to have continued till at least 1593,[28] the efforts of the Royal Commission being rendered ineffectual by the inability of the eastern clans to penetrate Lochaber.

Alasdair was next involved in the rebellion of the Earls of Huntley, Errol and Angus in their attempt to restore Catholicism in Scotland.[29] He led his clan at the Battle of Glenlivet where the Earl of Argyle, acting as the King's lieutenant was defeated. Despite this defeat the forces of the reformation were successful in crushing the rebellion. Alasdair was forced to make his peace with the Earl of Argyle. The manrent agreement took the usual form in which both parties bound themselves to mutually supporting each other against all foes excepting only the King and their own kinsmen. There were a series of special conditions attached to this agreement which emphasise the dominance of Argyle in this relationship. Alasdair gave his younger son, Angus, as a hostage,[30] Alasdair was to travel under safe conduct to Inveraray to wait upon the Earl on or before Christmas 1595. It also stated that if the Earl regarded it necessary Alasdair was also to surrender his eldest son, Ranald, as a hostage.

This bond of manrent was clearly regarded by Alastair as a matter of expediency. As soon as the Gordon Earl returned from banishment in 1598, Alasdair re-affirmed his clan's allegiance to him. Later in the same year Alastair joined Sir James MacDonald's rebellion in Kintyre.[31] It is clear that the feud between the MacDonalds of Keppoch and the MacKintoshes continued to erupt in outbreaks of violence. In April 1602 the Commissary of Inverness[32] raised letters against Alastair and the Privy Council duly pronounced Alastair a rebel, as he was held responsible for his brothers[33] raiding and fire-raising at Moy. In the spring of 1602 the central highlands were in the grip of endemic raiding as along with Alasdair, the Gordons, MacDonalds of Glengarry, the MacGregors and the MacKintoshes were also pronounced rebels. Alasdair's response to the Privy Council was to lead his clansmen in a large raid on the MacKintosh lands of Strathardale.

The Privy Council responded to this defiance of its authority by ordering the Earl of Huntley to capture Alasdair and his brothers and to "exhibit" them in Edinburgh. It is remarkable that at this late date (the summer of 1604) there was still such anarchy in this relatively accessible region of the highlands. The Privy Council demonstrated a complete failure to understand the true political situation when they ordered the Earl of Gordon to apprehend Alasdair, who was, at least in part,

---

[28] In March 1593, Rose of Kilravock sought assurances from Alasdair that his lands would not be attacked.

[29] The MacDonalds of Keppoch were staunchly catholic during this period.

[30] It was stipulated that Angus was only to be held by a Campbell gentleman.

[31] Sir James's rebellion in Kintyre was a last desperate attempt to prevent the lands of the Clan Iain Mor's lands being overrun by the Campbells.

[32] John Campbell.

[33] Donald Glass and Ranald.

acting as an ally of the Gordons. It will come as no surprise that Alasdair was never captured and "exhibited" by the Earl of Gordon.

The Privy Council, having realized that the Earl of Gordon would make no serious attempt to apprehend Alasdair, ordered Alasdair to appear before Lord Scone in the summer of 1605. They demanded that he pay his Royal rents, which were predictably in arrears, and present the charters by which he held his lands. Alasdair failed to appear and was declared a rebel. The reason why Alasdair chose to defy the Privy Council was that, apart from the lands of Gargavach,[34] Alasdair had no legal title to his lands although his clan had been settled in Glen Spean for two hundred years. Calculating that he had little to lose, Alasdair plunged into an orgy of raiding and fire-raising. He led his clan in raids in Strathardle and Glenshee, even burning the house of the Commissary in Inverness. He then led the men of Keppoch on an extensive raid into Athol where a number of tenants of the Duke of Athol were slaughtered.

The anarchy of the central highlands during the early seventeenth century created an environment which led to an overriding need for self-interest. It was not a world of absolute moral right, each clan was attempting to maintain its position and to add to its power by any means possible. The clans used whatever instruments were available to them in their struggle for survival. Even the expansion of the Campbells, however sinister from their victims perspective, was only unique because of its scale, subtlety, and its relentless success for generation after generation under able chiefs.

Alasdair now became involved in an event which places him in a less than heroic light. For centuries the MacGregors had been gradually dispossessed of their ancient lands by various branches of the Campbells. They had bitterly resisted this encroachment by all means available to them. This violence had bought down further retribution both from the Campbells and the Scottish state. Eventually the MacGregors became a broken clan, the description; The Children of the Mist, now seemed to be particularly apposite.

A group of MacGregors had fled over Rannoch Moor and were hiding at a place near Tirnadrish only two miles from Alasdair's castle at Keppoch. Alastair gathered his men and attacked the unsuspecting MacGregors, a few managed to escape but most were killed. There was no love lost between the MacDonalds of Keppoch and the MacGregors since the dispute over possession of Rannoch Moor some fifty years before, in the time of Alastair's father Ranald Og. Alistair could not allow a hostile clan to settle in the heart of his clan's territory.

On the face of it, his actions seem entirely reasonable but there is evidence that Alasdair had more than the interests of his clan at heart. The MacGregors were fugitives and probably had no intention to settle permanently. For his services against the proscribed MacGregors Alasdair was paid £100 by the Government.[35]

---

[34] Gargavach was held on lease from Huntley.

[35] Records of the Privy Seal.

Alasdair was himself often under sentence of rebellion and it is remarkable that Alasdair should be paid "blood money" by the state for slaughtering a few hapless MacGregor fugitives. There is indeed the strong suspicion that Alasdair was in effect a bounty hunter on this occasion. This sorry episode is above all an indictment of the weakness and cruelty of the Scottish state even at this late date in a relatively accessible part of the highlands.

In 1615 Alasdair and Donald of Clanranald helped Sir James MacDonald to escape from Edinburgh Castle. Alasdair led his clansmen in support of Sir James's last desperate attempts to preserve some vestiges of the ancient patrimony of the Clan Iain Mor.[36] After the failure of the rebellion Alasdair fled to the western isles before eventually returning to Glen Spean. The Government placed a bounty of 5000 merks on his head; the reward would be paid for his capture whether dead or alive. The task of apprehending Alasdair was given to the Duke of Gordon who again made little effort to capture Alasdair. A second commission was given to Gordon and his son with the threat that there would be grave consequences if they failed to capture Alasdair. Alasdair's wife, Janet MacDougal was expressly forbidden to have any contact with her husband. This time the Privy Council was in deadly earnest and eventually Alasdair had to flee to Spanish Netherlands (Belgium) where he joined Sir James MacDonald in exile.

Alasdair returned to London in 1620 where he was pardoned by King James for his past offences and received a considerable pension from the King for some valuable services he had rendered the King while in the Spanish Netherlands.[37] Despite the objections of the Privy Council who described Alasdair as "a man whose bipast lyffe and conversatioun hes bene so lewde and violent in bloode, thift, reafe, and oppressioun that to this hour he never randerit obeydeyence", he was eventually allowed to return to his clan in Lochaber. In his old age Alasdair lived peacefully amongst his people,[38] he died in 1635, having led his clan for forty eight years. Alasdair belonged to the ancient tradition of highland chiefs which was becoming something of an anachronism by the early seventeenth century. Despite all his wild raiding and feuding and his loyal support of the Clan Iain Mor in its death agonies he maintained the MacDonalds of Keppoch in their ancient lands of

---

[36] See chapter 12.

[37] Alasdair had sent James detailed information on a proposed Spanish invasion of the British Isles.

[38] Alasdair learnt many conjuring tricks while in Spain and was described as "nan Cleas" or "of the tricks". On his return to London he was entertained by a wealthy Englishman who remarked that Alasdair could not match his sumptuous plate especially his giant candlesticks. Alasdair claimed that he had far superior candlesticks in Lochaber, and persuaded his host to bet three times their value that this was not the case. When the Englishman was a guest of Alasdair's he asked to see the candlesticks. Alasdair called in twelve clansmen each holding a flaming torch. Alasdair won his bet; this quick witted opportunism was a mark of this remarkable man.

Glen Spean and Glen Roy. He was buried in the churchyard of Cille Chaorail the ancient burial place of the MacDonalds of Keppoch.

Cille Chaorail

Alasdair was succeeded by his eldest son Ranald Og who became eleventh chief of the MacDonalds of Keppoch. Ranald had been involved with his father in the escape and rebellion of Sir James MacDonald. Instead of following his father to the Spanish Netherlands he hid on Lochtrieg side and evaded the best efforts of MacKintosh to capture him. After his father's return and pardon the charges against Ranald were also dropped. Ranald adopted a very different policy to his father; from a letter to Grant of Freuchie it is clear that he attempted to end the feud with the MacKintoshes. The letter is dated 1623 and in it Ranald asks that relations between himself and Grant should improve especially as he had even managed to make his peace with MacKintosh. The late 1630's were years of unusual peace and tranquilly for the MacDonalds of Keppoch. These happy years were ended by the maelstrom of the Civil War. Ranald was a fervent supporter of the King and called out all his clansmen to join Montrose's campaign. These actions led to Ranald incurring the wrath of Grim faced Archie the Campbell Earl of Argyle. In 1640 the Campbells invaded Lochaber they burnt Ranald's castle of Tom Beag and stripped Lochaber bare. Archibald left a garrison of two hundred men, the Campbells were relentlessly attacked by the MacDonalds of Keppoch; most were killed, the rest fled over Rannoch Moor to Argyle. There is no further mention of Ranald after 1640 and it is clear he died before 1641. Had Ranald not been embroiled in the Civil War it is probable that he would have been able to give his clan a generation of peace.

Ranald was succeeded by his brother Donald Glass, who commanded the MacDonalds of Keppoch during the campaigns of Montrose. Donald Glass led his clansmen at the Battle of Inverlochy in which the military power of the Campbells was temporarily destroyed. Donald Glass later joined Alastair MacColla in his devastation of the Campbell lands in Argyle. While the men of Keppoch were away campaigning with Montrose the lands of Keppoch were subjected to counter raiding by the Campbells. When the men of Keppoch and Glencoe returned from the royalist campaign laden with their own spoils they found their lands ravaged and the women and children living in destitution.

Under the leadership of Angus Og of Achnancoichean the MacDonalds of Keppoch and Glencoe made a sudden descent on the lands of the Campbells of Breadalbane, driving off a large herd of cattle. The Campbells were gathered for a wedding at Finlarig, they rushed to arms and immediately set out in pursuit. The Campbells intercepted the raiders at Stronachlachan. The wedding guests had been celebrating with gusto and as a consequence their fighting abilities were impaired. In the bloody encounter that followed the Campbells were heavily defeated leaving "32 of the laird's ablest tennentis and servands" lying on the field. The MacDonalds also suffered severely; the men of Glencoe lost their chief, Alasdair Ruadh, while the men from Keppoch lost their leader Angus Og.[39] Donald Glass survived the turbulent years of the civil war and died peacefully in bed in 1649.

Donald was succeeded by his brother Alistair Buidhe who acted as tutor to Donald's son Alexander, who was only a child at the time. Alistair Buidhe maintained the clan's tradition of royalism. He accompanied the Scottish army to Worcester where it was decisively defeated by Cromwell; he led his people through the difficult times of the protectorate and saw them safely into the time of the Restoration. He was succeeded by his nephew, Alexander, the eldest son of Donald Glass, when he came of age.

Alexander had been fostered on Skye under the protection of Sir James MacDonald of Sleat. Alexander and his brother had been sent to finish their education on the continent. Fostering was an ancient custom among the clans but educating the chief's sons abroad was a new fashion which aimed at increasing their knowledge of the wider world. In many cases the exposure to European ways merely emphasized the material poverty of life in the highlands and led many chief's sons to feel dissatisfied with their lot. This feeling of "otherness" was

---

[39] Angus Og's death was celebrated by Iain Lom in one of his great battle poems. In this poem Iain Lom compares himself to a tree stripped of its bark without sap or fruit, as he stood weeping beside the dying man. Ian Lom accompanied Donald Glass during the epic campaigns of Alistair MacColla.

allowed to gain in strength as the need for the clan to provide an army began to diminish. There was a widening gulf between the chief and his clan which was to lead to a breakdown in the cohesiveness of clan societies. This in its turn allowed the British state to exert greater influence in the highlands and further undermine Gaelic culture.

Alexander returned to his clan barely able to hide the contempt with which he regarded his "children". His own pride and arrogance and lack of traditional values deeply offended the clan. An early indication of his future conduct was given when Alasdair Budhe asked how he was to be rewarded for his tutorship of the clan. Alexander replied that the tutorship itself should be reward enough. With ominous deliberation Alasdair Budhe remarked, "if that is how it is, we shall remember you." Tension inside the clan built up with various factions forming around Alexander and Alasdair Budhe.

The MacDonalds of Inverlair, a sept of the MacDonalds of Keppoch, had taken a tenancy directly from the Duke of Gordon, Alexander was enraged as he felt that they had bypassed the traditional authority of the chief. He gathered some sixty adherents and attacked the MacDonalds of Inverlair. In his complaint put before the Privy Council in January 1662 MacDonald of Inverlair states that Alexander "to the number of sixty persons, all armed, came to the complainer's lands of Inverlair, and there having brocken up the doors, violently entered, destroyed and took away the plenishing, pulled down some houses, drove away his nolt, sheep, and horses, and the said Alexander MacDonald boasts that he shall route out the said complainer from his possession, and that before his heart is satisfied one of them two must die." Alexander failed to appear before the Privy Council and was subsequently declared a rebel.

There are two versions of the events that follow, the most plausible one is that the MacDonalds of Inverlair, supported by the sons of Alasdair Budhe murdered Alexander and his younger brother Ranald.[40] Alasdair Budhe was not directly involved in the murder, it is likely that he used the MacDonalds of Inverlair as instruments of revenge and that he was deeply implicated in the plot.

Alexander of Inverlair and his six sons along with Alastair Budhe's two sons broke into Keppoch Castle in the early hours of the fifth of September 1663. Once inside they cornered the unsuspecting Alexander and his brother Ranald, Alexander soon lay dead having being hacked to pieces by the Inverlairs. Ranald ran to one of his assailants and clinging to his legs begged him to save his life. He was however shown no mercy and his mutilated corpse soon lay next to his brother's.

In the morning the scene was visited by the famous poet of the clan, Iain Lom. The sight of his slaughtered chief inspired him to compose the poem "Mort na

---

[40] The other version places the blame for the murders on the descendents of Iain Aluinn, the deposed chief. It is possible that they had nursed a desire to re-establish the chiefship in their family. This version seems less plausible as the MacDonalds of Inverlair had a more immediate reason for desiring revenge.

Ceapaich" which describes the mutilated corpses and lays the blame firmly at the door of the MacDonalds of Inverlair. There was no general outcry among the clan at the murder of their chief which in itself is testament to the loathing which the clan had towards Alexander. The perpetrators of the murders met at Torran nam Mion (the Hillock of Oaths), in Glen Roy, and there swore on their dirks that they would not divulge their parts in the plot.

Iain Lom appealed to the clan for revenge of their murdered chief but his eloquence fell on deaf ears. Realizing that he would not be able to obtain redress from his own clan Iain Lom determined to seek it elsewhere. He first travelled to Invergarry Castle where he appealed to Angus Lord MacDonald and Aros ninth chief of the MacDonalds of Glengarry. At this time Angus was attempting to establish himself as the leader of Clan Donald, and Iain Lom calculated that interfering in the affairs of the MacDonalds of Keppoch might further his ambition. Angus turned down his request for intervention on the grounds that he did not wish to become embroiled in an internal feud of his neighbours.

The disconsolate poet then asked the MacKenzie Lord of Kintail for justice but was again refused. Iain Lom finally made his way to Skye and went to Duntulm Castle and received an audience with Sir James ninth chief of the MacDonalds of Sleat.

"Where do you come from?" asked Sir James.
"From Laodicea," came the reply.
"Are they hot or cold in that place?" asked Sir James.
"Abel is cold, and his blood is crying in vain for vengeance; but Cain is hot and red-handed, and hundreds around are lukewarm as the black goat's milk."

This piece of theatre was played out to add drama to the scene; both Iain Lom and Sir James would have been well prepared before the meeting. Sir James agreed to avenge the murdered Alexander and applied to the Privy Council for a commission of fire and sword.[41] Sir James appointed his brother Archibald[42] to lead a force of fifty men to enforce justice in the lands of Keppoch. Due to favourable winds the party made good progress and arrived in Lochaber after four days. News of their approach had preceded them to Keppoch; the conspirators retreated to Inverlair and barricaded the house. Alistair Budhe's sons fled Keppoch, one never to return. The other returned after a long exile.

The MacDonalds of Inverlair led by Alistair Ruadh put up a desperate defence against the attacks of the men of Sleat. They resisted all attempts to storm the house and many of the besiegers were killed. Eventually the house was set on fire

---

[41] By this date (June 1665) it was no longer possible for a chief to act independently of the power of the state in matters of feuding.
[42] Archibald who was better known as An Ciaran Mabach was also a poet and had to be summoned from his home on North Uist.

and the MacDonalds of Inverlair were forced to sortie from the house. Once in the open they were quickly cut down as they attempted to reach safety. Iain Lom cut off the heads of the murderers using the dirk which had been used to murder young Ranald, and then set out with his heavy burden to confront Angus of Glengarry. On his way he stopped at a well by the shore of Loch Oich where he washed the heads. This was a symbolic act of rebuke to Angus. The well was known afterwards as Tobair nan Ceann (the Well of Heads), and later a monument was erected here in memory of these events.

Well of Heads

There is no record of the meeting between Iain Lom and Angus but it would be reasonable to suppose that the old poet was unsparing in his use of words. The heads were sent to Edinburgh as evidence that for once a directive of the Privy Council had been carried out to the letter.

Alistair Budhe had assumed the chiefship after the murder of Alexander. Although many suspected that he was deeply implicated in the murder there was no proof. The fact that his leadership was not challenged by the clan demonstrates that they acquiesced to the murder of Alexander. The MacDonalds of Inverlair and the family of Alistair Budhe were unlucky in facing such a distinguished and eloquent opponent as Iain Lom, whose views were not supported by the majority of the clan. These bloody events are typical of an internal power struggle within a clan, what is remarkable about them is that they should take place at such a late date when even in the remote western isles these types of atrocities had not occurred for fifty years.

The long running feud between the MacDonalds of Keppoch and the MacKintoshes continued to erupt into violence. In September 1667 a raiding party of MacDonalds entered Glenesk and removed a large herd of cattle. Glenesk belonged to Lindsay of Edzell whose daughter had become MacKintosh's wife only a few weeks before. No doubt this raid was to demonstrate to Lindsay that he had acquired new enemies as well as allies from his recent marriage.

Lachlan Mor MacKintosh had recently come to terms with the Camerons over the disputed lands in Lochaber, he had also patched up the relationship between the MacKintoshes and the Clan Chattan. The neutrality of the Camerons and the support of the Clan Chattan (albeit luke warm), gave Lachlan Mor a uniquely favourable opportunity to successfully invade Keppoch. Despite attempts by the Gordons to deflect him he swept down on Keppoch and left the population utterly destitute.

Two years later Alistair Budhe was dead; his second son Archibald became the fifteenth chief of the MacDonalds of Keppoch. Alistair Budhe has gone down in history as the architect of the murder of his chief, his sons and allies (the MacDonalds of Inverlair) paying a full price for their involvement. The story of how Iain Lom sought justice for his murdered chief places the conspirators in a dark light, their fate seen as just retribution. Alexander's character was not suited to leading a clan which still adhered to the old ways and who deeply resented his open contempt for them. There are many examples of the enforced deposition of chiefs by their clan most of which were violent.[43] All the evidence suggests that Alistair Budhe had the support of the clan and had it not been for the determination of Iain Lom to seek justice for Alexander, the clan itself would have been content with the situation. Alistair Budhe survived as chief and his stance was ultimately rewarded by the fact that it was his progeny who were to become the future chiefs of Keppoch.

Archibald is described as a wise and resolute chief by the clan historians. He was also an accomplished poet, the poems of his early years are described as "masterpieces of wit and humour", while a more serious work which he wrote on his death bed is admired for its perceptive contemplation.[44] All of these characteristics were especially admired in Gaelic culture and as a consequence Archibald was much loved by his clan. During his first few years as chief it is clear that the MacDonalds of Keppoch were still cattle raiding far and wide.[45] Archibald was not directly responsible for these raids, although it seems likely they had his

---

[43] An example of this is the murder of Dougal of Clanranald who was judged to be unfit by the gentlemen of the clan. See chapter 3.

[44] The poem is to be found in MacDonald Collection of Gaelic Poetry.

[45] Some raids were carried out as far away as Perth.

tacit support. The chiefs of the MacDonalds of Sleat and Glengarry were ordered to stand surety for them, but they were unable to prevent the endemic raiding.

For several years after 1675 Archibald became embroiled in the last multi-clan feud between the MacLeans and the Campbells. The MacDonalds of Keppoch supported their cousins the MacDonalds of Sleat and Glengarry in their efforts to assist the MacLeans in defending Mull against the seemingly inexorable rise of Campbell power. This support resulted in Glen Roy and Glen Spean being devastated by the Campbell Earl of Breadalbane. In 1681 Archibald was forced to give his bond of manrent to the Earl by whom he pledged to become the Earl's man in exchange for his protection.

During these years the feud over possession of Glen Roy and Glen Spean with the MacKintoshes continued to simmer. In 1672 Lachlan Mor MacKintosh sued for a commission to eject the MacDonalds from Keppoch. The legal process faced endless delays, thanks in part to the representations of the Earl of Moray who did not wish to see MacKintosh power increase. After five years of delay MacKintosh decided to invade Keppoch without the legal issues being resolved. The invasion eventually came to nothing, MacKintosh was thwarted by the influence of the Gordons on some of his clansmen and by disputes with the Clan Chattan.

The MacDonalds of Keppoch had, after their involvement with the MacLeans and their continual cattle raiding fallen into severe disfavour with the Privy Council. MacKintosh attempted to seize this opportunity to apply to the courts to break the clan by a legal declaration that Archibald was no longer "master" of his "tenants". This absurd piece of legal theatre was obviously rejected by the MacDonalds of Keppoch. This latest dispute was put to arbitration under the Earls of Moray and Caithness and Sir George Munro. This arbitration completely failed with neither Archibald nor Lachlan Mor accepting their findings. The feud with the MacKintoshes was destined to continue beyond the lifetime of yet another chief of Keppoch, Archibald died in December 1682. Archibald left behind him four sons and no less than nine daughters.[46]

The much lamented Archibald was succeeded by his son Coll, known to his clan as Coll of the cows. Coll was a student at Saint Andrews University when he heard that his father had died. While resting at Inverness on his way home, Coll sent a message to MacKintosh offering to submit their differences to the law courts. MacKintosh, being a magistrate of Inverness exercised his power, and immediately imprisoned Coll. MacKintosh who had been thwarted all his life in what he considered his rightful possession of Keppoch, was unable to control his bitterness. He would not charge or release Coll who thus became a prisoner in a state of limbo. Coll appealed to the Privy Council who ordered MacKintosh to release him on bail. Coll failed to meet the conditions of his bail (which no doubt he regarded as unjust), he was summoned to appear before the Privy Council. Coll duly appeared and met the conditions of his bail.

---

[46] One of whom was the noted poetess Silis Nic Raghnaill.

Coll was filled with resentment at the treatment he had received at the hands of MacKintosh. It had taken a great deal for a young, proud, highland chief to submit his clan's future to the slow grinding of the law. Coll now sucked up the long history of feud between the two clans and resolved to defy MacKintosh at all cost. Within a few years (1685) of his obtaining the chiefship he was declared a rebel for failing to appear before the Privy Council on charges of raiding. At the time when he was condemned he was leading his clan and some Gordons in his favourite hunting ground of Argyle.

Lachlan Mor MacKintosh was by now an old man. He decided to make one last great effort to gain possession of Glen Roy and Glen Spean. Since the original gift of these glens to his ancestors by Alexander third Lord of the Isles over two hundred years before the MacKintoshes had been denied them by the MacDonalds of Keppoch. On the first of March 1688 Lachlan was granted a commission to occupy Keppoch by the Privy Council. The Council ordered the town of Inverness to supply him with food and transport and they also provided a company of regular soldiers under the command of a certain Kenneth MacKenzie. Lachlan appealed to all the branches of Clan Chattan as well as his own MacKintoshes. With the notable exception of the MacPhersons[47] the MacKintoshes were joined by the whole Clan Chattan confederacy. In late July 1688 a vast clan army of over one thousand men, supported by the regular army company invaded Keppoch. Surprisingly Coll was taken unawares and narrowly escaped capture as he fled from the old castle of Tom Beag.

Lachlan immediately started building a small fort near Tom Beag which was to be a cornerstone of permanent MacKintosh occupation. In a letter written a few days after his arrival Lachlan describes how the MacDonalds of Keppoch are coalescing in the surrounding hills and that he was delayed from dealing with them due to being pre-occupied with building the fort and the fact that all the rivers are in spate, (not an unusual occurrence in a Scottish summer). Coll had also been busy since fleeing to the hills. He had sent out the fiery cross to summon the entire fighting strength of his clan. This ancient call to arms was then sent to the MacDonalds of Glencoe and Glengarry as well as the Camerons.[48] Coll's own clan rallied to him to a man,[49] and he was heartened that a significant number of men came in from the neighbouring clans.[50] On the fourth of August Coll was ready to make a counter attack, he was leading a force of seven hundred men.

---

[47] There had long been tension between the MacPhersons and the MacKintoshes over whether the latter held primacy over Clan Chattan.

[48] Coll's wife was a Cameron.

[49] At this late date many chiefs were beginning to experience problems in raising the whole clan for war.

[50] The Camerons who joined him were from his wife's immediate family; they came without the permission of their chief who wanted to keep his people out of any new conflict with MacKintosh.

Coll took up position among the hills to the east of the river Roy, he planned to sweep down on MacKintosh at daybreak. Lachlan had also decided to attack the next morning. Due to his age Lachlan was unable to lead his clan and had to wait anxiously in the gardens of Keppoch for the results of his plan. Before dawn both armies were on the move, Coll moving down the hills of Mulroy to fall on an unsuspecting MacKintosh host. The MacKintoshes supported by the regular company were moving up the slopes of Mulroy with a similar plan. As the dawn broke the two clan armies came in sight of each other. Coll ordered his men to halt and draw up on a ridge of the hill.

The MacKintoshes rushed forward to attack their ancient enemies. The MacDonalds successfully resisted the initial onslaught. For over an hour the hillside of Mulroy was a boiling caldron of slaughter as eighteen hundred men hacked and slashed at each other with broadswords, dirks and Lochaber axes. Eventually the MacKintoshes broke and fled down the hillside, leaving dozens of dead and wounded behind them. Amongst the dead was Kenneth MacKenzie the commander of the company of regular troops. Coll had given express orders that the regular troops were to be avoided if at all possible, no doubt fearing future Government wrath. In the mayhem of this vast hand-to-hand combat it would have been impossible for clansmen to be discerning in who they encountered.

There is a surviving written account of the battle by one of the participants which is worth quoting.[51] "Both parties (the MacKintoshes and the regular troops) ordered their men to march up the hill. A company being in front, we drew up in a line of battle as we could, our company being on the right. We were no sooner in order but there appears double our number of MacDonalds, which made us then to fear the worst; at least, for my part, I repeated my former wish (that he had been back in Inverness spinning tobacco). The MacDonalds came down the hill upon us, without either shoe, stocking, or bonnet on their head; they gave a shout, and then the fight began on both sides and continued a hot dispute for an hour. Then they broke in upon us with their sword and target and Lochaber axes, which obliged us to give way. Seeing my captain sore wounded, and a great many more with their heads lying cloven on every side, I was sadly affrighted, never having seen the like before. A Highland man attacked me with sword and targe and cut my wooden handled bayonet out of the muzzle of my gun; I then clubbed my gun and gave him a stroke with it which made the butt end to fly off. Seeing the Highland men to come fast upon me, I took to my heels and ran thirty miles before I looked behind me. Every person I saw or met I took him for my enemy."

It is clear from this account that in the heat of battle the MacDonalds made no attempt to avoid engaging the regular troops despite Coll's orders. As the MacKintoshes broke, their standard bearer, who was being hotly pursued by a party of MacDonalds, leapt across a chasm and thus saved the standard from capture. The Battle of Mulroy was the last clan battle ever fought in the highlands.

---

[51] This witness was Donald McBane who had enlisted in the regular company.

It is remarkable that as late as 1688 this type of encounter was still possible. Putting aside the presence of the Government company and the use of muskets the battle was very similar to the first clan battles two centuries before.

Lachlan Mor was captured in the pretty garden of Keppoch. Coll compelled Lachlan to draw up a document in which he gave up any claim to the Keppoch lands in exchange for his own life and that of the many prisoners. Coll's victory was celebrated by the clan's poet. The poem is in the ancient archaic style with lines which are reminiscent of the celebration of the Battle of Inverlochy so many years before.

"keen broadswords uncovered the marrow, and who, like brave dogs, held at the mountain cats and regardless of their sharp claws took the mewing out of their nose."[52]

Scott records a local tradition that Coll released Lachlan when he heard of the approach of the MacPhersons, and that Lachlan had the indignity of not only being captured by Coll but also being released by the MacPhersons on the same day.[53] Coll probably released Lachlan having achieved his objectives of a military victory and a signed document in which Lachlan waived the ancient MacKintosh claims to Keppoch.

The Privy Council was outraged at this eruption of ancient hatred and Coll's rough handling of government troops. The council resolved on the extermination of this troublesome clan. It first called for a massive invasion of Keppoch by the neighbouring clans. These clans were largely sympathetic to the cause of the MacDonalds and even if more inclined towards the claims of the MacKintoshes they were certainly not prepared to risk conflict with Coll on behalf of them. The Council then called up a large force of dragoons who were given orders to kill all men, women and children they came across in Keppoch. It is ironic that these barbaric instructions were issued on behalf of James II, a Stuart King. It was for the restoration of the Stuart Kings that so many MacDonalds of Keppoch were to lose their lives in the next sixty years. Coll led his people into the remote fastnesses of their territory, and kept them out of the reach of the dragoons. The army units were withdrawn shortly afterwards to meet the threat posed by the invasion of England by William of Orange.

Lachlan after brooding on his humiliation was still determined to gain possession of Keppoch, in February 1689 he obtained another commission of fire and sword against Coll. Coll decided to pre-empt Lachlan and swept down on the MacKintosh territories with over a thousand men. It is clear from a petition for

---

[52] One of the mottos of the Clan Chattan was "beware the cat."
[53] This story seems to be incorrect as it is not mentioned in Lochiel's contemporary memoirs or in those of Aeneas MacPherson who surly would not have failed to record this humiliation of his old advisory.

compensation presented to the Scottish Parliament that Coll was very thorough in his attentions. "…..and did harrie and robb his haille lands in Babzenoch, Strathnairn and Strathearne, thereby exposing the petitioner to a vast loss and his tennents to beggarie, wherby his haill lands are laid waste and will so continue…."

The town of Inverness had always been closely associated with the MacKintosh interest, it had provided men and provisions for the last MacKintosh invasion of Keppoch. Coll's opinion of the town can not have been improved by his memories of when he was held in the town jail at the behest of the town's magistrate, Lachlan MacKintosh. Coll swept into the town to the dismay of the inhabitants. He ordered the burgesses to pay him a large fine for their part in the invasion of Keppoch. For several days the population were in abject terror of these hostile highlanders; they were forced to bow on sight of a MacDonald tartan. This explosive situation was diffused by Viscount Dundee's arrival.[54] Dundee acted as an intermediary between Coll and the Burgesses and they were soon able to come to terms. Coll then headed south with Dundee to the Battle of Killiecrankie, and to face the grim Cameronians[55] at Dunkeld.

After the disintegration of the rising, Coll made his way back to Keppoch. It was clear to him that the world was changing, William was firmly on the throne, and of more immediate concern a Government fort had been built at Inverlochy placing Keppoch within easy reach of Government troops. Prudently Coll submitted when the amnesty of 1691 was offered. Coll now made every effort to live peacefully on his clan lands. He is described as "quyett, and in a condition to live without stealing," only old Lachlan MacKintosh still railed against his antagonist, describing Coll as, "that notorious and signall robber, murderer, and rascal."

It was suggested by interested third parties that the Government should purchase the lands of Keppoch and then rent them to Coll. Lachlan firmly rejected these attempts at mediation, complaining bitterly to the Privy Council that Coll had been allowed to escape the fate of all rebels. He again asked to be given a commission of fire and sword so that he could invade Keppoch and slaughter the population. The fact that Lachlan was not given his commission was largely due to the benign influence of Colonel Hill the Governor of Fort William.

Colonel Hill's successor, Brigadier Maitland was more inclined to Lachlan's point of view; claiming to be "resolved to be very uneasy to Coll until he get him apprehended," Eventually Lachlan was once again granted a commission of fire and sword against Coll. Lachlan invaded Keppoch with a large following of MacKintoshes with material support from Maitland. Under the cover of a blanket of fog Lachlan seized a large number of cattle, he then constructed a number of small wooden forts in Glen Roy and Glen Spean. Coll had again withdrawn to the safety of the hills. Lachlan returned to Castle Moy convinced that he had finally

---

[54] Dundee was leading a rising in support of the deposed James II.
[55] The Cameronians were strict covenanters mainly drawn from the south west of Scotland. They fought the highlanders to a standstill in the narrow streets of Dunkeld.

established a firm grasp on the lands of Keppoch. Coll travelled to the shores of Loch Oich and asked for help from Glengarry in the face of this new invasion. Before the combined forces of the MacDonalds of Keppoch and Glengarry could encounter the MacKintosh garrisons they melted away and returned to their own country. It was now clear to all the involved parties, even the recalcitrant Lachlan, that this long running feud could not be settled by force. Under Maitland's protection Lachlan and Coll met at Fort William on the twenty second of May 1700. Lachlan was accompanied by several MacKintosh gentlemen while Coll had Sir Donald MacDonald as his cautioner. With the help of a shrewd lawyer who acted for both parties, after lengthy and no doubt vitriolic debate the two bitter enemies reached an agreement. The gist of this agreement was that Coll was to retain the Keppoch lands of Glen Roy and Glen Spean on condition that he paid MacKintosh a regular rent. The subtle details of the wording of this agreement allowed both chiefs to maintain their dignity. Thus Coll "granted" to Lachlan the disputed lands while Lachlan retained his former rights by leasing these lands back to Coll. Of critical importance was the right that Coll established to pass the ancient lands of the MacDonalds of Keppoch to his descendents.

It was in this way that the longest feud in highland history came to an end. The feud had continued intermittently for two hundred and fifty seven years. It had caused immeasurable suffering to generation after generation of MacDonalds and MacKintoshes alike. The MacDonalds of Keppoch had managed to maintain their ancient right to Keppoch against all comers for two and a half centuries. They had maintained occupation of Glen Roy and Glen Spean with no legal right under either feudal or Gaelic law.[56] They had resisted claimants who were more powerful and numerous than themselves and who were backed by legal right. This successful defiance demonstrates an enduring and tight social cohesion which can only be matched by the MacGregors amongst all the clans of the highlands. It is a sad irony that these glens, which had been held by a strong sword arm for centuries passed out of possession of the MacDonalds with hardly a whimper due to debt, the clan itself being replaced by sheep.

---

[56] The grant of Keppoch to the MacKintoshes by Alexander Lord of the Isles was certainly valid under Gaelic law.

THE MACDONALDS OF GLENGARRY TO 1680

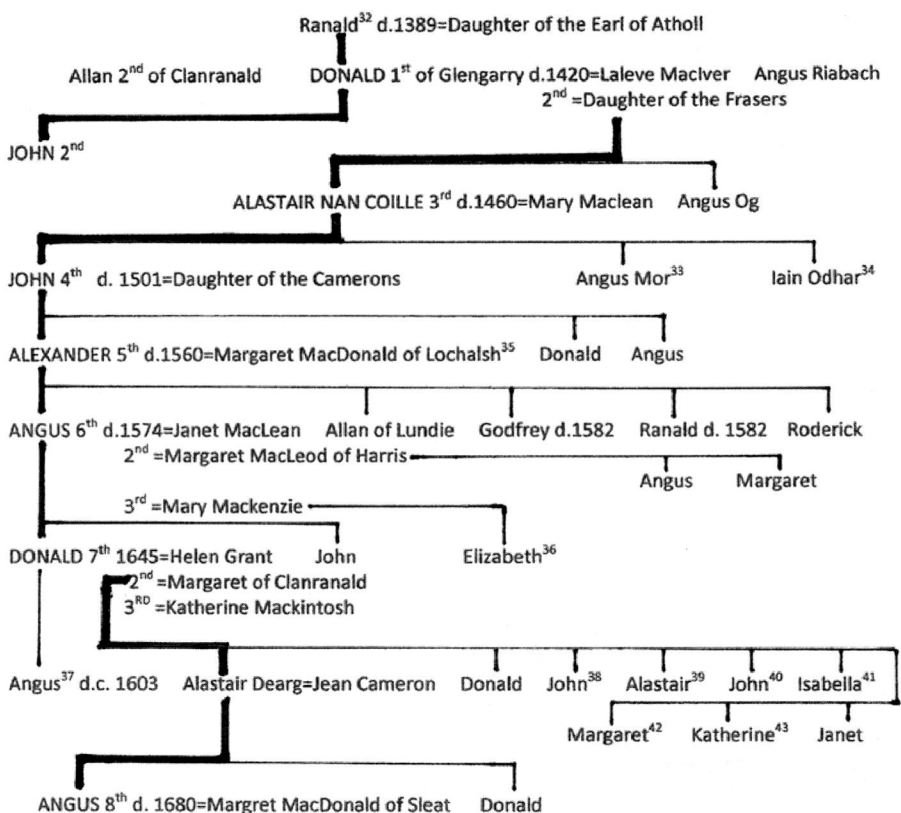

---

[32] Ranald was the eldest son of John 1st Lord of the Isles by his first wife Amie MacRuari

[33] Angus Mor's descendants are the MacDonalds of Shian.

[34] Iain Odhar's descendents are the Clan Iain Uidhir.

[35] Margaret was one of the two heiresses of the MacDonalds of Lochalsh.

[36] Elizabeth married Mackenzie of Gairloch.

[37] Angus married Margret Mackintosh

[38] John's descendants are the MacDonalds of Ardnabie.

[39] Alastair's descendants are the MacDonalds of Aberchalder and Culachie.

[40] John's descendants are the MacDonalds of Leek.

[41] Isabella married Roderick Mor MacLeod of Dunvegan.

[42] Margaret married Torquil MacLeod of Lewis.

[43] Katherine married Duncan Grant

Chapter 9

The Bitter Legacy of Lochalsh

This chapter describes the history of the MacDonalds of Glengarry,[1] from their emergence as an independent clan in the mid-sixteenth century to the ending of their feud with the MacKenzies in the first half of the seventeenth century. The MacDonalds of Glengarry held the most easterly possessions of any of the clans of their house. This distribution of their possessions and their relatively late emergence as an independent entity led them to have a distinctive series of relationships with both the eastern clans, like the MacKenzies and Grants, and with the western highland seaboard. To a lesser extent the same could be said for the MacDonalds of Keppoch and the MacDonalds of Glencoe whose possessions were also on the mainland.

The MacDonalds of Glengarry were the last of the MacDonald clans to emerge as an independent and cohesive clan society.[2] By this date the Lordship of the Isles had been proscribed for fifty years. Although the desire for its re-establishment still burnt in the hearts of its faithful adherents, the risings to restore it were becoming more spasmodic, and their scale was diminishing. As a result of their late emergence and the location of their possessions they play a far less prominent part in the events which occurred in the western isles, while they were more involved in the struggles for power and survival on the mainland. The possessions of the MacDonalds of Glengarry originally comprised of Morar and Glengarry, but were later to include lands in Lochalsh, Loch Carron and Loch Broom. After these last three were lost to the MacKenzies they established control over Knoydart.

Glengarry formed part of the ancient Lordship of Lochaber which was held by the Comyns until the wars of independence in the fourteenth century. After the fall of the Comyns and their MacDougal supporters most of Lochaber was gifted to Angus Og MacDonald, the father of John first Lord of the Isles by Robert the Bruce.[3] The lands of Glengarry and Morar were thus in possession of the MacDonalds from the early fourteenth century.

Ranald the eldest son of John first Lord of the Isles and progenitor of the Clanranald had two sons, Alan and Donald. The former became the second chief of the Clanranald, while Donald was given the Stewardship of Lochaber and the lands of Morar. The Glengarry chiefs styled themselves as "of Morar and Glengarry", which may suggest that Donald was originally gifted Morar and that it was through his position as Steward of Lochaber that he established a claim to Glengarry.

---

[1] More properly known as the Clanranald of Knoydart and Glengarry.
[2] They previously formed part of the Clanranald.
[3] See chapter2.

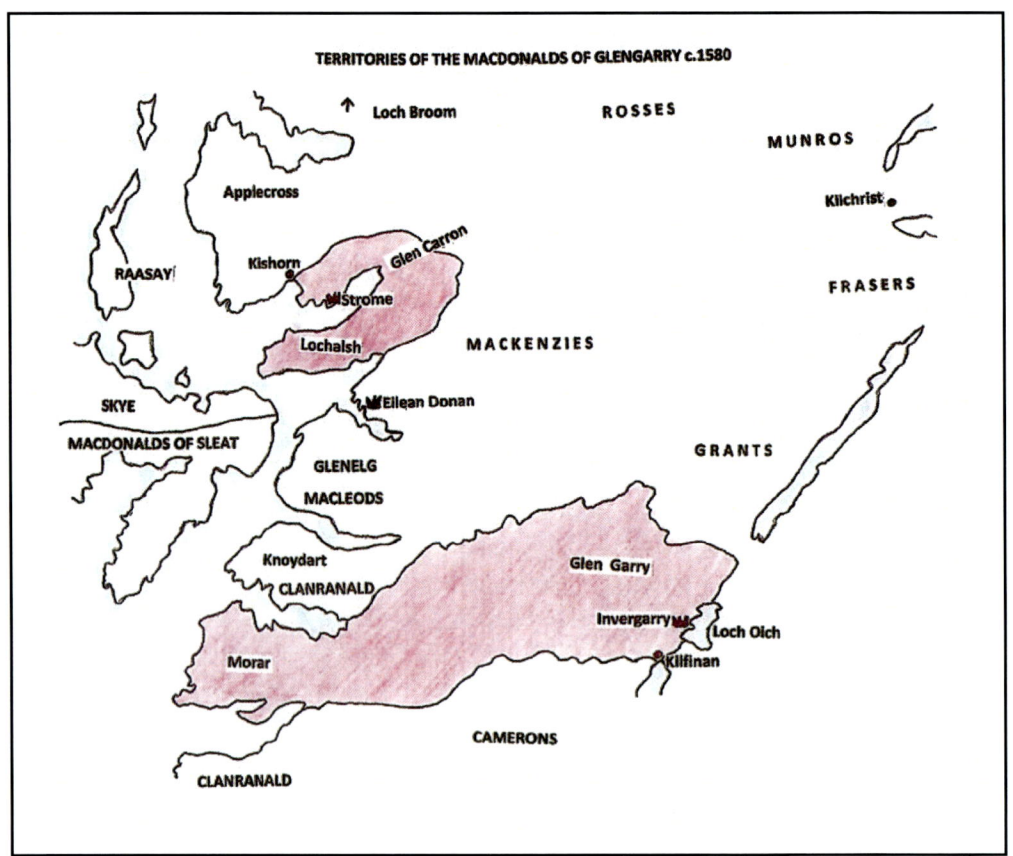

There are no charters from the Lords of the Isles to any chief of Glengarry, the earliest Royal charter being in 1538. It is clear from this charter that by 1538 the MacDonalds of Glengarry are an independent clan. It is however unclear at what date they first became a distinctive entity in their own right. The most likely scenario is that during the Lordship they were an important cadet family of the Clanranald and that their history is the history of the Clanranald until sometime in the first decade of the sixteenth century, and that they only developed their own independent policies some fifty years later.

Donald died in 1420 and left a surviving son Alexander who was described by MacVurich as "a powerful, bold, warlike Lord of the Clanranald". This description demonstrates that at least in the 1430's the family of Glengarry were part of the Clanranald. Alexander died in 1460, leaving his son John, who became the fifth chief of Glengarry. MacVurich records that this John was murdered by Fraser of Lovat in 1501 at Archteraw in Abertaff. In the resulting feud the Frasers were defeated and were forced to concede Abertaff to the MacDonalds of Glengarry. Clearly Abertaff did not stay long in MacDonald hands, because during the campaigns associated with the Battle of Kinlochlochy the 1540's, it was firmly under Fraser control. John in his turn was succeeded by Alexander the sixth chief of Glengarry.

It was during the chiefship of Alexander that the MacDonalds of Glengarry make the transition into being a fully independent clan, not only in terms of their territorial possessions but also in their relationships with other clans. Within a few months of his accession Alexander was summoned by the Crown for occupying his lands of Morar and Glengarry without a Royal charter. It is clear that Alexander had no written charter for his lands from the Lords of the Isles, and that his sympathies lay with the ancient MacDonald hegemony which had fallen only seven years before. His lands were leased out by James IV to the Gordons. This lease was ineffective as neither James nor the Gordons and any means to enforce the King's will in Glengarry.

Alexander, although in dispute with the King over his legal title, had the good sense to avoid becoming involved in the first rebellion of Donald Dubh which ended in 1505.[4] In 1513 James IV fell under the blows of the English bill men at Flodden. The dislocation that was caused by the death of such a high percentage of the Scottish nobility and such an able ruler presented Sir Donald Galda of Lochalsh with an opportunity to attempt to re-establish the Lordship of the Isles under his rule. Sir Donald Galda claimed the Lordship because he was the grandson of Celestine who would have become the fifth Lord of the Isles on the abdication of his brother John had the Lordship not been forfeited by James IV.

Sir Donald Galda was Alexander's brother in-law, as Alexander had married Margaret, Sir Donald's sister. When this close relationship was combined with the prospect of a major raid on Alexander's neighbours, the Grants, the temptation was too much and Alexander joined Sir Donald's rebellion. Alexander mustered his clan at the MacDonald castle of Invergarry, and then joined Sir Donald's forces as they swept up the Great Glen. The rebels stormed Castle Urquhart and then systematically plundered the lands of the Frasers and Grant of Freuchie. Large tracts of the Great Glen were stripped of any object of value; some idea of the thoroughness of this despoliation can be demonstrated by the fact that the rebels occupied Castle Urquhart for three years. Alexander supported Sir Donald Galda until he died in 1519 and the rebellion petered out.

Sir Donald's three sons had predeceased him and his lands in Lochalsh, Loch Broom and Loch Carron were divided equally between his two daughters, Margaret and Janet. Margaret's portion included the Castle of Strome which controlled the entrance to Loch Carron. Finally, on the sixth of March 1539 Alexander was confirmed by royal charter, in possession of Morar and Glengarry, and also half of Lochalsh, Loch Broom and Loch Carron through his wife Margaret. Alexander could never have expected that such a promising inheritance would turn into such a poisoned chalice for his descendents.

---

[4] See chapter two.

Invergarry Castle

In May of the same year Alexander was again in rebellion. This time he is supporting Donald Gorm MacDonald of Sleat in his attempts to claim the Lordship. It is possible that both chiefs were also interested in curbing the ever growing power of the MacKenzies, a clan which had always been hostile to MacDonald interests.[5] This rebellion quickly withered away with the death of Donald Gorm under the walls of Eileen Donan.[6] In an attempt to overawe the western clans JamesV made an expedition to the western highlands. While at anchor of Portree on Skye he invited all the chiefs to a council. Alexander was among those who attended and was with many other chiefs clapped in irons and taken to Edinburgh. There he was imprisoned in the castle where he was to remain until shortly after the death of James V in 1542. Before his death James had forfeited Alexander's lands of Glengarry and bestowed them on John, chief of the MacKenzies. The MacKenzies did not gain actual possession of Glengarry, however, that such a powerful and antagonistic clan should have legal title to the heartland of their possessions was a real threat to the MacDonalds of Glengarry.

---

[5] The MacKenzies had always resisted MacDonald claims to the Earldom of Ross, primarily because they would then become the feudal superiors of the MacKenzies.
[6] See chapter 6.

Alexander along with his fellow MacDonald chief John Moydartach made their way back to their clans after being freed by the Regent Arran. Many chiefs in the western highlands were full of resentment at the way they had been personally treated by James V. There was however a more fundamental reason for their anger; this was the ever increasing power of the state, and the almost continual expansion of the Campbells and to a lesser extent the MacKenzies who acted as the instruments of the state in the western highlands. The power of the state was most clearly manifest in the necessity for the clans to have royal charters for their lands in order to have security of tenure.

There were many other factors which in the 1540's created a potentially explosive situation in the Gaelic west. The Lordship had only been broken for less than fifty years and was not yet a distant memory. Donald Dubh the direct descendent of the Lords of the Isles was still alive, although held prisoner in Edinburgh Castle. The chiefs of many of the western clans were still secure from retribution from the state especially in its weakened state after the disaster of Flodden. Backed by the significant military power of their clan and that of many of their neighbours the dream of the re-establishment of an independent Gaelic state seemed a very real possibility. The spark that lit the fuse to this powder keg of dissatisfaction was the escape of Donald Dubh from his confinement.

Alexander joined the large scale rebellion which erupted throughout the western highlands after the escape of Donald Dubh; he was among the seventeen chiefs who formed Donald Dubh's council. In 1544 he led the men of Sunart and Glengarry to the bloody field of Kinlochlochy in support of John Moydartach in his bitter feud with Hugh Lord Lovat.[7] The Grants of Urquhart and Glenmoriston had supported the Frasers. Alexander seized his opportunity and led his clan and the Camerons in a raid on the Grants. In the following year of 1545 they again swept through the Grant lands, storming Urquhart Castle and "swept the land of every hoof and article of food or furniture which they could find, sparing only the Barony of Corrimony whose owner had no part in Blair-na-Leine".[8]

The scale of this raid is shown by the large sum of £11,400 Scots which was claimed by the Grants in compensation. A list of the stolen livestock, agricultural goods and possessions is listed in Mackay's work, Urquhart and Glenmoriston. Of course no compensation was ever received by them from either Alexander or the Camerons. There was however a more serious consequence of these raids, the Grants received charters to all the lands of the MacDonalds of Glengarry including those of Lochalsh. Even with the support of the Scottish executive the Grants were never able to enforce any form of control over these regions, nor were they able to extract any rents from the inhabitants. Despite the successful resistance to the Grants, the MacDonalds of Glengarry had been legally dispossessed of all their lands. This was a serious threat to the clan with such astute and powerful

---

[7] See chapter 3.
[8] Clan Donald. Blair-na-Leine is here called Kinlochlochy.

neighbours as the MacKenzies, who it will be remembered had been granted a set of charters to Glengarry a decade before.

The Scottish state, having failed to bring any of the rebellious chiefs, amongst whom was Alexander, to obedience again exhibited its weakness by giving them a pardon in 1548. Alexander along with John Moydartach of the Clanranald and the Camerons continued to defy the state and their powerful instruments, the Gordons and the Campbells. The Dowager Queen Mary was driven to write of them "perseuerand in thair evil and vickit myndis, oppressis oure derrist dochteris subjectis, committand slauchteris, reiffis and vthiris odious crymes;" The MacDonalds of Glengarry, the Clanranald, and the Camerons had all lost their charters to their land (or had never had any) and were all being pressed by the legal owners. As a consequence they formed a loose alliance and not content that they would assist each other in the defence of their ancient heritage they made plans to go onto the offensive against their oppressors. This threat caused an equal and opposite affect, in that the MacKenzies, Grants and MacKintoshes also formed a bond of mutual defence. There were a series of raids and counter raids between the two opposing groups of clans; the ordinary people on both sides suffering losses of material they could ill afford.

Alexander known as Mac Iain Mhic Alistair to his people died in 1560 and was buried at Kilfinnan[9] overlooking the battlefield of Kinlochlochy at the head of Loch Lochy. He was succeeded by his son Angus who became seventh chief of Glengarry. As has been seen the Grants were unable to derive any benefit from their legal right to the lands of the MacDonalds of Glengarry, so they adopted a new and more subtle approach to ensuring their security from their lawless neighbours. The new chief of the Grants attempted to find security for his people by forming alliances with his neighbours through marriage. The first was with Colin Cam MacKenzie, eleventh of Kintail. Colin married Barbara Grant the chief's daughter who bought half of Loch Broom to the MacKenzies as part of her dowry. As part of the marriage contract Colin agreed that the MacKenzies would assist the Grants if they were attacked by any of their neighbours. The chief of the Grants then married his other daughter, Helen, to Angus MacDonald of Glengarry, again on condition that Angus would also assist the Grants against all enemies excepting only the royal authority. In exchange for this marriage and alliance the Grants gave up any claims they had to the MacDonald territories, both in Glengarry and Lochalsh.

Angus enjoyed a rare period of tranquillity in the history of the MacDonalds of Glengarry. He became a favourite at the Scottish court, and was even appointed as bailiff to oversee the fisheries of Loch Broom and Loch Carron. Angus died in 1575 and followed his father up the peaceful lane to Kilfinnan.

---

[9] Kilfinnan was by now the traditional burial ground of the chiefs of Glengarry. The original burial ground was submerged by the rising waters of Loch Lochy after the Caledonian Canal was built in the nineteenth century.

Angus was succeeded by his son Donald as eighth chief of Glengarry. Donald was to live to the extraordinary age of one hundred and two; he was to be tested in one of the most deadly and long lasting feuds ever recorded in the highlands. His rule as chief began peacefully enough; the first reference to him is in a dispute with the Frasers over them preventing him from floating his timber to Inverness. Soon however he was presented by a most unusual threat. Colin Campbell had just succeeded his brother Archibald to the chiefship of the Campbells. Colin developed a taste for committing raids on his neighbours, leading two against the MacLeans and the Clan Iain Mor. Colin's attention then turned to the lands of the MacDonalds of Glengarry. Under the guise of suppressing "broken" and lawless men he made preparations to invade the Great Glen. Donald made an urgent appeal to the Privy Council who immediately ordered that the Grants, MacKenzies, Frasers, Chisholms, MacKintoshes and Rosses should band together to defend the MacDonalds of Glengarry. What the chiefs of many of these clans made of been ordered to defend a clan which had long been a thorn in their side can only be imagined; one can only marvel at the ever fluid dynamics of political relationships in the highlands in the sixteenth century. On seeing such a powerful confederation built up against him, Colin thought better of his plans and abandoned his expedition.

The relationship between the MacDonalds and the MacKenzies had always been problematic. The MacKenzies interests had always been opposed to those of the MacDonalds; they had resisted any expansion of MacDonald power into the central northern highlands. In the fifteenth century they had done their utmost to prevent the Lords of the Isles gaining a firm control over the Earldom of Ross. Later they had acted as an effective instrument of the state in thwarting the ambitions of the house of Lochalsh in its attempts to re-establish the Lordship.

As has already been mentioned the MacDonalds of Glengarry came into possession of half the lands of Lochalsh, Loch Broom and Loch Carron through the marriage of Alexander to Margaret the daughter of Sir Donald of Lochalsh. The other co-heiress was Sir Donald's other daughter Janet. Janet brought her half of the Lochalsh inheritance into the family of the Dingwalls of Kildun when she married into that family. Colin Cam MacKenzie purchased these lands from the Dingwalls; he already possessed the other half of Loch Broom through his marriage to Barbara the daughter of the chief of the Grants. Having acquired half of the lands of the Lochalsh inheritance by marriage or purchase he now cast envious eyes over the remainder. It may well have been that his principal interest lay in the Castle of Strome which controlled the entrance to his new possessions in Loch Carron and the MacKenzie hinterland. The storm clouds of war and subtle intrigue were gathering around the unsuspecting Donald of Glengarry.

From a MacDonald perspective there is a major problem in recounting the details of this bitter feud. The details do not exist in any extant MacDonald manuscripts; they are only to be found in the histories of their enemies the MacKenzies. Clan histories were written by members of the clan, and were written primarily for the edification of the gentlemen of that clan. They are all clearly partisan in favour of their own people and it is often remarkable how the same event is described in the histories of the clans involved, at its worst it is hard to recognize that they are referring to the same event. Apart from the rather dry state manuscripts the MacKenzie sources are the only ones available and although there has been an attempt at objectivity this must always be born in mind.

The territories of the MacDonalds of Lochalsh had been gifted to Celestine by his brother John, the fourth Lord of the Isles, in the middle of the fifteenth century. This was a relatively late acquisition of the MacDonalds and the land was already occupied by the Mathesons in Lochalsh and the Clan Iain Uidhir in Glen Carron. The Mathesons had no tradition of being followers of the Lordship; rather they had close ties with their neighbours the MacKenzies and in earlier times to the Earls of Ross[10] before the Earldom was claimed by the Lords of the Isles. The Clan Iain Uidhir were descended from Iain Odher the third son of Alexander na Coille (of the woods) third chief of the MacDonalds of Glengarry. It is interesting to note that MacDonalds were settled in Glen Carron by the middle of the fifteenth century. The MacKenzie historians imply that the MacDonalds of Glengarry were latecomers to the lands of Glen Carron when clearly their immediate relatives had been settled there long before the arrival of the MacKenzies.

The MacKenzie chroniclers state that the MacDonald owners treated their tenentry very badly especially if they found any evidence of friendly contact with their relatives living further up Loch Carron under the sway of the MacKenzies.[11] It is clear that considerable bitterness built up between the MacDonald population whether they were incomers from Glengarry, or had been settled there under the family of Lochalsh and some of the ancient inhabitants namely the Mathesons. The gentlemen of Glengarry are accused of raiding their own tenentry and " lie in their houses yea, force their women and daughters" even though they paid the rents that were due. The Mathesons resented being under the hegemony of the MacDonalds when their relations enjoyed a more peaceable existence under the rule of the MacKenzies. Due to the increased tension in the district both internally and with the MacKenzies, Donald took up residence on the shores of Loch Carron and placed a garrison in Strome Castle. The Lochalsh possessions of Donald were very remote from his power base in Sunart and Glengarry and in close proximity to that of the MacKenzies. It was no doubt because of this that Donald decided to bolster his position by living on the shores of Loch Carron.

Donald MacDonald eighth chief of Glengarry and Colin Cam MacKenzie the ninth of Kintail were to become embroiled in a bitter feud after a series of minor incidents which led to a major conflagration between the two clans. One of Donald's tenants, a certain Duncan Uidhir, was caught killing deer in Colin's forests by the MacKenzie gamekeeper. When Duncan and his companion refused to allow

---

[10] The Earls of Ross were the progenitors of Clan Ross.
[11] Caution must be taken when reading this description of the situation in Glen Carron as it forms part of the MacKenzie justification for their appropriation of this region.

themselves to be taken before Colin a fierce altercation broke out, the result of which was that the two poachers were killed and buried in secret on the hillside. The gamekeeper and his gillie were suspected of being involved in the disappearance of Duncan Uidhir and his companion, but although they were put on trial by both Colin and MacKenzie of Gairloch no proof was forthcoming that they were guilty. A friend of Duncan Uidhir searched for any sign of his friend for two years, eventually coming across his remains on the remote hillside.

This member of Clan Iain Uidhir gathered some companions and set out to exact revenge. Arriving at Inchlochell in Glenstrathfarrar they came across the brother of the gamekeeper and killed him while he was unsuspectingly ploughing his field. The murdered man was a tenant of Rory Mor MacKenzie of Redcastle, a man known to be of a proud and warlike disposition. Rory Mor sent a messenger to Donald demanding redress for the murdered tenant's family and the punishment of the raiders. Donald refused any attempt at redress for the murder; no doubt he felt that there had been murder on both sides, nor would he have wanted to be seen handing his own tenant over to the tender mercies of the MacKenzies. It is somewhat ironic that Donald and his clan were to become embroiled with the MacKenzies on behalf of members of the Clan Ian Uidhir[12] who according to the MacKenzie historians he was persecuting in Lochalsh. There must be severe reservations as to the veracity of these claims of persecution by the MacKenzies.

Rory Mor was determined to have redress for the murder of his tenant, despite the advice of his friends. Rory Mor went to Applecross to consult with his friend Dougall MacKenzie, and soon the conspirators had hatched a plan. Dougall sent a messenger to Donald saying that he had something of the greatest importance to tell him and could they arrange a meeting. Once the place and time had been agreed Dugall informed Rory Mor. Rory Mor had also been busy; he had had meetings with senior members of the Clan Ian Uidhir who, despite close ties of marriage and blood (they were MacDonalds) agreed to abandon their support for Donald and support Rory Mor. This treachery by the Clan Uidhir is made more bitter from a MacDonald perspective as Donald was becoming embroiled in this feud on behalf of members of the Clan Ian Uidhir.

On the appointed day in 1581 Donald sailed from Strome to the rendezvous at Kishorn accompanied by his new wife Margaret, a daughter of Allan of Clanranald. Donald's first wife Helen Grant had been abandoned a few years earlier thus bringing her fathers plans to an end while Donald retained legal title to his lands.[13] The unsuspecting Donald met Rory Mor at Kishorn where they conferred for some time and attempted to settle the disputes between the two clans. As Donald was going down to his waiting galley, Dugall advised Donald not to sail back in such a clumsy craft, when he had only two miles to walk if he went overland. Dugall also

---

[12] Who were themselves MacDonalds.

[13] It may be that the union between Donald and Helen Grant was only a "handfast" marriage.

suggested that his wife may be uncomfortable in the boat, and he offered to put her up for the night and to escort her home in the morning.

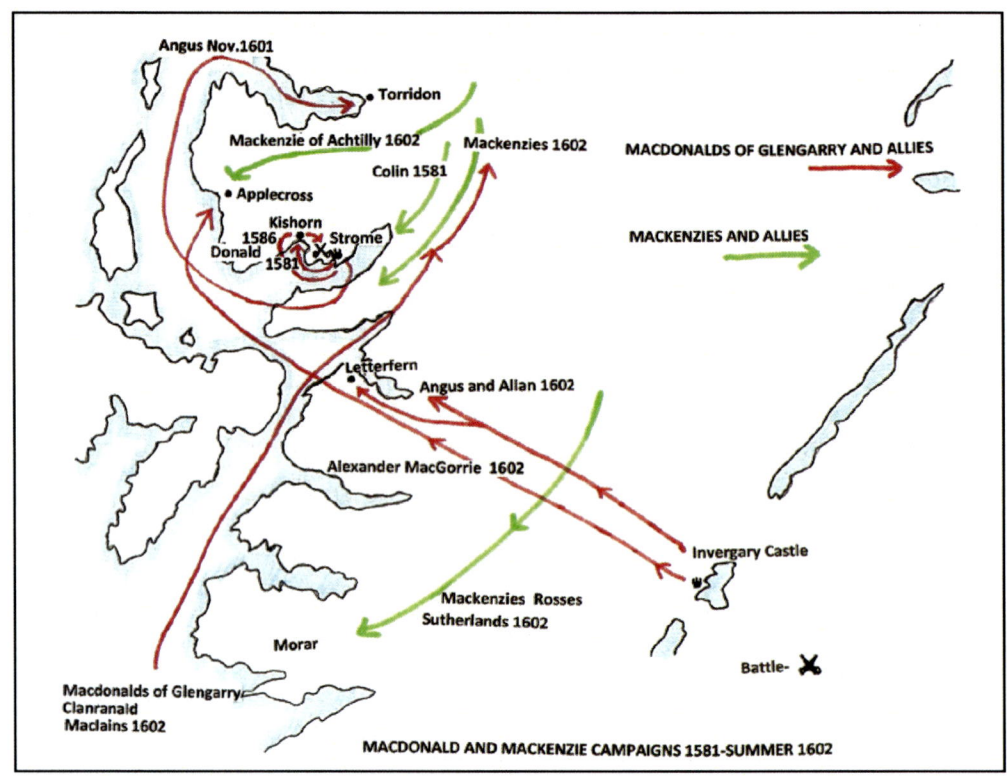

MACDONALD AND MACKENZIE CAMPAIGNS 1581-SUMMER 1602

Donald declined this rather lame reasoning and sent his wife home in the galley with four attendants while he and the rest of his retinue walked back along the shore line. Rory Mor was waiting with his men at a place still called Glaic nan Gillean; the unsuspecting Donald walked straight into the ambush. Donald and his clansmen were surrounded by a vastly superior force of MacKenzies who were armed for war. When Donald was called upon to surrender one of the MacDonalds fired an arrow at Rory Mor which just missed piercing his shoulder but did transfix his plaid. The MacKenzies attacked the lightly armed MacDonalds and soon none but Donald was left alive. MacKenzie historians relate how Donald threw down his sword and rushed into the arms of Rory Mor begging that his life be sparred. This description does not fit well with the ingrained behaviour of a highland chief, especially one from the proud and warlike MacDonalds of Glengarry. Such behaviour would have meant that he would almost certainly have been deposed as chief by a shamed clan, after all Ranald Galda was rejected by the Clanranald for the far less serious offence of parsimony.

When one examines the evidence as to the causes of this feud, even though it is recorded from a MacKenzie standpoint, there is little doubt about who was at fault. Whether or not the Matheson's and the Clan Ian Uidhir were mistreated by the

MacDonalds is not relevant to the cause of this feud. The lands which they occupied undistbutably belonged to the MacDonalds of Glengarry and were outside the remit of the MacKenzies. The two incidents that then occurred, the murder of the poacher and the murder of the ploughman, are minor events and were typical in the highlands during the sixteenth century. In any event the second murder was carried out by members of Clan Ian Uidhir, a people who were said to be victimized by the MacDonalds and desperate to be under the bounteous rule of the MacKenzies. There is an argument that the feud begins with the treacherous attack by Rory Mor MacKenzie on Donald of Glengarry at Kishorn, where he was taken prisoner and his clansmen all murdered.

MacKenzie power had been expanding for over a century, by a heady mix of political skill, legal astuteness and military power. These attributes were wielded by able and ruthless chiefs, and this is best exemplified by how the MacKenzies ensnared, dispossessed and ultimately annihilated the MacLeods of Lewis. It is not inconceivable that the MacKenzie Lords of Kintail had also prepared the way for the entrapment of the proud and hot headed MacDonalds of Glengarry.

There is a divergence in the descriptions given of the next events. When Donald appeared before the Privy Council he claims that the MacKenzies then attacked and captured Donald's uncle, three of his sons, and other clansmen and "they caused the hands of these persons to be bound with their own sarkis (clothes) cruelly slew them, and appointed that they should not be buried like Christian men but cast forth to be eaten by dogs and swine". The MacKenzie account blames this incident on members of the Clan Iain Uidhir who bore Donald a grudge for what they considered to be the dispossession of their land. Donald then recounts how he was taken first before Colin Cam MacKenzie and then exhibited before the walls of Strome Castle. The garrison was ordered to surrender or their chief would be butchered in front of them. Lastly Donald recounts how the MacKenzies captured Donald Makmorach Roy one of his close relatives and "bait thame in his blude and be a strange example to satisfie their cruell and unnaturall heartis, first cut of his handis, nixt his feit, and last his heid, and having cassin the same in a peitpott, exposit and laid out his carcage to be a prey for doggis and revenues beistis.". Allowing for the propaganda value of exaggeration, it is clear that many MacDonalds were brutally murdered on the shores of Loch Carron in the summer of 1581.

Having heard this dreadful indictment the Privy Council, in the absence of Colin Cam MacKenzie, ordered that the Castle of Strome should be returned to Donald (it having been surrendered by the garrison as a condition of Donald's release). Colin Cam was ordered to find caution (a form of bail) for his subsequent good behaviour. If he failed to abide by either of these two conditions he would be denounced as a rebel. Within a month Colin Cam had protested at the Council's decision claiming that he had received no notification of the proceedings against him. He then went on to state that he was ignorant of the events which had taken place in Lochalsh.

Colin Cam was able to sow considerable confusion in the minds of the Council over what was the exact status of the rights of possession of the Castle of Strome. They eventually decreed that it should be put into the custody of Argyle; certainly this would have pleased neither Donald or Colin Cam. Certainly the Privy Council were convinced of Colin Cam's guilt as Donald of Glengarry received a charter from James VI confirming him in all his lands in Lochalsh and Loch Carron. This is reinforced by another Royal confirmation that Donald is heir to all his grandmother's lands in Lochalsh. Colin Cam's guilt in the events in Lochalsh is confirmed (at least in the eyes of the council) by a remission granted to Colin Cam in 1586, which amongst other crimes, for being art and part in the cruel murder of Roderick, Donald's uncle.

Strome Castle

Donald's position seemed unassailable, he had charters confirming him in his lands both in Glengarry and Lochalsh and the Privy Council were convinced of the guilt of Rory Mor and by association with him, Colin Cam. He further secured himself by an agreement with George Earl of Huntly in which, in exchange for the Earl's protection he would support the Earl in all his enterprises, with the usual caveat that he was to be exempted from opposing the King or his own kindred.[14]

---

[14] A manrent agreement.

Some of the gentlemen of the MacDonalds of Glengarry thirsted for revenge for the massacres which had taken place on the shores of Loch Carron in 1581, and in February 1588 invaded the MacKenzie district of Kishorn and slaughtered Dugald MacKenzie and his servant. Dugald's widow appealed to the Council for justice. Donald was held to be responsible for the actions of his clansmen; and when he failed to appear before the Council he was declared a rebel, which meant that he lost legal title to his clan's lands.

Donald had abandoned Helen Grant the daughter of the chief of the Grants of Glenmoriston in favour of the daughter of Allan chief of the Clanranald. Naturally Helen's father was not pleased that his daughter had been spurned and that his efforts to safeguard his people had been thrown into jeopardy, while Donald had legally recovered his lands. In 1586 Grant gave the land charters of Lochalsh to MacKintosh, MacKintosh made no effort to put his new claim into effect realizing that any gain would be outweighed by the losses caused by the inevitable feud with the MacDonalds of Glengarry. Having failed to enmesh the MacKintoshes in his dispute with Donald the chief of the Grants allowed the matter of the lands of Lochalsh to lie dormant for over ten years, except for the painfully slow actions he undertook in the Scottish courts. Eventually in 1597 he achieved legal title to the lands of Loch Carron and Lochalsh, while Donald was confirmed as his tenant. The two chiefs then agreed a mutual bond of manrent, in which they agreed to support each other against all their enemies, the exceptions for the MacDonalds of Glengarry being the King and the Clanranald.

Donald was not destined to live out his life in peace, his son Angus who is described even by his own clan's historians as of "a warlike and restless disposition" gathered a large force of his own people and a "grit nowmer of brokin and disorderit Hielandmen" and in November 1601 fell on the MacKenzie lands of Torridon with fire and sword. Angus destroyed the small clachan of Cro, killing several of the inhabitants and carrying off large booty of cattle and household goods. When Angus returned to Invergarry Castle with his considerable spoils, Donald's pride in his son and his pleasure at obtaining further material redress from his MacKenzie enemies overcame his sense of judgment and he gladly accepted the spoils of the raid.

Kenneth MacKenzie twelfth chief of his clan and Lord of Kintail was imbued with all the intelligence and ruthlessness of his predecessors and while preparing a counter stroke against his MacDonald enemies, set his lawyers to work in the courts. Donald and Angus failed to grasp the significance of these manoeuvres and did not appear in Edinburgh to defend themselves against the charges laid before the court. Kenneth had already encompassed the fate of the MacLeods of Lewis and soon established the legal groundwork for his counter stroke against the MacDonalds. An eighteenth century manuscript describes how Donald and Angus were "inexpert and unskilful in the laws of the realm, the Clan-Chenzie intrapped and insnared them within the compass thereof". Kenneth soon obtained a commission of fire and sword against the MacDonalds of Glengarry; Donald having been declared a rebel because of his failure to appear before the court.

Armed with his commission Kenneth prepared his counterstroke. Leaving enough men to guard the MacKenzie territories, he mustered an army of seventeen hundred men among whom were a contingent of one hundred and eighty Rosses under the command of Ross of Invercharron and one hundred and twenty Sutherlands under the command of Gordon of Embo. By the scale of these preparations it is apparent how MacKenzie power had expanded since the fifteenth century as one of many clans in Wester Ross. The army was accompanied by a herd of three hundred cows which were to sustain the men in the remote fastnesses of the passes into Morar.

When the MacDonalds of Morar heard of the approach of this large force they drove all their cattle into a remote glen and prepared to attempt to halt Kenneth's forces at the passes which gave access to Morar from Ross. Here, badly outnumbered they were driven back and the MacKenzies poured into this remote and isolated MacDonald territory. The MacKenzies and their allies stripped Morar of every living domestic animal and all the chattels of the unfortunate inhabitants. The plunder from this raid was said to have been the largest ever taken in the highlands, "both of cows horses, small bestial, duin-uasals, and plenishing, which he (Kenneth) distributed among his soldiers, and especially among the strangers that were with them[15]..."). This raid would have been a disaster for the population of Morar, many would have fled to Donald and Angus for support, while others would have died of starvation in their remote and beautiful homeland.

Kenneth now seized his opportunity and swept through the MacDonald lands of Glen Carron and Lochalsh. Here he activated a policy of "ethnic cleansing", he evicted the entire population, the exceptions being the Mathesons and any of the Clan Iain Uidhir who would irrevocably commit themselves to the MacKenzies by "imbrowing their hands in the enemies blood." The only possession of the MacDonalds of Glengarry which survived this onslaught was the Castle of Strome which held out against Kenneth.

While the MacKenzie host was occupied in Morar, Angus gathered his men and invaded the MacKenzie lands of Lochalsh and Applecross, carrying death and terror in his wake. This raid into Applecross caused consternation in the highlands as the area was regarded as having holy sanctity second only to Iona. The inclusion of the Applecross district into this feud gives some hint as to the bitterness that had boiled up between the contending clans.

In the following autumn of 1602 Alexander MacGorrie, a redoubtable warrior of the MacDonalds of Glengarry, led another raid on the MacKenzie territories of Wester Ross. Ignoring the advice of his friends he again raided Applecross, and killed several MacKenzies and pillaged the district. During the early part of 1602 Donald and Angus had been busy forming a series of alliances with their kindred,

---

[15] Presumably the Rossses and Sutherlands.

the Clanranald and the MacIains of Ardnamurchan, as well as some of the dispossessed members of the Clan Ian Uidhir who had not been willing to commit atrocities against their MacDonald neighbours at Kenneth's behest. The forces of the MacDonalds of Glengarry, the Clanranald, the MacIains of Ardnamurchan and some members of the Clan Iain Uidhir now coalesced and invaded the MacKenzie districts of Loch Carron and Lochalsh. These districts were only their initial targets, ultimately their ambition was to ravage all the western MacKenzie territories.

The MacDonald coalition of thirty seven galleys then prepared to sail for Applecross. Alexander MacGorrie decided to scout ahead on his large galley and landed on Applecross. At this time Kenneth MacKenzie was visiting his kinsman MacKenzie of Gairloch whose house was on Island Rory in Loch Maree, when word reached him that Alexander had again landed in the vicinity. He immediately ordered that lookouts should be placed on the entire MacKenzie coast to determine the size and destination of the next MacDonald attack.

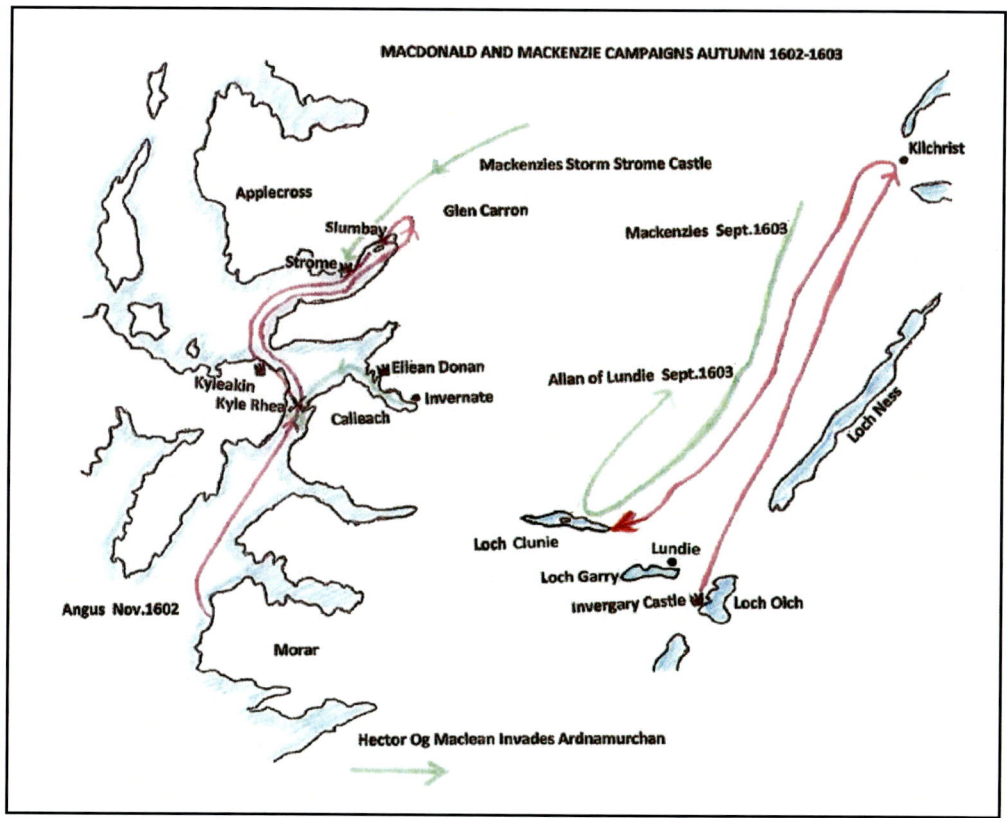

MACDONALD AND MACKENZIE CAMPAIGNS AUTUMN 1602-1603

Kenneth also dispatched a small galley under the command of MacKenzie of Achtilly to find the location of the MacDonald fleet. On their way south by the merest chance they landed on a peninsular on the coast of Applecross. They were told by a local woman who was gathering shellfish on the shore that earlier a large galley had landed on the other side of the peninsular. Achtilly immediately ordered the galley to sail round the peninsular while he set off on foot with eighteen men across the peninsular. The party of MacKenzies came across a MacDonald sentry who was sleeping peacefully in the heather; he was quietly sent to his eternal rest before they moved on. The sentry had had a pair of bagpipes by his side in order to warn of any approaching danger, these the MacKenzies took with them.

When Achtilly led his men to attack the unsuspecting MacDonalds accompanied by the rant of the pipes he caused panic among Alexander's men and they fled for the safety of their galley. Alexander swore an oath that he would never retreat before the MacKenzies and drawing his broadsword rushed forward alone to meet the enemy. The eighteen MacKenzies attacked him furiously and Alexander, defending himself with great skill withdrew to a large rock which protected his back. The MacKenzie historian describes how Alexander fought with great bravery and skill, keeping the enemy at bay. The MacKenzies withdrew a short distance to try to kill him from a distance with arrows, Alexander deflected the arrows collecting them like porcupine quills on his targe. Eventually Alexander was wounded by an arrow below the belt, yet none of his assailants dared approach him. One MacKenzie skirted round behind the rock and lifting a large boulder dropped it on the unsuspecting Alexander. Alexander's skull was crushed and he died instantly. The MacKenzie historian comments that had Alexander possessed as much wisdom as he did courage he would have been a very formidable opponent even for the wily Kenneth. The death of Alexander was a severe blow to all his clan as they now needed more than ever the leadership and courage he could have offered in this desperate feud with such a subtle and powerful neighbour.

Alexander had rekindled the feud and although he had paid with his life his actions had exposed all the MacDonalds of Glengarry including the women and children to poverty, insecurity, death and possible starvation whether they supported him or not.

The MacKenzies then met up with their own galley and went in pursuit of Alexander's men who were making for the safety of their own fleet. This description by the MacKenzie historian seems somewhat stretched as by his own account there were eighty MacDonalds and only some thirty MacKenzies. However, it is the only surviving account we have available to us. He does allow that when Achtilly saw the whole MacDonald fleet baring down on him he ordered his men to turn and row for their lives. The MacKenzies managed to keep ahead of their pursuers and reached the shore only a few minutes before the MacDonalds. In the gathering gloom of evening a local man led the MacKenzies over a ford between two rocks. The MacDonalds continued up the glen unaware that they had turned off. When the MacDonalds were returning to their galleys they came across Alexander's mutilated body, his death had profound implications for his clan. When they had bought the corpse back to Invergarry Castle the MacDonald forces were disbanded as one of the main driving forces of the feud in the form of Alexander was no more.

Mackenzie of Achtilly returned to Gairloch's house on Loch Maree and told Kenneth what had happened. Kenneth; once the withdrawal of the MacDonalds had been confirmed, returned to Kintail to prepare for the next round of the struggle. When he arrived home he found that the two clans had arraigned a truce as both clans were exhausted by the continual warfare. Donald MacDonald, who was by now in his mid-sixties, had arranged the latest truce. He would now have settled for peace with the MacKenzies even if it meant the loss of his lands of Loch Carron and Lochalsh; his proud and warlike son was not in the least persuaded. Donald begged Angus to let the dust settle, but Angus and the young men of the clan were not to be dissuaded and they prepared to re-open hostilities. This example of Angus's defiance of his aging father is another instance in which a clan was divided between those that adhered to the old chief's authority and those that followed the vibrant eldest son, who to them represented the future. This type of power struggle was not uncommon, for example, the civil war that was caused in similar circumstances during the Lordship of the Isles between Angus Og and his father John fourth Lord of the Isles.

The MacDonalds of Glengarry raised every available man and invaded the MacKenzie country with two separate forces. One led by Angus ravaged Glenshiel and Letterfearn while the other under Allan MacDonald of Lundy took fire and sword to Glenelchaig. The MacKenzies were caught off guard and had to retreat before the unexpected attacks. The MacDonald raiding parties withdrew with considerable plunder before the MacKenzies had had time to coalesce and resist the incursion.

After this raid Angus exhibited a different aspect of his character, that of the politician. He knew that by breaking the truce he had committed his people to a new struggle with the MacKenzies and their allies the Rosses and Sutherlands. Angus needed allies of his own. Travelling extensively on the western highland seaboard he visited the chiefs of the other MacDonald clans including those of Sleat, the Clanranald, the Maclains of Ardnamurchan, the MacDonalds of Keppoch and the Clan Iain Mor in the south. When word reached Kenneth of Angus's attempts to rally the whole of the MacDonald polity to his cause he became apprehensive, because although MacKenzie power and influence had expanded greatly it would still be no match for the combined power of all the branches of the house of Somerled.

Kenneth's sister had married Hector Og MacLean of Duart. Kenneth who was resident at this time at Eilean Donan Castle on the western periphery of his territories, sailed immediately for his brother-in-law's castle of Duart on the island of Mull. The MacLeans had been involved in their own bloody feud with another branch of the MacDonalds, the Clan Iain Mor over the Rinns if Isla.[16] Their interests were also threatened by any expansion of MacDonald power. The MacKenzie and the MacLean interests were mutually reinforcing and this was strengthened by

---

[16] See chapter 11.

Kenneth's marriage to Hector Og's sister. Kenneth and Hector Og met and soon agreed to form an alliance between the two clans. Hector Og's decision to aid his brother-in-law was made easier when Kenneth explained to him that he had a commission of fire and sword against the MacDonalds of Glengarry, which meant that any actions the MacLeans took against the MacDonalds were sanctioned by the state. The agreement the two chiefs made was both defensive and offensive in that Hector Og undertook to invade the territories of the Clan Iain Mor, the MacDonalds of Keppoch or the Maclains of Ardnamurchan should they send men to aid Angus in his struggle with the MacKenzies.

The MacKenzie manuscripts mention that Donald, still nominally head of the MacDonalds of Glengarry, made every effort to persuade his son not resume the feud with the MacKenzies. However, Angus's star was rising and he was supported by a considerable number of the gentlemen of the clan.

Taking advantage of Kenneth's absence on Mull, Angus made his preparations for a counter stroke. At the end of November 1602 Angus sailed with a considerable fleet of galleys and in the afternoon twilight landed on the shores of Loch Carron. Most of the Mathesons and MacKenzies escaped up the steep sides of the glen, those that stayed to resist were put to the sword and Angus stripped the entire area of anything of any value. He then withdrew to the Island of Slumbay to reorganize his forces and to allocate the spoils. The fiery cross had been sent out by the appalled inhabitants of Loch Carron and soon MacKenzies and Mathesons were rushing to Loch Carron to resist the raiders. Angus ordered his men to set sail and as the fleet made for the open water a shower of arrows from MacKenzie archers was discharged at them. They were however by now too far out to sea, and the arrows fell harmlessly into the water.

The MacKenzies sent twelve of their fittest men to alert the garrison at Eilean Donan, and to intercept Angus as he was sailing back to the safety of Morar. At Invernate near the head of Loch Duich was a newly constructed twelve oared galley belonging to one of the MacKenzie tenants. Having alerted the garrison of Eilean Donan they ran on down the loch side and sailed the galley back to the castle just as the main force of MacKenzies had arrived from Loch Carron. Kenneth's wife Lady MacKenzie organized the preparations for the interception; she stripped the castle of its supply of gunpowder and supplied her clansmen with two small brass cannons. She then appointed Duncan MacGillechriost to command the clan and gave them a short oration which fuelled their thirst for revenge. Lady MacKenzie stood on the battlements of the castle and watched her fleet disappear into the darkness, her emotions being a heady mix of hatred, fear, excitement and a lust for revenge. As the MacKenzie fleet sailed towards Lochalsh they met one of their own scout galleys which informed them that Angus's fleet had reached Kyleakin. Learning this they sailed forward cautiously hugging the south shore of Loch Duich.

It was a calm moonlight night, with occasional showers of snow, the tide had turned so that it was speeding their progress and would hinder Angus as he sailed past this dangerous choke point. Duncan Gillechroist guessed that Angus would wait for the tide to turn again before attempting to sail through with all possible speed. Duncan ordered his fleet to sail slowly and quietly to the narrows of Kylerhea, to reduce any chance of detection he ordered that the rowlocks be bound with seaweed to reduce the noise of the oars. Soon they saw a small MacDonald scout ship rowing with all possible speed to Kylerhea to check that the way was clear. To avoid detection the MacKenzies allowed it to pass unmolested and proceeded up the straits to ambush Angus. As they neared Cailleach, a low rock midway between the shores, they saw a large galley at anchor covered in a dusting of snow. Angus for some reason had positioned his own galley some way in front of the MacDonald fleet and it was this ship that the MacKenzies were bearing down on.

When the sentries saw the MacKenzie galleys they challenged them three times and on each occasion they received no answer. The MacKenzie galleys were by now only a few yards from Angus's ship, they fired a devastating broadside from their two brass cannons. Angus's galley was severely disabled and thrown on the Cailleach Rock. The MacDonald crew rushed to arms and pored over to one side of the galley to engage the enemy. The stricken galley now capsized with this sudden redistribution of weight and many of the MacDonalds were thrown into the icy waters. Some of the crew attempted to swim for the shore while others were quickly slaughtered as they struggled in the water. Duncan ordered a galley to sail to the shore and wait for any survivors to reach land. As the exhausted MacDonalds crawled up the beach they were dragged back into the sea and drowned.

The only survivor from the MacDonald galley was Angus himself, he had been wounded twice in the head and once in the body by shrapnel from the cannons and was hauled aboard Duncan's galley. Angus died of his wounds just as dawn was breaking. The remainder of the MacDonald fleet withdrew after the loss of Angus and beached their ships on Sleat and here they were under the protection of Donald Gorm Mor chief of the MacDonalds of Sleat. They eventually sailed for Morar. Angus was taken to Eilean Donan and was, on the instructions of Lady MacKenzie buried at Kilduich amongst his MacKenzie enemies. Some accounts say he was buried in the doorway of the church so that his remains were continually walked on by the coming and going congregations. Sir Robert Gordon in his Feuds of the Clans hints at a different set of events when describing the death of Angus he says, "not without slaughter of the Clan-Chenzie likewise." There is a suggestion here that the circumstances of Angus's death may have been very different from the events recorded in the MacKenzie manuscripts.

When messengers arrived at Duart and informed Kenneth about the circumstances of the death of Angus of Glengarry, he immediately set sail for Eilean Donan, in Hector Og's largest galley, his own being judged to small if there was an attempt to intercept him. Such an attempt was indeed made presumably by the Clanranald or the Maclains. Kenneth's galley managed to outmanoeuvre the ambushers, and Kenneth returned safely to his own people.

Hector Og invaded Ardnamurchan to prevent the Maclains from assisting Angus; for this he incurred the wrath of the Campbell Earl of Argyle as he was by this date the feudal superior of the Maclains of Ardnamurchan. During the consequential legal proceedings Kenneth supported Hector Og and eventually the Earl of Argyle was placated and the issue was forgotten.

Angus died amidst uproar and violence; an end which fitted his turbulent nature. It was said that although he was imbued with the characteristics of courage and pride, qualities admired by his clan, he lacked any political skill and the subtlety of his adversary Kenneth MacKenzie of Kintail. This description of his character does fit the facts with the benefit of hindsight, but had he succeeded in his ambition to reclaim the lost lands of Lochalsh, Loch Carron and Loch Broom his epitaph would have been very different. As the eldest son of the chief of such a proud clan it was not possible for Angus to accept the loss of his people's inheritance from the Knights of Lochalsh. Angus was outmatched by Kenneth in political, economic and military power; his life is only recorded by his bitter enemies and had fate dealt him a different hand he would have been seen in a more favourable light and to his own people he would have been a hero to rival John Moydartach.

The only remaining outpost of the MacDonalds of Glengarry in Wester Ross was the Castle of Strome which was still garrisoned by Donald's clansmen. Kenneth knew that the MacDonalds would thirst for revenge after the death of Angus and that his clan's possessions in the whole of Wester Ross were threatened so long as Strome Castle could be used as a place of refuge for MacDonald raiding parties. Kenneth resolved upon the destruction of Strome, to secure his western flank.

In the late 1602 Kenneth laid siege to Strome Castle. Although now cut off from their own people the MacDonald garrison resisted the MacKenzie attempts to storm the castle with great bravery. No clan army was temperamentally suited to lengthy sieges, and Kenneth's was no exception; soon the MacKenzies began to lose heart and prepared to abandon the siege.

One dark night shortly before the besiegers left some women were sent out of the castle to draw water from the well which was situated just outside the entrance. When they returned to the store house they poured the water into the barrel containing the gunpowder, having missed the water butt in the darkness. In the morning when the garrison went to replenish their powder they found it ruined. A MacKenzie prisoner who was allowed to roam the castle overheard the men abusing the water drawers and complaining that all the gunpowder was ruined. When the prisoner climbed onto the battlements he saw that the besiegers were packing up and were about to leave, he knew that he must act immediately. He threw his plaid over the guard that was with him and ran along the battlements till he came to a place where there was a large dung heap up against the wall. He jumped over, his fall being broken by the soft manure and then darted for the safety of the MacKenzie camp. There he told Kenneth that the MacDonald garrison had lost all their gunpowder and that their food was running low.

Kenneth rallied his clansmen and prepared for an all out assault. The garrison knew that the MacKenzies were now aware of their predicament and watched with increasing anxiety as the scaling ladders were bought closer to the walls. Their resolve to resist soon collapsed and they asked to parlay with Kenneth. The garrison's terms were that they would surrender the castle if they were granted safe passage with their goods back to Glengarry. Kenneth immediately agreed to these terms and was soon in possession of Strome. This ancient castle had been a centre of MacDonald power for centuries, first under the Lords of the Isles, later under the MacDonalds of Lochalsh and for the last sixty years the MacDonalds of Glengarry, it was lost to the MacDonalds forever. Kenneth had once before seen this castle slip from his grasp, he resolved that it would not happen again. Strome Castle was destroyed in a series of massive blasts; its shattered ruins were no longer of service to their ancient masters. With the fall of Strome the MacDonalds of Glengarry had lost their last foothold on the coast of Wester Ross; they were never to be reinstated in this part of the ancient MacDonald patrimony.

While the final acts of this feud were being played out in Wester Ross the Scottish Council in Edinburgh were attempting to halt the conflagration, by a series of legal actions. On the sixth of August 1602, Stewart of Grantully was fined five thousand merks; this being the amount that he had stood surety for Donald's good behaviour. On the ninth of September Donald of Glengarry and Kenneth MacKenzie were both bound to keep the peace till May 1603; if they failed to do so they would both be declared rebels. It was at this time that Donald relinquished his clan's rights to all the lands in Wester Ross. The lands of Loch Broom, Loch Carron and Lochalsh were lost and from this time fell within the orbit of the ever expanding grasp of the MacKenzie Lords of Kintail.[17]

There was however one last act to be played out in this long running tragedy. The MacDonalds of Glengarry nursed a great sense of resentment for the illegal usurpation of their lands and were unable to let the matter rest. In September 1603 Allan MacRanald of Lundie (a gentleman of the MacDonalds of Glengarry), gathered a large force of clansmen and struck deep into MacKenzie territory in Easter Ross. This fertile and prosperous region had escaped the endless blood letting which had occurred in the west. The MacKenzies were taken by surprise as the raiders drove quickly to the east.

There was some resistance by the MacKenzies, but due to the speed of the MacDonald advance it was quickly swept aside as the braes of Ross were covered in the smoke from burning homesteads, and resounded to the bellowing of stolen cattle and the weeping of the dispossessed. The principal tenant to suffer was Mr. John MacKenzie who later put in a claim to the Privy Council for compensation for the destruction of twenty seven houses, numerous barns and kilns, his library, four hundred bolls of oats and some seventy head of cattle. The size of the claim,

---

[17] N. H. MacDonald has pointed out that the legal transfer of these territories did not take place till the 17th of March 1607.

demonstrates that this raid was on a fairly modest scale and would not normally have been considered of much significance. The unique aspect of this raid was the alleged atrocity committed at the church of Kilchrist not far from the ancient market town of Dingwall.

Church of Kilchrist

The traditional story is that the MacDonalds came down on Kilchrist on a Sunday morning while the MacKenzie congregation were at prayer. Allan ordered that the door be blocked and that the church should be set alight. The entire congregation were burnt to death while the MacDonald piper composed a new pibroch and proceeded to march around the burning church playing with all his might to drown out the screams of the dying. This tale has all the bitter qualities of previous feuds; for example, the burning alive of the MacLeod congregation of the church of Trumpan.[18]

The story was first bought to a wider audience by Donald Gregory in his work "The History of the Western Highlands and Isles"; he quotes a number of sources, none of whom actually mention this terrible event. Johnson takes up the story in his book on his travels in the highlands but transfers the scene to Culloden Moor in 1746. The story is taken up with gusto by MacKenzie historians. There is however

---

[18] See chapter 4.

one comment that implies that the whole episode did not take place. Alexander MacKenzie in his "History and Genealogies of the MacKenzies" does remark that "it is somewhat startling to reflect that this terrible instance of private vengeance should have occurred in the commencement of the seventeenth century, without, so far as we can trace, any public notice being taken of such an enormity." It is inconceivable that such an outrage which allegedly occurred in 1603 in an area of the highlands which was not at all remote could have passed without comment in any state papers. This massacre was committed on the tenants of one of the greatest magnates in the north of Scotland, a magnate who had an intimate knowledge of the working of the state apparatus and if such an event had occurred would not have failed to drag the perpetrators through the legal process. The MacKenzie Lords of Kintail were also in possession of considerable military recourses. Kenneth had clearly demonstrated in the events in Wester Ross that he was prepared to use them with ruthlessness should the need arise. Again, if this massacre had taken place is it conceivable that Kenneth would not have mustered his clan and attempted to exact revenge on the MacDonalds of Glengarry?

In the MacDonald brothers "Clan Donald" they take the argument on further by examining the evidence in more detail.[19] The parish of Kilchrist had been joined to that of Urray in 1574, and in 1603 all that remained of the church of Kilchrist was its bare walls, which given that there was as yet no tradition of open air worship meant that at the time of the raid the church was abandoned. Mr John MacKenzie, the principal plaintiff against Allan of Lundie was the minister of the parish of Killearnan, not of Kilchrist. It was true that he was the lay tenant of the lands of Kilchrist, and that he lived in the parish; although having no ecclesiastical connection with the derelict church. The question should also be asked, if he was the minister of Kilchrist why he was not consumed in the flames along with his congregation?

The most important evidence that the massacre at Kilchrist was a mere folk tale that took on a life of its own comes from the MacKenzies themselves. When John MacKenzie claims compensation from Allan of Lundie, mentioning exactly how much oats was carried off, why is there no mention of the loss of his entire congregation or even his destroyed church? The tale of the massacre of Kilchrist may have started as some local folklore which was taken up and expanded upon by people that could see its propaganda value or individuals who were merely prurient. Once Gregory had let the tale slip through as fact, it then took on a new lease of life as it was re-recorded by later historians.

There are differing accounts of the aftermath of the raid on Kilchrist. Here we will follow the MacDonald tradition[20] which was enjoyed for many generations in

---

[19] The first person to publicly question the veracity of the story was K. MacDonald in 1888.
[20] N. H. MacDonald in The Clanranald of Knoydart & Glengarry.

Glengarry.[21] Shortly after the raid, a large party of MacKenzies from Kintail surrounded Loch Lundie hoping to take Allan by surprise. Allan was alerted to their presence and he started calling out to non-existent clansmen to surround the MacKenzies and prevent them from escaping. The MacKenzies, fearing that they were about to be encircled, immediately attempted to escape. They were pursued by Allan and his men who killed many of them when their silhouettes showed up as they crossed a ridge and stuck out on the skyline.

The raid on Kilchrist was the last gasp of this long and bitter feud, Donald of Glengarry and Kenneth MacKenzie finally managed to settle down to an uneasy peace.

The MacDonalds of Glengarry were involved in some minor feuds during the next few years, the principal one being with the MacDonalds of Knoydart, a cadet house of their own kinsmen the Clanranald. The feud began with a raid by the Knoydart men on Laggen in Glengarry, which destroyed a considerable number of houses. This attack may have been caused by the desperate poverty of this clan's people, who were at the time under severe pressure from the encroachment of the Camerons. Donald appealed to the Privy Council and obtained a commission of fire and sword against the Knoydart men. He was backed by a formidable array of allies, including the Grants of Glenmoriston and the MacLeods of Harris. Initially the Knoydart men attempted to resist the formidable forces gathering against them, but realising their position was hopeless submitted to the inevitable and Donald of Glengarry was given possession of Knoydart. This acquisition by one branch of the MacDonalds of another branch's lands reflects the new "real politic" which pervaded the early years of the seventeenth century. Now it was more often the case that each clan pursued its own interests with little regard for the affiliations of the past. From this date the MacDonalds of Knoydart ceased to be an independent entity and this cadet branch of the Clanranald was absorbed into the MacDonalds of Glengarry.

In the 1620's Donald is found acting for the government in suppressing "broken men" and is employed in the persecution of the Clan Greggor as well as keeping the Camerons in check. The extant papers are addressed to Donald as chief of the clan; however it is highly likely that Alasdair Dearg, Donald's second son was the acting head of the clan by this time due to Donald's extreme old age. Alasdair Dearg understood how the political environment had changed and was attempting to adjust to the new conditions by acting as a willing instrument of the state. He died

---

[21] The MacKenzie tradition asserts that Allan was pursued by two parties of MacKenzies, one group came across some of Allan's men drinking in an ale house and killed them all except one who pretended to be the landlord. The other party surprised Allan and the remainder of his men by the banks of Aultsaigh burn; they killed all the MacDonalds except for Allan who made his escape by jumping over a chasm. N. H. MacDonald has pointed out that there is no such chasm on the Aultsaigh.

in the late 1630's and was succeeded by his son Angus as the effective chief of the MacDonalds of Glengarry.

Donald having reached the remarkable age of one hundred and two died in 1645. It is said that he died on the same day that the Campbell army was utterly defeated at Inverlochy by Alistair MacColla, a redoubtable warrior who sprung from one branch of the Clan Iain Mor[22] to bring terrible devastation to the Campbells, the persecutors of his clan. The MacDonalds of Glengarry were heavily involved in Montrose's campaigns and in the later attempts to restore the Stuart monarchy to the throne. They suffered great hardship for their loyalty to the old order, eventually in 1746 seeing their ancient castle of Invergarry destroyed by Hanoverian troops.

It was with the death of Alexander Ranaldson MacDonald fifteenth chief, in 1828 that the ancient lands of the MacDonalds of Glengarry passed forever out of their hands. Alexander set much store in keeping the old traditions of the highlands alive, including the "dignity" of a chief. He often travelled with the Luchd- crios, or body-guard, and set sentries when he stopped for the night. These and other eccentricities led to the accumulation of massive debts against which the ancient estate was heavily mortgaged. When his son Aeneas succeeded to the chiefship he was left with no option but to sell all the possessions of the MacDonalds of Glengarry to meet his enormous debts. Aeneas and a large number of the clan transported themselves to Canada where a new Glengarry was established. Clearances from the Glengarry estates had been occurring for decades; a large body of clansmen had already being cleared in the late eighteenth century when Duncan fourteenth chief was introducing large scale sheep farming.

When one stands on the raven's rock and take in the atmosphere of Invergarry Castle, or one drives through the desolate conifer forests of Glen Garry it could be easy to forget that on this land were once dozens of clachans, thousands of people who spoke only Gaelic and whose eyes were turned to the west from where their ancestors came many centuries before.

---

[22] The MacDonalds of Colonsay.

THE MACDONALDS OF GLENCOE TO 1714

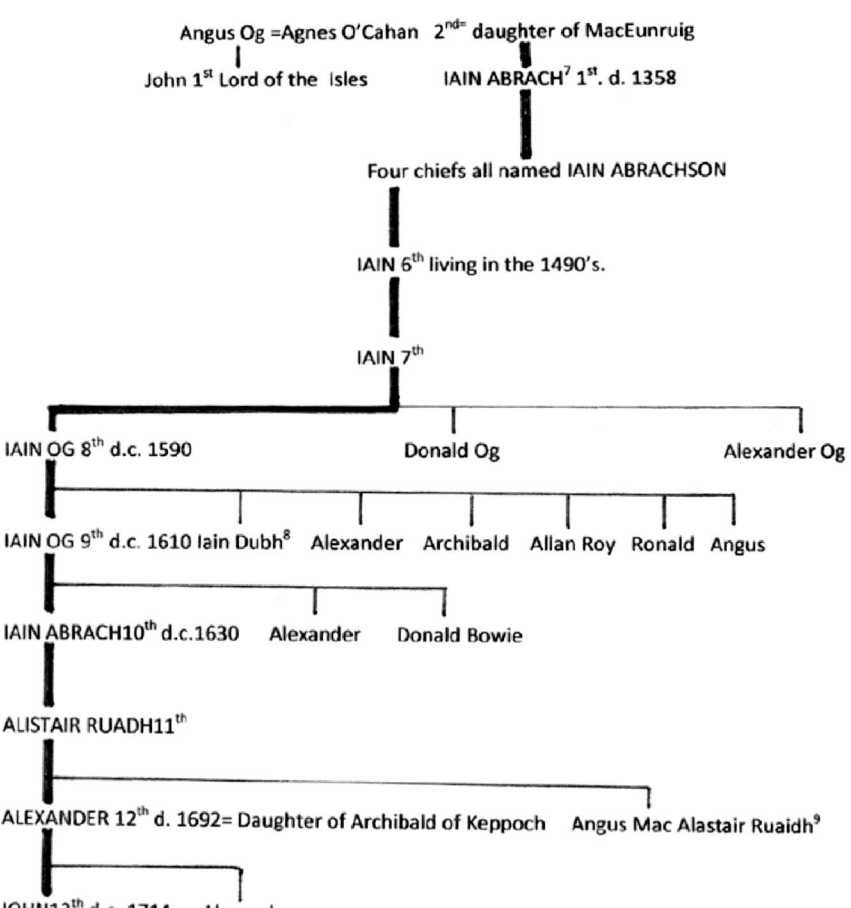

Angus Og =Agnes O'Cahan   2nd= daughter of MacEunruig

John 1st Lord of the Isles   IAIN ABRACH[7] 1st. d. 1358

Four chiefs all named IAIN ABRACHSON

IAIN 6th living in the 1490's.

IAIN 7th

IAIN OG 8th d.c. 1590   Donald Og   Alexander Og

IAIN OG 9th d.c. 1610 Iain Dubh[8] Alexander Archibald Allan Roy Ronald Angus

IAIN ABRACH10th d.c.1630   Alexander   Donald Bowie

ALISTAIR RUADH11th

ALEXANDER 12th d. 1692= Daughter of Archibald of Keppoch   Angus Mac Alastair Ruaidh[9]

JOHN13th d.c. 1714   Alexander

---

[7] Iain Abrach was also known as Iain Fraoch.
[8] Iain Dubh founded the septs of Dalness, Achtriochtan, Laroch, Inverigan and Achnacon.
[9] Poet.

Chapter 10

The Lowlanders Great Hatred

This chapter is concerned with the extant history of the MacDonalds of Glencoe, a considerable amount of it is taken up with the massacre in Glencoe in the late seventeenth century. This event was not part of a feud but more the terrible consequence of the state exacting retribution on a society which it had no understanding off.[1]

The MacDonalds of Glencoe were the smallest of all the independent clans of the house of Somerled. When their fighting strength is recorded, the number of clansmen that their chiefs could raise was about one hundred and fifty men. This would give a population of approximately five hundred souls for the entire clan. They lived for centuries in their isolated glen, their culture being as rich and diverse as their larger cousins.

The Herdsmen of Glencoe

---

[1] The massacre has been included because some readers will expect it to be here as they believe that it was as a consequence of a feud between Campbells and MacDonalds.

Glencoe was known by the MacDonald poets as the Glen of Dogs, after the great hunting dogs of Fingal.[2] The glen runs from east to west for seven miles, the north wall rises to three thousand feet and is known as Aonach Eagach. On this side of the glen there is only one difficult trail which is called The Devil's Staircase, this path climbs from Lock Leven and flanks Aonach Eagach for six miles before it descends to Rannoch Moor at the eastern entrance to Glencoe. The Devil's Staircase would have been completely inaccessible for most of the long winter months. The southern edge of the glen is formed by five mountains which join at Bidean nam Bian, the highest mountain in Argyle. Two of the other mountains are called The Great and Little Herdsmen of Etvie after the ancient cattle economy of the MacDonalds. On this south side of the glen is the pass of Glen Etvie, in which was the clachan of Dalness; the only settlement of the clan outside Glencoe. There are three other narrow passes on the south side but all of these end in mountain peaks where snow is only absent for a few weeks of the year. For all practical purposes Glencoe is inaccessible from the north and south, even during the summer months.

The entrance at the eastern end was protected by Rannoch Moor, a quaking floor of moss and heather which would be hidden in winter by several feet of snow. Apart from the MacGregors and the McDonalds of Keppoch and Glencoe few men knew the paths which could bring them across the moor. The only accessible route into Glencoe was at the western end where the River Coe spills into Loch Levin. Even here the landward approaches are long and tortuous being partially blocked by the Ben Nevis massif to the north and the Fhionnnnlaidh Massif to the south. By far the easiest access to Glencoe before the eighteenth century was by sea from the west. This meant that the MacDonalds of Glencoe were not isolated from the other western clans, but were virtually immune to the influence of the Scottish Kings or their vassals. The grandeur and majesty of the glen was a fitting backdrop to the terrible events which were to engulf the MacDonalds at the close of the seventeenth century.

Glencoe was part of the ancient patrimony of the MacDougals[3] who were forced to relinquish the glen and many other territories to Angus Og,[4] father of John first Lord of the Isles. While Angus Og's eldest son, John, succeeded his father as superior to the extensive and expanding MacDonald territories, his younger son Iain Fraoch (of the heather) or Abrachson[5] was given Glencoe. Iain Fraoch was born

---

[2] In Gaelic tradition the glen was originally inhabited by the Feinn, who's chief Fingal led them to victory over the Norse at Loch Levenside at the western end of Glencoe.

[3] The MacDougals were stripped of most of their possessions because they supported the Balliol faction against Robert the Bruce.

[4] Amongst which were Glen Roy and Glen Spean which passed to the MacDonalds of Keppoch.

[5] Abrachson denotes that Iain Fraoch had been fostered in Lochaber.

from a "handfast" [6]marriage between Angus Og and the daughter of Dugall MacEanruig, the ancient occupier of the glen. The most likely scenario as to how the MacDonalds of Glencoe came by their inheritance is that; while Angus Og was on a progress of inspection of his vast territories he met and fell in love with the daughter of Dugall MacEenruig. They had a "handfast" marriage, or an even less formal arraignment, the result of which was Iain Fraoch. Iain was then brought up by his mother's people; hence the name Abrachson, meaning that he was fostered in Lochaber. Angus Og recognized his son Iain Fraoch by giving him and his descendents the lands of Glencoe. Dugall MacEanruig's people would have been amongst Iain Fraoch's most loyal supporters and many would have changed their name to MacDonald.

After the death of John first Lord of the Isles, Glencoe came into the possession of the Stewarts of Appin and later during the minority of Mary Queen of Scots Appin itself passed into the hands of the Campbells. The Campbells were from this time the feudal superiors of the MacDonalds of Glencoe. As "mere" feudal tenants they are absent from all the early charters, and there is no trace of them as an individual clan during the rest of the Lordship. One can be sure that this small clan played its part in supporting their relatives the MacDonald Lords of the Isles in all their struggles with the Scottish state. Their position as tenants of the Dukes of Argyle means that they are absent from many documents of the sixteenth century as they were not regarded as an independent social and political entity. They appear only fleetingly in the historical record; however these descriptions allow us to have a clear idea of their political inclinations and their way of life. The MacDonalds of Glencoe and the other highland clans understood that the feudal tenure of the Campbells counted for nothing in Glencoe and that this clan was in effect as independent as any other.

Iain Fraoch died at Knapdale in 1358; he was buried alongside his father on Iona. Later generations were buried on the sacred island of Munde[7] which lies in the middle of Loch Levin a few hundred yards from Invercoe.

Iain Fraoch was succeeded by five chiefs in succession all called Iain Abrachson; it can only be assumed that son followed father to lead the clan. The MacDonalds of Glencoe re-emerged into the light in 1500 when Archibald Campbell, Earl of

---

[6] Handfast marriages were contracts between couples for a specified period, usually a year and a day. This type of union was widely practised in late medieval Scotland and lingered on for centuries north of the highland line. It was possible for the offspring to be recognized by their clans as chiefs, however under feudal law they were considered to be bastards, and thus had no right to the succession. This in turn meant that should a clan "elect" a chief from a handfast marriage this chief would hold no legal title to the clan land as far as the state was concerned.

[7] The MacDonalds of Glencoe, the Stewarts of Appin, and the Camerons all laid claim to this island. They each cropped it for hay in rotation and resolved their disputes on the nearby Island of Discussion. All three clans brought their dead to a specific landing place before burial in the island cemetery.

Argyle attempted to evict the Stewarts of Appin and the MacDonalds of Glencoe. Despite the full weight of the law behind him Archibald failed to remove the ancient possessors of Glencoe. There is no mention of the MacDonalds of Glencoe in the one hundred and forty two years between the death of Iain Fraoch and this attempted eviction.

In 1501 the MacDonalds of Glencoe were chosen to attempt the rescue of Donald Dubh the heir to the Lordship of the Isles. They were chosen for their intimate knowledge of the paths across Rannoch Moor and their generally excellent knowledge of the tracks to Loch Awe.[8] Donald Dubh was held in the forbidding castle of Inchconnel by the banks of Loch Awe. It was already a Campbell boast that it was a "far cry to Loch Awe", by which they meant that it was difficult for any hostile clan to penetrate as far as Loch Awe which was in the Campbell heartland. The hundred or so MacDonalds quickly reached Loch Awe, broke into Inchconnel and released Donald Dubh. They then escaped back to the relative safety of Glencoe before the Campbells could catch up with them. It is a testament to their speed, courage and determination that such a small clan was able to penetrate to the heart of Campbell territory, break into one of their most secure strongholds and release such a valued captive. Then having alerted the Campbells, they managed to evade their pursuers and thus let loose the vengeful Donald Dubh.[9]

The MacDonalds of Glencoe sink back into obscurity for another fifty years before emerging in a manrent document dated May 1563, in which Iain Og (probably the seventh chief), binds himself to serve the Campbell Earl of Glenorchy in exchange for secure tenure of Glencoe. In this document there is a specific stipulation that Iain Og will loose his tenancy if he does not immediately serve against the MacGregors, who were still trying to maintain possession of Rannoch Moor.[10]

This agreement did not last long; in 1582 the MacDonalds of Glencoe and Keppoch descended on Breabalbane and invaded the lands of the Campbells of Glen Orchy, Glen Lyon and Lawers. This raid met with disaster at the hands of Mad Colin Campbell of Glenlyon. Mad Colin captured thirty-six of the raiders and hanged them in rows outside the walls of his castle of Meggernie. When Colin was asked by the Privy Council to confirm that he had acted within the bounds of the law, he replied that, not only would he put his hand to a document affirming his legal right of "pit and gallows" but that he would add his foot.

---

[8] Their knowledge of the geography of Argyle was due to their continual cattle raiding.
[9] All the clans belonging to the original Lordship of the Isles rose in support of Donald Dubh and the western highlands were again in open rebellion (see chapter two).
[10] In this same year the MacDonalds of Keppoch signed a very similar bond of manrent which included the same stipulation with regards to the MacGregors. During the previous century the MacGregors had been displaced from their possessions in Breadalbane by the Campbells; they were now reduced to living amongst the wastes of Rannoch Moor.

The rich glens of Breadalbane were an irresistible magnet for the MacDonalds of Glencoe and Keppoch. In the summer of 1583 they again swept down from Rannoch Moor, this time they were more successful. Mad Colin complained to the Council, "...with bow, quiver and other weapons invasive, upon the twenty fourth of June last by the break of day, and masterfully reft, spulzied and took away from the said complainer and his servents, four score head of kye, eleven horses and mares, together with the whole insight and plenishing of their houses; and also not satisfied with the said oppression committed by them as said is, struck and dang the women of the said lands and cutted the hair of their heads." This last act of casual abuse clearly demonstrates that by this date there was a festering, generalized contempt between the two great houses of Gaeldom.

Two documents, one a commission, dated 1588, granted to the Gordons and Grants to act against the MacDonalds of Glencoe and another dated 1589, a bond of mutual support between the Camerons and Grants against the depredations of the inhabitants of Glencoe imply that the MacDonalds of Glencoe were extensively raiding a wide area. These two documents demonstrate that they were roaming far and wide in the sixteenth century, stealing cattle from even their most powerful neighbors, and driving the herds back to Glencoe and hiding them in the high blind glens of The Great and Little Herdsmen. It is remarkable that such a small clan was able to bring fear to such powerful neighbors without retribution. The topography of Glencoe must have delivered security from invasion and counter-raiding, and clearly the MacDonalds of Glencoe were regarded as a lawless and restless community even by their Gaelic neighbors.

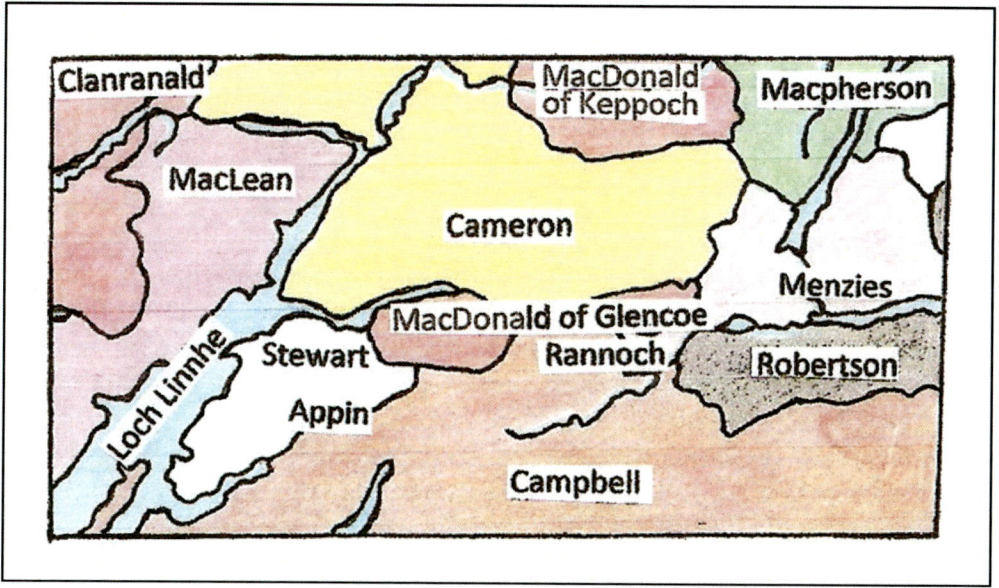

Territories of the MacDonalds of Glencoe and neighbouring clans c.1600

In 1591 the MacDonalds of Glencoe were caught up in a feud between the Campbells and Ogilvies. Campbell of Persie was a guest at an Ogilvie wedding, a quarrel broke out and Campbell insulted the bride and stabbed her father. The Ogilvies drew their weapons and Campbell was soon disarmed. He narrowly escaped hanging and was driven from the celebrations in a most undignified way. Campbell of Persie's disgrace was felt as a personal affront to his dignity by Grim Faced Archibald Campbell, Earl of Argyle. Archibald called in the obligations of service the MacDonalds of Keppoch and Glencoe had signed up to in the bonds of manrent.

Certainly neither clan of MacDonalds would have obeyed this summons if it had not suited them. Here was an opportunity too good to miss; they were called upon to raid a rich clan under the protection of the Earl of Argyle. In his complaint to the Privy Council Lord Ogilvie states that his clan were unexpectedly attacked by five hundred raiders and that he was "nocht able to resist them, but with grite difficultie and short advertisement he his wyffe and bairnis eschaiped."

In the same year the MacDonalds of Glencoe raided the lands of the Drummonds of Blair, this time on their own initiative. After crossing Rannoch Moor they swept down on the Drummond lands and made off with a large haul of cattle. Amongst those cited in the complaint to the Privy council are Iain Abrachson ninth chief, and his brothers. John Stewart of Appin was, as their feudal superior cited to appear before the Privy Council. There is no record of him ever having done so, nor do there appear to have been any later consequences for his failure to appear to answer for his recalcitrant tenants. Glencoe contained no more than a few hundred acres of land which were viable for cereal production and a few thousand acres of grazing in the short summer growing season. These limited resources were unable to support the five hundred people of the clan. This led to the clan having to risk the enmity of their more powerful neighbors to supplement their food supply as the glen itself was unable to sustain them.

In 1599 they were again brought to the attention of the Privy Council, for raiding Lennox. In the complaint to the Privy Council the MacDonalds of Glencoe were led by their chief and gentlemen to the woods of Ardinacple which belonged to the MacAulays. As they moved stealthily towards Ardincaple House they took hostage several MacAulys to prevent them from giving the alarm. They waited till MacAulay came out of his house and then chased him through the woods, MacAulay narrowly escaping the raiders. The MacDonalds then proceeded to set fire to several houses before stealing a number of prized cattle and slaughtering some others. On their return journey they relieved the Duke of Lennox of thirty two horses and twenty four cattle, Grim Faced Archibald must have been extremely annoyed that he, as their feudal superior, was fined a considerable sum of money for failing to control his tenantry. The continual raiding of the MacDonalds of Glencoe at this late date must have built up a store of resentment among their Campbell neighbours who were often their victims or held responsible for their depredations.

This resentment against the MacDonalds of Glencoe did not prevent the Grim Faced Archie from using a contingent of Glencoe clansmen. He persuaded them to join with the MacGregors and others in a full scale assault on the Colquhouns of Luss. In the bitter winter of 1603 they came down through the Pass of Arrocher and encountered the Colquhuons and their Buchanan allies and Lowland levies in Glen Fruin. The Colquhouns were overwhelmed and their lands stripped of a vast haul of livestock and goods. Among the Glencoe contingent was a notorious villain called Allan Og. He was left in charge of some forty prisoners. Irritated that others were making off with all the spoil; he cut their throats and joined in the looting. When MacGregor of Glenstrae asked him where the prisoners were, he drew his dirk and said "Ask that, and God help me." It was six years before he was captured, condemned to death and executed. This was the last time that the men of Glencoe allowed themselves to be drawn into the machinations of the Campbells; the reason lay in the bitterness of the whole of Clan Donald over the ruthless extirpation of the Clan Iain Mor.[11]

In the early years of the seventeenth century a feud broke out between the MacDonalds of Glencoe and their neighbours, the Stewarts of Appin.[12] One of the consequences of this feud was the deaths of John and Alexander Stewart. A commission was given to the Colquhouns, MacLeans and Camerons to capture Alastair MacIain of Dalness. Alastair was the brother of the Iain Og ninth Chief of Glencoe, Alastair is described as a "common and notorious theif and sorner, and oppressor, for many years a fugitive and an outlaw." Alastair was eventually captured and imprisoned in Edinburgh. During this feud the MacDonalds of Glencoe are said to have killed more Appin Stewarts than in any other feud in which the later were involved. Shortly after the murder of Walter Stewart the MacDonalds invaded the lands of Stewart of Strathgarry in eastern Rannoch. After killing the herdsmen they drove off his entire herd which had been grazing on the summer shielings.

The Stewarts of Appin appealed to their powerful cousins the Stewarts of Athol and Balquhidder, who obtained Letters of Fire and Sword against the MacDonalds of Glencoe. The Stewerts gathered at the western end of Glencoe by Loch Levenside. By now it was high summer and the MacDonalds were dispersed throughout Glencoe tending to their cattle in the high mountain pastures. The Stewarts marched up Glencoe and surrounding each shieling in turn, fell upon their enemy with sword, dirk and axe. The MacDonalds attempted to resist the invaders at Carnoch but were overwhelmed by the enemy. Iain Abrach and his brother fell at the head of their clan; their heads were cut off and pickled in a barrel. A simple minded Stewart clansman was given the task of taking these grisly trophies to

---

[11] During the early sixteenth century the Clan Iain Mor, after a desperate struggle, lost possession of their ancestral lands in Kintrye and Isla to the Campbells (see chapter 12).
[12] These two clans, who were a similar size, were usually allies against the ever present threat of Campbell expansion.

Edinburgh to bear witness that the orders of the Privy Council had been carried out. On his way south the messenger stopped at Strathgarry and showed his cargo to the lady of the house. He knocked the heads together inside the barrel saying, "Why are you making such a noise in there? Aren't you friends?" Her reaction is not recorded, but it is likely that in the true highland tradition she enjoyed the spectacle of seeing those who were responsible for ruining her husband being treated in such a way.

By the early seventeenth century an uneasy calm had descended over many regions of the highlands. The MacDonalds of Keppoch and Glencoe were amongst the last clans to submit to the requirements of the increasingly powerful state apparatus. There is an ever growing sense that the MacDonalds of Glencoe are beginning to be seen as bandits not only by the authorities but also by their neighbours who were abandoning the old ways. It is significant that the powerful and warlike Clan Cameron is appearing ever more frequently in commissions issued by the Privy Council to punish the MacDonalds of Glencoe. MacDonald and Cameron had in turn been at feud with each other or been allies against other clans ever since the disintegration of the Lordship of the Isles over a hundred years before. By this date even the Camerons were adapting to the new environment while the MacDonalds of Glencoe are clinging to the old ways with their continual raiding. They were caught in a conundrum, Glencoe could not support the population and yet the remedy of raiding was making them increasingly isolated, even from their ancient allies. As the years went by this small clan was unable to expand either by military conquest or political intrigue. The chief and gentlemen of the clan would have been well aware of their difficult position but were unable to do anything about it.

For seventeen years there is no mention of the MacDonalds of Glencoe in the records of the Privy Council. But in 1634 they were raiding the lands of the Chrichtons in north-west Aberdeenshire. The Glencoe men were, along with many Gordons and "broken" men plundering, burning and stealing in this distant land. At this time the Gordons were at feud with the Chrichtons and it was only with the connivance of the Marquis of Huntley that the MacDonalds were able to raid so far from home. This raid took place in November, where the dates of these raids are accurately recorded; it is remarkable how many took place in the early winter months. This was because the MacDonalds of Glencoe needed to ensure that they had an adequate supply of cattle to get them through the hard winter months.

Alastair Ruadh, eleventh chief of Glencoe was forced to appear before the Privy Council and was ordered to remain in Edinburgh as part of his bail conditions, Alastair was not permitted to travel more than one day's journey from the capital. On suspicion that he was about to escape his mentors and return to Glencoe, Alastair was imprisoned in Edinburgh jail. Alastair was released from jail after several months and after spending a year in Edinburgh, was allowed to return home. Within a few years the Glencoe men, allied to the MacDonalds of Keppoch, raided the Campbells. Although the raid was successful, their chief, Alastair Ruadh, lost his life while holding at bay the Campbells who were attempting to recover their cattle.

This raid took place while the Campbells were celebrating the marriage of the daughter of Campbell of Breadalbane to the chief of Clan Menzies. As the MacDonalds were driving the stolen cattle around the slopes of Sron a'Chlachain they were intercepted by the Menzies and Campbells. The latter had poured out of the wedding reception and rushed to arms while still drunk from the celebrations. Archibald MacPhail a champion of Glencoe uttered a short prayer in which he implored God to stay out of the fight if He could not bring himself to side with the MacDonalds. Archibald then charged down the hillside firing his bow at the Campbells and Menzies who were struggling up the slope. Afterwards Archibald boasted that he had shot an arrow into the groin of the Menzies chief ending his hopes of becoming a father. In less than ten minutes fifteen Campbell gentlemen from Glenorchy lay dead, but the running fight continued with losses on both sides. The fighting drew to an exhausted stalemate in the Corrie of the Bannocks. The small stream there was known afterwards as The Bloody Burn.

As their attackers drew off, the MacDonalds made stretchers for their wounded and slowly made for Rannoch Moor with their plunder. The Campbells and Menzies were reinforced by fresh contingents and renewed their attack. There was a running series of skirmishes, in which Menzies of Culdares[13] killed young Angus of Keppoch.[14]

In 1655 The MacDonalds of Glencoe were again tempted by the riches of Bredalbane. They crossed the twenty or so miles of Rannoch Moor and poured down into their old plundering grounds. Soon they were burning clachans and driving off the cattle. A Campbell girl called MacNee, who was tending some of the cattle, was forced to go along with the raiders. When they reached the narrow pass of Glen Moran which led up onto Rannoch Moor she broke the legs of some of the calves which delayed the MacDonalds long enough for the pursuing Campbells to catch up with them. There was a vicious struggle on the shores of Loch Lyon in which the Campbells managed to rescue some of their cattle. The girl was killed in the encounter, but she had partially achieved her objective in saving the cattle. This sad episode clearly demonstrates the value placed by highlanders on their herds of cattle. Although MacNee died in this skirmish, she was remembered for centuries in a song the Campbell women sang their children.

> Colin's cows of my heart, John's cows so dear,
> They'll give milk on the heather with nothing to fear,
> Colin's cows of my heart, Colin's cows of my love,
> Like the wing of the moor-hen, brown-speckled above.

---

[13] Menzies of Culdares was the bridegroom at the wedding.
[14] The grief stricken poet Iain Lom composed a moving poem describing his feelings as he watched the young man die.

During the civil war, the MacDonalds of Glencoe played their part in Montrose's campaigns. It was their intimate knowledge of Argyle which was used to such devastating effect during the terrible depredations of Alastair MacColla, which left vast swathes of Argyle desolate. These were years of plenty for the people of the clan; Glencoe was full of Campbell cattle and possessions of all types filled the round houses of the calchans. For a time Campbell power was broken and there was no immediate risk of retribution from their old enemy. During this period the clan was led by a redoubtable warrior, Ranald MacDonald of Achtriachtan. He was known as Raoull na Sgeithe, or "Ranald of the Shield."

There is a story of Ranald which demonstrates why he was held is such high regard by his clansmen. An English dragoon was captured during the campaign; he was heard saying that the highlanders were poor swordsmen as they needed a targe to defend themselves with. Ranald indignantly offered to dual with the dragoon, he being armed with a dirk and targe while the dragoon was to be given his sword. Ranald promised the Englishman his liberty if he was able to kill him. At this point, Another Glencoe man, Aillean dubh nam fudh (Black Allan of the Deer) interrupted Ranald and offered to take his place as he was a better swordsman. He warned Ranald the sword was much better than the dirk, and asked him to listen to his advice or there was no knowing what would happen to him. Ranald would have none of it, exclaiming, "there is no knowing what may happen to me, but the very devil will happen to him."There is no record of the consequences of the dual but as there is no mention of the dragoon's release and we know that Ranald lived to be an old man we may be sure that targe and dirk triumphed on this occasion. Ranald was not only a clan warrior but also a poet of some distinction;[15] he will appear in a later sadder context.

The history of the MacDonalds of Glencoe is obscure for most of the sixteenth century; the character of individuals and even their campaigns have been lost. In the mid-nineteenth century an old woodsman from Argyle recorded some of the local folk memories of his region.[16] Amongst these tales are two which tell of famous highlanders from Glencoe, Archibald MacPhail and Iain MacAllein.

Archibald MacPhail was a hero to the people of Glencoe; he accompanied his clan on all their raiding expeditions in the early seventeenth century. He was an expert and fearless swordsman but even his own clan admitted that he lacked the finer sensibilities. He once met a lowlander at Achnacone and greeted him in Gaelic in the traditional way, "God's blessing on you, Sir." The lowlander, having no Gaelic replied that it was indeed a fine day. Archibald, angered at this unintelligible and to him disrespectful response replied; "Foolish man, do you despise the word of God?" Archibald drew his sword and killed the unfortunate traveler on the spot. When he recounted the events to the local Stewart laird he failed to appreciate that his actions might be regarded as somewhat criminal, merely observing that the

---

[15] Ranald composed a haunting lament after the execution of Charles I.
[16] John Dewar, whose manuscripts are in the archives of Inveraray Castle.

man's clothes would fetch a good price.[17] There was never any question of bringing Archibald to justice for his crime. Whether the murder of a lowlander was regarded as of little consequence or because to attempt to hang a well respected member of this clan was considered unwise.

Archibald was next embroiled in a raid on the Campbells of Glenorchy. Duncan Stewart of Appin had married Jean Campbell, a daughter of Campbell of Glenorchy. Stewart firmly believed that he had not received his dowry from Glenorchy. He mustered his clan and accompanied by MacDonald of Dalness and his men, amongst whom was Archibald, invaded his father-in-law's lands. Glenorchy withdrew to his forbidding castle of Kilchurn driving all the cattle into the courtyard. However some of the calves had been overlooked. Some of the Stewarts began to torment the calves and their blaring was heard by the cows inside the courtyard. MacDonald of Dalness pointed out that if any man could now break down the castle door it would be to their advantage. Archibald rushed forward to the gate ignoring the fire of arrows, muskets and even some small cannon. He broke down the gate, and the maddened cows rushed out to reach their calves. When asked by his brother why he had risked his life Archibald replied that, "It were all the same to me to be dead as to refuse my gentleman."

When Archibald was visiting his son in Glen Orchy he fell gravely ill; he made his son swear to take his body back to his own people. "When it is death with me, if it happens here, strike a blow of the dirk in my back,[18] put me across the piebald mare and she will carry me to Glencoe, and the people shall bury me on the Island of Munde. By all that you have ever seen, dare not lay me but beside the MacDonalds. Put a sword in my fist and my face to the Camerons. I have never turned my back on them!"This last request whether pure fabrication for the enjoyment of the listeners or containing a kernel of truth hints at a mindset which would not have been out of place in the pre-Christian world of his ancient Irish and Norse ancestors.

Archibald MacPhail had a nephew Iain MacAllein; they would often accompany each other on raiding forays. One summer's day, Iain, Archibald and three companions went raiding in Strathspey. Strathspey had long been settled by the Clan Grant who had no love for any of the branches of the MacDonalds. This small group managed to steal some cattle and quickly set off for home across Badenoch. The next evening they stopped by a small lake, they secured the cattle on a promontory which jutted out into the water. They then started a fire and began to roast one of the calves. As they had made their way towards the safety of Glencoe they had been followed by the chief of the Grant's son with sixty clansmen. On seeing the Grants silhouetted against the skyline the companions rushed to arms to

---

[17] The laird, knowing more of lowland custom returned to the corpse and on searching the victim's trousers found sixty gold guineas.

[18] This was a common practice to confirm that an individual had indeed died; in the 1930's doctors were still paid a fee to bleed a corpse to ensure death.

face their pursuers. Archibald prayed aloud as they moved forward. He called upon the Almighty for aid, stipulating that should his request be granted, he would never bother him again. Iain approached the chief's son holding his sword by the blade in a gesture of surrender. As the Grant reached for it, Iain spun his sword in the air, caught it by the hilt, and cut him down with one stroke. Archibald and the other MacDonalds rushed forward to support Iain. Some of the Grants fled, while the others advanced to avenge the mutilation of the chief's son. After a brief struggle, the Grants were defeated and fled.

The next morning the small party continued on their way, heading for the hidden tracks across Rannoch Moor and safety. The fate of the young man he had cut down began to play on Iain's mind. Telling his friends that he would catch them up, Iain turned back and on coming across his wounded victim went down to the lakeside to fetch him some water. As he returned to the young man, he was shot by the Grant. The pistol ball shattered Iain's thighbone and the two men lay together in a pool of blood. Iain then suggested that they should continue their struggle, the young Grant agreed. As the youth struggled to his feet he saw that Iain could not stand and not wishing to take advantage of his crippled foe he suggested that they should become friends. Iain agreed and they lay together in the heather till some Grant clansmen returned and carried them to the chief's house. Here Iain was cared for by the Grants for a year, until he was able to return to his own people.

It does not really matter if elements of these stories have been embellished in the telling. What is certain is that both Archibald and Iain were regarded as great men by their clan, who admired their courage, strength and stoicism. Even at this late date, the MacDonalds of Glencoe still maintained their passion for the ancient values of their forefathers. The stories of Archibald and Iain were told for two hundred years around the peat fires, which demonstrates how much they must have been enjoyed by teller and listener. Highlanders admired the mixture of brutal violence and gentle gallantry which this last tale exemplifies. There is a sense in which these tales show us how the MacDonalds of Glencoe thought; and how they aspired to emulate them. It was this antiquated outlook which was to contribute to their being so utterly overwhelmed by the scheming of more "modern" men.

Alasdair MacDonald became the twelfth chief of the MacDonalds of Glencoe, when his father Alasdair Ruadh died in 1650. It is likely that he led his clan into England in support of Charles II. The Scottish army was virtually annihilated in the streets of Worcester; there is no record of how Alasdair and the other survivors, including Ranald of the shield escaped the vengeance of Cromwell's New Model Army; or of their long journey home.

In his later years there is evidence that Alasdair was faced with serious unrest within the clan. Amongst the Inveraray papers is a small scrap written by the ninth Earl of Argyle which records that Alasdair's cousins, the gentlemen of the clan, butchered several members of their own clan. It may well be that this incident was an example of Alasdair exercising his powers of "pit and gallows" to the full.

Alasdair who was now in his sixties was captured and to the great delight of many Campbell lairds imprisoned at Inveraray. Alasdair, much to the chagrin, of the Campbells and the Government managed to escape.

After the restoration of Charles II, the MacDonalds of Glencoe were involved in the daunting of the western shires of the Lowlands. The enforced billeting, along with the predictable pillaging, caused grate resentment amongst these lowland Scots and did untold damage to the highlanders. It created an environment which meant that many lowlanders could sit back with equanimity or even pleasure as the highlanders were later massacred and evicted.

In a rare miscalculation of Campbell policy the Earl of Argyle rose in rebellion against James II and with three thousand clansmen declared his support for the Duke of Monmouth. Monmouth and the Campbells were defeated; the Campbell chief meeting his death with quiet stoicism under the heavy blade of the Maiden.[19] Argyle's instincts had been correct but he was three years too early. James had called for the ancient enemies of Clan Campbell to suppress them. The MacDonalds of Glencoe had joined the highland host which had been drawn up to oppose them. With the defeat of the Campbells, Argyle was invaded from the north, south and east by various clans who had been the victims of Campbell expansionism. This invasion of Argyle was no mere raid; it was a state sanctioned act of retribution against rebels. Alasdair had the pleasure of consigning Campbell gentlemen to the prison at Inveraray before stripping the lands of Campbell of Asknish, Brabeck and Ardkinglass. Interestingly Alasdair was joined in this sanctioned plundering by Campbell of Lochnell who was related by marriage to Alasdair and who had remained loyal to James.[20] Alasdair was unable to resist this golden opportunity to extend his activities to the fertile lands of Campbell of Knockderrie, who later complained bitterly to the Privy Council, as he had also remained loyal to James.

James was forced to flee to Ireland after he had been deposed by William of Orange in 1689. He again appealed to the clans for help.[21] Alasdair joined Dundee's rebellion not from a strong sense of loyalty to James, but from a hope that there would be yet more state sanctioned plundering.

There is a contemporary description of Alasdair in his old age,[22] written by the standard bearer of Dundee's army before the Battle of Killiecrankie in 1689. "Next came Glencoe, terrible in unwonted arms, covered as to his breast with new hide, and towering far above his whole line by head and shoulders. A hundred men all of gigantic mould, all mighty in strength, accompany him as he goes to war. He himself turning his shield in his hand, flourishing terribly his sword, fierce in aspect,

---

[19] The Maiden was the Scottish name for the newly imported guillotine.

[20] This is a rare example of the breakdown of the cohesion of the Campbells.

[21] In the previous year he had appealed to his subjects to "....concur in suppressing and rooting out the said barbarous and inhuman traitors (the MacDonalds of Glencoe), to their utmost power....". These were hardly the words of a King worth hazarding your clan for!

[22] This description is in a poem called the Grameid, by James Philip of Almerclose.

rolling his wild eyes, the horns of his twisted beard curled backward, seems to breathe forth wherever he moves."Clearly, even allowing for the hyperbole, Alasdair was a physically imposing character. This description of a clan chief would not have been unfamiliar to onlookers a thousand years before.

Killiecrankie proved a hollow victory, for although General Mackay's army was cut to pieces by the onslaught of the highland clans, Dundee was killed. The clans were fought to a standstill at Dunkeld, and the highland host dispersed. Alasdair returned home to Glencoe through Glenlyon, over the Black Mountain and across Rannoch Moor. As they passed through Glenlyon they stripped the glen of all its livestock.[23] By the feast of Samhain[24] the men of Glencoe had returned with their plunder to the safety of Glencoe. This raid left the local Campbell lairds in a state of near bankruptcy and their people destitute. Their suffering only added to the long history of hatred between the two clans.

For his part in Dundee's campaign Alasdair was declared a rebel and his lands were forfeit to the Crown. On the eleventh of September 1690 a Commission was given to Argyle to invade Glencoe and take possession of it for the Crown. This was the first direct step which was to lead to the terrible events of the massacre of Glencoe.

The clans who were loyal to James remained obdurate in their defiance of William, initially taking the view that they could only be relieved of their loyalty to the former king by written affirmation of their release by James himself. William had little interest in the affairs of Scotland, let alone the highlands. William's overriding concern was the security of the Netherlands and the interests of his new kingdom were a poor second. He was happy to allow affairs in the highlands to be dealt with by ministers who were corrupt and self-serving.

The Campbell Marquis of Breadalbane was entrusted with a large sum of money,[25] with a view to bribing the recalcitrant chiefs to take an oath of allegiance. The Marquis was tainted by the suspicion that he was corrupt, and all elements of Scottish society were convinced that a great deal of this money would find its way into his own pockets. Worse still, as a Campbell whose lands had been ravaged repeatedly over the last fifty years, he was extremely partisan. Although he had been appointed to bring peace to the highlands through conciliation, his first pronouncement was to inform Alasdair that he would keep the money earmarked for him in compensation for the cattle stolen from his lands when the Glencoe clansmen were returning from Dundee's rebellion. Breadalbane soon informed the Secretary of State for Scotland that "the money has been spent; the Highlands were quiet, and that was enough between friends."

As well as the inducement of the bribes, William issued a proclamation that if the chiefs made their submission to the Crown before the thirty first of December

---

[23] The Campbells assessed their losses at £7540; a vast sum for one glen.
[24] Samhain was feast day which marked the end of summer.
[25] £12,000 sterling.

1691 they would be pardoned, while those clans which did not submit would be regarded as traitors and thus exposed to the full extremity of the law.

Sir John Dalrymple, Master of Stair, Principal Secretary of State of Scotland, was the man in charge of the pacification of the highlands. Even amongst his lowland contemporaries Dalrymple was both despised and feared for his cunning and duplicity. He was lampooned anomalously by his detractors,

That slippery Stair goes unstraight, stoops and high,
Do like his neck turn his whole course awry.
That trap, for public place, that's Jacob's ladder...

Sir John was charged with administering the activities of Breadalbane and ensuring that William's proclamation was adhered to. For centuries the Scottish state had issued letters of "fire and sword" against law breakers and rebels in the highlands. It had issued commissions to the most powerful magnates in the country to carry out its edicts.

With very few exceptions the clans had been able to treat the state's authority with contempt and had pursued their own self interest in open defiance of the state. Sir John was determined to finally end this state of affairs. He assumed that the chiefs would remain defiant and gave orders to his commanders in the field, "Your troops will destroy entirely the country of Lochaber, Lochiel's lands, Keppoch's, Glengarry's and Glencoe's. Your power shall be large enough. I hope the soldiers will not trouble the Government with prisoners." These types of orders had been issued many times before over the centuries. The great difference this time was that the state had the power to implement them.[26] Sir John was determined that this time there really would be a wide scale massacre of highlanders which would instill fear and obedience in the others.

The commander of the garrison at Fort William, Colonel Hill,[27] took the oaths of loyalty of some of the clans. The Camerons and the MacDonalds of Sleat, Keppoch, Glengarry, Clanranald and Glencoe stood aloof still stating that they needed James to release them. An envoy had been sent to the Court of Saint Germains, some months before, to obtain James's signature. James finally signed the document on December 12th 1691; all sides had let time run short. By his vacillation James had allowed time to drift away, it was highly unlikely that those chiefs which were waiting for his release would receive the document and be able to act on them before the end of the year. Major Menzies, the envoy, made all possible speed and reached Dunkeld on the twenty third of December. He instantly sent messengers to

---

[26] Government forts were being built or rebuilt all over the highlands, its ships were regularly sailing in the western islands and the clans loyal to William, amongst whom were the Campbells, were reaching the apogee of their power.

[27] Colonel Hill was a far sighted and moderate officer who had a clear appreciation of how to treat the recalcitrant clans.

the Privy Council begging them to postpone their plans as the chiefs needed more time to receive the release, by which time the day of grace (31st of December) may well have passed. On the fifth of January the Privy Council sent a copy of the release to London.[28]

Sir John Dalrimple became ever more impatient as December wore on; he was under pressure from the King to pacify the highlands so that valuable regiments could be released from their garrison duties in the highlands and redeployed to protect the Netherlands. In the middle of December Sir John wrote to Breadalbane urging him to be more vigorous in his attempts to cajole the chiefs to submit. He then states that he would like to begin the massacres even before the end of the month, as in his opinion the oaths will not be worth the paper they are written on anyway. There is a sense in which he is anxious that the clans should not evade "justice." By the end of December all the chiefs or their representatives had signed the oath except Glengarry and Glencoe. They had signed with great alacrity. Was it possible that they knew that this time the Government was quite capable of carrying out its threats?

Sir John had been refining his plans of slaughter as the situation evolved; in the end he decided that Alasdair and the MacDonalds of Glencoe should be the only victim of this malicious policy. He would have reasoned that this small clan which was notorious throughout the highlands for their raiding had few friends outside of their own kin, who were preoccupied with trying to save themselves. In a letter of late December to Colonel Hill at Fort William, Sir John, gives the Colonel permission to give young Alasdair Dubh of Glengarry every chance to take the oath and to compromise with him so long as he takes it in the end. There is also an extant letter from Sir John to Lieutenant-Colonel Hamilton an officer of the Fort William garrison. The letter refers to the affection this minister of the Crown holds for Hamilton and how, if Hamilton carried out his duties he would be rewarded. The letter finishes with a clear hint as to what these duties might be, "....for the wintertime is the only season in which we are sure the Highlanders cannot escape us, nor carry their wives, bairnes, and cattle to the mountains." The relationship between Sir John and Hamilton is unclear. Did Sir John have some hold over Hamilton or was Hamilton simply overawed by authority? Either way it was Hamilton who had been selected as one the Sir John's instruments.

Four weeks before the expiry date for the oath taking, Sir John is writing to Breadalbane "....The madness of these people makes me plainly see there is no reckoning with them; delanda est Carthago[29] (Carthage must be destroyed). Even if

---

[28] By being sent to Court it is highly likely that William would have been aware of this release.

[29] Cato the Elder would finish any speech he made to the Roman Senate with the words "ceterum censeo Carthagineum esse delendum" which translates as, "for the rest, it is my opinion that Carthage must be destroyed." Within a few decades Carthage was wiped from the face of the earth.

some were to take the oath by the day set they deserved no kindness and hostages should be taken from them. All must be taught a harsh and brutal lesson, and the victims of it, quite plainly, should be Clan Donald, the Gallows Herd whose deaths none but their own kinsmen would morn."

Here we have, at the end of the seventeenth century, Sir John Dalrymple, the Master of Stair and Secretary of State for Scotland writing letters which gleefully talk of cold blooded murder and even of the massacre of women and children. His loyalty to the state and his hatred of Dundee go no way to explaining the evil machinations of this statesman. Was it that, the MacDonalds of Glencoe, with their endless raiding, Catholicism, their violence and strangeness simply deserved to be massacred? Was Sir John simply overwhelmed by Mi-run morn an Gall, the Lowlanders great hatred of the Highlander?

Breadalbane soon left the highlands and made his way to London where he joined Sir John Dalrymple, at Kensington Palace. Had Breadalbane; that crafty and subtle politician become alarmed at the vitriolic and hysterical letters from his superior? Did he want to make sure that if there was to be a massacre that he was far from the scene?

Alasdair would have received James's release about four days after Major Menzies had reached Dunkeld on the twenty third of December. Within a few days, Alasdair was standing before Colonel Hill at Fort William asking the Governor to witness the swearing of the oath to William. Alasdair must have already made his mind to give the oath before receiving James's release, as within a day of its arrival he had set out for Fort William. Alasdair had seen all his neighbors submit, or knew they were going to take the oath to the new order and knew that he must also follow the pragmatic path of submission. The proclamation of loyalty, clearly states that the oath must be taken in front of a sheriff, "...in the presence of the Sheriffs, or their deputies, of the respective shire where any of the said persons shall live." Hill informed Alasdair that he was unable to administer the oath. Alasdair had run out of time and knew that he could not reach Inveraray in a day especially as there were frequent snowstorms which would have made any crossing of Rannoch Moor a slow and hazardous process. He would also have preferred to take the oath in front of a respected professional soldier rather than a Campbell sheriff.

For Alasdair to go into the heart of Campbell country, to a town where he had been imprisoned and many of his clan hanged, and there to offer his submission to the chief of a clan which had been replacing his own was a bitter pill to swallow. Colonel Hill must have found the meeting difficult as he saw the proud old chief before him; he knew of the plans to encompass the MacDonalds of Glencoe and knew that troops were already on the move.

Alasdair immediately set out for Inveraray; he carried with him a letter from Hill to Ardkinglas asking him to overlook Alasdair's late arrival. As Alasdair watched the blizzard rage around him, he knew that the quickest route to Inveraray over Rannoch Moor would be impassable so he took the torturous coastal route. As Alasdair watched, his attendant clansmen landed on the shores of Loch Creran where they were arrested by a nervous troop of newly raised militia. Alasdair was detained for twenty four hours at Barcladine Castle before being allowed to go on his way. It was January the first before the company of MacDonalds were allowed to go on their way to Inveraray, the date for taking the oath had passed. It was dawn on the second of January before the exhausted company arrived in Inveraray.The MacDonalds must have felt a sense of foreboding on entering the Campbell capital, passing the prison and the court house, with the vast grey walls of Invararay Castle in the background. In front of them was Doom Hill where so many of their race had drawn their last breadth as they were suspended between heaven and earth.

Ardkinglas was staying with his family on the other side of Loch Fyne when Alasdair arrived. It was three days before he summoned Alasdair to meet him at the court house. Sir Colin Campbell of Ardkinglas had a reputation of a stern but fair administrator. After reading Hill's appeal he wrote, "... he has been with me, yet slipped some days out of ignorance, but it is good to bring a lost sheep at any time, and will be an advantage to render the King's government easy." He told Alasdair that the time had passed and that he would not administer the oath. He was then presented with the extraordinary sight of Alasdair twelfth chief of the MacDonalds of Glencoe the ancient enemies of his clan standing before him weeping openly. This proud old chief knew that his people were in mortal danger from forces he could not fully comprehend. Ardkinglas relented when he saw his old foe so broken.[30]

The next day, after a lecture on his late arrival, Ardkinglas administered the oath to Alasdair in front of the town dignitaries. He did state for the record that he could give no assurance that the Privy Council would accept Alasdair's submission because he was out of time. Alasdair returned to Glencoe believing that he had secured "his children" from the wrath of the state. On a large rock near his house of Carnoch he addressed his clan, he told them that he had signed the oath and that so long as they remained within the law they were safe. Alasdair's belief that his clan were safe was reinforced when he received a letter from Hill assuring him that he was now under the protection of the garrison at Fort William. [31]

Ardkinglas sent a document with a list of all those who had taken the oath, to his kinsman Colin Campbell of Dressalch, in Edinburgh, and asked him to place the document before the Privy Council. Ardkinglas also included Hill's letter and a letter of his own asking the Privy Council whether Alasdair oath was to be accepted. Dressalch had been one of the victims[32] of Alasdair's raiding and was not pleased to see Alasdair's name on the list. Dressalch took it upon himself to consult with

---

[30] For all their mutual hatred Ardkinglas was also a Gael, and clearly the plight of Alasdair stirred some sympathy in his heart.

[31] Both Hill and Ardkinglas were under the impression that the MacDonalds were safe even though Alasdair had been late in taking the oath.

[32] Dressalch was still petitioning for £240 in compensation for some stolen cattle.

several lawyers, many of them Campbells, as to whether Alasdair's name should be scratched from the list. The opinion that he received was that Alasdair submission could only be accepted with the express consent of the King, his signature was duly scratched from the list.

Events were now being determined by Sir John Dalrymple, Master of Stair, in Kensington Palace. The Earl of Breadalbane, spent many days in his waiting room. From his correspondence it is clear that he was vacillating between trying to distance himself from forthcoming events and wanting to be part of the decision making process. The initial reports from Scotland intimated that Alasdair had saved his clan by signing the oath on time. Sir John could hardy contain his anger as his attention turned to the Camerons and MacDonalds of Glengarry. When the true picture emerged[33] he could not hide his pleasure and excitement, "....Lord Argyle tells me that Glencoe hath not taken the oaths, at which I rejoice. It's a great work of charity to be exact in rooting out this damnable sept, the worst in all the Highlands."

At Fort William, Colonel Hill, had reason to feel pleased with the way he thought events were unfolding. All the branches of Clan Donald had agreed to take the oath and it seemed as though the clans would peaceably submit to the new order in London. In London Sir John presented his written plans for the extirpation. An example was to be made of this small clan; he expected to suppress the warlike and independent spirit of the western clans for good. William needed soldiers for his continental wars and felt that while the other clans may be valuable recruiting grounds the MacDonalds of Glencoe would be little loss. Despite the fact that other larger clans had not yet signed (the Camerons and MacDonalds of Glengarry), this small clan was to suffer the full and literal interpretation of the penalty of being an enemy of the state. They were judged to be significant enough to instill fear in the others yet small enough to be no real loss. The MacDonalds of Glencoe had, by their continual raiding and archaic outlook become isolated. William signed the papers which would give authority for Sir John's plans to be put into effect.

By the end of January, Sir John's detailed requirements backed by William's signature had arrived on Colonel Hill's desk. Hamilton's Argyle militia were already in place, being garrisoned in and around For William, Hill was now powerless to prevent events unfolding; as this old soldier was prevented from any ameliorating action by the signatures of the Secretary of State for Scotland and the King.

Sir John had selected the man who was to have his hand on the trigger with great care. Captain Robert Campbell fifth laird of Glenlyon was sixty years old when he led his men into Glencoe. He was a gambler an alcoholic, and a bankrupt. He was tall, with a florid complexion and in his youth had been considered handsome. Robert Campbell was also reckless and brave, two characteristics which would be essential if he was to successfully carry out his orders in full. His drinking and

---

[33] He received the news that Alasdair had been late in taking the oath from the Lord of Argyle in person.

desperate financial situation led to outbursts of rage and he was regarded as being extremely unstable, his relative the Earl of Breadalbane was once heard to remark that Robert "...ought to be sent to Bedlam."[34]

His clan had occupied Glen Lyon for nearly two hundred years, among his ancestors was Mad Colin who had hung so many Glencoe clansmen from the walls of Meggernie Castle. Now the only part of Glen Lyon left to him was the estate of Chesthill, the rest having being lost to some of his many creditors. Robert had had to submit to "comhairl'-taigh" or guidance from his overlord the Earl of Breadalbane, to whom he owed a vast sum of money. His dire financial situation had been exacerbated by Alasdair's raid on Glen Lyon when he was returning from Dundee's campaign. The MacDonalds of Glencoe had stripped his estate of Chesthill of all its livestock and chattels and now this last remaining land could not long stay in his family. Clearly this unstable and desperate man who had been reduced to utter poverty, the final blow being given by the MacDonalds of Glencoe, was the ideal man to carry out the dreadful machinations of Sir John.

The Argyle militia companies were ferried across the narrows to Ballahulish. A mile before reaching Invercoe, at the western end of Glencoe, the Government companies were met by a few dozen MacDonald clansmen, under the command of Iain MacDonald, Alasdair's son. Alasdair had been alerted when the boats of soldiers were still crossing to Balahulish. He assumed that the soldiers had come to disarm his clansmen and wanted Iain to divine their purpose and delay them while the clan's weapons were well hidden. A junior officer told Iain that the soldiers came in peace and that the Government required the MacDonalds to quarter these two companies of troops. Glenlyon then came forward and greeted Iain asking after his niece Sarah, who had married Alasdair Og, who was Iain's brother. The meeting between Iain and Glenlyon was full of tension, each man harbouring his own resentful thoughts. After a few moments Iain welcomed them and gave them unopposed access to Glencoe; after all he had been assured by regular army officers of their peaceable intentions, and he had seen the written request from the Government for quarter.

Iain led the companies of soldiers to Alasdair's house of Carnoch; the soldiers were watched anxiously by small groups of MacDonalds as they entered the glen. Alasdair welcomed Glenlyon, offered him and his men the clan's hospitality, he was relived that this maintenance of two companies was all that was required of him. If Glenlyon recognized any of his cattle grazing on the southern slopes of the glen, or saw his red stallion in Alasdair's yard he had the good sense to say nothing. The soldiers were to spend thirteen days living with their unsuspecting hosts, they were dispersed among the clachans from Carnoch to Archtriachtan;[35] Glenlyon saying he

---

[34] Bedlam was a well known "hospital" for the insane.
[35] They lived three or four to a cottage.

would stay at Inverrigan.[36] All the houses in the glen were full to bursting, each being occupied by MacDonald clansmen and Campbell militia.

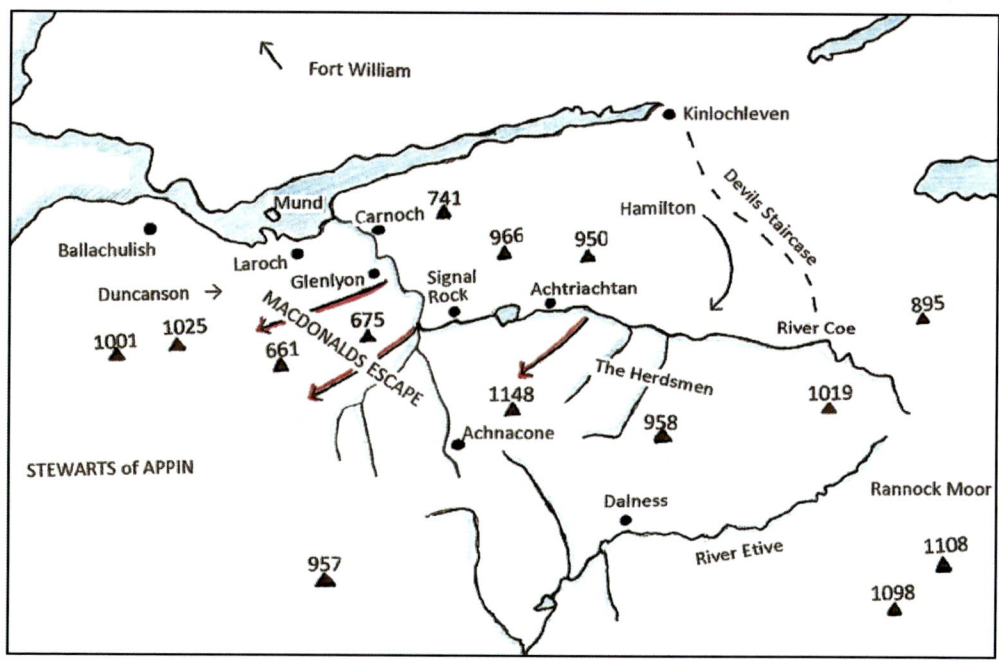

Initially there was a considerable sense of unease amongst the MacDonalds and within a few days of the arrival of Glenlyon a deputation of a hundred people went to complain to Alasdair about the presence of the soldiers. Alasdair angrily told them to accept the situation[37] and that they were quite safe as he had "broken bread" with the officers and by ancient tradition, he had offered, and they accepted his hospitality. It was a central part of their culture that once hospitality had been offered both host and guest were safe under any circumstances. As the days past the Campbell soldiers and the MacDonalds began to form relationships of cordiality if not friendship; only the lowland soldiers were kept at arm's length. During the short winter days they played camnachd (shinty) and wrestling. After dusk they gathered round the smoking peat fires and told stories well known to them all because of their shared heritage.[38]

Glenlyon spent his time either drinking with Alasdair at Carnoch or gambling with Alasdair's sons and his officers at Alasdair Og's house. Glenlyon would always be the last man sitting at the card table, returning after sun rise to Inverrigan.

---

[36] Glenlyon may have wanted to avoid having to live amongst pots and pans stolen from his own house.

[37] He was well aware that the situation could have been a lot worse than having to quarter two companies of soldiers for a while.

[38] Many stories would have been avoided to prevent an outbreak of violence.

Glenlyon had been carefully selected for this terrible mission but it is most unlikely that he knew what would be asked of him in a few days time. He was a quarrelsome drunkard; subject to fits of rage and for these reasons it is unlikely that his superiors would have told him of his true mission until the last moment.

The massacre was delayed by Hill's refusal to sign the final orders. He wrote again to Sir John asking him if it really was his intention to massacre a population which was unsuspecting and law abiding. Sir John's reply left no room for doubt, "You cannot receive further directions... be as earnest in the matter as you can... be secret and sudden... be quick...". Colonel Hill was devastated by the reply, he was a professional soldier with a keen sense of duty, he was old, poor and had two dependent daughters, and he knew that he would be instantly replaced if he failed to sign the order. With a heavy heart he wrote to Hamilton, "You are with four hundred of my regiment, and the four hundred of my Lord Argyll's regiment, ...to march straight to Glencoe, and there put in due execution the orders you have received from the commander-in-chief (the King)."

Hamilton was ready; he gave orders for fourteen companies[39] to take up positions with would enable them to trap and exterminate the MacDonalds of Glencoe. Hill's regiment was ordered to proceed to Kinlochlevinside and then take the path known as The Devil's Staircase which emerges at the eastern end of Glencoe. They were to seal off any attempt to escape up onto Rannoch Moor and then drive down from the eastern end of Glencoe killing all in their path. They were to be in position by seven in the morning. Hamilton ordered major Duncanson, who was in command of Argyle's regiment to block the escape routes through the western end of the glen as well as the high passes of Gleann an Fiodh, Gleann eac na Muidhe and Lairig Gartain. Hamilton's letter to Duncanson is most explicit, "....that the old fox and none of the cubs get away. The orders are that none are spared, nor the government troubled with prisoners...".

Duncanson, in his turn wrote to Glenlyon, "You are herby ordered to fall upon the rebels, the MacDonalds of Glencoe, and to put all to the sword under seventy. You are to have a special care that the old fox and his sons do upon no account escape your hands. You are to secure all the avenues that no man escape. This you are to put in execution at five of the clock precisely; and by that time, or very shortly after it, I'll strive to be with you with a stronger party. If I do not come to you at five, you are not to tarry for me, but to fall on. This is by the King's special command, for the good and the safety of the country that these miscreants be cut off root and branch. See that this be put in execution without feud or favor, else you may expect to be dealt with as one not true to King or Government, nor a man fit to carry Commission in the King's service..."

Duncanson had been ordered to close the western and southern escape routes at seven, yet in his letter to Glenlyon he twice orders him to begin the massacre at five. The most likely explanation for this discrepancy is that Duncanson hoped that

---

[39] Fourteen companies represented over nine hundred officers and men.

by the time he arrived the killing would be over, and that he would not then be made a scapegoat for the decisions of powerful politicians.

That Friday another storm was breaking and most clansmen and soldiers were huddled around the fires of the smoky round houses. Despite his bitterness, drunkenness and hopelessness, Glenlyon as a highlander himself would have understood the terrible implications of breaking the trust he had accepted from Alasdair and his clan. That he was then to command his men to murder every man, woman and child was unspeakable, it is not known whether Glenlyon was tormented by his orders, the chances are that he was, although he was unable to extricate himself from the fast flowing events. Whatever inner turmoil Glenlyon was going through he managed to hide it well from Alasdair as they played their usual game of cards that night.

As the storm began to rage through the glen, Glenlyon sent word to his officers in the scattered clachans throughout Glencoe. The ordinary solders were not to be told till the last minute. [40] It is quite possible that at some houses the news did leak out well before five and that some of the soldiers felt compelled to warn their hosts. At Brecklet in Glean an Fiodh a family called Robertson were warned by their Campbell guest. Staring hard at the family he said, "Were this plaid mine, I would put it on my shoulders and I would take my family out to drive my cattle to a safe place." The story then goes on to relate how this family took his advice.

In the early hours of Saturday morning Iain MacDonald was woken up by shouting outside in the darkness. On looking out the window he saw small groups of soldiers moving about in the swirling snow storm. After reassuring his wife he went to Inverrigan to ask Glenlyon what all the activity meant. Glenlyon explained that they had had orders to march against Glengarry. Seeing that Iain was still suspicious he said the one thing that would reassure him, "You think we intend Glencoe some ill? Man, if that were my orders do you think I would have given my niece and your brother no warning?"

Iain returned home not knowing that in the next room Inverrigan and eight members of his household lay bound and gagged awaiting "justice". The hands of Glenlyon's watch reached five, and the killings began. Duncan Rankin was the first to die; he was shot while attempting to cross the Coe, his body was found floating in Loch Levin. Alasdair was woken by a servant saying that the Campbell soldiers wished to say goodbye as they were leaving for Glengarry's country. Alasdair was attempting to get dressed when the Campbells burst in; he was shot in the back by an officer called Lindsay and then shot in the head as he lay face down on the bed.

---

[40] There was a tradition amongst the MacDonalds of Glencoe that the soldiers knew, on the Friday. One of these stories is of a warning given by a Campbell soldier to his hosts. He had been silent all evening, finally he addressed the families dog, "If I were you, grey dog, my bed tonight would be in the heather." His hosts slipped out when he pretended to sleep and they escaped the massacre.

Alasdair's wife was robbed of her jewelry and left naked and traumatized. Along the entire length of the glen shots ran out, the massacre had begun in earnest.

Iain MacDonald guessed immediately what was happening. As he opened his eyes, he saw the look in his servant's eyes and heard the musket fire mixed with the screams of his people. He saw a group of soldiers approaching his house; he quickly gathered his frightened family and led them to the safety of the wood on the slopes of Meall Mor. His brother, Alasdair Og also escaped with his family and servants; they also made for the safety of Meall Mor. The MacDonalds could hear the shots ringing out in the darkness above the howl of the storm. They could smell the acrid smoke which was pouring from their burning homes. Iain and Alasdair realized that dawn was not far away and that their wives and children would run the risk of been discovered. They asked them to climb to the safety of Gleann an Fiodh and Gleann Leac na Muidhe, despite the fact that in these high passes they would be exposed to the bitter cold of the blizzard, but at least they would be hidden from the eyes of the soldiers. Alasdair's sons made their way to Inverrigan. Here they came across more terrified women and children. They told them to seek the safety of Glean Leac.

At Inverrigan Glenlyon ordered his hosts to be thrown on a nearby dung hill. Here they were methodically murdered with musket and bayonet. When it came to the last of the family Glenlyon seems to have sickened at the slaughter and ordered his soldiers to stop. Soon afterwards another officer, called Drummond came up, and on seeing the frightened young man still alive shouted at Glenlyon, "Why is he still alive? What of our orders? Kill him!" When none of Glenlyon's company moved, Drummond drew his pistol and shot the youth in the head. A boy ran out of the darkness and flung himself at Glenlyon's feet begging for mercy, saying that he would follow Glenlyon anywhere if he would spare him. As Glenlyon stood transfixed, Drummond barked out an order and the boy was hauled away and shot. The slaughter at Inverrigan was terrible, MacDonalds were bayoneted in their beds and quick quiet murder was secretly done amongst the swirling snow and howling wind.

Sergeant Barber was in charge of the detachment which had been quartered at Achnacone, which was the most easterly of all the clachans in Glencoe. Barber's men were ready at five; they surrounded all the houses in the little community. MacDonald of Achnacone and his brother Iain MacDonald of Achrtiachtan had been woken by the movement of the soldiers; they were gathered round the fire with their clansmen. The door was suddenly forced open and at the same time muskets shattered the small pains of glass in the windows.[41] Eighteen muskets fired instantaneously, Achtriachtan and four others were killed instantly. Achnacone although badly wounded lay on the floor still alive. He asked Barber if he would finish him off outside. Barber replied that since he had received hospitality from

---

[41] Glass windows were still a rare phenomena in the highlands and few men below the level of a tacksman (gentleman) had access to this expensive commodity.

Achnacone, he would grant him his wish. Achnocone was dragged outside and propped up against the wall of his house. Having reloaded the solders moved up close to the wounded man; after all this was execution not sport. As they cocked their muskets Achnacone threw his plaid over them and rushed out into the darkness where his figure was soon obscured by the heavy snowfall. Inside the house the wounded survivors broke through the back wall and also escaped into the darkness.

Barber's men killed many MacDonalds as they ran out of their burning houses, one family of fourteen who could not bring themselves to face the soldiers were burnt to death in their house. Among the victims at Achnacone was an eighty year old man and a young boy. In desperation the MacDonalds turned on their persecutors and three of the soldiers were killed on the hillside. They were later furtively buried where they had fallen.

Sergeants Hendrie and Purdie were in command of the men based at Achtriachtan;[42] at five they began their own grisly work. There were some among the soldiers who found their orders distasteful but there were also those who reveled in their work. One Campbell who had been a victim of the raiding of the men of Glencoe particularly relished his work. With each thrust of the bayonet he would shout, "There's for Catherine's blanket and that's for Colin's cows." It is possible that the redoubtable warrior Ranald of Shield was still alive, if he was, he died at Archriachtan on that terrible morning. Iain MacRaonuill Og, a respected Glencoe poet was saved by his son who carried his father to the east up the glen towards Rannoch Moor.

The survivors of Achriachtan could only flee to the east as they were hemmed in by the glen itself and to the west they could hear the massacre was in full spate. Some of the young men climbed over the steep rocks and made their way to Dalness and Appin. The women and children were too weak and exhausted to attempt this arduous route in the storm. They climbed three hundred feet to Coire Gabhail (the Hollow of Capture), and blocked the entrance with a fallen tree.

As dawn broke the blizzard blew itself out and Glenlyon's soldiers could see Duncanson's companies marching up the glen.[43] The killing had stopped and there was an unnatural quite among the ancient clachans of the MacDonalds. It was said that Glenlyon's piper played a Breadalbane pibroch as Duncanson approached.

---

[42] The clachan of Achtriachtan was known amongst the MacDonalds as the "village" of the poets.

[43] If Duncanson had planned to avoid the killing, by telling Glenlyon to begin the massacre at five, then this ruse had been successful.

Listen, then, to my pibroch,
It tells the news and tells it well
Of slaughtered men
And forayed glen,
Campbell's banners and the victor's joy!

Duncanson became more and more agitated as he searched in vain for the bodies of Alasdair's sons; he could only hope that they had been caught by Hamilton's soldiers who were to have sealed off the eastern end of Glencoe.

Hamilton's companies had reached the head of Loch Levin in the middle of the night. Due to the blizzard and their exhaustion it was impossible for the soldiers to attempt the Devil's Staircase. When one considers the route which Hamilton's companies were being expected to take, that they were to do it in the dark and to be in position by five one must consider the possibility that Hamilton also intended to arrive late. Hamilton's troops did not reach the eastern end of Glencoe till mid-morning after an arduous journey along the Staircase. They made contact with some of Duncanson's patrols at Achrtiachtan. The troops left Glencoe in the afternoon; they took with them all the livestock and left the glen quiet and full of swirling smoke from the burning houses. The troops had stripped every house of all its valuables, no doubt many of the Campbell troops from Argyle would have felt justified in looting so many possessions which had originally come from their people. Did Glenlyon recover his cattle and his fine red stallion?

The Eastern End of Glencoe

In the dusk of late afternoon the MacDonalds who had survived the cold came down the steep sides of the glen to search amongst the smoldering ruins for their loved ones. Alasdair was buried with many others of his clan in the graveyard of the chapel on the Island of Mund. Alasdair's sons found their mother; they wrapped her in a plaid and took her to join the other survivors of the clan. With the murder of Alasdair, Iain MacDonald became the thirteenth chief of his clan. He gathered the survivors together and took them over Gleann Leac to Appin to seek sanctuary among the Stewarts. As the pitiful party made its way over the high passes the wind got up again and the temperature dropped. It was here, on the high southern crags of Glencoe that Iain's mother died of cold and exhaustion. Some of the young men lurked on the inaccessible sides of Glencoe while some families fled to their summer shielings high on Rannoch Moor. Many of the young and old did not survive till the spring, dying of hunger and cold in the bleak late Scottish winter.

The massacre at Glencoe on the thirteenth of February 1692 has left an indelible stain on those responsible for this crime. Only some few dozen MacDonalds were murdered on the day of the massacre and the question why this event, terrible as it was, should have become so infamous?

Glenlyon's Campbell militia were in the end, not the troops most suited to the task. Despite the impoverishment caused by the continual raiding of the MacDonalds of Glencoe, the Campbell element in the companies were themselves highlanders and sprung from the same Gaelic culture. In the tales that were handed down from mouth to mouth there were several examples of kindness or at least evasion of duty. The fact that there were so few victims must have meant that many soldiers turned a blind eye to fleeing figures in the dark, or that, people found hiding were left unmolested. The most famous story of this compassion is of a Campbell soldier who was ordered to kill a woman and her child who were hiding under the bridge at Alt-na-Muidhe at the western end of the glen. When the soldier went over to the woman he noticed they had a dog, he bayoneted the unfortunate creature and showed the officer the bayonet. The officer was suspicious and ordered him to go back and kill the couple, threatening him with execution if he failed to obey him. The soldier returned to the woman and cut off the child's finger smearing its blood on his bayonet.

Many years later the old soldier was traveling through Appin when he stopped at a cottage for the night. As the company talked that night the soldier was asked to name the most terrible thing he had done, he told his hosts that he had been present at the massacre of Glencoe. The cottagers were MacDonalds and they planned to murder him in the morning. Over breakfast the soldier recounted the story of the woman under the bridge. As he finished his story his host raised his hand to show that he had a finger missing and told the soldier that he was that child. There is a very similar story which casts some doubt on the accuracy of either. However that these stories exist, and were told by the MacDonalds about their persecutors must mean that there were instances when Campbell soldiers risked their lives to save some of their ancient foes. It is certain that if other regiments had been used, like the Cameronians,[44] the slaughter would have been much worse.

The events in Glencoe did have the desired effect of bringing the remaining defiant clans to take the oath, although the massacre caused shock and resentment throughout Lochaber. In August, William gave his permission for the survivors to return to Glencoe. They were helped to re-establish themselves by their neighbors, the MacDonalds of Keppoch, the Camerons and the Stewarts of Appin. When news of the massacre reached the remote island of Heskier in the Outer Hebrides, Alasdair MacDonald loaded his boat with meal and set sail for Loch Leven to give aid to his fellow clansmen.

There was considerable public anxiety over the massacre which was continually fanned by Jacobite sympathizers, who had their own agenda in wishing to damage William's reputation. Eventually, in April 1695 a Royal Commission was appointed to examine the events in Glencoe, three years before. Surprisingly the Commission carried out its work quickly and succinctly, its report was put before Parliament in June. To varying degrees all the principal actors in the tragedy were found to be guilty of causing or taking part in the massacre. The one exception to this indictment was King William; Parliament bent over backwards to exonerate him. Although Sir John Dalrymple, Master of Stair was the prime mover of events,

---

[44] The Cameronians were drawn from the populations of south west Scotland and were known not only for their extreme Protestantism but also their brutal toughness.

William cannot escape the part he played in the tragedy. He did, after all, sign the final order for the massacre to take place. Suspicion of his guilt (i.e. he knew exactly what he was signing) is increased by William granting Sir John a remission for his crimes despite strong popular opposition. Was he afraid that unless Sir John was guaranteed immunity he would let some uncomfortable truths come out?

Hill was acquitted; Duncanson, Drummond, Glenlyon, Lundie and Barbour were all found guilty of "slaughter under trust". William left for Ireland and then Flanders, before leaving he retired Sir John Dalrymple from public office for a while; none of the others were ever brought to trial for their crimes. William and Parliament clearly did not want this sordid matter to receive another public airing.

Why is it that the massacre at Glencoe has left such a strong impression on the public imagination? After all there were many incidents in highland history in which many more people were massacred; for example, the events on Eigg.[45]

The massacre in Glencoe took place on the thirteenth of February 1692. By this date the world of feud and massacre had long passed in almost all of the highlands.[46] By the late seventeenth century Britain was a partial democracy, with a sophisticated market economy and a highly developed sense of the rights and worth of the individual. At this late date, massacre simply could not be tolerated, even when committed by the state on the wild and strange inhabitants of the northern mountains. The fact that the Government apparatus, from the King to the sergeants in Glencoe, were instrumental in planning and then carrying out this brutal act was profoundly shocking to the vast majority of the population.

For many the worst aspect of the massacre is summed up by British law itself, when it condemns some of the perpetrators of "being guilty of murder under trust". This betrayal of hospitality was particularly shocking in the Gaelic societies north of the highland line. It confirmed that their freedom to act as quasi-independent clans who could feud with each other and defy the state was over. Moreover for the more perceptive amongst them it was a clear warning that the British state would act ruthlessly and mercilessly if its interests were threatened by them.

The MacDonalds of Glencoe recovered quickly from the events of 1692. In 1745 Alasdair's grandson joined the Prince's army with a hundred fighting men. The implication of this is that by this period there were five to six hundred souls living in Glencoe who were still ready to risk all for their chief.

Glencoe was held by the descendents of Iain Fraoch till the nineteenth century when it was sold by the trustees of the daughter of Ewen MacDonald seventeenth chief of his clan. "The Gallows Herd" were replaced by sheep and Glencoe fell silent; the struggle by generations of MacDonalds to maintain themselves in the Glen of Dogs had ended.

---

[45] See chapter 4.

[46] An exception was the long running feud between the MacDonalds of Keppoch and the MacKintoshes over Glen Spean (see chapter 8).

THE MACDONALDS OF CLAN IAN MOR

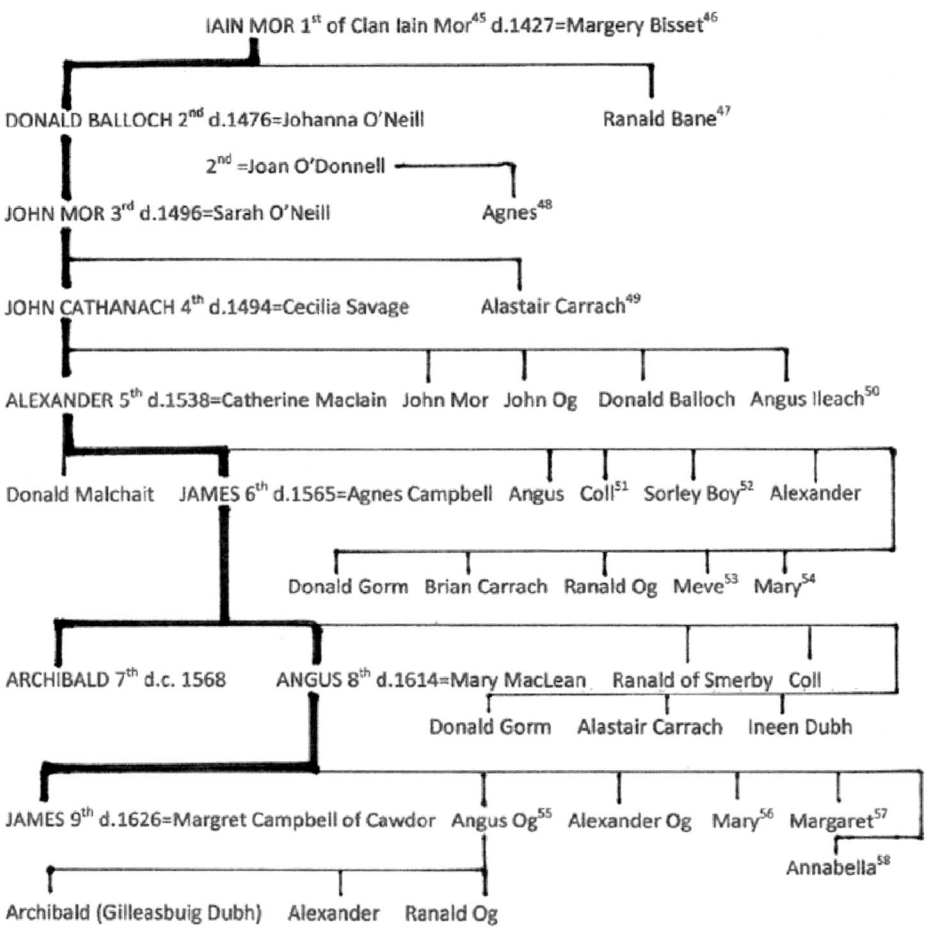

IAIN MOR 1st of Clan Iain Mor[45] d.1427=Margery Bisset[46]

DONALD BALLOCH 2nd d.1476=Johanna O'Neill   Ranald Bane[47]

2nd =Joan O'Donnell

JOHN MOR 3rd d.1496=Sarah O'Neill   Agnes[48]

JOHN CATHANACH 4th d.1494=Cecilia Savage   Alastair Carrach[49]

ALEXANDER 5th d.1538=Catherine Maclain   John Mor   John Og   Donald Balloch   Angus Ileach[50]

Donald Malchait   JAMES 6th d.1565=Agnes Campbell   Angus   Coll[51]   Sorley Boy[52]   Alexander

Donald Gorm   Brian Carrach   Ranald Og   Meve[53]   Mary[54]

ARCHIBALD 7th d.c. 1568   ANGUS 8th d.1614=Mary MacLean   Ranald of Smerby   Coll

Donald Gorm   Alastair Carrach   Ineen Dubh

JAMES 9th d.1626=Margret Campbell of Cawdor   Angus Og[55]   Alexander Og   Mary[56]   Margaret[57]

Annabella[58]

Archibald (Gilleasbuig Dubh)   Alexander   Ranald Og

---

[45] Iain Mor was the second son of John 1st Lord of the Isles by his second marriage to Princess Margaret.
[46] Margery Bisset was the heiress to the Glens of Antrim.
[47] Ranald Bane's descendants are the MacDonalds of Largie.
[48] Agnes married Thomas Bannatyne.
[49] Alastair Carrach founded the MacDonalds Kinbane.
[50] Angus's descendants are the MacDonalds of Sanda.
[51] Coll nan Capull's descendants are the MacDonalds of Colonsay.
[52] Sorley Boy's (Somhairle Buidhe) descendants are the MacDonalds of Antrim.
[53] Meve married Hector MacLean of Coll.
[54] Mary married Hector Mor MacLean of Duart.
[55] Angus Og married Katherine Campbell of Danna.
[56] Mary married Donald of Clanranald.
[57] Margret married Ranald MacDonald of Benbecula.
[58] Annabellla married Archibald MacDonald of Largie.

Chapter 11

Dubh Sith

The Clan Iain Mor[1] is also known as the Clan Donald South,[2] or the MacDonalds of Dunnyveg and the Glens.[3] Of all the clans of MacDonalds which emerged as independent entities after the fall of the Lordship, they were regarded as the most senior branch and were the most powerful until they passed out of history. The cause of the utter ruin of this great clan at the beginning of the seventeenth century lay partly in their inability to adapt to an evolving political landscape and the fact that their possessions lay directly in the path of Campbell expansionism.

The clan derive their name from their progenitor Iain Mor who was the second son of John, first Lord of the Isles and Princess Margaret of Scotland; his elder brother Donald[4] became the second Lord of the Isles. John gave Iain Mor extensive possessions on Kintyre and Isla; these possessions were to form the nucleus of the clan's lands in Scotland. In the late fourteenth century he married Margery Bisset,[5] as a dowry she bought with her the Glens[6] of Antrim. From this time the Clan Iain Mor held extensive possessions on both sides of the Irish Sea. This meant that they could move with consummate ease between Ireland and the western highlands reinforcing either part of the clan as circumstances dictated. It also meant that they could evade the wrath of Scottish Kings by removing themselves to Ireland.

Iain Mor was known by the people of the Lordship as Iain Mor Tannister.[7] From an early period Iain Mor is found to be in correspondence with several English monarchs,[8] knowing several of them personally. This international contact at such an early date is remarkable. Iain Mor supported his brother Donald in all his attempts to maintain and increase the power of the Lordship of the Isles; he was present at the Battle of Harlaw in 1411. The death of Iain Mor in 1427, and the events which led to his murder are contentious, the MacDonald tradition will be

---

[1] The anglicized "Mor" has been used throughout the book but the more correct spelling is Mhoir.

[2] This name derives from the fact that all their Scottish territories were in the southern Hebrides and Kintyre.

[3] Dunnyveg was the ancient castle which they occupied from the fifteenth century, while the appellation of the Glens is derived from their first possessions in Ulster.

[4] Iain Mor supported Donald's pro-English policy in the struggle between England and Scotland. Like his brother, Iain Mor's motive was to maintain a Gaelic polity independent of Scotland.

[5] The Bissets were an old Anglo-Norman family, Margery was the last of her line.

[6] The Glens are on the extreme north-eastern tip of Ulster, they were often referred to by the clan as, na seachd tuathaibh Glinneach or the heritage of the Glens. The Glens were delineated by the rivers Inver and Boyse.

[7] Tannister roughly translates as the one who had the right to succeed.

[8] Amongst whom were Richard II and Henry IV.

followed here.[9] James I had been involved in a bitter struggle with Donald second Lord of the Isles for control of the western highlands.

With the death of Donald in 1423, Iain Mor assumed the role of leader of the Lordship in his capacity as Alexander's uncle.[10] James attempted to break up the cohesion of the Lordship by offering Iain Mor large tracts of the Lordship. Iain Mor refused the gift; he remained loyal to his nephew, the child Alexander, who would, in due course become the third Lord of the Isles. James's emissary, James Campbell proposed that he and Iain Mor should meet at Ard Dubh on Isla. Iain Mor arrived at Ard Dubh accompanied by only a small following of MacDonald gentlemen; he was surprised to see that James Campbell had brought a considerable number of supporters. Iain Mor again refused the King's offer, after which James Campbell attempted to take Iain Mor prisoner. The MacDonalds were greatly outnumbered but resisted the Campbells ferociously until they were overwhelmed and Iain Mor lay dead. James Campbell was later led to the scaffold for the murder, till the last maintaining that he had been acting under James's instructions. Many people suspected that Campbell was indeed acting on orders; the wily James denied this and allowed the truth to die with Campbell.

The belief that James had treacherously murdered the loyal Iain Mor was widespread in the territories of the Lordship and his duplicity in Iain Mor's death increased their sense of alienation from Edinburgh. The clans of the Lordship rose as one when Alexander raised the standard of revolt. Alexander's army was unable to confront the full power of a Royal army and he was forced to submit and face imprisonment in Tantallon Castle.[11]

Iain Mor's eldest son was Donald Balloch, a ferocious warrior, who commanded the respect of the clans of the Lordship. Donald Balloch led a large island host (including men from the Glens of Antrim) to once again challenge the power of James I. The clan levies of the Lordship overwhelmed the Royal army at Inverlochy. James was incensed at this humiliation and mustered the whole force of the Kingdom to suppress the rebels. Donald Balloch was unable to resist the assembled might of Scotland and was forced to seek safety amongst the Glens of Antrim. Here he remained till James died in 1437.

With the death of Alexander, third Lord of the Isles in 1449, Donald Balloch assumed the same role as his father, as tutor for Alexander's young son John. As fourth Lord of the Isles; John lacked the political astuteness of his great-grandfather the first Lord of the Isles. With the earls of Crawford and Douglas he plotted to dismember the Scottish state.[12] Through a lack of co-ordination and decisiveness the plot failed. Donald Balloch led the forces of the Lordship on a devastating

---

[9] Boardman makes the case that the date of Iain Mor's murder may well be later and was a consequence of James Campbell acting independently.

[10] Alexander, third Lord of the Isles was still a minor.

[11] For the details of this campaign see chapter 2.

[12] Treaty of Ardtornish.

invasion of the islands of Arran and Bute, which were of particular significance as they had once belonged to the descendents of Somerled, but had passed into the hands of the King's family, the Stewarts. In the eyes of the Scottish court Donald Balloch's actions were clearly treasonable. However, from his perspective it was the feudal Kingdom of Scotland which was attempting to usurp the ancient hegemony of the MacDonalds in the west.

Donald Balloch survived the bitter struggle of the Lordship to establish itself as an autonomous Gaelic polity and died peacefully of old age on Isla in 1476. He was succeeded by his son John Mor who became the third chief of the Clan Iain Mor. There is little mention of John Mor in Scottish history; the most plausible explanation is that John was busy in Antrim, attempting to expand his clan's interests into the Route[13] against his Irish rivals. John kept the Clan Iain Mor out of the rebellions of the Lochalsh MacDonalds which followed the forfeiture of the Earldom of Ross.[14] John Mor made his peace with James IV after the fall of the Lordship in 1494. In exchange for John's acquiescence to the new situation, James made John Mor a knight, but more importantly gave him charters to all the lands he had held from the Lords of the Isles.

There was however the problem of Kintyre which belonged to the Clan Iain Mor. Kintyre dominated the Clyde estuary an area vital to Royal interests. James felt he could not leave such a strategic peninsula solely in the hands of a powerful clan which had such a long history of opposition to Royal authority. Encouraged by many western magnates he placed Royal garrisons in the castles of Tarbert and Dunaverty. For John Mor and his son John Cathanach this was a serious erosion of their power throughout Kintyre, Tarbert Castle was built on the narrow isthmus where Loch Tarbet nearly cuts the peninsular in half; the castle thus controlled any movement up or down Kintyre. Dunaverty was on the extreme southern end of Kintyre and kept watch on any ships sailing from the Antrim coast and Argyle. This was of critical importance as this narrow stretch of water was the route used by the streams of redshanks[15] which poured into Ireland from the western highlands each summer.

Sir John mobilized his clan and stormed Dunaverty; the governor of the castle was hung. As James was returning home with his fleet he faced the humiliation of seeing his governor hanging from the battlements. For the proud James this humiliation was unforgivable. James declared John and his son John Cathanach, rebels and thus prey to any man able to take them. John and his son sailed to Isla assuming that there they were safe from the reach of the King.

---

[13] The Route was a fertile area adjacent to the Glens.

[14] See chapter 2.

[15] Redshanks were the mercenary soldiers which were drawn from most of the west highland clans. They offered their services to the Irish tribes in their continual wars. The Clan Iain Mor used Dunaverty as one of their main embarkation points when sending reinforcements to their possession in Antrim.

John Brayach, chief of the MacDonalds of Ardnamurchan arranged a meeting with John. When the two parties met, John Brayach captured John, John Cathanach and some of his sons and took them to Edinburgh to face the King's justice. On the Boroughmuir three generations of the Clan Iain Mor danced their last jig under the direction of the hangman. Sir John had gravely miscalculated that he would be safe having a meeting with a fellow MacDonald. The surviving sons of John Cathanach fled to the glens of Antrim and begun a feud with the MacDonalds of Ardnamurchan (who had been given charters to extensive territories on Isla by the King) which was to ultimately lead to the latter's total defeat.[16]

Dunaverty Castle

Alexander, one of John Cathenach's surviving sons, had become chief of the Clan Iain Mor. When the news reached Alexander that James IV had fallen with most of the Scottish nobility at the battle of Flodden he returned to his Scottish possessions. Alexander joined the savage and reckless Sir Donald of Lochalsh in his rebellion to re-establish the Lordship. The rebellion failed after the death of Sir Donald at Cairnburgh Castle on the remote Treshnish Isles. Alexander asked for

---

[16] See chapter 5.

terms from the Council[17] and with remarkable leniency, the Council, returned all the Clan Iain Mor's lands to Alexander even adding some new possessions to them. The Council's leniency was an expression of their inability to control this powerful clan with its wide interests in Scotland and Ireland.

It was during Alexander's chiefship that the Clan Iain Mor became entangled in the first strands of the legal web which the Campbells were to successfully weave around them.[18] Alexander led his clan against the Campbells and campaigned in Ulster against both the Irish and the English.[19] In his later years he became a loyal friend and supporter of James V; he died in 1538 leaving the Clan Iain Mor in a position it was never again to have in Scotland.

Alexander left three remarkable sons behind him; the eldest was James MacDonald who was to become the sixth chief of the Clan Iain Mor. The second son was Coll MacDonald who established a branch of the family on Colonsay. The third son was Sorley Boy[20] MacDonald who became responsible for the clans possessions in Ireland[21] and whose descendents are the Earls of Antrim.

James MacDonald inherited extensive possessions, both in Scotland and Ireland yet due to an unhappy series of interconnecting elements which included the political and military aspirations of the English and Scottish states, the MacLeans the Campbells and the Irish tribes he was, despite his best efforts, unable to prevent a gradual erosion in Clan Iain Mor's power. Although James had been educated at the Scottish court, where he was held to ensure his father's good behaviour, he had the proud and independent blood of his ancestors coursing through his veins. He kept the Clan Iain Mor out of the rebellion of Donald Dubh, but with the death of James V in 1542, and despite the best efforts of the Regent Arran, James began to drift into the world of Gaelic politics and aspirations. James flirted with the idea of claiming to be the rightful heir to the Lordship, but shrewdly judging that the Lordship could not now be resurrected he re-affirmed his loyalty to the Crown. In an attempt to neutralize the ever growing power of the Campbells, James married the remarkable Lady Agnes Campbell daughter of Colin Campbell third Earl of Argyle.

The next decade saw James and his brothers deeply involved in politics and warfare in Ulster. In Ulster there was a continual three cornered struggle for control of different parts of the province between the native Irish, the English and the Clan Iain Mor. James's ambition was to gain firm control of the Route; an area of land between the rivers Bann and Bush. James concentrated much of Clan Iain

---

[17] The Council was dominated by Archibald Douglas, sixth Earl of Angus. The lenient treatment of Alexander may well have been part of Archibald's attempts to halt the growing power of the Campbells.

[18] Appendix.

[19] See chapter 12.

[20] Sorley Boy was the English attempt to pronounce Somhairle Buidhe.

[21] See chapter 12.

Mor's strength on Ulster as it offered an opportunity for colonization[22] and conquest neither of which were available by this date in Scotland.

The seeds of the great feud between the Clan Iain Mor and the MacLeans were sown in the 1550's, this feud weakened both of these clans and in the end only facilitated further Campbell expansion. The MacLeans had been loyal supporters of the Lords of the Isles; they had taken part in all their campaigns and rebellions of the last two centuries. The MacLeans world view was identical to that of their MacDonald neighbours, they also dreamed of a restoration of the Lordship and longed to be an important element in an autonomous Gaelic kingdom. With each failed rising it became clearer to the gentlemen of the clan that the Lordship could not be revived. As independent clans,[23] the MacLeans changed their policy by the middle of the sixteenth century and were determined to strike out on their own. Like so many other western clans they now took every opportunity to expand their clan's possessions.

The maps of the clan territories used in this book are to give the reader an idea of the areas over which different clans had influence. Clan lands and populations were not delineated by neat lines drawn on maps and the distribution of clans was considerably more complicated. There were areas of overlap with some members of different clans living in each others territory, and the land ownership pattern was a complex web of feudal and Gaelic land rights. Often, not only did these overlap but more than one clan had rights to the same land under the same legal framework. This chaotic system of tenure was at the heart of this feud.

In July 1539 Ailein nan Sop MacLean, brother of the chief of the MacLeans of Duart, Hector Mor, was given the tenancy of the Island of Gigha and some lands in the Rinnes of Isla.

The possession of these lands was confirmed by a grant to Hector, Ailein nan Sop's son, in 1552. Two years later Neil MacNeill of Gigha sold the island to Sir James MacDonald chief of Clan Iain Mor. The MacLean historians themselves confirm that MacNeill had the right to sell Gigha in its entirety, and that by implication Hector MacLean was merely a tenant. Hector refused to give up his lands on Gigha to Sir James, and appealed to his uncle Hector Mor chief of the MacLeans.[24] Sir James MacDonald and Hector Mor MacLean had an extremely acrimonious meeting; they did not part on good terms. The two chief's attention then turned to the Rinnes of Isla, where the MacLeans were in occupation of a large part of the peninsular. James had recently received a Royal charter which

---

[22] For the Gaelic population of Scotland there was always a need for some emigration as the impoverished natural resources of the highlands always struggled to keep pace with the demands of the population. Emigration to the rest of Scotland at this date was very unusual ,while settlement in Ulster was much easier due to a similar culture and language.

[23] Like the MacDonalds there were several independent clans of MacLeans by the sixteenth century, including the MacLeans of Coll and Lochbuie and Duart, the MacLeans of Duart being the most powerful.

[24] In this chapter references to the MacLeans will be taken to mean the MacLeans of Duart.

confirmed him as being the sole owner of Isla. Hector Mor disputed James's claims to the MacLean farms in the Rinnes; he refused to ask his people to remove from the Rinnes.

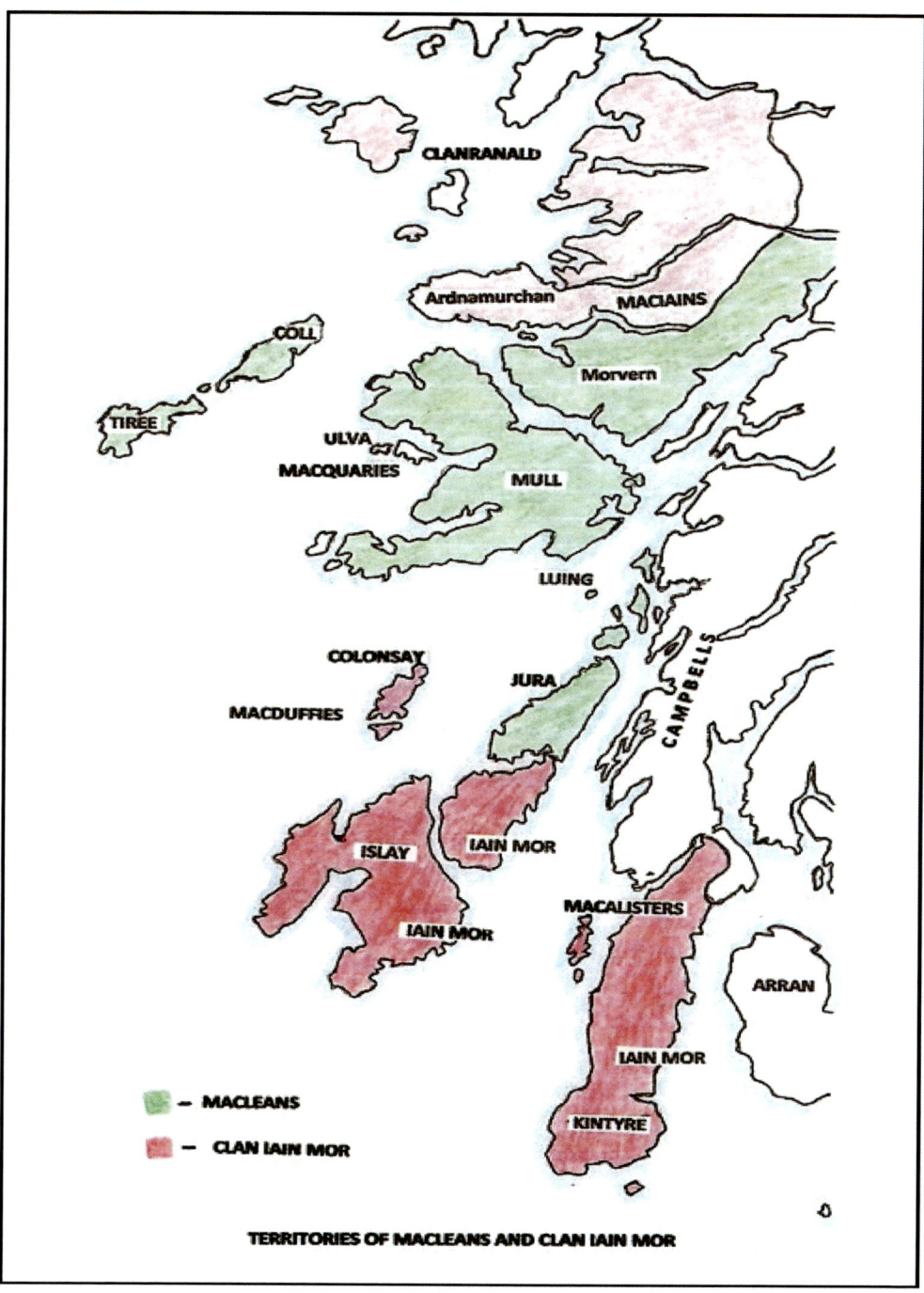

TERRITORIES OF MACLEANS AND CLAN IAIN MOR

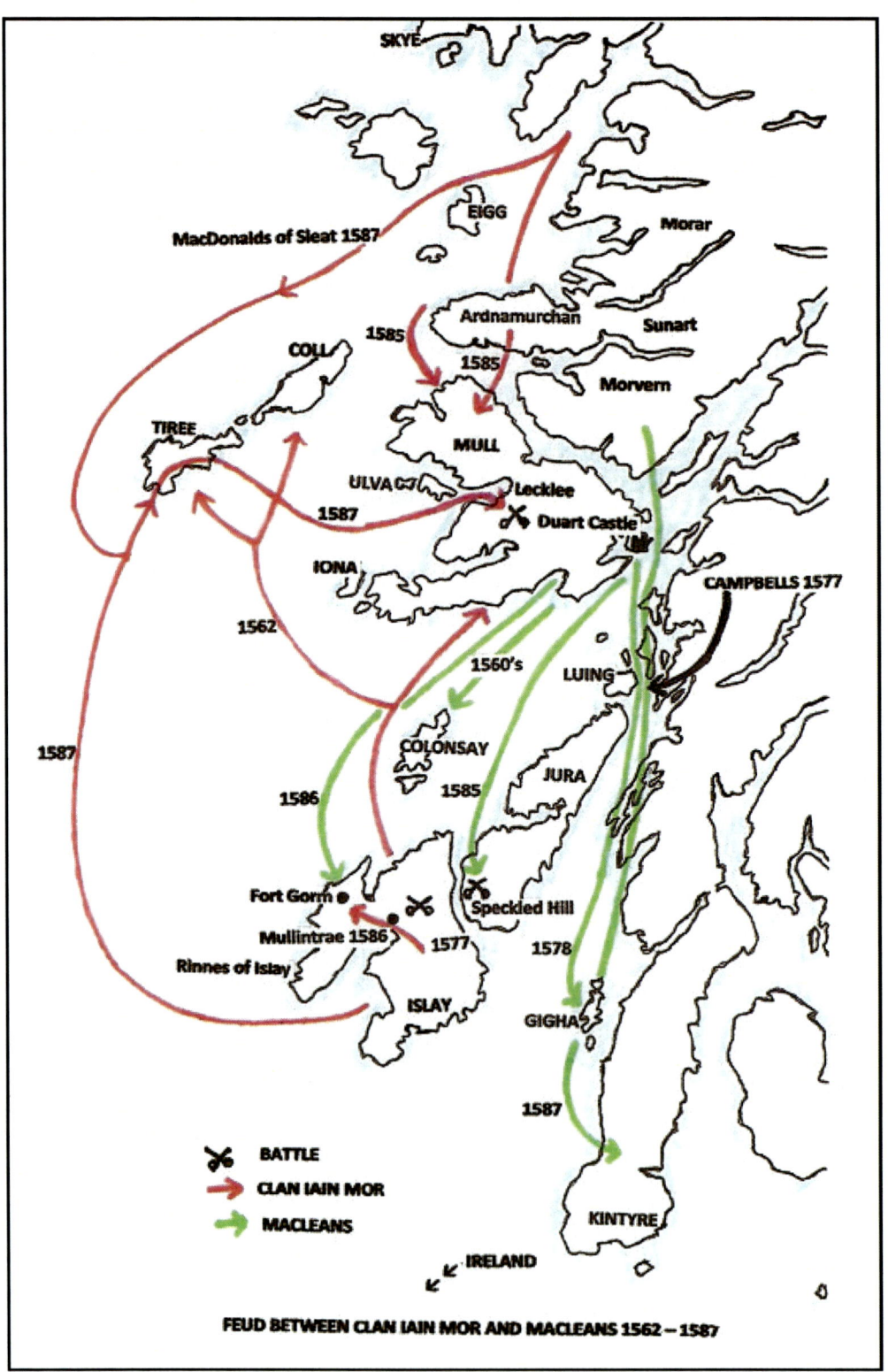

FEUD BETWEEN CLAN IAIN MOR AND MACLEANS 1562 – 1587

- 264 -

Both clans began a series of raids on the territories of each other; these raids were launched from the galley fleets which they both possessed. The raiding caused a viscous cycle of violence in which each loss caused a lust for further revenge.[25] The people of both clans were reduced to utter destitution by the endemic violence. Eventually in 1565 both chiefs were summoned to appear before the Privy Council and were bound over to keep the peace, failure to do so resulting in a huge fine. Within a few months Sir James fell mortally wounded while commanding the Clan Iain Mor at the battle of Glentaisie in Ulster. His clan army was overwhelmed by a vastly superior force led by O'Neill.[26] The death of Sir James was considered a great loss to the whole of the Gaelic west, although we may be sure that Hector Mor MacLean did not mourn his passing. In Ireland the Annals of the Four Masters describes him as "….a paragon of hospitality and prowess, a festive man of many troops, a bountiful and munificent man. His peer was not to be found at that time among the Clan Donald of Ireland or Scotland; and his own people would not have deemed it too much to give his weight in gold for his ransom," Clearly James was a man whose character was much admired in the Gaelic west; he had upheld the rights and dignity of his clan and had paid the ultimate price.

James was succeeded by his eldest son Archibald. His career as chief of the Clan Iain Mor was uneventful; no doubt a blessing for the men and women of his clan. Archibald died in 1569 after leading the clan for four years. He was succeeded by his brother Angus who became the eight chief of the Clan Iain Mor. The early years of Angus's chiefship were peaceful, with the Clan Iain Mor occupying Kintyre, Isla, Gigha, the southern half of Jura and the Glens and Route of Antrim. MacDonald historians have expressed the situation beautifully, "The fortunes of the family were at this time at the zenith of their prosperity. Both in Scotland and in the North of Ireland the Clann Iain Mhoir exercised a sway which bade fair to rival the splendour of the ancient House of Isla. But all the time there was a canker gnawing at the root of the goodly tree which was destined to lay its proud luxuriance in the dust."[27]

Angus's character is complex, but he was ruled by pride, he was undiplomatic, rash and violent. These characteristics, could in different circumstances, have been used to the Clan Iain Mor's advantage. But the Clan Iain Mor was threatened on all sides by powerful enemies and it required a chief who had a firm and intelligent grasp of the political environment and who would wait patiently to strike at his

---

[25] Grieve recorded descriptions of several battles fought on Colonsay between the MacDuffies and MacLeans as he heard them from Sir John MacNeill in 1881. The MacDuffies of Colonsay supported the Clan Iain Mor throughout its long struggles with its opponents until its final destruction. It is probable that the battles described took place during this period.

[26] See chapter 12.

[27] The Reverend MacDonald brothers.

enemies. In Ireland the Clan Iain Mor was faced with the threat of English and O'Neill invasion of the Route and Glenns. In Kintyre there was the ever present threat from the Campbells, who with their political and military power continually expanding would seize any opportunity to deprive the Clan Iain Mor of its ancient patrimony. Then to the north were the MacLeans who were now led by Lachlan Mor MacLean. Lachlan Mor was a man of great ambition. He was intelligent, proud, and violent and it was known throughout the Hebrides that he suffered from "land hunger". Lachlan Mor still maintained his right to the Rinns of Isla. The personalities of Lachlan and Angus were to make a difficult situation catastrophic. Angus's unsubtle and rash nature was ultimately to bring the Clan Iain Mor to extinction.

One of the most interesting aspects of the coming feud were the roles played by the mothers of Angus and Lachlan. Angus's mother was Agnes Campbell, daughter of the third Earl of Argyle, while Lachlan's mother was Janet Campbell daughter of the fourth Earl of Argyle. So the mothers of the two chiefs were both Campbells and further more they are closely related as Agnes was Janet's aunt. Sadly the role these two powerful women played in the coming struggle is obscured. What was their relationship like? To what extent were they torn between the interests of their sons and their clans and the interests of the Campbells? Was it even possible that they encouraged their sons to fight on, knowing that both clans would be weakened and thus facilitate Campbell expansion? This intriguing web of marriage connections can be taken one step further, when Angus, later married Mary MacLean, Lachlan's sister, so making the two contending chiefs brother-in-laws.

In the summer of 1577 the Clan Iain Mor and the Campbells formed an uneasy alliance against the MacLeans. The MacLeans were still occupying much of the Rinns of Isla and Angus considered them the most immediate threat to the interests of the Clan Iain Mor. Angus led an army of twelve hundred clansmen, supported by two hundred and fifty Campbells against the fort on Loch Gorm which was occupied by the MacLeans. Simultaneously the Campbells invaded the MacLean possessions of Luing. Angus failed to storm the fort and the MacLeans continued to hold this strategic position. This failure to capture the fort at Loch Gorm, despite the overwhelming numerical superiority of the MacDonalds is not surprising as clan armies were notoriously bad at storming fortifications. They lacked all the technology required for reducing walls and sieges were rare as the besiegers rarely had enough food to last for a prolonged period of inactivity. The methodical and patient reduction of castles did not suit their view that war should be heroic, and should be resolved quickly in brutal hand-to-hand encounters.

In the winter of 1578 John Dubh MacLean[28] of Morvern descended on the island of Gigha. The island was devastated; the houses were burnt and everything of any

---

[28] John Dubh had acted as the leader of the MacLeans while Lachlan Mor was returning from the lowlands after the death of his father Eachann Og.

value was plundered.[29] The Clan Iain Mor and the MacLeans continually invaded each others lands for the remainder of the year; this was not just a struggle between Lachlan and Angus but a war which was entered into by the entire population of both clans. The violence reached such a pitch that eventually the Privy Council ordered Lachlan and Angus to become reconciled with each other; failure to do so would result in severe penalties for them both. In an attempt to shore up the peace Angus married Lachlan's sister, Mary MacLean, in the early months of 1579. The peace was to last for six years, but in 1585 Lachlan's violent and impetuous nature led him into being tricked into renewing the feud with greater ferocity than ever.

On the island of Skye, the MacDonalds of Sleat had been embroiled in viscous internal feuding;[30] an infamous villain called Hugh MacGilleasbuig Chleirich MacDonald had had to share control of the MacDonalds of Sleat during the minority of the young chief Donald Gorm Mor. Hugh deeply resented the fact that he was forced to share control of the clan which he regarded as his sole right, and his alone. Hugh was forced into exile for various crimes he had; or was suspected of committing.[31] This evil and embittered man took to piracy in the southern Hebrides.

In the summer of 1585 Donald Gorm Mor (who had achieved his majority and become the seventh chief of the MacDonalds of Sleat) sailed from Skye to visit Angus MacDonald chief of the Clan Iain Mor. Donald Gorm Mor sailed south in several galleys accompanied by a large retinue of nearly one hundred men. Owing to a severe storm that blew up, the MacDonalds were forced to take shelter at Speckled Hill Inlet in the southern part of Jura.

That same night, Hugh who was on one of his piratical expeditions was also forced to sail for the shelter in a neighbouring bay. Hugh and his accomplices[32] slaughtered or drove off a large number of cattle belonging to the MacLeans knowing that Donald Gorm Mor and his party would be blamed. Hugh then slipped away from Jura unobserved by the MacDonalds. On discovering the loss of their cattle the Macleans immediately sent word to Lachlan who was at his castle of Duart on Mull. The hot headed Lachlan immediately called his clan to arms and sailed for Jura.

The unsuspecting party of MacDonalds had lingered a few days in Jura; it was the custom for these summer visits to be leisurely so they could be enjoyed by all the party after the long confinement of winter. Led by their incensed chief the

---

[29] The haul included, 500 cows, 300 horses and 2000 sheep and goats. The number of horses is remarkable. They were unlikely to have been heavy draft horses for ploughing as they would have required too much food. Possibly they were breed for meat as horses convert fodder into meat more efficiently than cattle.

[30] See chapter7.

[31] See chapter 7.

[32] The most notable of whom was Angus MacDonald of Griminish, a descendant of Donald Hearaich.

MacLeans fell upon the resting MacDonalds and within a few minutes sixty lay cut down on the shores of Innes Knock Breck, (the grazing field of the speckled hill). Donald Gorm Mor had slept on his galley and thus was spared in the initial onslaught. He gathered together the survivors and sailed back to Skye, he was outraged at this unprovoked (as far as he was concerned) and treacherous attack on his clan and swore to have vengeance on the MacLeans. By his ill-considered and reckless violence Lachlan had now embroiled his clan in a feud with the MacDonalds of Sleat as well as the Clan Iain Mor.

When Donald Gorm Mor returned to his castle of Duntulm he sent messengers to all the chiefs of Clan Donald telling them what had happened and asking them to assist him in taking his revenge on the MacLeans. A powerful confederacy of the Clan Iain Mor and the MacDonalds of Sleat, Ardnamurchan, Glengarry and the Clanranald was formed. Mull was continually ravaged by the MacDonalds; Lachlan was unable to protect his people from such a powerful combination of enemies. Eventually the King intervened to save the MacLeans and ordered the MacLeods of Harris to assist the MacLeans. The coalition of MacDonald clans accepted an uneasy peace, not wishing to defy the ever growing authority of the King.

The next year, Angus with his retinue visited Donald Gorm Mor on Skye. By this time both chiefs knew what had really happened on Jura and Angus consulted with the gentlemen of the Clan Iain Mor and those of Sleat as to how he should deal with Lachlan Mor MacLean. Against the opinion of the majority of his advisors he decided to visit Lachlan in his lair and see if the feud could be truly ended. On his arrival at Duart Castle, Angus and his retainers were welcomed by the MacLeans and invited to a feast. Lachlan now saw an opportunity to finally gain control over his long desired prize; the Rinnes of Isla. In the early dawn all the MacDonalds were seized and thrown into the castles dungeon. Lachlan announced to Angus that he would remain there until he signed over his rights to the Rinnes. Eventually Angus agreed to Lachlan's terms, he was forced to leave his young son James and his brother Ranald behind as hostages until the titles to the Rinnes had been completed.

Angus left Mull with his heart full of hatred for Lachlan. His anger was magnified by the fact that Lachlan had broken the sacred laws of hospitality, which were held to be sacrosanct by all highlanders. Now there could be no peace between the two chiefs or indeed their clans till either Angus or Lachlan were dead.

In July 1586 Lachlan Mor sailed to Isla to take possession of the Rinnes of Isla. Angus's brother was left in chains at Duart while he took Angus's son, James, with him as security. The MacLeans headed for the ruined fort on Loch Gorm and began to rebuild its defences.[33] Within a few days he received word from Angus, inviting him to stay at his residence of Mullintrae. Lachlan naturally hesitated before going into the heart of Isla where he would be deep within the territory of the Clan Iain

---

[33] It is unclear when the MacLeans had been forced to abandon this fort after their successful defence of it during the outbreak of the feud.

Mor. Eventually, after receiving the most solemn of assurances and being reminded that he held both Angus's son and brother hostage, Lachlan agreed to visit Angus's residence at Mullintrae.

Mullintrae

Lachlan arrived at Mullintrae with James and a large bodyguard of eighty six MacLeans. That afternoon and evening the MacLeans were entertained to a large feast by the MacDonalds. During the feast, Mary, Lachlan's sister, suspected her husband of plotting against Lachlan. Despite her best efforts she was unable to speak to Lachlan alone. In desperation she leaned across the table and said to her brother, "the night is stormy, and every shepherd should have an eye on his flock." Lachlan took the hint and refused Angus's offer of a room in his house, preferring one of the out houses surrounded by his men.

When Angus heard that Lachlan was on his way he had sent messengers out to all the districts of Isla calling on his clan to assemble at Mullintrae by nine o'clock.

That night the MacLeans, who were somewhat the worse for wear, retired to the huddle of small houses which surrounded Mullintrae. Lachlan kept James within easy reach as he bedded down for the night. A jovial and apparently drunk Angus called to Lachlan to have one last drink with him. Lachlan placed James on his shoulders and went apprehensively to the door. When he opened the door he was greeted by the sight of hundreds of armed men who had surrounded Mulintrae, at their front was Angus fully armed for battle.

James, who was no more than five, begged his farther to spare Lachlan, Angus, was moved not to kill Lachlan on the spot[34] and imprisoned him in a secret chamber till dawn. The men of the Clan Iain Mor then called on the MacLeans to surrender. They were assured that if they came out of the houses peacefully they would not be harmed. However two men of Lachlan's party were excluded from this offer of surrender. One was John Dubh MacLean who had led the devastating raid on Gigha and the other was Angus MacDonald of Griminish who was known to have been one of Hugh's companions when he had ensnared Donald Gorm Mor on Jura. The two men knew they could expect no mercy, they stood in the door of the building where they had been sleeping, and fortified by their despair defended themselves against overwhelming odds. Eventually the house was set on fire and they died in the flames.

When news reached Mull that Lachlan had been taken prisoner, a close relative of Lachlan's called Allan MacLean disseminated a rumour that Angus's brother had been put to death in the dungeons of Duart Castle. Allan was driven to encompass the fate of Lachlan by his desire to become the chief of the MacLeans during the minority of Lachlan's son.[35] In due coarse the rumour came to Angus's attention, believing the story Angus's lust for blood knew no limits. He ordered the jailor of the MacLeans, a certain Coll MacJames, to behead the prisoners. Angus instructed that they were to be executed a couple at a time each day, to draw every last drop of satisfaction from his revenge. He ordered that MacJames was to start with the least significant captives leaving Lachlan to last. For the next forty days two MacLeans were taken out and beheaded in front of the jeering Clan Iain Mor until only Lachlan was left. Angus did not wish to miss the execution of his hated rival and appeared on his horse to witness Lachlan's execution. Just before Lachlan faced the axe, Angus's horse threw him to the ground. Angus broke a leg and ordered the execution to be postponed until he was well enough to enjoy it.[36] This mass murder was not only fuelled by the desire for revenge, among the eighty or so dead would have been many of the leading MacLean gentlemen. Their loss would have seriously damaged the cohesion of the MacLeans and greatly reduced their effective ability to make war.

News of these events had reached the King, who immediately asked the Campbells to mediate between the two clans. Angus rejected any mediation and the Campbells were unable or unwilling to force him to obedience. James VI then sent a Royal herald to parley with Angus. On hearing that a herald was on his way from Edinburgh, Angus forbade any of his clan from helping the nervous herald sail to Isla. The herald, unable to find any means of getting to Isla returned to

---

[34] Angus may well have been concerned as to his son's safety.

[35] As tanist to the clan he would also be entitled to the revenues from Lachlan's estate.

[36] There is an alternative story as to why Lachlan was not beheaded; this MacLean tradition suggests that Lachlan was spared so that he could be traded for Angus's brother Ranald who was still held at Duart.

Edinburgh. During this period the MacLeans were still active. They managed to capture Angus's cousin who with his brother they hoped to exchange for Lachlan.

Eventually, due to pressure from the King and the Campbells, Angus agreed to terms. It was agreed that Lachlan should give up his claims to the Rinnes of Isla and to leave the Clan Iain Mor in peaceful possession of them. Lachlan agreed to release both Angus's brother and cousin. Taking advice from the Campbells, the King agreed that Angus would receive a full pardon for any outrages he had committed. The most remarkable aspect of this pardon was that Angus was to be given eight hostages by the King from some of the most important clans in the western highlands, until the King forfilled his promise. The hostages were, Hector MacLean (Lachlan's son), a brother of William MacLeod of Harris, two sons of MacKinnon of Strathordill, two sons of MacNeill of Barra and the sons of MacLean of Ardgour and Cairnburgh. The King appears to have had doubts about the wisdom of leaving such distinguished hostages in Angus's hands. He later ordered that they were to be held by the Campbells on behalf of Angus. Angus refused to hand over such a valuable prize and kept a close watch on his esteemed "guests". In due course Lachlan returned to Mull and the feud appeared to have ended with the release of all the prisoners and hostages.

With the terrible atrocities which had been committed on both sides, both chiefs knew that this period of peace could only be a brief interlude before open war was resumed. Within a few months Lachlan returned to Isla at the head of his clan, the MacLeans laid waste much of the island. They killed any man they came across who was capable of bearing arms. At this time Angus was in Ulster attempting to repair his authority with the Clan Iain Mor in Ireland after the death of his brothers[37] and the rise of the influence of his uncle, Sorley Boy.

Angus immediately returned to Isla. Earlier in the year, Angus had signed a treaty with Donald Gorm Mor and Lachlan MacKintosh committing these three clans to a defensive alliance.[38] A combined clan army of the Clan Iain Mor and the MacDonalds of Sleat devastated the small MacLean population on the island of Tiree. They then turned their attention on the MacLean heartland of Mull. For some reason Lachlan was taken by surprise and ordered his clan to abandon their coastal settlements and drive their livestock into the mountains. Angus sailed into Loch-nan-Gall and landed at Derryguaig at the foot of Ben Mor.

The MacLeans resolved to make a stand at Lecklee, behind Geradu. The MacDonald host halted at Sron-na-Cranalaich about three miles from Lecklee. The MacLeans were commanded by John MacLean of Inverscadle who was considered to be one of his clan's best warriors. They were drawn up on the sides of a narrow pass which led to the interior of the island. Had John had the patience to wait for the MacDonalds to attack, the MacLeans would have been able to hold their

---

[37] Alasdair Carragh and Donald Gorme, See chapter 12.

[38] The inclusion of MacKintosh may have been because Angus wanted a counter weight to the Gordons who often acted as the King's Lieutenants in the North.

ground with ease. John, however, was unable to control his impetuosity and led the outnumbered MacLeans in a charge against the enemy. John survived the encounter but left most of his clansmen lying on the field.

The victorious MacDonalds still felt it was unwise to attempt to force the pass. They set off along the coast, ravaging less well defended targets. When they were returning to their galleys they were ambushed by the MacLeans and lost a few men in the resulting skirmish. The hatred which had built up during this feud led to acts of barbarism which were unusual even in the deadly feuds of the western highlands. The MacDonalds killed every MacLean they came across and wantonly slaughtered all the livestock they could find.

As Angus could not be halted in Mull, Lachlan ordered his gentlemen from Morven to invade Kintyre. In due course many districts of that peninsular were burnt and laid waste by the MacLeans. Angus was forced to abandon Mull so that he could go to the relief of his people in Kintyre. There now followed a series of charters and directives which show James VI's highland policy at its most fatuous. In October 1587 Angus was declared a rebel for failing to release his hostages and as a consequence, Lachlan and his son Hector MacLean were given charters for much of the land of Clan Iain Mor. This legislation was hopelessly partisan and although it is true that Angus had refused to surrender his hostages to the Campbells, it is clear that Lachlan Mor MacLean had instigated this latest round of bloodletting. The reason for this unjust and explosive set of decisions lay with the Earl of Glencairn, who had a great deal of influence at the Scottish court. The Earl was Lachlan's father-in-law. Yet again the corrupt environment of the Scottish legislature would be one of the main external elements which would cause a great deal of sorrow in the western highlands.

The struggle between the MacLeans and the Clan Iain Mor now took on a regional significance. Almost all the clans of the western seaboard of the highlands aligned themselves with one or other of the contending parties. On one side were all the clans of MacLeans, the MacQuarries of Ulva, the MacNeils of Barra, the MacKinnons of Skye and the MacLeods of Harris. While on the other were the Clan Iain Mor, the Clanranald, the MacDonalds of Sleat, Ardnamurchan, and Glengarry, the MacAlisters of Kintyre, the MacNeils of Gigha, the MacDuffies of Colonsay and the MacLeods of Lewis. Most of these clans kept out of the bloodshed, merely keeping an eye on one or other of their opponents in the opposing power block.

As the region was being rent in two a different emotion was stirring in the heart of John MacIain ninth chief of the MacDonalds of Ardnamurchan. Lachlan's mother, Janet Campbell the daughter of the fourth Earl of Argyle, had recently become a widow again. She was now a woman of considerable wealth and MacIain knew that she would bring a substantial dowry with her if they were to marry. Janet had married Hector MacLean of Torlisk after the death of her first husband Hector Og. Finding herself a widow again (on the death of Hector), she petitioned her son that he might agree to the union. Initially Lachlan was strongly opposed to the idea that his mother might marry one of the chiefs who were aligned against him. Later, perhaps after consultation with the gentlemen of his clan, Lachlan could see that by allowing his mother and Maclain to marry he might be able to detach this clan from their alliance with the Clan Iain Mor. Lachlan wrote to Maclain giving his blessing to the couple. Janet and Maclain were married at Torloisk House.

The evening was spent with both parties enjoying the traditional feasting. Lachlan was the jovial host and after much whisky had been consumed led the happy couple to their room. Most of the rest of Maclain's party also retired to a nearby barn to sleep. A few of the MacDonalds stayed up and continued drinking with Lachlan and his men. During one of the drunken conversations, one of Maclain's men let slip that Maclain had married Janet for her wealth and not because he loved her. He compounded his indiscretion by going on to say that Maclain would continue to support the Clan Iain Mor and the MacDonalds of Sleat in their struggle with the MacLeans.

A MacLean who was sitting next to him was outraged at the insult that Lachlan's mother had received and shouting, "drunken men always tell the truth," reached for his dirk and stabbed his indiscreet drinking companion in the heart. The stabbing ignited an outbreak of explosive violence; the MacLeans rushed upon their guests and killed them all. With Lachlan at their head they ran over to the barn and quickly slaughtered all of the sleeping MacDonalds. Within a few minutes eighteen of Maclain's men were dead, and Lachlan was leading his men to the wedding room to deal with John Maclain.

Lachlan's actions were not only fuelled by his own innately violent temperament but also by his frustration when he realized that Maclain, despite marrying his mother, was not going to abandon his MacDonald cousins. As soon as Lachlan knew that he could not detach Maclain from his alliances, he decided to deal a crippling blow to the MacDonalds of Ardnamurchan by butchering their chief and leading gentlemen.

Maclain had been woken by the screams of his dying clansmen, sword in hand he awaited the arrival of the MacLeans; he was determined to sell his life as dearly as possible. The MacLeans burst into the room and there was a violent struggle before Maclain was overpowered. Janet was distraught at the idea of losing her new husband and desperately begged her son not to kill him. Lachlan relented and imprisoned Maclain with two of his surviving clansmen. Through his lawyer[39] Maclain appealed to the Privy Council also complaining that he was being tortured by Lachlan. When Lachlan failed to appear before the Council to answer the charges bought against him, he was declared a rebel on eighteenth of June 1588. Later that summer Lachlan had a change of heart and released his prisoners.

By his treacherous and homicidal behaviour Lachlan had managed to create a situation in which the MacLeans were now at deadly feud with the Clan Ian Mor, the MacDonalds of Sleat and the Maclains of Ardnamurchan. This powerful alliance

---

[39] MacGill of Nesbitt.

was now joined by the Clanranald who were outraged at Maclain's treatment, and the casual murder of his clansmen.

In the autumn of 1588 the Florida, one of the largest galleons belonging to the Spanish Armada, was compelled to seek shelter in Tobermory Bay. The ever enterprising Lachlan made a deal with the Spanish captain; in exchange for provisioning the galleon the captain would provide one hundred Spanish soldiers to assist Lachlan in his struggles with the MacDonalds.[40] Lachlan knew that he could not resist the combined force of his enemies so he decided to go on the offensive.

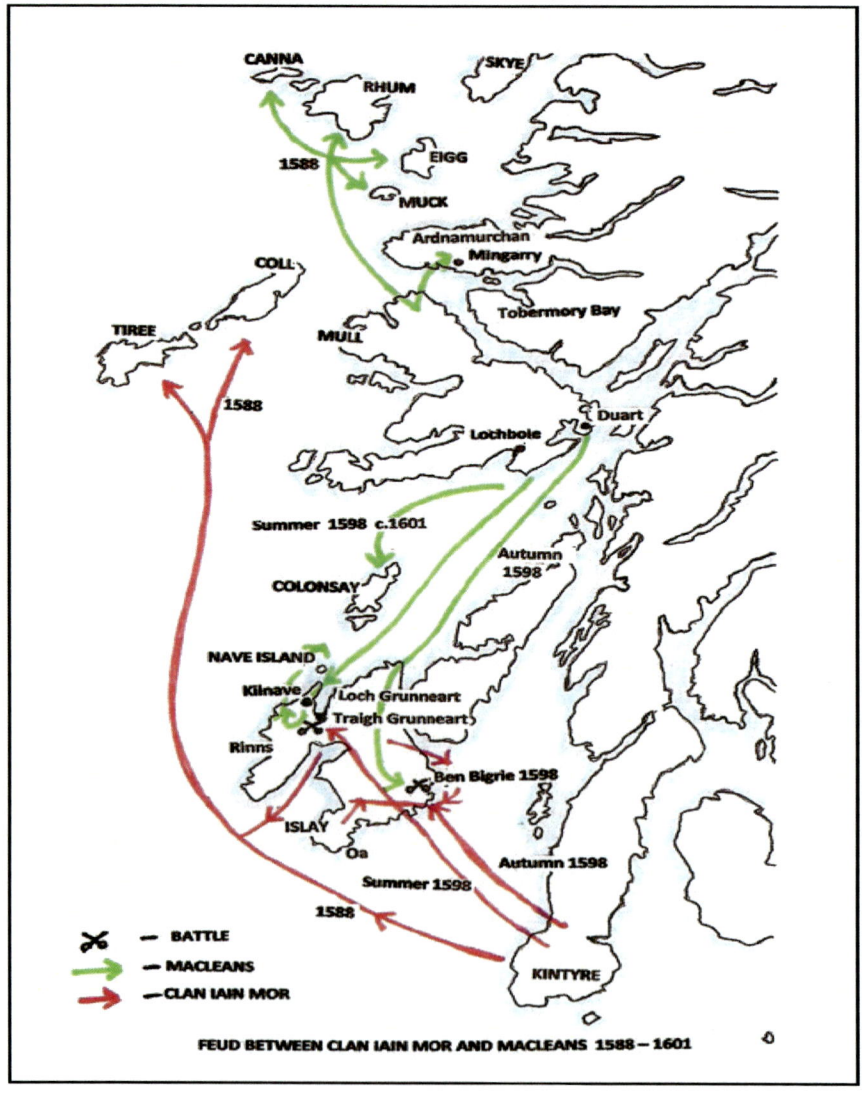

---

[40] The Spanish galleons of the Armada carried soldiers as well as sailors.

With the combined force of his own clan and the Spanish he invaded the islands of Canna, Rum, Eigg and Muck whose population belonged to the Clanranald. He burnt many houses and slaughtered most of the livestock and according to the MacDonald petioners to the Privy Council, "...he slaughtered in the most barbarous, shameful, and cruel manner, all the men, women, and children."[41] Allowing for the usual exaggeration it is clear that a significant number of innocents were slaughtered during Lachlan's incursion. It was during this period that almost the entire population of Eigg was massacred for a second time.[42]

Lachlan then invaded Ardnamurchan and committed it to the flames. For three days he laid siege to Mingarry Castle and devastated the surrounding area. Unable to take Mingarry, Lachlan returned to Mull. While Lachlan had been devastating the lands of the Clanranald and Ardnamurchan, Angus had not been idle. Angus retained some one hundred English mercenaries in Kintyre to help him resist Campbell and Royal pressure. Angus invaded the MacLean islands of Coll and Tiree with a mixed force of mercenaries and the Clan Iain Mor. The hapless population of these islands suffered the same fate as those on the Clanranald islands.

Shortly after Lachlan returned from Ardnamurchan the Florida exploded with the loss of all the crew except for three or four stunned survivors. There are several differing accounts as to how and why the Florida exploded.[43] It is likely that both Lachlan and the Spanish captain, Don Fareija, were planning on betraying each other. Don Fareija would have wanted to obtain what supplies he needed and then sail for Spain. It is inconceivable that he would have wanted to stay as a guest and "ally" of Lachlan's any longer than was absolutely necessary. Lachlan had in the Florida a supply of well armed and trained men, and a source of gold coins for his supplies. If Lachlan had been able to capture the Florida he would have been able to obtain a vast quantity of material including, clothes, gold, weapons, artillery and even the ship's timber would have been extremely useful to such an impoverished society. If Lachlan had learned that Don Fareija was planning on setting sail it would not of been beyond him to order the ship to be blown up. The man responsible for destroying the Florida was either George Smollet[44] or his brother John, by setting fire to the ship's powder magazine.

The Clan Iain Mor and the MacLeans had been in a state of open warfare for over two years. Large tracts of their territories had been laid waste and a high

---

[41] In 1577 the population of Eigg had been massacred by the MacLeods.

[42] See chapter 4.

[43] The Ardgour MS. States that the Florida was blown up by Donald Glas, a MacLean gentleman. Donald had been sent on board by Lachlan to ask for the settlement of outstanding bills owed by the Spanish. When he was refused he set fire to the powder magazine. Local folklore tells that Lachlan was able to bring about the destruction of the Florida with the help of a local witch called Doideag Mhuileach. Here Martin's version has been followed as he was writing only seven years after the event.

[44] George Smollet governed the island of Luing for Lachlan.

proportion of their populations were utterly destitute. Both clans were exhausted by the continual warfare and even Angus and Lachlan knew they needed peace. At a "Parliament of peace" which was attended by many of the western clans including the Campbells they agreed to end their feud. Angus released his distinguished hostages while Lachlan released Maclain and the other two survivors from the events at Torloisk. Both Angus and Lachlan received remissions for their past actions from King James, in March 1589.

A few months later the two chiefs were induced to pay a visit to Edinburgh, ostensibly to give their views to the Privy Council as to how peace and stability could be established in the western isles. As soon as Angus and Lachlan arrived in Edinburgh they were arrested and thrown into prison. At the beginning of 1591 they were put on trial for their activities over the last few years. This treacherous and cunning behaviour was unworthy of any king or any state, it again demonstrated the weakness and corrupt dishonesty of the Scottish political system. Angus was likely to leave Edinburgh with feelings of contempt and resentment for those who claimed the right to rule his clan.

Angus and Lachlan were released after they agreed to pay a heavy fine and that they would leave hostages till the fine was paid. Angus left his two young sons, James and Angus at the Scottish court when he set out for the west in the summer of 1592. As soon as Angus reached the safety of remote Isla, his confidence was restored and he defied the King and refused to pay the fine imposed upon him.[45] By June the Scottish Parliament had declared that they would "punish and repress all the treasonable and barbarous rebels of the Highlands and islands." It further declared that Angus and Lachlan were to appear before them before July the fourteenth. Unsurprisingly Angus and Lachlan failed to make their appointment. By late 1594 Angus was confirmed as a rebel and had had all the Clan Iain Mor possessions stripped from him.

In 1596 James VI made preparations to "daunt" the western highlands with an invasion by a Royal army.[46] All the western chiefs were summoned to meet James at Dumbarton on August the first. Despite the inefficiencies of the Scottish state's processes of government, its power had greatly increased over the course of the sixteenth century. Almost all the chiefs could see that it was no longer wise to defy the King and made their submissions to James. Angus delayed his submission to James and thus became the object of the sovereign's attention. Did Angus still believe that he could ride out the storm by retiring into his possessions in Antrim? In any event his treatment at the hands of the state's apparatus would not have disposed this proud and headstrong chief to willingly go to Dumbarton. With his feud with Lachlan still unresolved, with the threat of continual Campbell expansion

---

[45] It is possible that his devastated territories were simply unable to raise sufficient money.
[46] This "daunting" of the Clan Iain Mor, as with so many earlier Royal threats came to nothing.

into the ancient possessions of the Clan Ian Mor and the threat from the English in Ulster, it was most imprudent of Angus to defy James.

James had reached the end of his patience with the recalcitrant Angus. As Angus was under forfeiture as a rebel all the lands of the Clan Iain Mor were forfeit and he could dispose of them as he willed. James gave Lachlan a grant to the long desired Rinnes of Isla. It is clear that James VI intended to end the anarchy in the southern Hebrides by breaking the ancient MacDonald hegemony over Isla, in the same document in which he grants the Rinnes to Lachlan. He also states that, "..... to disponee upoun the landis of Ilay noch set to Maklane, and also upoun the haill ilis of Jura and Colonza and upoun the said fourtie merkland adjacent to Kilkarrane, as his Majesties all think gud for planting of burrow townis with civile people, religioun, and traffique of merchandice thairupoun." James was mesmerized by the alleged potential of the western isles.[47]This attempt to colonize the western highlands with more amenable subjects came to nothing, however some districts of southern Kintyre were successfully settled by farmers from south western Scotland within a few decades. He had been persuaded that under the right tenantry the islands could produce large quantities of agricultural produce and thus pay him high rents.

Angus then completely lost his head and entered into negotiations with his kinsman James MacDonald of Dunluce[48] with a view to obtaining his aid in expelling the Royal forces from Kintyre. It is clear that by the last decade of the sixteenth century the Clan Iain Mor in Ireland had established its own independent identity and Angus's authority no longer held sway over them. The folly of this plotting was exacerbated when Dunluce reported Angus's plan to the King. Time was running out for Angus, who now had to contend with the ambitious Dunluce who wished to take possession of the Clan Ian Mor's Scottish territories.[49]

During the late summer of 1596 Angus was visited by his son James who, although he had been a hostage at the Scottish Court, had become a great favourite of King James. The King had even gone so far as to give the young heir to the Clan Iain Mor a knighthood. James had learnt the values of diplomacy and intrigue while growing up at court. He used all his powers of persuasion to make Angus see reason. The attitude of the gentlemen of the clan is unknown although it is likely that they were as divided as father and son, and were thus not able to give Angus uniform and consistent advice. Angus agreed to abject surrender and placed himself at the mercy of the King. Angus declared that his son could still be a hostage at court and take control of the Clan Iain Mor and his extensive territories.

---

[47] An example of these absurdly over optimistic evaluations of the potential of the western isles is Munro's report of 1549.

[48] Sorley Boy's son.

[49] Dunluce also claimed that Angus was illegitimate and that he was the rightful heir to the chiefship of the Clan Iain Mor.

He volunteered to quit Kintyre with his immediate family,[50] that he would keep "good" rule in Isla, Colonsay and Gigha, he would deliver his castle of Dunnyveg to one of the King's men and finally that he would present himself before the King by the end of December to hear the King's will.

In due course Angus appeared before the Privy Council to hear the King's decision. The Council were unable to decide how to deal with Angus because although he had submitted he was still under forfeiture from the events of 1595, they postponed any decision till a later date. Angus left Edinburgh infuriated that he had been left in limbo even after he had made such an abject submission.Once back in Isla he slipped back into his more comfortable attitude of defiance towards Royal authority.

In 1598 young James MacDonald was sent by the King to reason with his father, Angus. Angus by now regretted agreeing to hand over the possessions of the Clan Iain Mor to his son, especially as he had received no pardon from the King. The events that followed are discussed more fully in chapter twelve, it is enough to say here that, father and son quarrelled bitterly and that Angus was badly injured in a fire which had been deliberately started.

The young Sir James MacDonald had overthrown his father and become the ninth and last chief of the Clan Iain Mor. He inherited a dire situation. The chiefs of Clan Iain Mor had had their authority supplanted in Antrim by the descendents of Sorley Boy, the MacDonalds of Dunluce, the King laid claim to Kintyre and Lachlan Mor Maclean had been granted legal tenure of the Rinnes of Isla.

Initially Sir James formed a tenuous alliance with Lachlan to co-operate in gathering an army of red shanks to invade Ulster and support English interests. This alliance soon fell apart when the parsimonious Elizabeth failed to pay the chiefs the money they had asked for. Lachlan's eyes once more turned to Isla whose lands he had so long desired. Driven by a hunger to possess the Rinnes, Lachlan mustered the whole might of his clan which after the heavy losses of the previous years, still numbered some six hundred clansmen.[51] A popular folk tale on Isla recounts how, Lachlan, before leaving Mull, consulted with a witch who told him that to cheat death he must not land on Isla on a Thursday. She also told him to avoid Loch Gruinneart and not to drink from Tobar Niall Neonaich (the well of strange Niall).

---

[50] This probably included most of the gentlemen of the Clan Iain Mor.

[51] There is a real problem with the events that followed, there are several nearly contemporary accounts of the Battle of Gruinneart. These include the Ardgour MS., Tytler's History of Scotland which uses a letter written by Nicholson the English ambassador to the Scottish Court five days after the battle. The other main source is The Conflict of the Clans which was written within a few years of the battle in the later years of James the sixth's rule. To exacerbate the problem there are also some oral traditions concerning the battle, which were recorded on Isla in the nineteenth century. This book will follow the description in the Conflict of the Clans and also include some of the oral traditions of Isla.

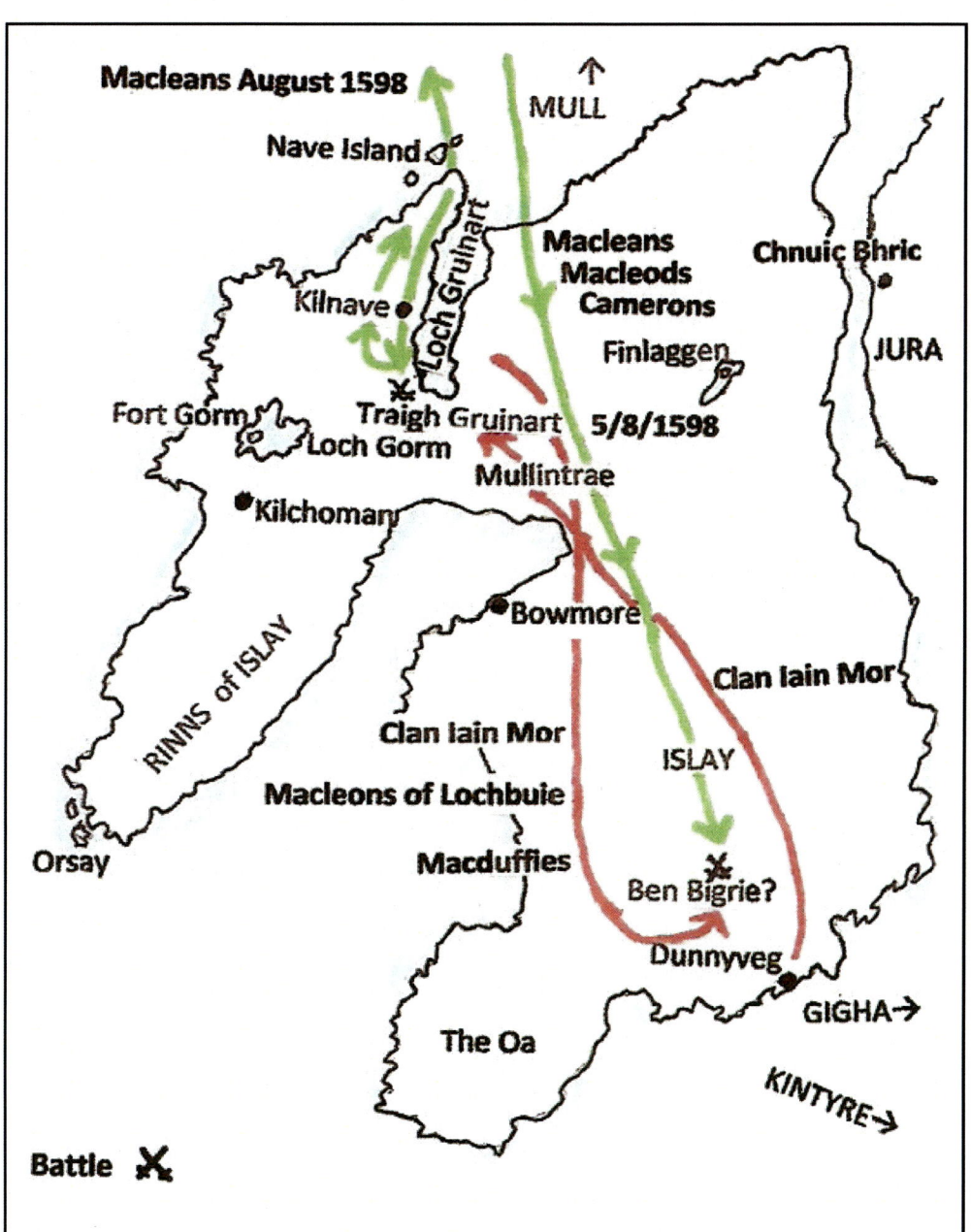

Macleans August 1598

MULL ↑

Nave Island

Macleans
Macleods
Camerons

Chnuic Bhric

JURA

Kilnave

Loch Gruinart

Finlaggen

Fort Gorm

Traigh Gruinart

5/8/1598

Loch Gorm

Mullintrae

Kilchoman

Bowmore

Clan Iain Mor

ISLAY

RINNS of ISLAY

Clan Iain Mor

Macleons of Lochbuie

Macduffies

Ben Bigrie?

Orsay

Dunnyveg

GIGHA →

The Oa

KINTYRE →

Battle ✗

The Macleans were delayed by a storm and happened to land on Isla, at the head of Loch Gruinneart, on a Thursday. Sir James MacDonald was in Kintyre when he heard that Lachlan had landed on Isla. He gathered what men he could and sailed to the island. Sir James attempted to avoid open war by diplomacy.[52] He proposed that Lachlan should have possession of the Rinnes for his lifetime holding the land as a tenant, and to submit the dispute to the King. Lachlan would have none of it, rightly claiming that the King had granted him the Rinnes, but also Lachlan then claimed the rest of Isla. Lachlan may have gambled that Sir James would submit to these demands because he would want to avoid open war as the Clan Iain Mor was already regarded by the King as rebels. It is more likely that Lachlan was attempting to provoke Sir James into committing his clan to open war, a war that Lachlan was confident he could win. If the latter is true then Lachlan was not to be disappointed by Sir James's response.

Sir James moved across Isla with his clansmen from Kintyre gathering the Isla men on route. When the two clans faced each other at Traigh Gruinneart at the head of Loch Gruinneart there were six hundred MacLeans facing seven hundred men of the Clan Iain Mor. Many of the MacDonalds were veterans of their clan's continual struggles in Ulster against the Irish and the English.

Local traditions assert that as the two clans were preparing for battle, Lachlan Mor was approached by a dark-skinned, hunch-backed, hairy dwarf called Dubh Sith (Black Fairy). It was said that his father was a Shaw and his mother a fairy from the island of Jura. Livingstone the distinguished Isla poet describes him as having being "hatched by the devil in the hollow of Jura."[53] Dubh Sith offered his services to Lachlan Mor as an archer. Lachlan, who was seven feet tall must have towered over this insignificant little man, rudely declined Dubh Sith's assistance. The folk tale describes how Dubh Sith turned his twisted face to look up at Lachlan and then turned and left without saying a word.

---

[52] Having being brought up at court James would have known the value of delay, deceit and compromise.

[53] Mac Dubh Sith translates as The Dark Shaw, it is also the Gaelic route of MacDuffie who were the small clan who occupied Colonsay and remained loyal to the Clan Iain Mor after the fall of the Lordship. The fact that local folklore claims that Dubh Sith's mother was a fairy and that he was "hatched by the devil" was a common way in which highlanders explained deformity.

Loch Gruinneart

Dubh Sith made his way over to the Clan Iain Mor and looked for Sir James who was busy marshalling his troops. He offered his services to James who gratefully received him into the ranks of his clan. Dubh Sith told a no doubt incredulous Sir James, that if the MacDonalds would deal with the other MacLeans he would deal with Lachlan Mor. Dubh Sith then walked off and climbed a rowan tree by a well and waited.

It was the fifth of August 1598, the sun blazed down on the golden sands of Loch Gruinneart; on this day both clans wanted to make an end to the dispute over the Rinnes of Isla. Sir James ordered his men to withdraw a short distance so that they could occupy the ridge of a small hill. The Clan Iain Mor had the sun to their backs and the enemy below them.

The imposing figure of Lachlan Mor towered over his clansmen as he led them up the hill in their "regiments" each commanded by his gentlemen. The leading groups of MacLeans were thrown back on their main body after a violent engagement. The battle then became a swirling mass of screaming men who slashed wildly at each other with their basket hilted swords and Lochaber axes. As the battle wore on the clashes became more intermittent as the protagonists quickly became exhausted by the extreme exertion involved in hand to hand combat.

Isla tradition asserts that during a lull in the fighting Lachlan Mor made his way to a well to quench his thirst.[54] Lachlan knelt down by the edge of the well and removed his helmet. Seizing his chance Dubh Sith aimed his cross bow and fired a bolt at Lachlan. The bolt went threw the back of Lachlan's neck, and passing through his brain, the tip just protruding out of an eye socket. Lachlan died instantly and with him the long held MacLean ambitions on the Rinnes. With the death of their charismatic chief[55] the MacLeans were disheartened and began to waver. Soon they were in headlong retreat and making for the safety of their galleys which were at the other end of the loch.

As they retreated along the shores of Loch Gruinneart some of them sought sanctuary in the little church of Kilnave. Their maddened pursuers set fire to the thatch roof and MacLeans perished in the flames. Only one man, MacMhuirich, escaped and according to local tradition he ran down to the shore of the loch and plunged into a reed bed. He broke off a reed and used it to breathe as he submerged himself in the Loch. The MacDonalds thinking he had drowned carried on up the loch shore. MacMhuirich emerged from the reeds and was taken in by a local family.[56]

Kilnave Church

---

[54] It is unclear whether this was the well of Strange Neill or whether he drank from this well soon after landing at Gruinneard. In any event it is said that by the time of his death he had done the three things the witch on Mull had told him to avoid.

[55] Other traditions assert that Lachlan was mortally wounded in the stomach during the battle.

[56] MacMhuirich's descendents live in Bowmore to this day.

The surviving MacLeans reached their galleys which had been beached at the entrance to Loch Gruinneart and on the nearby Nave Island. They launched their galleys and sailed for Mull. During the struggle Sir James had been pierced by an arrow, his wound was so severe that his clansmen assumed that he had been killed, he lay among the dead and wounded through the night. It was only the next morning, when his men were burying the dead that he was found to be still alive. He was carried from the battlefield with great care and looked after till he recovered.

The MacDonalds also found the body of Lachlan Mor; they buried him with respect at Kilchoman churchyard, six miles from the battlefield. His huge frame was laid in the soil he had so long desired by the southern wall of the church.

Kilchoman Church

Lachlan Mor MacLean was only forty one when he died; this great highland chief had led his clan in many wars in his short lifetime. He was an expert swordsman of great physical strength who had great courage, charisma and who commanded the total loyalty of his clan. Lachlan was violent and impetuous, stubborn and acquisitive. In a different age he could well have become a national hero but at the end of the sixteenth century he was mourned only by his own people. MacLean losses were heavy at the Battle of Gruinneart, sixty gentlemen and two hundred clansmen were killed. Clan Iain Mor's losses were considerably less with thirty dead and sixty wounded.

Lachlan's son Hector Og MacLean survived the battle and in the weeks that followed travelled widely in the western highlands enlisting support for a counter attack against the Clan Iain Mor. Hector Og soon formed a powerful confederation of the Camerons, MacLeods of Harris and the MacNeils of Barra.[57] With the aid of these clans and the MacLeans who had survived Gruinneart he invaded Isla to avenge his father.

Sir James knew that the MacLeans were planning to return and gathered what support he could in the few weeks that were available to him. Apart from the Clan Iain Mor from Kintyre and Isla he was joined by the MacDuffies of Colonsay and the MacLeans of Lochbuie. The MacLeans of Lochbuie had been at deadly feud with their more powerful cousins the MacLeans of Duart for some time. The powerful element of the Clan Iain Mor in Antrim was unable to join him either because there was no time or because by this date this branch of the clan was an independent entity with its own commitments in Ireland.

Sir James was unable to resist the invaders and retreated towards his castle of Dunnyveg. At Ben Bigrie the Clan Iain Mor made a stand. There is little recorded of this battle other than it was fought without mercy and that the clansmen of the Clan Iain Mor were overwhelmed and they fell fighting against great odds to a man. At some point during the engagement Sir James was severely wounded by an arrow and although he survived he was unable to be with his men at the end. Hector Og MacLean and his allies now ravaged the island, the helpless population being subject to casual murders, rape and robbery. By the autumn of 1598 Isla had been devastated with a population living in utter destitution amongst the charred ruins of their houses. There can be little doubt that the next winter carried off more of the weak, the old and the young.

The last recorded acts of this feud occurred in the next few years when Hector Og carried fire and sword to the MacDuffies of Colonsay, who had always been loyal supporters of the Clan Iain Mor. In 1602 Hector Og was ordered to appear before the Privy Council for "touching the slaughters, herships, and depredations committed by him upon the King's own tenants in the Isles of Oronsay and Colonsay." In time honoured fashion, Hector failed to put in an appearance and was declared rebel.

This deadly feud seems to have petered out at this time; for a few brief years the Clan Iain Mor kept possession of Isla, including the Rinnes. Both the MacLeans and the Clan Iain Mor were exhausted by the huge losses of manpower they had incurred during their many encounters. Equally serious was the economic devastation to their territories and the impoverishment of their populations. There were no new direct repercussions for either Sir James or Hector Og for this feud which had taken the lives of many hundreds of people including the great Lachlan Mor. It is likely that King James and the Privy Council rejoiced at witnessing these

---

[57] It is probable that both the MacLeods of Harris and the MacNeils of Barra joined Hector because of Angus MacDonald's refusal to give up his hostages which included their sons.

two powerful and belligerent clans tear themselves to pieces. The King would not have mourned the death of Lachlan Mor as shortly before his death Lachlan was prepared to intervene in Ireland on behalf of the Queen Elizabeth.

The King and his ministers were not the only party to enjoy the spectacle of these two clans fatally weakening each other. Grim-faced Archibald the seventh Earl of Argyle, chief of Clan Campbell was watching and waiting at Inveraray Castle. With the military might of his clan and his close connection to the reigns of power in Edinburgh there were so many opportunities laid at his feet.

Chapter 12

No Joy With Out Clan Donald

This chapter describes the extinction of the Clan Iain Mor[1] in Scotland and the usurpation of their ancestral lands by the Campbells. The Clan Iain Mor played a significant role in the history of the Lordship of the Isles,[2] in which they supported every attempt by the Lordship to challenge the authority of the Scottish kings in the western highlands. In the later efforts to re-establish the Lordship their position became more ambivalent; where their own interests clashed with a given rebellion they would remain neutral.[3]

With the anarchy which developed in the western highlands as a result of the collapse of the Lordship the Clan Iain Mor was involved in two desperate feuds with its neighbours. The first was with another branch of the MacDonalds; the Maclains of Ardnamurchan. Under the leadership of their ambitious chief, John Brayach, the Maclains attempted to wrest control of Isla from the Clan Iain Mor. This attempt ultimately failed and ended with John Brayach, and two of his surviving sons and the majority of his clansmen being slaughtered at the battle of Creag-an-Airgid in 1518.[4]

An even more terrible feud erupted between the Clan Iain Mor and the MacLeans in the middle of the sixteenth century.[5] This struggle was over the two clan's rival claims to the Rinnes of Isla. The MacLeans and MacDonalds under their bellicose chiefs, James MacDonald and Lachlan Mor MacLean, fought each other for several decades in the second half of the century. Amidst astonishing levels of violence the two clans carried on their war in most of the south western highlands. While these clans were exhausting themselves the Campbells power had been inexorably rising from its already substantial base in the 1550's. This bitter feud left both the MacDonalds and the MacLeans weakened and more vulnerable when they were faced by Campbell encroachment.

Under an almost unbroken succession of subtle and able chiefs the Campbell star had been rising since their early days when they were one of the clans who lived by the shores of Loch Awe. The first major impetus to their domination of the western highlands was their backing of Bruce against the Balliols. They had, although to a lesser extent, like the MacDonalds benefited from the proscriptions of the MacDougals and Comyns who had supported the loosing faction. From this time on the Campbells developed a policy by which they acted as the only available instrument by which Royal authority could be implemented in the remote south-

---

[1] The Gaelic spelling is Mhoir.

[2] See chapter two.

[3] James (the sixth chief of the Clan Iain Mor) kept the clan out of Donald Dubh's rebellion in the 1540's.

[4] See chapter 5.

[5] See chapter 11.

western highlands. Unlike many of the western clans (including the MacDonalds) they were not bound by any sense of loyalty to the Lords of the Isles and a restoration of the Lordship did not suit Campbell policy. For centuries Campbell policy was to oppose the Lordship and eventually to supplant it as the dominant power in the western highlands. Campbell chiefs usually made sure that under the guise of carrying out Royal decrees they also served their own clan's interests. They understood from a very early date that they must have influence at the Scottish court and if possible the ear of the King. They were thus able to accurately assess the political scene at court and to make their own plans accordingly.

The Campbells also realized the importance of the feudal legal system as it made its first tentative steps into the western highlands during the fifteenth century. During the sixteenth century they constructed an intricate web of manrent agreements with many of the clans. These agreements essentially placed other clans under the "protection" of the Campbells in exchange for recognizing the Campbells as their feudal superiors. These agreements were signed as matters of mere expediency by their neighbours and it is certain that none of the other clans fully appreciated the full implications of these documents. In theory these manrents placed the Campbells as the feudal superiors of most of the western clans with the full backing of feudal law and thus ultimately, the full backing of the state. Despite their unrivalled (for a highland clan) understanding of the gradual shift in power during the sixteenth century the Campbells never lost touch with their Gaelic heritage and when necessary Campbell ambitions were backed by the armed might of their clan. It was the ability of the Campbell chiefs to express their policies by military as well as political means that made them so indispensible to the Scottish state.

In the early sixteenth century it was not yet clear that it was to be the Campbells who would replace the MacDonalds as the most powerful clan in the highlands. Most of the west highland chiefs had entered into bonds of manrent with the Campbells. The explanation as to why they should have so readily acquiesced to this involvement with the Campbells can only partly be explained by their dismissive attitude to these agreements. Was it that they saw it as a way of gaining some influence with the King by using the auspices of the Campbells?

Alexander, the fifth chief of the Clan Iain Mor was no exception. On the sixth of May 1520 he entered into a bond of manrent with Sir John Campbell of Cawdor in which he agreed to become Cawdor's "cuming man and a servand hym self and all the brance of the Clan Donyll that he is cumying of." In exchange for this submission Alexander was granted a five year lease of his ancestral lands on Isla, Jura and Colonsay. The wording of this document creates the impression that Alexander was to be the vassal of Cawdor but, based on future events, it is clear that to Alexander this document was of no significance. It is unclear how Cawdor come into possession of the feudal right to grant these leases; perhaps the superiority of these lands had been gifted to Colin the third Earl of Argyle by the King. Colin had then gifted these superiorities to Cawdor.[6]

During the period of the lease Cawdor invaded Colonsay and laid it waste. The reason for this action has been lost; was it that Alexander did not show Cawdor the respect he felt he was due? It is from this date of the early 1520's that the western clans began their struggle to resist Campbell encroachment. The reverend MacDonald brothers wrote "the cloven foot was seen and the Western Clans swore eternal enmity against the race of Diarmid[7]"; while the language is somewhat colourful it does express a common view among many highland neighbours of the Campbells down to the nineteenth century.

When James V achieved his majority he revoked all the Royal land grants granted by the Regent Albany.[8] This act led to outbreaks of rebellion in the western highlands, amongst which was the open rebellion of Alexander at the head of the Clan Iain Mor. The Clan Iain Mor had been granted leases to their ancestral lands by the regent. These lands formed part of the territories of the Lords of the Isles and had been confiscated by the Crown with the fall of the Lordship in 1493 when John fourth Lord of the Iles had been declared forfeit by James IV. Alexander prepared his clan for war against the Campbells as they were, in his opinion, to blame for these revocations. Alexander was joined by the MacLeans who had their own score to settle with the Campbells. Their chief Lachlan had been stabbed to death by Cawdor who wanted revenge for Lachlan's attempted murder of his wife who was Cawdor's sister.

The Clan Iain Mor and the MacLeans invaded the Campbell lands of Rosneath, Lennox and Craignish and destroyed everything in their path. The inevitable retaliation followed with the Campbells raiding the MacLean lands of Mull and Tiree. In 1529 Cawdor appealed to King James V for assistance on behalf of his ailing brother. James suspected that a significant amount of the current unrest had been caused by Campbell intrigues and in response to Cawdor's appeal sent him a cannon and two falconets[9] and three barrels of gunpowder. This miserly contribution to the Campbell armoury reflected his general distaste for all the participants in the unrest. James also sent a herald to order Alexander to halt his assault on the Campbells and order him to come to court to make his submission. Alexander sent the herald unceremoniously packing.

James's next step was to prepare for an invasion of the south western highlands to bring the recalcitrant chiefs to heal. By the spring of 1530 James was ready with the levies called up from most of western Scotland. James then sent word to the

---

[6] While the clans believed that their lands were inalienable to the people, Scottish law was clear that the King had the right to dispose of any lands in the Kingdom as he saw fit.

[7] The Campbells.

[8] Due to his weak position Albany had been forced to grant many feudal charters to the western clans for their territories in an attempt to placate them.

[9] Falconets are a type of very small cannon.

rebellious clans offering them an amnesty if they would submit. The threat of a royal army proved an effective instrument for bringing the rebel clans to submit, all except the Clan Iain Mor came in. Due to the death of Colin Earl of Argyle and other external factors the invasion was called off till 1531. Archibald Roy Oig, the fourth Earl of Argyle, was appointed leader of the expeditionary force. When Alexander realized that an invasion was imminent and was to be led by the Campbells he appeared before James with a retinue of thirty clansmen to make his submission. James and Alexander soon established a close personnel rapport the result of which was that Alexander was granted a remission for his part in the recent violence. James also renewed the royal leases to the Clan Iain Mor's territories and even gave him one hundred pounds. In exchange Alexander was expected to become James's man in the lands he had influence over, "in eschewing of trouble and in quietation of the Kingis lieges and heirschip of the countrie." James, however, still insisted that Alexander hand over his heir, the young James MacDonald, as a hostage who would stay at the Scottish court when Alexander returned to Isla.

For Archibald Campbell this friendly bond between the King and Alexander was a direct threat to his authority in the western isles and threatened his ability to act as an intermediary between the King and the western clans. Archibald presented a long petition to James accusing Alexander of committing a series of new crimes against the Campbells. Alexander was ordered to appear at court to answer the charges. Alexander immediately set off for court to face his accuser. After Alexander arrived he waited for thirteen days to face Archibald. When Archibald failed to appear, Alexander submitted a written deposition to James in which he laid counter claims which included laying the blame for the recent unrest at the door of the Campbells. He accused the Campbells of acting out of malice and in their own self-interest with regards to the Clan Iain Mor. Alexander also promised James that he could bring more men to assist the King than Archibald could and that if asked he would force Archibald "to duell in ane uthir parte of Scotland... quahir the Kingis Grace may get ressoun of him."

James had been carefully observing the behaviour of Archibald and Alexander[10] and could see through Archibald's plotting. He summoned Archibald to appear before him and when the Earl gave no satisfactory answers to his questioning stripped him of all his offices and threw him in jail. Alexander died in 1538 while on his way to visit the James at Stirling.

The significance of the relationship between the two men can hardly be overstated. James had the shrewdness and intelligence to see through the

---

[10] Alexander remained on good terms with James until his death. The two men corresponded frequently with each other throughout their lives and Alexander was able to assist James in his anti-English policies in Ulster. With the Clan Iain Mor's large territorial possessions in Isla, Kintrye and the Glens of Antrim no highland chief was better placed to advance Scottish policy in Ireland.

machinations of Archibald and the strength of character to manage his affairs in the highlands without the power of the Campbells to assist him. He understood that by using one clan to put down another it created enormous resentment which was a reservoir for further trouble. James could see that it was in the Campbell interest to act as a filter between the King and the other western clans and that they could serve their own desire for expansion under the guise of carrying out the King's commands. It is also probable that in part Archibald's schemes unravelled so badly because James simply did not like him. Alexander was unique among the chiefs of the Clan Iain Mor in that he knew when to use force and when to use diplomacy. He was the only chief of his clan who managed to accomplish the complete rout of Campbell policy at the Scottish Court. If there had been just one more king as perceptive as James and one more chief of the Clan Iain Mor like Alexander it is likely that the history of the western highlands would have been very different.

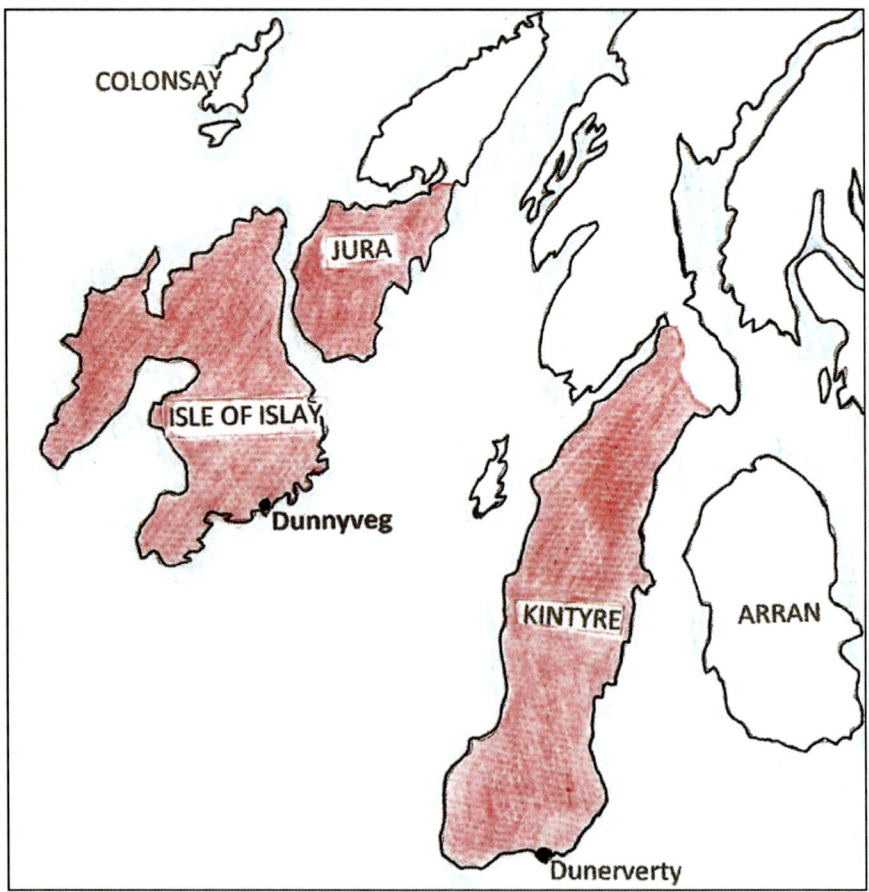

Terratories of the Clan Lain Mor c.1550

Alexander was succeeded by his eldest son James who became the sixth chief of the Clan Iain Mor. James had grown up at the Scottish court, where he had been a hostage for his father's good behaviour. In July 1539 James had to stand surety for some of his own clan and for the MacAlisters of Loupe[11] who had become involved in a small scale but bloody feud with the MacNeills of Gigha. The causes and consequences of this feud have been lost, however, the surviving evidence attests to the usual misery being inflicted on the participants. Despite the close friendship between James and the King, James was still required to give his brother, Coll,[12] as a hostage. Clearly the King wanted some control over James now that he had inherited his vast Gaelic patrimony which stretched from Antrim to Isla.

In the 1540's James was regarded as chief of the most senior branch of the MacDonalds,[13] and as such could command support from them. He was on good terms with James V; the Campbells were out of favour with the King while Sorley Boy was extending the clans possessions in Ireland by conquering the Route in Antrim.[14] James also had the support of many of the smaller clans in the south western highlands, for example, the MacNeills of Gigha, the MacAlisters of Loupe and the MacDuffies of Colonsay. With the fall of the Lordship these clans had transferred their loyalties to the Clan Iain Mor. James also had the ability to call upon the support of several thousand redshanks who were in essence mercenary soldiers who came from most of the clans of the south western highlands. These redshanks were usually only available during the summer months and were, in general, favourably disposed towards the Clan Iain Mor and the Gaelic heritage it represented. Less than a century later the Clan Iain Mor had been annihilated (in Scotland) and the MacDonalds had been dispossessed of all their ancestral lands in Kintyre, Isla and Jura.

With the untimely death of James V in 1542, the Clan Iain Mor lost the first vital element in the maintenance of their security. Scotland was then ruled by the Regent Arran who made every effort to maintain the loyalty of James. Arran even gave James feudal title to his clan lands; in other words the lands of the Clan Iain Mor could be passed from generation to generation without any outside interference. James's loyalty always lay with his own clan, with the interests of the Scottish state coming a poor second. It is ironic that the absolute legal right to the clan's land fell into James's lap while in Ireland his younger brother Sorley Boy was

---

[11] The MacAlisters of Loupe were the first family to develop a separate identity from the rest of the MacDonalds. They are descended from Alasdair Mor(died 1299) the younger brother of Angus Mor who was the grandfather of John first Lord of the Isles. The MacAlisters possessed the "Loupe", which is a district of Kintrye to the south of Loch Tarbert, for many centuries. The history of this ancient family is relatively obscure but was intimately bound up with the history of the Clan Iain Mor in Scotland. MacAlisters would have been present beside their MacDonald kindred at most of the bloody encounters in which the Clan Iain Mor were involved.

[12] Coll was the progenitor of the MacDonalds of Colonsay.

[13] This is because through their founder, Iain Mor, they were the most closely related to the Lords of the Isles.

[14] Appendix.

to spend a lifetime immersed in bloodshed to obtain a similar title to the clan's lands in Ireland (from Elizabeth). During Donald Dubh's second rebellion in the 1540's, James managed to keep his clan neutral, although we can be sure that many individuals from his clan joined the rebellion.

When Donald Dubh died in 1545 James accepted the offer of the rebels to become the next "Lord of the Isles." By this date the cohesion of the rebellion was already starting to disintegrate and James shows a startling lack of political judgment in accepting this by now anachronistic title. With the western clans at odds over the leadership of the rebellion and disputes over the distribution of the English subsidies the rebellion petered out. James had gained nothing by becoming the Lord of the Isles except that he had shown his hand to Arran. Meanwhile the Campbells had been rewarded for their loyalty by being granted many of the lands which had belonged to the Earl of Lennox.[15] James soon found himself in dispute over claims to some of his clan lands with the Campbells; however these were patched up in the presence of Arran. To cement their reconciliation James married Lady Agnes Campbell sister of Archibald the fourth Earl of Argyle.

For the next twenty years till his death in 1565 James was fully committed to the continual struggle of the Clan Iain Mor to maintain and expand its possessions in Ireland against both English and Irish opposition.[16] The 1550's also saw the opening rounds in the feud with the MacLeans over the Rinnes of Isla.[17] James died of his wounds after his clan was overwhelmed by the O'Neills at the Battle of Glentaisie in Antrim.[18] James's campaigns in Ireland, which were, as far as he was concerned, purely a matter of clan politics, had some unexpected consequences for his political relationships in Scotland. Despite his lapse of loyalty after the death of Donald Dubh he regained the trust of the Dowager Mary and Mary Queen of Scots. This was because fortuitously his policies for the Clan Iain Mor were the same as those of the Scottish state. Both monarchs did not wish to see English power expand into Gaelic Ulster, and there is a friendly correspondence between James and the Scottish court over these years as well as Royal grants to uphold his right to his clan lands. His friendship with Mary Queen of Scots was reinforced by their Catholicism and their consequent mutual opposition to the reformation, which was then sweeping through the Lowlands of Scotland.

During these years the relationship between the Clan Iain Mor and the Campbells also became relatively friendly. The Campbell Earls of Argyle had a strained relationship with both Marys as by this date the Earls had espoused Protestantism. However the Earls of Argyle still maintained their support for Scottish policy and therefore their relationship with James was also cordial during

---

[15] The Earl of Lennox had intrigued with the English and had invaded the south western highlands on their behalf.

[16] See appendix.

[17] See chapter 11.

[18] See appendix.

these years. In fact James's ability to raise redshank armies in Scotland to assist the Clan Iain Mor in Ireland were in part only possible with the connivance of the Earls of Argyle as the redshanks were often raised from lands under his direct control.[19]

James was succeeded to the chiefship of the Clan Iain Mor by his eldest son Archibald. Archibald's brief chiefship was uneventful, although interestingly he did receive assistance from the Earl of Argyle in attempting to get Sorley Boy released after his capture at the Battle of Glentaisie. By 1569 Archibald was dead and leaving no legitimate heirs his younger brother Angus became chief of the Clan Iain Mor. Nothing is known about Archibald's character, but by inference it can be assumed that he was unusual amongst the chiefs of his people in that he was of a peaceful disposition. The four year period that he led his people was plenty long enough for him to have had a much fuller representation in the clan history.

The young Angus MacDonald who had become the eighth chief of the Clan Iain Mor was made from different clay to Archibald. Angus's temperament was volatile and he lacked the political subtlety of his ancestors. It may well have been, that as a younger son he had not been tutored in the arts of diplomacy by the gentlemen of the clan as he was not expected to assume the chiefship. His unbounded energy and bellicose nature appealed to his people who readily supported him through all his struggles to maintain the clan's patrimony. In the Gaelic culture of the western highlands Angus was an ideal chief; however the world was changing and clans needed more from their chiefs than energy, bravery and loyalty to his "children".

Angus's mother, the strong willed Lady Agnes Campbell, now a widow had married Turlough O'Neill the son of Shane O'Neill who had temporarily destroyed the Clan Iain Mor's military strength in Ulster at the battle of Glentaisie. It is clear from Turlough's correspondence that Angus did not pay his step-father the respect he felt he was due. The marriage of Angus's mother to the chief of the O'Neills by which it was possible for Campbell and O'Neill interests to coalesce was potentially a major threat to the Clan Iain Mor. The clan was also threatened by MacLean claims to the Rinnes of Isla; this threat was heightened by their chief, the ambitious and warlike Lachlan Mor. Later when the Clan Iain Mor was fighting for its very existence, Scotland was ruled by James VI whose cunning, avaricious and cowardly nature led contempries to describe him as "the wisest fool in Christendom". James's character and his lack of sympathy for the Gaelic west of his Kingdom allowed Campbell policy to go unchecked. There was to be no safety net for the Clan Iain Mor enemating from Royal authority, in fact James allowed the power of the state to support Campbell ambitions.

Angus spent the next fifteen years re-building the Clan Iain Mor's power in Ireland;[20] with the vital help of his uncle Sorley Boy he was eventually successful. With the help of his mother, Lady Agnes Campbell, he was granted title to the

---

[19] It is interesting to speculate as to how many of the redshanks who fought in Ulster on behalf of the Clan Iain Mor during this period were Campbells.

[20] See appendix.

Glens by Elizabeth I, while Sorley Boy was granted title to the Route. In the early years of Angus's chiefship there was an uneasy alliance between Angus and the Campbells. In 1574 Angus signed a bond of manrent with Colin the sixth Earl of Argyle in which Angus acknowledged Colin as his feudal superior in exchange for Campbell support. In view of later events this alliance seems strange. However highland politics was extremely fluid and for a time Campbell and the Clan Iain Mor's policies were united in mutual interest. Angus probably signed this document, which to him was of no great significance, in order to gain Campbell support against the MacLeans. When Angus attacked MacLean settlements on Isla he was indeed supported by two hundred Campbells under the command of Campbell of Lochnell.[21]

In 1580, during the Regency of Morton, a Royal decree was issued which ordered Colin Campbell Earl of Argyle to surrender any claims he might have on the lands of the Clan Iain Mor. A document was duly signed agreeing that Angus held his clan lands free of any Campbell interest The document ends with the two men agreeing that the Campbells and the Clan Iain Mor would mutually support each other against all others excepting only the King. This document affirms clearly that the Campbells had no hold over Kintrye or Isla under feudal law. Certainly under Gaelic law the Clan Iain Mor would have considered it impossible for any of their chiefs to have the power to sign any document which disinherited them. In the 1580's the feud between the Clan Iain Mor and the MacLeans erupted with renewed violence.[22] The slaughter and violence of this clan war spread to most of the western highlands and was eventually brought to the attention of James VI.

James sent a herald to Isla where Angus held Lachlan Mor Maclean captive. The herald was to order Angus to hand over Lachlan to the Campbells and to desist from any further feuding. The herald was unable to reach Isla because Angus had removed all the boats from the shores of Kintrye. Soon after this Angus and Lachlan patched up a truce which conformed to the King's wishes. Lachlan was handed over to the Campbells, but before he was released he agreed to release Ranald, Angus's brother from Duart Castle. Angus also took hostages from the clans which had supported the MacLeans, the MacLeods of Harris, the MacNeills of Bara, the MacKinnons and other branches of Clan MacLean. Angus ensured that he received a royal pardon for his various acts of violence. James later ordered Angus to hand these hostages over to the Campbells; Angus failed to comply with this order and kept the hostages in Isla.

In his feud with Lachlan Mor, Angus had been supported by the MacDonalds of Sleat and the Clanranald as well as the MacLeods of Lewis and many of the smaller

---

[21] In 1578 the Campbells were also at feud with the MacLeans and Campbell forces invaded the island of Luing and essentially cut the MacLeans off from the lowlands by preventing the MacLeans from travelling through Argyle.
[22] See chapter 11.

clans of the south-western highlands.[23] At this period he also entered into a pact with the MacKintoshes in which both clans agreed to support each other. Almost immediately Angus invaded Ireland only to meet with a disastrous defeat at the Battle of Ardnary in which the Clan Iain Mor is said to have lost one thousand fighting men and a thousand women and children.[24] Amongst those killed at Ardnary were Angus's two brothers, Donald Gorm and Alastair Carragh. The terrible losses the clan suffered at Ardnary were to prove irreplaceable when Angus needed every man to defend his Scottish possessions against the inroads of the Campbells and MacLeans.

When Angus returned to Scotland he found that Lachlan Mor MacLean had invaded the Clan Iain Mor's lands with fire and sword paying no regard for the hostages which Angus still held. It is to Angus's credit that none of the hostages were harmed. Many districts of Isla and Gigha had been laid waste. Angus no less violent than his adversary raised his clansmen from Kintrye[25] and proceeded to ravage the MacLean islands of Mull and Tiree.[26] Eventually the MacLeans and MacDonalds encountered each other at the Battle of Benmore where the MacLeans were defeated with terrible losses.[27] James intervened again, Lachlan Mor was pardoned for his offences and granted a life rent of many of the Clan Iain Mor's lands in Isla, and these included the long disputed Rinnes of Isla. Angus was declared a rebel for failing to hand over his hostages to the Campbells. Clearly James's decisions were unjust and would only serve to fuel the Clan Iain Mor's resentment against the MacLeans.

To the impartial observer the feud between the Clan Iain Mor and the MacLeans over the Rinnes was a clan war in which both sides had committed terrible atrocities, but it is indisputable that the Rinnes were the ancient patrimony of the Clan Iain Mor since the fall of the Lordship a century before. James's unjust decision, which favoured the MacLeans, is attributable to the Earl of Glencairn who had great influence at the Scottish court. The Earl of Glencairn was Lachlan Mor's father-in-law. The unjust and arbitrary policies emanating from the Scottish court only served to add to the bitterness in the western highlands and were to lead the Clan Iain Mor to defy James and thus to encompass their doom at the hands of the Campbells.

---

[23] These included the MacNeills of Gigha, the MacDuffies and the MacAlisters.

[24] That so many non-combatants were massacred by the English implies that many had come as spectators to the battlefield, a similar thing happened at Culloden.

[25] These included some English mercenaries he kept in his pay.

[26] On the surface this feud was caused by the bellicose chiefs of the two clans. However, it should be remembered that that the fundamental causes of many feuds were: Gaelic culture, insufficient resources and attempts to reduce the power and prestige of a rival clan's chief by reducing his ability to provide for his people.

[27] See chapter 11.

In 1589 Angus and Lachlan Mor attended a "parliament of peace" which was also attended by the Earl of Argyle, Angus's mother Lady Agnes and his uncle Sorley Boy. The adversaries patched up their differences and Angus was pardoned on condition that he release his hostages; which he duly did. Angus then left Scotland to visit his step-father Turlough O'Neill in Ulster. The two men became firm friends and exchanged many gifts including Irish horses and highland plaid. By this date (1590) James VI was well aware that he could inherit the English crown on the death of Elizabeth. Therefore he no longer wished to have a vibrant and independent Gaelic Ulster as part of the Irish equation. James could well have suspected that the friendship of Angus and Turlough did not bode well for peace in Ulster.

James invited Lachlan Mor and Angus to attend him in Edinburgh. When the two chiefs arrived in Edinburgh he threw them both into prison. Angus was only released in 1592 on condition that he paid his crown rents and a heavy fine. Angus was forced to provide James VI with his two sons, James and Angus as hostages. As soon as Angus returned to his people he refused to pay the crown rents or the fine that had been imposed upon him. To a highland chief James's behaviour was inexcusable in that he had betrayed Angus's trust and broken the laws of hospitality.[28] James duly declared Angus a rebel and in June 1594 the Clan Iain Mor's lands were declared forfeit, which in effect meant that they were at the disposal of the King. However bitter Angus had become at his treatment by James it was a serious miscalculation to defy the King. James's power was often weak and disorganized, but the days when the monarch's writ did not run in the western isles were gone. One can imagine the delight with which Grim Faced[29] Archibald 7th Earl of Argyle would have greeted the news that the King had declared Kintrye and Isla were forfeit.

Angus's eldest son James had been growing up at the Scottish court; he became a favourite of the King. Under a permissive license the young James visited Isla and Kintrye where he entered into a bond of manrent with the MacNeills of Gigha. This bond demonstrates that, in the eyes of the King; James was now the chief of the Clan Iain Mor because his father had been declared forfeit. His status was confirmed when James was knighted by the King and was known as Sir James MacDonald of Smerby. Although James was recognised as been the chief of his clan it is clear that the gentlemen and commonality of the Clan Iain Mor still recognized Angus as their chief.

---

[28] In highland culture it was considered a heinous crime to harm anyone who you had offered hospitality to. There are many examples where the host endured the presence of a man who had killed his brother or father.

[29] Archibald got the epithet of "grim faced" from his demeanour. During his minority there had been plots within Clan Campbell to put him to one side and one of his tutors had been murdered. He had learnt to trust no one and was a hard and ruthless individual.

In 1596 King James decided to put an end to the disturbed and rebellious nature of the south western highlands. He summoned the recalcitrant chiefs to make their submission to him at Dumbarton while he struggled to raise the finances to equip and maintain the proposed expedition.[30] All the chiefs, except for Angus, made their submission and by October the King was ready to invade Kintrye. Angus's reluctance to appear before James is understandable when he had been treated so disgracefully by James a few years before. However it was a serious miscalculation which the proud and rash chief made. Angus had been in communication with James MacDonald of Dunluce who had inherited the Route in Ulster from his father Sorley Boy. He had asked for Dunluce's help in removing the Royal garrisons from Kintyre. Dunluce promptly told James of Angus's plot.[31] Dunluce's betrayal of Angus's trust was duplicitous and cynical; however it did reflect a better understanding of the political environment in the highlands in the late sixteenth century. The old order of things in which highland chiefs could defy Royal authority with equanimity were gone and defenders of Dunluce's character could suggest that he was merely demonstrating the pragmatism which was so clearly lacking in Angus.

When James heard of Angus's plots he immediately granted a new lease to the MacLeans for the Rinnes of Isla and prepared to invade Kintrye. Sir James asked the King's permission to visit his father before the Royal army invaded. It is unclear whether James was sent with any demands from the King or whether he acted on his own behalf. At the meeting between father and son it was made clear to Angus how dire his situation was and of the catastrophic threat to the Clan Iain Mor. Angus duly sent a letter back to the King with Sir James. In it he bound himself to accept whatever Sir James agreed on his behalf, and he renounced his right to the chiefship and all the lands of the Clan Iain Mor in favour of his son. This last offer was so that if Angus himself could not be saved the ancient patrimony of his clan could pass to his son.

When Sir James had an audience with the King, he agreed to remain at court (essentially as a hostage), and to pay any outstanding rents and debts to the King. The King accepted these conditions with the proviso that Angus and his clansmen would leave Kintrye and Gigha and go to Isla. He also stated that Angus was to hand over his Castle of Dunnyveg to a Royal garrison and that later Angus was to submit to the King's will with regards to Isla. The King sent Sir William Stewart to inform Angus of the additional terms which he had stipulated. Angus had no choice; he agreed to the terms offered by the King and gave his submission to the

---

[30] In the late sixteenth century, Scotland had an undeveloped economy and even a small scale military expedition required an enormous effort.

[31] By this date the Clan Iain Mor's lands in Ireland were becoming detached from those in Scotland and in practise the Irish part of the clan recognized James of Dunluce as their chief. It is probable that Dunluce betrayed Angus's trust because he understood the threat to the Clan Iain Mor's position in Scotland, and wanted to be in a strong position to pick up the pieces.

King. Angus had promised to hand over the Clan Iain Mor's patrimony to his son; in feudal law they were not his to give as they had already been declared forfeit to the King. However this offer was understood by all the parties to have significance as only by Angus relinquishing power would the Clan Iain Mor accept Sir James as their new chief with all that that implied. The potential loss of Kintrye would have caused enormous distress and anger amongst the whole of the Clan Iain Mor as it had been in the hands of the MacDonalds since time immemorial. Generation after generation had farmed its poor soils and their ancestors had shed their blood for it in countless battles.

Early in the following year Angus's cousin, Dunluce, visited James VI in Edinburgh. Dunluce was not finished with his own plans for aggrandisement; he claimed that Angus was illegitimate and that he was the rightful heir to the lands of the Clan Iain Mor in Scotland. A less likely, but more charitable, interpretation of his motives would be to suggest the Dunluce was attempting to save Isla and Kintyre for the clan by disassociating them from Angus. Dunluce's allegations were dismissed; however he was granted a considerable acreage in the peninsular.

Once Angus returned from his submission to the King, he sat tight in Kintyre and refused to vacate his ancestral lands. Angus's continual defiance and subsequent submission to James VI was a disaster for the Clan Iain Mor. With each round of this cycle the clan's position was weakening while their enemies were waiting in the wings. Angus failed to understand that highland chiefs could no longer pursue their own policies with impunity in the western isles. He was hoping to lie low for a year or two till things blew over and then he could resume his old ways. Earlier in the century this strategy had usually been successful; the inability of the Scottish executive to act decisively in the highlands had been shown time and again. Angus's situation was entirely different; while James VI still struggled to launch an invasion of the Isles; his power was becoming more effective than previous monarchs. James also had at his command the willing might of Campbell military and political power. The Clan Iain Mor was itself divided, with his cousin (Dunluce) seeming to undermine his position; it was no longer possible for Angus to flee to the clan's lands in Ireland till the situation had improved as his ancestors had done. Angus fulfilled none of his promises to the King and waited in Kintrye.

In 1598 Sir James was allowed to visit his father to see if he could persuade Angus to fulfil his promises. The inaction of the King had encouraged Angus to rescind on the terms of his agreement. He was no longer willing to surrender his birthright to his son. There is no way of telling whether he was influenced in this decision by the gentlemen of his clan, but there would have been many conferences between the senior members of the clan during this lull in events.

At the time of the meeting between Angus and Sir James an internal power struggle developed amongst the MacAlisters of Loupe. Young Gorrie MacAlister was destined to become the next chief of the MacAlisters when he achieved his majority; in the meantime the clan was led by his tutor. The cause of the friction has been lost; suffice it to say the tutor was killed by Gorrie and his supporters.

Angus had supported the tutor's cause and subsequently sheltered the tutor's sons at his house of Askomull. Sir James had taken the part of young Gorrie. In the early summer of 1598 they (James and Gorrie) surrounded Askomull with three hundred clansmen and demanded that Angus hand over the tutor's sons. Angus refused so the besiegers set fire to the house, Angus and his wife[32] escaped from the house although both of them received severe burns. Sir James put his father in chains and took him as a prisoner to Smerby. This incident demonstrates not only the rift which had developed between Angus and his son, but also the struggle between the two for control over the Clan Iain Mor. It is likely that the King only allowed Sir James to go to Kintyre on condition that he either bring Angus to obedience or he apprehended him. The feud between the MacAlisters and the opposing sides that father and son espoused can be seen as merely a pretext for the struggle between the two men for control over the Clan Iain Mor. It is also possible that the King was playing a deeper game; future events suggest that the King not only wanted Sir James to deal with his father but that he would then use Sir James's actions as an excuse to move against him also.

The King subsequently ordered that a new army should be raised from the western shires to invade Kintrye. This invasion also came to nothing and the uneasy status quo continued. The problems between the Clan Iain Mor and James VI were rudely interrupted by that old adversary of the clan, Lachlan Mor MacLean, who had invaded Isla. Sensing the weakness of the Clan Iain Mor; Lachlan was no longer content with his tenancy of the Rinnes. Lachlan wanted the whole of Isla. Sir James, who was by now the unquestioned head of his clan knew that he could not ignore the challenge to his clan's right to Isla. The events which led up to the Battle of Gruinneart and Lachlan Mor's death are described elsewhere (see chapter 11). Suffice it to say that although Sir James was badly wounded and thirty of his clansmen killed in battle, the MacLeans were defeated with the loss of not only their chief but also many gentlemen and scores of clansmen.

Sir James does not appear in the historical record for a year till he meets with Sir David Murray, the King's Comptroller, to agree terms for the future of the Clan Iain Mor. The reason why Sir James appears so inactive between August 1598 and the following August is that he was recovering from his wound. James offered on behalf of himself and his clan (he must have secured the agreement of at least the gentlemen of the clan) to surrender Kintrye and the Castle of Dunnyveg on Isla and enough land to sustain the garrison, while the Clan Iain Mor was to rent the rest of Isla from the crown. Sir James offered to pay £600 rent for the island as well as a further payment of £650 to maintain Angus in his old age. The rent offered the King for Isla was a large sum for such poor land and reflects the clan's desperation by this stage. Sir James also offered to submit his brother, Angus Og, as a hostage and even to pay for his upkeep. Sir James's offer to the King was accepted on his behalf by the majority the Privy Council in September 1599. Despite the terrible loss of

---

[32] Mary MacLean of Duart.

Kintyre and the humiliating terms their chief had been forced to offer James VI, it looked to the gentlemen of the clan that the Clan Iain Mor still had a future on its ancient lands.

During 1599 Sir James married Margret Campbell the daughter of Sir John Campbell of Cawdor. Whether or not it was marriage based on love it was certainly a political marriage. Sir James was using a well tried strategy for forming an alliance with a powerful neighbour; no doubt he hoped that the marriage would blunt any expansionism on the part of the Campbells. Traditionally marriage between two clans had been used to cement an alliance, confirm a friendship or end hostilities. As Sir James was married to Cawdor's sister he had every reason to believe that Cawdor would act as his friend and offer him the best advice he could. Cawdor, no doubt taking his lead from Grim Faced Archibald Earl of Argyle, urged Sir James not to confirm the approval of the Council of his own proposals. Sir James foolishly let the offer of the possession of Isla in perpetuity lapse presumably in the hope of gaining better terms; he clearly did not see that Cawdor's advice suited only the Campbell interest.

From 1599 onwards the Campbells began to spin their web in which, in the end, the Clan Iain Mor however it struggled was enmeshed. Angus was supported and encouraged in every foolish act by Grim Faced Archie. Archibald hoped that by using Angus's rash and unsubtle character against his son he could fatally weaken the Clan Iain Mor. Angus was encouraged to enter into a bond of friendship with Campbell of Auchinbreck. Auchinbreck worked on the credulous old man and persuaded Angus that Sir James was plotting against him. Angus captured the unsuspecting Sir James and handed him over to Auchinbreck who in his turn surrendered him into the hands of Grim Faced Archibald. Archibald brought him before the Council for not acknowledging their acceptance of his terms. By the early months of 1604 Sir James was imprisoned in Blackness Castle. With the help of some of his clansmen Sir James nearly succeeded in escaping. The plot failed because of the treachery of one of the accomplices. For greater security Sir James was secured in Edinburgh Castle.

Archibald's schemes against Sir James were facilitated by not only the rift between Angus and his son but also the political environment in Scotland in 1604. Archibald as Earl of Argyle held enormous influence with the Council, who during this period wielded great power in Scotland as by this date James VI had accepted the English crown on the death of Elizabeth. James was much more interested in his new patrimony than in affairs in Scotland. The interminable disputes of the south western highlands must have seemed truly insignificant to him and a world away from London and his affluent new Kingdom.

Angus resumed his chiefship of the Clan Iain Mor in the summer of 1605. Angus was summoned by Lord Scone, the Lord Comptroller, to appear before him. He was to bring his title to the Clan Iain Mor's remaining lands and to find surety for his Crown rents, which rather predictably he had not paid. Failure to meet either request would result in Angus being declared a rebel and Isla being invaded with fire and sword. Angus was in a hopeless position because clearly he had no legal title to Isla. Angus failed to appear before Lord Scone who immediately called out the men of Argyle to assemble at Tarbat and bring forty days supply of provisions with them. He also passed decrees forbidding any removal of boats from Kintrye so as to prevent Angus from isolating himself. Hepburn, an officer in the King's guard was immediately sent to Isla to order Angus to surrender Dunnyveg Castle. After the usual tardy assembly of the Scottish levies Lord Scone was ready. Fearing an imminent invasion Angus capitulated and paid his back rents in full; he surrendered Dunnyveg and handed over two of his sons as hostages, (Angus Og and Archibald MacDonald of Gigha).[33]

Dunnyveg Castle

By his surrender Angus had again averted disaster. However, the internal situation in the political framework of the Clan Iain Mor must have been catastrophic. There was the terrible rift between Angus and Sir James. Clearly Sir James was fit to be chief, however without being deposed by the gentlemen of the clan, Angus was the rightful chief. This situation must have led to divided loyalties amongst the gentlemen of the clan. The loss of Kintyre resulted in not only significant losses of manpower and economic recourses but also a loss of prestige

---

[33] Archibald MacDonald of Gigha was a "natural" son.

for the Clan Iain Mor. This loss would have been keenly felt by the whole clan and would have led to much dissatisfaction and demoralization. It may not be going too far to say that the Clan Iain Mor was beginning to fall apart due to internal stresses as much as external factors.

Even Angus was aware that the existence of his clan was hanging by a thread, and in the autumn of 1606 he wrote to the Council again promising to pay his rents and to submit himself to the laws of the land. He then wrote a letter to James VI "beseeching your Majesty for the cause of God to respect my age and poor estate, and to let me know your highness's own mind signed with your Majesty's own hand." It is clear from this pathetic letter that Angus knew that he could expect little mercy from the council, which was heavily under the influence of Archibald Earl of Argyle. Archibald made sure that Angus's letter to the King never left Scotland. He could not allow Campbell plans to be thwarted by any direct contact between a Scottish King and the Clan Iain Mor as it had been in the past. Now that Sir James was safely out of the way in the dark recesses of Edinburgh Castle, Grim Faced Archie could withdraw any pretence of support from Angus.

In November 1606 Archibald was ready to make his move. He proposed to the Council and Lord Scone that he become the crown tenant in Kintyre. Kintyre had been held directly by the crown since Angus had been forfeited. With the prospect that the Campbells were to be granted Kintyre the Clan Iain Mor stirred itself once again. Sir James made an unsuccessful attempt to escape from Edinburgh Castle and then tried to influence the Duke of Lennox and the King by a series of letters. To the Duke of Lennox he wrote that he would accept banishment if only the King would release him. While to James he wrote " For Christ's cause, sir, once forgive me my past offences, and with God's grace I shall ever behave myself dutifully." There is no evidence that either Lennox or the King ever replied to these pitiful letters. Archibald MacDonald of Gigha did manage to escape from imprisonment and returned to the west to aid his people.

In the early summer of 1607 Archibald Campbell Earl of Argyle received the royal tenancy to Kintrye and the MacDonald lands on Jura. He immediately began to oust the Clan Iain Mor from his newly acquired lands. It was with a sense of bewilderment and anguish that the people of the Clan Iain Mor left the little clachans where they had lived all their lives and where their ancestors had lived for many generations before them. It was not just the loss of their homes and the means of supporting themselves, it was the loss of Kintrye a cornerstone of the identity of the Clan Iain Mor.

Angus realized that this time Kintrye was really going to be lost to his clan. He broke out into open rebellion; he gathered up the strength of the Clan Iain Mor from Isla, Jura and the refugees from Kintrye. He also assembled a fleet of galleys. Archibald had settled the more fertile districts of Kintrye with Lowlanders. When they heard of Angus's preparations they fled their newly acquired lands. Ironically many of them fled to Ulster where they were given protection by James MacDonald of Dunluce and settled in the Route. The Clan Iain Mor faced its many foes alone apart from support from the MacDonalds of Sleat under their chief Donald Gorme. Angus's army disbanded a few months later. Had the gentlemen of the clan been able to persuade Angus as to the folly of encountering not only the Campbells but also James VI?

In the winter of that year, Sir James again attempted to escape from his gaolers. He overpowered his guards and jumped from the castle wall. His legs were still in fetters and when he landed the chains injured one of his legs. Sir James was soon recaptured and returned to his dungeon. Within a few weeks the King issued a warrant for Sir James to stand trial for his misdemeanours.

Due to the slow grinding of the law James was not brought to trial till May 1609. He was accused of setting fire to his father's house at Askomull and of attempting to escape from his prison. The prosecution called for the death sentence if he was found guilty, as Sir James would have committed "maist high and manifest treason." By 1609 there was a hysterical hatred of those that represented the remnants of the Gaelic traditions of the highlands. Sir James was facing a show trial in which he could expect no justice. The prejudice against Sir James is demonstrated by the opening words of the indictment against him. "Forsamekill as, frome your verrie youthe, ye be tranit up in all manner of crewall barbarities and wiketnes, and following the pernitious examill of your godless parentis, kynmen and countrie people....". The language used by the court shows a contempt for, and ignorance of, Gaelic culture emanating from highly educated Scotsmen. The fact that Sir James had been brought up at the Scottish court and that his grandmother and wife[34] were Campbells was wilfully overlooked by the prosecutors. Sir James was appointed Mr Russell as his defence lawyer. The poor man would not take up this poisoned chalice unless he received a warrant signed by the King himself.

Sir James answered his accusers with dignity and prudence. He denied setting fire to Askomull, which technically he may well not have done, but did admit to apprehending his father and attempting to escape gaol. He had a warrant in his possession which was signed by the King, expressly authorising his apprehension of his father and approving his subsequent actions. Putting aside the evidence of the King's connivance in the seizure of Angus, as shown by the warrant, one must wonder why the King had let five years elapse since the events Askomull before acting. Was it that circumstances had changed and Sir James and the Clan Iain Mor were to be condemned? Sir James had the circumspection not to use the warrant in his defence, if he had implicated the King then he would have been executed immediately. While he held the warrant back, the king knew he possessed it. Knowledge of this warrant might restrain the prosecution for fear that the King's shabby actions might be made public. Sir James also admitted to attempting to escape jail but denied harming any of his gaolers in his attempts to escape.

Sir James was enmeshed in a situation in which Grim Faced Archibald held all the cards, the judge was subservient to the Earl of Argyle, as Archibald was the

---

[34] Lady Agnes Campbell and Margaret Campbell.

Chief Justiciar of Scotland. The prosecution witnesses, who included Sir James's father and mother were not cross-examined. All the written evidence passed through Archibald's hands before it was shown to the court. In his defence Sir James argued that any evidence procured against him which was influenced by Archibald should be ignored because Archibald wanted his conviction so that he could further his own interests and those of the Campbells. His arguments were, of course, ignored. Sir James was duly convicted of treason and condemned to death. The sentence was not carried out,[35] and Sir James was taken back to gaol.

What were Sir James crimes against the King? It is true that he had failed to ratify the Council's acceptance of his offer of submission to the King.[36] It is also true that he had attempted to escape from gaol, in an attempt to save his clan from destruction at the hands of his imbecilic father and the machinations of the Campbells. Amongst the long litany of rebellion, mayhem and murder committed by so many of the King's subjects his "crimes" do not seem that heinous. Clearly he and the Clan Iain Mor stood between the King achieving higher rents and the Campbells long held desire for expansion into Kintrye and Isla. Some Campbell historians have claimed that the lands of the Clan Iain Mor fell into the lap of the Campbells who were mere spectators, as the Clan Iain Mor tore itself apart. The pitiful correspondence issuing from members of the Clan Iain Mor to the King amongst others, begging to be judged by anyone other than the Campbells, belies this rather bland interpretation of Campbell policy in the early seventeenth century.

In 1610 Lord Ochiltree was ordered to surrender Dunnyveg Castle to Bishop Knox who was appointed its Constable for life and Steward of Isla. The Bishop was also entitled to arrears of rent which Angus had still failed to pay. On the first of January 1612 old Angus MacDonald eighth chief of the Clan Iain Mor sold his clan's patrimony in Isla to Campbell of Cawdor for the paltry sum of six thousand marks.[37] Angus was by now destitute and desperate for money in his old age. He had no right to sell Isla as it was still forfeit to the King, and thus Cawdor had no right to buy the island. No doubt the transaction suited both parties; Angus received his money, while Cawdor could lay claim to Isla with a semblance of legality.

That their chief should sell them to their foes was incomprehensible to the Clan Iain Mor and was of course unacceptable. The Clan would have been well aware of its struggles to maintain its identity against the Maclains of Ardnamurchan a century before, and its continual wars in Ireland. Many of them would have fought and suffered for their clan in the bitter feud with the MacLeans and their relatives

---

[35] Because of his possession of the warrant from the King.

[36] Under the influence of Campbell of Cawdor.

[37] At the time of the union there were approximately 2 marks to the Scots pound and approximately 9 Scots pounds to the English pound, so that during this period there were about 18 marks to the English pound. Isla was sold for £333. This pitiful sum was little recompense for all the blood that the Clan Iain Mor had shed in their struggles to maintain possession of the island.

lay in the churchyard so that the pretensions of Lachlan Mor MacLean were resisted. In their Gaelic law it was not possible for any individual, even the chief, to simply sell the clan's lands. The survivors of the Clan Iain Mor would not accept Campbell occupation without a struggle.

Angus spent the remainder of his life among the Stewarts of Bute. Angus's relationship with this branch of the Stewarts had been cordial for many years,[38] and his continued ties with them is attested to by the fact that John Stewart of Bute was a witness to his sale of Isla. Angus Macdonald eighth chief of the Clan Iain Mor died on the twenty first of October 1614. Angus's character would have been better suited to simpler times. His undoubted courage and stamina had stood him in good stead in a life of almost ceaseless campaigning and bloodshed. Although a valiant leader of his clan, Angus was rash and lacked the political acumen to steer his clan through the complex and dangerous political environment of his later years. He failed to understand all the significant changes which were taking place at the end of the sixteenth century, the rise in power of both Campbell and Royal authority. His vacillation between abject submission and defiance of James VI placed the Clan Iain Mor in a hopeless situation. His stubborn and ill-considered persecution of his son to serve his own petty interests not only meant that he failed to fulfil his duties as a father but, more importantly as a chief to his "children". When writing his eulogy the MacVurich historian of Clanranald describes him as "the best of the MacDonalds in his own time," not an epitaph that any of the Clan Iain Mor would have been able to agree with.

Towards the end of 1614, the Castle of Dunnyveg was captured from its Royal "garrison" by half a dozen men of the Clan Iain Mor. The "garrison" consisted of Robert MacGilchrist and his family,[39] hardly an effective force when one considers how many great men had bent their wills to the problems of Isla. The leader of the MacDonalds was Ranald Og, who, local gossip had it was a bastard son of Angus's. Ranald Og is described as being a vagabond with no fixed residence.

Angus Og, the brother of Sir James, was elected to lead the clan after the death of his father Angus. When Angus Og heard that Dunnyveg had been seized he immediately sent round the fiery cross to raise his clan so that they could restore control of the castle to Bishop Knox. Angus Og besieged Dunnyveg for six days. On realizing that he did not command the support of the Clan Iain Mor, Ranald Og and his accomplices slipped away during the night. Angus Og then occupied Dunnyveg in the name of the King.

The actions of Ranald Og and Angus Og show that there were two opposed views within the Clan Iain Mor. The majority of the clan followed Angus Og and were prepared to do what they must to avoid the wrath of the King and his vengeance through his instruments the Campbells. Ranald Og clearly represented a

---

[38] Many years before he had entered into a bond of manrent with them.
[39] It was not unusual for highland castles to be garrisoned by a handful of people however given the tension on Isla it is surprising that the authorities had allowed this situation to arise.

differing strand of opinion which viewed the occupation by Knox as an affront to the dignity of the Clan Iain Mor. The fact that Clan Iain Mor was losing its cohesion is indicative of the strain the clan was under.

Angus Og soon captured Ranald Og and his accomplices; Angus executed several of Ranald's men and interrogated Ranald. Ranald claimed that, Donald Gorm, who was an illegitimate son of Sir James's, had told him that Dunnyveg was to be given to a third party and that Isla was to pass to another owner and the Clan Iain Mor banished from the island. Donald Gorm promised to support Ranald if he captured Dunnyveg and protect Ranald from any consequences which might arise from his actions. Ranald also claimed to have a letter which would explain his actions, but when Angus pressed him for it Ranald destroyed it. This rather complex and confused story suggests that the MacDonalds on Isla were susceptible to any wild rumour they came across in their efforts to make sense of their situation.

Angus Og held Dunnyveg ostensibly in the name of the King, and professed his readiness to surrender the castle to Bishop Knox on certain conditions. These were that Angus and his men should be pardoned for any previous offences they had committed including the execution of the followers of Ranald Og. The garrison consisted of members of the Clan Iain Mor, including Donald Gorm, and some MacAlisters from Kintrye.

As the summer of 1614 wore on reports reached the council that Angus had still not handed Dunnyveg over to the Bishop and that he appeared to be preparing for a siege. Sir James petitioned the Council that they might order his release. In this letter he describes his suffering and, if released, offers to live wherever the King commanded and to appear before the council when they should call him. He also expressly states that he would not return to his clan without the permission of the King. Unable to decide on Sir James's fate the Council sent the letter to London for the King to decide Sir James's fate. Before any reply could be received the correspondence had to travel down the poor roads to London where it had to be put before the King and then a reply sent back to Edinburgh. James,[40] as King of both Scotland and England, was swamped with the administration of his two kingdoms. The fate of Sir James and events in Isla could only have commanded a moment's consideration and the fate of the Clan Iain Mor hung on a whisper in the ear and few seconds thought. By the early seventeenth century Sir James and his clan were only able to communicate with the King through a series of intermediaries who were following their own interests and could manipulate what the King heard. The King's own prejudice against the clans of the western highlands were reinforced by the views and wealth of his new Kingdom; he had little time or inclination to see that the Clan Iain Mor received justice.

The Council, suspecting that Sir James was encouraging the MacDonald garrison of Dunnyveg increased the closeness of his confinement, this probably meant that he was put back into leg irons, they also searched his miserable possessions to find

---

[40] James the VI of Scotland and James I of England.

evidence of his treason. The correspondence they found proved that Sir James had been encouraging Angus Og to surrender Dunnyveg and that he was innocent of any plotting against the authorities. A letter was also found which had been written by Angus Og for the attention of the council; which confirmed that he was willing to surrender the castle to the Bishop on condition that he was pardoned. This letter must have only been in Sir James's possession for a very short time as it was clearly vital that it reached the Council as soon as possible. When the Council was made aware of Angus's willingness to surrender Dunnyveg they decided to put his words to the test. They ordered Angus to surrender the castle and granted Bishop Knox a commission of fire and sword should he fail to do so.

It emerged later that during the summer of 1614 Angus had received secret correspondence from Archibald, Earl of Argyle. Angus Og had heard from the ancient allies of the Clan Iain Mor, the MacNeills of Gigha, that Archibald had said in public that, "he was a friend Angus Og and his friends would give up the castle and that , if they did so, it would turn to their utter wreck." When MacNeill asked the Earl if he might tell Angus what he had heard, Archibald replied that he had spoken thus in order that his words would be repeated to Angus.[41]

Grim faced Archie encouraged Angus to resist any attempt by the Bishop to occupy Dunnyveg as this would lead to the ruin of Angus and the Clan Iain Mor. Archibald's subtle letters played on Angus's clearly credulous nature. Angus allowed himself to be persuaded that once the Bishop had gained control of Dunnyveg the Council planned to drive the Clan Iain Mor from Isla. Clearly Archibald was encouraging Angus to resist Royal authority so that he would be asked to use Campbell power to enforce the will of the Council. It is a sad reflection on the gullibility of Angus and his advisors that he accepted the advice of the chief of a clan which had so long desired Isla. The surviving elements of the leadership of Clan Iain Mor were probably illiterate, they had little understanding of how the processes of state functioned and their isolation from the main body of decision making left them vulnerable to Archibald's advice which was to lead their clan to catastrophe. However none of these reasons as to why they listened to Archibald fully explain their gullibility.

On the sixteenth of August 1614, at the instigation of Bishop Knox, the Council granted a remission to Angus Og for the execution of Ranald's accomplices and his seizure of Dunnyveg. This remission was conditional that Angus should surrender Dunnyveg to the Bishop when he arrived on Isla. Angus agreed to surrender the castle, but only to the Bishop who was to give Angus a letter of "friendship". The Bishop duly arrived in Isla accompanied by fifty hired men and twenty MacAulays and a contingent of the MacDonalds of Sleat led by their chief Donald Gorm

---

[41] Archibald's complicity in the downfall of the Clan Iain Mor was accepted by many of his contemporaries, Sir Alexander Hay wrote to a friend, " by many it is thought that if good deeds will did second the duty which they (the Campbells) employ are bound to do, these frequent island employments would not occur so often."

MacDonald. Donald Gorm, had offered to accompany the Bishop and to negotiate the surrender of the castle. Donald Gorm would have been aware of the precarious situation of the Clan Iain Mor and would have wished to save them from destruction.[42] Donald Gorm went ahead and had an interview with Angus, when he learnt that Angus would not surrender Dunnyveg to the Bishop, he abandoned the Bishop and returned to Skye. Donald Gorm had been unwilling to back the Bishop against fellow MacDonalds even if it was in the Clan Iain Mor's interests in the long run. He sailed from Isla with a heavy heart.

As the Bishop's depleted force made its way across the island, Angus had sent a small raiding party to destroy the Bishop's four boats. Bishop Knox found himself cut off from the mainland on what to him was a remote and desolate island. His depleted force was greatly outnumbered by the Clan Iain Mor who he could observe gathering on the hillsides. Being in effect, a hostage, he was forced to agree to Angus's terms. The Bishop promised to obtain a seven year lease of Isla for Angus from the Council as well as acceptance of his right to occupy Dunnyveg. The Bishop was forced to surrender his son and nephew as hostages to Angus. Before returning to Edinburgh Bishop Knox wrote a letter to the Council in which he implicates Archibald Campbell, Earl of Argyle; "Angus Og, their captain, affirms, in the hearing of many witnesses, that he got direction from the Earl of Argyle not to surrender the castle and that he (the Earl) should procure for Angus the whole lands of Isla, and the house of Dunnyveg."

Bishop Knox returned to Edinburgh in disgrace for his failure to implement the Council's policy. They ignored the Bishop's assertion that the Campbells were behind Angus's intransigence and that he had been forced to leave hostages. They appointed Campbell of Cawdor[43] to retake the island for the King. The terms of his instructions sheds light on some of their motives. The council were to provide Cawdor with some artillery and ammunition, but the subjugation of Isla was to be purely at his own expense. The Council were no doubt encouraged in choosing Cawdor because he had offered to pay high rents to the King should he be given the commission. The savings on the public purse, the future high rents and the strong Campbell influence amongst the council led to this extremely inappropriate choice. It was already clear to the Council that the Campbells had been encouraging Angus's intransigence; they knew that any Campbell occupation of Isla was bound to lead to great resentment amongst the Clan Iain Mor and that the ancient inhabitants of Isla could expect little mercy from the Campbells. The Council had even been expressly warned by Bishop Knox, "neither can I, nor any man who knows the estate of that country think it either good or profitable to his Majesty, or this realm, to make the name of Campbell greater in the Isles than they

---

[42] The Clan Iain Mor were not only brother MacDonalds but also these two clans had recently been allies in the feud with the MacLeans.

[43] Cawdor's sister, Margaret was married to Sir James MacDonald, it would be fascinating to know where she stood in this struggle between her brother's clan and that of her husband.

are already; nor yet to root out one pestiferous clan, and plant in another little better.....". This warning came from a man who had no reason to be partial to MacDonald interests. In the end the King's council in Scotland decided on this disastrous course of action because it was easy and it was cheap.

On hearing of this new threat to the Clan Iain Mor's possessions Sir James made a new appeal to the Council. He offered a huge rent of eight thousand merks (£4000 Scots) a year for Isla, in exchange for a seven year lease. He also offered to transport himself and his clan to Ireland or wherever else the King decided. If the King found this unacceptable he offered to take the Clan Iain Mor out of the King's dominions on condition that all of his clan receive a pardon. Sir James even went so far as to suggest that the clan settle in Holland with the proviso that he could raise his clan for the service of that country if they accepted him. His failure to understand the depths of Campbell involvement is demonstrated by his insistence that his brother-in-law, Campbell of Cawdor would stand surety for him. It is doubtful if these desperate offers were ever put to the King and were never seriously considered by the Council. No highland chief had ever offered to remove his clan from their lands let alone to remove them from Scotland. These quixotic and fanciful offers showed the desperate circumstances which Sir James knew the Clan Iain Mor to be in.

Cawdor began his preparations for an invasion of Isla while the Council offered a pardon to those who would submit to the Council's will.[44] The Earl of Dunfermline, who was the Scottish Chancellor, in an effort to obtain the release of the Bishop's hostages employed Graham of Eryns to act as a negotiator with Angus Og. Without any official sanction Graham set out for Isla. Graham convinced the hapless Angus Og that if he released the hostages and surrendered the castle, Graham had the authority to halt the threatened Campbell invasion. After some hesitation Angus surrendered the hostages and castle to Graham. Graham then offered the castle back to Angus on condition that he hold it for the King until further instructions were received from the Earl of Dunfermline.[45] Angus was completely taken in by this consummate liar. When a Royal herald arrived before the walls of Dunnyveg demanding that Angus surrender the castle to the King, Angus not only refused but threatened the herald with violence. This added layer of intrigue may well have been a last minute effort on behalf of the Chancellor to stop Isla falling into the hands of the Campbells and obtaining the island for himself.

On the first of October 1614 Cawdor expressed anxiety about this proposed invasion of Isla. He was concerned as to the fate of the hostages and (more importantly) the reaction of the rest of the Scottish nobility to any further expansion of Campbell power. These "sensibilities" were dismissed by the Council and Cawdor was ordered to proceed against the Clan Iain Mor. By mid-October,

---

[44] Even Angus Og was included in this offer provided that he give up the hostages he had taken from Bishop Knox and surrender prominent members of his clan to be hostages.

[45] These discussions were witnessed by Angus Og's wife, Katherine Campbell of Danna.

Campbell levies had invaded Isla; they were joined by Cawdor towards the end of November. Although Isla was quiet, Angus Og still held out in Dunnyveg the besiegers having made little impression on the ancient walls built so many years before by his ancestors. With his men exposed to the harsh winter weather and running low on supplies Cawdor returned to Duntroon to organize more provisions for his clansmen. Two days after Cawdor had left, a fleet of four ships arrived with reinforcements for the besiegers led by Sir Oliver Lambert and Campbell of Glencarradale.

Lambert called upon Angus Og to surrender Dunnyveg. Angus Og still insisted that he had a Royal warrant to hold the castle, given to him by Graham on behalf of the Chancellor. When a copy was produced for Lambert's inspection he declared the warrant invalid and warned Angus Og that the siege would continue when Cawdor returned. Due to contrary winds Cawdor did not manage to return to Isla till the fifth of January 1615, with provisions and two hundred reinforcements. The next day he was joined by Campbell of Barbreck-Lochawe at the head of three hundred men and the artillery. Within a few days the Campbell forces were augmented by regular troops from Ireland which included cavalry. The Campbell forces in Isla now had an overwhelming superiority to the forces available to the Clan Iain Mor. On the twenty first of January Angus Og's uncle, Ranald MacJames surrendered the newly fortified position on Loch Gorm.

By the twenty seventh of January the artillery was ready to force a breach in the walls of Dunnyveg. In the initial phases of the bombardment Angus's men managed to kill one of Lambert's officers and one of Cawdor's Campbells. Angus then attempted to parley, but the besiegers would accept nothing but unconditional surrender. Worried that the tiny garrison might attempt to escape by sea the castle was watched from both land and sea twenty four hours a day. The next day Angus himself came out to seek terms, he explained to Lambert that he had been duped by Graham and agreed to surrender Dunnyveg. However when he returned to the castle he was persuaded by Coll Coitach[46] to continue the unequal struggle. Coll Ciotach MacDonald was the chief of the MacDonalds of Colonsay.[47] Angus delayed his surrender as long as he could but realising that the walls were in imminent danger of collapse, he surrendered to Cawdor without conditions in the first few days of February.

The night before the surrender, Coll Coitach and some of his men escaped by boat from the castle, the boats were rotten and leaked badly. The fugitives were

---

[46] Coll Coitach otherwise known as Colkitto was the chief of the MacDonalds of Colonsay. He was the father of Alasdair MacCholla who was to take a terrible revenge on the Campbells during the civil war.

[47] Colkitto's (Coll Coitach) grandfather was Colla nan Capull also known as Colla Maol Dubh who was a brother of James, the sixth chief of the Clan Iain Mor, who died of his wounds after the Battle of Glentaisie. Colla Coitach's name has been taken to mean Colla the sinister where a more accurate translation would be Colla the ambidextrous.

forced to land on the shores of Isla. Coll Coitach escaped[48] but six of his men were not so lucky, they were caught by Campbell search parties and were summarily executed. On taking possession of Dunnyveg, Cawdor held a justice court. Fourteen MacDonalds from the Dunnyveg garrison and six from the fort on Loch Gorm were tried, condemned and hung. Unlike the grander players in this tragedy, who at least had some understanding of the larger forces at work, these poor souls had merely obeyed their chief and had lost their lives for defending their clan from Campbell aggression. Campbell of Glencarradale roamed Isla with his clansmen destroying any references to Catholicism and calling for the islanders to make their submission to Cawdor at Dunnyveg. Although the islanders were cowed by the overwhelming military might of the Campbells they were still defiant; only one man duly made his submission to Cawdor.

Angus Og was brought before the Council, he was told of Archibald's plotting and those of the Chancellor. Although Graham was disgraced it will come as no surprise to read that neither the Earl of Argyle nor the Chancellor were in any way blamed for the events on Isla. For Angus Og and his surviving clansmen there was to be a different ending; they were found guilty of treason and "justified". When Angus died resistance to the Campbells on Isla erupted again. He died before seeing the final destruction of the Clan Iain Mor. Angus Og like his father before him was ill-equipped to deal with complex manoeuvrings of the early seventeenth century. He was no match for Grim Faced Archibald Campbell and although he strained every nerve to preserve his clan's inheritance, his actions only played into the hands of his persecutors.

On the twenty third of May 1615 Sir James escaped from prison. He later claimed that he was forced to escape on hearing that Cawdor was obtaining a warrant for his execution. His real motive was to go to Isla to resist the Campbell occupation. With the help of the sons of the chiefs of the MacDonalds of Keppoch and Clanranald he slipped across the Forth and into Perthshire. The Council acted immediately by offering £2000 Scots for his capture and the Duke of Atholl and the Camerons were ordered to intercept him.[49] Sir James passed through Atholl hotly pursued by his oppressors. Near Loch Rannoch Sir James only escaped capture by abandoning his horses and luggage.[50] The fugitive was only able to draw breath when he reached Glen Spean which was in the lands of the MacDonalds of Keppoch, who were led by Alasdair who sympathized with Sir James. Sir James

---

[48] "Colkitto" allied himself with other "broken" men amongst whom were many MacLeods of Lewis whose clan would receive a similar fate to the Clan Iain Mor. His piratical wanderings took him throughout the Hebrides, he even visited the remote island of Saint Kilda.

[49] The Dukes of Atholl and the Camerons had their own reasons to resent Campbell expansionism, it is unlikely that they carried out the Council's instructions with any enthusiasm or diligence.

[50] Amongst his possessions were a number of books; clearly James had wanted them enough to bring them with him.

then made his way through Lochaber and the lands of the Clanranald to the territories of the MacDonalds of Sleat on Skye. The chiefs of these two clans[51] while sympathetic to Sir James plight were unable to show any open support for the Clan Iain Mor for fear of retribution from the powerful axis of the Council and the Campbells. While on Skye Sir James was joined by a small band of clansmen.[52]

Sir James then sailed to the island of Eigg, the ancient rallying place of the MacDonalds in the northern part of their territories. The news of his escape and travels through the highlands spread from clachan to clachan. Many MacDonalds must have reflected on their past glories and with their hearts wanted to join him in one last attempt to establish a vibrant MacDonald hegemony in the west. Even the less well informed amongst them knew that the days of the Lordship had passed and most stayed at home. However there were those with nothing to lose. Sir James was joined by members of his own clan who had fled Isla or Kintyre, he was joined by the remnants of the Maclains who had also lost their ancient patrimony of Ardnamurchan to the Campbells. Under the command of Donald MacDonald who was tutor to the young chief Alexander they returned to Ardnamurchan and captured the castle of Mingarry and held it on behalf of Sir James. Within a few days his small force was supplemented by the arrival of Coll Coitach and his band of MacDonalds and MacLeods of Lewis.[53] The small army celebrated in time honoured fashion with oxen roasting on the spit while Sir James's adherents marched around him shouting and firing their muskets. It was to be last time that Eigg played host to such a gathering. The small force sailed to Colonsay and then on to Isla.

Meanwhile the Council demonstrated their inability to act decisively in the western isles. They sent commissions to many of the western clans ordering them to send contingents to suppress the rebellion. These commissions were to demonstrate to the King that they were taking all possible measures to suppress the rebellion. They knew that only the Campbells could be expected to answer the summons; the other clans had their own grievances against the instruments of Royal authority. The Council raised the price on Sir James head to £5000 Scots,[54] and appealed to the King to order Archibald Earl of Argyle to return to Scotland. The Council only permitted Campbell of Cawdor and Lundy to go to speak with Argyle on condition that they would be liable for a fine of £1000 Scots each if they did not return. That an "army" of a few hundred men in the western highlands should induce such apprehension in the ruling body of Scotland is a testament to the legacy of the Lords of the Isles.

---

[51] Sir Donald and Donald Gorm Mor.

[52] These men were unlikely to have espoused Sir James's cause without the tacit approval of Donald Gorm Mor.

[53] The MacLeods of Lewis had lost their lands to the MacKenzies in an even more tragic set of circumstances.

[54] It is interesting that the Council were prepared to pay a bounty for Sir James which was considerably greater than the amount that Cawdor had paid for Isla.

At this time Archibald was in London avoiding his creditors and continuing that long practised Campbell policy of being intimately in touch with the Royal court. They begged the King for Argyle's return with words which demonstrate the impotence of their authority in the western highlands without Campbell assistance, referring to Argyle "as being the special person of power and friendship in the Highlands". Archibald's satisfaction must have been immense when he was begged to carry out the pacification of Isla on behalf of the King, after which it was to be occupied by the Campbells.

Sir James's arrival on Isla went unobserved by the Campbells; his clansmen were able to ambush the garrison of Dunnyveg, and twelve men were killed including the Constable of the castle. The survivors managed to reach the castle's keep while the MacDonalds occupied the courtyard. However after their water supply was cut off the garrison were forced to surrender. Unlike so many of his predecessors, Sir James exercised considerable restraint, and sent the survivors back to the mainland. Sir James was now joined by the remnants of the Clan Iain Mor on Isla, while his forces were supplemented further by a steady trickle of men who were either still loyal to him or disaffected "broken" men from the fragments of other clans. He ordered that the fort on Loch Gorm be re-fortified by building a turf wall and ditch.

Coll Coitach was sent to Kintrye to raise the Clan Iain Mor's dwindling fighting strength on the peninsular while messengers were sent to Jura and Colonsay. Within a few weeks Sir James's forces were augmented by the arrival of Donald Gigach Maclain who led the Clan Iain Mor on Jura and by MacDuffie at the head of the Colonsay men.

It is clear from a letter written by Campbell of Ardchattan to the Council that many of the population of the territories now in the possession of the Campbells were still sympathetic to Sir James's cause and were refusing to muster on behalf of the Campbells. Despite the steady increase in the numbers of his men and the passive support of many districts in the south western highlands, Sir James knew that his position was hopeless unless he could get the King to alter his policy. He wrote a series of letters to his few remaining friends and acquaintances that were in a position to plead his case. To Lord Bining he wrote, "My Lord- if his Maiestie be not willing that I sall be his heighnes tennent in Ila, for Goddis cause let his Maiestie hauld it in his awin haund; for that is certain, I will die befoir I sei a Campbell posses it." He even wrote to Bishop Knox offering him Isla on condition that the Campbells had no influence on the island.

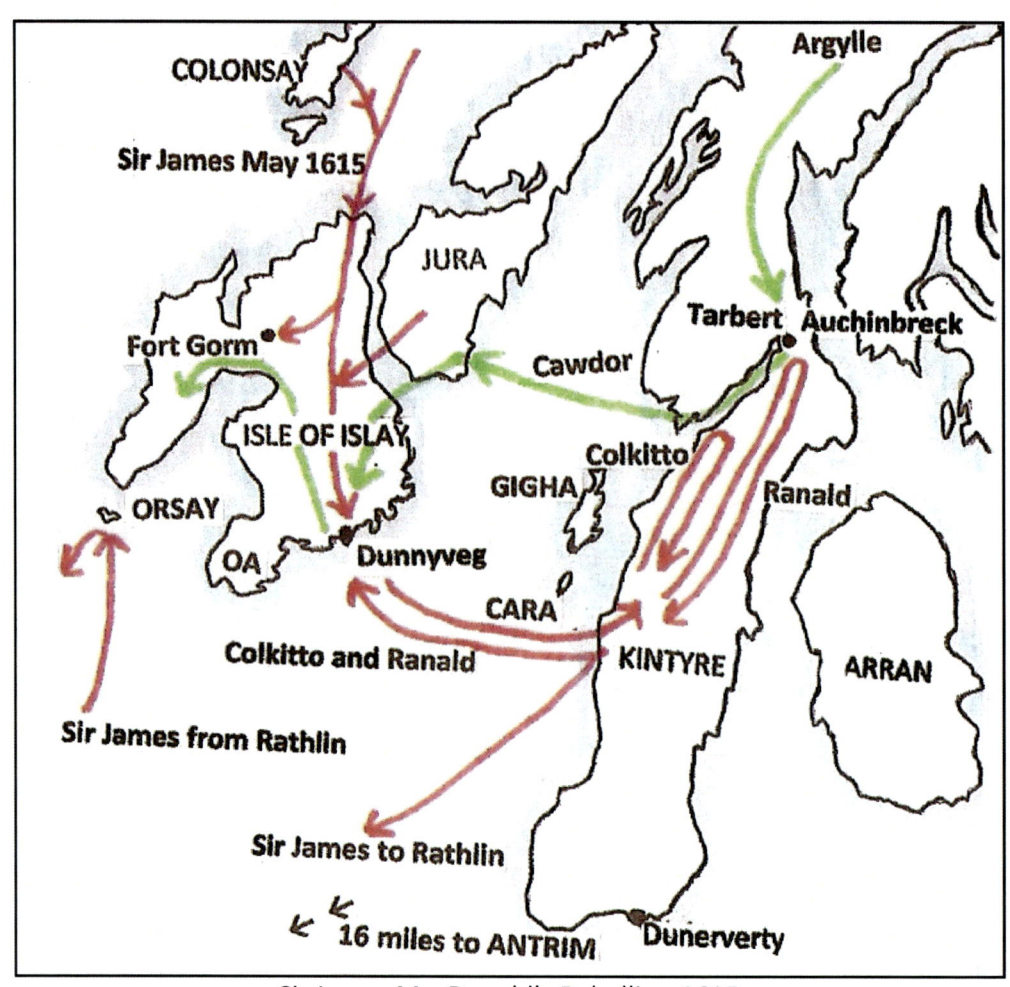

Sir James MacDonald's Rebellion 1615

Loch Gorm

James VI had already decided that Argyle was to be his instrument in suppressing this rebellion. Archibald was offered the tenancy of all the ancient lands of the Clan Ian Mor when he had "pacified" the region. In his instructions to Archibald his tone towards the rebels is more conciliatory than in past proclamations. There were to be no summary executions and Archibald was instructed to protect the property of any of the inhabitants not directly involved with Sir James. He instructed the Council to offer an amnesty to any who should lay down their arms. But despite these moderate instructions, James had made up his mind that the Clan Iain Mor had to go to make way for a new order. He finished his instructions to Argyle stating that he was to proceed in such a way "that civil manners and customs might be established in these Iles, and all their old, barbarous customs utterly abolished."

With the might of the Campbells and the levies from the western shires of Scotland ranged against him, Sir James made his dispositions for a last stand of the Clan Iain Mor. Sir James and a thousand men took up position on Kintrye opposite Cara. Sir James sent his uncle, Ranald with four hundred men to block any move by Campbell of Auchinbreck who was in charge of large force at Tarbert. Colkitto was sent with a small force to West Loch Tarbert to give early warning of the approach of Argyle. Argyle had been mustering his army at Duntroon. He ordered the Campbells of Barbreck-Lochawe, Cawdor and Lochnell along with the MacDougals to sail to Cara by night to take the MacDonald galleys by surprise. Argyle marched down the eastern side of Kintyre accompanied by two companies of regular troops, the Campbells of Kilmichael, and Ardkinglass as well as the Lamonts and MacLachlans.[55]

When Coll Coitach heard of the imminent arrival of Argyle's large force he abandoned his position and retreated to the south, his only success was to capture Campbell of Kilberry who he took with him. He then heard that Campbell of Cawdor had overrun the island of Gigha. When he went to investigate the veracity of this report he nearly fell into Cawdor's hands. During the pursuit Coll Coitach had to abandon some of his boats.

Sir James was alerted to the approach of the Campbells by beacons which were set alight on their approach by the MacAlisters of Largie. Faced by overwhelming superiority, Sir James's vanguard led by Ranald retreated and soon Sir James's position became untenable. Sir James fled to the island of Rathlin,[56] so long a refuge for the Clan Iain Mor, while Coll Coitach and Ranald escaped to Isla where they garrisoned the fort on Loch Gorm and Dunnyveg. Sir James then sailed to Isla and made camp on the south-western extremity of the island at the Point of Rinnes close to the small island of Orsay.

Argyle sailed to Jura and cowed the local populace. It was while he was on Jura that he was joined by some ships of the Royal Navy. This latest edition to his forces meant that he was the undisputed master of the sea. His control of the sea meant that Isla was indefensible and that the rebel leaders would be lucky to escape.

Sir James knew that the end had come; he proposed a truce for four days at the end of which time he would surrender unconditionally. Argyle, suspecting that he was playing for time hoping to get favourable winds to take his ships to Ireland insisted that Sir James hand over Dunnyveg and the fort at Loch Gorm within twenty four hours. Sir James agreed, but when he ordered Coll Coitach to surrender Dunnyveg, Coll refused to surrender the castle, but he then sent a message to Argyle confirming he was willing to hand over the ancient walls. Argyle had by now gained total control of Isla as well as having control of the sea. He decided that he would not wait while the leaders of the Clan Iain Mor danced their last jig. He set off with a thousand men to capture Sir James. The MacDonalds were alerted to the Campbell movements by fires lit by their kin on the Oa.[57] Sir James and the remnants of the leadership prepared to escape to Ireland, with the exception of Coll Coitach who was still holding out in Dunnyveg. As Sir James was waiting on the beach he was approached by the local populace who said that as his "children" they had risked everything for their chief. They begged him not to leave them as they could expect no mercy from the Campbells. One can only imagine how Sir James felt as he looked back on his people, abandoned, defenceless. After a lifetime of suffering he was leaving his ancestral lands in the hands of the

---

[55] These clans owed the Campbells "service" under feudal law.
[56] Just of the coast of Antrim.
[57] The Oa is the southern peninsular on the opposite side of Isla to the Rinnes.

Campbells. The Clan Iain Mor had fallen, never again would the clan celebrate at Dunnyveg or sail in their galleys between Kintyre and Antrim. The medieval Gaelic glory of the western highlands which the clan had struggled to uphold had passed into history with their eclipse.

It is no joy without Clan Donald
It is no strength to be without them
The best race in the round world
To them belongs every goodly man

A race the best for service and for shelter
A race the best for valour of hand ill
Ill I deem the shortness of her skein
By whom their thread was spun

Alas for those who have lost that company
Alas for those who have parted from their society
For no race is as Clan Donald
A noble race strong of courage

In the van of Clan Donald learning
Was commanded and their rear
Were service and honour and self respect

MacVurich

THE MACDONALDS OF ANTRIM TO 1696

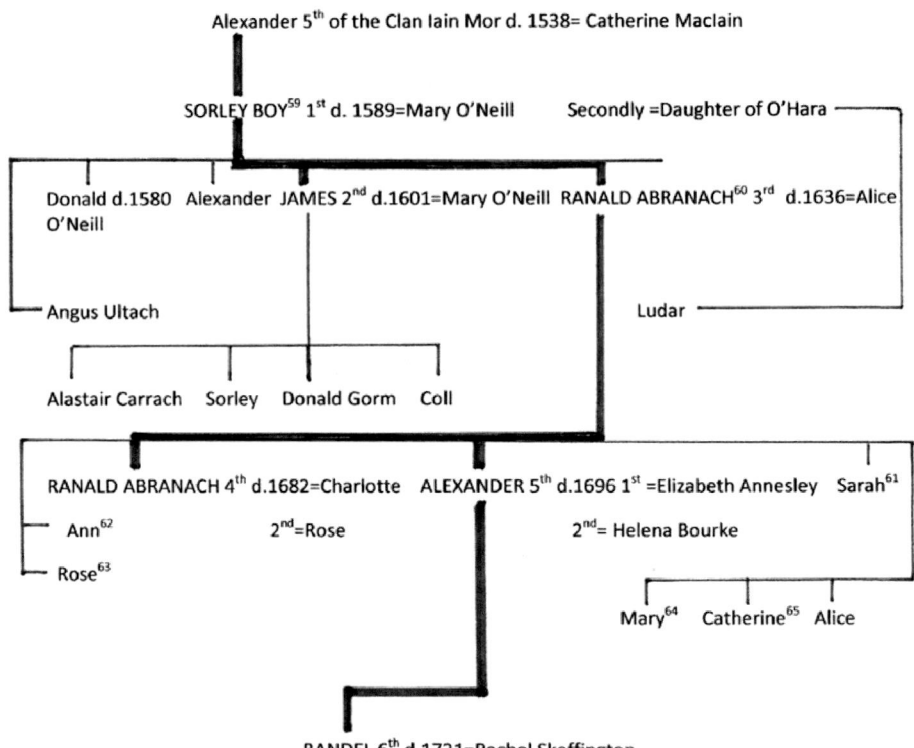

Alexander 5th of the Clan Iain Mor d. 1538= Catherine Maclain

SORLEY BOY[59] 1st d. 1589=Mary O'Neill   Secondly =Daughter of O'Hara

Donald d.1580   Alexander   JAMES 2nd d.1601=Mary O'Neill   RANALD ABRANACH[60] 3rd d.1636=Alice
O'Neill

Angus Ultach   Ludar

Alastair Carrach   Sorley   Donald Gorm   Coll

RANALD ABRANACH 4th d.1682=Charlotte   ALEXANDER 5th d.1696 1st =Elizabeth Annesley   Sarah[61]

Ann[62]   2nd=Rose   2nd= Helena Bourke

Rose[63]

Mary[64]   Catherine[65]   Alice

RANDEL 6th d.1721=Rachel Skeffington

---

[59] Sorley Boy (Somhairle Buidhe) was the fourth son of John Cathanach.
[60] The sobriquet of "Abranach" derives from the fact that he was fostered on Arran.
[61] Sarah married Neill O'Neill.
[62] Ann married Lord Delvin.
[63] Rose married George Gordon.
[64] Mary married Viscount Dillon.
[65] Katherine married Lord Dunsany.

Appendix

Ireland the Maelstrom

The clan Ian Mor was unique among the Scottish clans in having extensive possessions in Ulster. It was however not the first involvement by the western highland clans with Ireland. From at least the thirteenth century waves of Galloglachs,[1] more commonly known as "Gallowglasses",[2] had descended on Ulster in the spring and returned to the western highlands in the autumn. The Gallowglasses were professional heavy infantry who hired themselves out for pay and food and shelter. They were often known in Ireland as "bonaghts", after the name given to the system[3] by which they were maintained by the lesser Irish chiefs on behalf of the tribal[4] leader who hired them.

The Gallowglasses were picked men marked out by their superior size and strength. They wore mail shirts studded with iron nails and rings and were armed with long swords and broad battle axes called "spares". Each Gallowglass was accompanied by a youth who carried three short throwing spears to be used by the Gallowglass in skirmishing before the hand-to-hand fighting. They formed the backbone of every Irish tribal army and were clearly distinguishable from the Irish Kerns who were more lightly armed and clad. The Gallowglasses fought in dense masses with great ferocity inflicting terrible casualties on their opponents. Due to their prominence in the western highlands the MacDonalds furnished a high proportion of these professional soldiers. Gradually some of the Gallowglasses began to settle permanently in Ireland, either at the behest of the Irish chieftain or because it was to their own advantage to do so for political or economic reasons.

The first well documented MacDonald Gallowglass settlements were created by the consequences of the struggle for the Scottish crown between the Bruces and Balliols. This conflict not only led to a great enhancement to MacDonald power by the gift of many territories by Robert the Bruce to his supporter, Angus Og, but also the disinheritance of the family of Alastair Og.[5] Alastair Og was the eldest son of Angus Mor and the elder brother of Angus Og. He succeeded his father to the Lordship of the Isles in about 1295. Throughout the Bruce-Balliol struggle Alastair was the inveterate opponent of the Bruces, being steadfastly loyal to the Balliols and to the claims of Edward I. Edward rewarded him for his loyalty by appointing Alastair High Admiral of the Western Seas. From a modern perspective Alastair's stance seems self-serving and quite possibly treasonable, however his position could also be interpreted as an attempt to prevent any further encroachment by a

---

[1] Not all Gallowglasses were from the western highlands; some were of native Irish extraction.
[2] Gallowglass is the anglicized version of Galloglach and will be used in this text.
[3] Bronaght.
[4] Tribal is used instead of clan, to differentiate between the Irish and Scottish Gaels.
[5] See chapter two.

strong, feudal Scottish state. Did he hope that rule from distant England would be weak and ineffective and this in turn would allow his own Gaelic Kingdom to grow and flourish?

Alastair was eventually captured by Bruce with the fall of Castle Swen and imprisoned in Dundonald where he died. Alastair had six sons, Black John, Reginald, Somerled, Angus, Godfrey and Charles. All of their inheritance was gifted to their uncle Angus Og and they were dispossessed of all the lands their father had held sway over. From this point on all the branches of the MacDonalds that emerged in later centuries were descended from Angus Og the younger son of Angus Mor.

All the sons of Alastair Og fled to Ireland and became Gallowglass captains. They found themselves enmeshed in a world of utter anarchy the like of which was unrivalled even in the disturbed state of the western highlands after the fall of the Lordship in the sixteenth century. Ireland had always had a propensity for violence and chaos under the ancient Celtic societies, but this had been exacerbated by the dislocation caused by Norman intervention. Black John and his descendents became the Gallowglass constables of the O'Neills; the family established a seat at Cnoc-na-Cluith (the hill of sport), in the barony of Dungannon in county Tyrone. One can only speculate how this senior branch of exiles would have sat by the fireside and brooded on their lost claim to hegemony over the great Clan Donald. Both Black John and his son Somerled were killed by the MacMahons who were at deadly feud with the O'Neills. The family's claim to be the senior line of MacDonalds is recognized in the Irish Annuls which laments the death of Somerled, "Woe the world and the land and water wherein was submerged the noble and well –born offspring to wit, one who was born to be king of Innse-gall, namely, the son of Black John the son of Alasdair".

The descendents of Black John continued to serve the O'Neills for many generations, their numbers increasing despite the fact that none of the Gallowglass captains died in their beds. In a Scottish manuscript of 1450 they are even referred to as Clan Eoin Dudh (the Clan of Black John). Black John's descendents fought and died for their O'Neill lords in dozens of desperate encounters with MacMahons, O'Donnells, the Roes and others. In the mid-sixteenth century there is evidence of conflict between the O'Neills and their MacDonald Gallowglass captains. This may not only reflect a temporary weakening of O'Neill power but also the ever increasing pressure from the English authorities in Dublin.

Eventually the MacDonald Gallowglasses agreed to abandon their support for the O'Neills and to serve English interests. As a result of this they were forced to abandon Cnoc-na-Cluith where they had been settled for two hundred years. The English authorities gave them Grene Castle in what was then the empty wastes of Mourne in South Down. After twenty years of serving English interests, in what must have been an uneasy relationship for both parties the MacDonalds returned to their ancient relationship with the O'Neills. They are again found slaughtering and being slaughtered in their master's quarrels. It is likely that it was at this time that they resumed their ancient seat of Cnoc-na-Cluith. The last named captain of this branch of Alastair Og's descendents was Arthur MacDonald who could bring into the field twenty horsemen and three hundred Gallowglasses. This implies that by the 1570's the MacDonald community of Cnoc-na-Cluith would have been in the order of one thousand people.

In the early seventeenth century the ancient practice of hiring Gallowglasses was abolished by the English government, who found that although the Gallowglasses could be hired by the state they were unreliable and their heart always remained with the remnants of Gaelic Ireland. The Gallowglass captains were pensioned off and ended their days as an impotent subsidized anachronism. However, the long line of Gallowglass captains descended from Alastair Og had become extinct before this sorry fate overcame them.

Somerled another of Alastair Og's sons was the progenitor of various Gallowglass communities in Connaught and Leinster. In Connaught, Somerled's descendents served as Gallowglass captains to the O'Conners. The fact that four of his sons acted as Gallowglass captains for the O'Conners successively and that each in turn died on the battlefield is testament to the endemic violence in Ireland during the fourteenth and fifteenth centuries. The MacDonald Gallowglass families of Connaught fall into obscurity; however it is reasonable to assume that they continued to play a bloody role in the violent anarchy of Connaught till the sixteenth century.

One of Somerled's sons, Marcus MacDonald who fell in battle against the O'Donnells in 1397 was the progenitor of the MacDonald Gallowglasses of Leinster. Marcus's son Charles settled his Gallowglass community in Wicklow on the edge of the Pale. That Charles was able to settle his people in an area so far from the MacDonald power base was facilitated by the desolation caused by the Scottish invasion of Edward Bruce and by the acquiescence to the settlement by the English settlers in the Pale. These two threatened communities formed an alliance against the hostile Irish and Charles's descendents became Gallowglass constables of the Pale, or as the English preferred to call them, the wardens of the marches. The MacDonalds occupied the strong castle of Tynekill and it was from here that the Gallowglasses protected their own and the English settlements.

The relationship between this community of MacDonalds and the English was based on self-interest as is shown by the steady flow of pardons and forfeits emanating from the Lord Deputy in Dublin. In 1597, Hugh O'Neill assumed the title of The O'Neill, which in many respects had the same connotations in Ireland as the Lord of the Isles had in the western highlands, and broke out in rebellion against English authority in Ireland. He was joined by many of the Irish tribes and the Gaelic Scots in one of the last significant attempts by the Gaelic inhabitants to re-establish an independent Irish kingdom in Ireland. He was joined by the MacDonald Gallowglass community of Tynekill along with many others. After the failure of the rebellion their leader Hugh Boy MacDonald was again granted a pardon. This toleration of disloyalty owes more to English weakness than to any attempt at reconciliation between the two traditions. The Tynekill MacDonalds eventually lost their lands at Tynekill for their enthusiastic role in the in the Great Rebellion of 1641.

All the MacDonald Gallowglass communities which were descended from Alastair Og whether shrouded in obscurity, or being well recorded in the historical record were immersed in the chronic violence and anarchy of Gaelic Ireland in the fifteenth and sixteenth centuries. The endemic violence of Ulster was caused by a number of factors including a scarcity of resources, the nature and construction of Gaelic societies and the instability caused by a continual struggle for power between many different groups including the O'Neills the MacDonalds and the English. The Gallowglass communities played an important role as the backbone of various Irish tribal armies in their interminable struggles for power and land. Much like the early English settlers in Ireland, in the medieval period, they went "native" and became an integral part of Irish society. Despite their origins, being descended from the senior line of the Lords of the Isles, there is no evidence that they involved themselves in the struggles of their MacDonald cousins, the Clan Iain Mor, either in Ulster or in their bitter feuds with the MacLeans or Campbells. It is clear that after Alastair Og's flight to Ireland this branch of the MacDonalds was immersed in their own Irish world and had no ties with other branches of the clan.

It was another branch of MacDonalds, the Clan Iain Mor (Mhoir), which were to establish large territorial possessions in Ireland. These they were to occupy for centuries and it was from these possessions that the MacDonald Earls of Antrim were to emerge.[6] The origins of the clan Iain Mor and their feuds and struggle for survival in Scotland have been discussed elsewhere (chapters five, eleven and twelve). Their possessions in Ulster made them unique among the highland clans in that they had permanent and extensive territories in Ireland.

These possessions were both a blessing and a curse to the Clan Iain Mor. They provided a source of manpower for the clan's struggles in the western isles and a place of refuge from the ire of the Scottish Kings. These possessions, although often wild and desolate, were in parts more fertile than the storm swept western isles and on occasions offered more potential for expansion than the crowded and impoverished western highland seaboard. But they also embroiled the clan in the murderous environment of Irish politics in the fifteenth, sixteenth and seventeenth centuries. On balance the clan's struggles in Ireland led to a draining of manpower from its Scottish possessions and areas of influence. The clan was involved in a three way power struggle in Ulster between themselves, the Irish tribes, especially the O'Neills, and the growing power of England. Three way relationships are notoriously unstable, and the Clan Iain Mor in Ireland was in a state of almost continual war in its attempts to maintain and expand its possessions.

The Irish tribes were involved in prolonged internecine conflict amongst themselves as well as attempting to keep the MacDonalds in check and resist the spasmodic, but steady, encroachment of the English. Under the leadership of The

---

[6] To this day they are large landowners in Antrim, their seat being at Glenarm Castle.

O'Neill there was an almost nationalistic element to some of their campaigns, whether against the MacDonalds or the English. The English with varying degrees of enthusiasm, were bent on establishing their authority over Ulster; this policy was intimately connected to their political relationships with Scotland and Spain. Above all they feared that this lawless, Gaelic and Catholic region would be used by either Scotland or Spain as a base to strike at English interests in the Pale or even to invade England itself.

The Clan Iain Mor was driven by more modest policies but these were vital to clan interests in Ireland. Their objectives were to secure their possession of the Glens, while expanding into, and securing the Route. To achieve these objectives they had attempt to foil the policies of the Irish and English.

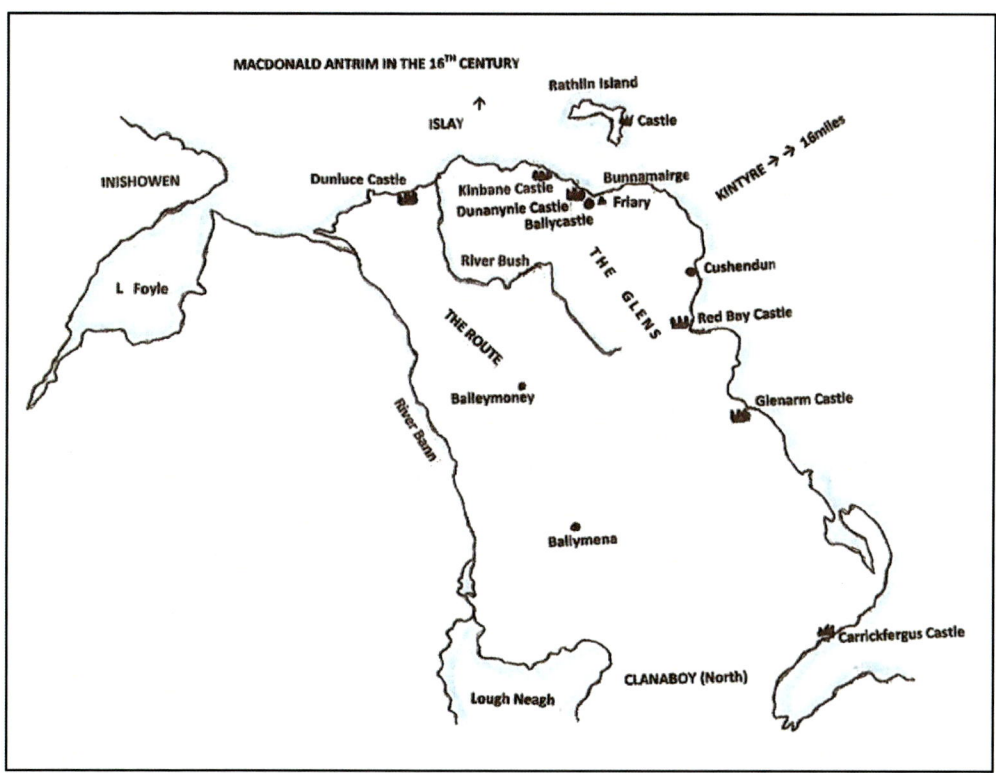

This chapter will concern itself only with the Irish aspects of the history of Clan Iain Mor although this history is not in itself directly about clan feuds. The events in Ireland were so intimately linked with the clan's struggles with the Maclains of Ardnamurchan, the MacLeans and the Campbells that to ignore the clan's history in Ireland would lead to a failure to understand the Clan Iain Mor's situation.

From its inception as an independent entity the Clan Iain Mor held possessions in Ireland. The progenitor of the clan, Iain Mor, the second son of John first Lord of the Isles, acquired the glens of Antrim as a dowry when he married Marjory Bisset. The Glens extended from the river Inver to the Boyse and the chiefs of Clan Iain

Mor often styled themselves as Lord of Dunnyveg and the Glens. Marjory Bisset was the daughter of Hugh Bisset and was the heiress to the Glens. The Bissets were an Anglo-Norman family who had obtained the Glens from the de Courcy earls of Ulster. It may well have been that the birth of a son (Donald) to his elder brother[7] had encouraged Iain Mor to make such an advantageous marriage. His new possessions in Antrim might provide scope for territorial expansion of his own family beyond the remit of the Lords of the Isles.

By the time of Iain Mor's death in 1427 the MacDonalds were firmly established in the remote, steep, wooded valleys of the Glens. Although the Glens were the first lands to be controlled by the MacDonalds in Ireland, Ulster was a much more familiar land to them than lowland Scotland. For over one hundred years the province had been densely settled with Gallowglass communities many of whom were descended from Alastair Og MacDonald the elder brother of Angus Og who was the grandfather of Iain Mor.[8] There was a particularly close association between the Clan Iain Mor and the O'Cathans over a long period of time; this is attested to by the name of one of Iain Mor's great grandsons, John Cathanach who derived his name from having being fostered with the O'Cathans.

Iain Mor followed the example of his brother, Donald second Lord of the Isles, in developing a close relationship with England in an attempt to halt the growing power of the feudal Scottish state. His son Donald Balloch led the forces of the Lordship against the Royal armies at Inverlochy in 1431, where he overwhelmed them. He was however unable to resist the full weight of James I military power and had to flee to the Glens of Antrim for the rest of his reign. In 1437 he returned to Scotland and loyally served Alexander, third Lord of the Isles, till his death in 1449. This heroic warrior then assumed the role of chief of the MacDonalds during the minority of Alexander's son, John.[9]

Donald Balloch was succeeded by his son John Mor who became the third chief of Clan Iain Mor in 1476. There is little known about John Mor's activities in the eighteen years between his accession to the chiefship and his defiance of James IV in 1494. He did however manage to keep his clan out of the rebellions of the MacDonalds of Lochalsh and initially made his peace with James after the fall of the Lordship. It is likely that a good part of the "missing" years were spent in the Glens placing his clan's hold on their Irish possessions on a firm footing.

When James garrisoned Tarbert and Dunaverty castles in Kintyre, for what he considered Scotland's vital interests[10] it clashed with the interests of the Clan Iain Mor. Dunaverty was not only of huge strategic importance to the clan but it was also one of the main embarkation point for large bands of Gallowglasses in their

---

[7] John first Lord of the Isles.
[8] Iain Mor's grandmother was Agnes O'Cathan. The O'Cathans were one of the principal Irish tribes of Ulster.
[9] See chapter 2.
[10] See chapter 10.

seasonal journeys to Ulster. To have a royal garrison sitting astride the main route that connected the clan's Scottish and Irish possessions was, despite his astute cautiousness, intolerable to John Mor. In sight of the Royal fleet he stormed Dunaverty and hung the constable from the walls. James had been humiliated by John Mor and planned his revenge. He used Archibald Ruaidh Campbell to help him ensnare John Mor and his sons. At this time the Clan Iain Mor were at feud with the MacDonalds of Ardnamurchan under their able and ambitious chief John Brayach. Archibald encouraged John Brayach to capture John Mor and his sons and hand them over to James.[11] Amongst others John Mor and his son John Cathanach were executed in 1499.

Alexander MacDonald and his brother Angus Ileach, the eldest surviving sons of John Cathanach escaped the attentions of John Brayach and reached the relative safety of the Glens of Antrim. Here they managed to evade every attempt by John Brayach to capture them, MacVurich, the Clanranald historian wrote that John Brayach "expended much wealth of gold and silver in making axes for the purpose of cutting down the woods of the Glens, in the hope that he might be able to banish Alexander son of John Cathenach, out of the Glens and out of the world".

By 1500 the Clan Iain Mor had had its power base in the western isles destroyed. Their chief was a fugitive in Ireland and all their Scottish possessions were in the hands of John Brayach. It is possible that if Alexander had not been able to use the Glens as a refuge, the history of the clan would have ended at this date.

There was however one consequence of these events which was to greatly strengthen the clan's position in Ireland and ultimately to enable the clan to recover its Scottish possessions. This was a series of large scale emigrations from the ancient territories of the clan in Isla and Kintyre to escape the persecutions of John Brayach. Alexander was not only joined by his own clan but also other clans who had been adherents to the MacDonalds during the Lordship; they included, some MacDonalds of Largie, MacAlisters, MacNeills of Ghiga, MacKays and MacEacherns. Some of these migrants were encouraged to emigrate by the prospect of new lands to settle in, while others were escaping from the pressure caused by Campbell and Maclain expansionism. This large supplement to the MacDonald population not only secured the Glens against the ambitions of their neighbours but also allowed Alexander to think of expansion.

John Bryach MacDonald of Ardnamurchan continued his efforts to extirpate the Clan Iain Mor in the Glens. He sent a large party to the Glens to capture Alexander and his followers. They were defeated after the defection of some of the force who had been raised in Isla and regarded Alexander as their lawful chief. Alexander immediately led a small party of clansmen to Isla where the Castle of Dunnyveg was willingly surrendered to him by his own clansmen. Alexander then marched across Isla gathering reinforcements on the way and captured John Brayach who had taken refuge in the fort at Loch Gorm. John's life was spared on the condition

---

[11] See chapter 5.

that he cede the ancient possessions of the Clan Iain Mor to Alexander and the two chiefs attempted a reconciliation which was founded on the marriage of Alexander to John's daughter Catherine. Having secured the clan's Scottish territories Alexander turned his attention to Ireland.

Alexander's policy was to secure the sea crossing between the clan's Scottish and Irish possessions by establishing a series of strongholds on the Antrim coast. He first occupied Dunanynie Castle overlooking Ballycastle Bay. This bay was the traditional landing place for the Gallowglass hosts and their successors the Redshanks. By the later sixteenth century the type of highland mercenary adventurer had changed from the heavy infantry of the Gallowglass to a more mobile soldier who was equipped with bows, basket hilted sword, and targe. These Redshanks were more suitable to the mobile warfare evolving in Ulster among the Irish, MacDonald and English protagonists. Ballycastle Bay and Cushendun were where the Clan Iain Mor's galleys would land with troops and supplies from Isla, Kintyre and the southern Hebrides. They were not only the nearest landing place on the Irish coast from Kintyre, but also gave easy access to both the Glens and the Route. It was for these reasons that Alexander established Dunanynie Castle as the principal residence of the Clan Iain Mor in Antrim.

Dunanynie Castle

To secure the clan's communications with Scotland Alexander extended the clan's coastal settlements by establishing strongholds at Cushendun and Red Bay. To emphasize that the Clan Iain Mor intended that Ulster would from now on, form a pivotal role in the clan's policies, Alexander adopted Bunnamairge Friary as the new burial place of the chiefs of the Clan Iain Mor.

Bunnamairge Friary

With the successful establishment of a significant MacDonald presence in Ulster Alexander's importance to both James IV and Henry VIII increased considerably. Although James never forgave the Clan Iain Mor for his humiliation at Dunaverty he was far too pragmatic not to see that they could be a useful element in diverting English military power away from the Scottish borders. It seems that although Alexander never returned to Scotland during the lifetime of James, cordial relations were re-established between the chief and his monarch. James encouraged MacDonald emigration to Ulster; this had the dual advantages of weakening this powerful clan in Scotland while gradually increasing the pressure on the English garrisons in Ulster. With the death of James and most of the Scottish nobility at Flodden in 1513, Alexander's room for manoeuvre was considerably increased. The Scottish executive, who ruled Scotland during the minority of James V, due to the weakness of his Kingdom, wanted better relations with the Clan Iain Mor, while Henry's attention was focused on France where he was engaged against Francis I.

Alexander returned to Scotland, his hand greatly strengthened by his significant assets in Ulster.

It is from this period that the struggle between the Clan Iain Mor and Clan Campbell begins in earnest. The Executive had appointed Colin Campbell, third earl of Argyle, as "justiciar, sheriff, coroner, bailie, and chamberlain of Kintyre and Knapdale, south and north".   It was clear that due to its own weakness the Executive expected the Campbells to be the Crown's "policeman" in the Gaelic west. This struggle for supremacy was to lead ultimately to the extinction of the Clan Iain Mor in its ancient Scottish possessions.[12] Alexander supported Sir Donald Galda, chief of the MacDonalds of Lochalsh in his vain attempt to re-establish the Lordship. With the death of Sir Donald in 1519 the rebellion petered out and Alexander wisely made his peace both with the state and its agents in the west, the Campbells. During the rebellion Alexander was able to settle an old score; the Clan Iain Mor, amongst others, twice invaded the territories of the MacIains of Ardnamurchan. During the second invasion they ran John Brayach to ground at Creag-an-Airgid; both John and his two surviving adult sons were killed.

In 1528 James V achieved his majority; he immediately revoked all the charters bestowing large tracts of Royal lands which had belonged to the Lordship and which had been granted by the executive to various highland chiefs. The infuriated Clan Iain Mor and the MacLeans invaded the lands of the Campbells and laid large tracts of land waste. Gradually James was able to assemble a formidable army and Alexander decided to sue for terms. The King was also ready to come to an accommodation as, due to the weak state of the Kingdom, it did not suit him to lead a lengthy campaign in the remote western Isles.

On the seventh of June 1531 Alexander met James at Stirling and was duly pardoned. Alexander also received charters for the Clan Iain Mor's territories in Isla and Kintrye. The clan's ancient patrimony was, for the time being, secure against further Campbell encroachment. Alexander's eldest son, James was to stay at court to strengthen the Scottish states influence on the future chief of this important clan. The fact that James was in effect, a hostage, shows that although cordial relations between Alexander and the Scottish state had been re-established, there was still some doubt in the mind of James V as to the loyalty of Alexander. The subsequent struggle between Alexander and the Earl of Argyle for the favour of the King is discussed in chapter 12; suffice it to say that Alexander became a favourite of James V and the Clan Iain Mor was restored to all its ancient possessions.

To assist James's antagonistic policy towards England, Alexander, gathered a huge host of seven thousand men, drawn from the Clan Iain Mor and the redshank mercenaries of the southern Hebrides and attacked English settlements in Ulster. Although there were no long lasting effects of this invasion it is clear from English correspondence that the MacDonalds in Ulster were now a serious force to be

---

[12] See chapter 12.

reckoned with, "The Scottes also inhabit the now buyselley a greate parte of Ulster,......,and it is greatlie to be feared, oonless that in short tyme they be driven from the same, that they bringing in more nombre daily woll, by lyttle and little so far encroache in acquyringe and wynninge the possessions there, with the aid of the Kingis disobeysant Irishe rebelles,......, that at lengthe they will put and expel the King from his whole seignory there."

With the ever increasing power of the Campbells in the south west highlands, Alexander, judged that there was more potential for his expansionist policies in Ireland. During the 1520's the Clan Iain Mor aided the O'Neills in one of their interminable wars with the O'Donnells. This support for the O'Neills was no doubt part of Alexander's plans to extend his clan's influence into the hinterland of Ulster.

In 1538, during one of Alexander's visits to the Scottish court, Alexander died at Stirling and was buried in the High Church of the town. It is somewhat poignant that the chief who had determined that Bunnamairge Friary should be the burial place of the chiefs of Clan Iain Mor should be laid to rest so far from the Glens of Antrim. This remarkable chief had re-established his clan as a viable successor to the Lordship in the south west highlands. In Scotland, by his loyalty to James V, he had obtained legal feudal right to his clan's possessions. He was recognized as an important instrument of Scottish policy in Ireland. The fact that he could put an army of seven thousand men into the field in Ulster (perhaps half were his own clansmen, the remainder being made up of redshanks from disparate clans in Argyle who saw the Clan Iain Mor as the successor to the Lords of the Isles) meant that the Clan Iain Mor was, in the 1530's, at least as significant an element in Scottish national policy as the Campbells.

In the longer term it was to be his achievements in Ireland which were to be even more significant. Alexander had established a thriving and expansionist MacDonald community in the Glens of Antrim with secure lines of communication with the highlands. This allowed for a continual flow of redshank mercenaries to pour into Ulster each summer and further the ambitions of the Clan Iain Mor. This source of military power enhanced the importance of the clan in the eyes of all the protagonists in Ulster; the native Irish, and the Kingdoms of Scotland and England.

Alexander left five surviving sons behind him, James, Angus Uaimbreach (the proud), Alexander, Coll, and Sorley Boy[13] (the golden haired). While James was being educated in the ways of the Scottish Court, his younger brothers were actively involved in the maelstrom of Ulster's political and military events with their father. In 1538, when James assumed the chiefship of the Clan Iain Mor they were already battle -scarred veterans of their clan's struggle to survive and prosper in Ireland.

In the same year that Alexander died the Irish chiefs displayed a rare degree of unity in an attempt to drive the English garrisons out of Ulster. They were ostensibly supported in this effort by the Clan Iain Mor who were in their turn

---

[13] Sorley Boy is the anglicized version of Somhairle Buidhe and will be used in this text.

supported by two thousand redshanks from Scotland. The MacDonalds played a lukewarm part in this ultimately unsuccessful coalition, but with the aid of their redshank allies they strengthened their position in the Glens. With the defeat at Ballyhoe and the subsequent submission of the O'Donnells and the desertion of most of his gallowglasses Conn O'Neill was forced into a humiliating surrender to Henry VIII in the autumn of 1542. Conn was forced to become Henry's vassal and to give up his title of The O'Neill which (in Irish eyes) implied hegemony over Ulster.

In 1542 the Clan Iain Mor became involved in a feud between the MacQuillins and the O'Cahans, the MacDonalds supporting the former. The MaQuillins and their MacDonald allies were defeated near the river Bann. This minor episode would have little significance if it were not for the fact that this was the first time that a MacDonald army had campaigned in the Route, thus exposing its fertile features to the hungry gaze of Alexander's younger sons. When compared to the Clan Iain Mor's Scottish possessions, the Route held out the prospect of an easier and more rewarding region for conquest and settlement. While these sons were embroiled in the struggles in Ulster, James was fully occupied with the clan's Scottish possessions. The clan's Scottish and Irish territories were still under James's control, but even at this early date his younger brothers were acting semi-independently due to the pressing demands of politics and war in both Scotland and Ireland.

In the mid-sixteenth century, Ulster was still a purely Gaelic territory, only adulterated by the occasional English coastal garrison. Ulster was dominated by two great ruling families, the O'Neills of Tyrone and the O'Donnells of Tryconnel; they were known as the ceannfine (great ruling families). They were supported by lesser chieftains who were known as oir rioght, who controlled "countries" known as tuaths which were several hundred square miles in extent. The oir rioghts were either lesser branches of the main house or were smaller Irish tribes such as the MacQuillins, O'Cahans and Magennises. These Irish tribes were at almost continual feud with each other as well as attempting to prevent the spread of MacDonald, Scottish and English power.

By 1544 the situation in Ulster was, even by its own standards, extremely unstable. The Irish vassals of the O'Neills and O'Donnells were restive; in part due to their overlord's submission to the English and in part due to a dire economic situation caused by two consecutive cold wet summers. The O'Donnells had invaded the Route with fire and sword in support of the O'Cahans who were in their turn at feud with the MacQuillins who were supported by the Clan Iain Mor.

1545 saw the last great rebellion to re-establish the Lordship led by Donald Dubh, grandson of John, last Lord of the Isles. This rebellion caused the policies of the Scottish, the English, the western clans and even the French to become enmeshed in the already congested situation in Ulster. For their different reasons the Regent Arran, James and Argyll wanted to suppress the rising. Henry VIII and his Scottish ally Lennox (who was a bitter opponent of Arran) wanted to weaken Scotland by encouraging the rebellion. The French saw Donald Dubh's highland host as an ideal instrument for weakening or destroying English power in Ireland if it could be diverted there. Donald Dubh's advisors believed that if they made a foray into Ireland they would have access to English gold (by way of a bribe) and would be able to return to Scotland considerably enriched.

James stood aloof from this rebellion, despite his own inclinations and the pleas of his brother Angus who had joined the rebels. James was betrothed to Lady Agnes Campbell sister of Archibald Campbell the current Earl of Argyll and his intimate understanding of Campbell power and the workings of the modern Scottish state (from his many years spent at court), led him to the pragmatic conclusion that the time of the Lordship had passed.

The rebellion petered out after the death of Donald Dubh at Drogeda in 1545, in a welter of bickering over the distribution of the English gold and who should succeed Donald Dubh. James was offered the position as the most rightful claimant to the Lordship. James flirted with the offer but wisely declined it. During the rebellion he had managed to extract more charters to his clan's ancient lands from Arran and had finally received Agnes Campbell's hand in marriage, and as a dowry he was gifted some parts of Ardnamurchan, from Argyll. James continued his policy of co-operation with the Scottish state and led a large contingent of his clan to the Battle of Pinkie where the Scots were defeated by the English army led by the Protector Somerset.

No doubt in consultation with his brothers, it was now that James determined that the Clan Iain Mor would attempt to expand into the Route of Ulster by either political or military means. Due to his pro-Scottish policy this would not only be opposed by the Irish but also the English administrations in Dublin and London. The early years of the 1550's saw James having to commit his full attention to the clan's territories in Scotland, as the desperate feud between the Clan Iain Mor and the MacLeans, over the Rinnes of Isla, was beginning. So it was during this decade that his brothers began to act semi-independently of their chief, with Sorley Boy emerging as the pre-eminent brother. It was Sorley Boy who was to lead the clan's efforts to conquer the Route.

Sorley Boy's career as a semi-independent chief began inauspiciously when he was arrested by the English authorities and imprisoned in Dublin Castle in 1550. The English may well have arrested Sorley to prevent him causing them difficulties in Ulster and they may have hoped to make the Clan Iain Mor compliant by holding him as hostage. Sorley was released from English captivity in the autumn of 1551; his stay in Dublin had not encouraged any affection in him for his English hosts.

The English always feared that Ulster could be used by hostile powers, whether it was the French, Scots or Spanish, as a jumping off point for an invasion of England. This anxiety was exacerbated by the strong MacDonald presence in the Glenns, and their ever growing power which was primarily fuelled by the flow of redshanks from Scotland. Apart from the coastal fortresses of Carrickfergus and Olderfleet the English had almost no presence in Ulster, and these two isolated garrisons were utterly inadequate to the task of halting the flow of redshanks. Sir

James Croft the newly appointed Irish Lord Deputy invaded the north Ulster coast with the aim of capturing the Clan Iain Mor's stronghold of Rathlin Island. Rathlin Island was of great strategic importance to both the English and the Clan Iain Mor, because it sat astride the sea lanes by which the redshank bands crossed between Ireland and Scotland.

Once Croft was opposite Rathlin he despatched two of his lieutenants, Bagenal and Cuffe, with one hundred men (due to a shortage of boats) to capture the island. The small English force, being unaware of the treacherous currents, was swept ashore onto the island into the waiting arms of the MacDonalds. Colla MacDonald (one of Sorley's brothers) who had been left in charge of defending Rathlin had been reinforced by James who had sailed over from Kintyre with five hundred men. The English were forced to surrender; James would only agree to release his captives on condition that Sorley Boy was also set free. Croft's attempts to control the north coast of Ulster petered out with English exhaustion. Like so many English expeditions before and afterwards they were worn down by the weather, the poverty of the countryside and by an inability to bring their opponents to a decisive engagement.

During the winter of 1551-1552 Colla MacDonald invaded the Route at the head of elements of the Clan Iain Mor in support of his MacQuillin allies who were at feud with the O'Cahans. Colla drove the O'Cahans out of the Route, but then insisted on spending the rest of the winter there against the wishes of the MacQuillins. This winter sojourn was the first lengthy stay in the Route by the Clan Iain Mor. Looking at the larger political framework; Ulster was dominated in the early 1550's by a loose alliance between the Can Iain Mor and the O'Neills with a view to countering English aggression and to prevent any new English settlements.

Of the two English garrisons, it was Carrickfergus which lay closest to the Glens and was the most threat to the MacDonald settlements and lines of communication. On the orders of James, Sorley Boy attacked Carrickfergus and defeated the English garrison in battle in 1552. While dining with the captured constable of the castle Sorley Boy expressed his deep felt pan-Gaelic world view by saying that "Inglsghe men had no rygt to Yrland". Clearly it did not strike him as ironic that he was leading the Clan Iain Mor's own attempts at expansion. Perhaps he felt that it was different because the protagonists were Gaelic. At this point, James felt in a strong enough position to declare to the English that the Glens were the possessions of the Clan Iain Mor. Although his claim was rejected the English were at present unable to dislodge the MacDonalds from any of their possessions.

Having neutralized the threat from Carrickfergus, Sorley Boy then led the Clan Iain Mor into the Route where they defeated the MacQuillins,[14] the ancient possessors of the Route. After a bitter two year campaign Sorley Boy eventually drove the MacQuillins out of the Route. While MacDonald attention was focused

---

[14] The MacQuillins had been the allies of the Clan Iain Mor up to this period but now they stood in the way of further MacDonald expansion.

on the struggle for the Route, English policy towards Ulster was hardening. There was a shift away from the old policy of surrender and re-grant whereby the English attempted to maintain the loyalty of the Irish by controlling who had legal (feudal) title to the land. This policy which had the attraction of being cheap was also renowned for its ineffectiveness. Under the direction of Fitzwalter and Sidney the new English policy was one of conquest and occupation, with particular emphasis on breaking the power of the Clan Iain Mor and preventing the flow of redshanks from Scotland.

English aggression was first directed at the Clan Iain Mor, perhaps because unlike the Irish an attack on the MacDonalds had wider implications for English foreign policy with regards to Scotland. Fitzwalter and Sidney marched north from the Pale with a powerful force and crossed the border into Ulster on the first of July 1556. Shane O'Neill feigned submission to the English and did not contest their progress across his territories.[15] The English plan was to destroy the military power of the Clan Iain Mor in battle and then establish a series of coastal garrisons as well as a series of fortifications from Dundalk to Lough Foyle. Four ships were sent to patrol the North Channel; their mission was to prevent the MacDonalds from rushing large numbers of redshanks to Ulster from Scotland.

Once it was clear that an English invasion was imminent, James joined his brothers in Ulster. The Clan Iain Mor was prevented from receiving reinforcements by the English blockade, so, summoning all their available manpower the brothers set out to intercept the English before they reached the MacDonald heartland. The two armies met at the pass of Ballohe M'Gille Corrough on the eighteenth of July. The Clan Iain Mor was defeated with the loss of some two hundred men. Sydney's claims of an overwhelming victory were greatly exaggerated; he even claimed that James had been killed. It was however a serious reverse for the MacDonalds; James had to flee to his Scottish possessions and the English were able to occupy Glenarm Castle and gorge themselves on the local cattle.

Sorley Boy was appointed captain of the Route by James after the death of his elder brother Colla in 1558 and the refusal to accept the post by his other two elder brothers.[16] While English attention was focused on the Glens, Sorley was able to maintain and even strengthen the MacDonald hold on the Route from his base at Ballycastle. The landing sites which provided a continual flow of reinforcements were unmolested by the English, so that Sorley Boy could be reinforced from Islay with speed and ease.[17]

---

[15] There was no practical expression of pan-Gaelic unity during much of the sixteenth century; Shane no doubt hoped to see both his MacDonald rivals and the English weakened in the ensuing conflict.

[16] Angus and Alasdair.

[17] With favourable winds the MacDonald galleys could reach the Irish coast from Isla within three hours.

In June 1557 Fitzwalter[18] led another campaign against the Clan Iain Mor. The campaign lacked any clear objectives and like so many English campaigns before and afterwards foundered in the inhospitable fastnesses of Ulster. James and his brothers refused to encounter the English army in battle; the MacDonalds hovered on the English flanks picking off stragglers and denying the invaders supplies and rest. Despite the expenditure of large quantities of gold and blood, Ulster was still free of English domination by the closing months of 1557. The archbishop of Armagh wrote to London that Ulster was "...as far out of the frame as ever it was before, for the Scots beareth as great a rule as they do wish,....".

With the outbreak of war between England and France in 1558, English attention was reluctantly drawn back to Ulster and the O'Neills and the Clan Iain Mor. The volatile Shane O'Neill had been able to strengthen his position in Ulster by besting his O'Donnell and O'Neill rivals. He could now with some justification claim the title of The O'Neill. Despite the English assaults on them, the Clan Iain Mor continued to strengthen their grip on the northern Ulster coast. Both the O'Neills and the Clan Iain Mor were seen as a threat by the English in that they might be used by the French or Scots to threaten English interests in Ireland.

Sussex decided on a new strategy to break the power of the Clan Iain Mor, he resolved to strike at the clan's Scottish possessions. In September 1558 Sussex sailed with a fleet of twelve ships and a force of eleven hundred men from Dublin. After losing one ship in a storm Sussex landed on Rathlin Island taking the garrison by surprise. Sussex destroyed all the provisions which James had stored on the island and then occupied it with a small garrison. The English fleet then sailed on to Kintrye where they ravaged the coastline and destroyed James's residence at Saddell and the MacDonald stronghold of Dunaverty. Isla was spared the attentions of the English due to bad weather. In early November Sussex returned to Carrickfergus with the aim of invading the Route. Sussex had to abandon this plan because his army was severely weakened by losses and exhaustion.

Although Sussex's campaign had done significant damage to the clan's possessions in Kintrye, James had kept the clan's military power intact. Of more significance was the favour now bestowed on him by Mary Queen of Scots who confirmed James in all his Scottish possessions much to the chagrin of the Campbells. With the accession of Elizabeth to the English throne the pressure on the Clan Iain Mor eased, England was feeling the strain of sustaining a war on two fronts and was not able to finance any further attempts to reduce the Clan Iain Mor. However peace was to elude the clan in Ulster.

The original possessors of the Route, the MacQuillins, now made a desperate effort to drive the MacDonalds out of the Route. Sorley Boy's elder brother, Colla, (who had been Captain of the Route before Sorley Boy) had married Eveleen MacQuillin in an attempt to secure their loyalty. Colla's death in 1558 released the

---

[18] Fitzwalter had been created the Earl of Sussex and from now on will be referred to as Sussex.

MacQuillins from any restraint they had felt to the Clan Iain Mor. In the summer of 1558 they began their attempt to re-establish their possession of their ancient lands. The MacQuillins attacked Sorley Boy's forces, which were encamped at Beal-a-faula. They were repulsed with severe losses and retreated up Glenshesk to their camp on the banks of the river Shesk. Sorley led the MacDonalds in a counter attack and after a brutal encounter drove the MacQuillins towards Slieve-an-Aura. Here they were joined by the O'Neills of Clandeboy who had become alarmed at the growing power of the Clan Iain Mor.

Sorly Boy was reinforced by a small contingent of redshanks[19] in the spring of 1559 and then led the Clan Iain Mor in a skilful and highly mobile series of manoeuvres which culminated in an attack on the combined MacQuillin and O'Neill forces at Slieve-an-Aura on the thirteenth of July 1559. The MacQuillins and the O'Neills were well protected in a strong defensive position on the banks of the river Owennaglush, they were further protected from assault by the surrounding marshy ground. To lure the enemy out of this virtually impregnable position Sorley Boy devised a subtle stratagem. During the night he set his men to laying rushes across the bog, this activity was heard by the MacQuillins whose suspicions that Sorley was planning an attacked appeared to be confirmed when an O'Cathan[20] piper deliberately misinformed them that this was indeed the case. The allies decided to strike at the Clan Iain Mor before their preparations were complete. As they rushed out of their camp they became mired in the bog and fell easy prey to Sorley's archers and redshanks. The MacQuillins and O'Neills were cut to pieces as they struggled in the bog. After this decisive battle, Sorley Boy became the undisputed master of the Route.

MacDonald control of the Route was, in the short term, facilitated by the attention of the English being focused on the ever growing power of Shane O'Neill, who, since the defeat of his O'Neill and O'Donnell rivals had being extending his control over most of Ulster. The English were also concerned that the Scottish Queen Regent, Mary, (who was a staunch Catholic) would encourage French interference in Ireland. Mary, for her part, attempted to align herself with the Clan Iain Mor as a counter weight to Archibald Campbell, the protestant Earl of Argyle. The Clan Iain Mor rebuffed her advances as at this date Campbell ambitions on their Scottish possessions had not yet revealed themselves. Their chief, James, was married to Agnes, Archibald's sister, but of more significance was the fact that Archibald controlled many of the areas from which the Clan Iain Mor derived its supply of redshanks.

A situation in which three powers vie for control of one territory is by its very nature an unstable one. To the English, Shane was the greatest threat and their

---

[19] This contingent contained some pipers who were by now widely used both in the highlands and Ulster to martial and inspire clan armies.

[20] The O'Cahans had had close, if at times somewhat strained ties to the Clan Iain Mor since the fifteenth century through inter-marriage.

policy towards the Clan Iain Mor was to ensure that the two Gaelic powers did not combine. The Clan Iain Mor's policy was to initially stay neutral while being granted concessions by the English, the one they desired the most was legal title to the Route and the Glens. Ultimately they planned to pick up the pieces after the English and the O'Neills had exhausted themselves. By the late 1550's the Clan Iain Mor was in an extremely advantageous political position. They were being wooed by the Regent Mary of Scotland, the English and even Shane O'Neill; they even had a friendly Campbell Duke of Argyle on their side. By this date although James was the acknowledged chief of the clan, Sorley Boy was captain of the Route and his authority there was undisputed.

Shane O'Neill had managed to achieve something like hegemony over much of Ulster during this period. The expanding power of the Clan Iain Mor was no more acceptable to him than was the English presence. It is tempting to see the struggle in both the highlands and Ireland as a struggle by the Gaelic societies to maintain their culture and independence; in Ireland the Gaelic powers singly failed to follow policies which put this interpretation into practice. The previous chapters have amply testified that the same lack of Gaelic cohesion existed in the highlands of Scotland.

In the early 1560's the political landscape altered dramatically; England was at peace with France and assiduously courted Argyle as a Scottish counter weight to the Regent Mary. Argyle's position had been significantly improved by the continual rise of Protestantism in the lowlands of Scotland, and he agreed to assist the English in suppressing Shane O'Neill. The Clan Iain Mor attempted to remain neutral in the coming struggle having to weigh up the threat from their various rivals, Shane O'Neill, Argyle, and the English. Eventually James and Sorley Boy were lured into aligning the Clan Iain Mor with the English in exchange for legal title to the Glens and Route. There can be little doubt that Shane viewed this agreement as a hostile act.

By the summer of 1561 the English under Sussex were ready to take to the field from their base in Armagh. They launched a series of raids into Shane's lands; due to the dispersed nature of the O'Neill settlements and the paucity of targets these raids caused little lasting damage to Shane. Eventually an English army of one thousand men was defeated near Monaghan and the English offensive ground to a halt. In the late summer, Sussex launched another invasion of O'Neill territory but this also ended in failure amongst the bleak and rain soaked bogs of Ulster. Due to the failure of his two campaigns Sussex's aggressive policy towards Shane had fallen out of favour with Elizabeth who was now ready to negotiate with Shane. Elizabeth had also become disillusioned as to the usefulness of the Clan Iain Mor as they had determinedly sat on their hands during Sussex's campaigns.

The early fifteen sixties saw a significant deterioration in the political environment for the Clan Iain Mor. They had earned Shane's enmity because of their alliance with the English. The Campbells were beginning to flex their muscles due to their understanding with the English and their position as power brokers in the south west highlands. To make matters worse the Clan Iain Mor became involved in the bitter feud with the MacLeans over the Rinnes if Isla during these years, which kept James's attention focused on the clan's possessions in Scotland. The vital flow of redshanks was diminishing due to the strained relationship with Argyle and their use in the feud with the MacLeans.

After a tense but successful visit by Shane to London, Elizabeth reached an uneasy accord with Shane and began to focus her attention on the Clan Iain Mor who because of their Scottish connections she began to regard as more of a threat than Shane. When Shane returned to Ulster he again began to expand his power base and to threaten English and MacDonald interests alike. With the ever growing power of the O'Neills, James and Sorley Boy were forced to come to terms with Shane. In a letter from Sussex to Elizabeth he mentions that Shane has come to an agreement with James in which Sorley Boy agrees to "give him 500 kine and eight horsemen's furnitures....and serve him with 400 or 500 men in every journey..".

English policy once again went into reverse and Elizabeth began to court the Clan Iain Mor. She offered them permanent title to their possessions in Ulster in exchange for their active co-operation against Shane. James again tried to maintain his neutrality by claiming that he was unable to accept, as an agreement might be prejudicial to the interests of Mary, Queen of Scots. Elizabeth countered this evasion by stating that James could remove any aspect of the agreement which he judged might affect his position in Scotland. In effect Elizabeth was forcing James's hand. In their attempts to keep the Clan Iain Mor neutral, James and Sorley Boy had only succeeded in sowing suspicion in the minds of Shane and Elizabeth. The English became so desperate for the support of the Clan Iain Mor that they even considered a plan whereby two English pirates[21] would kidnap James and hold him hostage until he agreed to act in the English interest.

During the early 1560's Sorley Boy became the leader of the Antrim branch of the Clan Iain Mor. The extant letters concerning the Clan Iain Mor in Antrim are all addressed to or written by James. However, this does nothing to alter the fact that Sorley Boy acted as the clan leader in Ireland, his absence from the contemporary letters merely reflecting his illiteracy. It was during this period that James was fully occupied with the feud with the MacLeans and Campbell expansionism; it may well have been the only practical solution for James to delegate command of the clan in Ireland to Sorley Boy as he was fully stretched dealing with events in Scotland. It is clear that although the clan had different leaders in Scotland and Ireland it still acted as one entity (at this date) and that James was still the chief of the clan.

In the spring of 1563 Sussex was ready to face Shane on his home ground. The invasion was badly planned and equipped and as usual failed to find a suitable target as it drove into Tyrone. Shane avoided a pitched battle with the English army, which, with every passing day was growing weaker due to a shortage of provisions, the bad weather and the losses occasioned by sickness and desertion.

---

[21] Thomas Phettiplace and William Johnson.

Sussex's desperation is shown in his letters to England in which he repeatedly enquires as to the actions of the Clan Iain Mor; clearly he did not fully grasp that Sorley Boy had his own agenda. Like so many English invasions of Ulster, Sussex's expedition ended in failure after exhausting itself trying to come to grips with the native Irish. Sussex's discomfiture led to another volte face in Elizabeth's policy towards Ulster. She was exasperated by the failure of the Clan Iain Mor to aid Sussex despite being offered legal title to the Glenns and Route. She resolved to come to terms with Shane and eliminate the MacDonalds as a significant factor in the heady mix of Irish politics.

After lengthy negotiations, Shane signed a peace treaty with the English on the eleventh of September 1563 at Drum Cru. Shane was granted everything that he had fought for, he was recognized as the Lord of Ulster, English garrisons were to be withdrawn and he was to be allowed a free hand in his relationships with the O'Donnells.[22] He was also to be recognized as The O'Neill when he was addressed; this was a most important concession to the proud Gael. In return for all these concessions Shane agreed to become Elizabeth's man. Clearly this agreement would last as long as it suited both parties and was taken as a temporary expedient until either Shane or Elizabeth could seize an advantage over each other. This new alliance was to have near fatal ramifications for the Clan Iain Mor in Ireland.

Shane made his first move against the O'Donnells of Tryconnell in the early part of 1564. After a brief campaign he occupied Lifford Castle and captured the leading men of his ancient opponents. Shane's assault on the O'Donnells was to prevent them (with English support) from re-establishing their power base. This action and the subsequent one against the Clan Iain Mor had nothing to do with him being the Queen's man but everything to do with his own ambitions.

By September 1564 Shane was ready to begin his assault on the Clan Iain Mor. He had watched with growing anxiety, the continual flow of redshanks into the Glens and Route and the subsequent expansion of MacDonald power. Shane received the green light from the English authorities in Dublin who however refused Shane any aid in his invasion, no doubt because they did not trust him. Shane planned to strike hard and fast against the MacDonalds in the winter of 1564-65. This proud yet intelligent man knew that he must deal with the Clan Iain Mor during the winter when most of their redshank allies had returned to Scotland. He planned to strike quickly thus not giving the MacDonalds time to summon reinforcements from Scotland. Shane knew that he must bring his enemy to a decisive engagement and that the guerrilla tactics he had so successfully employed against the English had to be abandoned.

Shane began his campaign against the Clan Iain Mor with a series of diversionary manoeuvres on the banks of the river Bann. In September 1564 he began to re-fortify Culrath Castle near Colerain, and even sent a small force across the Bann to occupy a friary. These manoeuvres were designed to draw Sorley Boy's

---

[22] The O'Donells were the great Irish rivals of the O'Neills in Ulster.

attention away from his real target which was an invasion of the Glens from the south. In this he was entirely successful, as an invasion of the Route over the River Bann was the most obvious way for Shane to begin the destruction of the Clan Iain Mor's possessions in Ulster.

Sorley rushed a contingent of his clansmen to the friary and after a fierce engagement drove the O'Neills back across the Bann.[23] Despite being driven back across the river, Shane accomplished his objective by keeping Sorley Boy's attention focused on the Bann. James MacDonald had been kept well informed of the emerging threat from the O'Neills and had been busy attempting to thwart Shane's efforts to align the Campbells and the Scottish state against the Clan Iain Mor. Shane already had the passive support of Elizabeth and an O'Neill- Campbell alliance would be extremely dangerous for the Clan Iain Mor as it could interrupt the flow of the clan's reinforcements from Scotland. While Sorley Boy kept a close eye on the western approaches to the Route and James travelled back and forth to Edinburgh, the O'Neills began to put pressure on the Lecale MacDonalds whose settlements controlled the access to the Glens from the south.

By the beginning of 1565 Shane had managed to isolate the Clan Iain Mor, and although he had failed to get any active assistance from Elizabeth (who in her turn was planning to deal with Shane once he had destroyed the power of the Clan Iain Mor in Ulster) he had her acquiescence. His political manoeuvring in Scotland had created an atmosphere of uncertainty in which James and Sorley Boy were unsure whether the supply of reinforcements from Scotland could be guaranteed. It should also be remembered that the Clan Iain Mor had to keep a close watch on the MacLeans with whom they were at feud during this period.

James expected that Shane's invasion of his possessions was imminent by January 1565, so he sent Sorley Boy a reinforcement of three hundred Luchdtach; the Luchdtach were the elite fighting men of the clan, from Kintrye. The Luchdtach were sent to bolster the clan's defences in the Lecale region. During this period the Clan Iain Mor had a fighting strength of about one thousand men in Ulster, while Shane could muster at least two thousand men to his banner. Judging by future events it is clear that in the late winter months James and Sorley Boy failed to make adequate preparations for the coming storm. Knowing that Sorley Boy would start to receive redshank reinforcements in early May, Shane struck at the MacDonalds in April 1565.

When Sorley Boy heard that Shane was clearing a path through the woods which shielded Clandeboy from large scale invasion from the west, he gathered all his available forces and moved south to encounter Shane. After arriving at Edenduffcarrick, Shane halted for a few days to rest and reorganized his army. Sorley Boy concentrated both his own forces from the north and the local

---

[23] In September 1564 the Clan Iain Mor's fighting strength in Ulster was some seven hundred men; however this number was shrinking as their redshanks began to slip back to Scotland for the winter.

MacDonald contingents, including the Luchdtach, at Knockboy pass which controlled the access to the Glens. Despite a valiant resistance Sorley Boy's forces were driven from their defences in the pass by the overwhelming numbers of the O'Neills.

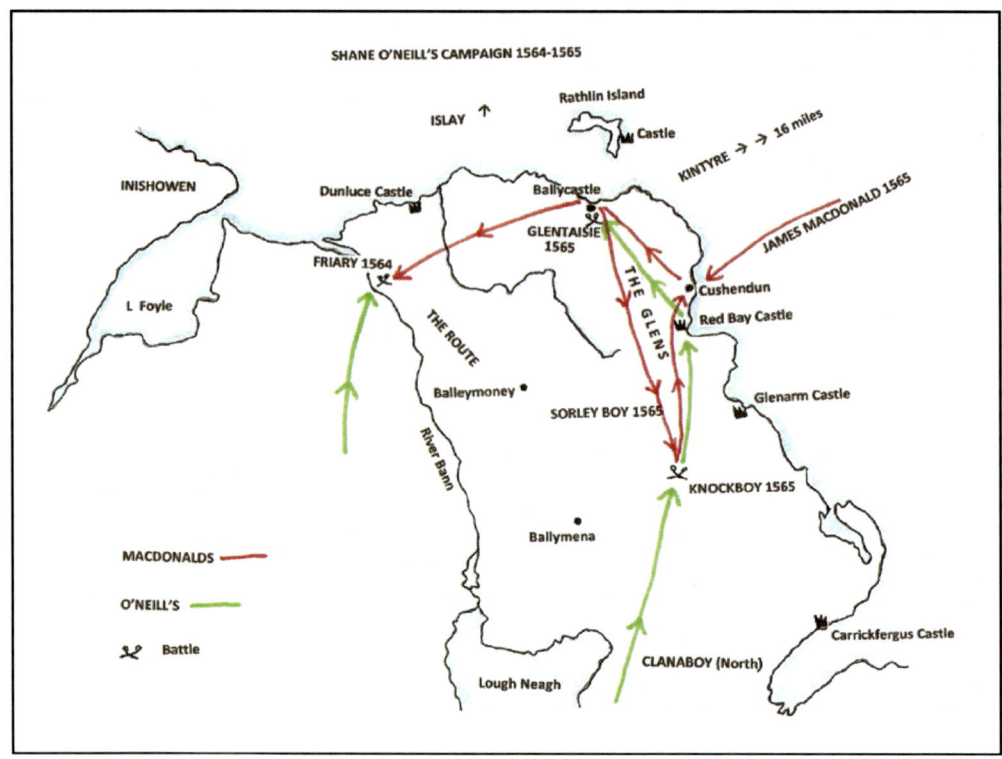

Once Sorley Boy realized that Shane had committed himself to a full scale invasion of the Clan Iain Mor's Irish possessions he sent runners to Ballycastle with instructions that the signal beacons should be lit. These beacons were at Torr Head, Murlough Bay and Fair Head; they were lit in extreme emergencies to summon the clan's reinforcements from Kintyre and Isla.

It was now clear to both Shane and Sorley Boy that time was of the essence; could Shane deal with Sorley Boy before James arrived from Scotland with large scale reinforcements? Shane pressed on, burning the MacDonald stronghold at Red Bay as he marched north. The loss of the castle at Red Bay exposed the entire southern boundary of the Glens as well as depriving the MacDonalds of a key redshank landing-place.

Torr Head

Once James had been told that the beacons in Ulster were alight he immediately summoned his clansmen to gather at his castle of Saddell. Wasting no time James sailed for Ireland that evening with those clansmen who had been able to reach the castle. James left his younger brother Alasdair Oge to lead the main force of reinforcements to Ulster as they came in from the outlying districts of Kintyre and the islands. It is testament to the Clan Iain Mor's efficiency that James was able to sail with the first contingent of reinforcements some twelve hours after the beacons had been lit on the Irish coast. At dawn the next morning James landed at Cushendun and was met by Sorley Boy, however their combined force was still significantly outnumbered by the O'Neills. Playing for time the MacDonalds retreated to Ballycastle which was of vital strategic importance to the Clan Iain Mor as it was the main redshank landing-place due to its proximity to Scotland. On the first of May Sorley Boy and James would have seen the rising plumes of smoke which signalled Shane's advance while watching a trickle of reinforcements landing on the beach at Ballycastle. All the time they would have been scanning the horizon looking out towards Kintyre and Isla; hoping to see the fleet that was due under the leadership of Alasdair Oge.

As Shane approached Ballycastle, James and Sorley Boy led their clansmen south up the glen of the river Tow. It is unclear whether they had been outmanoeuvred by Shane or whether this retreat from Ballycastle was a deliberate stratagem in which they hoped to catch Shane between themselves and the reinforcements of Alasdair Oge. Shane did not garrison Ballycastle but pressed on with his O'Neill host, hoping to bring the Clan Iain Mor to a decisive engagement before they received any more reinforcements from Scotland.[24] As dawn broke on the second of May 1565 the Clan Iain Mor faced their O'Neill adversaries in Glentaisie.

After years of political manoeuvring the two great Gaelic powers of Ulster were to strive for dominance of the province by force of arms. Apart from a few matchlock muskets[25] the two armies resembled those that had fought in Ireland for centuries. The heavy infantry whether gallowglass or redshanks were drawn up in the centre. They wore iron helmets and shirts of chain mail which covered them from their shoulders to their knees. They were armed with claymores[26] and Lochaber axes[27] while some of the redshanks may have been armed with a basket hilted sword and targe.[28] Both armies had swarms of skirmishers, known as Kerns, who hovered on the flanks of the heavy infantry. These light troops would skirmish with each other and attempt to disrupt the heavy infantry. They were unarmoured and were armed with bows and javelins as well as short swords and targes. Neither the Clan Iain Mor nor the O'Neills would have any significant numbers of cavalry as even the elite troops preferred to fight on foot.

Contemporary accounts[29] imply that Shane took the MacDonalds by surprise by attacking their camp very early in the morning. In any event it seems that the MacDonald battle line was barely formed when the O'Neills rushed upon them. The Battle of Glentaisie was a remarkably ferocious encounter even by the standards of Gaelic Ireland. The battle raged till well into the afternoon with the advantage swinging this way and that, the kerns rushing forward and firing their bows while the serried ranks of gallowglass stood and grimly hacked at each other.[30] The MacDonalds were outnumbered by two to one, in this type of conflict if both armies have equal moral then numbers become of vital significance. If one MacDonald faces two O'Neills and is hacked down then they can move on to their next target where the odds are now four to one and so on. It is a testament to James and Sorley Boy's leadership, as well as to the courage of the men of the clan,

---

[24] Shane would have been well aware that further reinforcements were on the way from Scotland.

[25] Gaelic armies only used muskets for skirmishing; broadswords, Lochaber axes, dirks and targes were relied on to deliver the decisive blow.

[26] Large two handed swords.

[27] A fearsome weapon which could roughly be described as a type of bill hook on a long wooden shaft.

[28] The mid-sixteenth century was a period of transition in weapons with the basket hilted sword (which was used till the end of the clan period i.e. 1746) gradually replacing the claymore.

[29] The Book of Howth and Dioness Campbell dean of Limerick.

[30] It was very unusual for Gaelic battles to last longer than an hour or two, with many being decided in a few minutes with the first furious onrush. Hand-to-hand combat for even a few minutes would require extreme physical exertion.

that they were able to resist the O'Neills for so long. Eventually in the afternoon the Clan Iain Mor was routed and they fled the field with the O'Neills in hot pursuit. It was during this phase of the battle that the majority of the MacDonald casualties would have been caused.[31] The O'Neills pursued their foes with great determination as they fled up the Glen. That the pursuit continued for several miles is demonstrated by the place where John MacDonald (one of Sorley Boy's captains) was cut down; on the other side of Knockland Hill.

Glentaisie

The battle of Glentaisie was a disaster for the Clan Iain Mor, of the thousand men involved in the battle six or seven hundred were killed or captured. Of this number, three to five hundred were killed. The brutal nature of this encounter is attested to by an English estimate of Shane's losses put at between three and four hundred.[32] The battle not only saw heavy losses amongst the commonality of the Clan Iain Mor but also amongst the leadership. James, who was severely wounded, and Sorley Boy were captured while Angus Uaibhreach, James's younger brother was left dead on the field. Shortly after the battle Alasdair Oge landed on Rathlin

---

[31] For a detailed discussion of hand to hand combat and its psychological aspects see, A. Goldsworthy's Cannae Hannibal's Greatest Victory.
[32] In a letter from Fitzwilliam to Cecil.

Island with nine hundred reinforcements, when he learnt of the disaster he led his force back to Kintyre.

For the time being the power of the Clan Iain Mor had been completely destroyed in Ireland. Their defeat may well have been caused by the few hours it had taken Alasdair Oge to reach Ballycastle from Kintyre. No doubt all the protagonists pondered how the battle would have turned out had the forces of James and Alasdair Oge been able to coalesce. The conflict between the Clan Iain Mor and the O'Neills can be seen in part as yet another feud between Gaelic societies and demonstrated the fragmentation of the Gaelic world after the fall of the Lordship of the Isles.

Immediately after the battle Shane marched his army into the Route; he soon captured the castle of Dunseverick before moving on to besiege Dunluce. After a bitter and protracted siege the warden was only persuaded to surrender the castle when Sorley Boy's emaciated and wounded body was exposed before the walls. The severely wounded James and the other MacDonald captives, with the exception of Sorley Boy were imprisoned at Shane's castle of Corcra in Tyrone. Sorley Boy was taken along with the O'Neill host as he campaigned in Ulster.

With one of the three power blocks in Ulster all but destroyed there was an almost inevitable rise in tension between Shane and the English. James's redoubtable wife Lady Agnes Campbell tirelessly worked for his release by putting what pressure she could on the Scottish court, as well as ensuring that her brother the Duke of Argyle would not attempt to interfere with the flow of redshanks when they were called upon by the Clan Iain Mor. The English, who had never trusted Shane, became increasingly alarmed at his sudden rise to prominence in the Gaelic world of Ulster. To reduce his hold over the province and to prevent a large scale MacDonald invasion the English worked tirelessly to persuade Shane to release James into their hands. With James's death in the dungeons of Corcra on the fifth of July 1565 both the English and Shane lost a valuable pawn in the dynamic and fluid world of Ulster politics. The Clan Iain Mor always believed the rumour that James was murdered by Shane to put an end to the demands of the English and Scottish governments for James's release. Although there is no proof that Shane murdered James many of his contemporaries believed this to be the case.

Dunluce Castle

James had led the Clan Iain Mor in a period of unequalled turbulence; he had had to contend with the ever growing power of the Campbells as well as resisting the restless Lachlan MacLean in their bitter feud over the Rinnes of Isla. He had spent much of his life expanding his clan's possessions in Ulster, ably assisted by Sorley Boy. He was a man of great personal courage as well as being in possession of a subtle political intellect. James was the most powerful individual to emerge from the MacDonalds since the fall of the Lords of the Isles; he was not only mourned by his own people but also by the wider Gaelic world. The scribes of the Four Masters wrote, "....he was a paragon of hospitality and prowess, a festive man of many troops, and a bountiful and munificent man. And his peer was not at that time among the clan-Donnell in Ireland or Scotland; and his own people would not have deemed it too much to give his weight in gold for his ransom, if he could have been ransomed."

The destruction of the Clan Iain Mor's power base in Ulster after Glentaisie completely altered the political landscape in Ulster. Shane attempted to placate the Clan Iain Mor by allowing them to re-occupy some of their coastal settlements as well as seeking an alliance with the Mary Queen of Scots and the Campbells so that he could withstand any onslaught from the English. He attempted to thwart or at least delay any English attack by continuing to pledge his loyalty to Elizabeth.

Alasdair Oge, who was now leading the Clan Iain Mor demonstrated a pragmatic and subtle policy of avoiding open conflict with Shane; he understood that the

O'Neills were not the only opponents of the Clan Iain Mor. Alasdair Oge's primary objective was to maintain and expand his clan's power base, and to do this he knew that he must avoid a death struggle with Shane. Both Alasdair Oge and on his release, Sorley Boy, demonstrated a surprising degree of ambivalence to Shane. Only James's widow Agnes Campbell was suffused with the thirst for revenge which was a more predictable passion in the Gaelic world of the sixteenth century.

Elizabeth was now concerned about Shane's domination of Ulster so she in her turn reduced her hostility to the Clan Iain Mor. She also took steps to counter Shane's power by forming a series of understandings with the ancient rivals of the O'Neills, the O'Donnells.

Mary Queen of Scots had always favoured the expansion of the Clan Iain Mor in Ireland as it concentrated English attention on Ireland rather than on her own borders. A powerful Clan Iain Mor also acted as a useful counter weight to the Campbells whose head; the protestant Earls of Argyle she distrusted.

Archibald or Gillasbuig Donn, as he was known to his clan, fifth Earl of Argyle was the brother of Agnes, James's wife. Like Alasdair Oge his overriding ambition was to see the extension of his clan's power. His position was complicated by his Protestantism which led him to be distrusted and disliked by Mary Queen of Scots. Archibald was only partially successful in his schemes as he attempted to placate both Mary and Elizabeth by promising various courses of action. Apart from his various jurisdictions over the south-west highlands, he also controlled much of the redshank recruiting grounds which meant that none of the other parties could ignore him. His policy was to prevent any of the other powers from gaining complete control over Ulster while expanding his own clan's power base in half-hearted efforts to placate his rivals.

With the appointment of Sydney as the Lord Deputy of Ireland English policy in Ireland took on a more hostile and aggressive stance towards Shane. One of the characteristics of this new approach was that the English were better disposed to the Clan Iain Mor who they no longer regarded as a threat. By the summer of 1566 Alasdair Oge found himself in the enviable position of being courted by both the English and Shane for the military strength of the Clan Iain Mor and their attendant redshanks. On learning of the English plans for an invasion of Ulster, Shane became desperate. He led an unsuccessful strike against the English garrison of Dundalk while pleading for aid from Alasdair Oge, promising him a complete restoration of the Clan Iain Mor's possessions in Ulster as well as tribute and the release of Sorley Boy. Alastair Oge rejected Shane's overtures and stood aloof from the immanent conflict. With this measured but essentially hostile stance, Alasdair Oge had made it clear to Shane that he could not hope for any assistance from the MacDonalds. Shane also had to keep a close eye on the O'Donnells of Tryconnell who were in close contact with the English and had been the greatest Irish rivals of the O'Neills.

With the support of his O'Donnell allies Sydney drove through the centre of Ulster in September 1566. Sydney's invasion was timed so that his army could destroy all the summer harvest which was to see the O'Neills through the winter.

The campaign settled into the normal pattern of Sydney marching back and forth destroying any fixed asset he could find with Shane avoiding an open set battle. Sydney was successful in diminishing support for Shane, as his prestige was greatly reduced by the English presence and the impoverishment of the countryside.

Alasdair Oge landed in Ulster in November at the head of twelve hundred men where his was joined by the surviving adherents of the Clan Iain Mor in Ulster. While Shane still possessed a large army he was threatened on all sides by implacable opponents and his position had been greatly weakened by his failure to lead the O'Neills into battle against the English. As the winter months wore on Shane situation deteriorated further, his army was plagued by desertion and all his settlements were occupied by the English or their O'Donnell allies. The final straw was the defeat of Shane's army at the hands of the O'Donnells at Farsetmore in May 1567. Shane had little option other than to see if he could come to terms with Alasdair Oge, whatever the risk.

Shane and Alasdair Oge met at Cushendun; Shane was accompanied by Sorley Boy and a small contingent of his followers while Alasdair Oge waited for him with six hundred of his clansmen. The two leaders attempted to hammer out an agreement, the gist of which was that, in exchange for Sorley Boy's release Alasdair Oge would provide a thousand redshanks to assist Shane while the Clan Iain Mor would take a position of benevolent neutrality. Negotiations were carried on for a couple of days, which were extremely stressful for both parties due in part to their critical nature and their bloody past.

Cushendun

The traditional story of Shane's death is that it was brought about by a drunken dispute between O'Neills and MacDonalds over the proposed marriage of Shane to Agnes Campbell[33] which was to have cemented the deal. The outnumbered O'Neills, including Shane were hacked down by a mob of enraged MacDonalds. While it is certain that Shane died at the hands of the Clan Iain Mor the reason for his death may well have been more calculated. It is likely that Alasdair Oge, on seeing Shane within his power knew that he could release Sorley Boy whenever he wished and that English and MacDonald political interests would both be served by his death. Shane's death would serve the Clan Iain Mor's interests in that it would result in the destruction of what was left of O'Neill power. It would also bring about the release of Sorley Boy as well as the possibility of obtaining legal title to the Glens and Route from Elizabeth. No doubt Elizabeth's large reward for Shane's head also played some part in Alasdair Og's actions.

In the ever shifting sands of Ulster politics the power of the O'Neills was, for the present, destroyed. Only the Clan Iain Mor stood between the English and their goal of dominating Ulster. Sorley Boy needed time to rebuild his clan's strength in Ulster, so while attempting to avoid confrontation with Elizabeth he made overtures to Mary Queen of Scots. These efforts were obstructed by Argyle and diluted by their attention being focused on the continuing feud with the MacLeans. Elizabeth had decided that the Clan Iain Mor must be finally removed from Ulster, and with them Scottish influence in Ireland. When Sydney returned to London she reluctantly agreed to meet the expense of a full scale invasion but then planned to reduce any further expense by settling English protestant migrants on the Antrim coast. These settlers would defend their own interests and those of Elizabeth by preventing any further re-settlement by the Clan Iain Mor. It was from this time that the Clan Iain Mor became two close but separate entities. The clan's Scottish possessions were protected by Alasdair Oge during the minority of Angus MacDonald, James's son. Meanwhile Sorley Boy became undisputed leader of the Antrim MacDonalds and it was from this period that they began to establish their own independent identity.

Sorley Boy left Ulster for Scotland to visit Archibald Campbell, Earl of Argyle; his aim was to have Archibald's acquiescence to him recruiting large numbers of redshanks to rebuild MacDonald power in Ulster. This mission was clearly successful, for by November it was estimated by the English that Sorley Boy had some fifteen hundred redshanks in Ulster with a further twelve hundred on their way. Sorley immediately re-asserted MacDonald control over the Route by cowing the MacQuillins and then sent out runners to the rest of the Irish Scots to come to him so that they may assist him in resisting the English threat. Amongst the communities these runners visited would have been the remnants of the ancient gallowglass MacDonalds whose ancestors had fled Scotland during the reign of Robert the Bruce.

---

[33] It will be remembered that Agnes was James MacDonald's widow.

While Sorley Boy was rapidly re-establishing the Clan Iain Mor as a major power in Ulster, the English garrisons were suffering from hunger and disease in their bleak forts and consequently English power was diminishing. Both Elizabeth and Sorley attempted to form an alliance with Turlough O'Neill who was Shane's cousin and had become The O'Neill on Shane's death. Turlough played both parties against each other and this led to none of the contending parties knowing where Turlough's loyalties lay.

By the early months of 1568 Sorley Boy had managed to greatly strengthen the Clan Iain Mor's position in Ulster by a series of alliances, with Turlough O'Neill and the clan's ancient opponents in the Route, the MacQuillins. Sorley could not rely on his new allies but these understandings did have the advantage of creating uncertainty in the minds of English policy makers. Throughout the late winter and spring the loose Gaelic confederation mounted hit and run attacks against the English garrisons who were as usual enfeebled by semi-starvation and poor living conditions. Sorley spent much of his time in Scotland aiming to achieve a close understanding with the Duke of Argyle. They arraigned that the Duke's redoubtable sister Lady Agnes Campbell would marry Turlough O'Neill,[34] and that the Duke would allow the flow of redshanks from Argyle to continue unabated.[35] Sorley's preparations for war were strengthened by a truce that was patched up between the Clan Iain Mor and the MacLeans in their long running feud.

In August Lady Agnes Campbell gave the blockading English fleet the slip and arrived in Ulster with over one thousand redshanks. In the same month she was married to Turlough O'Neill[36] and it seemed that for once there was a real possibility of a pan-Gaelic alliance to challenge English power. The bond between the Irish and the Scots was further strengthened by the marriage of Agnes's daughter Ineen Dubh (the dark girl) to the chief of the O'Donnells. Agnes and Ineen crossed and recrossed the Irish Sea in their efforts to raise redshanks for Turlough. With the tacit backing of the Campbells and the active support of the Clan Iain Mor they were able to raise several thousand redshanks to support him. Turlough now commanded an army of well over five thousand men and began to threaten English interests as far as Dublin. Partly due to his own vacillating nature and partly due to the inherent instability of Gaelic alliances, Turlough's army disintegrated in desertions and a welter of recrimination. Sidney withdrew many of the English garrisons from the borders of Ulster and concentrated them in the Pale.[37]Sorley

---

[34] This marriage was delayed because an English fleet which patrolled the channel between Ulster and Scotland prevented safe passage.

[35] The Duke's acquiescence to the flow of redshanks was part of his wider plans to be the only effective power broker in the western isles.

[36] From the outset it was clear that Turlough came a poor third in Agnes's loyalties, after her MacDonald sons and her own clan.

[37] The Pale was the area immediately surrounding Dublin. The expression "beyond the pale" originates from the English view that to go beyond the borders of the Pale was to go into a region which was lawless, anarchic and dangerous.

Boy took advantage of the preoccupation of the English and the native Irish with each other to extend MacDonald influence into Clandeboy.

Throughout this period Sorley Boy's relationship with his nephew, Angus MacDonald the chief of the Clan Iain Mor, was cordial[38] and having encouraged Turlough into open defiance of the English they, along with Angus's mother, Agnes, saw to it that Turlough received no more redshank reinforcements. They did not wish to see the O'Neills under Turlough becoming as powerful as his predecessor Shane. By 1571 Turlough had been reduced to being the head of one of the provincial powers of Ulster, he did not even have the company of Agnes who had failed to return to Ulster after a visit to Scotland. It was Sorley Boy at the head of the Clan Iain Mor in Ireland who now dominated Ulster. 1572 was the year in which Sorley Boy secured the dominant position of the Clan Iain Mor in Ulster.

It was also the year in which Elizabeth and her councillors resolved to establish a firm grasp on Ulster. They planned to plant vibrant protestant settlements in Ulster as a permanent counter weight to the Gaels. A prerequisite to the successful planting of settlements was the destruction of the military power of the Clan Iain Mor. Sydney was replaced by Essex who was determined to win the Queen's favour by finally destroying Sorley Boy and halting the annual flow of redshanks into Ulster. To buy time for Essex's preparations, Elizabeth granted Sorley Boy the legal right to live in Ireland in April 1573, while at the same time granting Essex complete political and military power over Ulster should he succeed in conquering it. Clearly there was to be no room for Sorley Boy and the Clan Iain Mor in Elizabeth's plans for the new Ulster.

Elizabeth's true intentions were revealed to Sorley Boy and the Irish leaders with the first English settlements in Clandeboy. It was now clear to all the Gaelic powers that Elizabeth intended to make a permanent end to their domination of Ulster, English settlement was perhaps the only factor which could unite the Gaelic powers; by early 1573 this duly came about. By the spring of that year the three great Gaelic powers of Ulster the Clan Iain Mor, the O'Neills and the O'Donnells were united in their opposition to English plantations, although they each pursued their own strategies and had their own differing agendas.

In August 1573 Essex landed with eleven hundred soldiers[39] and four hundred colonists at Carrickfergus, his aim was to strike at Sorley Boy before he could receive any assistance from the Irish. Essex failed to bring Sorley Boy to a decisive encounter and as Sorley Boy's forces melted away into the woods and bogs of Antrim, Essex found himself marching and counter marching with his army diminishing with the effects of desertion, and illness. Turlough managed to keep his nerve and both he and O'Donnell remained loyal to Sorley, who had also been reinforced by Angus MacDonald at the head of four hundred men. By the end of the year Essex had utterly failed to destroy Sorley Boy and was forced onto the

---

[38] It is clear that Sorley Boy wielded a great deal of influence over his young nephew.
[39] This force included Essex's own private troops as well as cavalry and engineers.

defensive. The sum of his achievements was that he shored up the defences of Carrickfergus.

During the winter months of early 1574 both sides attempted to strengthen their position for the coming struggle. Essex was reinforced with troops from England and the Pale as well as contingents from the settlers, bringing his army up to two thousand men. Sorley Boy had been in Argyle recruiting redshanks that were landing on the Antrim coast intermittently over the winter months with more committed to campaigning in Ulster in the spring. As the year wore on Essex's position became more desperate. The parsimonious Elizabeth was becoming exasperated at the expense of a campaign that had achieved nothing, Essex's efforts to detach the vacillating Turlough from his alliance with Sorley Boy had failed and redshanks continued to flow into Ulster to bolster Sorley's forces. As the summer months drifted bye time was running out for Essex to deal a decisive blow against the Clan Iain Mor. He chose instead to strike at Turlough O'Neill in an attempt to bring him to terms and leave Sorley Boy isolated. Turlough found some resolve to resist the English and using the traditional guerrilla tactics wore down Essex's forces as they struggled through Tryconnell. Essex's failure only increased his desperation as he knew that with every failed expedition, which of course cost Elizabeth ever more gold, he was incurring her displeasure and his position at court was being eroded. In the autumn the English army withdrew to Carrickfergus to recuperate over the winter.

By the summer of 1575 both Essex and Sorley Boy had completed their preparations for war. Both leaders had their unique problems, Angus MacDonald had had his plans for a massive redshank invasion of Ulster thwarted by the Duke of Argyle,[40] while Essex was trying Elizabeth's patience with every passing day of inactivity and expense. With all the English preparations for war, including the felling of woods which gave quicker access to the heart of his lands, Turlough lost his nerve and sued for peace. He met Essex at a newly constructed English fort on the Blackwater, where he agreed to support Essex against Sorley Boy in exchange for new titles to his lands from Elizabeth. Although Turlough's capitulation was a severe blow to any prospect of a united Gaelic resistance to Essex, Turlough had always been unreliable and his capitulation released a considerable number of redshanks from their obligations to Turlough and who now offered their services to Sorley Boy. With the summer wearing on time was running out for Essex so he struck at Sorley Boy.

---

[40] It is likely that Archibald did not wish to see the Clan Iain Mor successful in Ulster as this would be detrimental to his plans for Campbell expansionism.

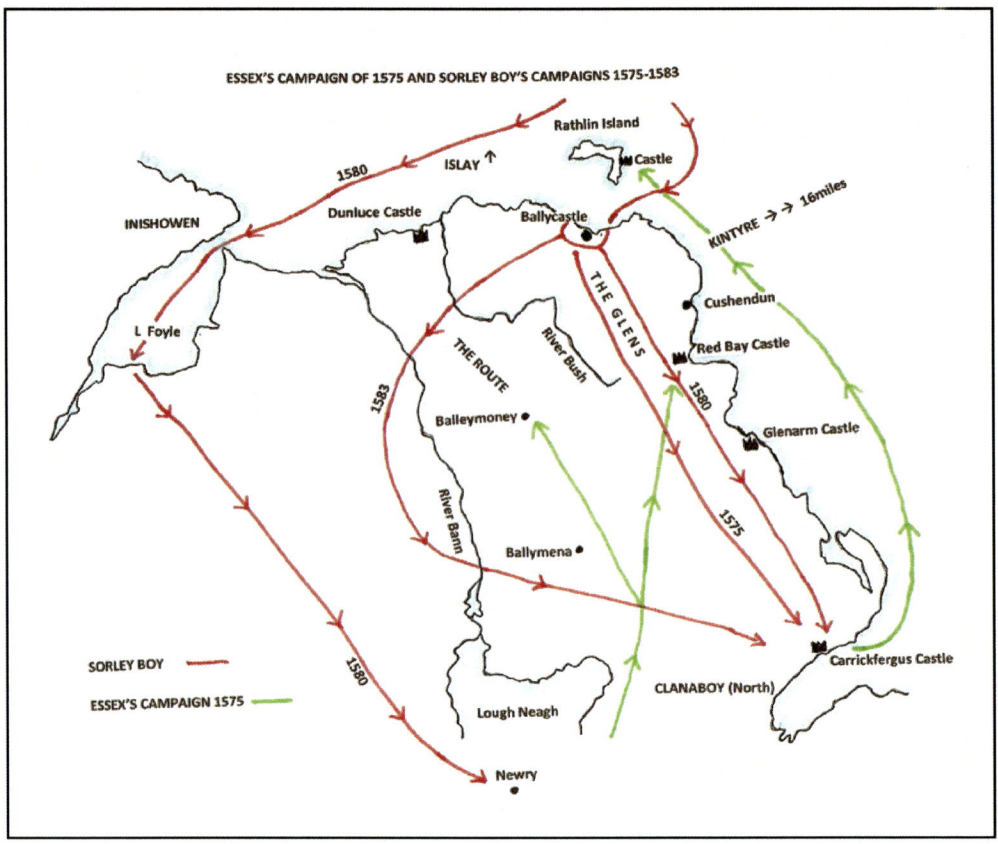

ESSEX'S CAMPAIGN OF 1575 AND SORLEY BOY'S CAMPAIGNS 1575-1583

Essex marched north through Clandeboy initially heading for the Glens. He then received intelligence that Sorley Boy had retreated to a fortified position on the banks of the Bann in the Route. When Essex came into contact with Sorley Boy's army there was a series of sharp skirmishes, which Essex claimed to have won, inflicting several hundred casualties on the MacDonalds. Whatever the truth of the engagements on the Bann, Essex was soon in retreat halting only when he reached Drogheda to reorganise his army. Clearly this invasion of the territories of the Clan Iain Mor was yet another failure of English military strategy in Ulster. Sorley Boy had been taken aback by the scale and speed of the English invasion, also no doubt he longed for peace having spent his entire life campaigning. He sent messages to Essex, in which he agreed to become a loyal subject of Elizabeth if she would grant him legal title to the Glens and Route. He was to be disappointed by the English response. With an ominous silence emanating from Dublin, Sorley Boy made his preparations for the decisive clash with Essex. Sorley sent the prominent non-combatant members of the clan to the relative safety of Rathlin Island. He then concentrated the Clan Iain Mor's available fighting strength at Ballycastle; this strategic position allowed him to cover both the Glens and Route.

Essex's position at court had been severely weakened by the failure of his most recent expedition against Sorley Boy, he resolved on a different strategy. He decided to capture and occupy the strategic island of Rathlin. If Essex's forces could hold Rathlin then they had a good chance of intercepting most of the redshank galleys after they had sailed from Kintrye to reinforce the Clan Iain Mor. Essex concentrated his forces at Newry which successfully drew Sorley Boy's attention away from his intended area of operations. Essex had left a force of three hundred infantry and eighty cavalry under the command of Captain John Norris at Carrickfergus. Norris was to sail with the three frigates based at Carrickfergus and occupy Rathlin, putting the population to the sword. In the light of future events these instructions were not meant to be the usual hyperbole so common in sixteenth century documents. When the winds blew in his favour Norris sailed for Rathlin, his immediate target was the small castle on the island which had been held by the Clan Iain Mor since the time of Robert the Bruce.

Rathlin Castle

The castle was held by a garrison of some forty redshanks, but within its walls were also two hundred women and children, many of whom were related to Sorley Boy. After a siege of two days the English managed to make a breach in the ancient walls of the castle. The English infantry rushed to storm the castle but were driven back with heavy losses by a charge from the courageous garrison. Accounts vary as to whether the garrison surrendered on terms or whether the castle was stormed; in any event the castle was soon in Norris's hands. There followed an appalling massacre not only of the survivors of the garrison but also of the women and children. Norris and his men hunted down every living soul in the castle and butchered them by cutting their throats. The fact that the castle had been captured, even if it was not under terms, and therefore the fate of the garrison was at the mercy of the victors and that the English soldiers were enraged at their heavy losses in their first attempted assault goes no way to excusing this appalling event.

Norris and his men were not yet satisfied, they proceeded to hunt down and slaughter the entire population of the island. The inhabitants of the island and other refugees from Antrim tried to hide where they could on this rugged and windswept island, many hid amongst the rocks and seaweed of the shore. The English were thorough in their work; they scoured the entire island, massacring every person they found, no one was sparred, "slaughtered them as if they had been seals or otters." The picture of women been cut down as they ran along the beach or children been butchered as they attempted to hide under the seaweed is a truly shocking one. The massacre on Rathlin was carried out in the name of a state which prided itself as being amongst the most civilized in Europe. The inhabitants of its capital listened to the beautiful and subtle plays of Shakespeare and Marlow, but within a few hundred miles of London English soldiers were hunting down and murdering children.

The massacre on Rathlin is one of the most disgraceful incidents in English history. In all about two hundred people were butchered in the castle with a further three to four hundred souls being murdered on the rest of the island. In terms of its cruelty and scale it far outweighs the massacre of Glencoe. Essex's instructions to Norris or their losses and depravations go no way to condone or explain the barbarous behaviour of the English soldiers. The events on Rathlin draw a very clear picture of the huge fissure between the Anglo-Saxon and Gaelic cultures. To most Englishmen there was something awful about these violent and strange people who inhabited the British Isles with them. To many they were as strange as any people from any part of the world that was emerging before them in the sixteenth century.

After destroying eleven redshank galleys and leaving a small garrison on the desolate island Norris returned to Carrickfergus. Sorley Boy had witnessed Norris's invasion from the mainland. In Essex's report to Elizabeth he was described as ".... likely to run mad with for sorrow, tearing and tormenting himself, and saying that he then lost all he had ever had." While the veracity of much of Essex's report can be called into doubt, there can be no question as to the agony Sorley Boy must have suffered, watching helplessly from the cliffs while his clan's women and children were massacred. Sorley Boy, despite his anguish kept a cool head and did not rush to the defence of the poor inhabitants of Rathlin. Had he done so he risked the annihilation of his forces at the hands of the English frigates and would certainly have exposed the whole of the Clan Iain Mor's possessions in Ulster to destruction from Essex's army which was still encamped at Newry.

When Elizabeth received Essex's initial report her first correspondence with him was congratulatory but when details of the massacre began to emerge she recalled him from Ireland and he was replaced by Sydney. Despite his aggressive policy of "fire and sword" Essex had only managed to bring disgrace upon himself and reinforced the fear and hatred the Gaelic powers had for their English opponents.

Rejecting English overtures of a truce the enraged Sorley Boy prepared for revenge. In September 1575 Sorley Boy fell upon Carrickfergus. The English garrison sallied out from the town to intercept the approaching Scots. They were ambushed and cut to pieces. Leaving over one hundred dead they fled back to Carrickfergus. Among the English casualties were some of the soldiers who had taken part in the invasion of Rathlin, no doubt their corpses were of some consolation to the embittered Sorley. Sorley Boy then proceeded to ravage the environs of Carrickfergus stripping the surrounding countryside of any movable valuables and livestock.

Sorley Boy and Sydney knew that their forces were exhausted. Sorley still needed legal title to his clan's possessions in Ulster as well as the removal of the English garrison on Rathlin; while Sydney recognized that with the forces available to him he would be unable to dislodge the Clan Iain Mor. As Sydney was negotiating with Sorley he was approached by Agnes Campbell, (who had been the wife of Sorly's elder brother James). Agnes was now styled, Lady Tyrone after her marriage to Turlough O'Neill. Agnes had noticed with an ever increasing sense of alarm the growing reliance of the Clan Iain Mor on Sorley Boy in Ireland. In legal terms it was beyond doubt that her children by James were the rightful heirs of the clan's possessions in Ulster. But it was also evident to the clan that with its commitments in Scotland[41] only Sorley Boy was capable of defending the clan's interests in Ireland. Agnes proposed that in exchange for her persuading Turlough O'Neill to come to terms with the English, Sydney would re-confirm her son's right to the Clan Iain Mor's Irish possessions. It is clear that Agnes's interest in the future of her sons overrode the interests of the Clan Iain Mor. The opportunity was too tempting for the wily old politician and Sydney accepted Agnes's offer. Secretly Sydney accepted Agnes's terms and sat back hoping to see the O'Neills and Clan Iain Mor tear each other to pieces. With some English aid the O'Neills attacked the unsuspecting Sorley Boy. In this encounter Sorley Boy lost a significant number of his best troops. The veteran Sorley Boy did not respond with the usual counter-attack but throughout 1576 kept on his guard while strengthening his clan's forces with another influx of redshanks. He had learnt the bitter lesson of Glentasie and was not prepared to hand Ulster to the English by becoming embroiled in a mutually destructive war with the O'Neills. With the encouragement of Agnes the weak willed Turlough screwed up his courage and launched another attack on the Clan Iain Mor. In one of the skirmishes between the O'Neills and MacDonalds,

---

[41] The feud with the MacLeans and the ever present threats caused by Campbell expansionist policies.

Sorley Boy's eldest son Donald was killed. Sorley still avoided a full scale confrontation with Turlough, knowing that Sydney was waiting in the wings to destroy both Gaelic powers.

1578 saw an uneasy peace in Ulster, with Sorley Boy and Sydney viewing each other with suspicion, Turlough had again sunk back into lethargic inaction while his dominating wife's attention was fully absorbed in the bloody feud between her son Angus and the MacLeans which had again erupted after the MacLeans had devastated the island of Ghiga in the early months of the year.

The following years were ones of relative quiet in Ulster. Turlough O'Neill's authority was being continually eroded by his vacillations and his cooling relationship with his wife Agnes. Although he was still supplied with redshanks with the connivance of the Earl of Argyle, they were of little avail to him as once they were in Ireland their first allegiance was always to Sorley Boy. Agnes was preoccupied with supporting her son Angus MacDonald in his struggles with the MacLeans, and during this period came to accept that although Angus was the nominal overlord of the clan's possessions in Ireland, it was Sorley Boy who led the Clan Iain Mor in Ulster. Sydney spent his time attempting to sow seeds of discord between the Gaelic powers while strengthening the borders of the Pale.

In the summer of 1582, Turlough O'Neill, fortified by massive reinforcements of redshanks,[42] invaded Connaught; Sligo was plundered and burnt to the ground. Sorley Boy had hoped that by encouraging Turlough to invade Connaught he would cause the English to weaken their grip on the borders of Ulster. The English held a series of garrison posts on the Carrickfergus- Newry Line which Sorley hoped would be weakened or even abandoned in face of the threat from Turlough. Turlough's invasion of Connaught rapidly lost momentum and the English maintained their grip on the borders of Ulster. Sorley continued to strengthen his clan's position in Antrim with a re-enforcement of two thousand redshanks during the summer of 1582. Unusually galleys were still disgorging redshanks onto the Antrim coast well after October, which was traditionally the end of the redshank "season". Sorley Boy not only intended to hold his clan's possessions against all comers but also intended to extend the reach of his people into new lands. The large numbers of redshanks available to Sorley Boy was partly due to the decline of the Clan Iain Mor in Scotland and the subsequent instability in Argyle.

Early in 1583 Sorley Boy crushed a MacQuillin attempt to gain control over the Route; the fact that they had been supported by some two hundred English troops, did not improve relations between Sorley Boy and Sydney. By May the armies of Sorley Boy and Turlough O'Neill had coalesced and some four thousand men were ready to advance on Dublin. Angus MacDonald was ready in Scotland with two thousand re-enforcements. The English situation appeared to be critical, the situation in Connaught was still unstable and the combined O'Neill MacDonald

---

[42] These redshanks had been provided by Angus MacDonald and Sorley Boy.

army looked more than a match for the English garrisons between Newry and Dublin.

At this critical juncture, Turlough again lost his nerve, he withdrew his followers from Sorley Boy's camp and wrote a series of letters to Dublin requesting a truce. Had he held his nerve it is interesting to speculate how differently Irish history might have developed. There was to be no strong pan-Gaelic alliance to drive the English back to the Pale. Shortly after the breakup of the Gaelic host, Turlough and Agnes promised fealty to the English authorities in Dublin. It is clear that Turlough was under the influence of Agnes, but why should Agnes submit to English domination when she had devoted her talents to supporting the ambitions of her sons, who, as leaders of the Clan Iain Mor were opposed to any further expansion of English power? The answer lay in the erosion of her influence with her sons, who would no longer be guided by her, Angus seems to have happily accepted that Sorley Boy was, to all intents and purposes, the chief of the Clan Iain Mor in Ireland. The two men were to co-operate with each other for many years in the interests of their clan.

In January 1584, Sir John Perrott was appointed Lord Deputy of Ireland. Elizabeth had given him instructions to maintain the status quo in Ireland while English efforts were concentrated on assisting the Dutch Protestants. The political situation in Ulster continued to change with its usual fluidity. Turlough O'Neill at first sent welcoming overtures to Perrott, but drew away from any accord with the English with the landing of fifteen hundred MacLean redshanks on the shores of Loch Swilly in August. Sorley Boy had also seen his forces supplemented by MacDonald redshanks. It is from this period that Sorley Boy seems to have finally abandoned any hope of getting any worthwhile support from the unreliable Turlough and decided that the Clan Iain Mor should go it alone in pursuing its ambitions in Ulster. Perrott believed that the MacLean and MacDonald forces would combine and thus pose a serious threat to English interests in Ireland. While an alliance of the two clans was probably encouraged by James VI to further Scottish policy in Ireland it seems most unlikely that Sorley Boy would have sought MacLean assistance because of the bitter feud between the two clans that intermittently raged in Scotland.[43]

The ambitious and hot-headed Perrott decided to make an all out effort to deal with the Clan Iain Mor before its power grew any further. Perrott sent Sir Richard Bingham to keep the MacLean redshanks in check while he struck north with the remaining English forces in August 1584. Perrott had received an assurance from Turlough that the O'Neills would not assist the Clan Iain Mor and in a further attempt to isolate Sorley Boy he had sent a naval squadron to patrol the north Antrim coast to prevent Sorley Boy receiving any further redshank reinforcements.

---

[43] This clan feud had been quiet since 1579 with the marriage of Angus to Lachlan MacLean's sister Mary. The feud was to erupt again in 1585 with Lachlan's attack on Donald Gorm Mor on Jura (see chapter 11).

The English army marched up the eastern side of Lough Neagh and then followed the river Bann towards Colerain. Perrott laid siege to Dunluce Castle, bombarding the fortress with artillery which had been landed at Portrush. After two days the garrison was forced to surrender to Perrott.[44] The timing of the English invasion had taken Sorley Boy by surprise; he quickly recovered his poise and sent messengers to Scotland with urgent requests for assistance. Sorley also ordered the MacDonalds to abandon their more vulnerable settlements and retreat into the fastnesses of Ulster with all their livestock. After garrisoning Dunluce Castle and sending out search parties to find and destroy the MacDonald livestock[45] Perrott returned to Dublin. In an attempt to break the cohesion of the Clan Iain Mor, Perrott granted Donald Gorm (who was Sorley Boy's nephew and a younger brother of Angus the current chief of the Clan Iain Mor) possession of The Glens; this stratagem failed as although Donald Gorm accepted the grant he never questioned Sorley Boy's leadership.

During the next winter Sorley Boy made preparations for the next round in the struggle with Perrott. Sorley travelled extensively in Argyle making sure that he would be supplied with significant redshank reinforcements during the next campaigning season while continually harrying the isolated and hungry English garrisons on the Bann. Sorley Boy mastered his impatience to recover the Route until the circumstances were more favourable. It is clear from his letters that Perrott believed that he had broken the power of the Clan Iain Mor by his occupation of the Route and the large plunder taken from it[46] and his appointment of Donald Gorm to The Glens, this was despite his failure to destroy Sorley Boy's army in battle.

During the early winter of 1584 Bagenal, who was one of Perrott's deputies led a force of six hundred into the Glens towards Red Bay. Bagenal was ambushed by a force of the Clan Iain Mor led by Donald Gorm. Clearly his appointment to the Glens by Perrott had not affected his loyalty to Sorley Boy. After a sharp skirmish[47] in which several English soldiers were killed and over a hundred injured Bagenal retreated to Carrickfergus. During these winter months there were several attempts by the English to assassinate Sorley Boy. The fact that all the attempts failed despite the acute poverty of the people that surrounded Sorley Boy attests to the loyalty of his clan to him and the tight social cohesion of the Clan Iain Mor at this time.

---

[44] The garrison numbered only some forty clansmen, clearly Dunluce was sacrificed to buy Sorley Boy time.

[45] The economy of Gaelic Ulster was based on cattle and their destruction would deal a severe blow to Sorley Boy's wealth and prestige.

[46] Irish sources say that of the fifty thousand cattle that belonged to the Clan Iain Mor only fifteen hundred survived the attentions of Perrott's men.

[47] Donald Gorme's force included over two hundred bowmen. It is interesting to note such a heavy reliance on bowmen in a clan army at this date.

In December reports came in of a MacDonald redshank army moving towards the Route; the English under Bagenal's command attempted to intercept and destroy it. These redshanks, lead by Donald Gorm, were attempting to link up with Sorley Boy who was returning to Ireland with a fleet of reinforcements. Donald Gorm engaged Bagenal's troops near Bunnamairge Friary, the battle was inconclusive after which the English forces divided with Bagenal returning to Dunanynie and Stanley moving towards Cushendun.

On the fifth of January Sorley Boy landed at Cushendun accompanied by Angus (the chief of the Clan Iain Mor) and two thousand fighting men. Sorley Boy threatened both Perrott's garrisons in the Route and the eastern end of his defensive line which was anchored on Carrickfergus. Perrott found himself outmanoeuvred by the arrival of the MacDonald army at Cushendun, Bagenal was ordered to abandon the Route and head south for Carrickfergus while Stanley had to retreat north from Cushendun towards Ballycastle as Sorley Boy's host stood between him and the relative safety of Carrickfergus.

Sorley Boy decided to strike at Stanley and recover the Route before considering any advance on Carrickfergus. Stanley continued his retreat before the MacDonald onslaught. Finally after gathering what outlying garrisons he could, he made a stand at Bunnamairge. Sorley Boy left a contingent of his host under the command of Donald Gorm to tie down Stanley while he headed for Red Bay (from where he threatened Carrickfergus) to prevent Bagenal offering Stanley any support. In a series of skirmishes, Donald Gorm was successful in driving off most of the English cavalry thus leaving Stanley stuck in a static defence and cut off from any source of support. In a few days Sorley had completely altered the military situation in Ulster, he had managed to separate and isolate the two English forces and then to threaten Stanley with annihilation. At this juncture Sorley again attempted to gain English recognition for the Clan Iain Mor's possession of the Route and The Glens. The English prevaricated, while once again the political landscape started to shift.

Turlough O'Neill began to show open hostility to Sorley's success by spreading his forces along the banks of the Bann thus threatening Sorley's western frontier, while an English force under Barkley invaded the southern Glens. To add to his difficulties Sorley's forces had been weakened by the return to Scotland of Angus and the contingent he had brought. Angus had to return to his Scottish possessions to face his old foe Lachlan Mor MacLean; this feud had erupted again after the events on Jura.[48] Sorley and Donald Gorm were forced onto the defensive eventually being forced to retreat to Scotland, when Barkley was reinforced by Bagenal. In a matter of a few weeks the Clan Iain Mor's position had deteriorated from one of military dominance to one in which only Sorley's son, Alexander and one hundred and twenty men were left in Antrim to defend the Clan Iain Mor's interests. Soon reports were reaching London that the Clan Iain Mor's power was finally broken in Ulster and that all that remained was to mop up a few pockets of

---

See chapter 11.

resistance, Elizabeth seized her chance to halt the endless drain on her exchequer and called a halt to English operations.

August 1585 saw Sorley Boy return to Ulster with an army of fifteen hundred clansmen. Sorley quickly rallied the O'Cahans, O'Kellys and the O'Neills of Clandeboy to his side as he prepared once again to face Perrott. The English garrisons were defeated in a series of skirmishes over August and September. Sorley's campaign culminated in the storming of Dunluce Castle in early November. Dunluce had been occupied by an English garrison since Perrott's campaign in 1584. Carie, the English constable of the castle was hung from castle rock while most of the garrison was massacred. To add to English woes, a regular company was overwhelmed by the O'Cahans a short time later.

At long last the environment was right for the English and Sorley Boy to negotiate for peace. Sorley Boy was by now an old man who no doubt felt the strain of defending his clan's interests against the native Irish and the English. He was aware of the dangers faced by his clan in Scotland with the disastrous feud with the MacLeans continuing and the ominous rise of Campbell power. The Clan Iain Mor had lost considerable manpower in the endless struggles both in Ireland and Scotland, the clan would have been desperate for some respite from the continual loss of life. The English faced a different set of problems, but they also needed addressing, while Perrott who was still advocating a continuance of the struggle had been discredited by Sorley's last return from Scotland and his subsequent victories. It was clear to Elizabeth that neither the English in Ireland nor James VI in Edinburgh were capable of containing Sorley Boy. She was also concerned about rumours of a Spanish invasion of Ireland and her own heavy commitments in the Netherlands. She was tired of the continual and indecisive warfare in Ulster which caused a steady outflow from her treasury.

Before Sorley Boy was able to achieve his long held ambition of obtaining legal possession of the Route and Glens he had to endure one final sorrow. In March 1585 his son, Alexander, was in Tryconnell with five hundred clansmen. Here he clashed with an equal number of English troops led by a Captain Merriman. As the two forces faced each other Alexander stepped forward and challenged Merriman to single combat. A gallowglass serving with the English claimed to be Merriman and engaged Alexander. After a bitter struggle, Alexander cleaved the gallowglass's head in two. He was then attacked by Merriman who managed to wound Alexander in the leg which prevented him from standing. Alexander was carried by his clansmen to a hiding place where they dug a small pit and laid him in it and then covered him in moss. Once they had hidden Alexander, the demoralized clansmen retreated. Merriman knew that Alexander would have been unable to walk and could not have left with the rest of Clan Iain Mor. After a long search Merriman came across the disturbed ground and pulling away the moss and turfs found the injured Alexander. Merriman cut off Alexander's head and sent it to Dublin where it was stuck on a pole in the castle. There are two striking features of the death of Alexander, the first is Alexander's challenge to Merriman. Even at this late date

Alexander is still steeped in the ancient culture of Gaelic heroes who fought as individuals in front of their hosts. Merriman's brutal killing of Alexander and the exposure of his head by the Dublin authorities demonstrates the gulf between English and Gaelic Ireland at the close of the sixteenth century.

Sorley Boy mastered his anguish at the death of his favourite son and overcame his thirst for revenge; a remarkable achievement for a man steeped in a blood feud culture. This restraint marks Sorley Boy out as not only a great warrior but also a great politician. Sorley had survived numerous battles, his wife,[49] his brothers and several nephews and now his son had died before him. He had witnessed the savage massacre of the women and children of his people on Rathlin Island, his entire life had been steeped in bloodshed and sorrow yet he continued on with his long held ambition of establishing the Clan Iain Mor as a powerful, and legal part of the political landscape in Ulster. Sorley's health was deteriorating, he was less mobile and he was losing his sight.[50] These afflictions would weaken his position in the eyes of the English. He knew that he must come to terms quickly before his health failed.

Sorley arrived in Dublin in June 1586; as he made his way into the castle he had to pass his beloved son's head still staring vacantly out at the passers by. By this date Angus's mother Agnes had already agreed a treaty with the English by which in exchange for the Clan Iain Mor's submission to Elizabeth the Clan Iain Mor was granted legal title to its ancient patrimony, the Bisset inheritance in the Glens. In exchange for Sorley's submission Elizabeth granted Sorley Boy the best two thirds of the Route and agreed that Sorley could hold the Glens from his chief Angus. Sorley was also appointed Constable of Dunluce Castle in exchange for providing a few dozen troops to serve Elizabeth when required. Although Angus was still the nominal overlord of the Glens it is clear that by this period the two branches of the Clan Iain Mor had gone their separate ways and were to go on to their very different fates. Sorley Boy retired to his favourite residence at Dunanynie where he died in 1590. His body was escorted to its final resting place by hundreds of grief stricken members of his clan. Sorley Boy was laid to rest amongst his ancestors at Bunamargie Abbey. Sorley Boy ranks amongst the greatest of all the MacDonalds throughout their illustrious history in terms of his achievements but above all in his unswerving dedication to the furtherance of his clan's ambitions.

Angus MacDonald was less content with the terms of the treaty established by his mother on his behalf. In particular he was infuriated that the MacQuillins[51] were left in possession of a small part of the Route. In July 1586 he again invaded Ulster at the head of a MacDonald-redshank army and ravaged much of Ulster, ranging as far as the Inishowan peninsula. He then descended on the MacQuillins slaughtering

---

[49] Mary daughter of Con O'Neill.
[50] In a letter written by Perrott to Elizabeth he describes how Sorley had had incisions cut in his forehead to help him recover his sight.
[51] The MacQuillins were the ancient possessors of the Route.

many of them and driving off their cattle. On the twenty third of September 1586 he faced the English army at Ardnary. His army of two thousand three hundred highlanders was cut to pieces and contemporary sources estimated that more than half of them fell on the battlefield. From the lack of any persecution of Sorley Boy's followers it is clear that he had managed to keep his part of the Clan Iain Mor out of the hostilities. Ardnary was a disaster to the Scottish moiety of the Clan Iain Mor as such huge losses could not be made good in time to face the impending Campbell threat to their ancestral lands in Kintrye and Isla. One thousand clansmen and as many women and children[52] were killed at Ardnary; including Angus's two brothers Donald Gorme and Alastair Carragh. What is remarkable about Angus's almost insane bellicosity was that this disastrous campaign in Ulster took place at the same time as his feud with Lachlan Mor MacLean had reached its height.

Sorley Boy had been succeeded by James MacSorley his eldest son, James took advantage of the destruction of the MacQuillins by Angus to occupy their part of the Route. James can be considered to be the first chief of the MacDonalds of Antrim as they now styled themselves. Gradually a schism developed between James MacSorley and the bellicose Angus. Their political manoeuvrings leave no doubt that by the late 1590's the Antrim MacDonalds and the Clan Iain Mor were acting as two separate clans following their own interests. The days when MacDonald armies sailed between Ulster and the Isles fighting as one clan were over. It is clear that it was the authority, charisma and subtle intelligence of Sorley Boy that had held the disparate Clan Iain Mor together.

The history of the MacDonalds of Antrim falls outside the scope of this book apart from where it impinges on the destruction of the Clan Iain Mor. The MacDonalds of Antrim were one of the great powers in Ulster; the origin of their possessions goes back to the marriage of John Mor Tannister to the heiress Marjory Bisset in the early fifteenth century. It was from this ancient legacy that they possessed the Glens. Their other great possession was the Route, this legacy they owed to the military and political skill and determination of Sorley Boy. The Irish legacy in terms of culture and blood was of paramount importance in forming the character of Alastair MacCholla who bought such terrible destruction to the Campbells during the civil war.

The Clan Iain Mor both gained and lost by its unique position, owning extensive territories in both Scotland and Ireland. This allowed the clan to evade their persecutors in either country when circumstances turned against them. It also meant that they could rush reinforcements to either possession by sailing their fleets over the short stretch of sea that divided them. Politically speaking it allowed the chiefs the possibility of playing off against each other the interests of the Scottish and English crowns. With the destruction of the Scottish branch of the clan

---

[52] It was common for non-combatants to watch clan battles and this continued up to Culloden where many townspeople from Inverness were cut down by English dragoons.

in the early seventeenth century it ensured the survival of the clan albeit under new leadership and a new name.

The desperate struggle of the chiefs and gentlemen of the Clan Iain Mor to defend and enhance their clan's territories was in the end only successful in Ulster. They were almost constantly embroiled with either the MacLeans, the Campbells, the Scottish and English states, the English administration in Dublin, the O'Neills and other lesser Irish tribes. Was it, in the end that their wide and disparate territories simply left them exposed to overwhelming odds?

Select Bibliography

Anon. Historical Account of the Clanranald. Edinburgh 1819.

Boardman S. The Campbells 1250-1513. John Donald 2006 an imprint of Birlinn Ltd.

Braudel F. The Structures of Everyday Life; Civilization and Capitalism, fifteenth to eighteenth centuries. New York 1981.

Brown K.M. Bloodfeud in Scotland, 1573-1625. Edinburgh 1986.

Bryne K. Colkitto! House of Lochar 1977.

Buchan J. The Massacre of Glencoe. London 1933.

Buchanan G. The History of Scotland. Edited and translated by Aikman. Glasgow 1827.

Campbell A. A History of Clan Campbell Volume 2. Edinburgh University Press 2002.

Connellan O. Annals of Ireland by the Four Masters (translation). Dublin 1846.

Cunningham A. The Loyal Clans. 1932.

Dewer J. Scottish West Highland Folktales. Edited by Meckechnie J, Glasgow, 1964.

Dressler C. Eigg The Story of an Island. Birlinn 2007.

Dodgshon R.A. From Chiefs To Landlords Edinburgh University Press 1998.

Donaldson G. Scotland James the Fifth to James the Seventh. Oliver and Boyd 1971.

Donaldson G. Scottish Historical Documents. Edinburgh 1970.

Eyre-Todd G. The Highland Clans of Scotland. Heath Cranton Ltd 1923.

Goldsworthy A. Cannae. Phoenix 2007.

Grant I.F. Highland Folk Ways. London 1961.

Grant I.F. The Lordship of the Isles. Edinburgh 1935.

Grant I.F. and Cheape H. Periods in Highland History. Shepheard-Walwyn Ltd 1987.

Gregory D. History of the Western Highlands and Islands. John Donald Publishers 1975.

Grieve S. The Book of Colonsay and Oransay. Edinburgh 1923.

Hill M.J. Fire and Sword: Sorley Boy MacDonnell and the Rise of Clan Ian Mor 1538-90. The Athlone Press 1993.

Jupp C. History of Islay. Museum of Islay Life 1994.

Kermack W.R. The Scottish Highlands. Edinburgh 1967.

Kingston S. Ulster and the Isles in the Fifteenth Century. Dublin 2004.

Lindsay I.G. and Cosh M. Inveraray and the Dukes of Argyll. Edinburgh 1973.

Lawson B. North Uist in History and Legend. Birlinn 2004.

MacDonald A. MacDonald A. The Clan Donald. The Northern Counties Publishing Co. Ltd. 1904.

MacDonald D.J. Slaughter under Trust. London 1965.

MacDonald D.J. Clan Donald. MacDonald Publishers 1978.

MacDonald H. History of the MacDonalds. Edinburgh 1914.

MacDonald J. Discovering Skye. J. MacDonald.

MacDonald N.H. The Clan Ranald of Gamoran.

MacDonald N.H. The Clan Ranald of Knoydart & Glengarry.

MacGrgor A.A. Behold the Hebrides. W. and R. Chambers Ltd 1925.

MacGregor A. The Feuds of the Clans. Eneas Mackay 1907.

Mackenzie A. History of the Camerons. Aberdeen University Press 1884.

Mackenzie A. History of the Frasers. Inverness 1896.

Mackenzie A. History of the Clanranald. Inverness 1881.

Mackenzie A. History of the MacDonalds and the Lords of the Isles. Inverness 1881.

Mackenzie A. History of the MacLeods. Inverness 1899.

Mackenzie A. History and Genealogies of the Mackenzies. Inverness 1894.

Mackintosh A.M. The Mackintoshes and Clan Chattan. Edinburgh 1903.

Mackintosh of Mackintosh. The History of the Clan Mackintosh and the Clan Chattan. Edinburgh 1948.

Maclean F. Highlanders a History of the Highland Clans. David Campbell Publishers1995.

Maclean Sinclair A. The Clan Gillean. Haszard and Moore 1899.

Martin F.X. Moody T.W. The Course of Irish History. Cork 1967.

Martin M. Description of the Western Isles (1695). Stirling 1934.

Miket R. Roberts D.L. The Mediaeval Castles of Skye and Lochalsh. MacLean Press 1990.

Moncreiffe I. The Highland Clans. Barrie and Rockliff 1968.

Monro Sir D. Description of the Western Isles of Scotland 1549. Glasgow, 1884.

Muir R. The Lost Villages of Britain. Michael Joseph 1982.

Newton N. Islay. Davis and Charles Ltd. 1995.

Nicholson A. History of Skye. Glasgow 1930.

Nicholson R. Scotland; The Later Middle Ages. Volume 2.Oliver and Boyd 1974.

Otway- Ruthven A.J. A History of Medieval Ireland. London 1968.

Paterson R.C. The Lords Of The Isles Birlinn Ltd. 2008

Prebble J. The Lion in the North. London 1971.

Prebble J. Glencoe. Penguin 1966.

Ranelagh, O'Beirne J. A Short History of Ireland. Cambridge 1983.

Sadler J. Clan Donald's Greatest Defeat. Tempus Publishing Ltd 2005.

Stevenson D.   Highland Warrior Alasdair MacColla and the Civil Wars. The Saltire Society 1994.

Skene W.F. The Highlanders of Scotland. Eneas Mackay 1902.

Stewart J. The Camerons. Clan Cameron Association 1974.

The Black Book of Taymouth. Ed. Innes C.